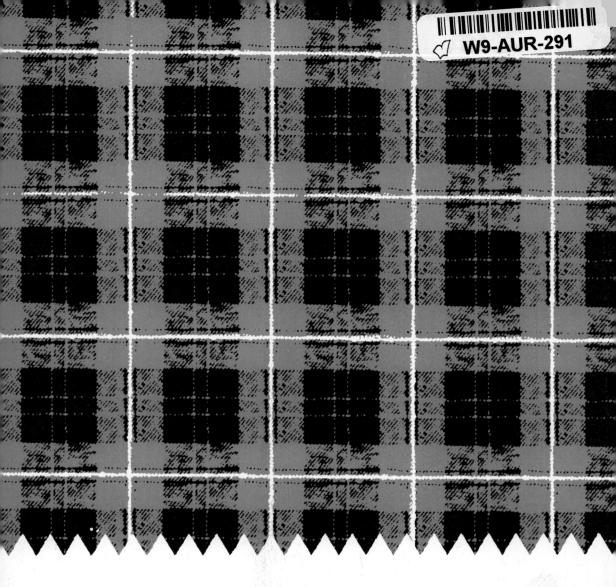

SWEET TOOTH BOOK TWO

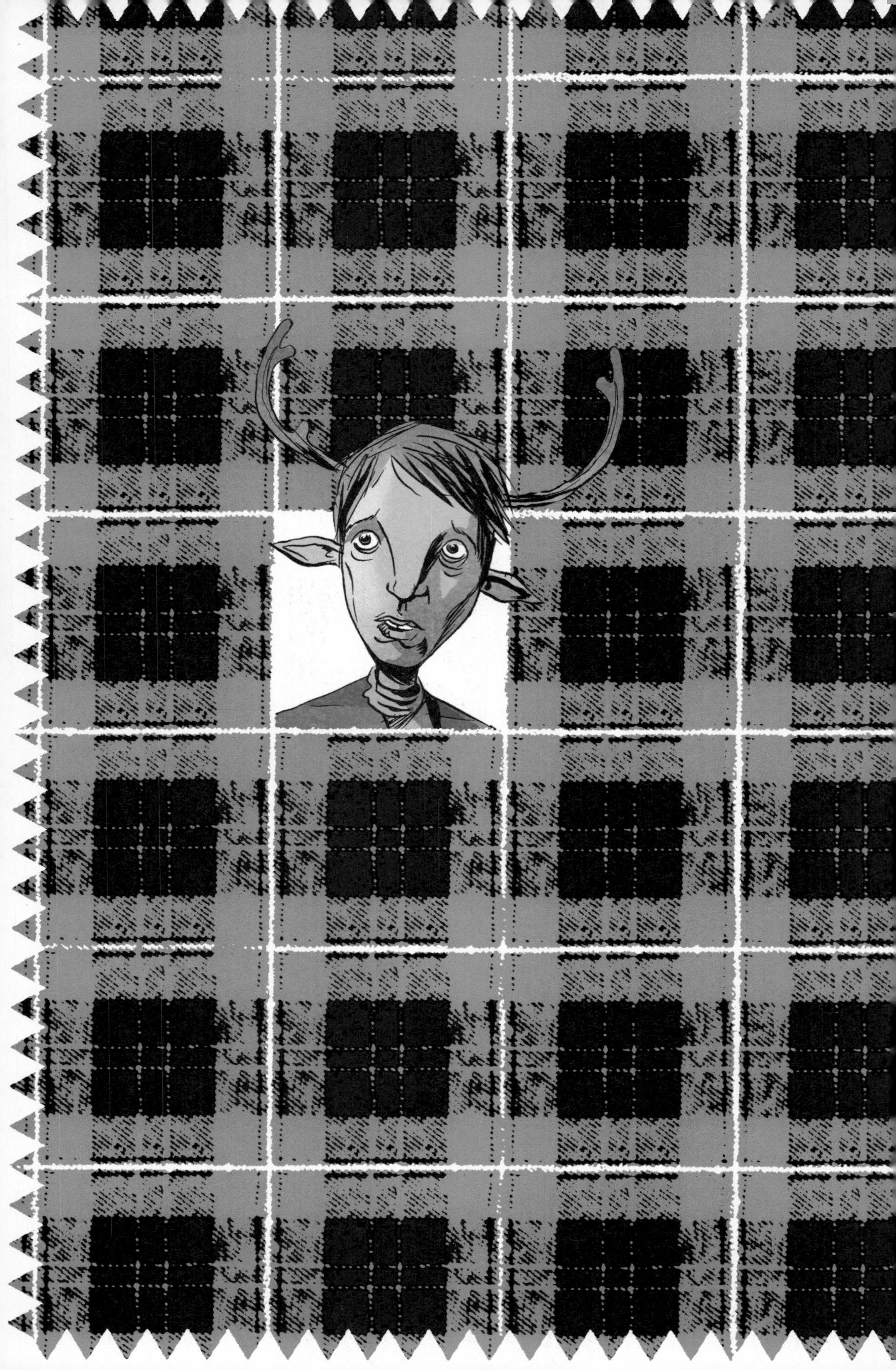

SWEET TOOTH

BOOK TWO
JEFF LEMIRE story & art
JOSÉ VILLARRUBIA JEFF LEMIRE colors
PAT BROSSEAU letters
NATE POWELL EMI LENOX MATT KINDT additional art
JEFF LEMIRE JOSÉ VILLARRUBIA collection cover
SWEET TOOTH created by JEFF LEMIRE

Pornsak Pichetshote
Mark Doyle Editors – Original Series
Jeb Woodard Group Editor – Collected Editions
Robin Wildman Editor – Collected Edition
Steve Cook Design Director – Books
Louis Prandi Publication Design

Bob Harras Senior VP – Editor-in-Chief, DC Comics
Mark Doyle Executive Editor, DC Black Label

Jim Lee Publisher & Chief Creative Officer
Bobbie Chase VP – Global Publishing Initiatives & Digital Strategy
Don Falletti VP – Manufacturing Operations &
    Workflow Management
Lawrence Ganem VP – Talent Services
Alison Gill Senior VP – Manufacturing & Operations
Hank Kanalz Senior VP – Publishing Strategy & Support Services
Dan Miron VP – Publishing Operations
Nick J. Napolitano VP – Manufacturing Administration & Design
Nancy Spears VP – Sales
Jonah Weiland VP – Marketing & Creative Services
Michele R. Wells VP & Executive Editor, Young Reader

SWEET TOOTH BOOK TWO

Published by DC Comics. Compilation and all new
material Copyright © 2018 Jeff Lemire. All Rights
Reserved.

Originally published in single magazine form in
SWEET TOOTH 13-25. Copyright © 2010, 2011 Jeff
Lemire. All Rights Reserved. All characters, their
distinctive likenesses and related elements featured
in this publication are trademarks of Jeff Lemire.
VERTIGO is a trademark of DC Comics. The stories,
characters and incidents featured in this
publication are entirely fictional. DC Comics does
not read or accept unsolicited submissions of ideas,
stories or artwork. DC – a WarnerMedia Company.

DC Comics,
2900 West Alameda Ave. Burbank, CA 91505
Printed by LSC Communications,
Owensville, MO, USA. Second Printing.
ISBN: 978-1-4012-8046-8

Library of Congress Cataloging-in-Publication
Data is available.

PEFC Certified

This product is from
sustainably managed
forests and controlled
sources

PEFC/29-31-337   www.pefc.org

FOREWORD
by JOSÉ VILLARRUBIA

The volume you hold in your hands is the *Empire Strikes Back* of the SWEET TOOTH series. After 12 issues of world setup and the introduction of the cast of characters, this is the part of the tale when things really get going. Jeff has established a cohesive universe and set the tone for the story—now it becomes an emotional roller coaster.

I have known Jeff for almost 10 years, ever since we were both part of the Top Shelf "family" that published both of us. Back then he was working in black and white only. When the opportunity to create an ongoing color series for Vertigo came about, Jeff contacted me right away and asked if I was interested in working with him. Of course, I jumped at the chance! Almost immediately, I could visualize how good Jeff's art would look in color, using a washy, moody palette. But when we sat down to actually do it, the first couple of issues were a little rocky. We both tried very hard to mesh line art and color, and I think the result looks fine, but it really improved in subsequent issues. And after a year, we were on fire!

Jeff would give me minimal notes. I worked almost intuitively, and he always liked the results. Oftentimes he would say, "This is not what I had in mind, but I like it so much better!" Which gave me the confidence to take bigger chances. I was able to do more experimental work here than in any of the mainstream comics I have worked on. At the same time, I avoided digital "special effects" like the plague (no pun on the story intended). Jeff's art is clearly hand-drawn, and I wanted to be consistent with it, not overwhelm it with Photoshop glows, bells and whistles.

Rereading these chapters, I realize that I painted a lot of turbulent watercolor skies in the first part of the story. This look was expanded by Jeff himself when he colored the dream sequences in his characteristic loose watercolor style. But by now, my one "iconic" contribution to the series is gone. Gus, the protagonist, is no longer wearing his trademark red plaid shirt. This was the only element in the colors that did not change perspective from panel to panel, and I believe it helped establish Gus in the beginning of the story. After a year, this was no longer necessary; he could wear anything. Gus was clearly the heart of the story.

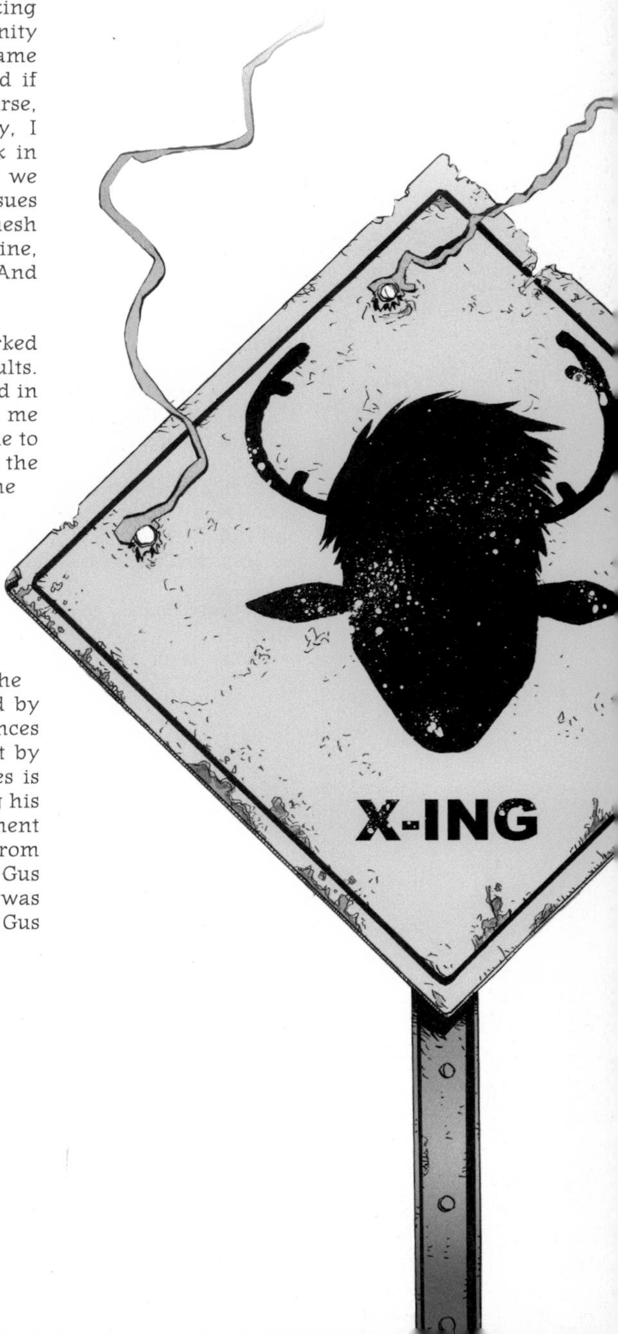
X-ING

When I look at the palette I used, I see how I used it to enhance the story's suspense. On almost every page, there is the possibility of imminent danger; any character may be injured or die without warning (and often it does happen). And the plot is peppered with violence that requires bold color choices (usually, obviously, red). I think the drab colors in the majority of the sequences achieve this effectively. The mostly flat, sometimes textured combinations reinforce that this is a tale of struggle and survival, but hopefully also offer hints that there is a light at the end of the tunnel.

SWEET TOOTH is the longest series I have ever colored. This allowed me to develop a special artistic relationship with Jeff and work in a large story arc for a complete long-format story (one could say a true graphic "novel"). While doing it, I did not know where the tale was going, but when I see it as a single work, I am very proud of how the color underscores its narrative pace and structure.

Jeff asked me to work with him again on the astonishing series TRILLIUM, this time sharing the color chores, and that was another extraordinary experience. But SWEET TOOTH and its unforgettable cast will always hold a dear place in my heart.

Now, if you have not yet, start reading the story...and if you already have, read it again. Gus will take your hand and hold it tight in your journey through his hazardous world. I am certain it will be a trip you'll never forget.

José Villarrubia,
Paris
February 2016

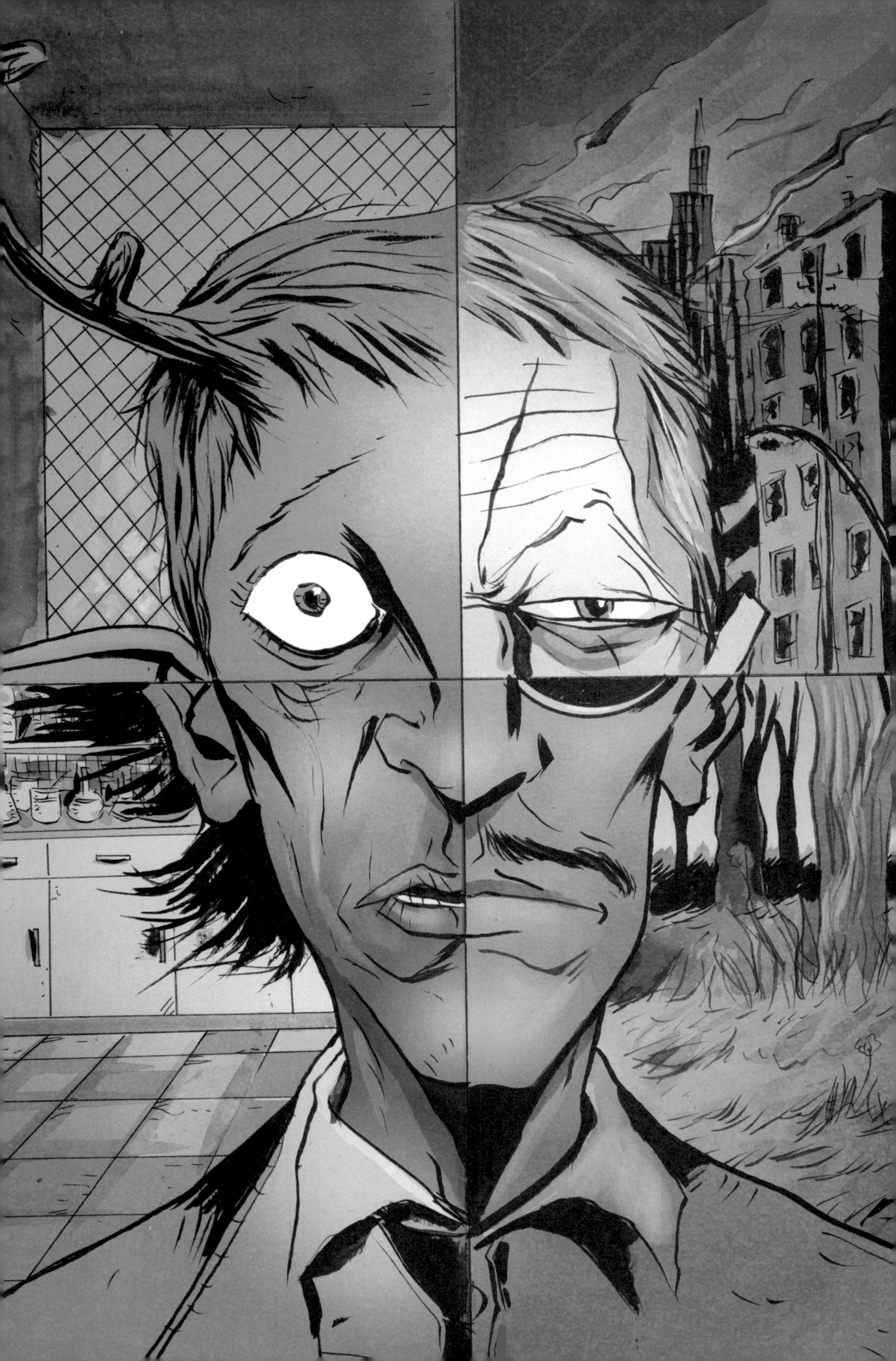

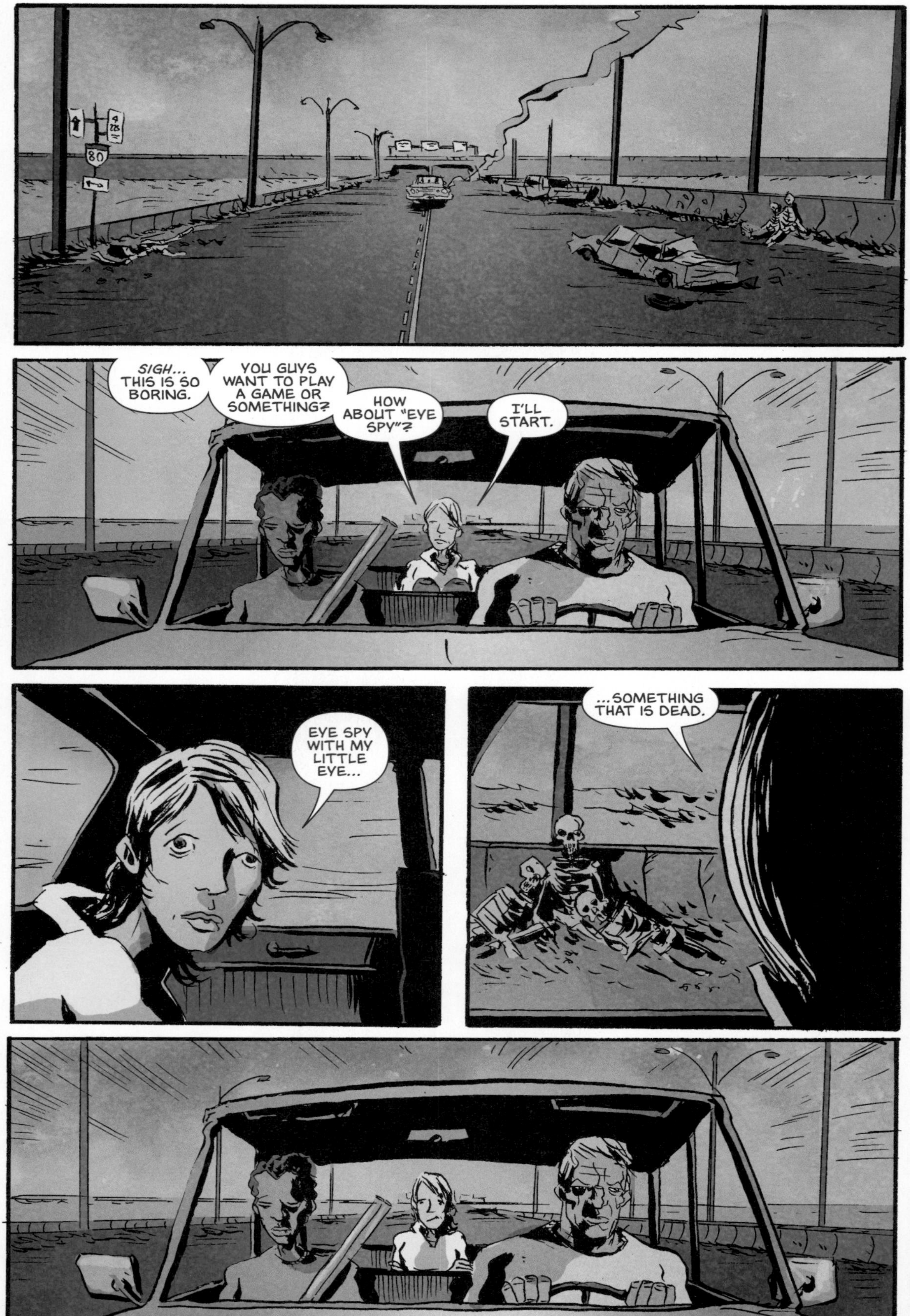
4
28
80
SIGH... THIS IS SO BORING.
YOU GUYS WANT TO PLAY A GAME OR SOMETHING?
HOW ABOUT "EYE SPY"?
I'LL START.
EYE SPY WITH MY LITTLE EYE...
...SOMETHING THAT IS DEAD.

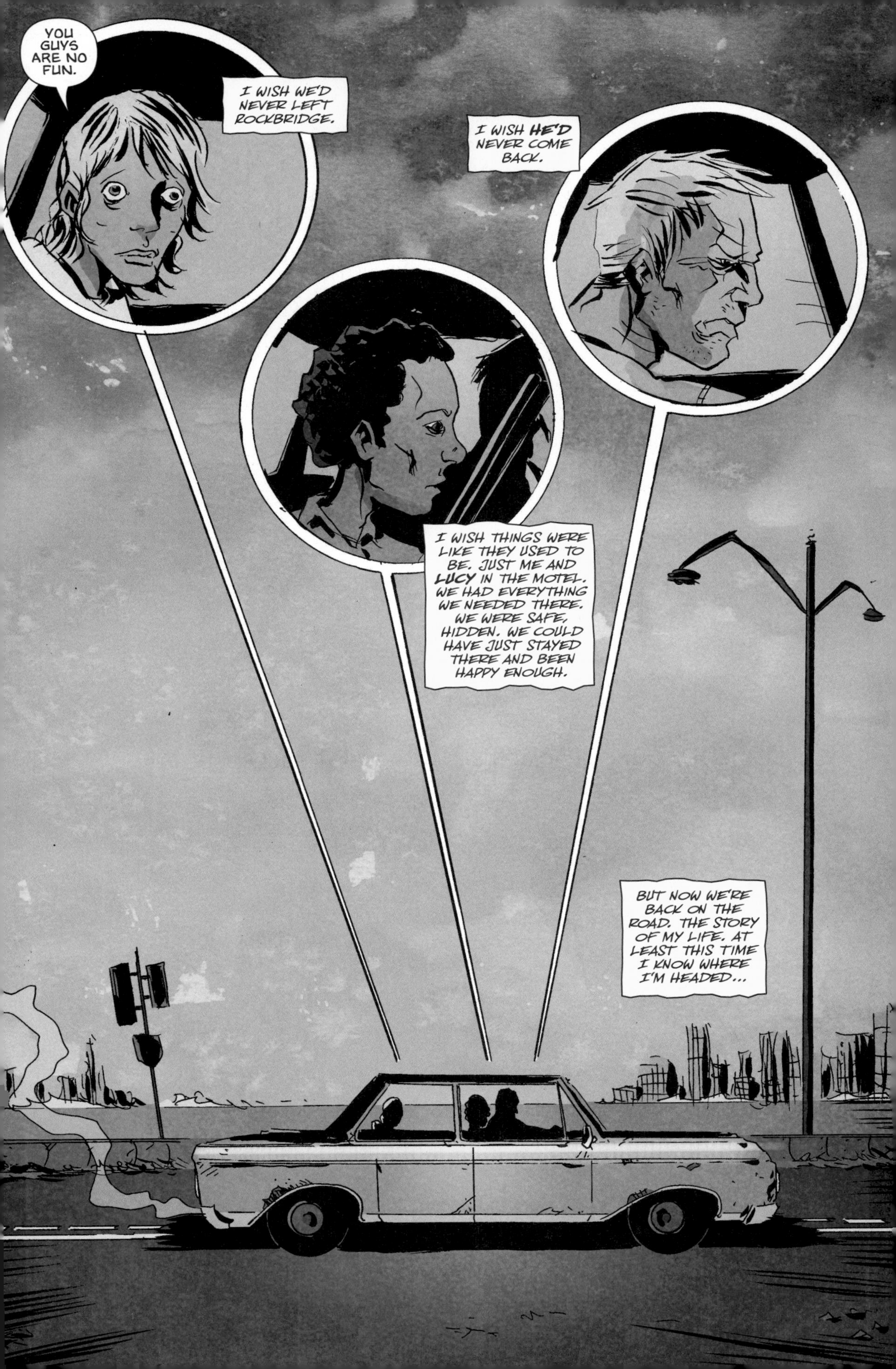
YOU GUYS ARE NO FUN.
I WISH WE'D NEVER LEFT ROCKBRIDGE.
I WISH HE'D NEVER COME BACK.
I WISH THINGS WERE LIKE THEY USED TO BE. JUST ME AND LUCY IN THE MOTEL. WE HAD EVERYTHING WE NEEDED THERE. WE WERE SAFE, HIDDEN. WE COULD HAVE JUST STAYED THERE AND BEEN HAPPY ENOUGH.
BUT NOW WE'RE BACK ON THE ROAD. THE STORY OF MY LIFE. AT LEAST THIS TIME I KNOW WHERE I'M HEADED...

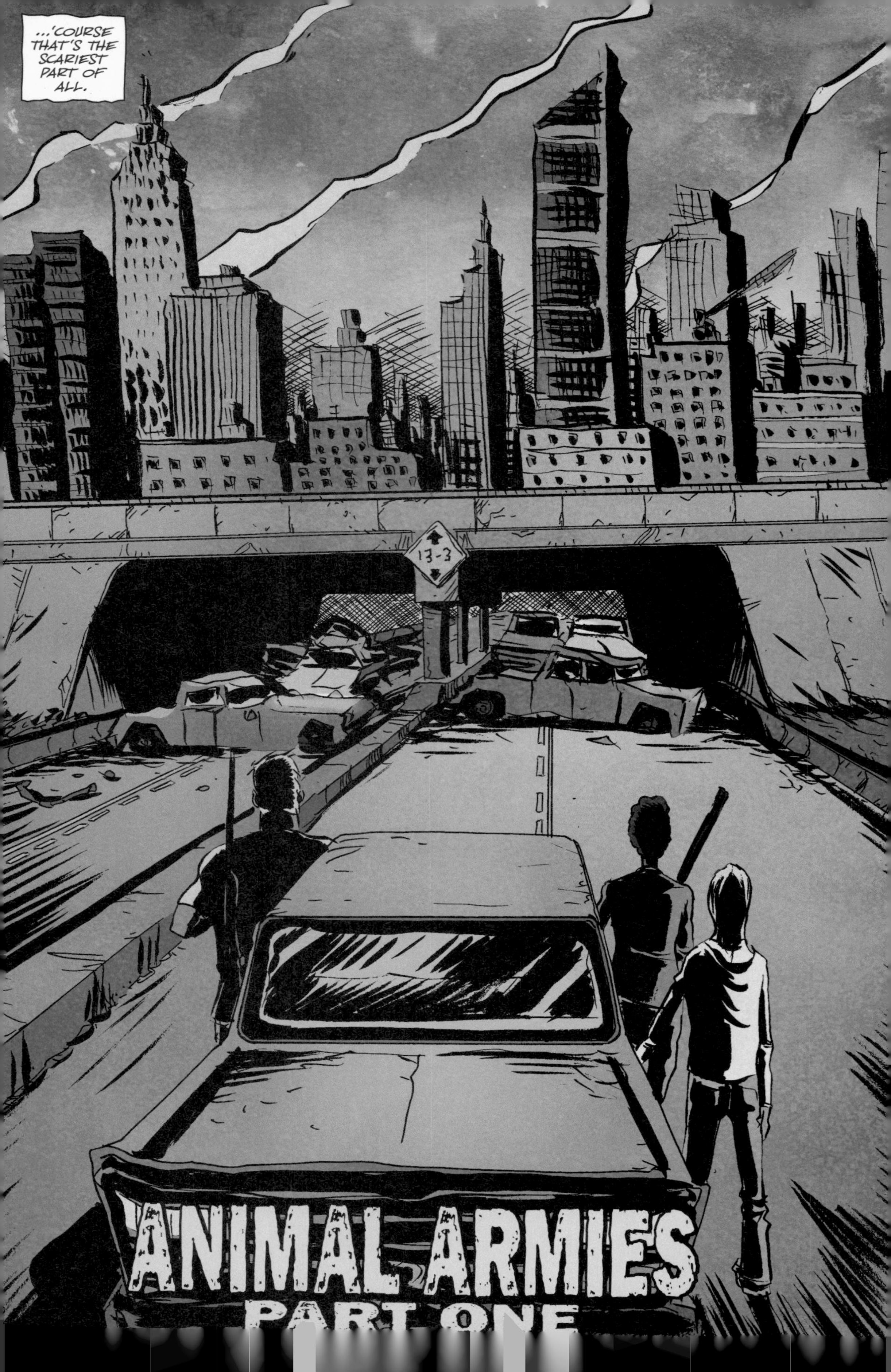
...'COURSE THAT'S THE SCARIEST PART OF ALL.
13-3
ANIMAL ARMIES
PART ONE

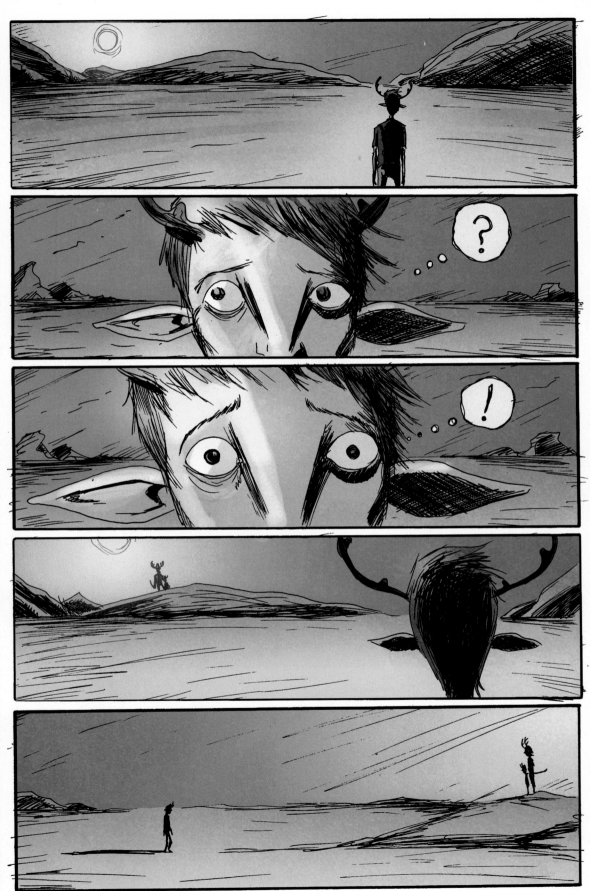

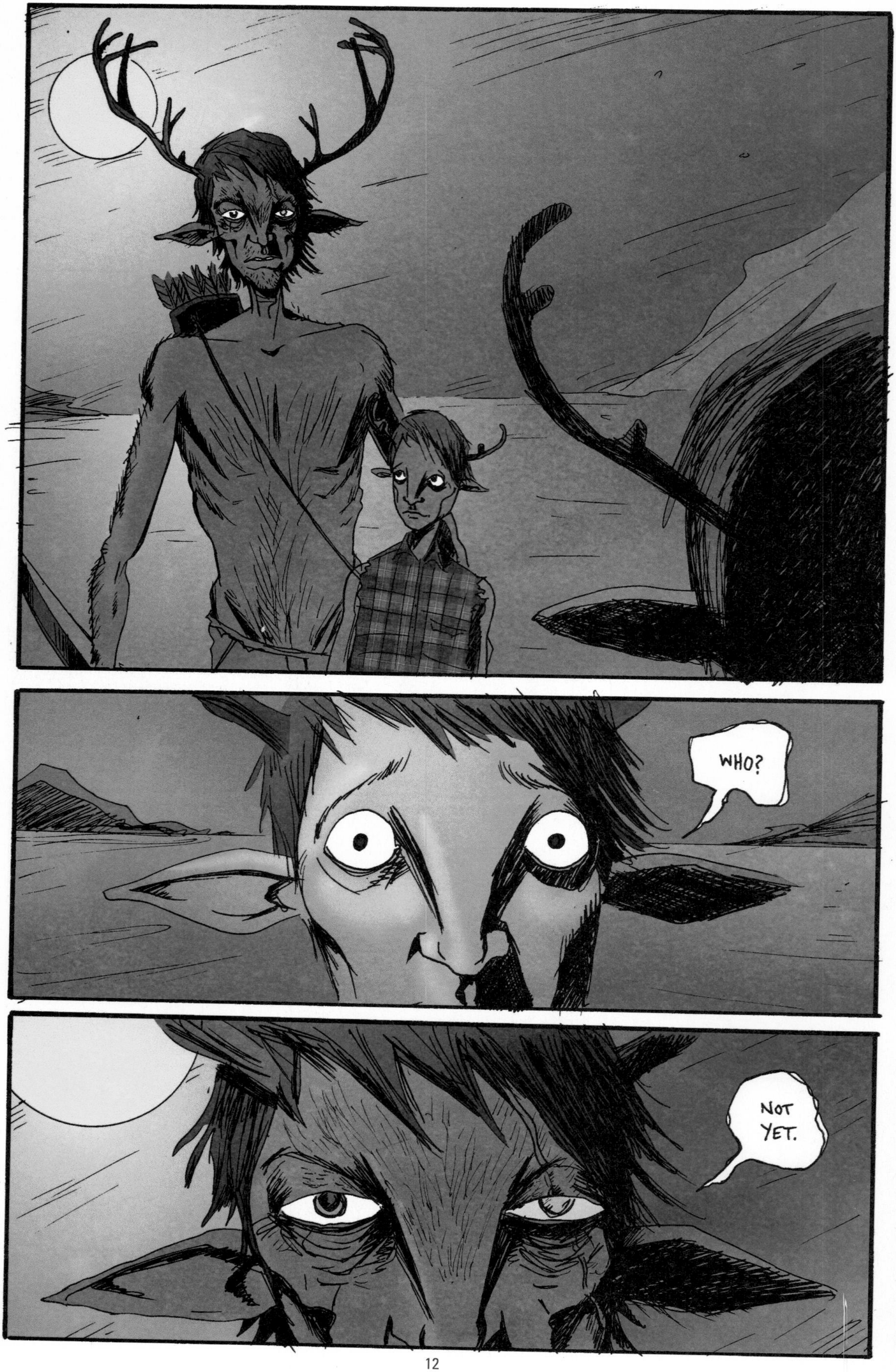
WHO?
NOT YET.

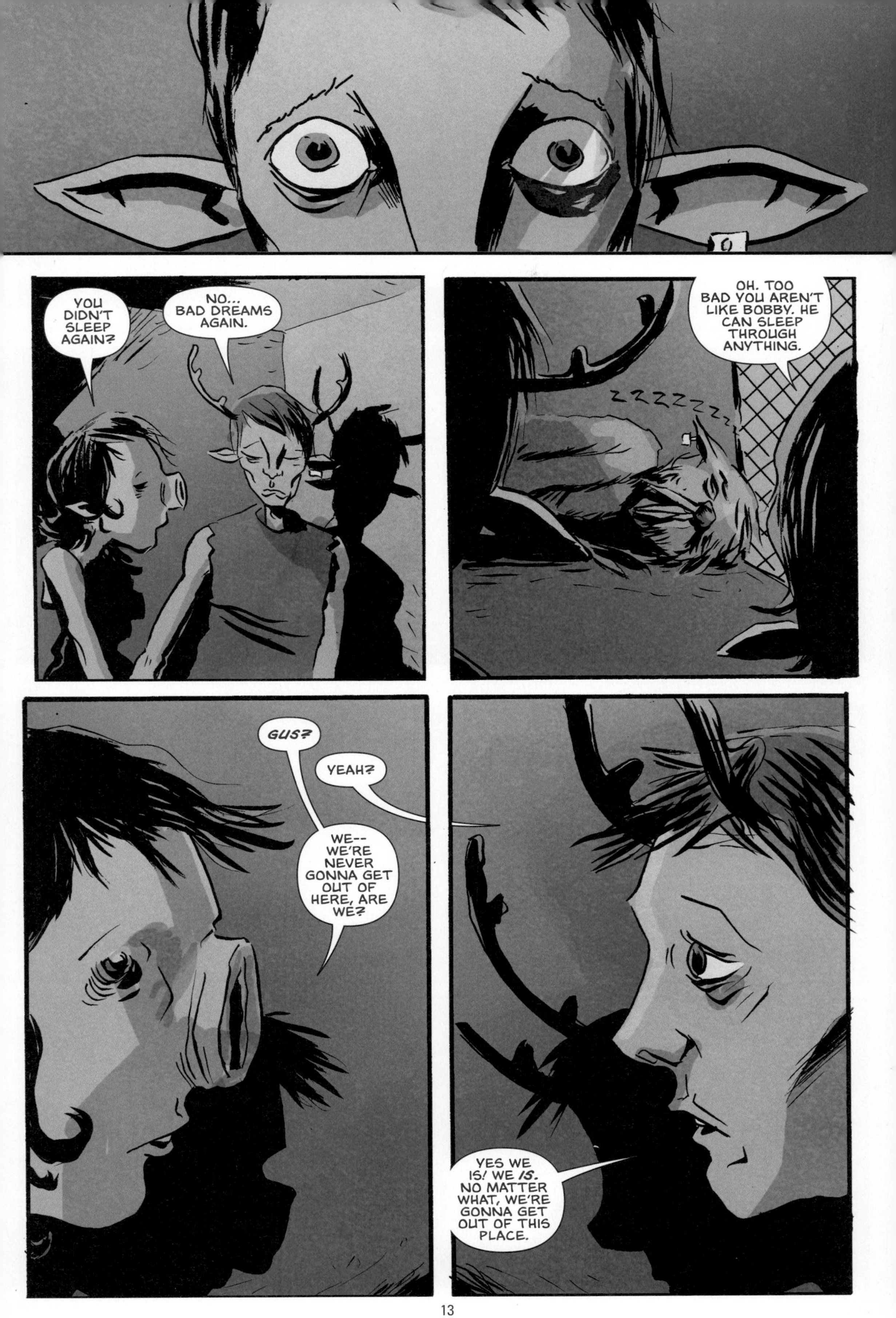
YOU DIDN'T SLEEP AGAIN?
NO... BAD DREAMS AGAIN.
OH. TOO BAD YOU AREN'T LIKE BOBBY. HE CAN SLEEP THROUGH ANYTHING.
ZZZZZZZZ
GUS?
YEAH?
WE-- WE'RE NEVER GONNA GET OUT OF HERE, ARE WE?
YES WE IS! WE *IS*. NO MATTER WHAT, WE'RE GONNA GET OUT OF THIS PLACE.

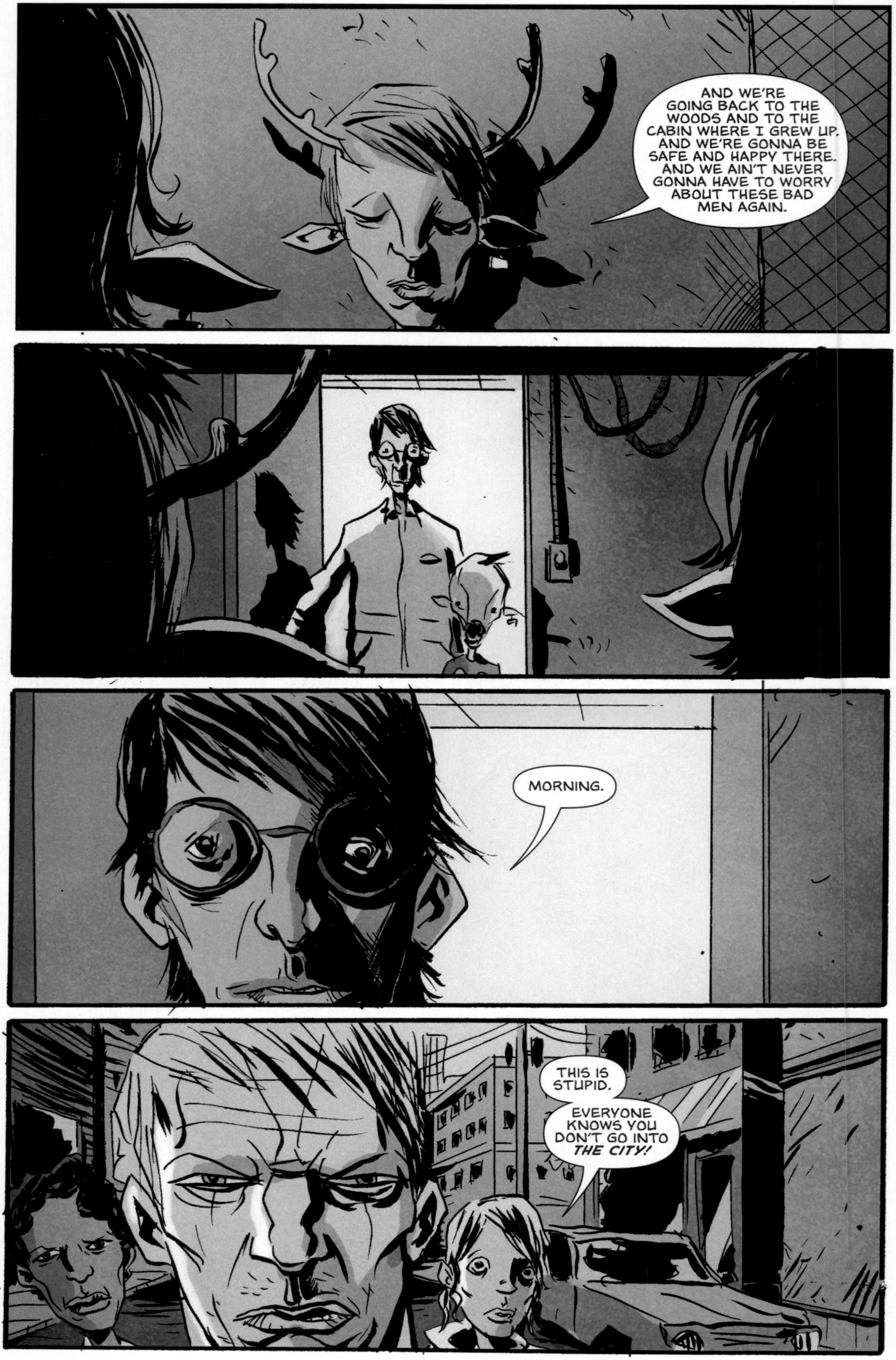
AND WE'RE GOING BACK TO THE WOODS AND TO THE CABIN WHERE I GREW UP. AND WE'RE GONNA BE SAFE AND HAPPY THERE. AND WE AIN'T NEVER GONNA HAVE TO WORRY ABOUT THESE BAD MEN AGAIN.
MORNING.
THIS IS STUPID.
EVERYONE KNOWS YOU DON'T GO INTO *THE CITY!*

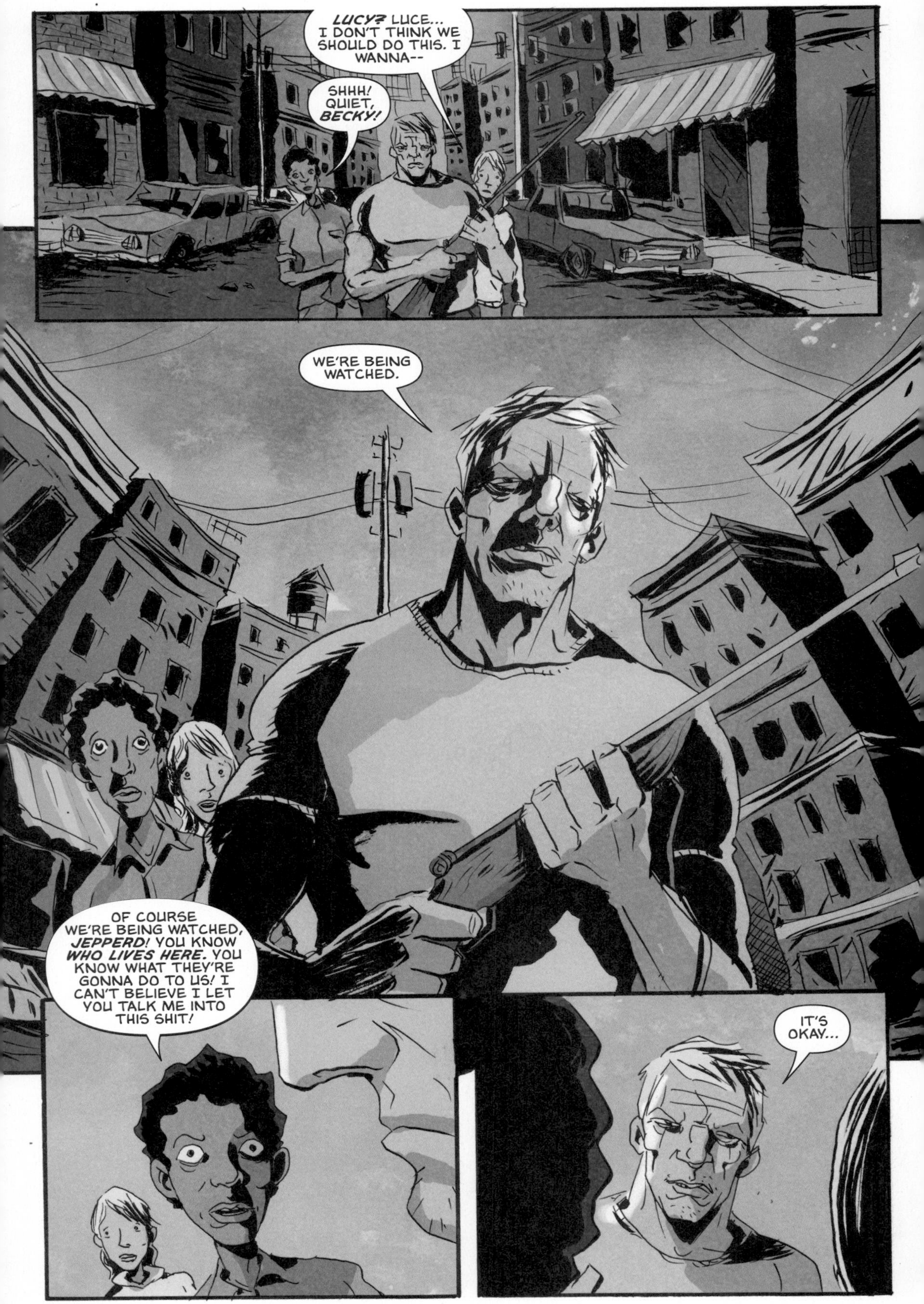
LUCY? LUCE... I DON'T THINK WE SHOULD DO THIS. I WANNA--
SHHH! QUIET, BECKY!
WE'RE BEING WATCHED.
OF COURSE WE'RE BEING WATCHED, JEPPERD! YOU KNOW WHO LIVES HERE. YOU KNOW WHAT THEY'RE GONNA DO TO US! I CAN'T BELIEVE I LET YOU TALK ME INTO THIS SHIT!
IT'S OKAY...

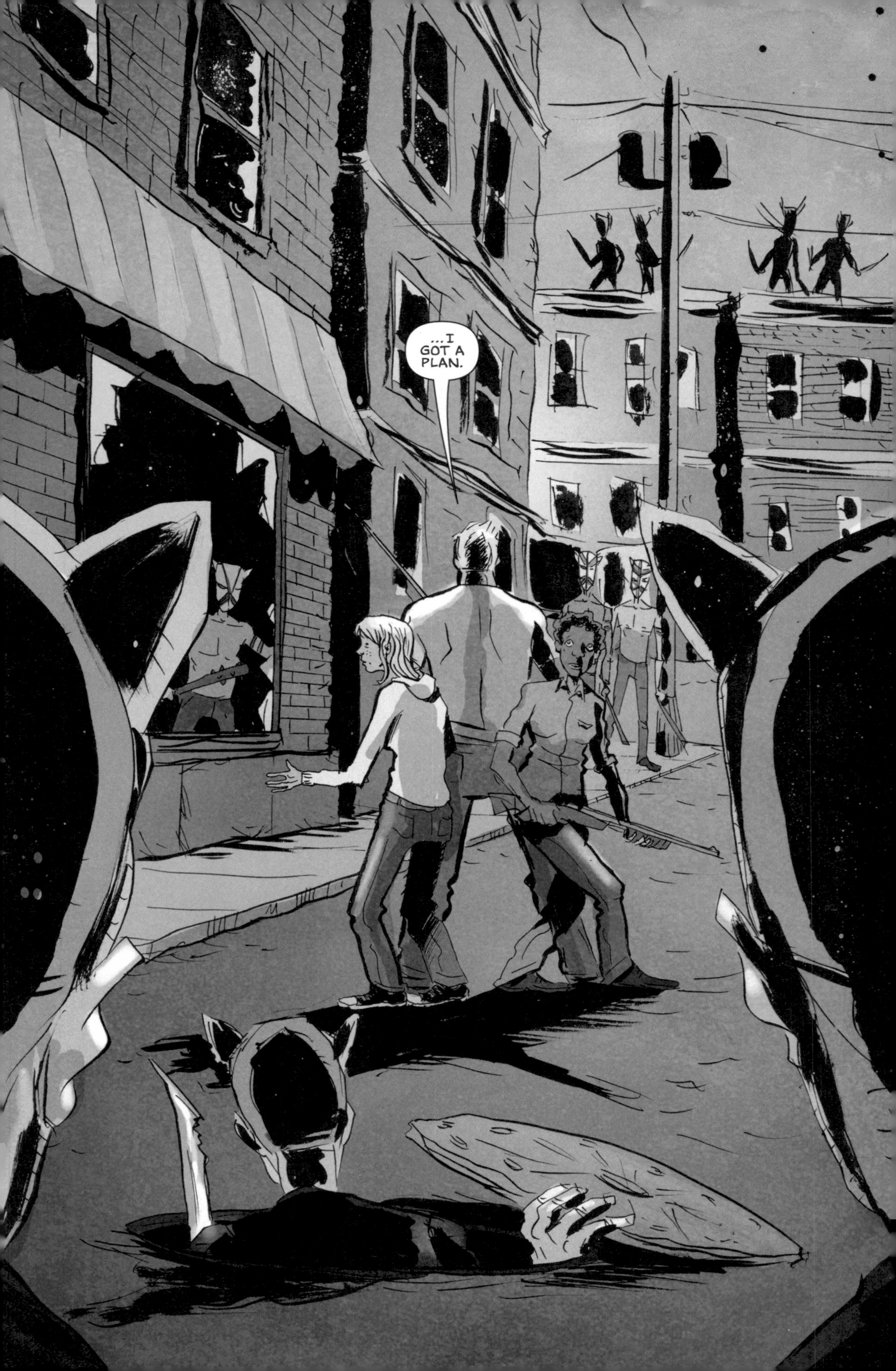
...I GOT A PLAN.

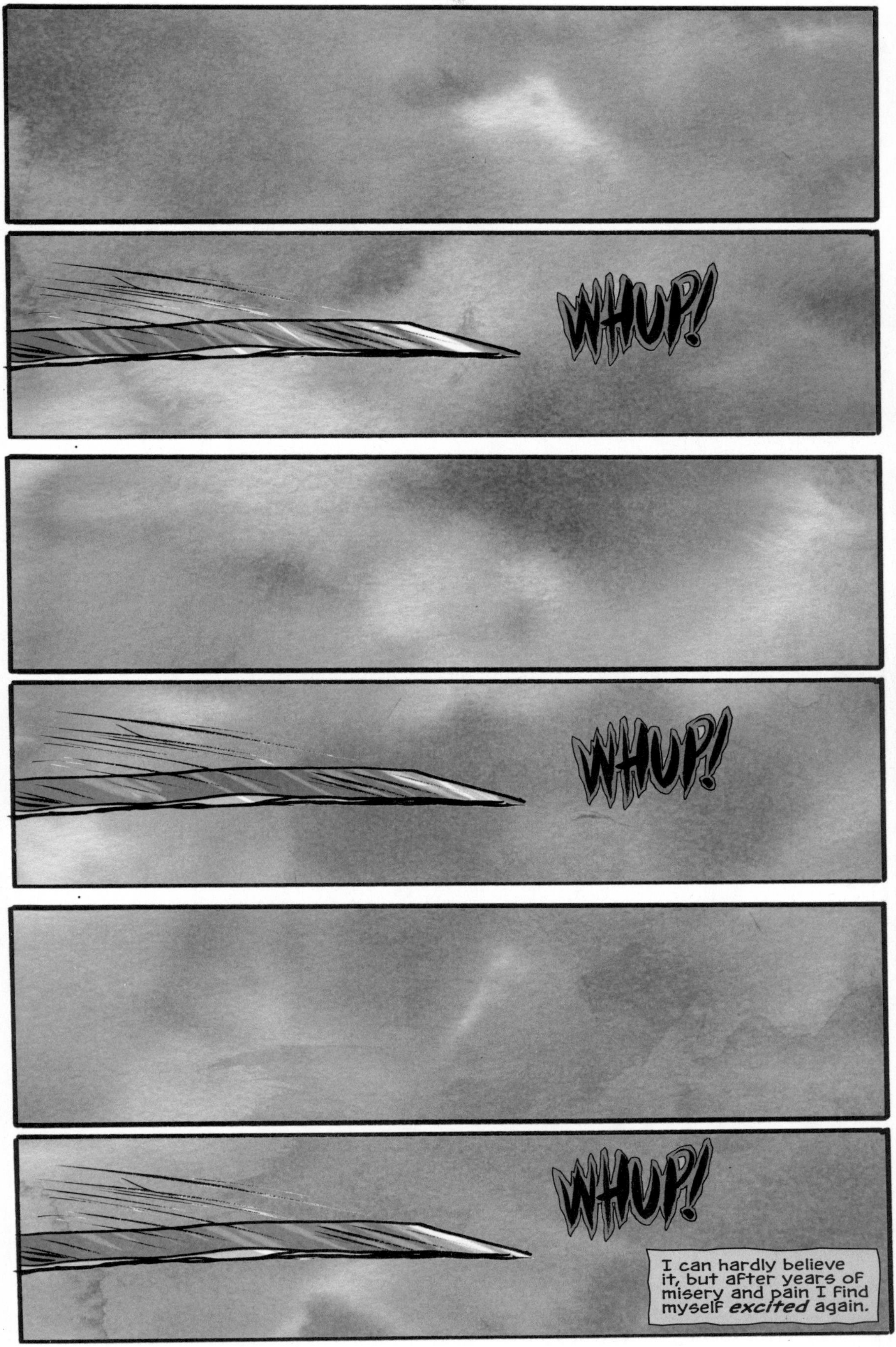
WHUP!
WHUP!
WHUP!
I can hardly believe it, but after years of misery and pain I find myself *excited* again.

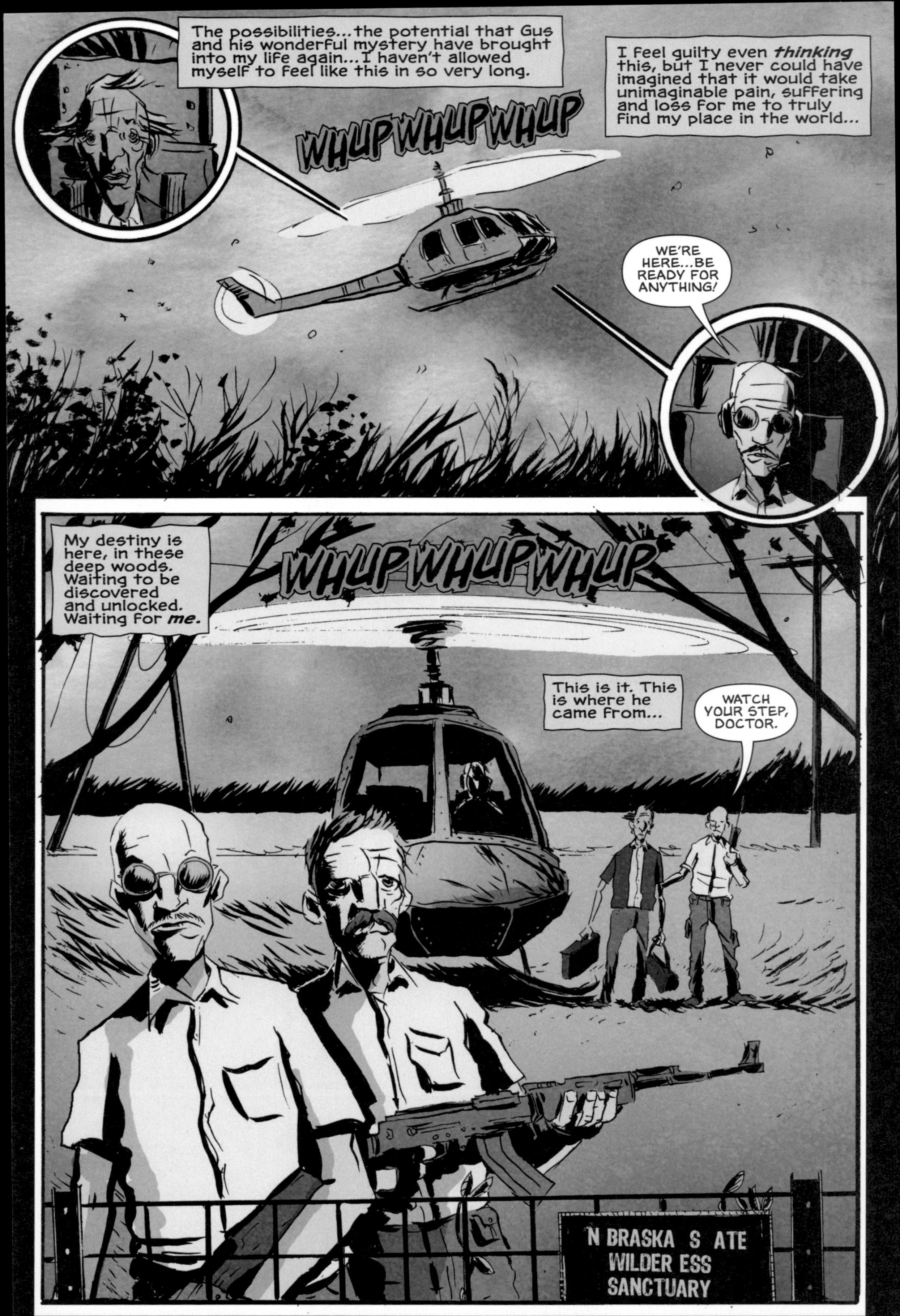

The possibilities...the potential that Gus and his wonderful mystery have brought into my life again...I haven't allowed myself to feel like this in so very long.
I feel guilty even *thinking* this, but I never could have imagined that it would take unimaginable pain, suffering and loss for me to truly find my place in the world...
WHUPWHUPWHUP
WE'RE HERE...BE READY FOR ANYTHING!
My destiny is here, in these deep woods. Waiting to be discovered and unlocked. Waiting for *me*.
WHUPWHUPWHUP
This is it. This is where he came from...
WATCH YOUR STEP, DOCTOR.
N BRASKA S ATE
WILDER ESS
SANCTUARY

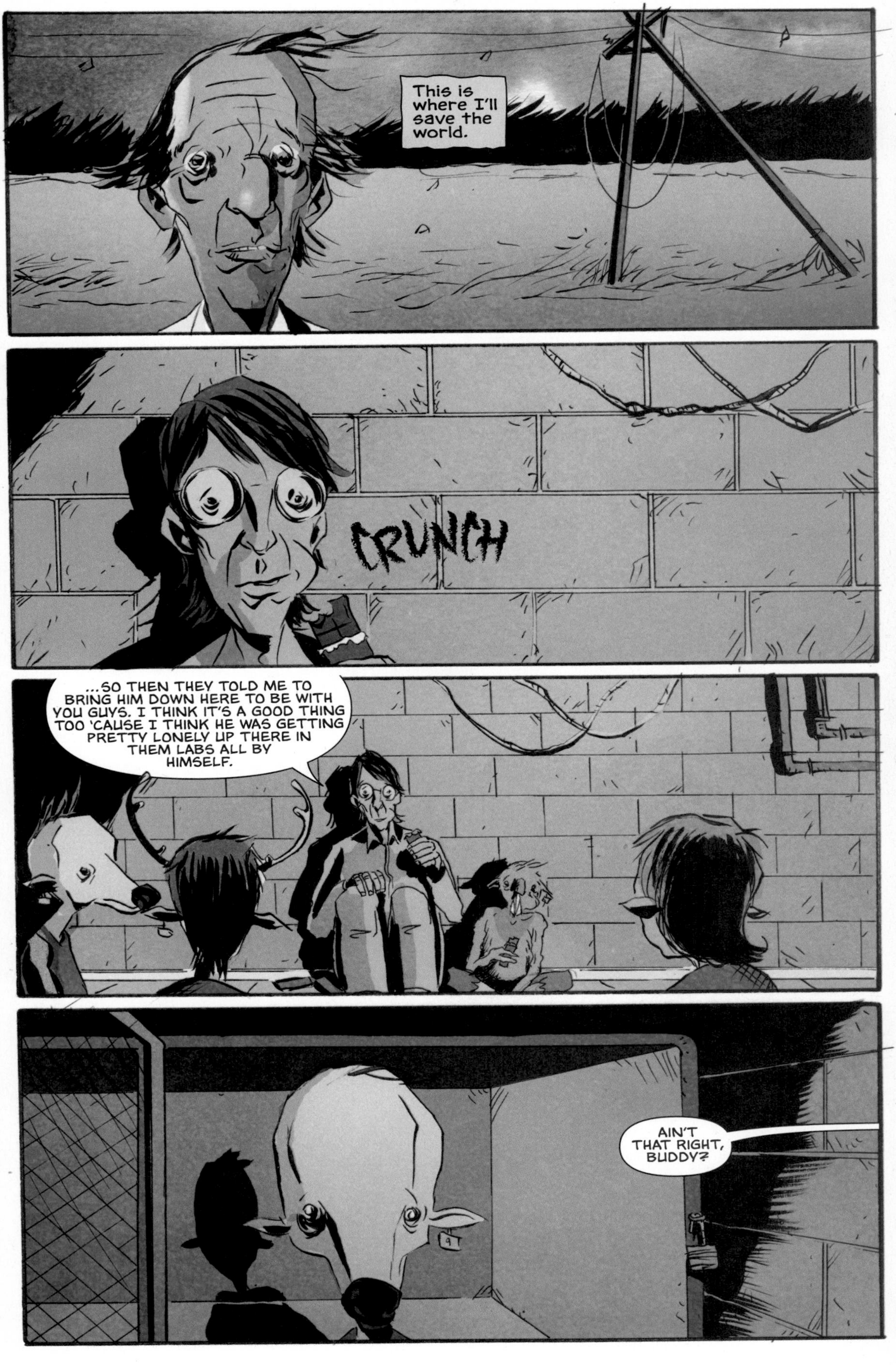
This is where I'll save the world.
CRUNCH
...SO THEN THEY TOLD ME TO BRING HIM DOWN HERE TO BE WITH YOU GUYS. I THINK IT'S A GOOD THING TOO 'CAUSE I THINK HE WAS GETTING PRETTY LONELY UP THERE IN THEM LABS ALL BY HIMSELF.
AIN'T THAT RIGHT, BUDDY?

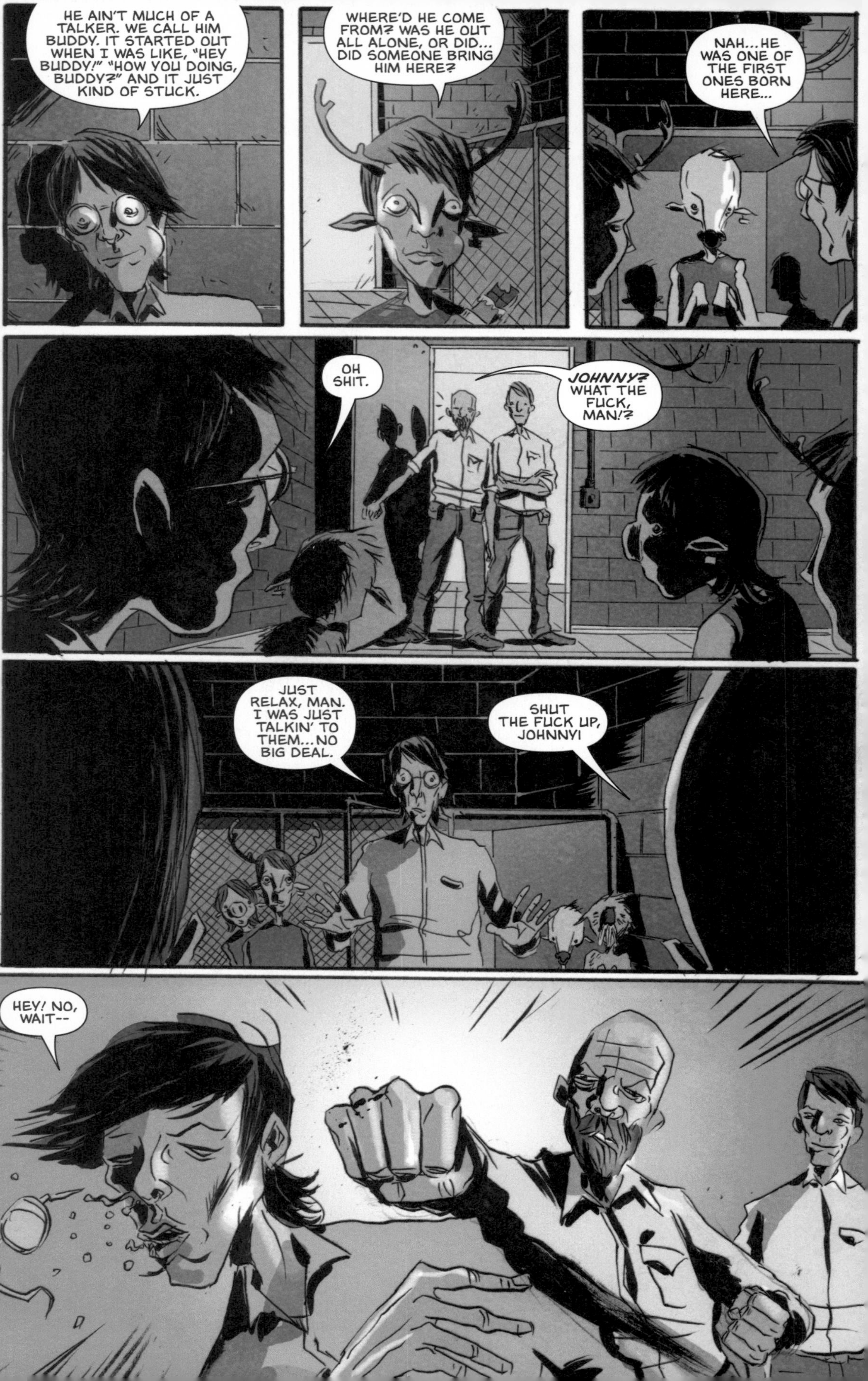

HE AIN'T MUCH OF A TALKER. WE CALL HIM BUDDY. IT STARTED OUT WHEN I WAS LIKE, "HEY BUDDY!" "HOW YOU DOING, BUDDY?" AND IT JUST KIND OF STUCK.
WHERE'D HE COME FROM? WAS HE OUT ALL ALONE, OR DID... DID SOMEONE BRING HIM HERE?
NAH... HE WAS ONE OF THE FIRST ONES BORN HERE...
OH SHIT.
JOHNNY? WHAT THE FUCK, MAN!?
JUST RELAX, MAN. I WAS JUST TALKIN' TO THEM... NO BIG DEAL.
SHUT THE FUCK UP, JOHNNY!
HEY! NO, WAIT--

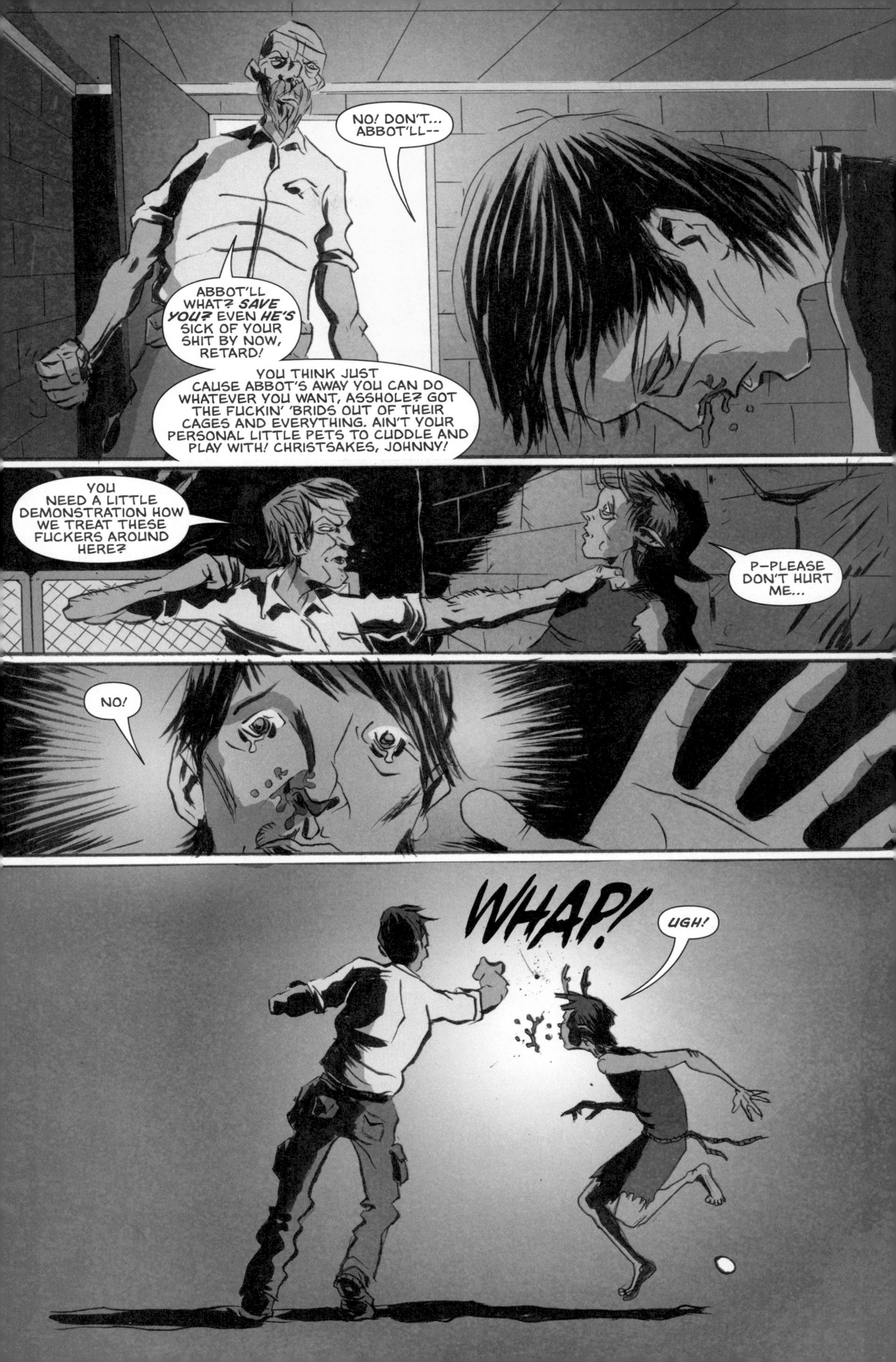
NO! DON'T... ABBOT'LL--
ABBOT'LL WHAT? **SAVE YOU?** EVEN **HE'S** SICK OF YOUR SHIT BY NOW, RETARD!
YOU THINK JUST CAUSE ABBOT'S AWAY YOU CAN DO WHATEVER YOU WANT, ASSHOLE? GOT THE FUCKIN' 'BRIDS OUT OF THEIR CAGES AND EVERYTHING. AIN'T YOUR PERSONAL LITTLE PETS TO CUDDLE AND PLAY WITH! CHRISTSAKES, JOHNNY!
YOU NEED A LITTLE DEMONSTRATION HOW WE TREAT THESE FUCKERS AROUND HERE?
P-PLEASE DON'T HURT ME...
NO!
WHAP!
UGH!

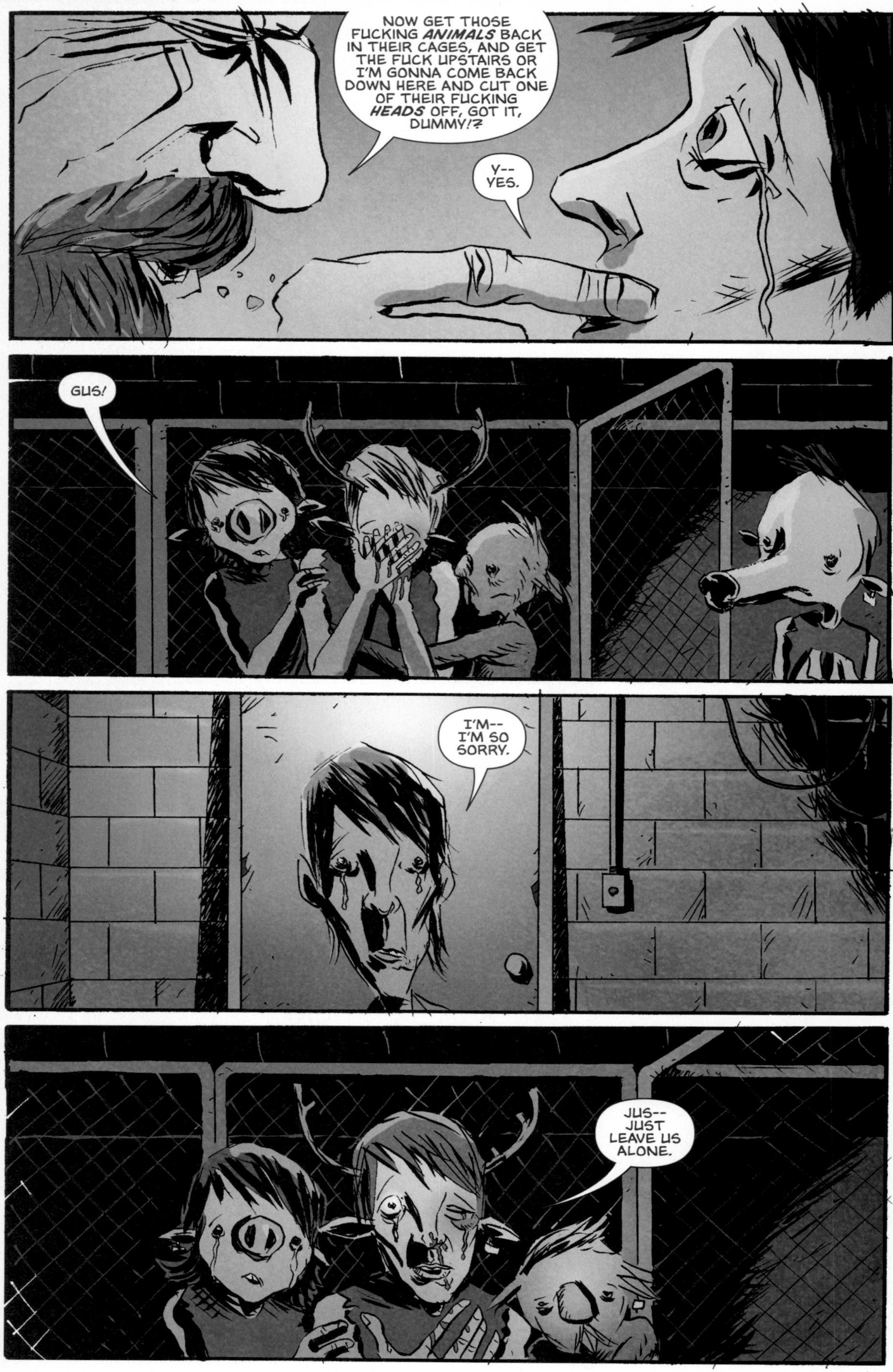
NOW GET THOSE FUCKING ANIMALS BACK IN THEIR CAGES, AND GET THE FUCK UPSTAIRS OR I'M GONNA COME BACK DOWN HERE AND CUT ONE OF THEIR FUCKING HEADS OFF, GOT IT, DUMMY!?
Y-- YES.
GUS!
I'M-- I'M SO SORRY.
JUS-- JUST LEAVE US ALONE.

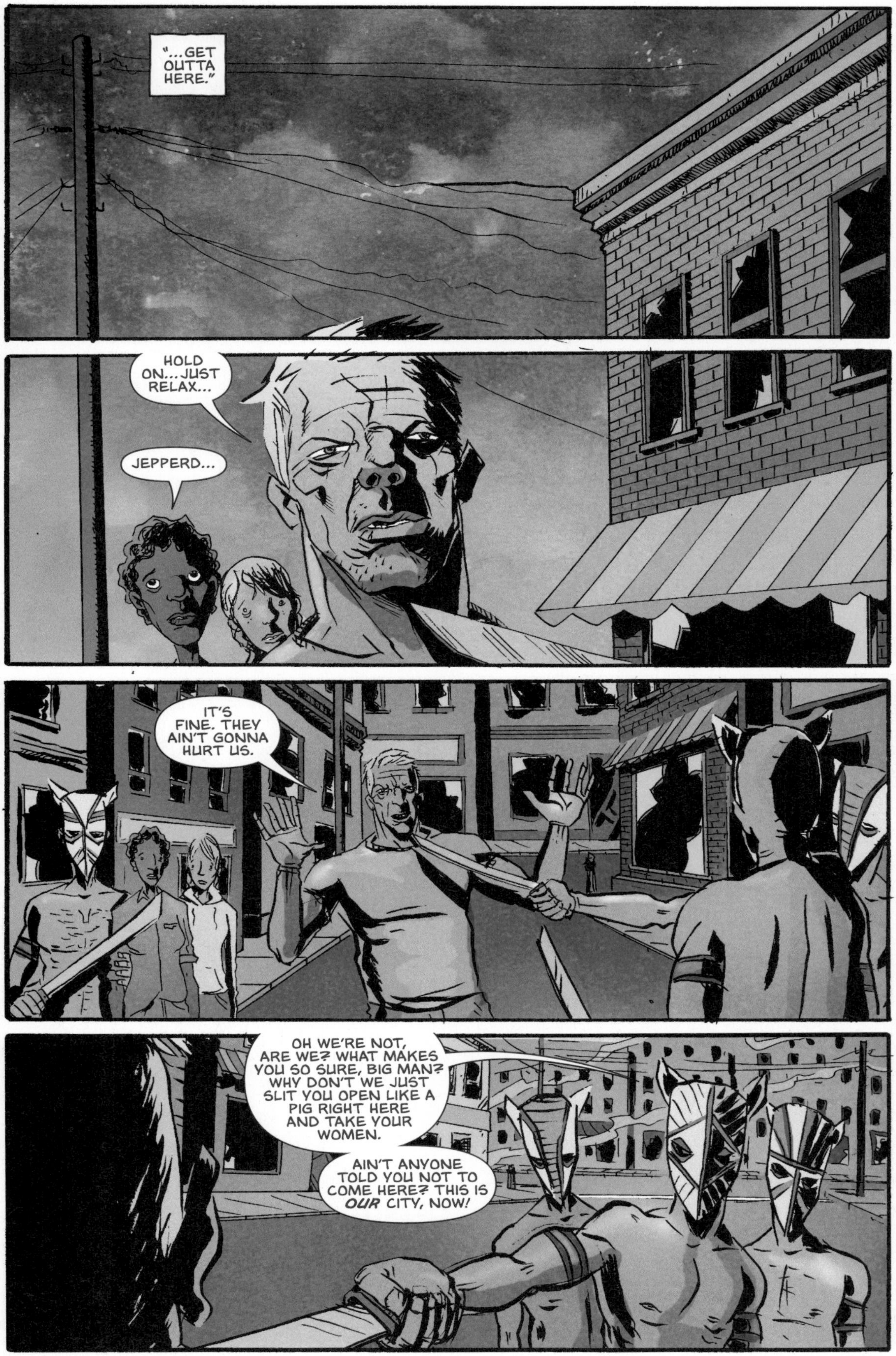
"...GET OUTTA HERE."
HOLD ON...JUST RELAX...
JEPPERD...
IT'S FINE. THEY AIN'T GONNA HURT US.
OH WE'RE NOT, ARE WE? WHAT MAKES YOU SO SURE, BIG MAN? WHY DON'T WE JUST SLIT YOU OPEN LIKE A PIG RIGHT HERE AND TAKE YOUR WOMEN.
AIN'T ANYONE TOLD YOU NOT TO COME HERE? THIS IS *OUR* CITY, NOW!

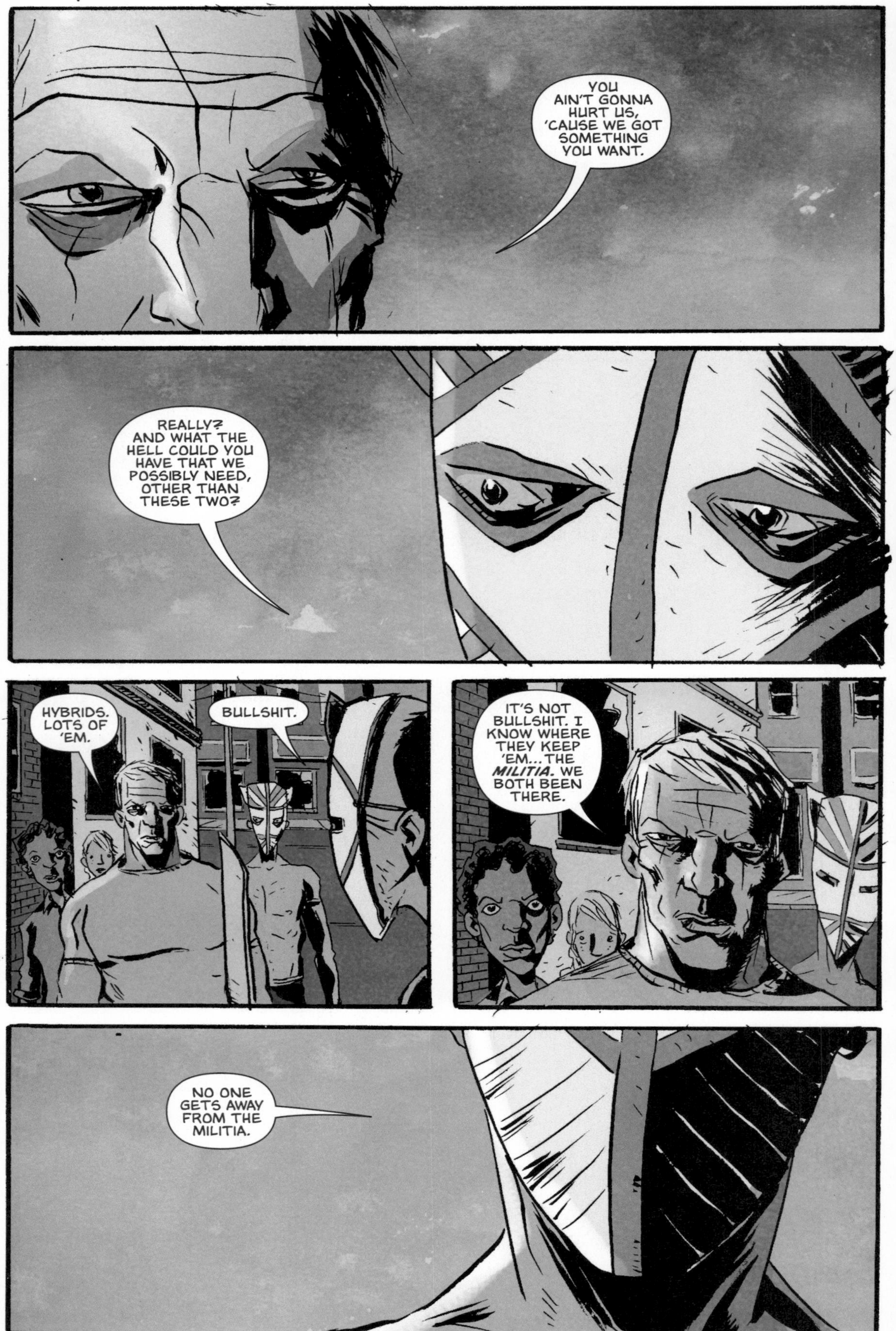
YOU AIN'T GONNA HURT US, 'CAUSE WE GOT SOMETHING YOU WANT.
REALLY? AND WHAT THE HELL COULD YOU HAVE THAT WE POSSIBLY NEED, OTHER THAN THESE TWO?
HYBRIDS. LOTS OF 'EM.
BULLSHIT.
IT'S NOT BULLSHIT. I KNOW WHERE THEY KEEP 'EM... THE *MILITIA.* WE BOTH BEEN THERE.
NO ONE GETS AWAY FROM THE MILITIA.

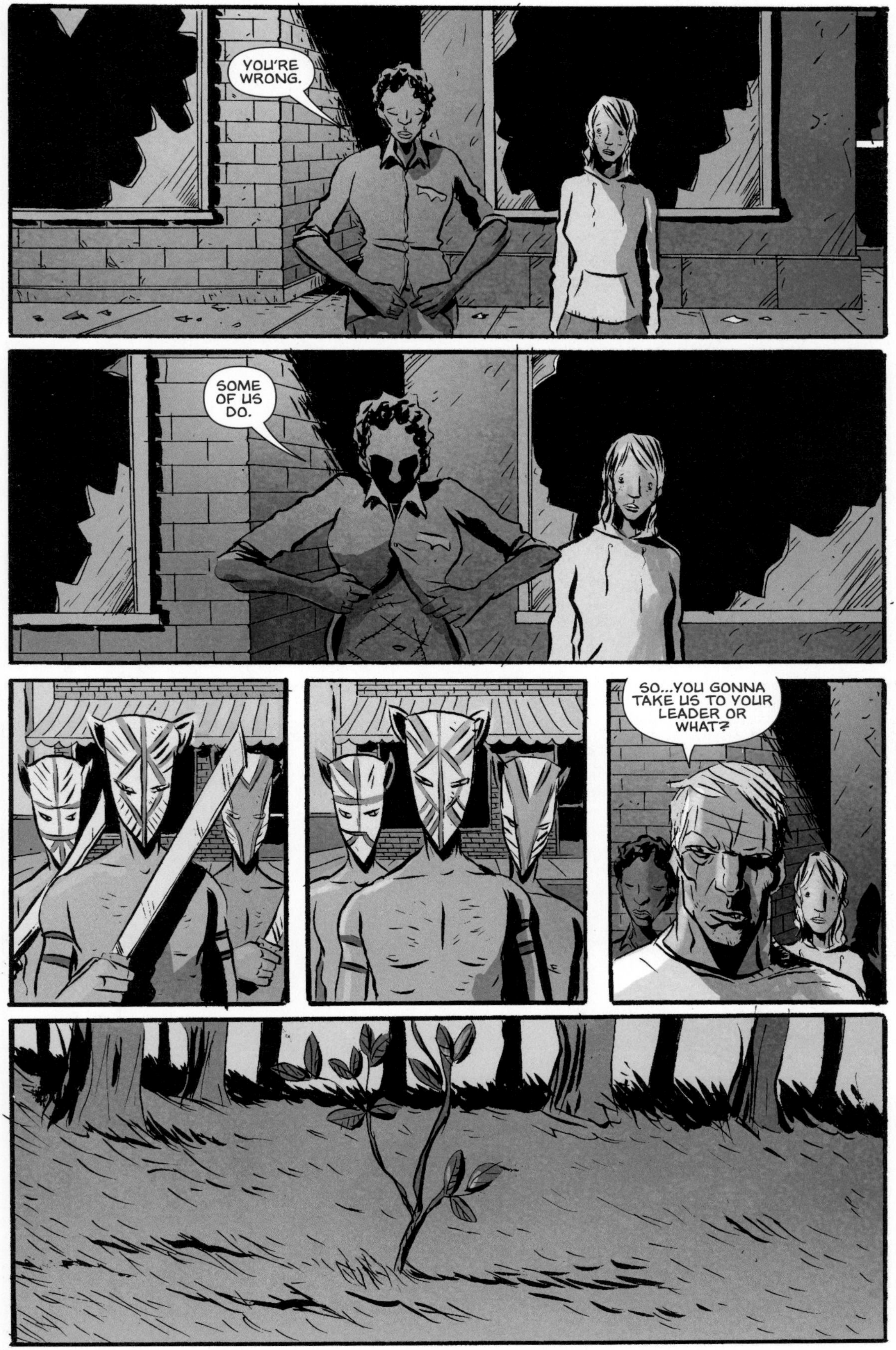
YOU'RE WRONG.
SOME OF US DO.
SO...YOU GONNA TAKE US TO YOUR LEADER OR WHAT?

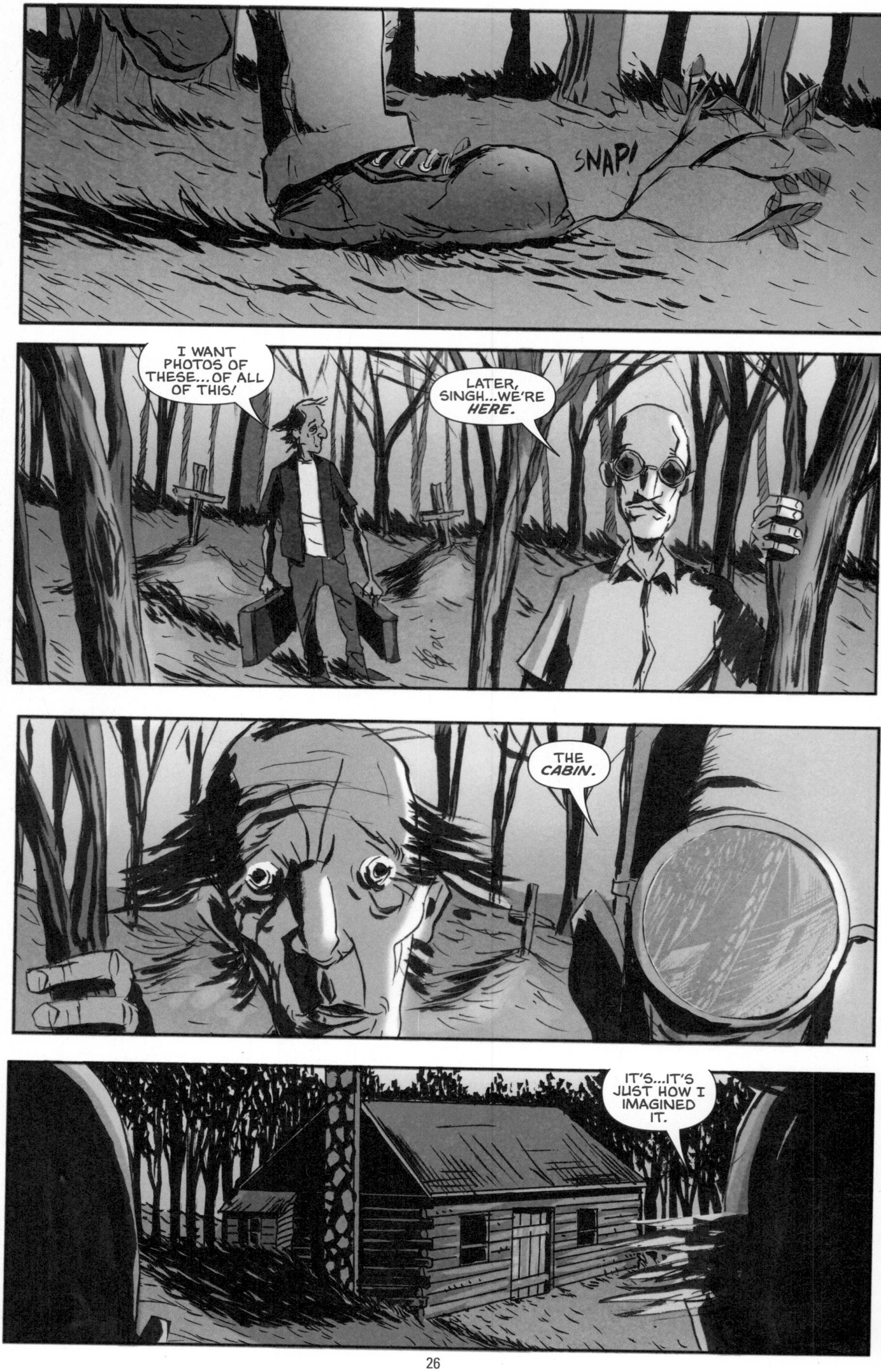
SNAP!
I WANT PHOTOS OF THESE...OF ALL OF THIS!
LATER, SINGH...WE'RE *HERE.*
THE *CABIN.*
IT'S...IT'S JUST HOW I IMAGINED IT.

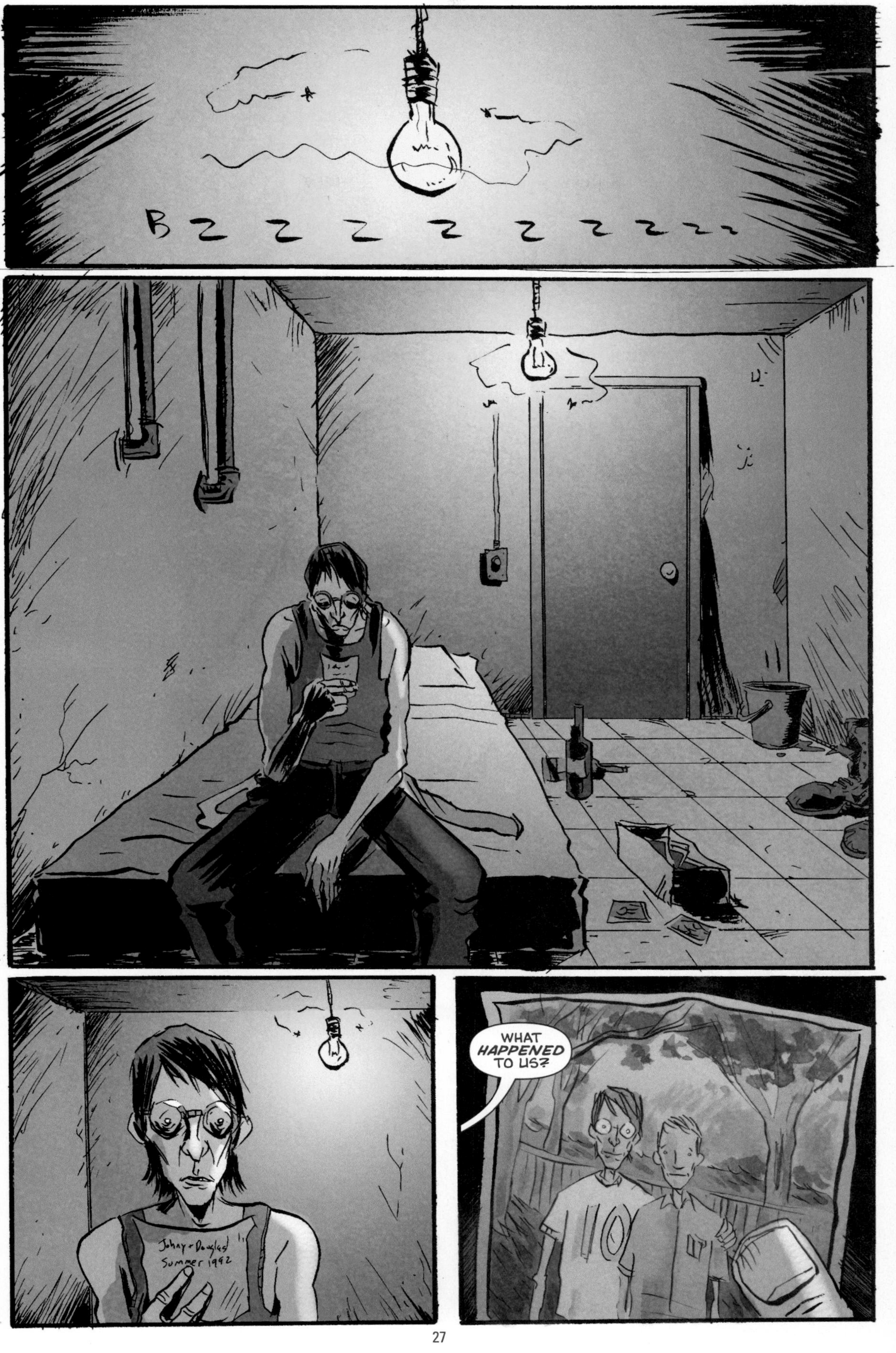

BZZZZZZZZZ
Johny + Douglas
Summer 1992
WHAT *HAPPENED* TO US?

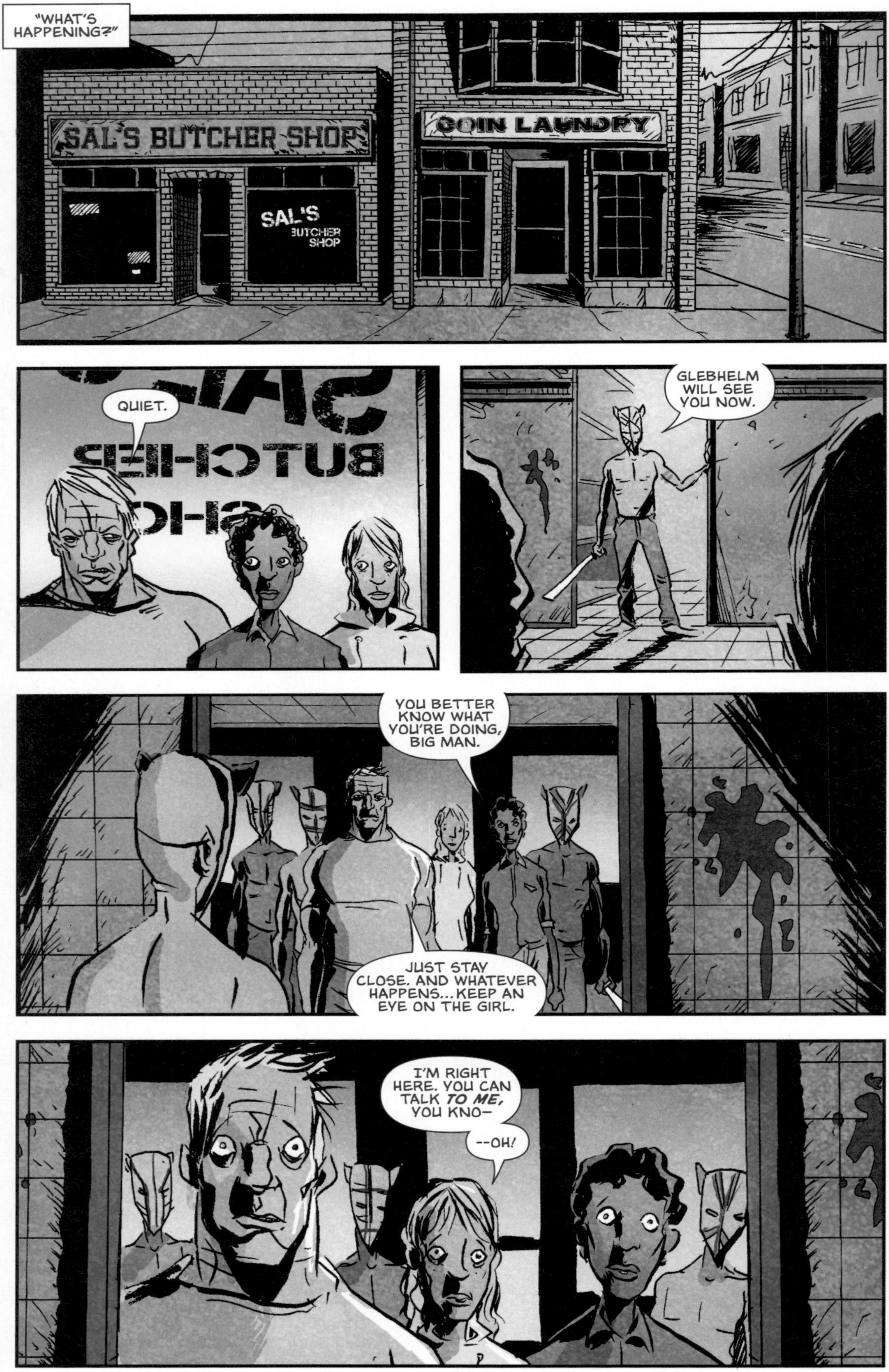
"WHAT'S HAPPENING?"
SAL'S BUTCHER SHOP
COIN LAUNDRY
SAL'S BUTCHER SHOP
QUIET.
GLEBHELM WILL SEE YOU NOW.
YOU BETTER KNOW WHAT YOU'RE DOING, BIG MAN.
JUST STAY CLOSE. AND WHATEVER HAPPENS... KEEP AN EYE ON THE GIRL.
I'M RIGHT HERE. YOU CAN TALK *TO ME,* YOU KNO—
--OH!

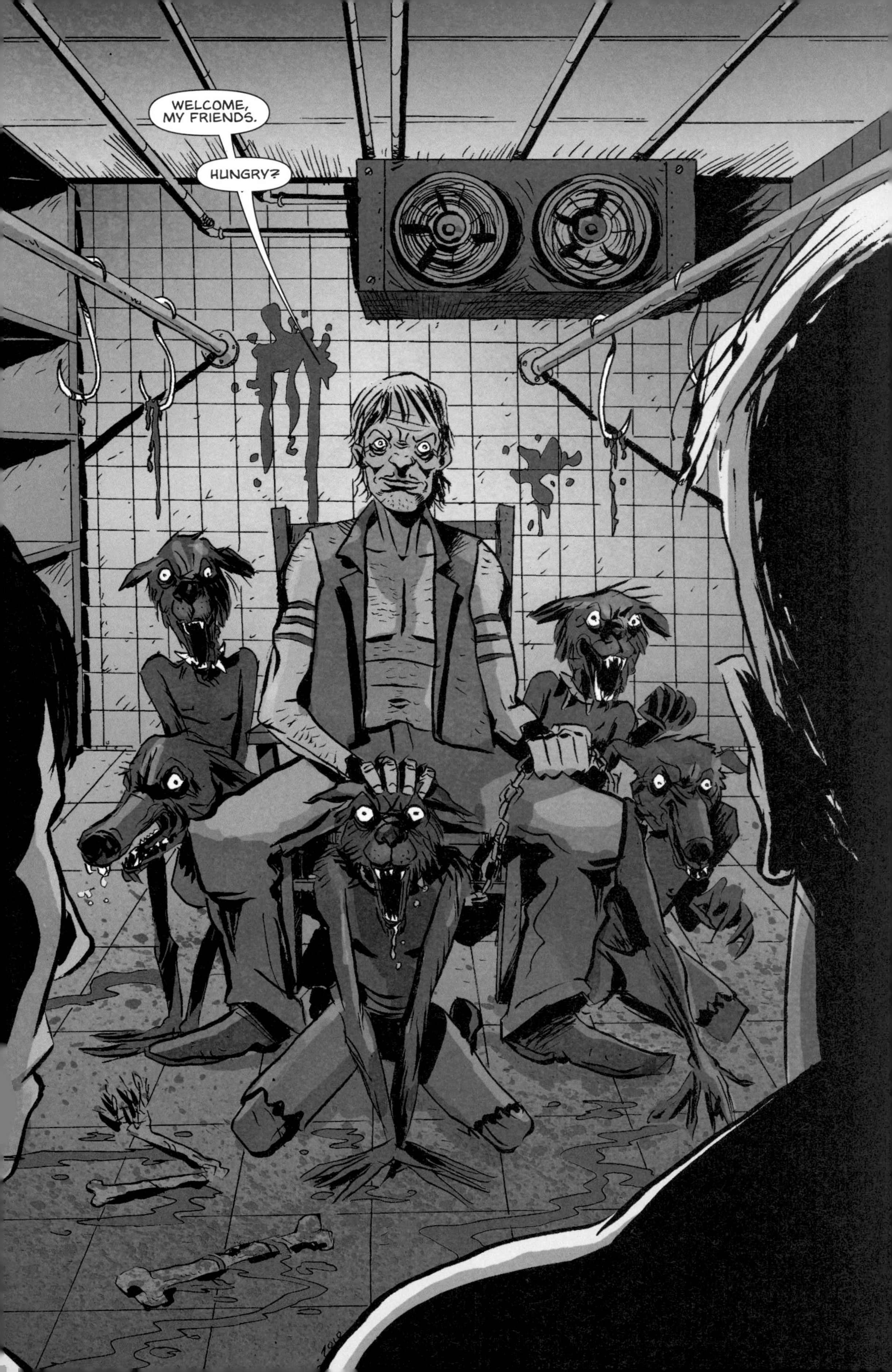
WELCOME, MY FRIENDS.
HUNGRY?

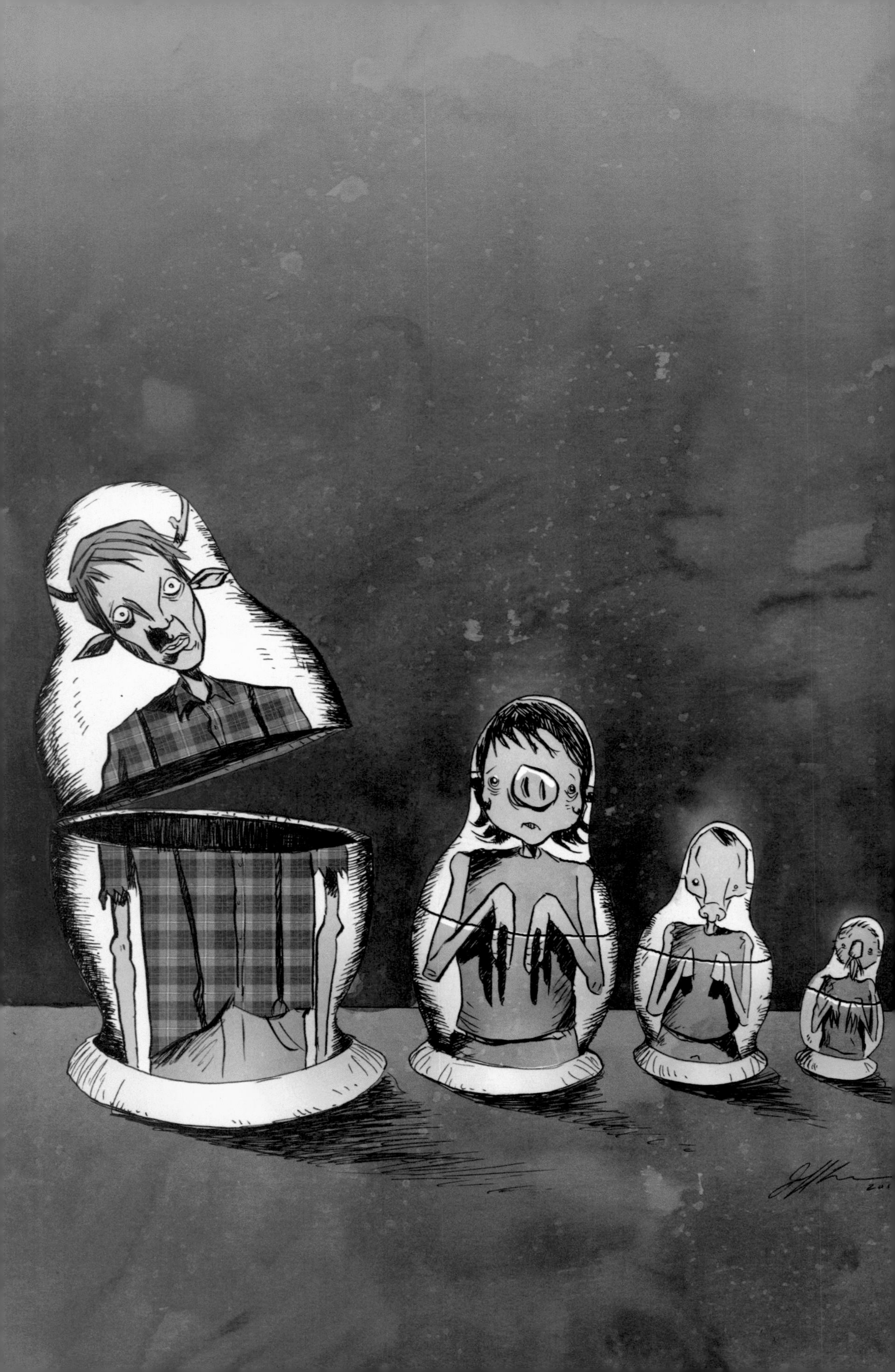

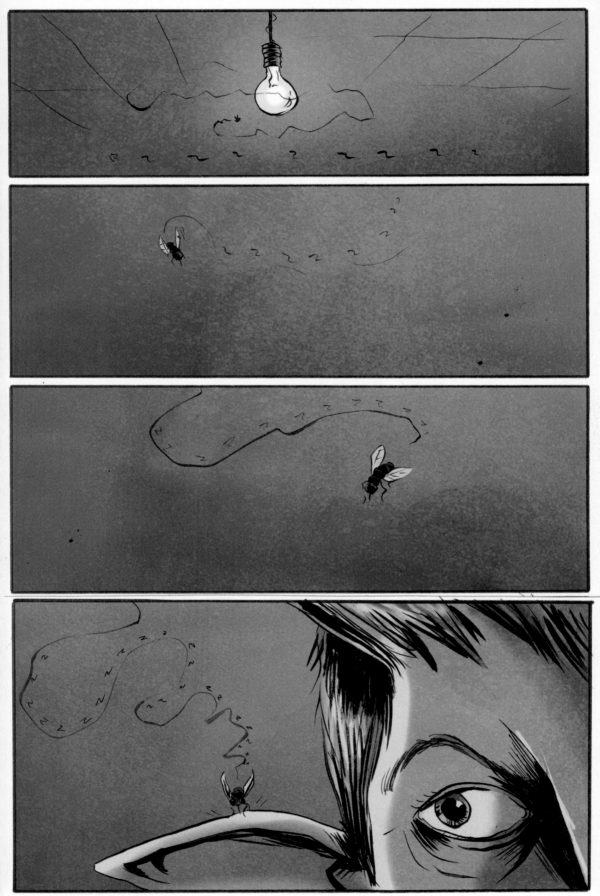

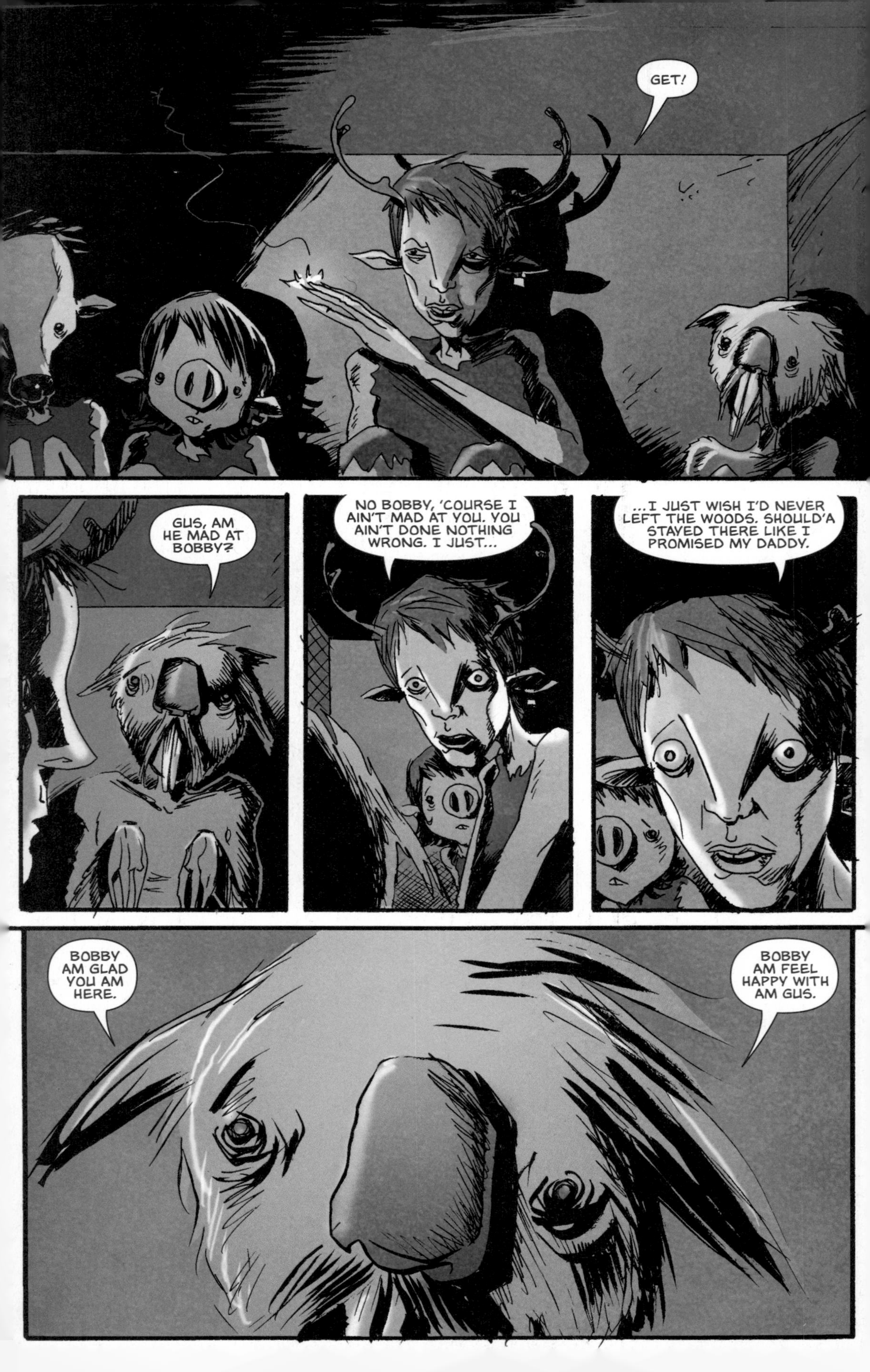
GET!
GUS, AM HE MAD AT BOBBY?
NO BOBBY, 'COURSE I AIN'T MAD AT YOU. YOU AIN'T DONE NOTHING WRONG. I JUST...
...I JUST WISH I'D NEVER LEFT THE WOODS. SHOULD'A STAYED THERE LIKE I PROMISED MY DADDY.
BOBBY AM GLAD YOU AM HERE.
BOBBY AM FEEL HAPPY WITH AM GUS.

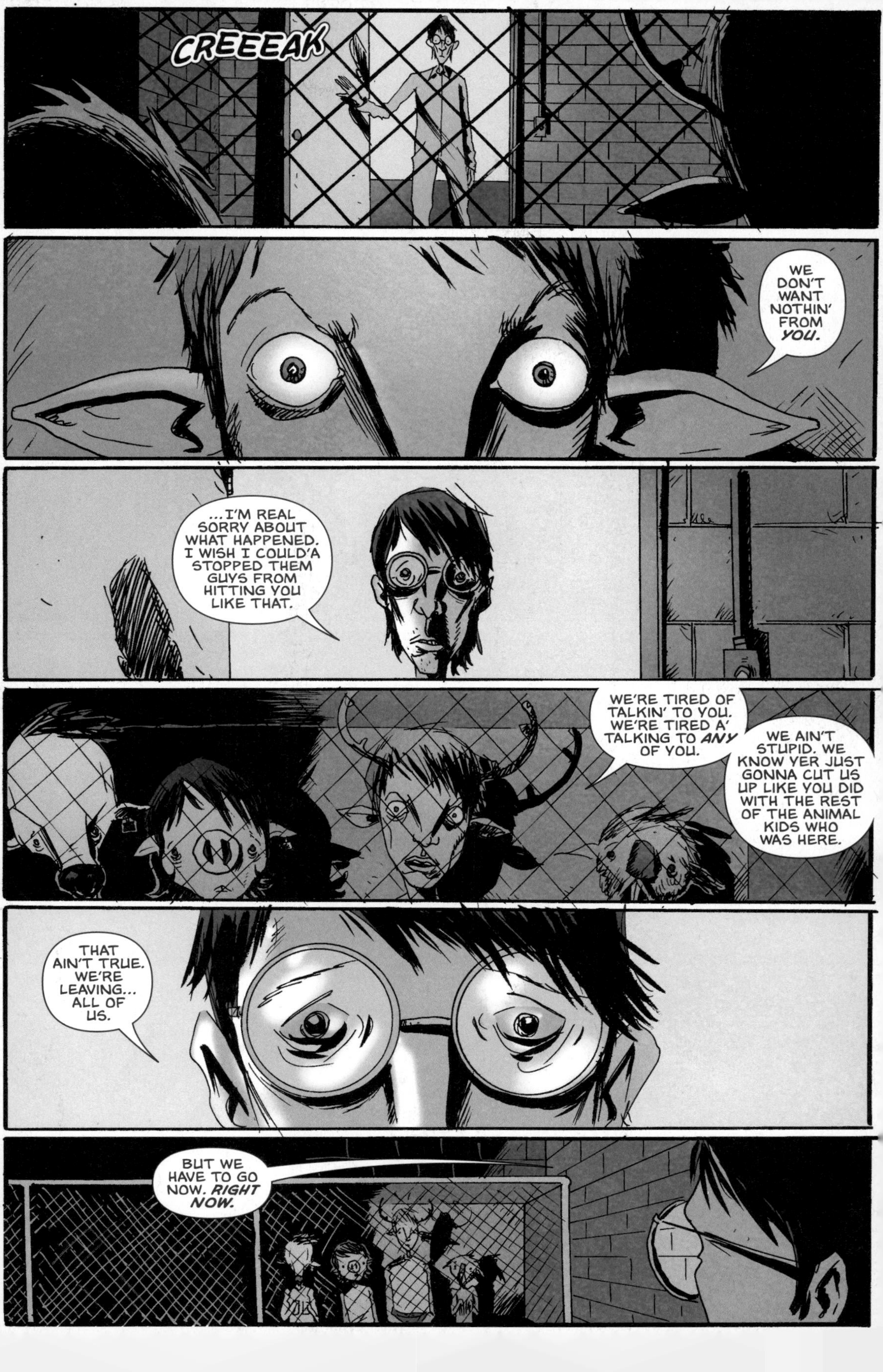
CREEEAK
WE DON'T WANT NOTHIN' FROM *YOU.*
...I'M REAL SORRY ABOUT WHAT HAPPENED. I WISH I COULD'A STOPPED THEM GUYS FROM HITTING YOU LIKE THAT.
WE'RE TIRED OF TALKIN' TO YOU. WE'RE TIRED A' TALKING TO *ANY* OF YOU.
WE AIN'T STUPID. WE KNOW YER JUST GONNA CUT US UP LIKE YOU DID WITH THE REST OF THE ANIMAL KIDS WHO WAS HERE.
THAT AIN'T TRUE. WE'RE LEAVING... ALL OF US.
BUT WE HAVE TO GO NOW. *RIGHT NOW.*

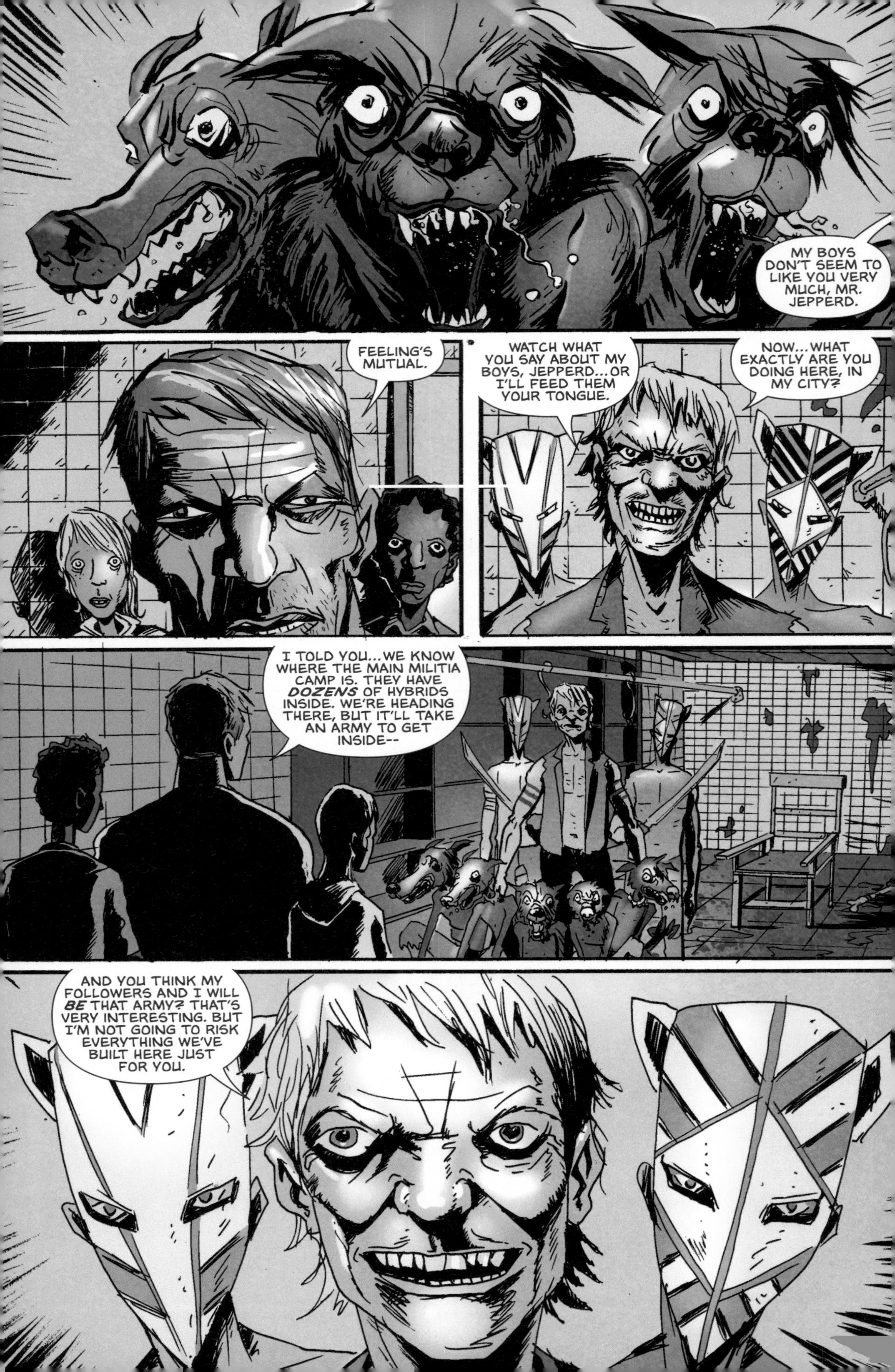
MY BOYS DON'T SEEM TO LIKE YOU VERY MUCH, MR. JEPPERD.
FEELING'S MUTUAL.
WATCH WHAT YOU SAY ABOUT MY BOYS, JEPPERD...OR I'LL FEED THEM YOUR TONGUE.
NOW...WHAT EXACTLY ARE YOU DOING HERE, IN MY CITY?
I TOLD YOU...WE KNOW WHERE THE MAIN MILITIA CAMP IS. THEY HAVE *DOZENS* OF HYBRIDS INSIDE. WE'RE HEADING THERE, BUT IT'LL TAKE AN ARMY TO GET INSIDE--
AND YOU THINK MY FOLLOWERS AND I WILL *BE* THAT ARMY? THAT'S VERY INTERESTING. BUT I'M NOT GOING TO RISK EVERYTHING WE'VE BUILT HERE JUST FOR YOU.

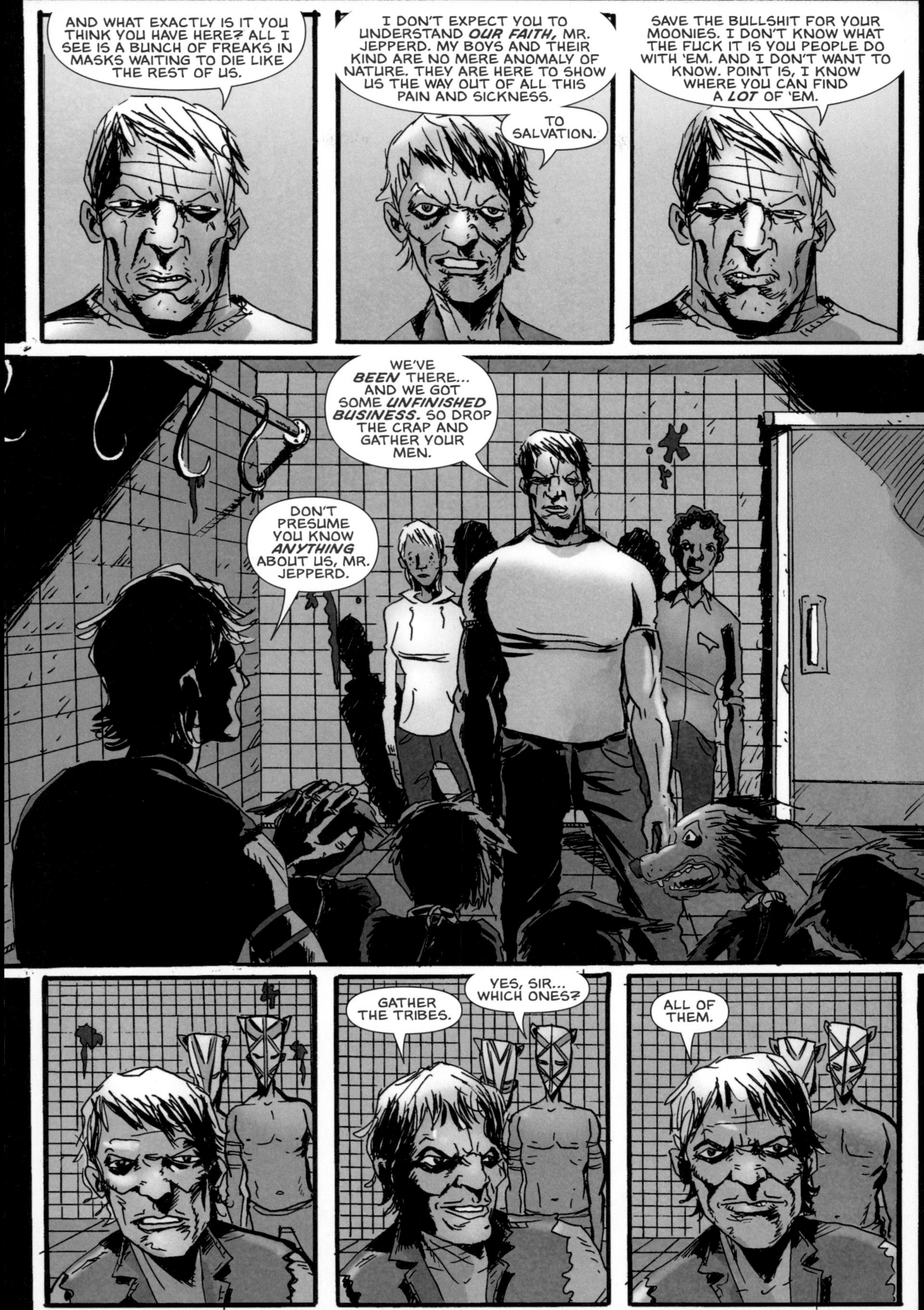
AND WHAT EXACTLY IS IT YOU THINK YOU HAVE HERE? ALL I SEE IS A BUNCH OF FREAKS IN MASKS WAITING TO DIE LIKE THE REST OF US.
I DON'T EXPECT YOU TO UNDERSTAND OUR FAITH, MR. JEPPERD. MY BOYS AND THEIR KIND ARE NO MERE ANOMALY OF NATURE. THEY ARE HERE TO SHOW US THE WAY OUT OF ALL THIS PAIN AND SICKNESS.
TO SALVATION.
SAVE THE BULLSHIT FOR YOUR MOONIES. I DON'T KNOW WHAT THE FUCK IT IS YOU PEOPLE DO WITH 'EM. AND I DON'T WANT TO KNOW. POINT IS, I KNOW WHERE YOU CAN FIND A LOT OF 'EM.
WE'VE BEEN THERE... AND WE GOT SOME UNFINISHED BUSINESS. SO DROP THE CRAP AND GATHER YOUR MEN.
DON'T PRESUME YOU KNOW ANYTHING ABOUT US, MR. JEPPERD.
GATHER THE TRIBES.
YES, SIR... WHICH ONES?
ALL OF THEM.

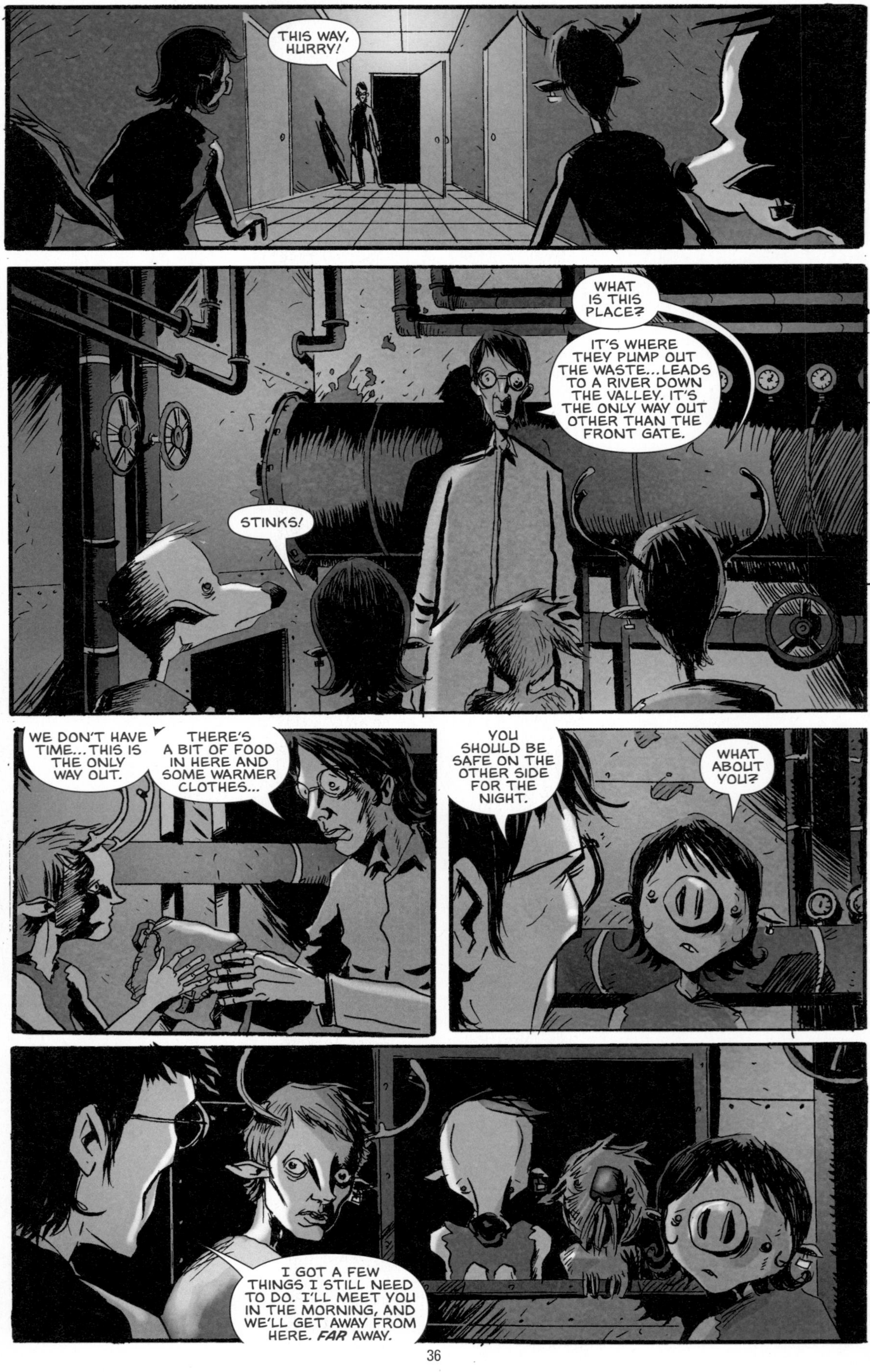
THIS WAY, HURRY!
WHAT IS THIS PLACE?
IT'S WHERE THEY PUMP OUT THE WASTE...LEADS TO A RIVER DOWN THE VALLEY. IT'S THE ONLY WAY OUT OTHER THAN THE FRONT GATE.
STINKS!
WE DON'T HAVE TIME...THIS IS THE ONLY WAY OUT.
THERE'S A BIT OF FOOD IN HERE AND SOME WARMER CLOTHES...
YOU SHOULD BE SAFE ON THE OTHER SIDE FOR THE NIGHT.
WHAT ABOUT YOU?
I GOT A FEW THINGS I STILL NEED TO DO. I'LL MEET YOU IN THE MORNING, AND WE'LL GET AWAY FROM HERE. FAR AWAY.

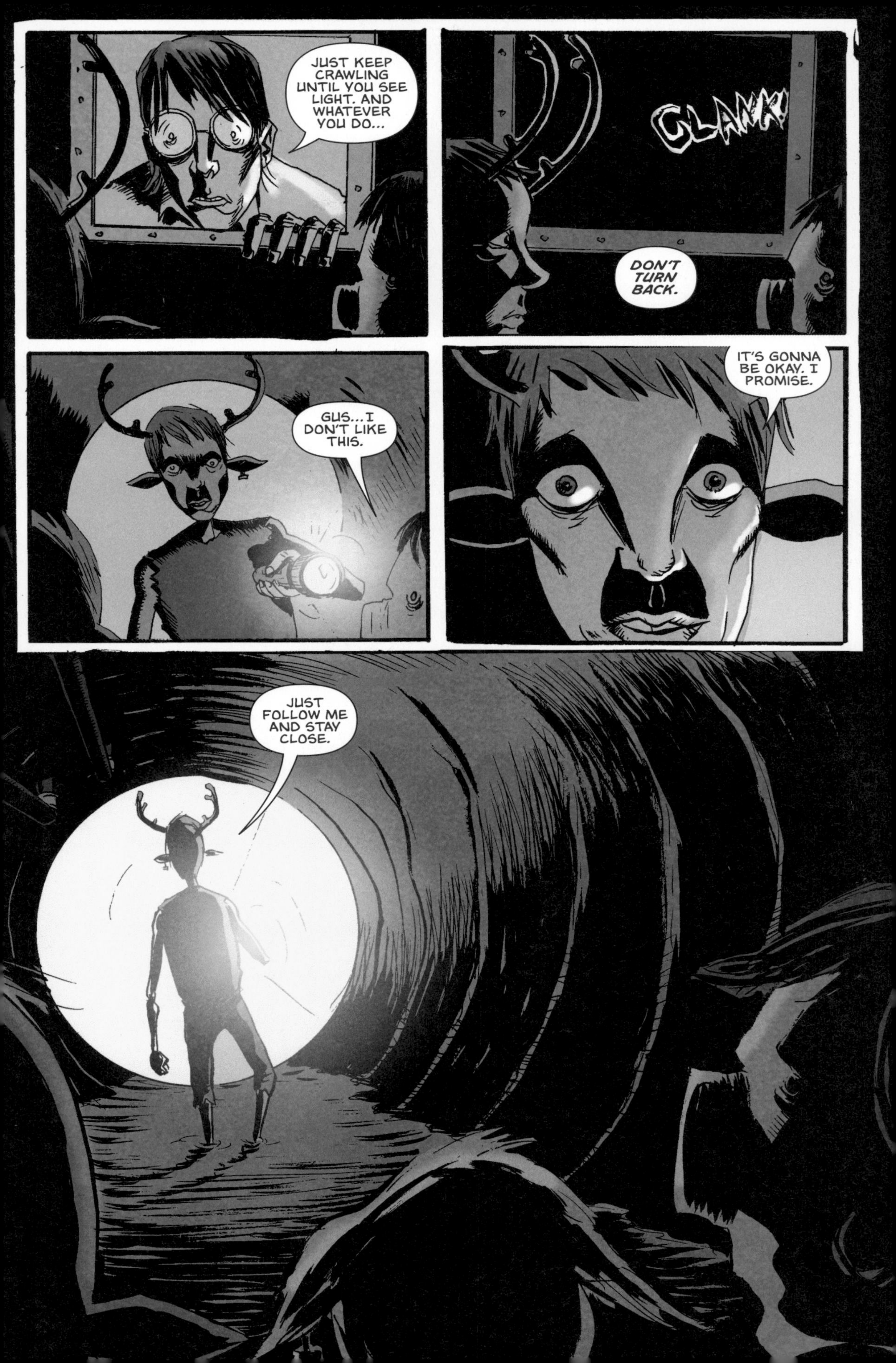
JUST KEEP CRAWLING UNTIL YOU SEE LIGHT. AND WHATEVER YOU DO...
CLANK!
DON'T TURN BACK.
GUS... I DON'T LIKE THIS.
IT'S GONNA BE OKAY. I PROMISE.
JUST FOLLOW ME AND STAY CLOSE.

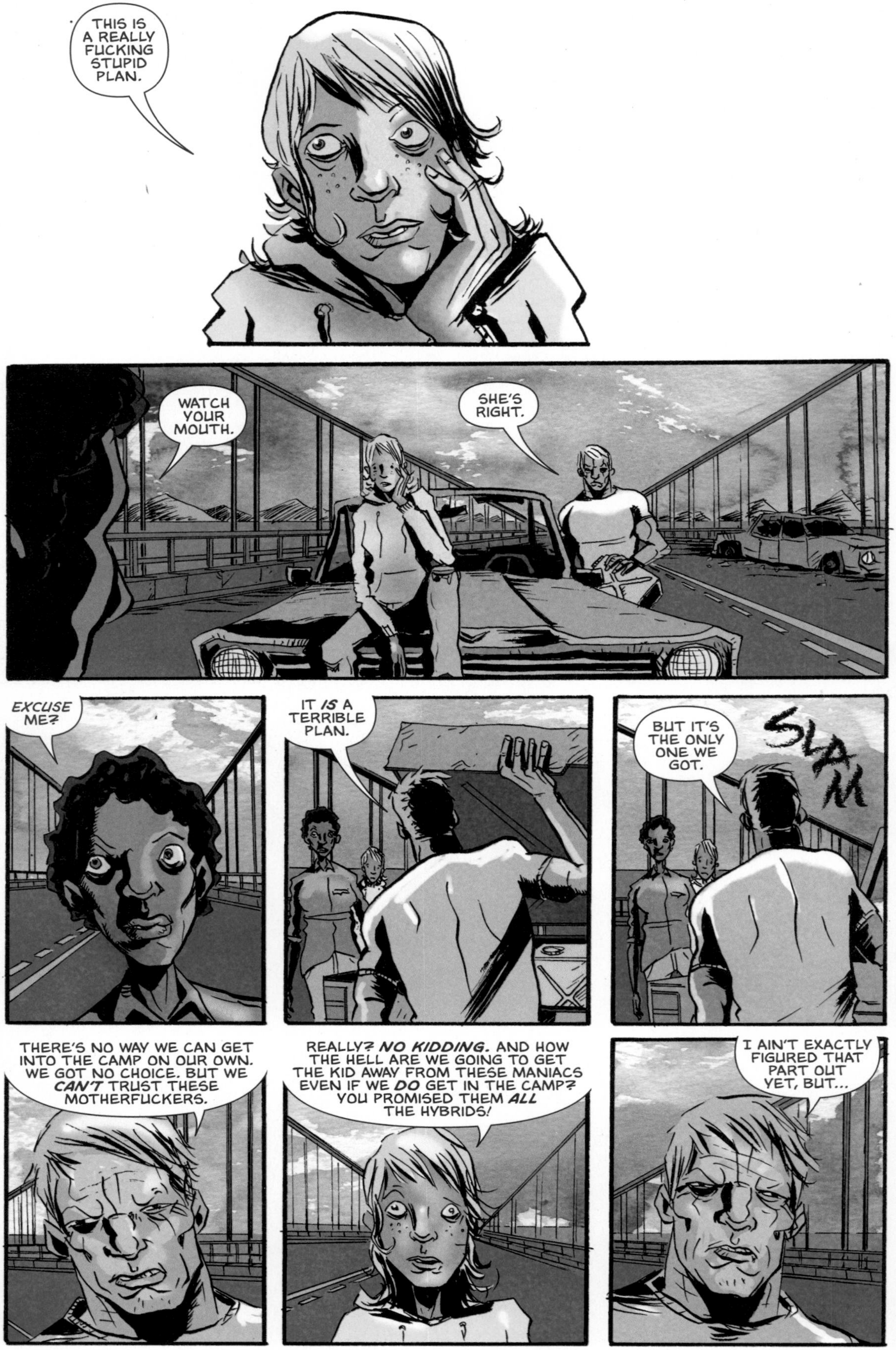
THIS IS A REALLY FUCKING STUPID PLAN.
WATCH YOUR MOUTH.
SHE'S RIGHT.
EXCUSE ME?
IT IS A TERRIBLE PLAN.
BUT IT'S THE ONLY ONE WE GOT.
SLAM
THERE'S NO WAY WE CAN GET INTO THE CAMP ON OUR OWN. WE GOT NO CHOICE. BUT WE CAN'T TRUST THESE MOTHERFUCKERS.
REALLY? NO KIDDING. AND HOW THE HELL ARE WE GOING TO GET THE KID AWAY FROM THESE MANIACS EVEN IF WE DO GET IN THE CAMP? YOU PROMISED THEM ALL THE HYBRIDS!
I AIN'T EXACTLY FIGURED THAT PART OUT YET, BUT...

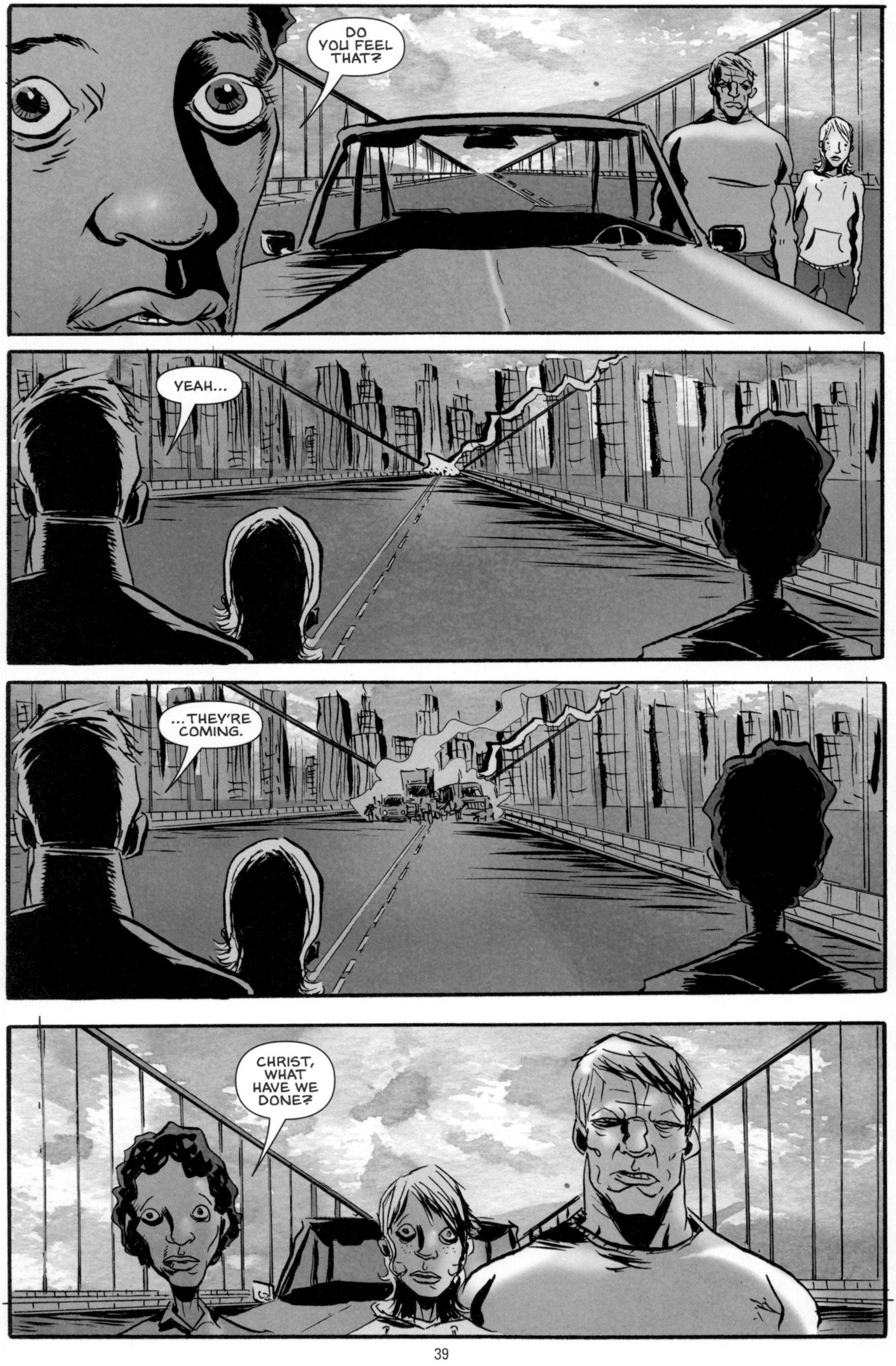
DO YOU FEEL THAT?
YEAH...
...THEY'RE COMING.
CHRIST, WHAT HAVE WE DONE?

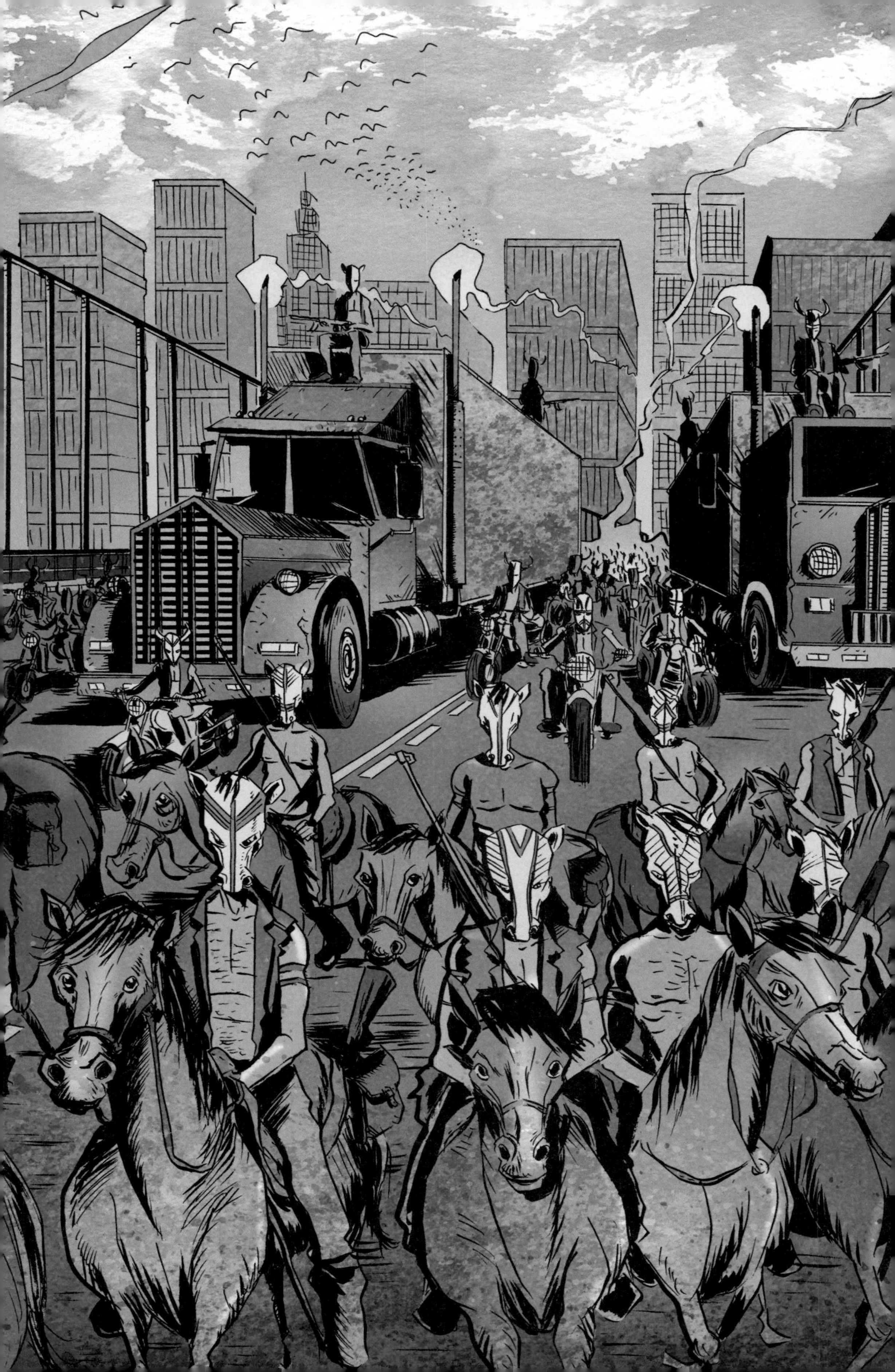

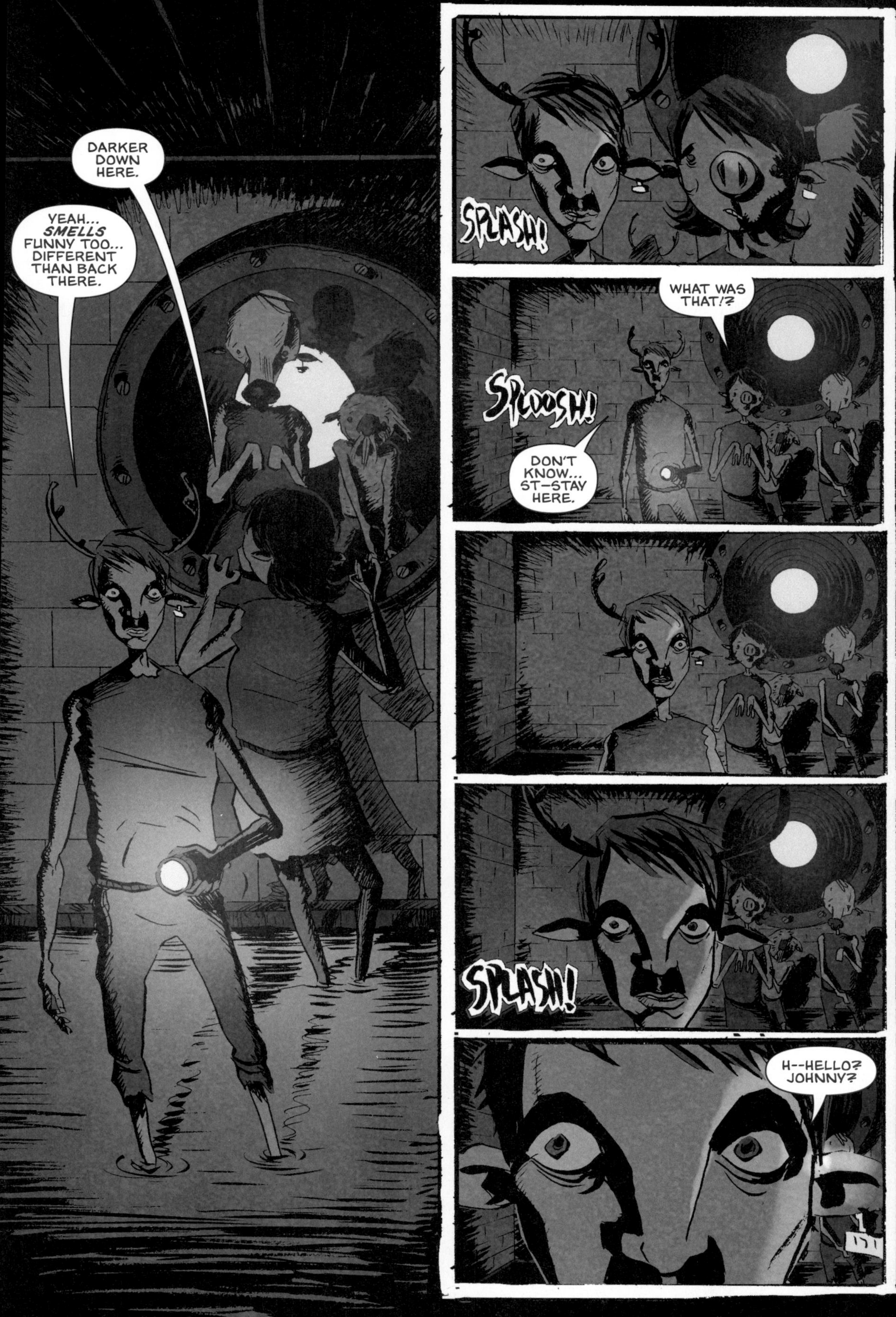
DARKER DOWN HERE.
YEAH... *SMELLS* FUNNY TOO... DIFFERENT THAN BACK THERE.
SPLASH!
WHAT WAS THAT!?
SPLOOSH!
DON'T KNOW... ST-STAY HERE.
SPLASH!
H--HELLO? JOHNNY?

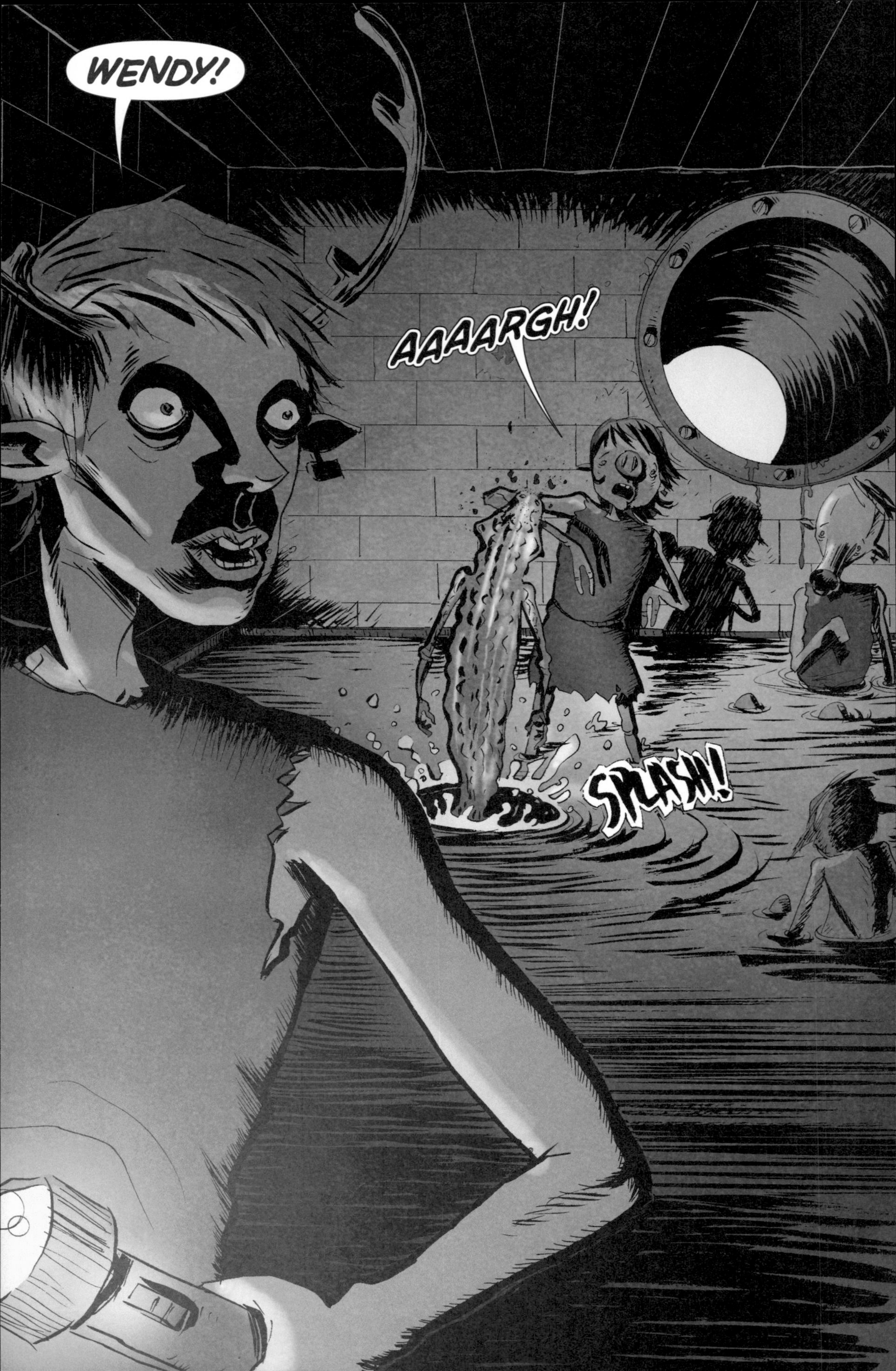
WENDY!
AAAARGH!
SPLASH!

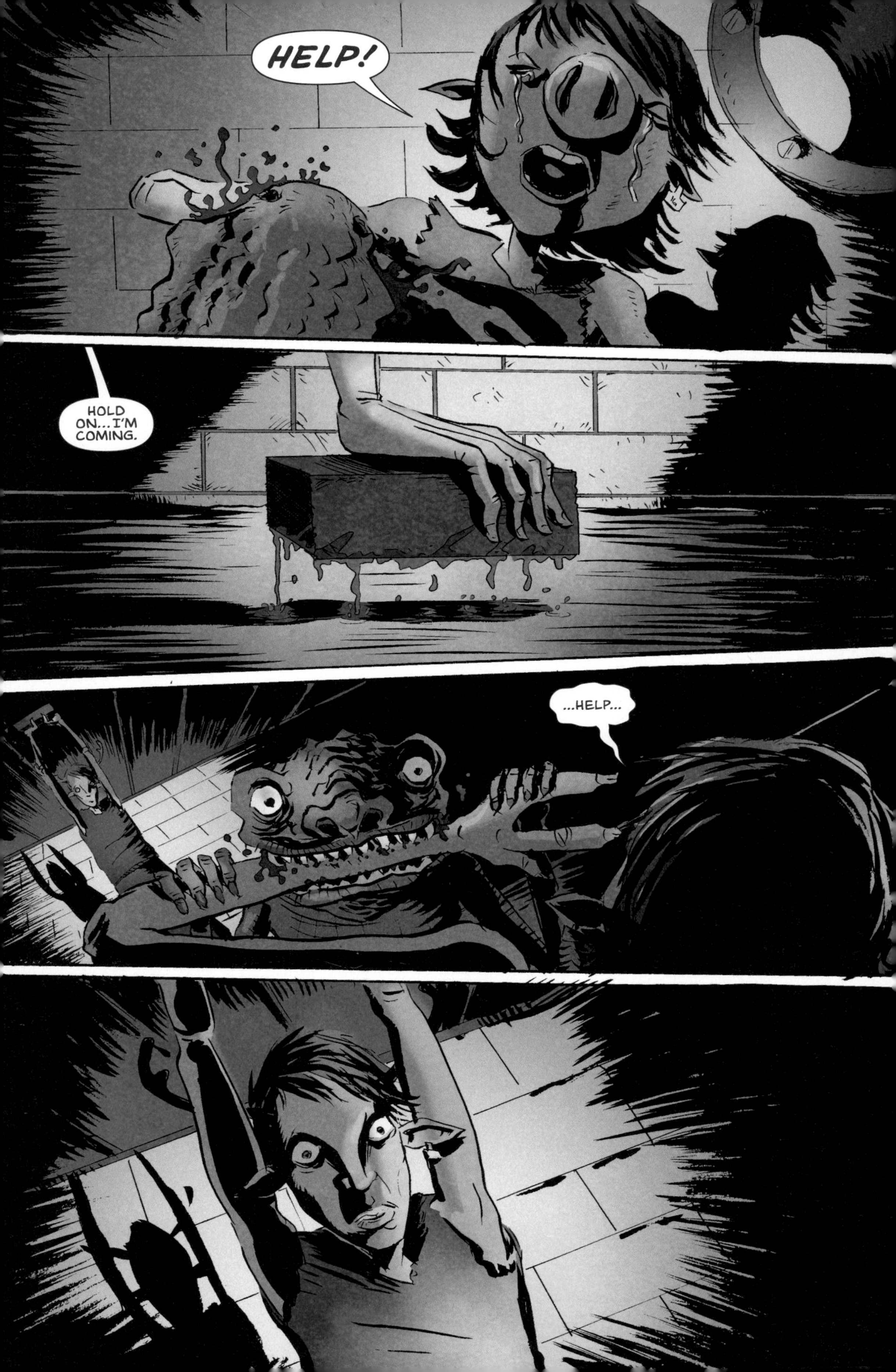
HELP!
HOLD ON... I'M COMING.
...HELP...

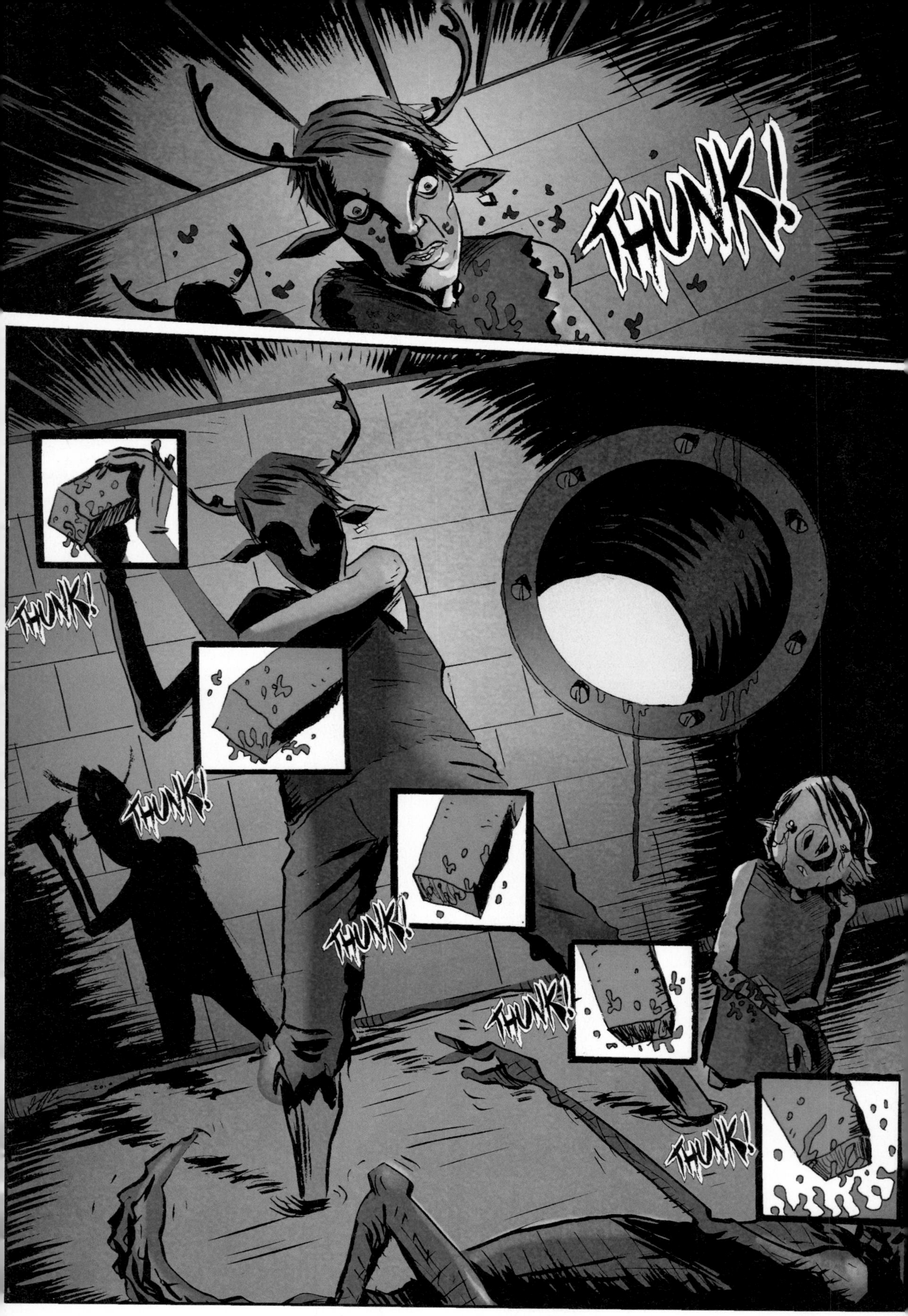
THUNK!
THUNK!
THUNK!
THUNK!
THUNK!
THUNK!

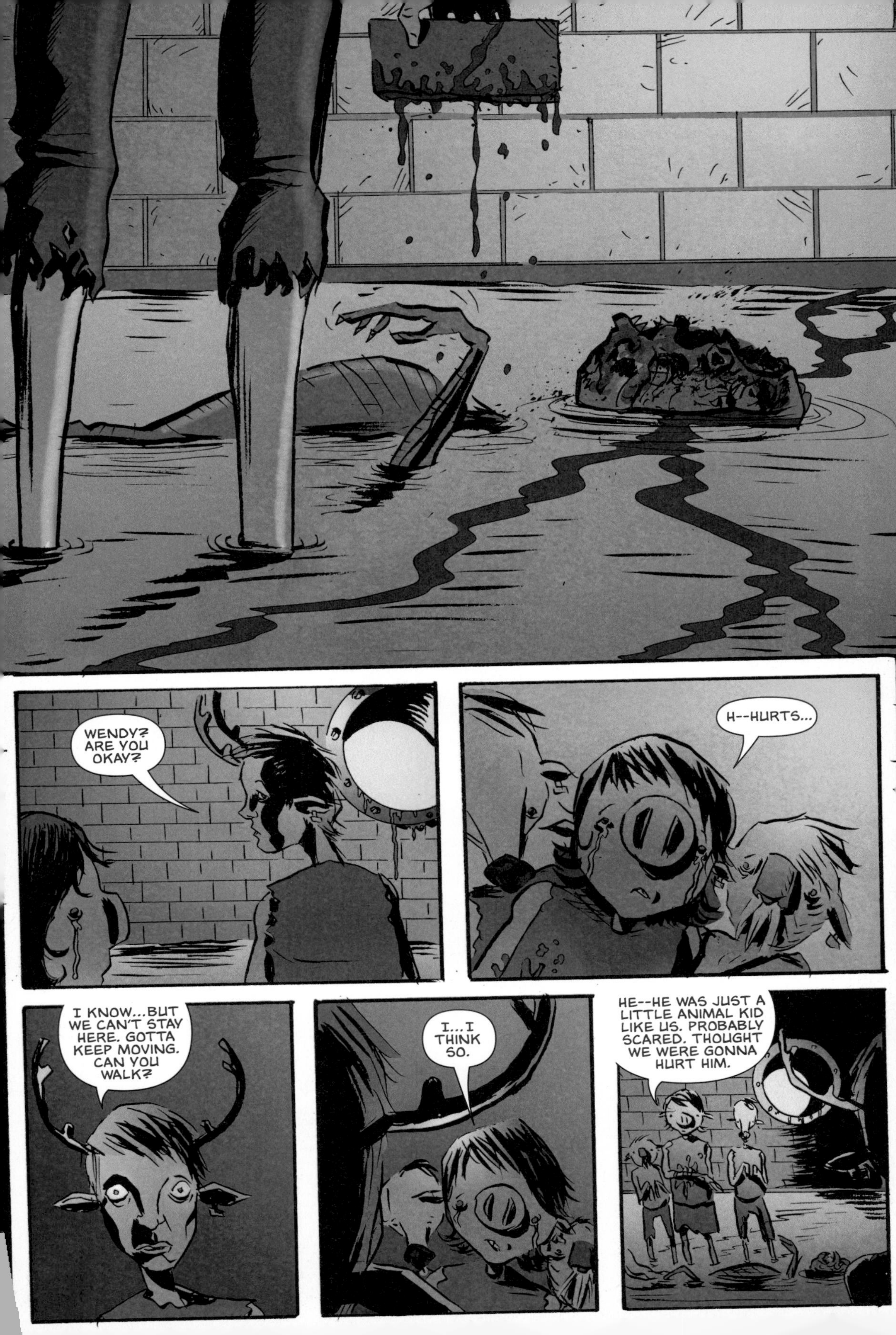
WENDY? ARE YOU OKAY?
H--HURTS...
I KNOW...BUT WE CAN'T STAY HERE. GOTTA KEEP MOVING. CAN YOU WALK?
I...I THINK SO.
HE--HE WAS JUST A LITTLE ANIMAL KID LIKE US. PROBABLY SCARED. THOUGHT WE WERE GONNA HURT HIM.

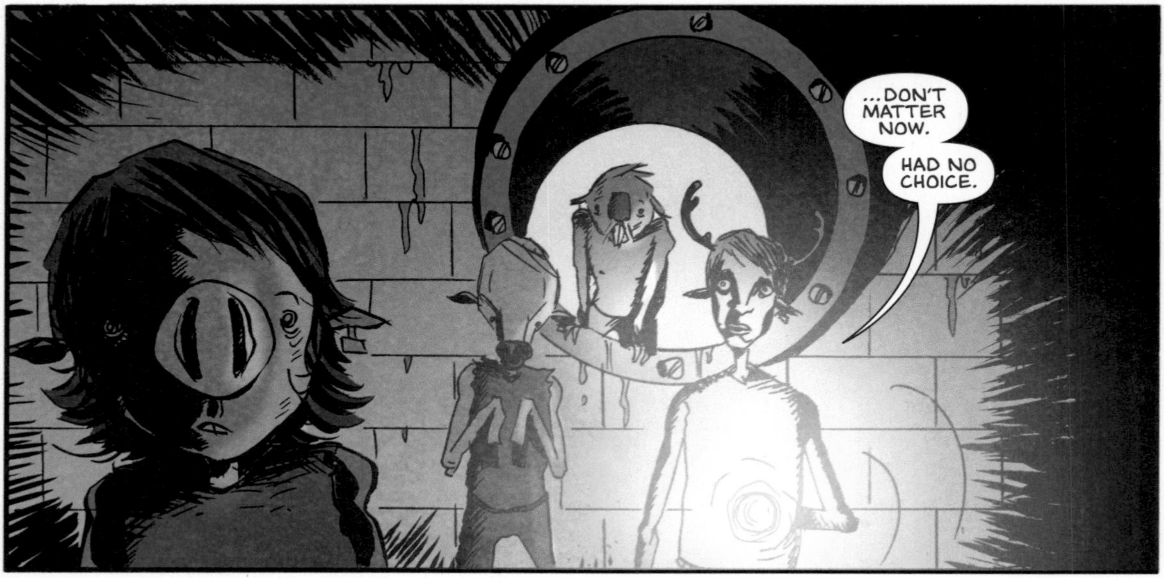
...DON'T MATTER NOW.
HAD NO CHOICE.

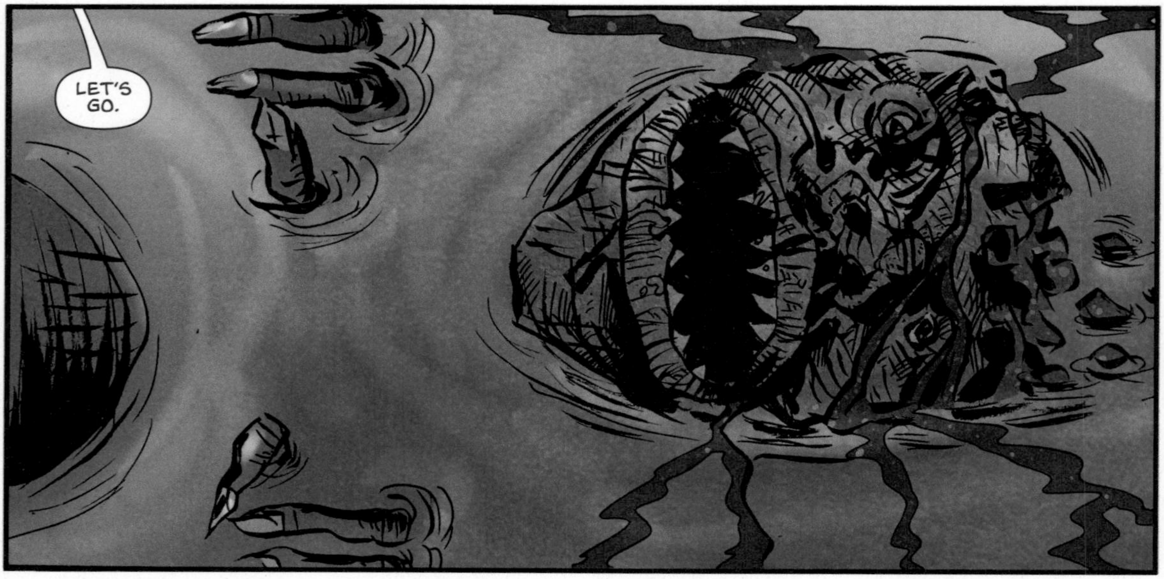
LET'S GO.

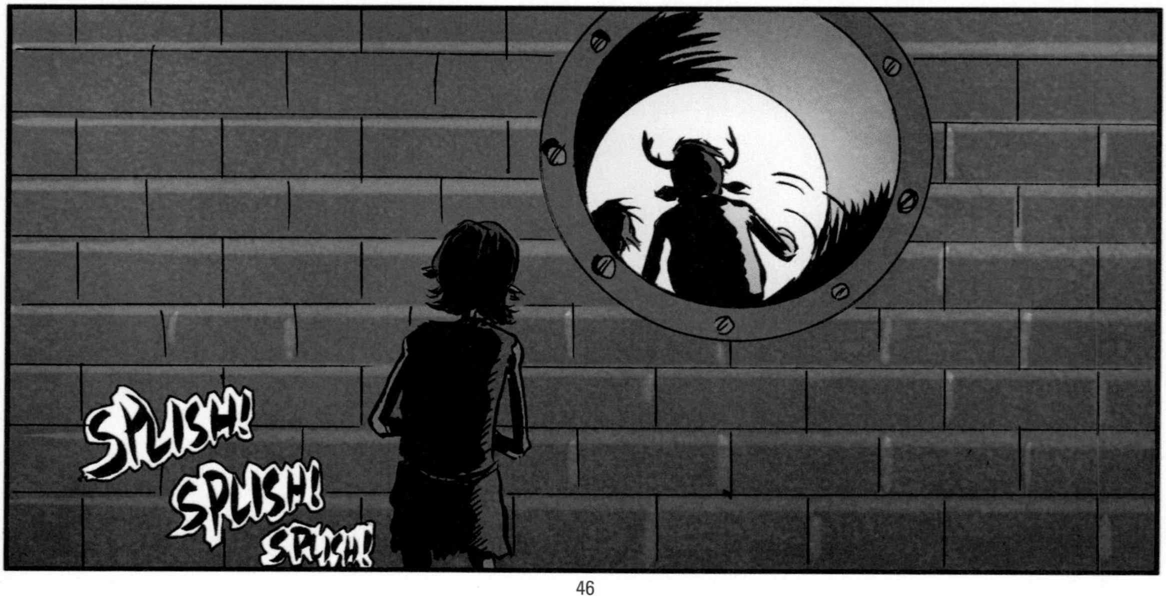
SPLISH!
SPLISH!
SPLISH!

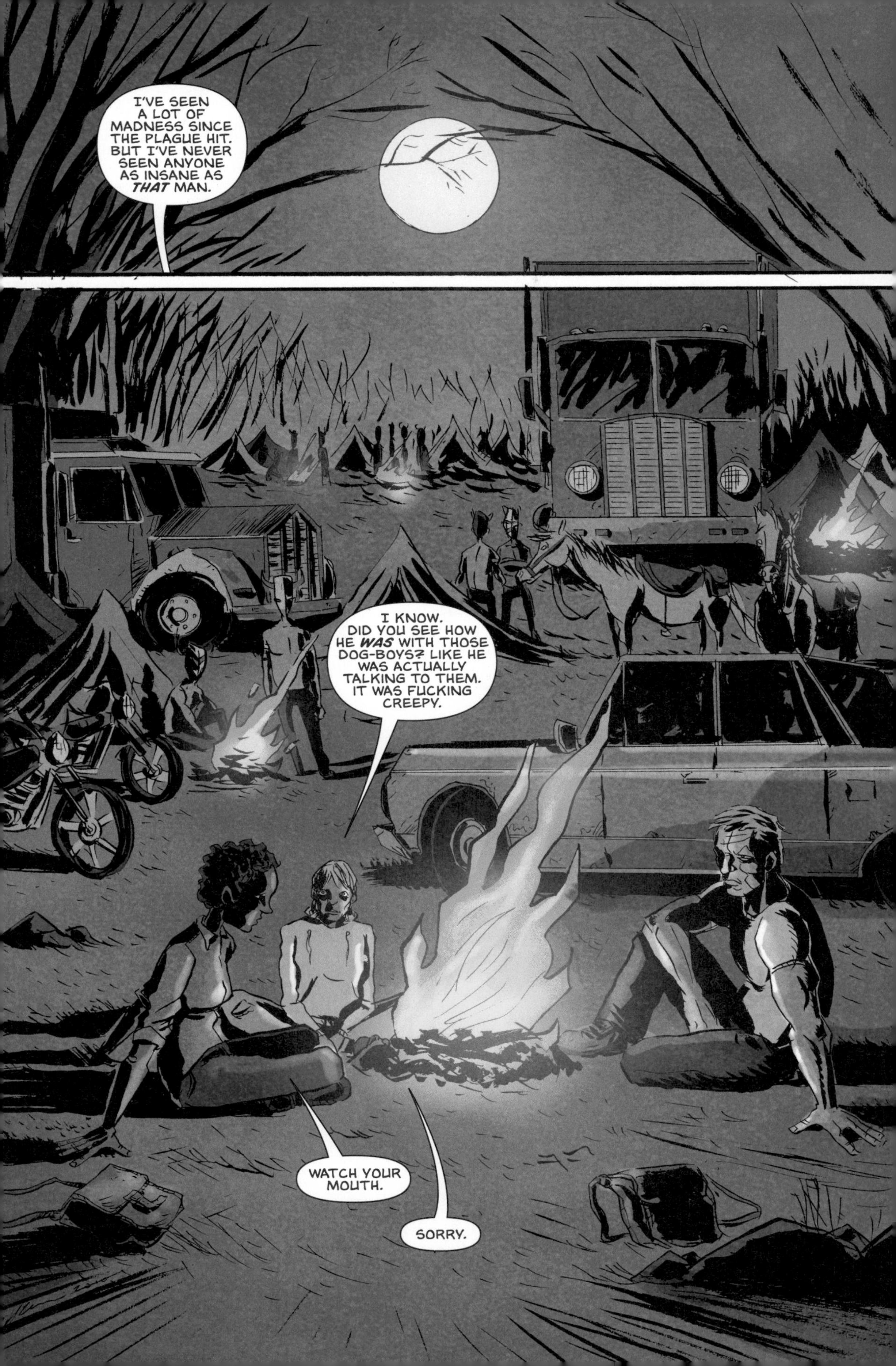
I'VE SEEN A LOT OF MADNESS SINCE THE PLAGUE HIT. BUT I'VE NEVER SEEN ANYONE AS INSANE AS *THAT* MAN.
I KNOW. DID YOU SEE HOW HE *WAS* WITH THOSE DOG-BOYS? LIKE HE WAS ACTUALLY TALKING TO THEM. IT WAS FUCKING CREEPY.
WATCH YOUR MOUTH.
SORRY.

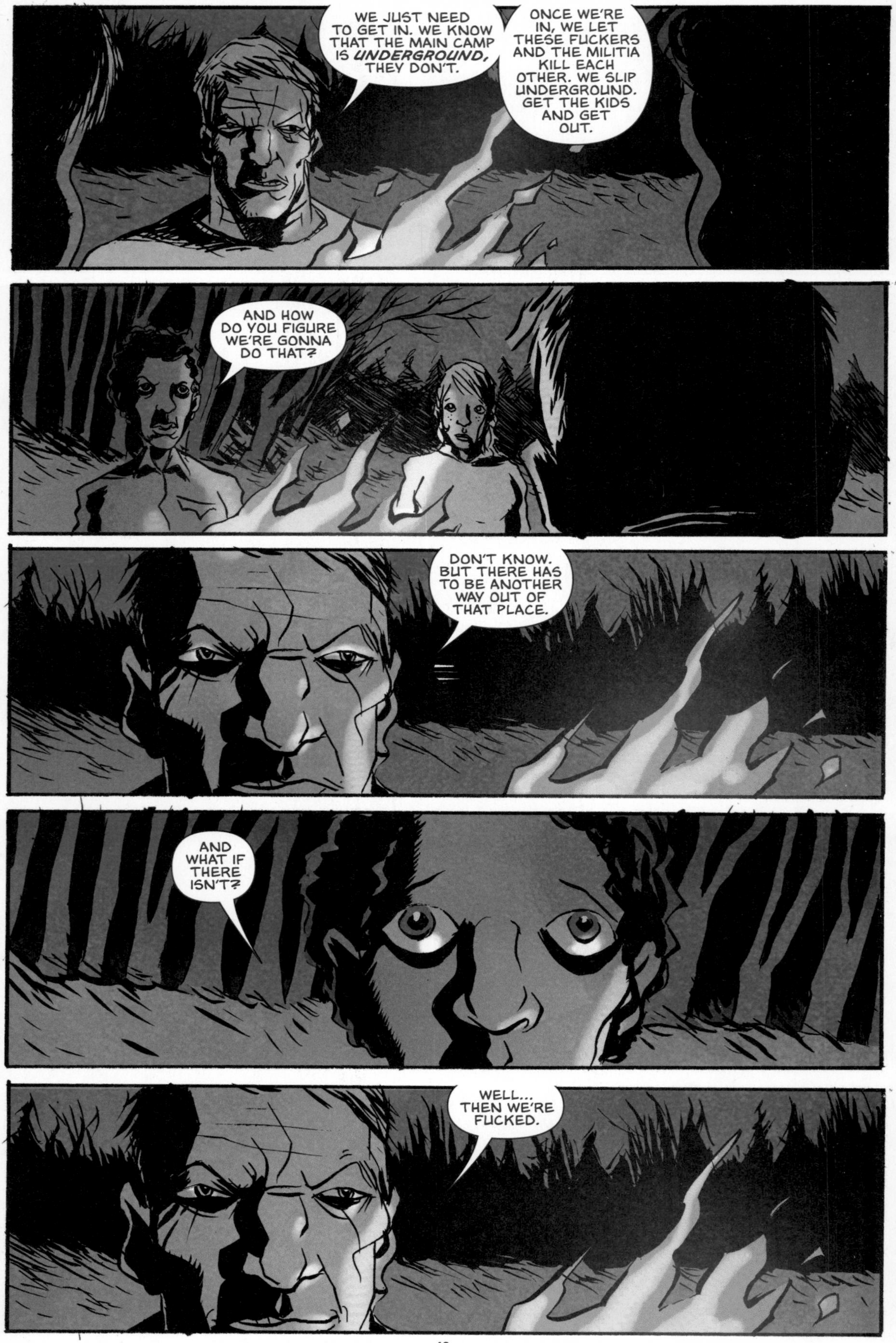
WE JUST NEED TO GET IN. WE KNOW THAT THE MAIN CAMP IS *UNDERGROUND,* THEY DON'T.
ONCE WE'RE IN, WE LET THESE FUCKERS AND THE MILITIA KILL EACH OTHER. WE SLIP UNDERGROUND. GET THE KIDS AND GET OUT.
AND HOW DO YOU FIGURE WE'RE GONNA DO THAT?
DON'T KNOW. BUT THERE HAS TO BE ANOTHER WAY OUT OF THAT PLACE.
AND WHAT IF THERE ISN'T?
WELL... THEN WE'RE FUCKED.

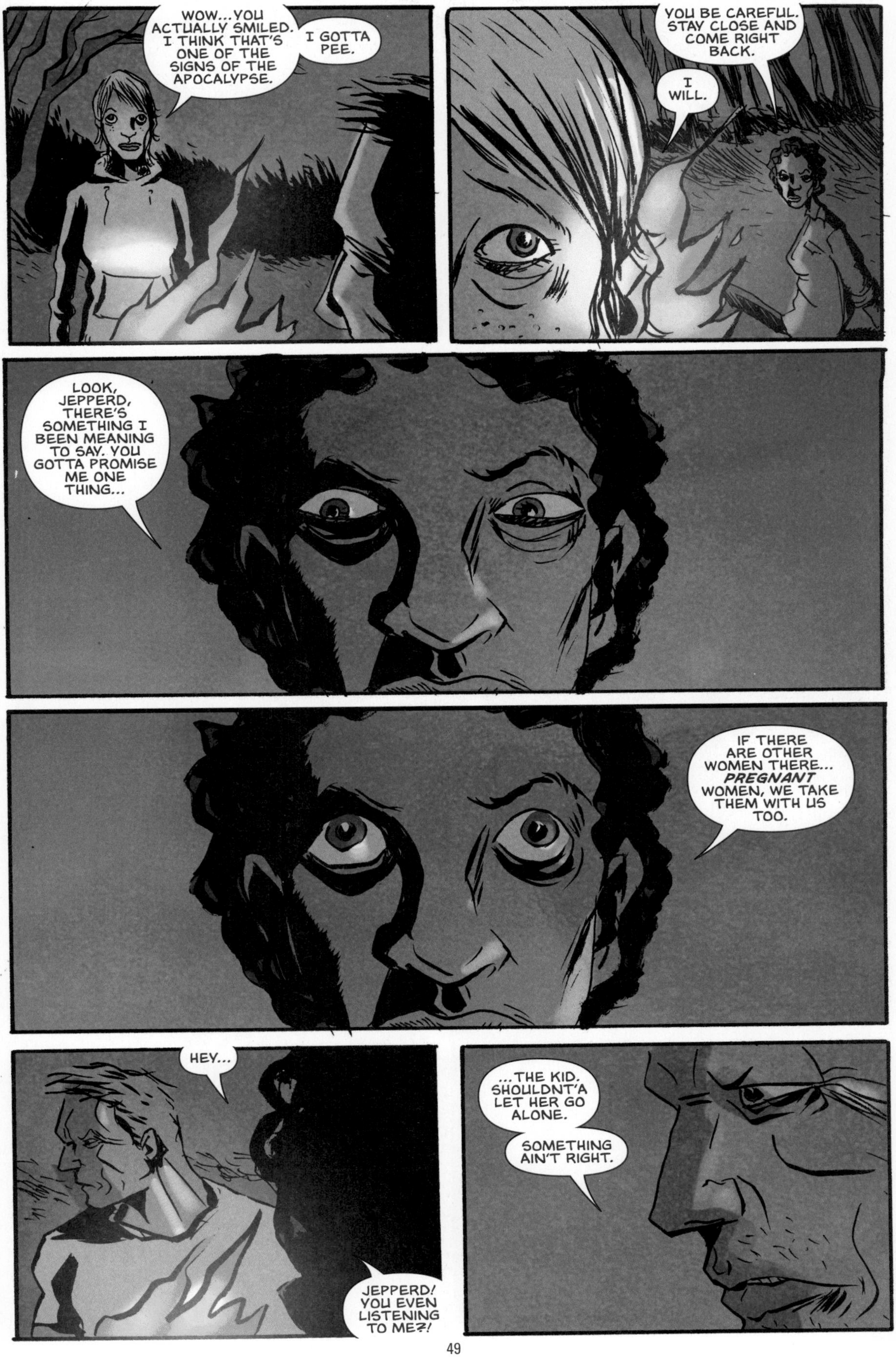
WOW...YOU ACTUALLY SMILED. I THINK THAT'S ONE OF THE SIGNS OF THE APOCALYPSE.
I GOTTA PEE.
YOU BE CAREFUL. STAY CLOSE AND COME RIGHT BACK.
I WILL.
LOOK, JEPPERD, THERE'S SOMETHING I BEEN MEANING TO SAY. YOU GOTTA PROMISE ME ONE THING...
IF THERE ARE OTHER WOMEN THERE... *PREGNANT* WOMEN, WE TAKE THEM WITH US TOO.
HEY...
JEPPERD! YOU EVEN LISTENING TO ME?!
...THE KID. SHOULDNT'A LET HER GO ALONE.
SOMETHING AIN'T RIGHT.

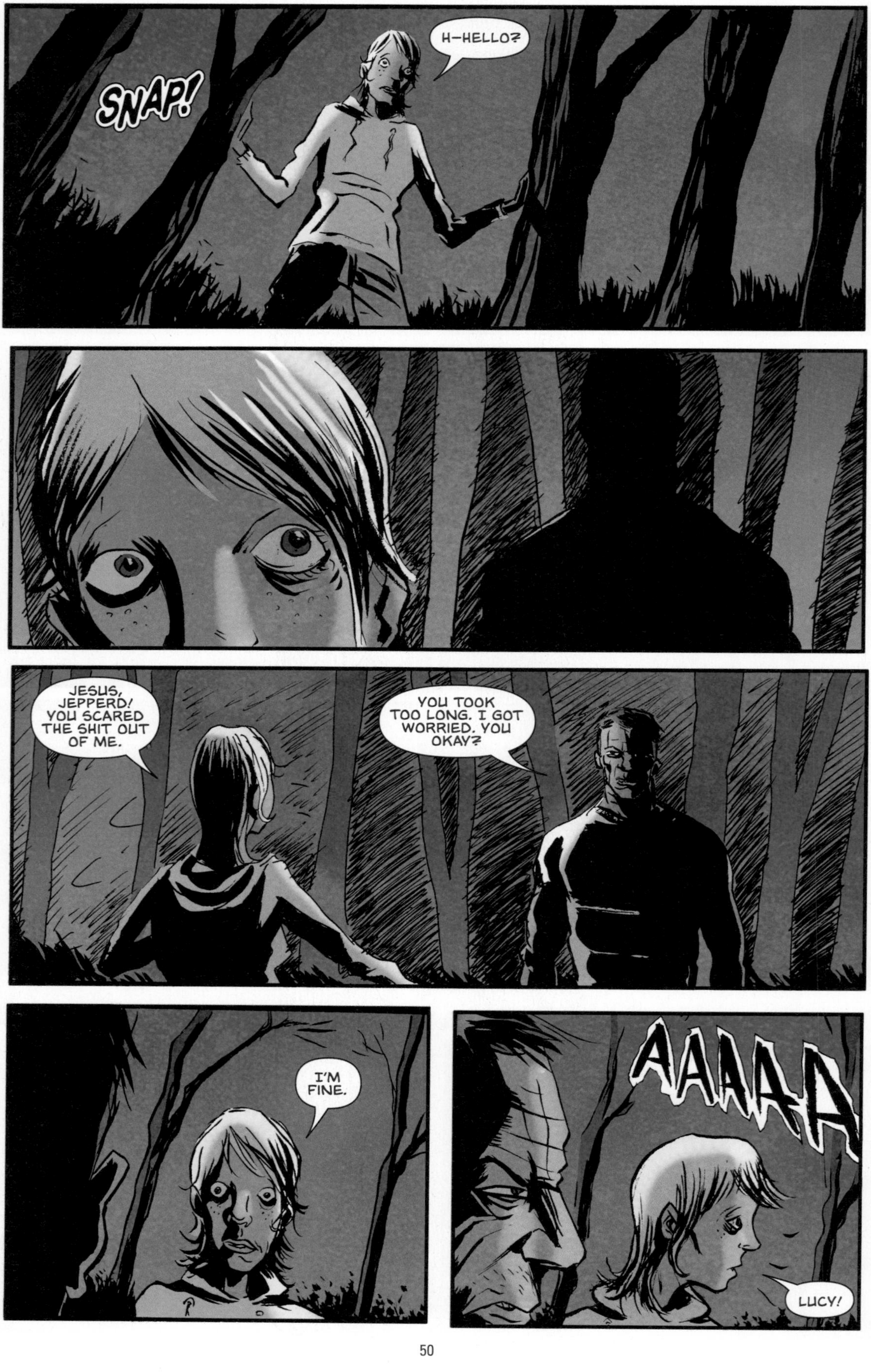
H-HELLO?
SNAP!
JESUS, JEPPERD! YOU SCARED THE SHIT OUT OF ME.
YOU TOOK TOO LONG. I GOT WORRIED. YOU OKAY?
I'M FINE.
AAAAA
LUCY!

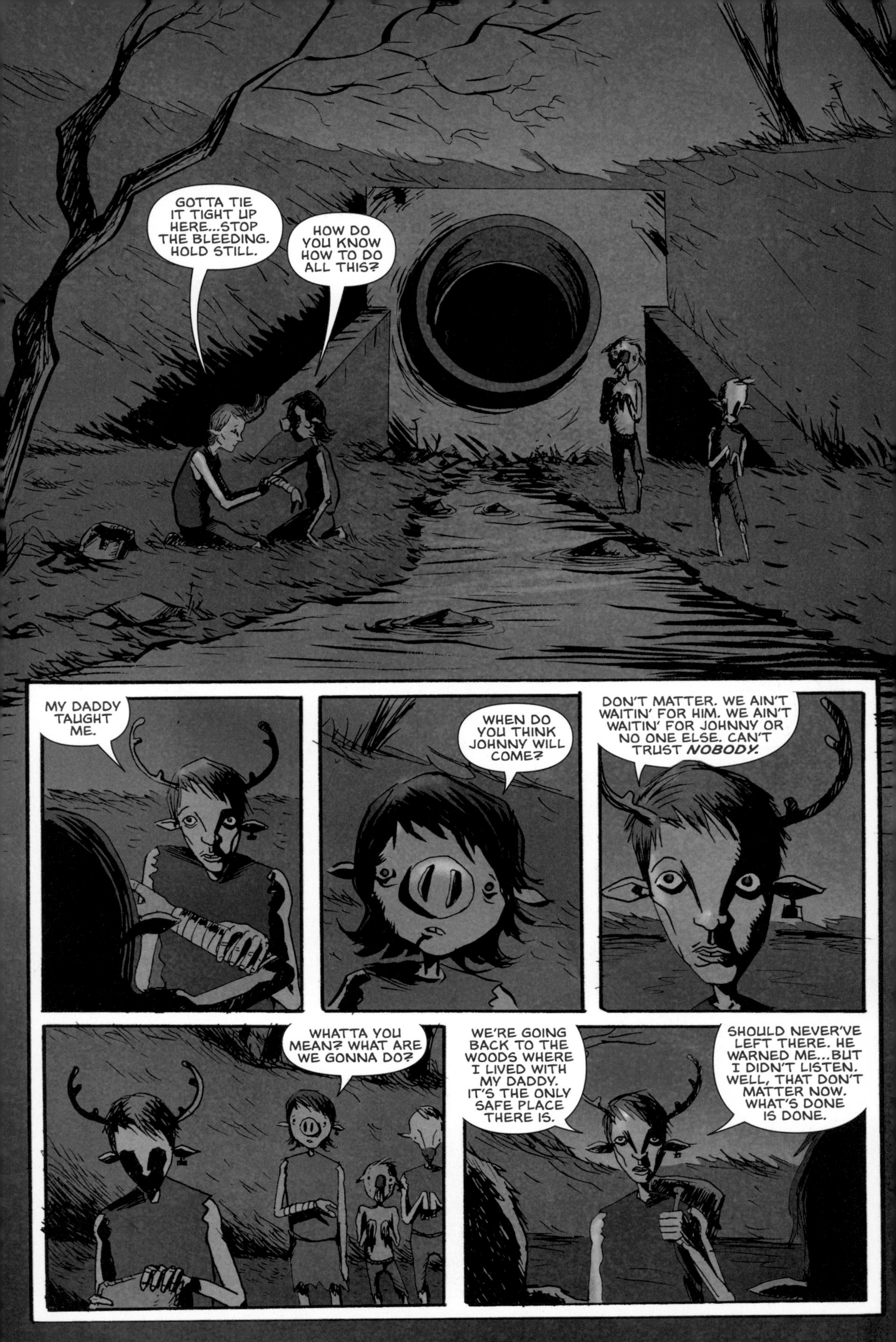
GOTTA TIE IT TIGHT UP HERE...STOP THE BLEEDING. HOLD STILL.
HOW DO YOU KNOW HOW TO DO ALL THIS?
MY DADDY TAUGHT ME.
WHEN DO YOU THINK JOHNNY WILL COME?
DON'T MATTER. WE AIN'T WAITIN' FOR HIM. WE AIN'T WAITIN' FOR JOHNNY OR NO ONE ELSE. CAN'T TRUST ***NOBODY.***
WHATTA YOU MEAN? WHAT ARE WE GONNA DO?
WE'RE GOING BACK TO THE WOODS WHERE I LIVED WITH MY DADDY. IT'S THE ONLY SAFE PLACE THERE IS.
SHOULD NEVER'VE LEFT THERE. HE WARNED ME...BUT I DIDN'T LISTEN. WELL, THAT DON'T MATTER NOW. WHAT'S DONE IS DONE.

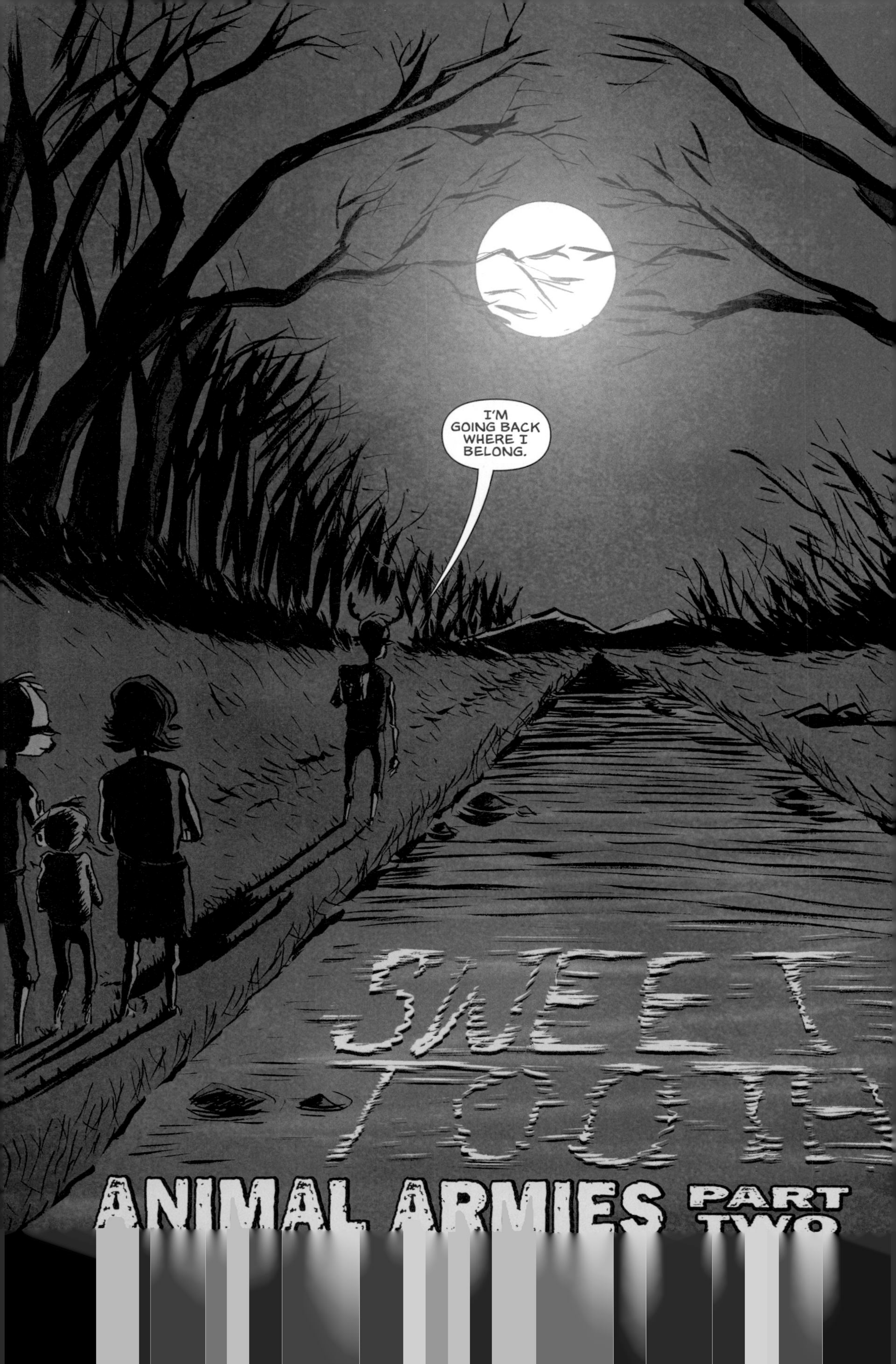
I'M GOING BACK WHERE I BELONG.
SWEET TOOTH
ANIMAL ARMIES PART TWO

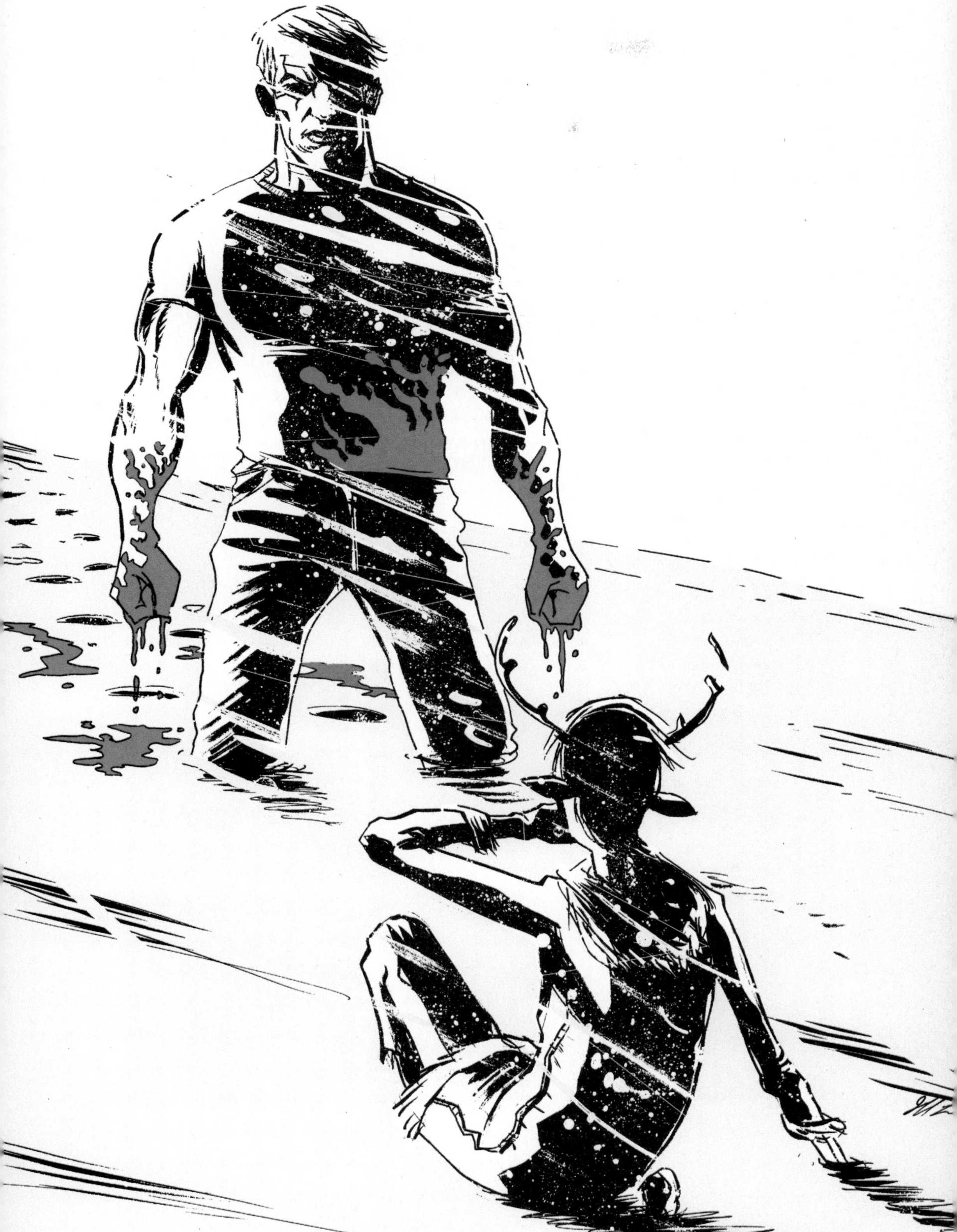

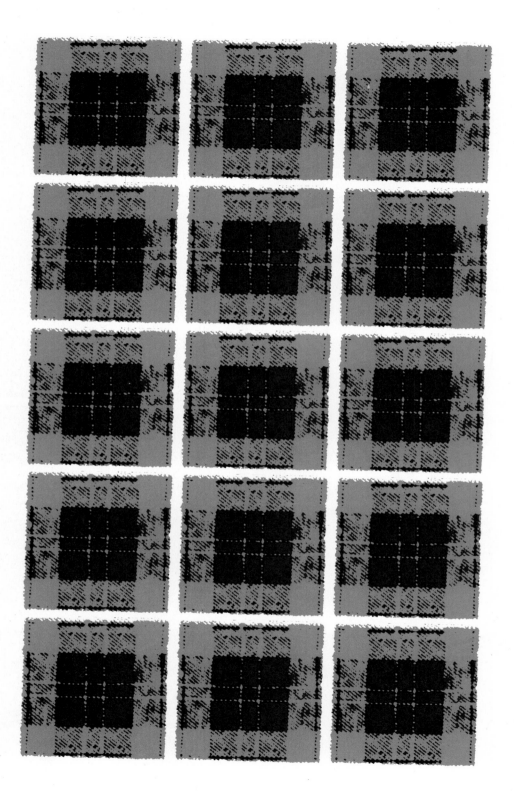

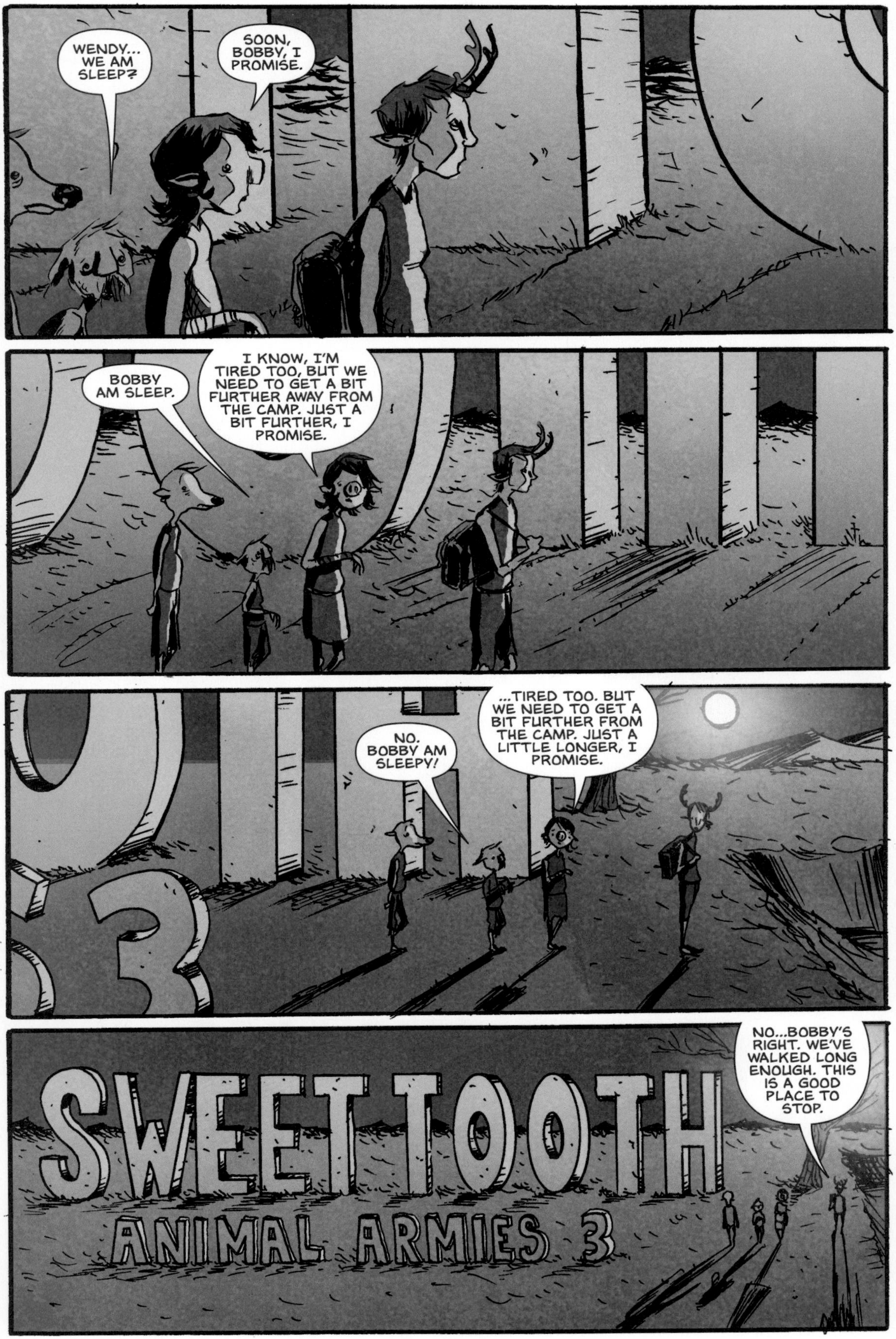
WENDY... WE AM SLEEP?
SOON, BOBBY, I PROMISE.
BOBBY AM SLEEP.
I KNOW, I'M TIRED TOO, BUT WE NEED TO GET A BIT FURTHER AWAY FROM THE CAMP. JUST A BIT FURTHER, I PROMISE.
NO. BOBBY AM SLEEPY!
...TIRED TOO. BUT WE NEED TO GET A BIT FURTHER FROM THE CAMP. JUST A LITTLE LONGER, I PROMISE.
SWEET TOOTH
ANIMAL ARMIES 3
NO...BOBBY'S RIGHT. WE'VE WALKED LONG ENOUGH. THIS IS A GOOD PLACE TO STOP.

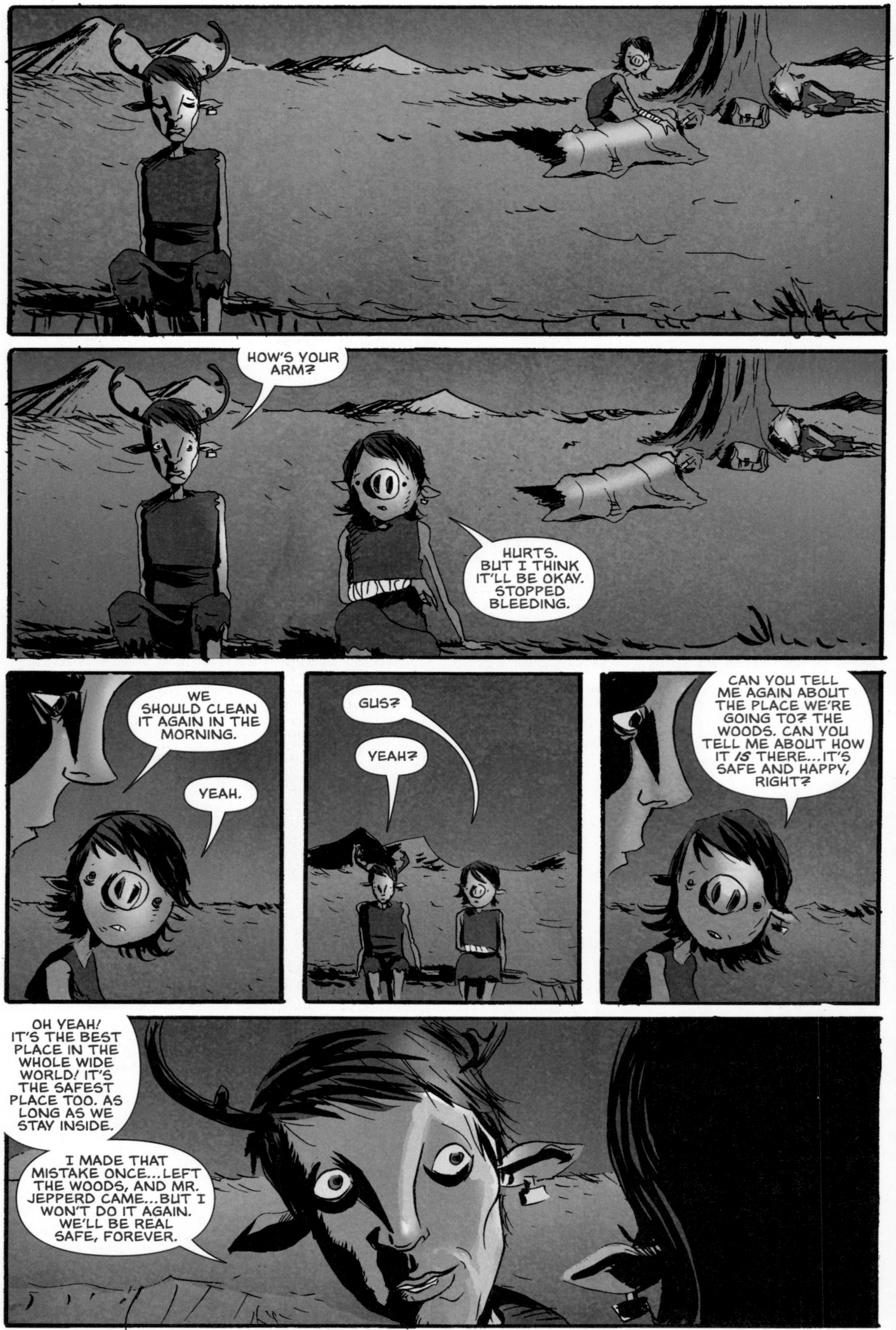
HOW'S YOUR ARM?
HURTS. BUT I THINK IT'LL BE OKAY. STOPPED BLEEDING.
WE SHOULD CLEAN IT AGAIN IN THE MORNING.
YEAH.
GUS?
YEAH?
CAN YOU TELL ME AGAIN ABOUT THE PLACE WE'RE GOING TO? THE WOODS. CAN YOU TELL ME ABOUT HOW IT *IS* THERE...IT'S SAFE AND HAPPY, RIGHT?
OH YEAH! IT'S THE BEST PLACE IN THE WHOLE WIDE WORLD! IT'S THE SAFEST PLACE TOO. AS LONG AS WE STAY INSIDE.
I MADE THAT MISTAKE ONCE...LEFT THE WOODS, AND MR. JEPPERD CAME...BUT I WON'T DO IT AGAIN. WE'LL BE REAL SAFE, FOREVER.

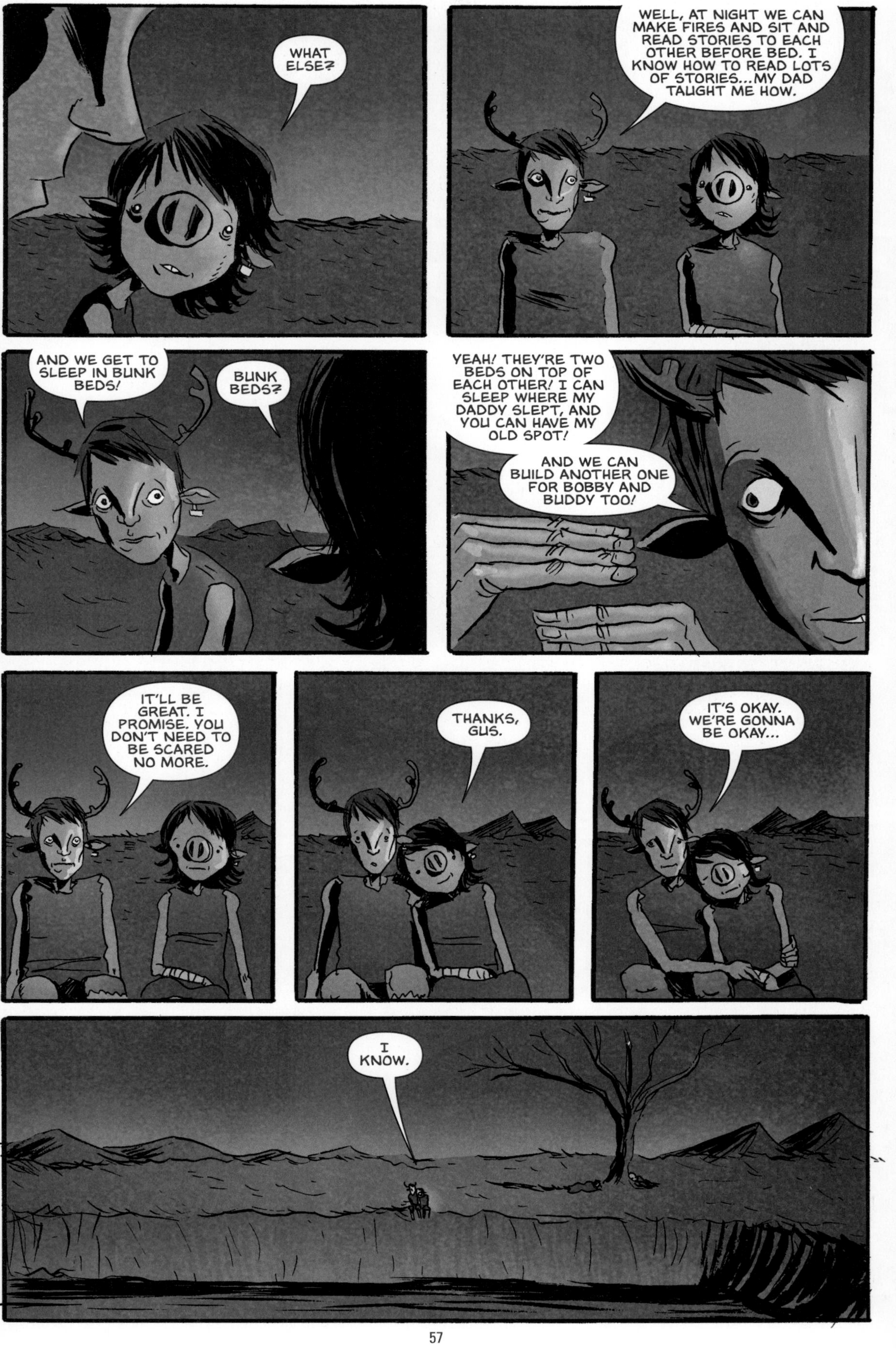
WHAT ELSE?
WELL, AT NIGHT WE CAN MAKE FIRES AND SIT AND READ STORIES TO EACH OTHER BEFORE BED. I KNOW HOW TO READ LOTS OF STORIES...MY DAD TAUGHT ME HOW.
AND WE GET TO SLEEP IN BUNK BEDS!
BUNK BEDS?
YEAH! THEY'RE TWO BEDS ON TOP OF EACH OTHER! I CAN SLEEP WHERE MY DADDY SLEPT, AND YOU CAN HAVE MY OLD SPOT!
AND WE CAN BUILD ANOTHER ONE FOR BOBBY AND BUDDY TOO!
IT'LL BE GREAT. I PROMISE. YOU DON'T NEED TO BE SCARED NO MORE.
THANKS, GUS.
IT'S OKAY. WE'RE GONNA BE OKAY...
I KNOW.

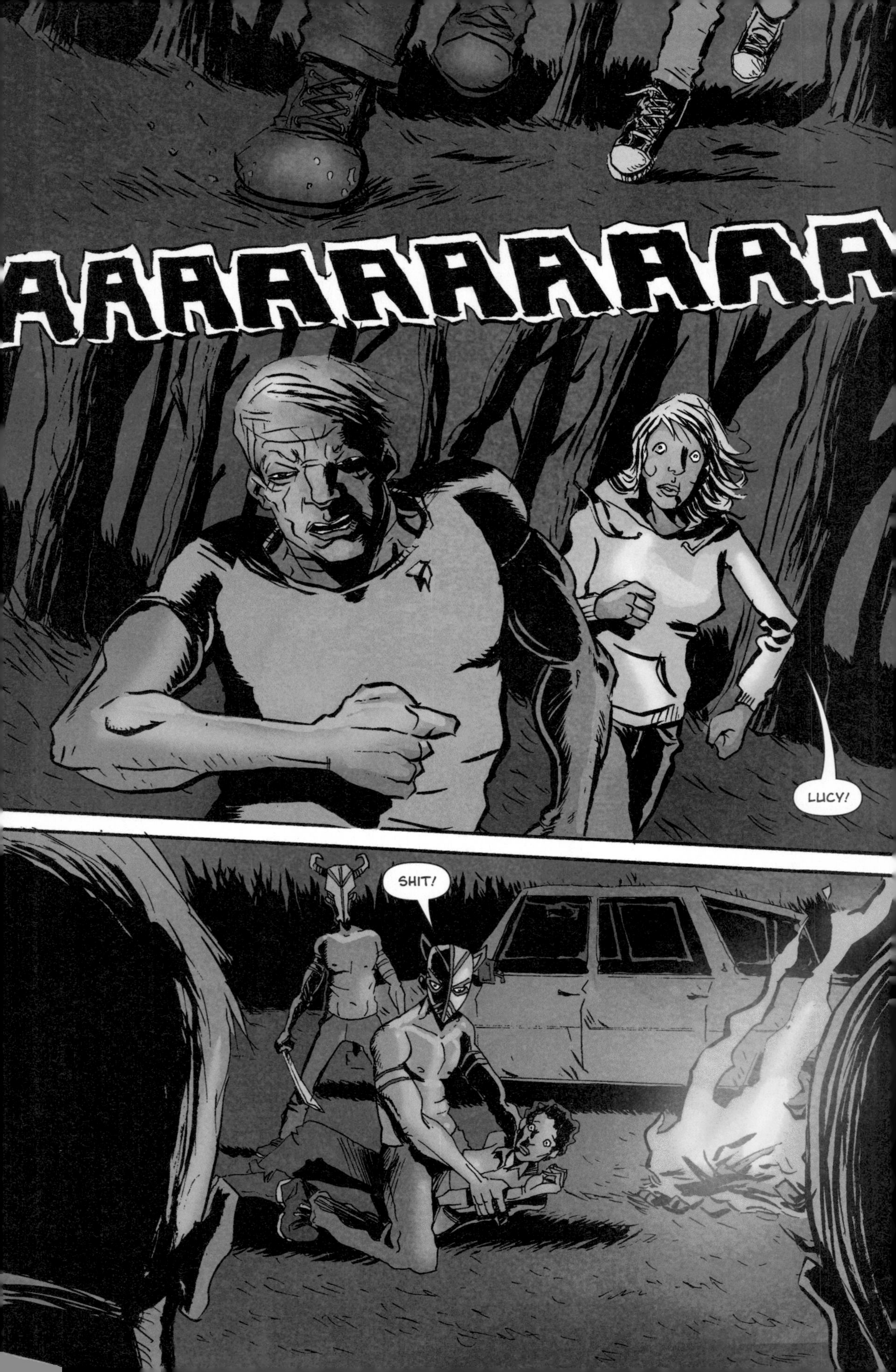
AAAAAAAAAAA
LUCY!
SHIT!

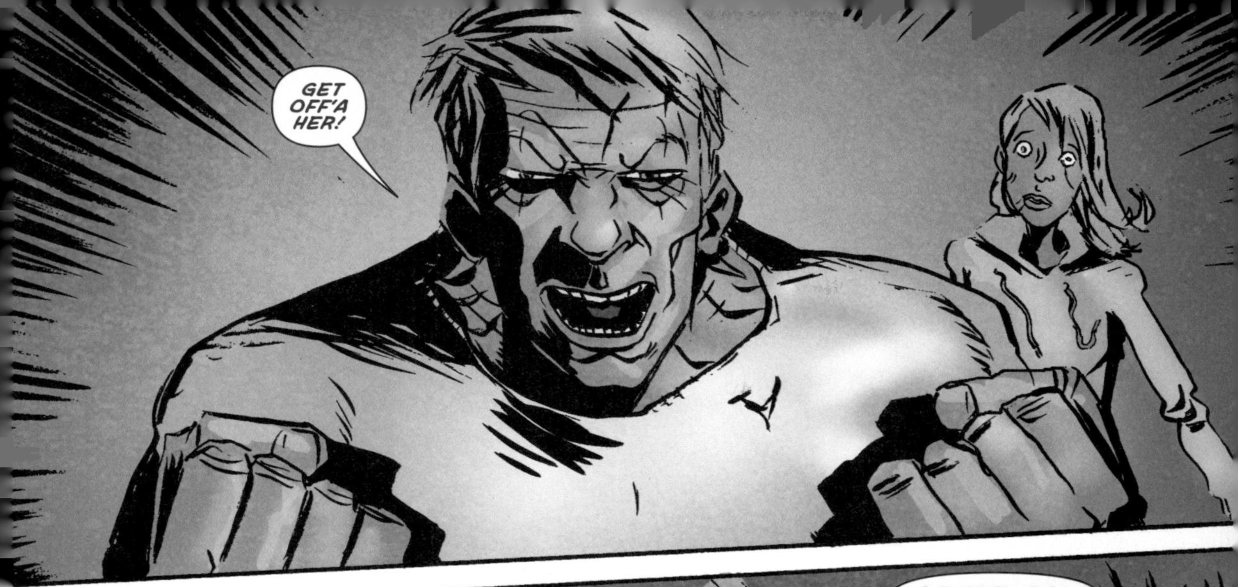
GET OFF'A HER!
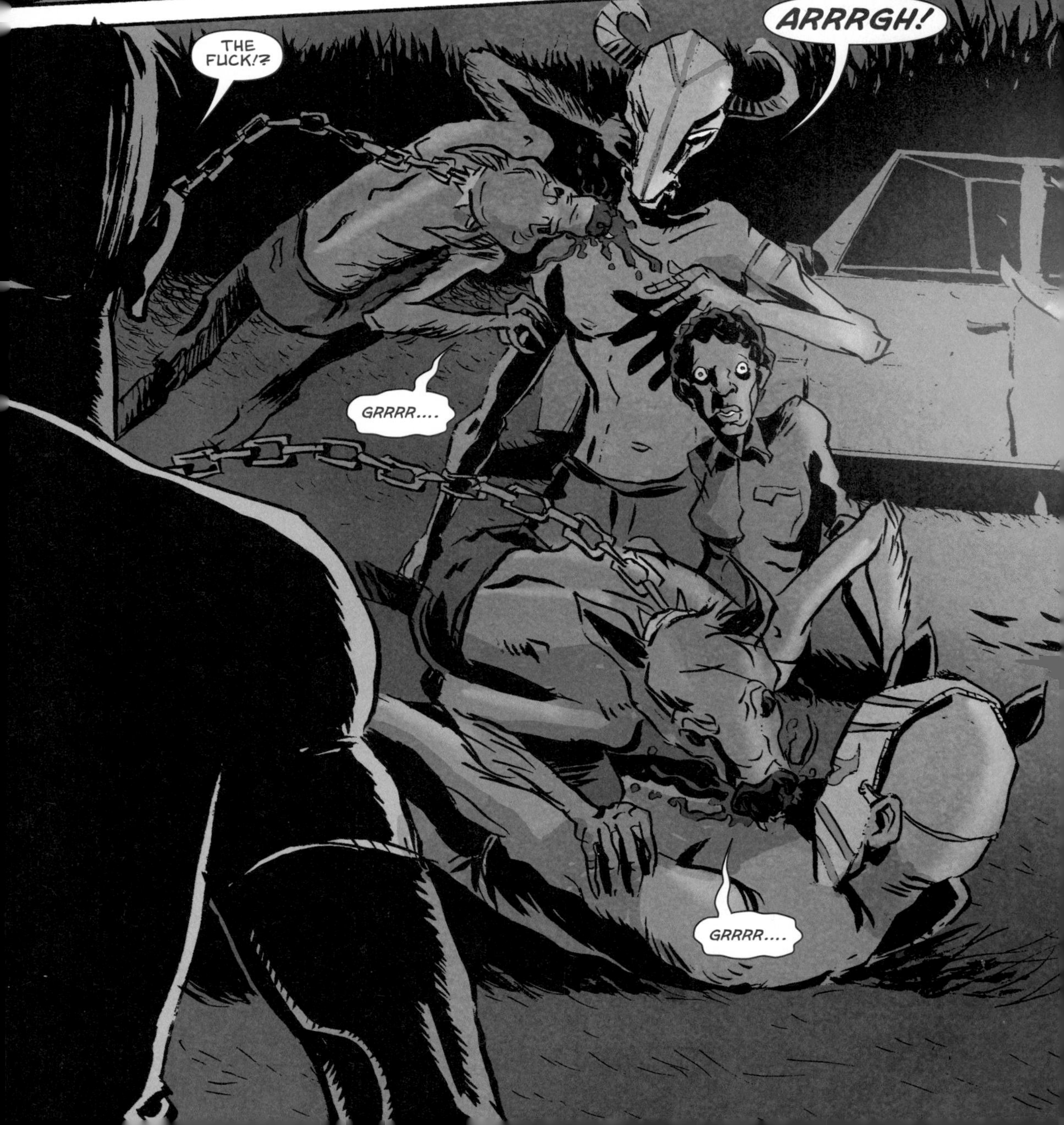
ARRRGH!
THE FUCK!?
GRRRR....
GRRRR....

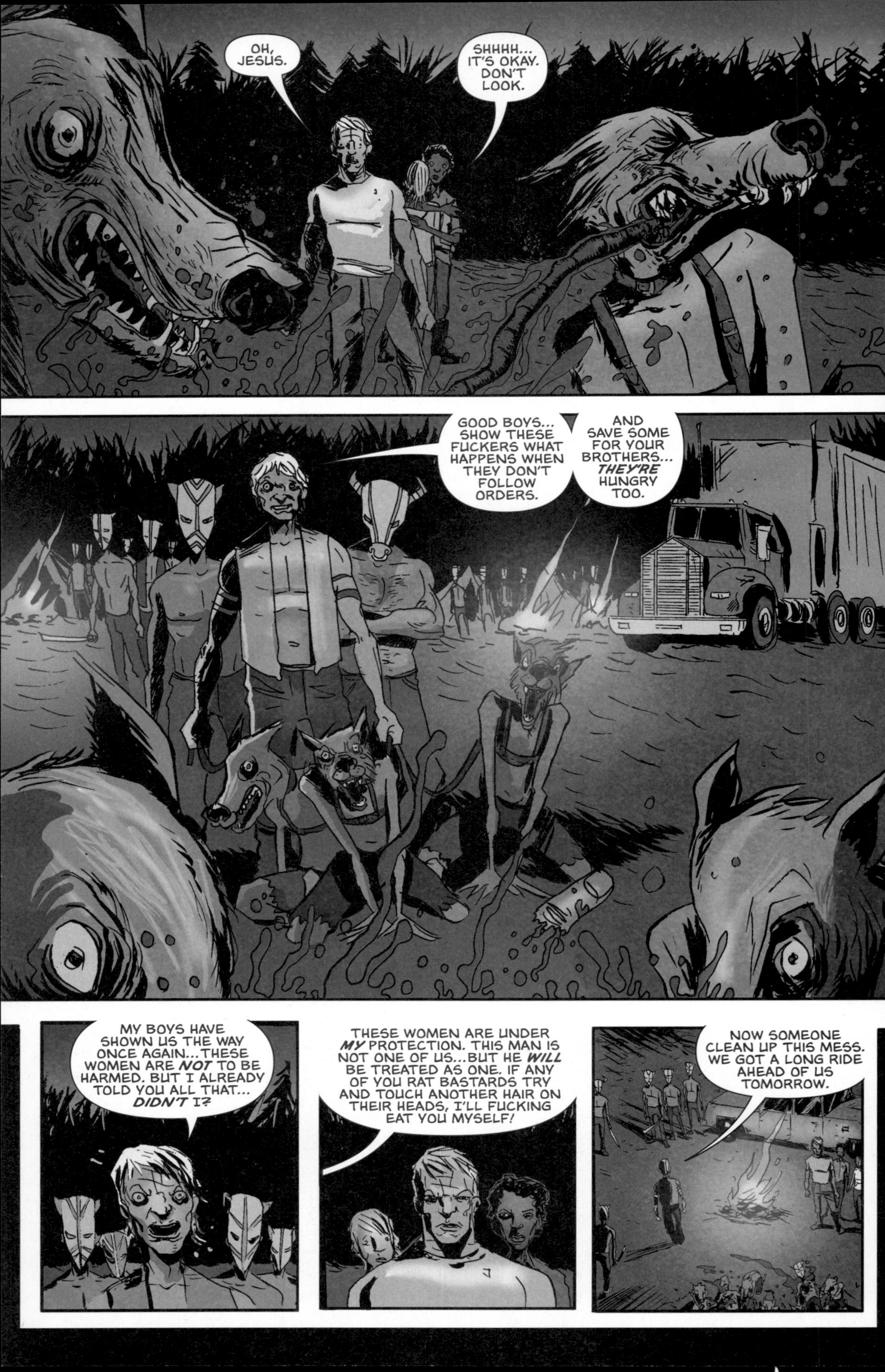

OH, JESUS.
SHHHH... IT'S OKAY. DON'T LOOK.
GOOD BOYS... SHOW THESE FUCKERS WHAT HAPPENS WHEN THEY DON'T FOLLOW ORDERS.
AND SAVE SOME FOR YOUR BROTHERS... *THEY'RE* HUNGRY TOO.
MY BOYS HAVE SHOWN US THE WAY ONCE AGAIN... THESE WOMEN ARE *NOT* TO BE HARMED. BUT I ALREADY TOLD YOU ALL THAT... *DIDN'T* I?
THESE WOMEN ARE UNDER *MY* PROTECTION. THIS MAN IS NOT ONE OF US... BUT HE *WILL* BE TREATED AS ONE. IF ANY OF YOU RAT BASTARDS TRY AND TOUCH ANOTHER HAIR ON THEIR HEADS, I'LL FUCKING EAT YOU MYSELF!
NOW SOMEONE CLEAN UP THIS MESS. WE GOT A LONG RIDE AHEAD OF US TOMORROW.

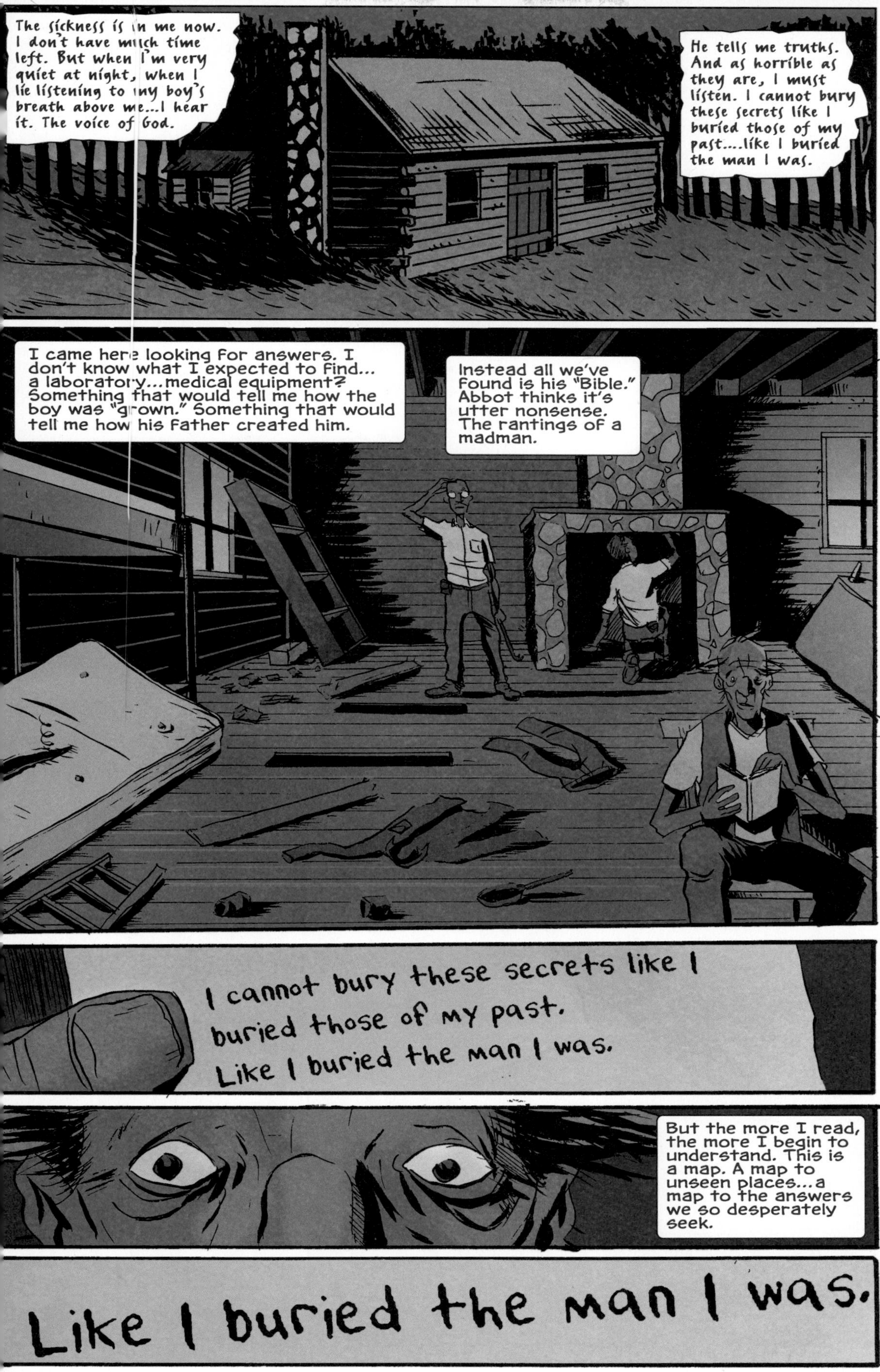
The sickness is in me now. I don't have much time left. But when I'm very quiet at night, when I lie listening to my boy's breath above me...I hear it. The voice of God.
He tells me truths. And as horrible as they are, I must listen. I cannot bury these secrets like I buried those of my past....like I buried the man I was.
I came here looking for answers. I don't know what I expected to find... a laboratory...medical equipment? Something that would tell me how the boy was "grown." Something that would tell me how his father created him.
Instead all we've found is his "Bible." Abbot thinks it's utter nonsense. The rantings of a madman.
I cannot bury these secrets like I buried those of my past.
Like I buried the man I was.
But the more I read, the more I begin to understand. This is a map. A map to unseen places...a map to the answers we so desperately seek.
Like I buried the man I was.

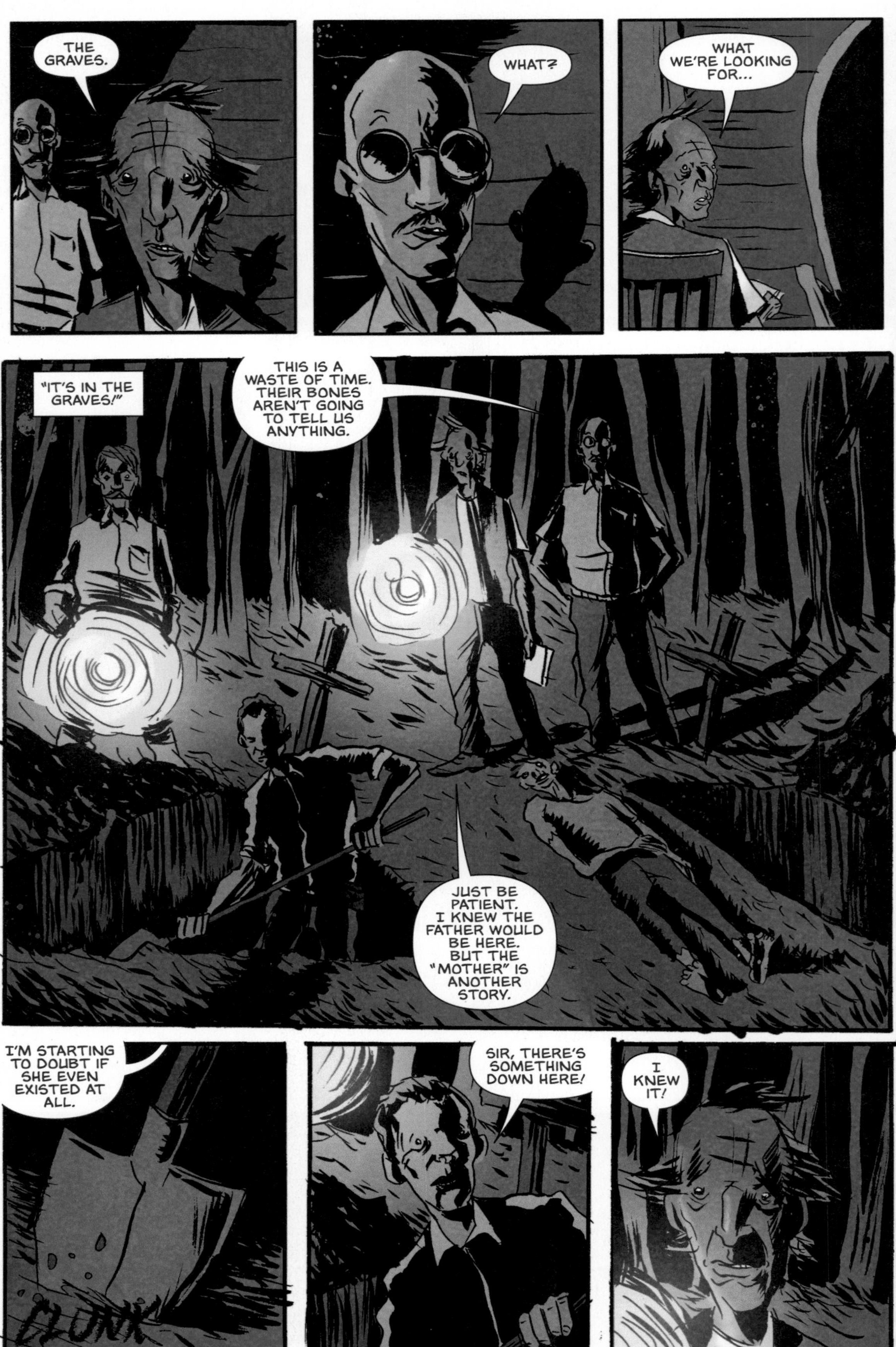
THE GRAVES.
WHAT?
WHAT WE'RE LOOKING FOR...
"IT'S IN THE GRAVES!"
THIS IS A WASTE OF TIME. THEIR BONES AREN'T GOING TO TELL US ANYTHING.
JUST BE PATIENT. I KNEW THE FATHER WOULD BE HERE. BUT THE "MOTHER" IS ANOTHER STORY.
I'M STARTING TO DOUBT IF SHE EVEN EXISTED AT ALL.
CLUNK
SIR, THERE'S SOMETHING DOWN HERE!
I KNEW IT!

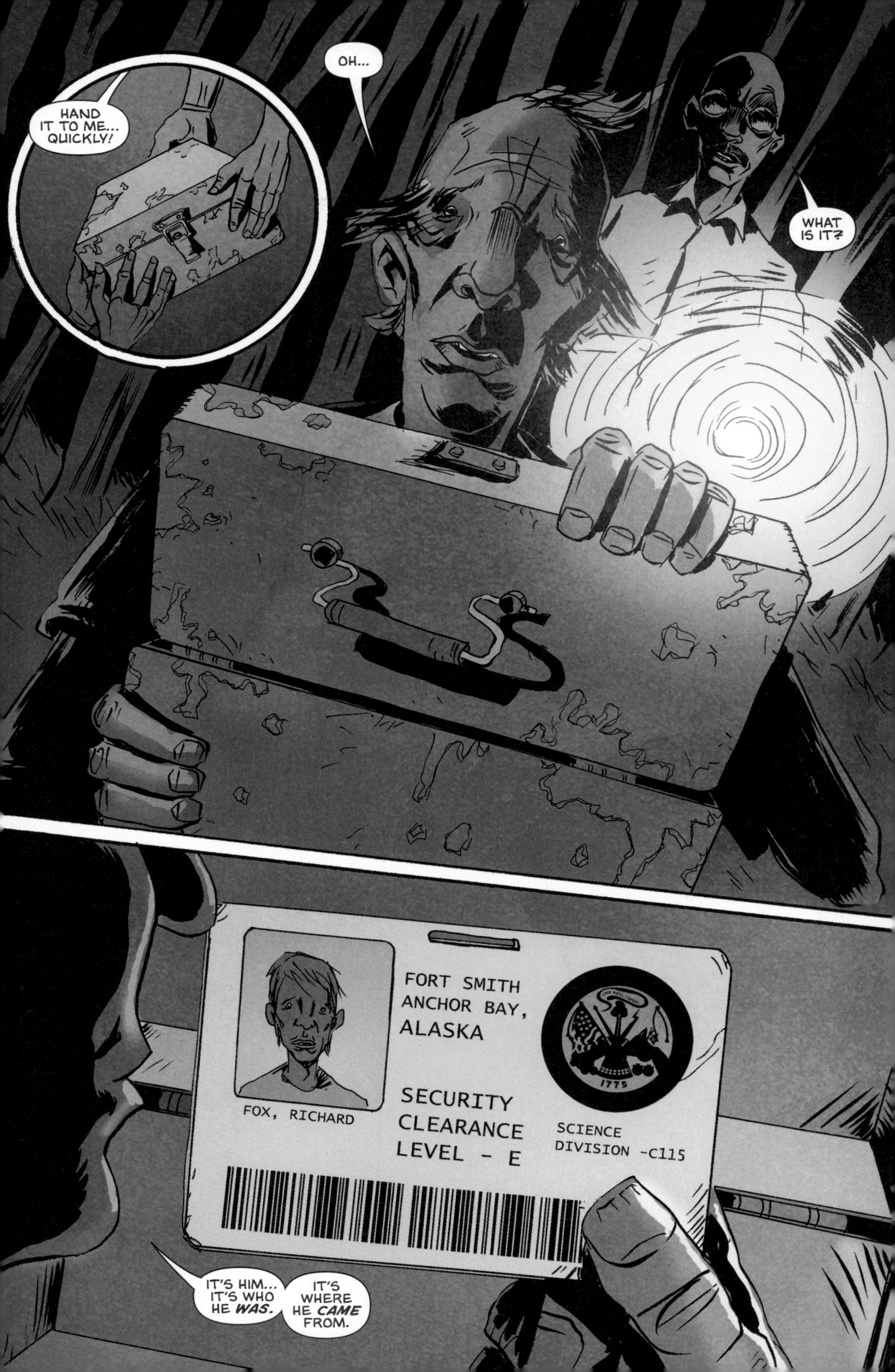
HAND IT TO ME... QUICKLY!
OH...
WHAT IS IT?
FORT SMITH
ANCHOR BAY,
ALASKA
1775
FOX, RICHARD
SECURITY
CLEARANCE
LEVEL - E
SCIENCE
DIVISION -C115
IT'S HIM... IT'S WHO HE *WAS*.
IT'S WHERE HE *CAME* FROM.

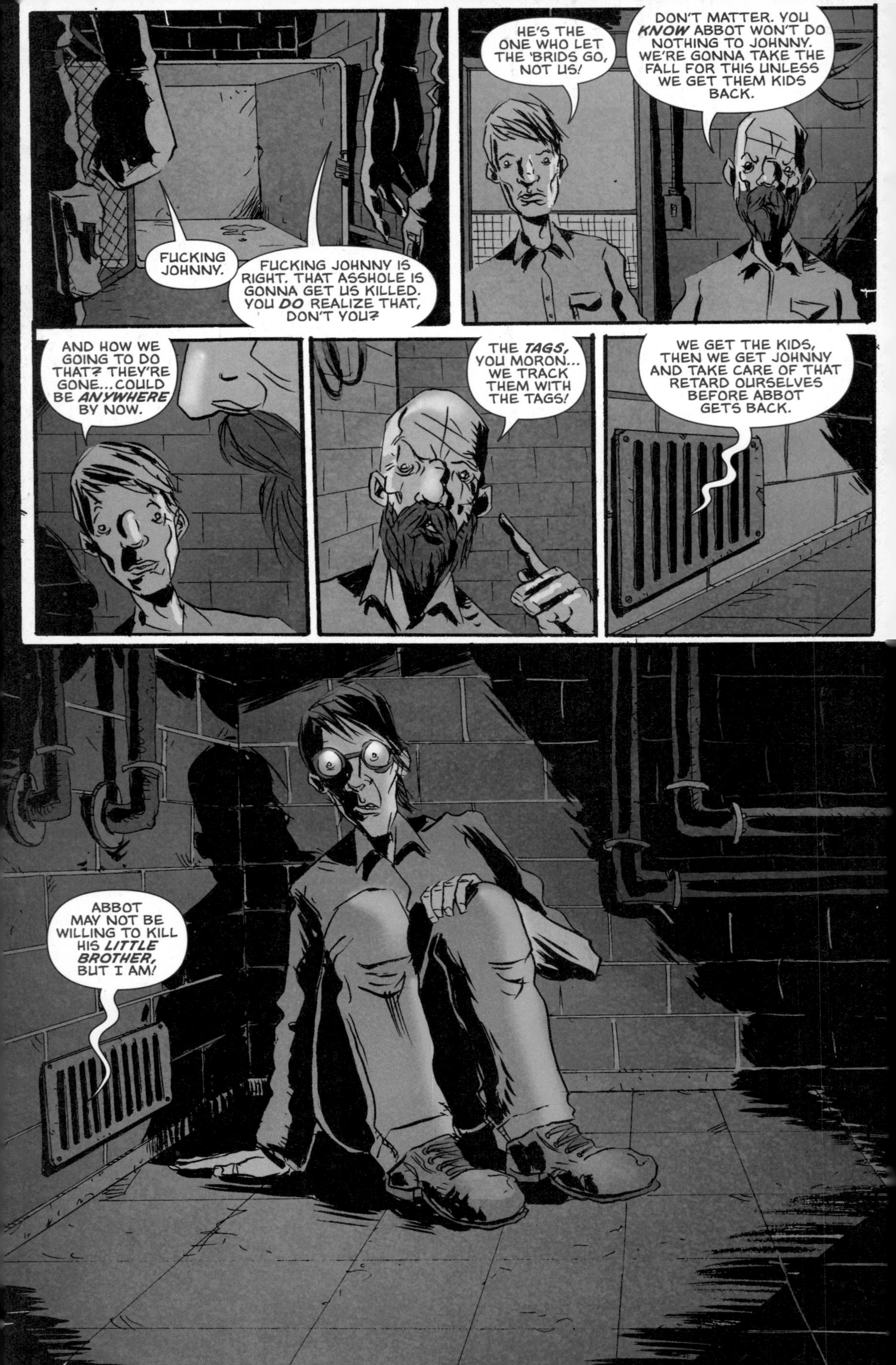
FUCKING JOHNNY.
FUCKING JOHNNY IS RIGHT. THAT ASSHOLE IS GONNA GET US KILLED. YOU DO REALIZE THAT, DON'T YOU?
HE'S THE ONE WHO LET THE 'BRIDS GO, NOT US!
DON'T MATTER. YOU KNOW ABBOT WON'T DO NOTHING TO JOHNNY. WE'RE GONNA TAKE THE FALL FOR THIS UNLESS WE GET THEM KIDS BACK.
AND HOW WE GOING TO DO THAT? THEY'RE GONE...COULD BE ANYWHERE BY NOW.
THE TAGS, YOU MORON... WE TRACK THEM WITH THE TAGS!
WE GET THE KIDS, THEN WE GET JOHNNY AND TAKE CARE OF THAT RETARD OURSELVES BEFORE ABBOT GETS BACK.
ABBOT MAY NOT BE WILLING TO KILL HIS LITTLE BROTHER, BUT I AM!

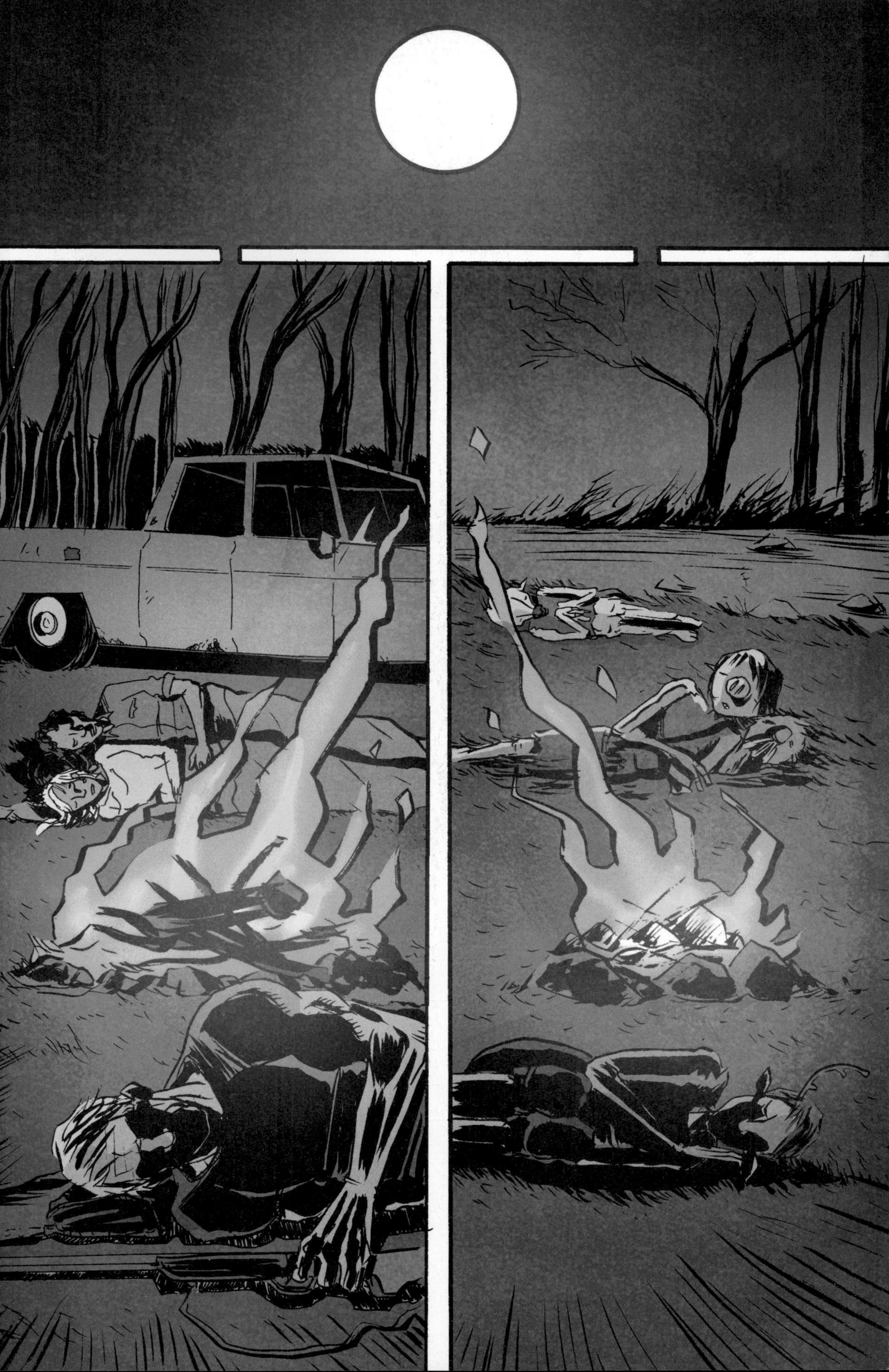

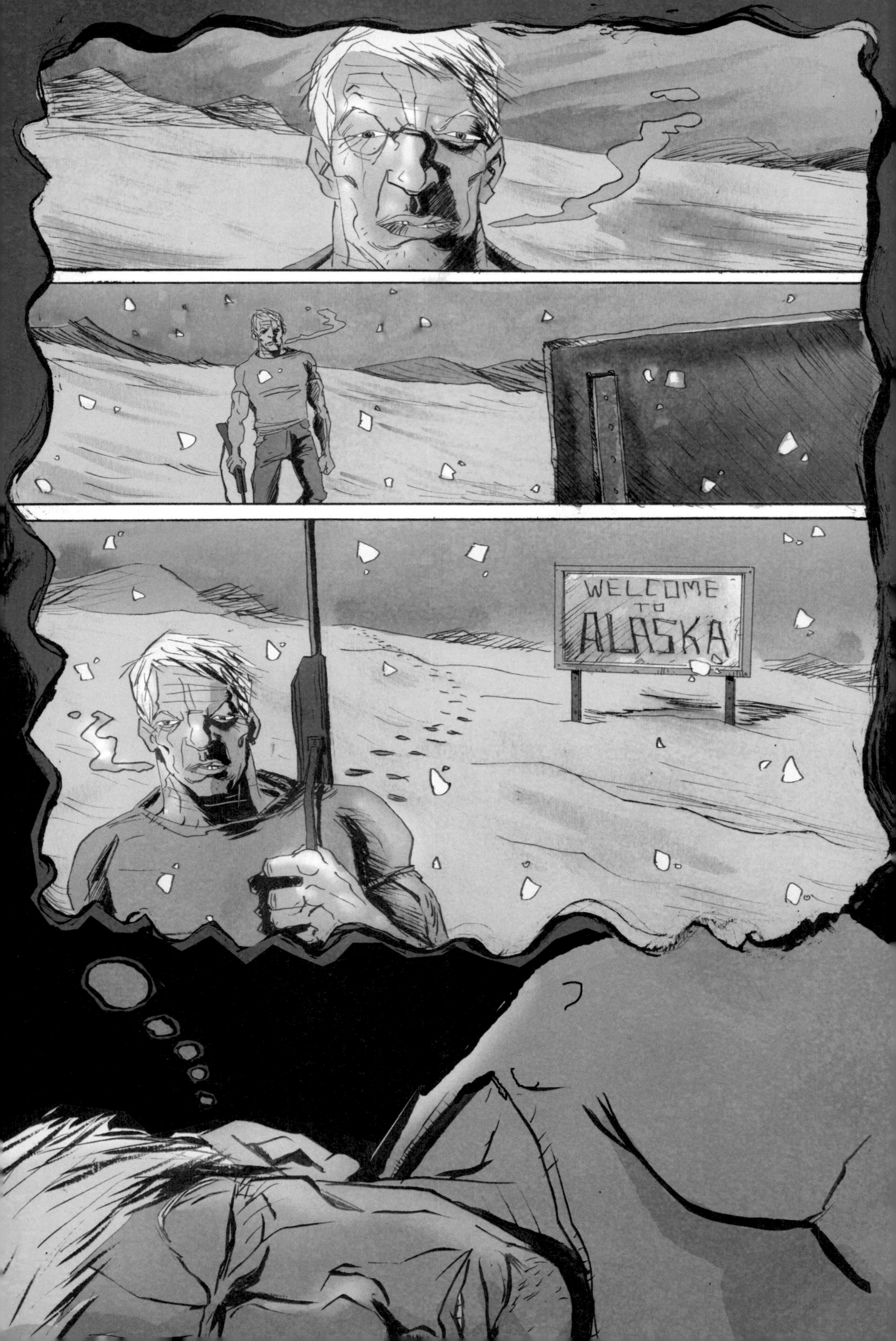
WELCOME
TO
ALASKA

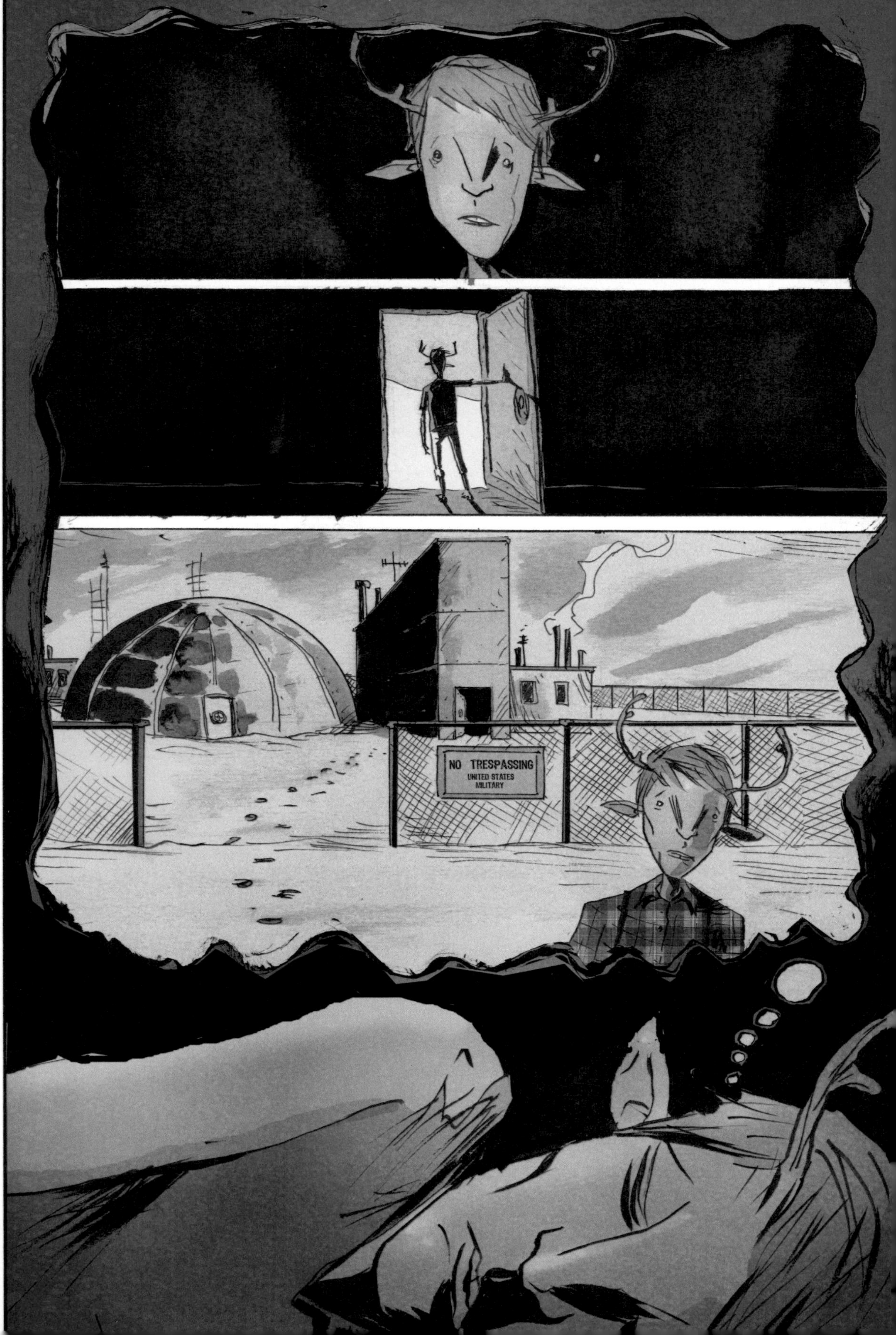
NO TRESPASSING
UNITED STATES
MILITARY

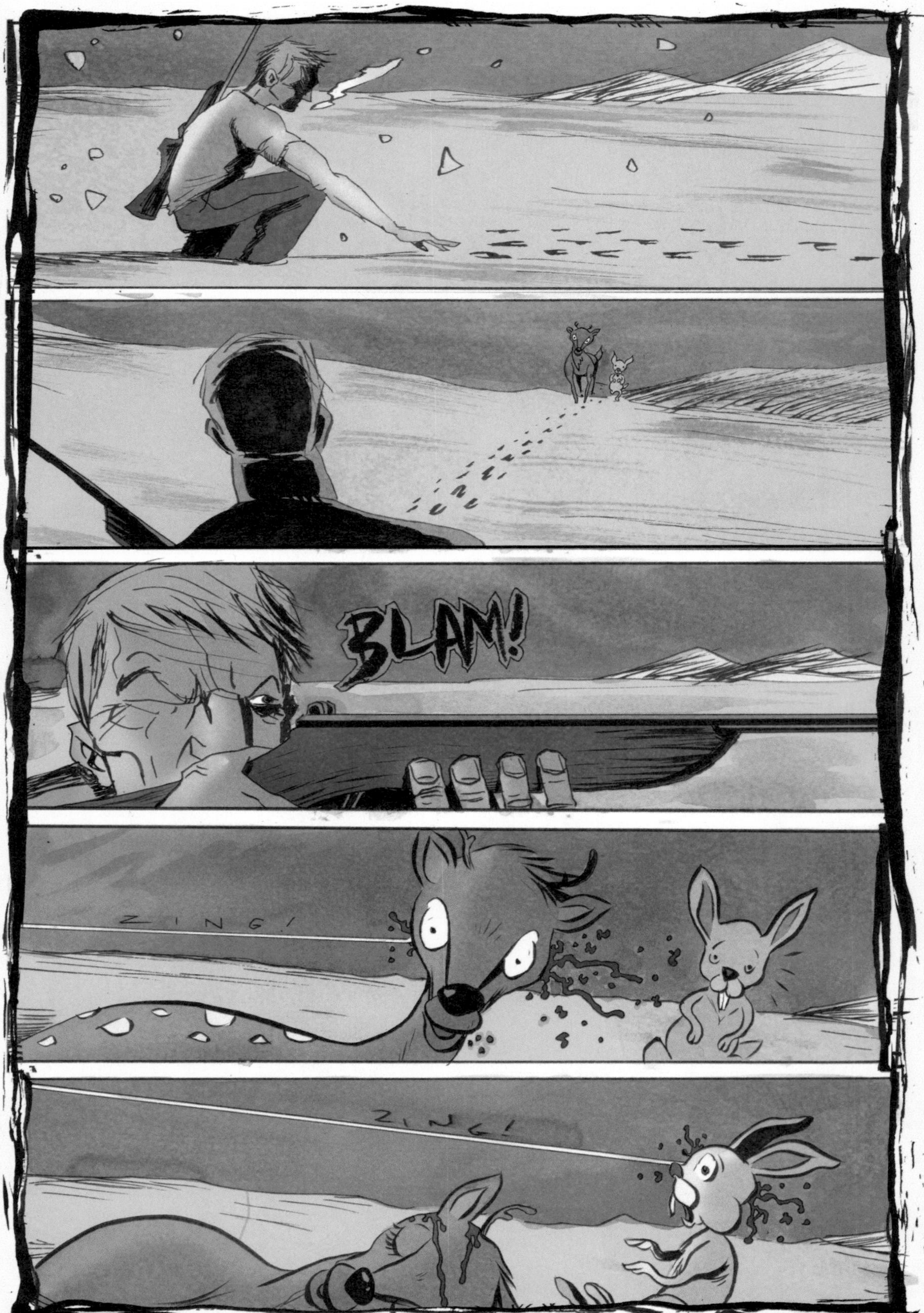
BLAM!
ZING!
ZING!

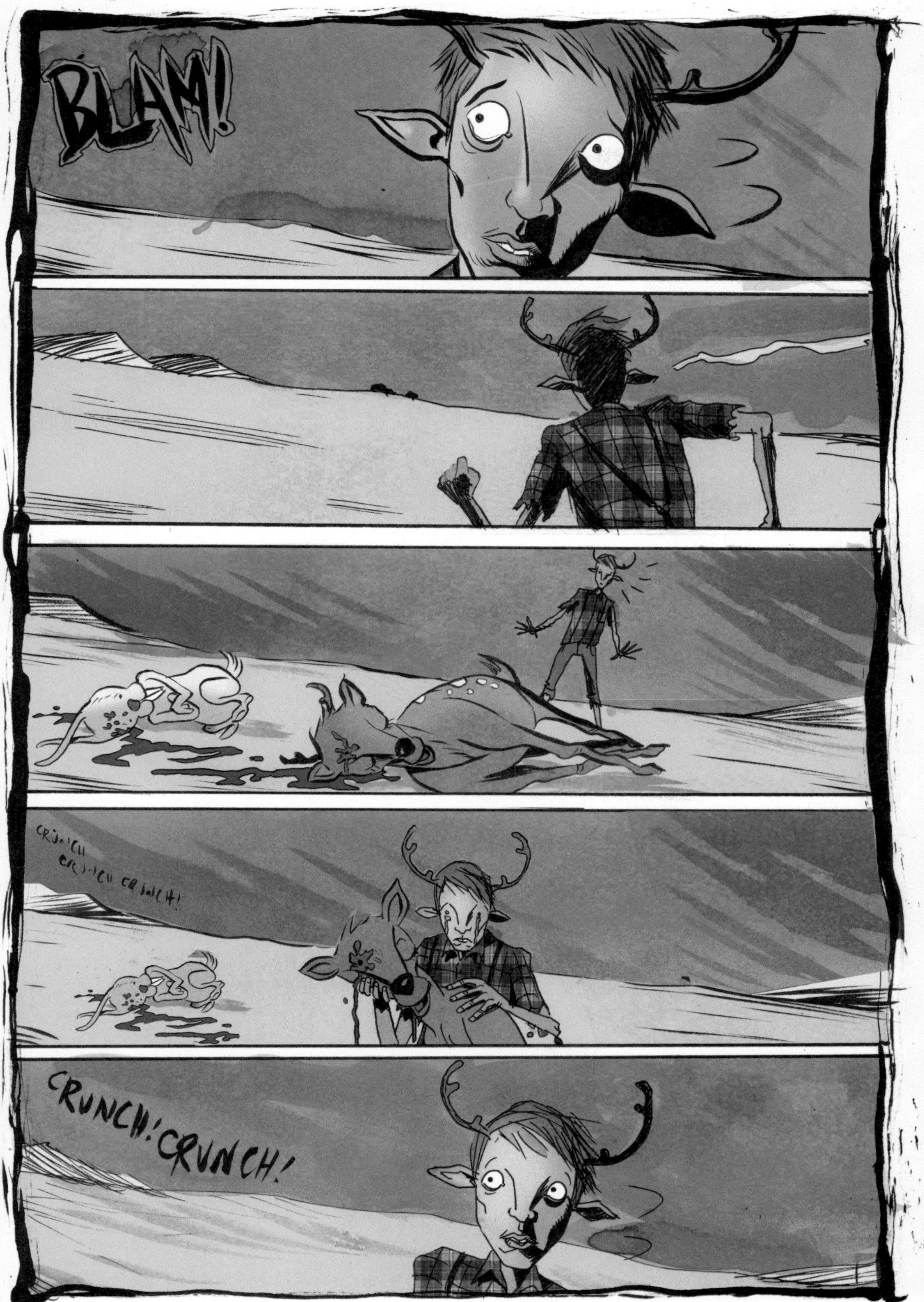
BLAM!
CRUNCH
CRUNCH CRUNCH!
CRUNCH! CRUNCH!

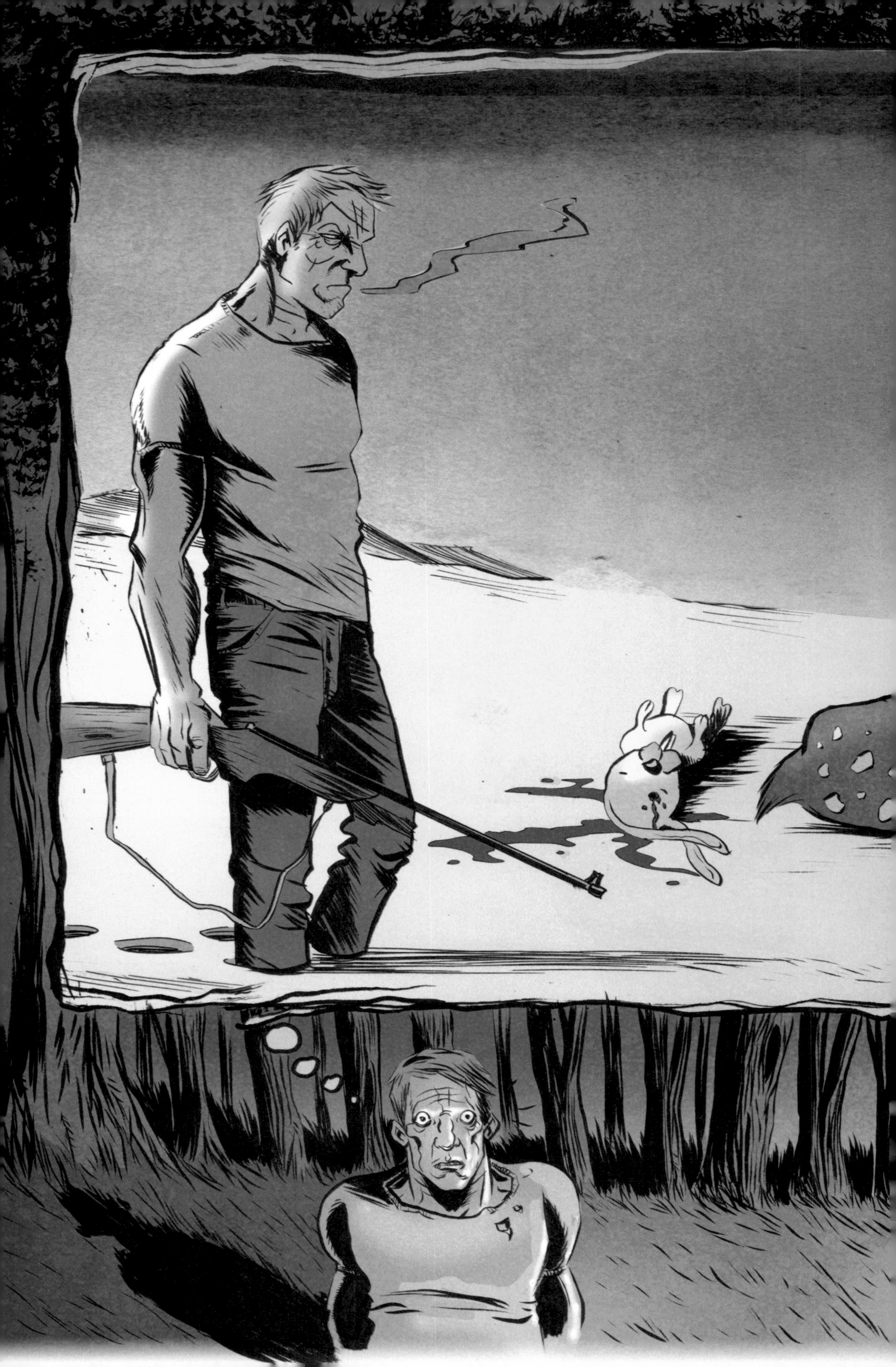

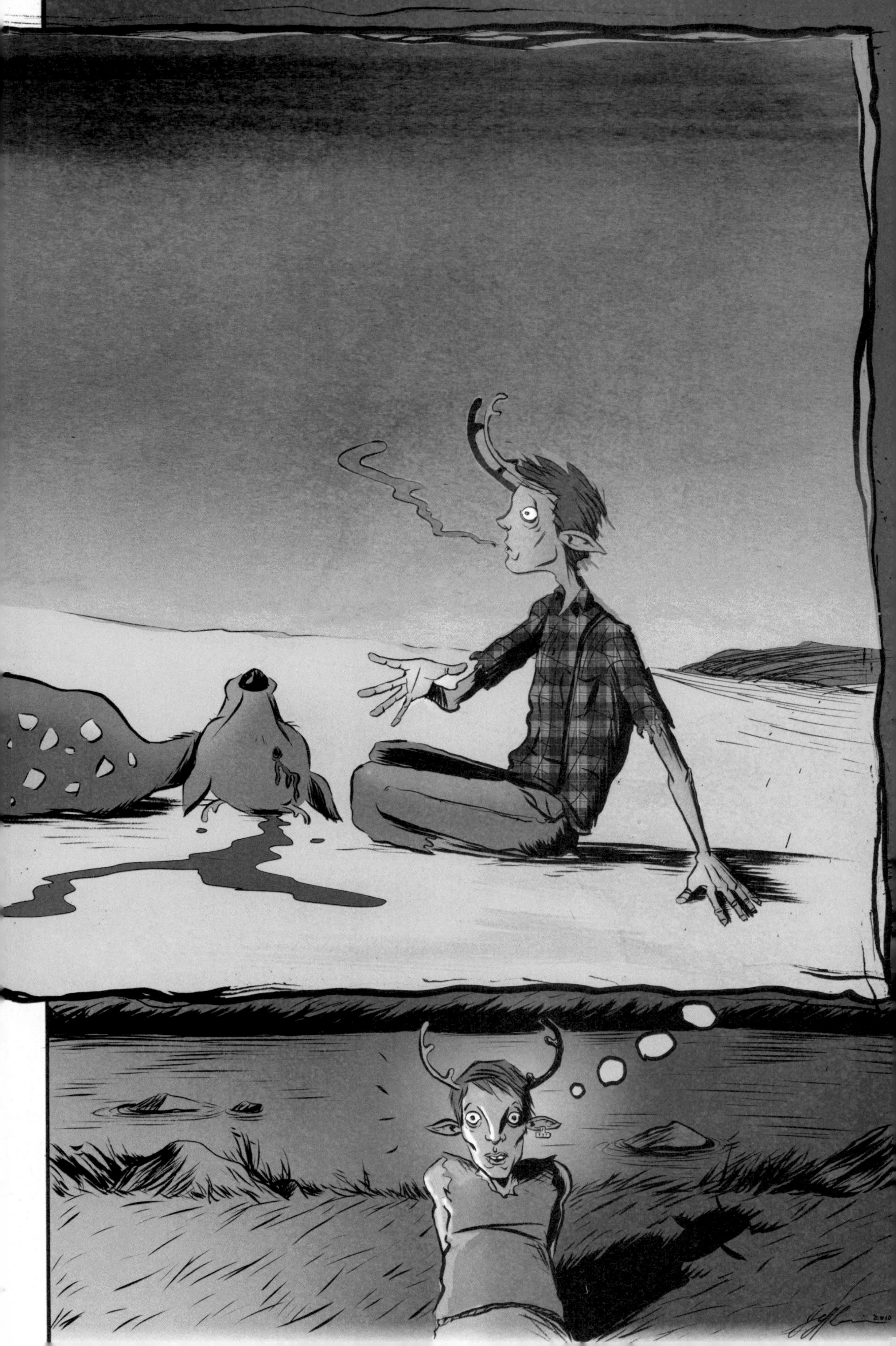

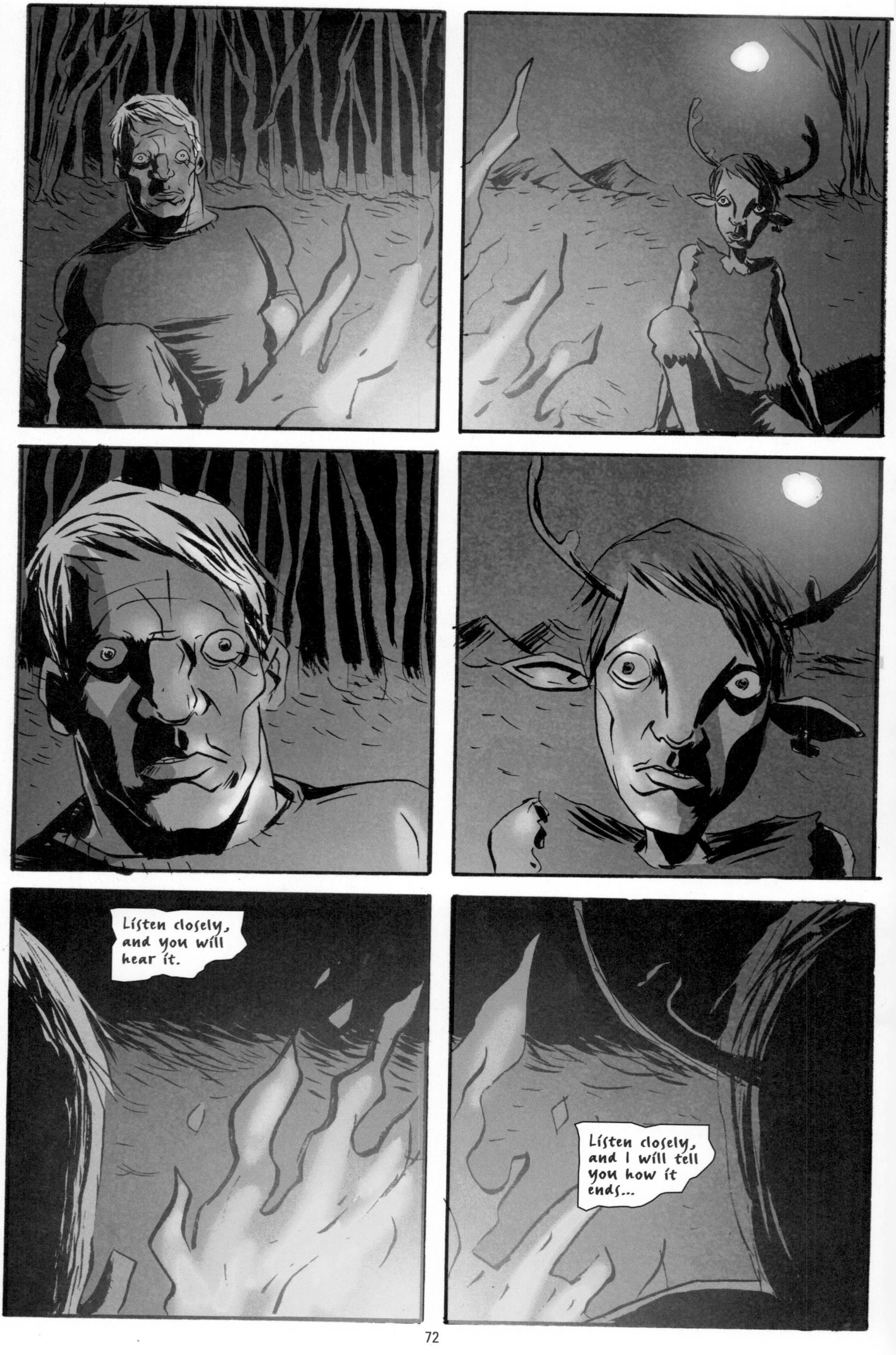
Listen closely, and you will hear it.
Listen closely, and I will tell you how it ends...

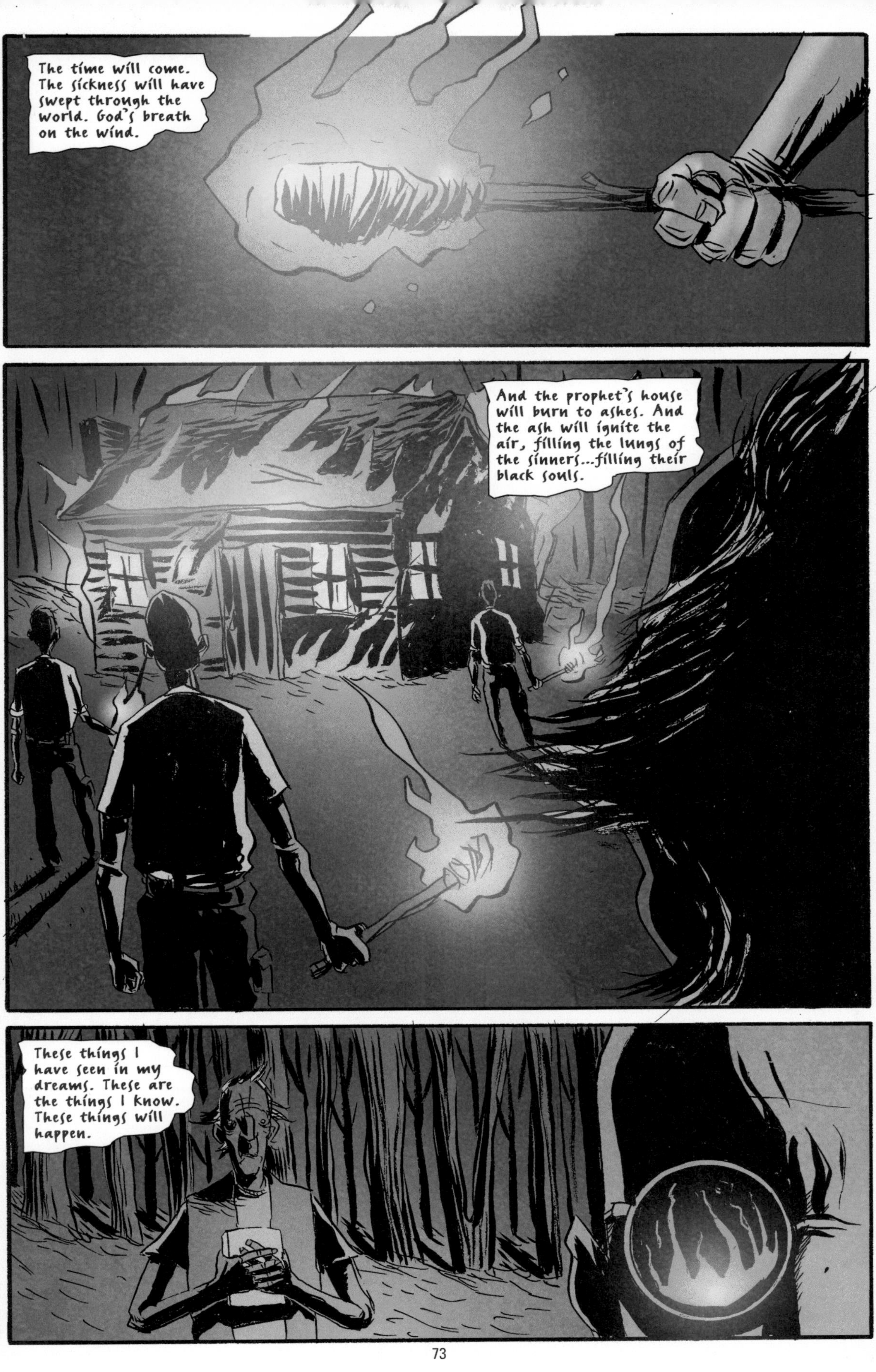
The time will come. The sickness will have swept through the world. God's breath on the wind.
And the prophet's house will burn to ashes. And the ash will ignite the air, filling the lungs of the sinners...filling their black souls.
These things I have seen in my dreams. These are the things I know. These things will happen.

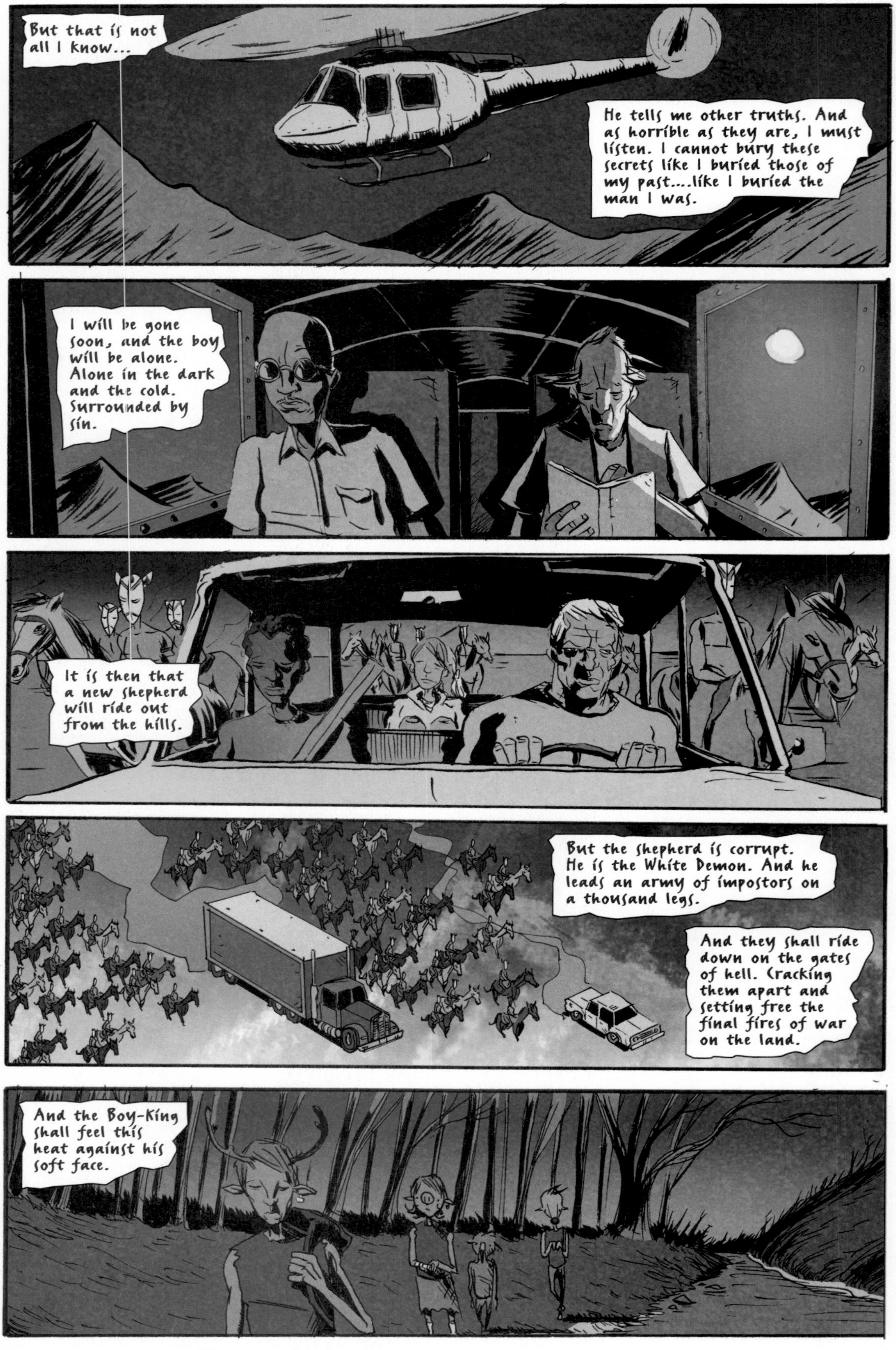
But that is not all I know...
He tells me other truths. And as horrible as they are, I must listen. I cannot bury these secrets like I buried those of my past....like I buried the man I was.
I will be gone soon, and the boy will be alone. Alone in the dark and the cold. Surrounded by sin.
It is then that a new shepherd will ride out from the hills.
But the shepherd is corrupt. He is the White Demon. And he leads an army of impostors on a thousand legs.
And they shall ride down on the gates of hell. Cracking them apart and setting free the final fires of war on the land.
And the Boy-King shall feel this heat against his soft face.

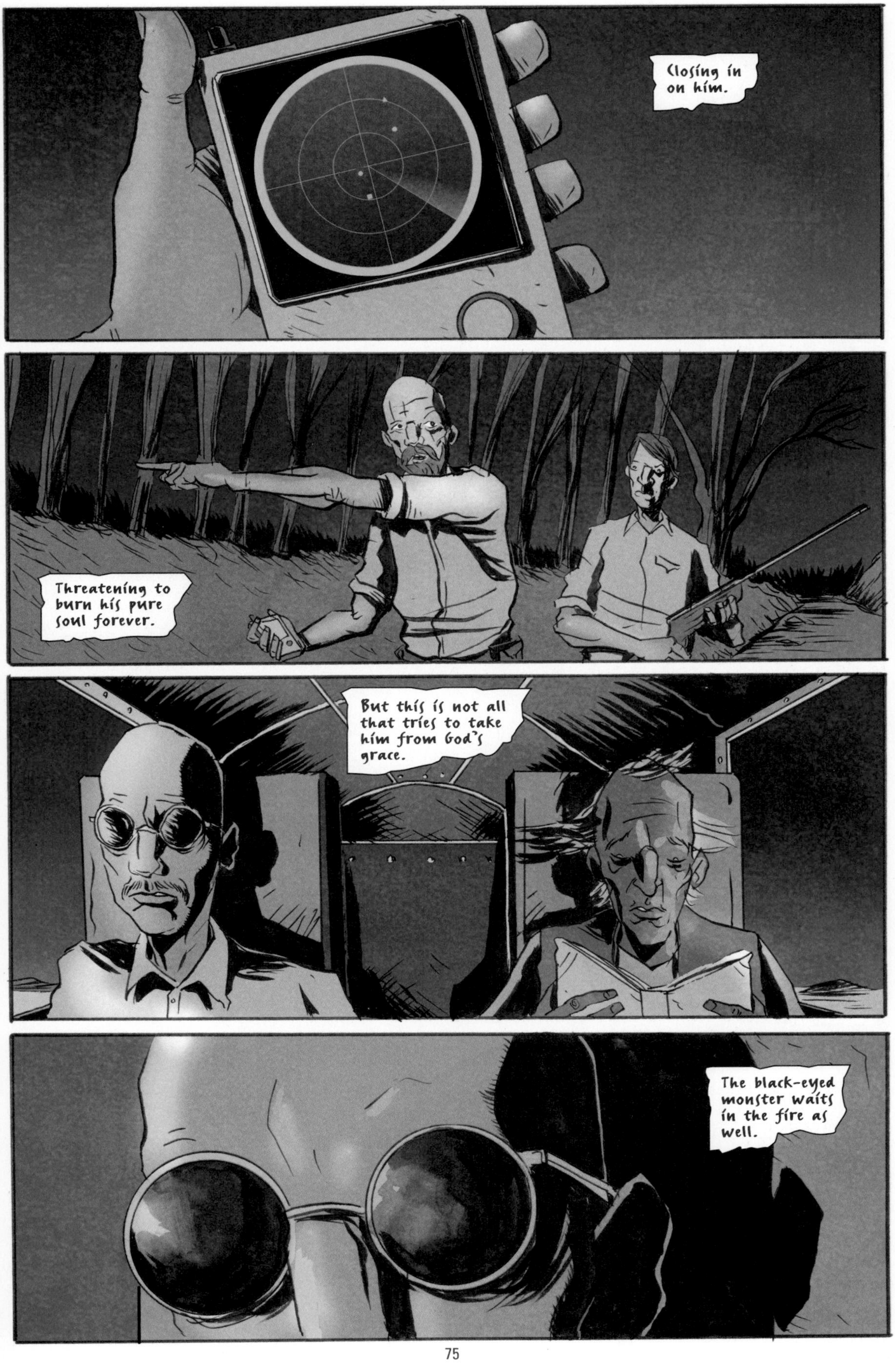
Closing in on him.
Threatening to burn his pure soul forever.
But this is not all that tries to take him from God's grace.
The black-eyed monster waits in the fire as well.

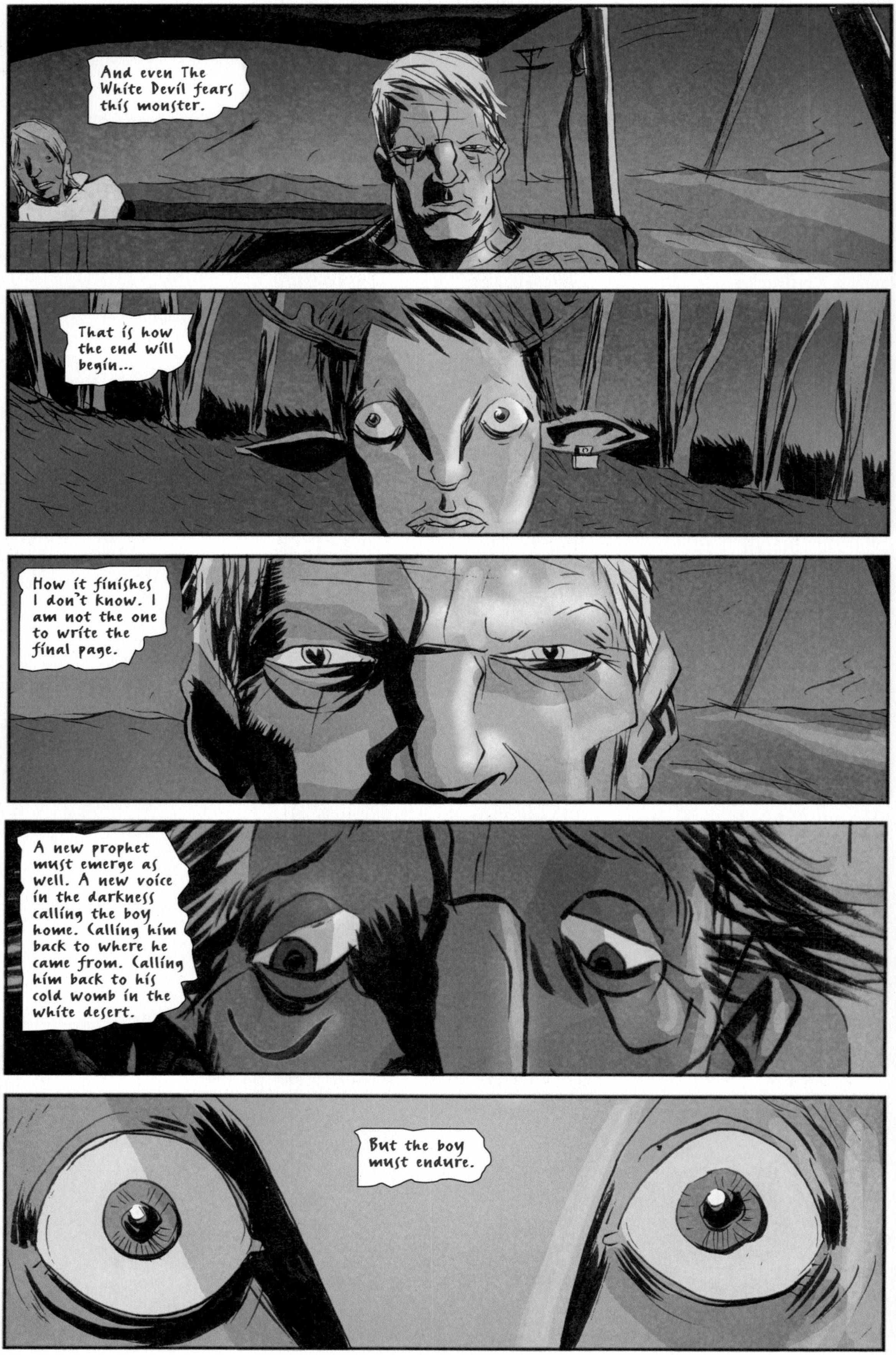

And even The White Devil fears this monster.
That is how the end will begin...
How it finishes I don't know. I am not the one to write the final page.
A new prophet must emerge as well. A new voice in the darkness calling the boy home. Calling him back to where he came from. Calling him back to his cold womb in the white desert.
But the boy must endure.

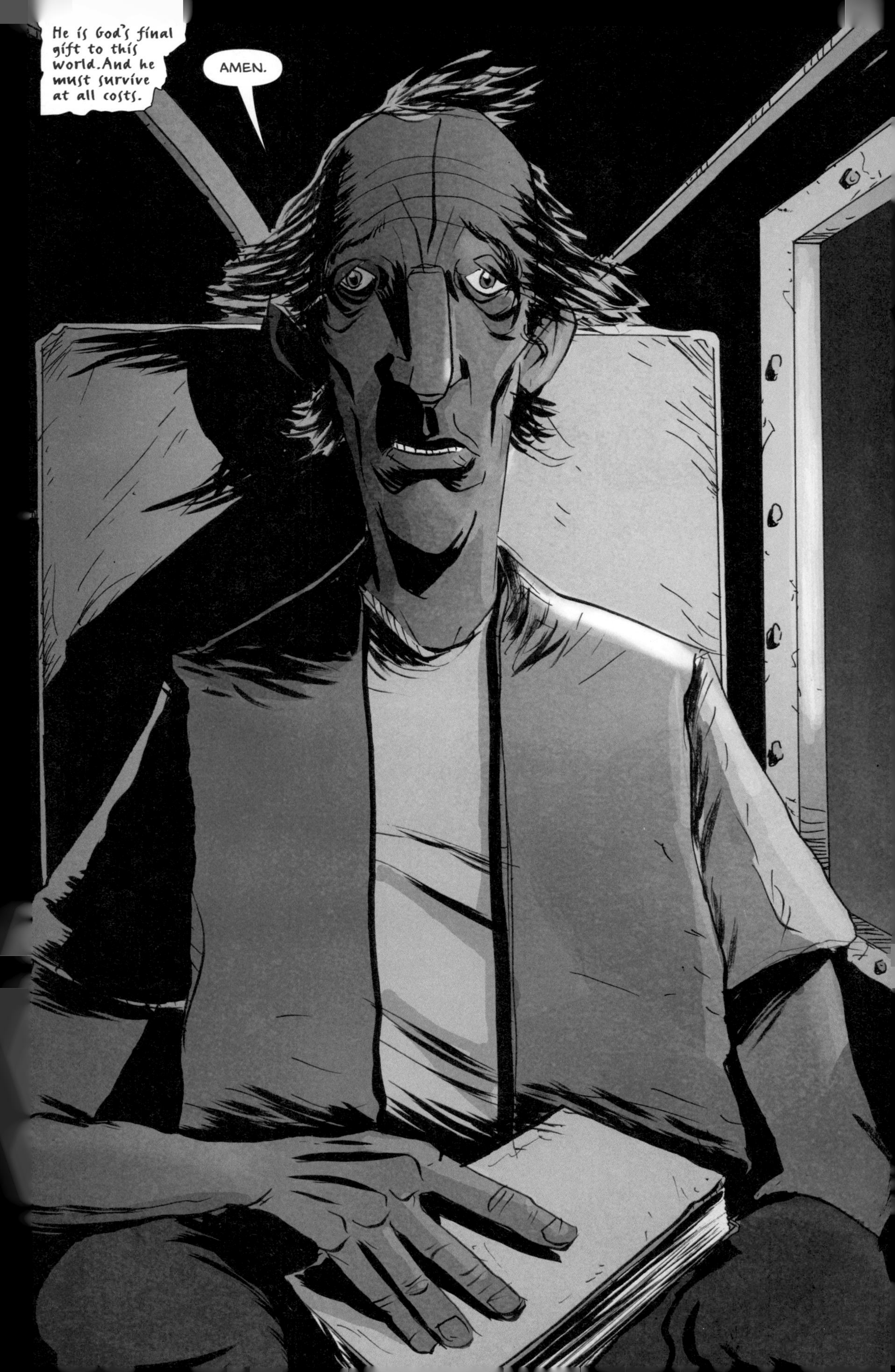
He is God's final gift to this world. And he must survive at all costs.
AMEN.

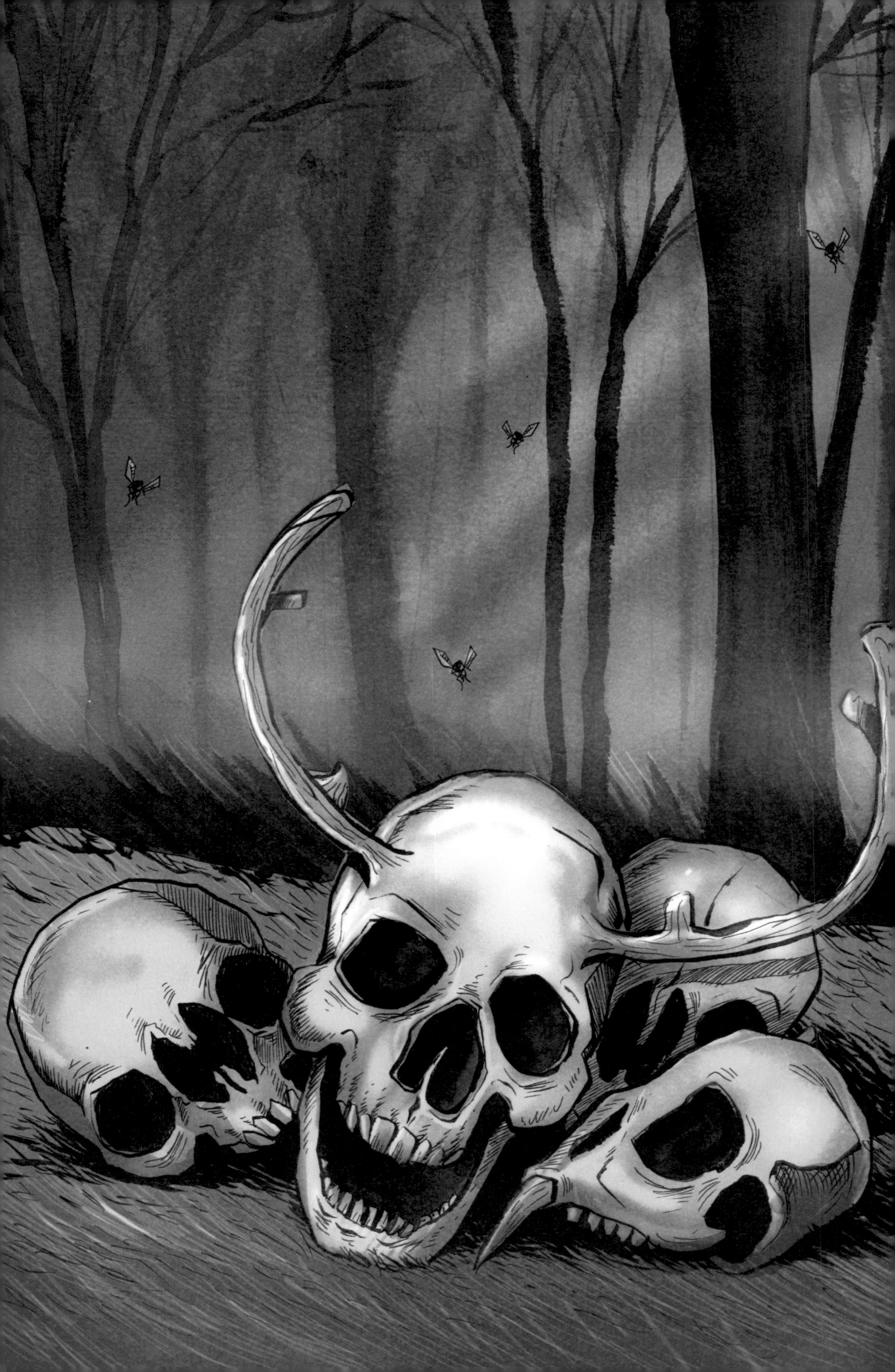

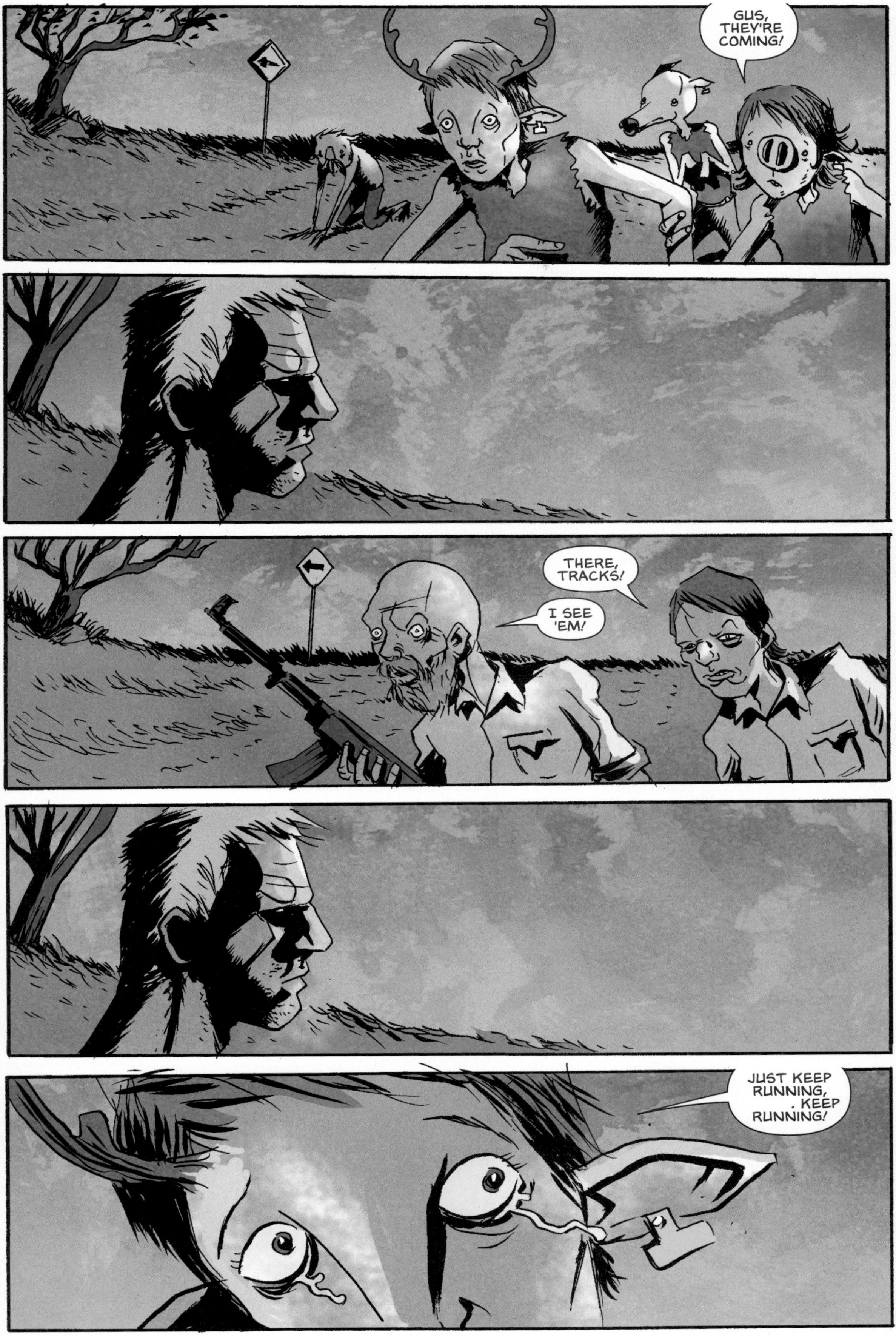
GUS, THEY'RE COMING!
THERE, TRACKS!
I SEE 'EM!
JUST KEEP RUNNING, . KEEP RUNNING!

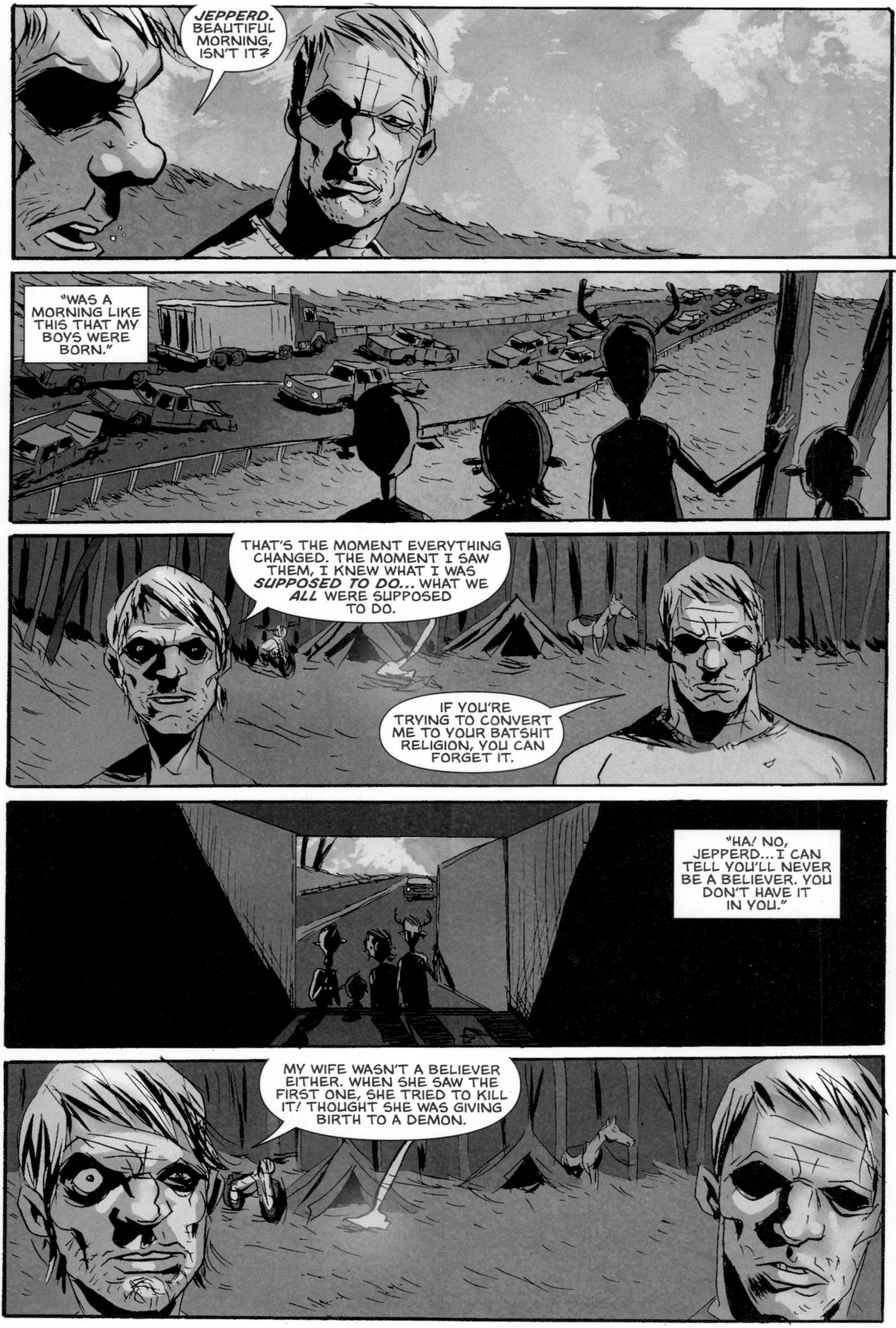
JEPPERD. BEAUTIFUL MORNING, ISN'T IT?
"WAS A MORNING LIKE THIS THAT MY BOYS WERE BORN."
THAT'S THE MOMENT EVERYTHING CHANGED. THE MOMENT I SAW THEM, I KNEW WHAT I WAS SUPPOSED TO DO... WHAT WE ALL WERE SUPPOSED TO DO.
IF YOU'RE TRYING TO CONVERT ME TO YOUR BATSHIT RELIGION, YOU CAN FORGET IT.
"HA! NO, JEPPERD... I CAN TELL YOU'LL NEVER BE A BELIEVER. YOU DON'T HAVE IT IN YOU."
MY WIFE WASN'T A BELIEVER EITHER. WHEN SHE SAW THE FIRST ONE, SHE TRIED TO KILL IT! THOUGHT SHE WAS GIVING BIRTH TO A DEMON.

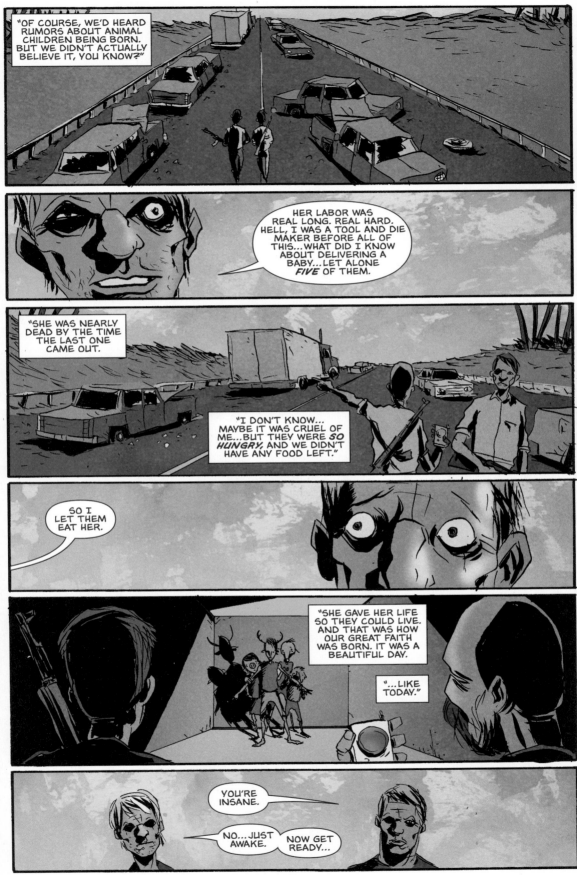

"OF COURSE, WE'D HEARD RUMORS ABOUT ANIMAL CHILDREN BEING BORN. BUT WE DIDN'T ACTUALLY BELIEVE IT, YOU KNOW?"

HER LABOR WAS REAL LONG. REAL HARD. HELL, I WAS A TOOL AND DIE MAKER BEFORE ALL OF THIS...WHAT DID I KNOW ABOUT DELIVERING A BABY...LET ALONE *FIVE* OF THEM.

"SHE WAS NEARLY DEAD BY THE TIME THE LAST ONE CAME OUT."

"I DON'T KNOW... MAYBE IT WAS CRUEL OF ME...BUT THEY WERE *SO HUNGRY*, AND WE DIDN'T HAVE ANY FOOD LEFT."

SO I LET THEM EAT HER.

"SHE GAVE HER LIFE SO THEY COULD LIVE. AND THAT WAS HOW OUR GREAT FAITH WAS BORN. IT WAS A BEAUTIFUL DAY.

"...LIKE TODAY."

YOU'RE INSANE.

NO...JUST AWAKE.

NOW GET READY...

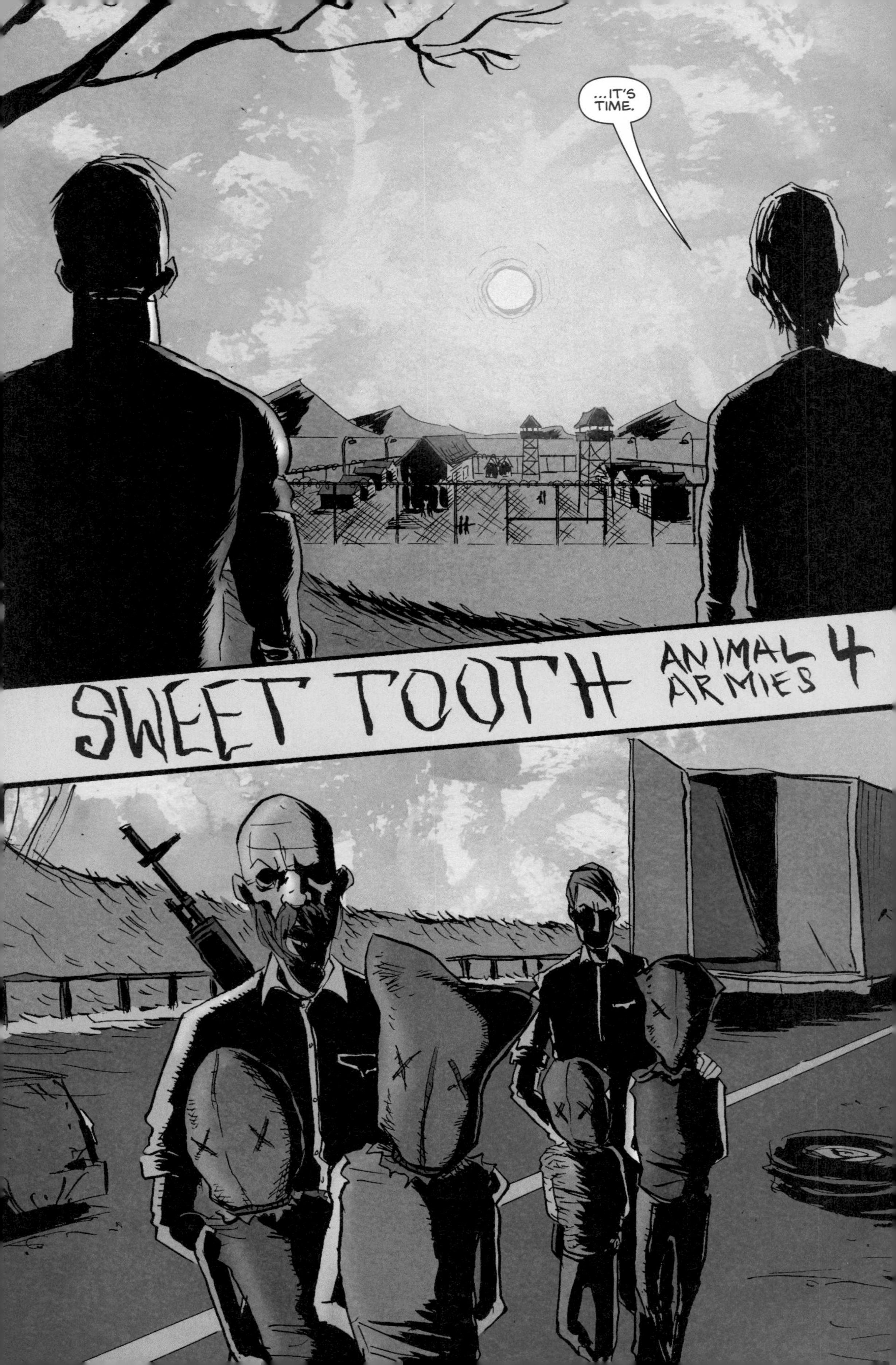
...IT'S TIME.
SWEET TOOTH
ANIMAL ARMIES 4

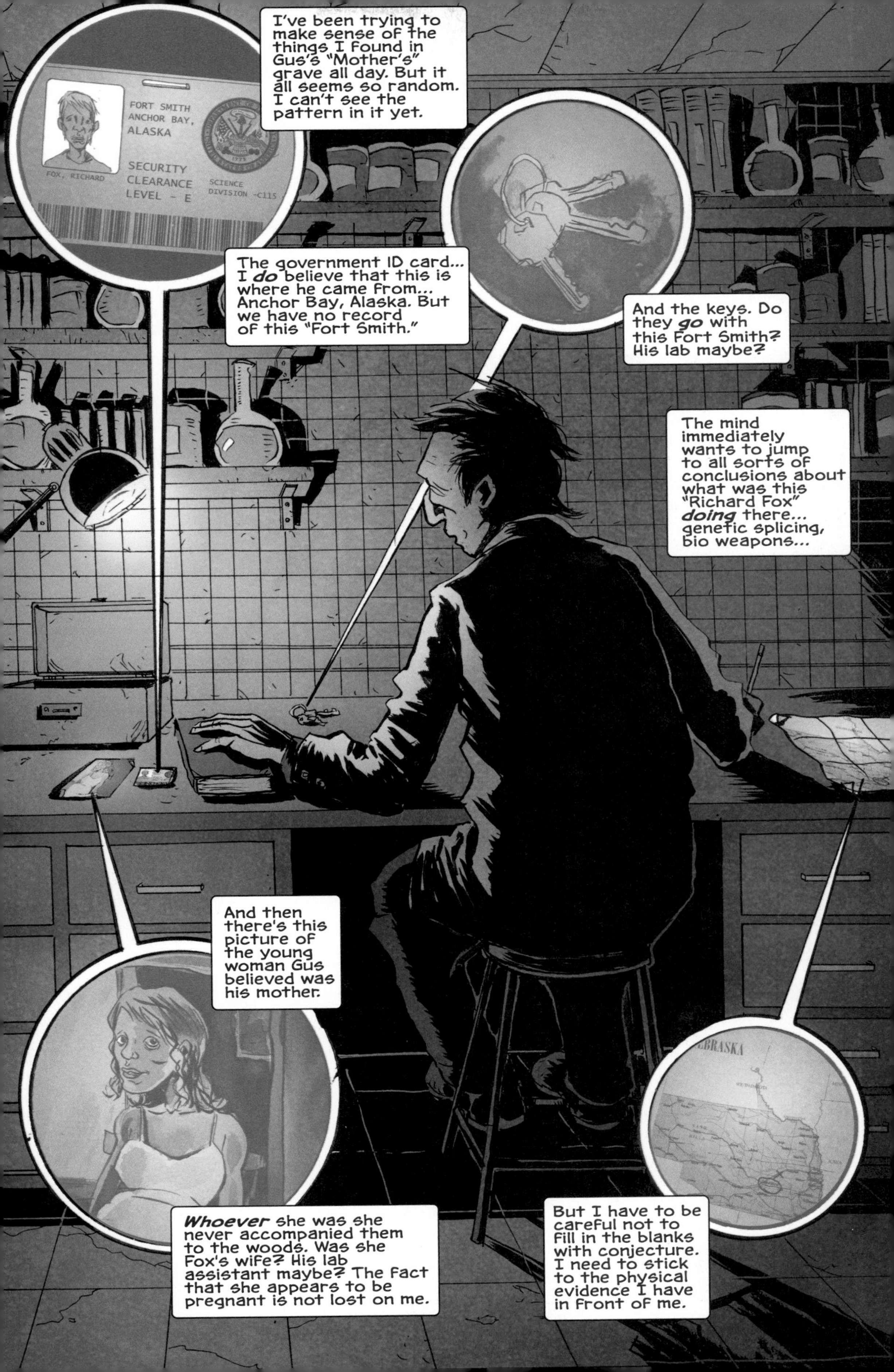
I've been trying to make sense of the things I found in Gus's "Mother's" grave all day. But it all seems so random. I can't see the pattern in it yet.
FORT SMITH
ANCHOR BAY, ALASKA
SECURITY CLEARANCE LEVEL - E
SCIENCE DIVISION -C115
FOX, RICHARD
The government ID card... I *do* believe that this is where he came from... Anchor Bay, Alaska. But we have no record of this "Fort Smith."
And the keys. Do they *go* with this Fort Smith? His lab maybe?
The mind immediately wants to jump to all sorts of conclusions about what was this "Richard Fox" *doing* there... genetic splicing, bio weapons...
And then there's this picture of the young woman Gus believed was his mother.
NEBRASKA
Whoever she was she never accompanied them to the woods. Was she Fox's wife? His lab assistant maybe? The fact that she appears to be pregnant is not lost on me.
But I have to be careful not to fill in the blanks with conjecture. I need to stick to the physical evidence I have in front of me.

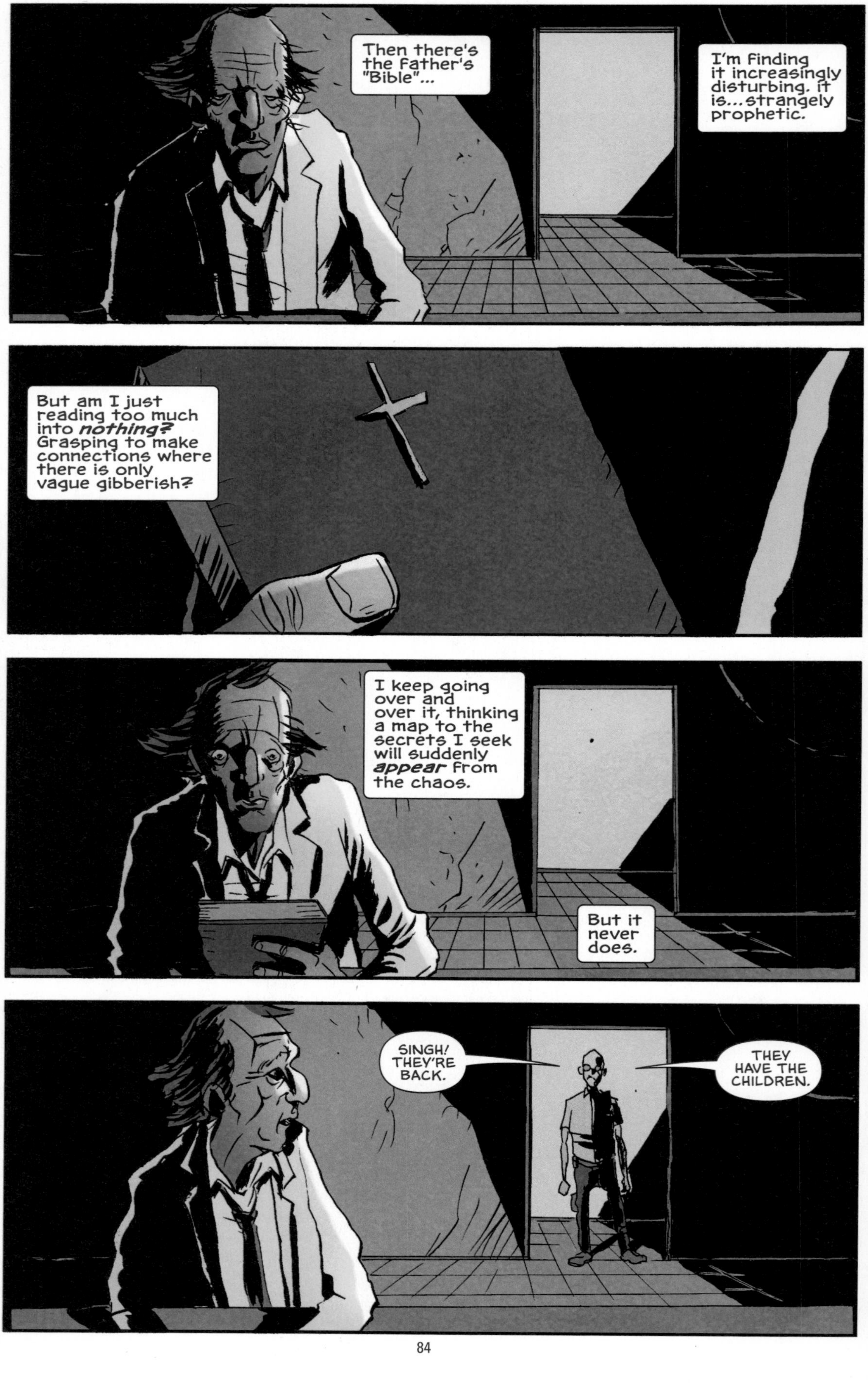
Then there's the father's "Bible"...
I'm finding it increasingly disturbing. it is...strangely prophetic.
But am I just reading too much into *nothing?* Grasping to make connections where there is only vague gibberish?
I keep going over and over it, thinking a map to the secrets I seek will suddenly *appear* from the chaos.
But it never does.
SINGH! THEY'RE BACK.
THEY HAVE THE CHILDREN.

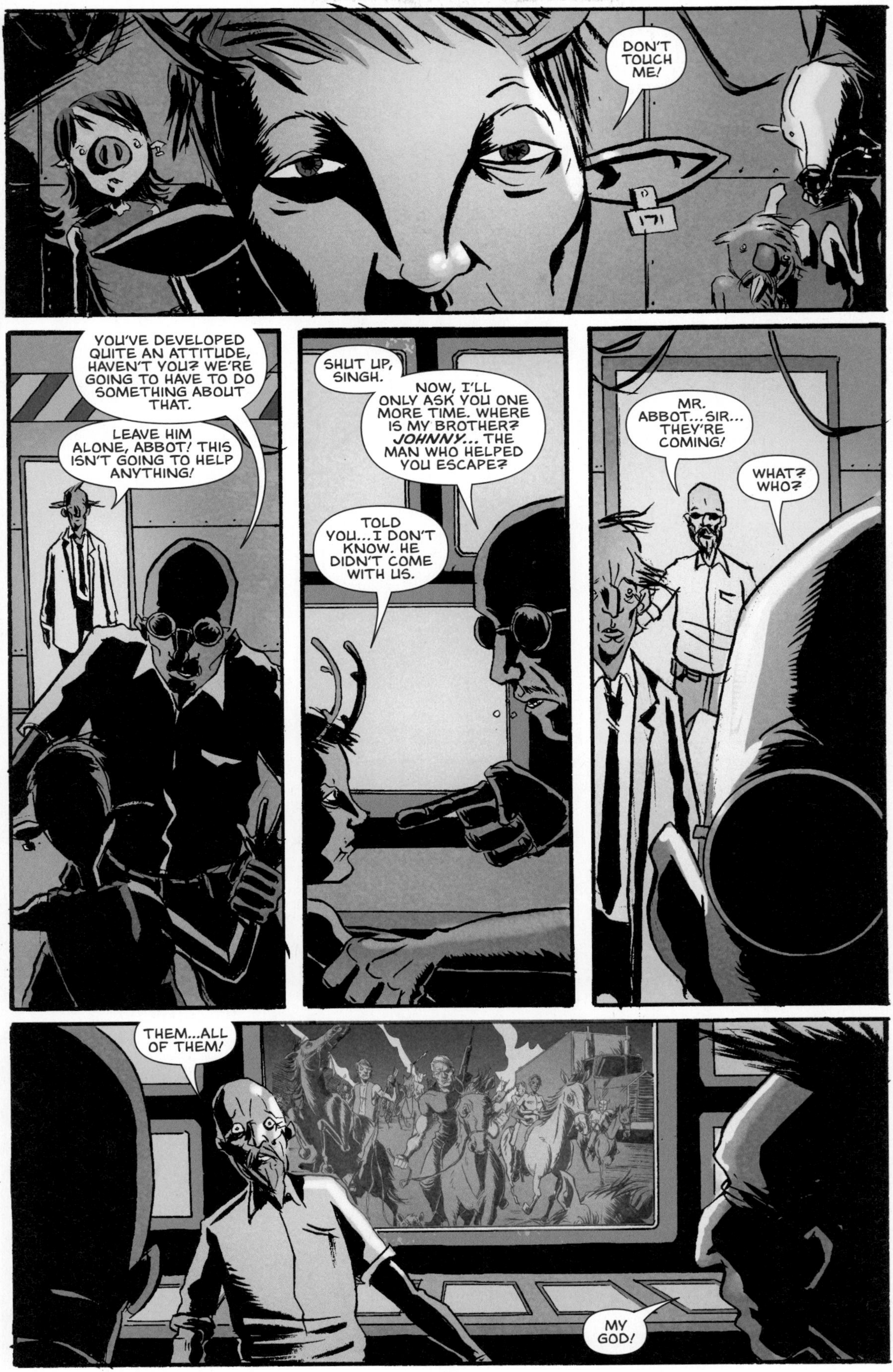
DON'T TOUCH ME!
YOU'VE DEVELOPED QUITE AN ATTITUDE, HAVEN'T YOU? WE'RE GOING TO HAVE TO DO SOMETHING ABOUT THAT.
LEAVE HIM ALONE, ABBOT! THIS ISN'T GOING TO HELP ANYTHING!
SHUT UP, SINGH.
NOW, I'LL ONLY ASK YOU ONE MORE TIME. WHERE IS MY BROTHER? JOHNNY... THE MAN WHO HELPED YOU ESCAPE?
TOLD YOU...I DON'T KNOW. HE DIDN'T COME WITH US.
MR. ABBOT...SIR... THEY'RE COMING!
WHAT? WHO?
THEM...ALL OF THEM!
MY GOD!

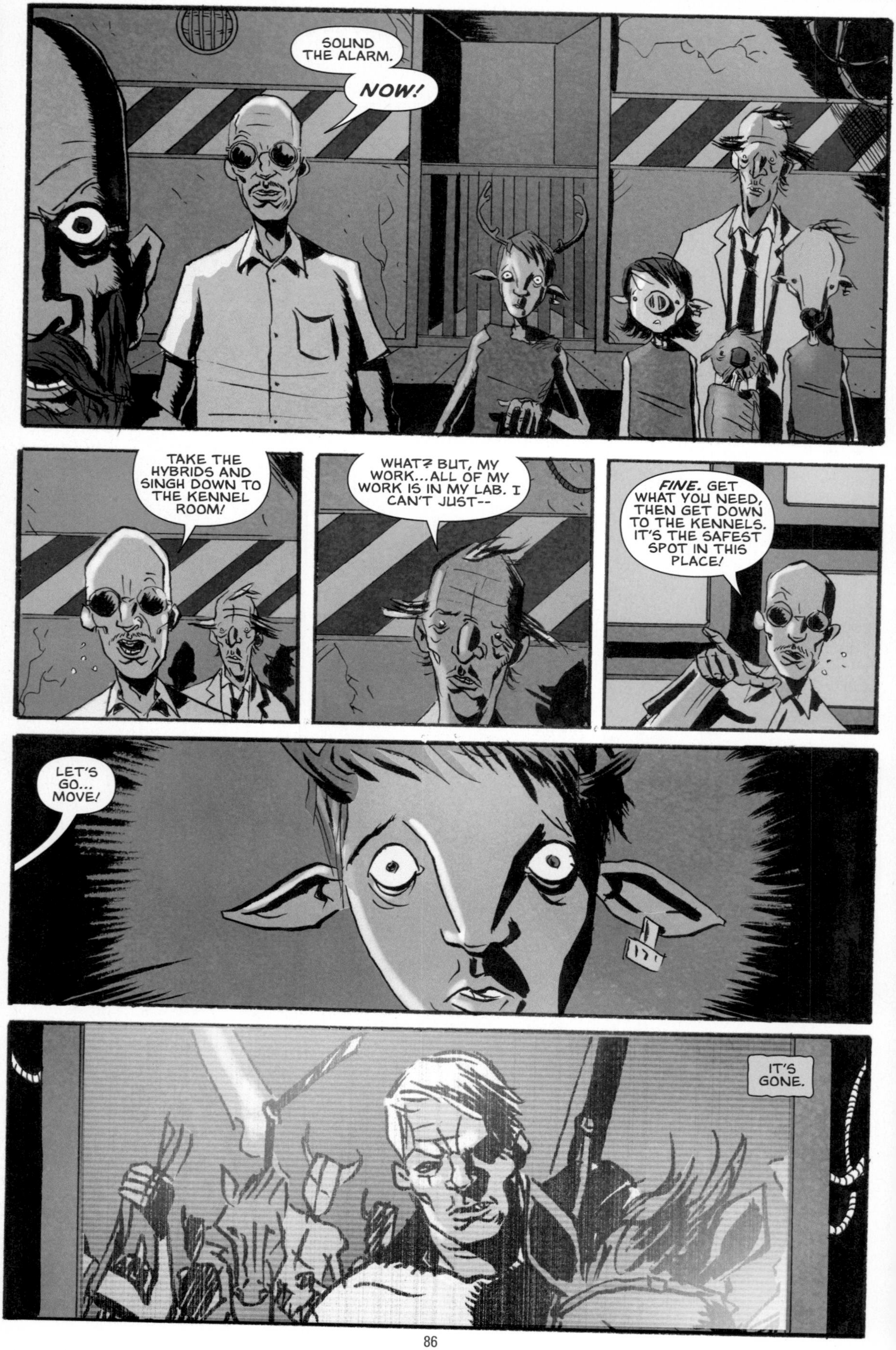
SOUND THE ALARM.
NOW!
TAKE THE HYBRIDS AND SINGH DOWN TO THE KENNEL ROOM!
WHAT? BUT, MY WORK...ALL OF MY WORK IS IN MY LAB. I CAN'T JUST--
FINE. GET WHAT YOU NEED, THEN GET DOWN TO THE KENNELS. IT'S THE SAFEST SPOT IN THIS PLACE!
LET'S GO... MOVE!
IT'S GONE.

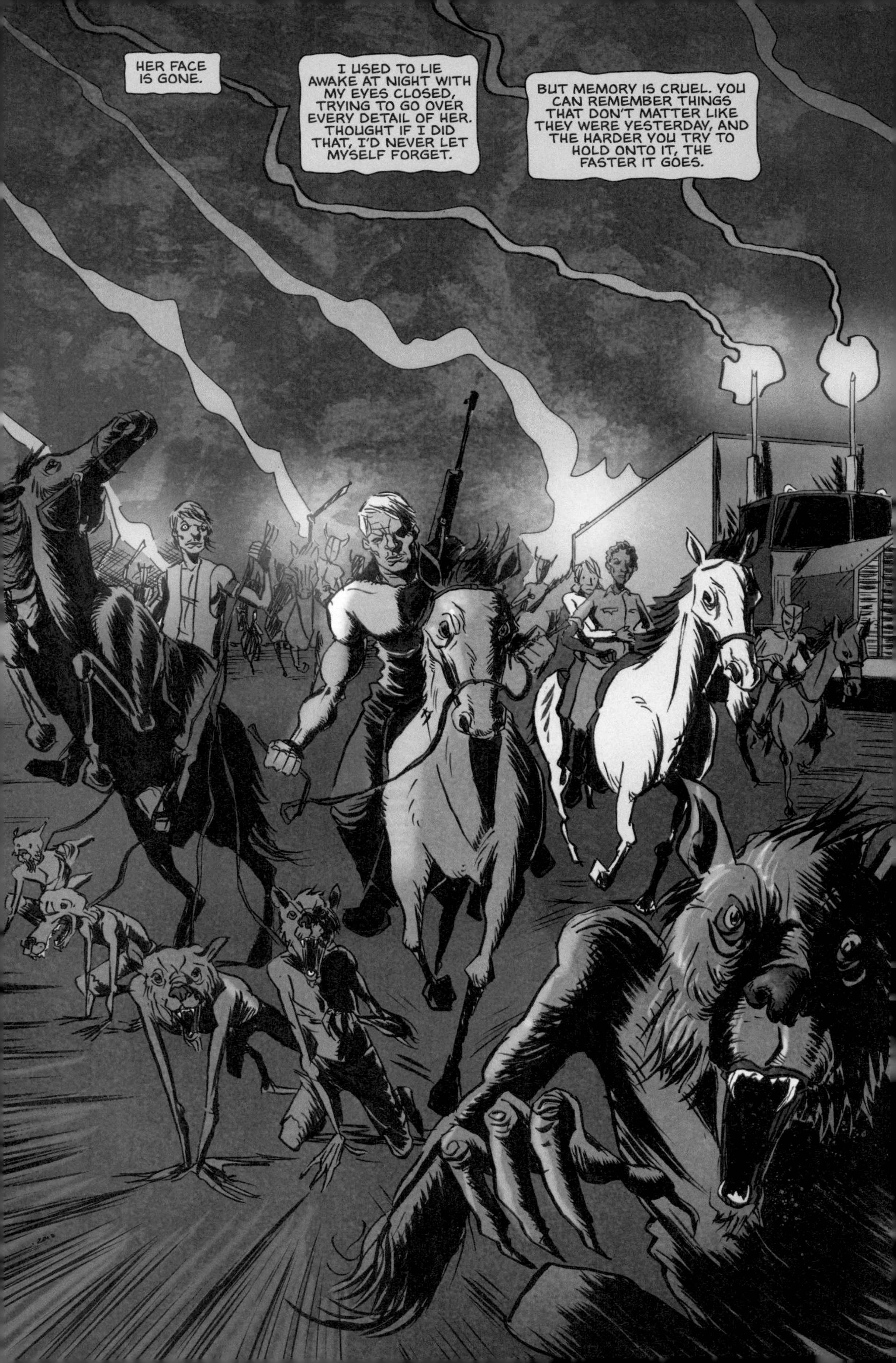
HER FACE IS GONE.
I USED TO LIE AWAKE AT NIGHT WITH MY EYES CLOSED, TRYING TO GO OVER EVERY DETAIL OF HER. THOUGHT IF I DID THAT, I'D NEVER LET MYSELF FORGET.
BUT MEMORY IS CRUEL. YOU CAN REMEMBER THINGS THAT DON'T MATTER LIKE THEY WERE YESTERDAY, AND THE HARDER YOU TRY TO HOLD ONTO IT, THE FASTER IT GOES.

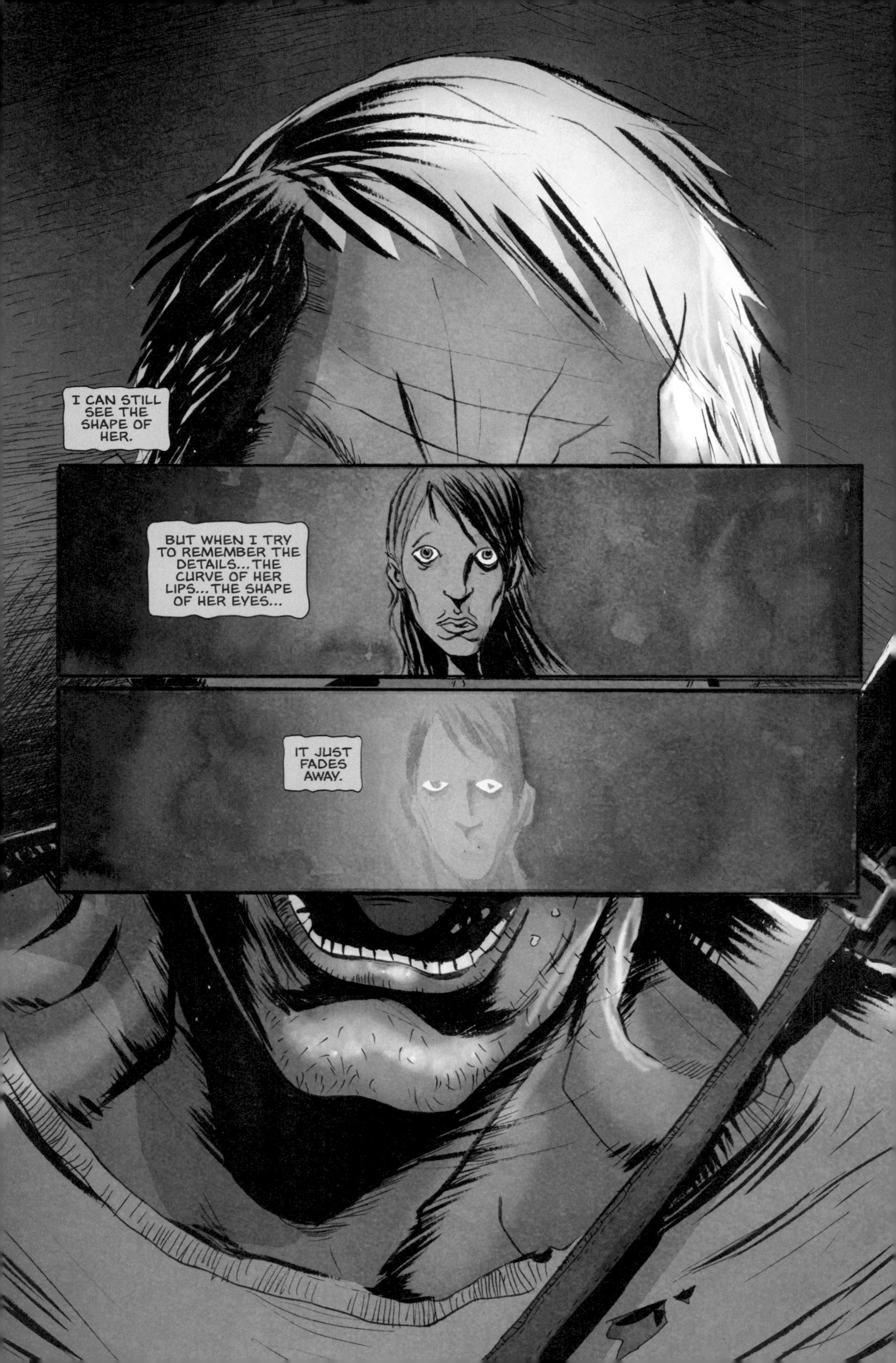
I CAN STILL SEE THE SHAPE OF HER.
BUT WHEN I TRY TO REMEMBER THE DETAILS... THE CURVE OF HER LIPS... THE SHAPE OF HER EYES...
IT JUST FADES AWAY.

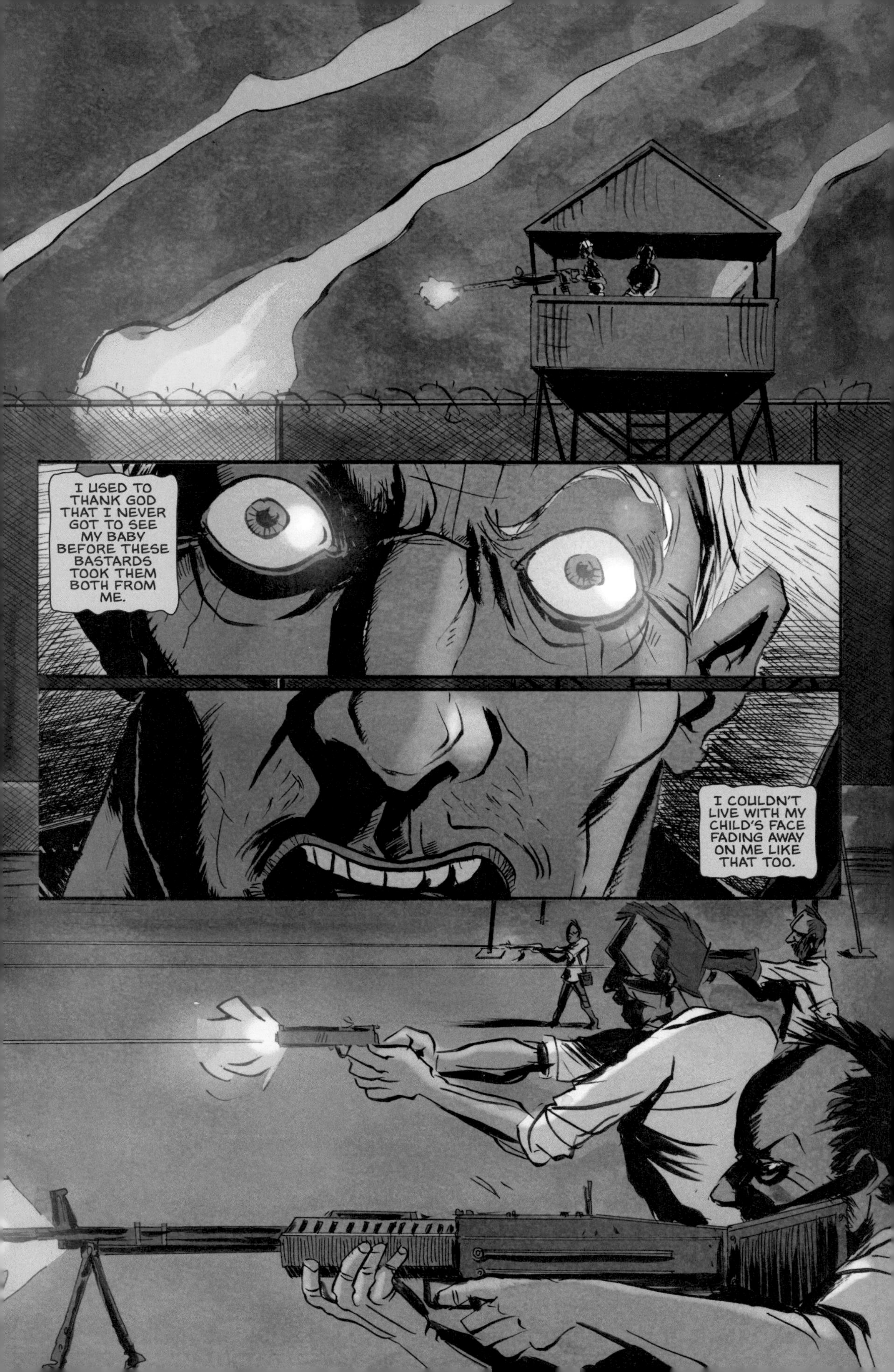
I USED TO THANK GOD THAT I NEVER GOT TO SEE MY BABY BEFORE THESE BASTARDS TOOK THEM BOTH FROM ME.
I COULDN'T LIVE WITH MY CHILD'S FACE FADING AWAY ON ME LIKE THAT TOO.

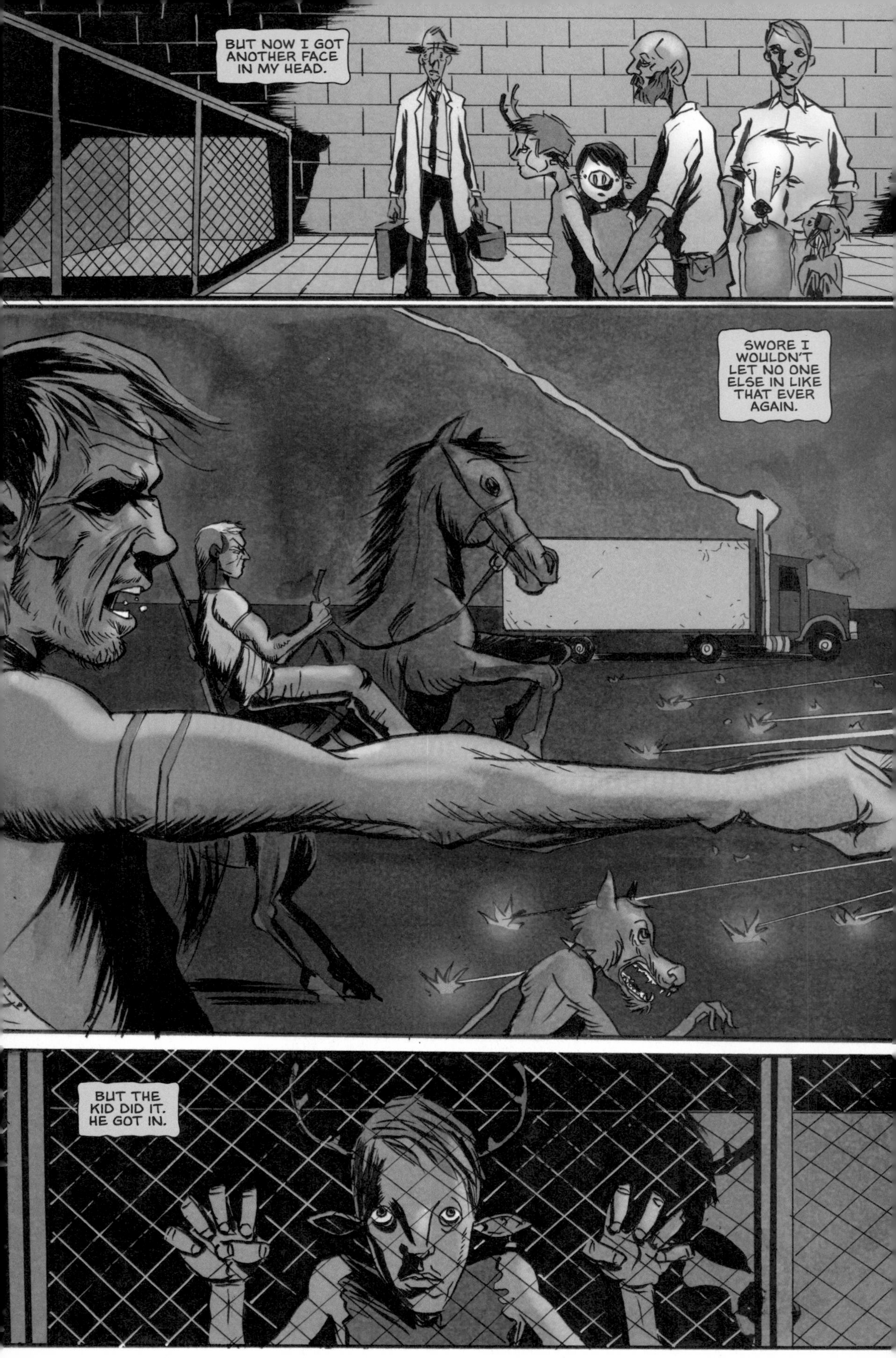
BUT NOW I GOT ANOTHER FACE IN MY HEAD.
SWORE I WOULDN'T LET NO ONE ELSE IN LIKE THAT EVER AGAIN.
BUT THE KID DID IT. HE GOT IN.

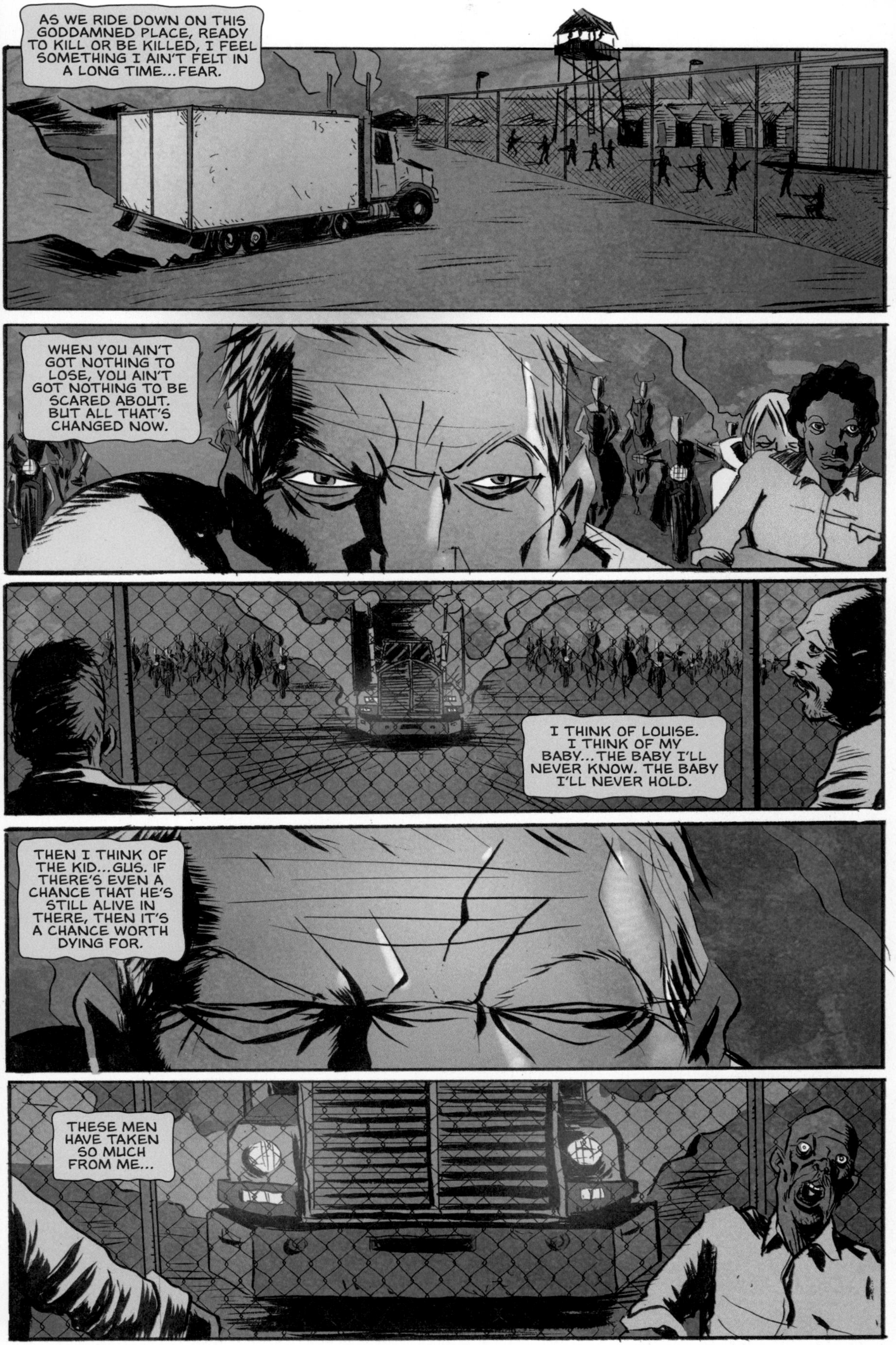

AS WE RIDE DOWN ON THIS GODDAMNED PLACE, READY TO KILL OR BE KILLED, I FEEL SOMETHING I AIN'T FELT IN A LONG TIME...FEAR.
WHEN YOU AIN'T GOT NOTHING TO LOSE, YOU AIN'T GOT NOTHING TO BE SCARED ABOUT. BUT ALL THAT'S CHANGED NOW.
I THINK OF LOUISE. I THINK OF MY BABY...THE BABY I'LL NEVER KNOW. THE BABY I'LL NEVER HOLD.
THEN I THINK OF THE KID...GUS. IF THERE'S EVEN A CHANCE THAT HE'S STILL ALIVE IN THERE, THEN IT'S A CHANCE WORTH DYING FOR.
THESE MEN HAVE TAKEN SO MUCH FROM ME...

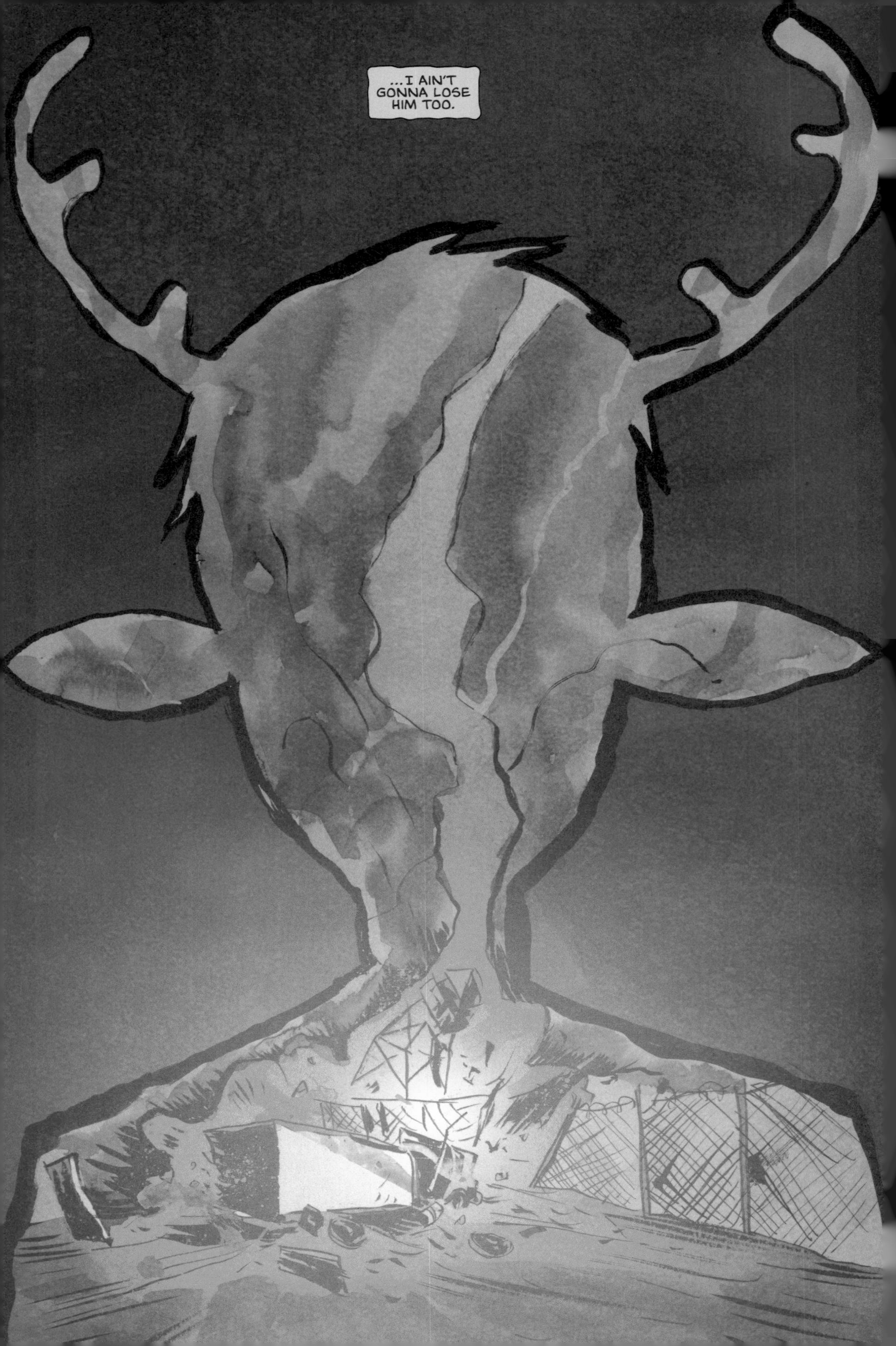
...I AIN'T GONNA LOSE HIM TOO.

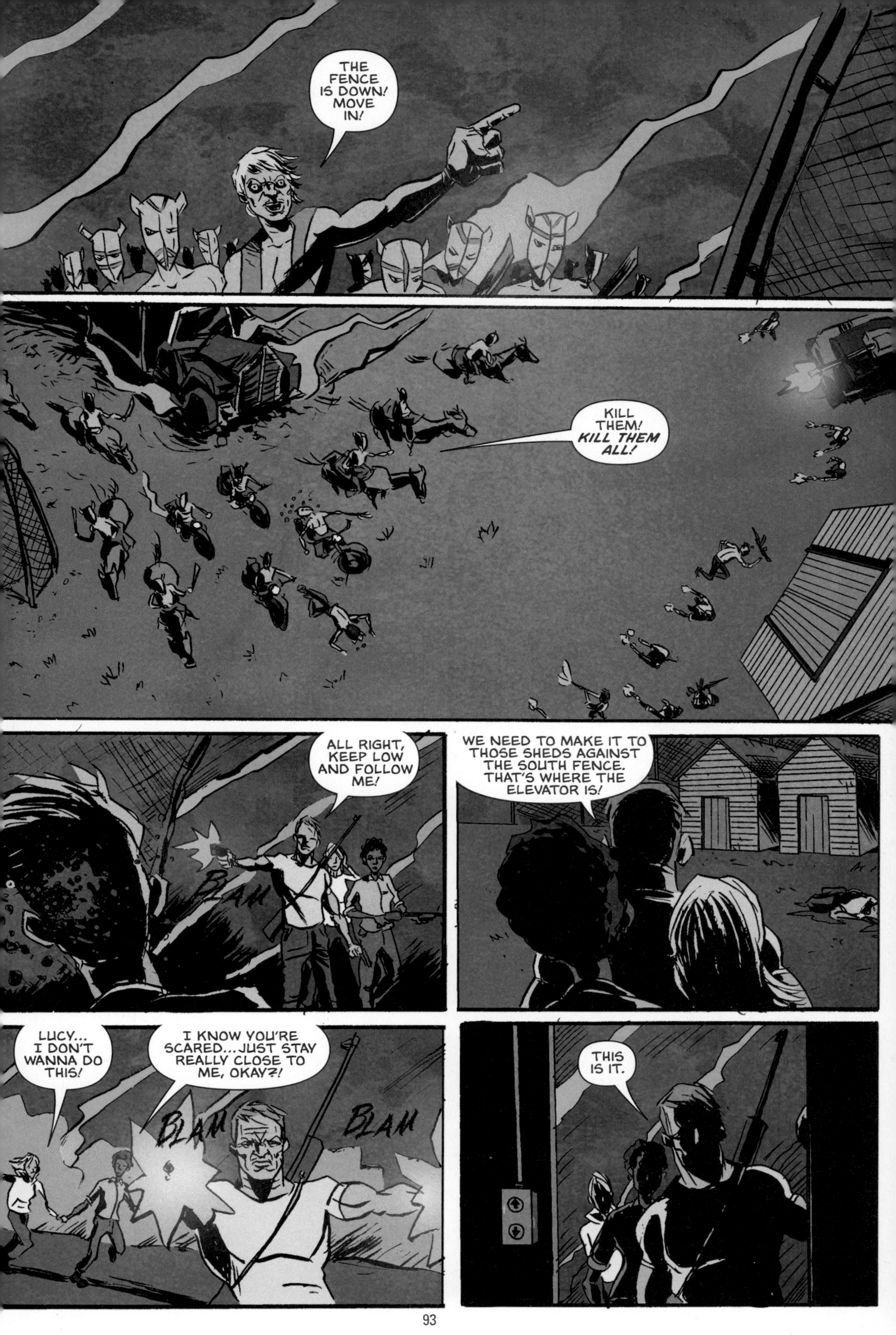
THE FENCE IS DOWN! MOVE IN!
KILL THEM! *KILL THEM ALL!*
ALL RIGHT, KEEP LOW AND FOLLOW ME!
BLAM
WE NEED TO MAKE IT TO THOSE SHEDS AGAINST THE SOUTH FENCE. THAT'S WHERE THE ELEVATOR IS!
LUCY... I DON'T WANNA DO THIS!
I KNOW YOU'RE SCARED... JUST STAY REALLY CLOSE TO ME, OKAY?!
BLAM
BLAM
THIS IS IT.

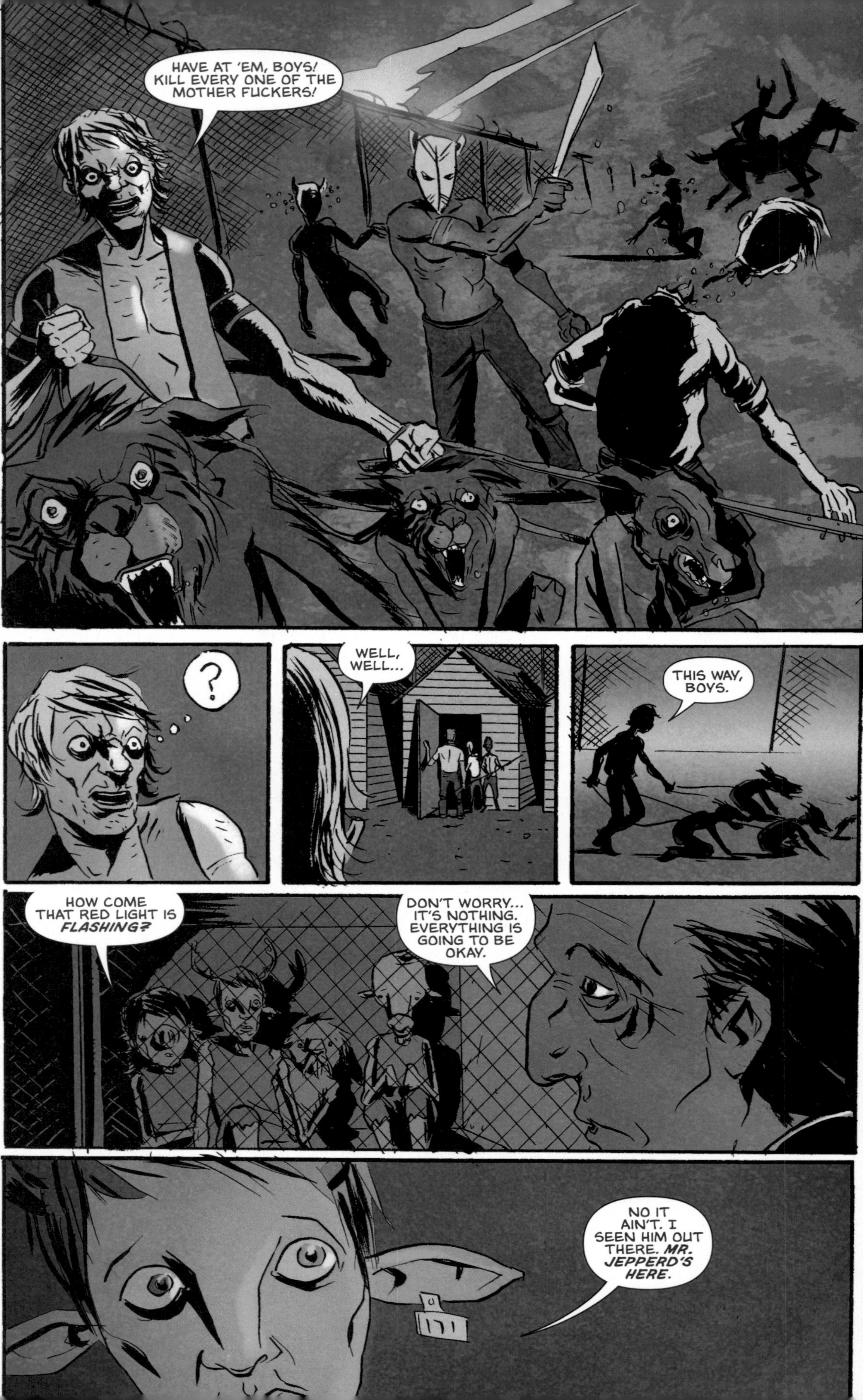

HAVE AT 'EM, BOYS! KILL EVERY ONE OF THE MOTHER FUCKERS!
?
WELL, WELL...
THIS WAY, BOYS.
HOW COME THAT RED LIGHT IS *FLASHING?*
DON'T WORRY... IT'S NOTHING. EVERYTHING IS GOING TO BE OKAY.
NO IT AIN'T. I SEEN HIM OUT THERE. *MR. JEPPERD'S HERE.*
171

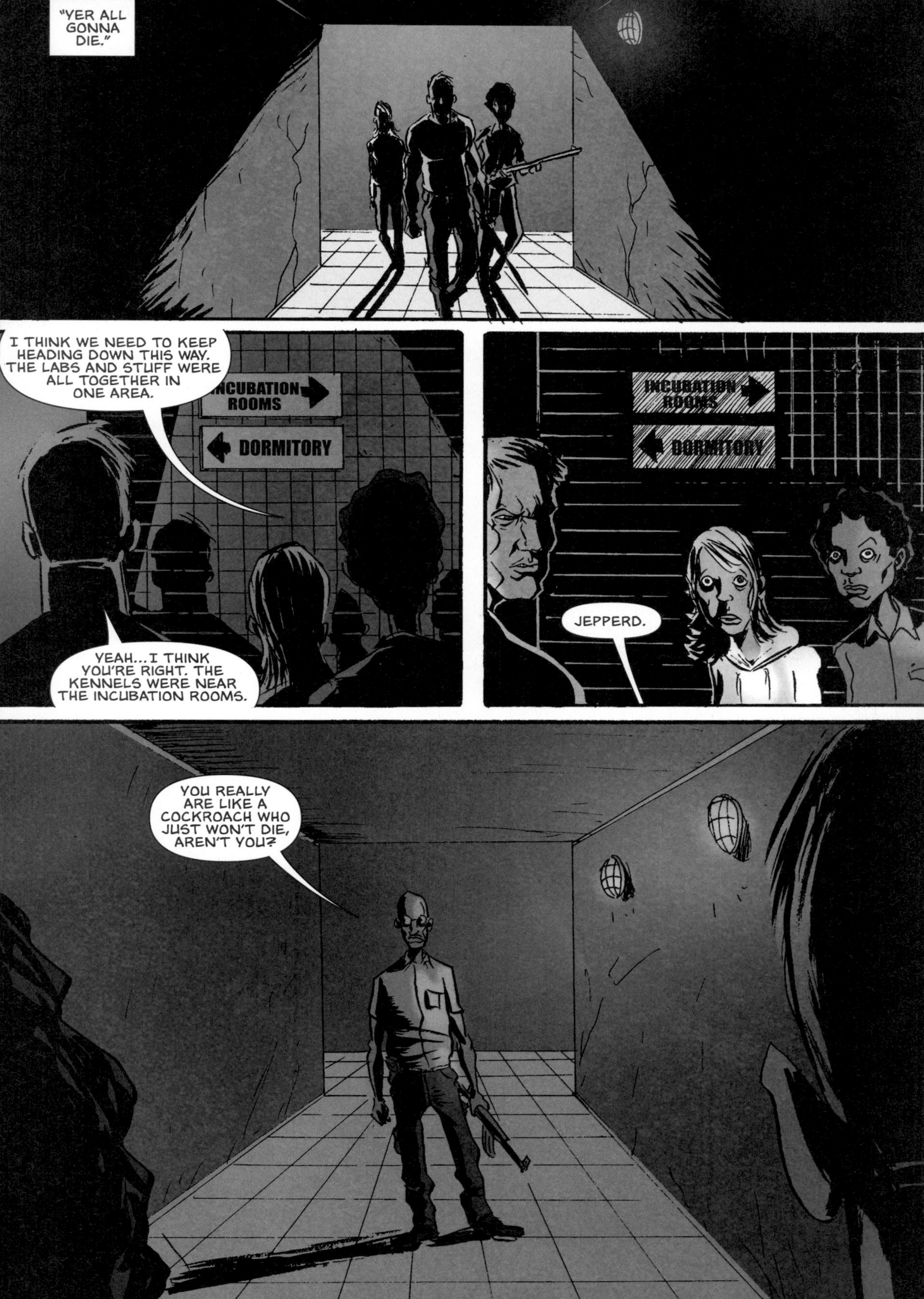
"YER ALL GONNA DIE."
I THINK WE NEED TO KEEP HEADING DOWN THIS WAY. THE LABS AND STUFF WERE ALL TOGETHER IN ONE AREA.
INCUBATION ROOMS
DORMITORY
YEAH...I THINK YOU'RE RIGHT. THE KENNELS WERE NEAR THE INCUBATION ROOMS.
INCUBATION ROOMS
DORMITORY
JEPPERD.
YOU REALLY ARE LIKE A COCKROACH WHO JUST WON'T DIE, AREN'T YOU?

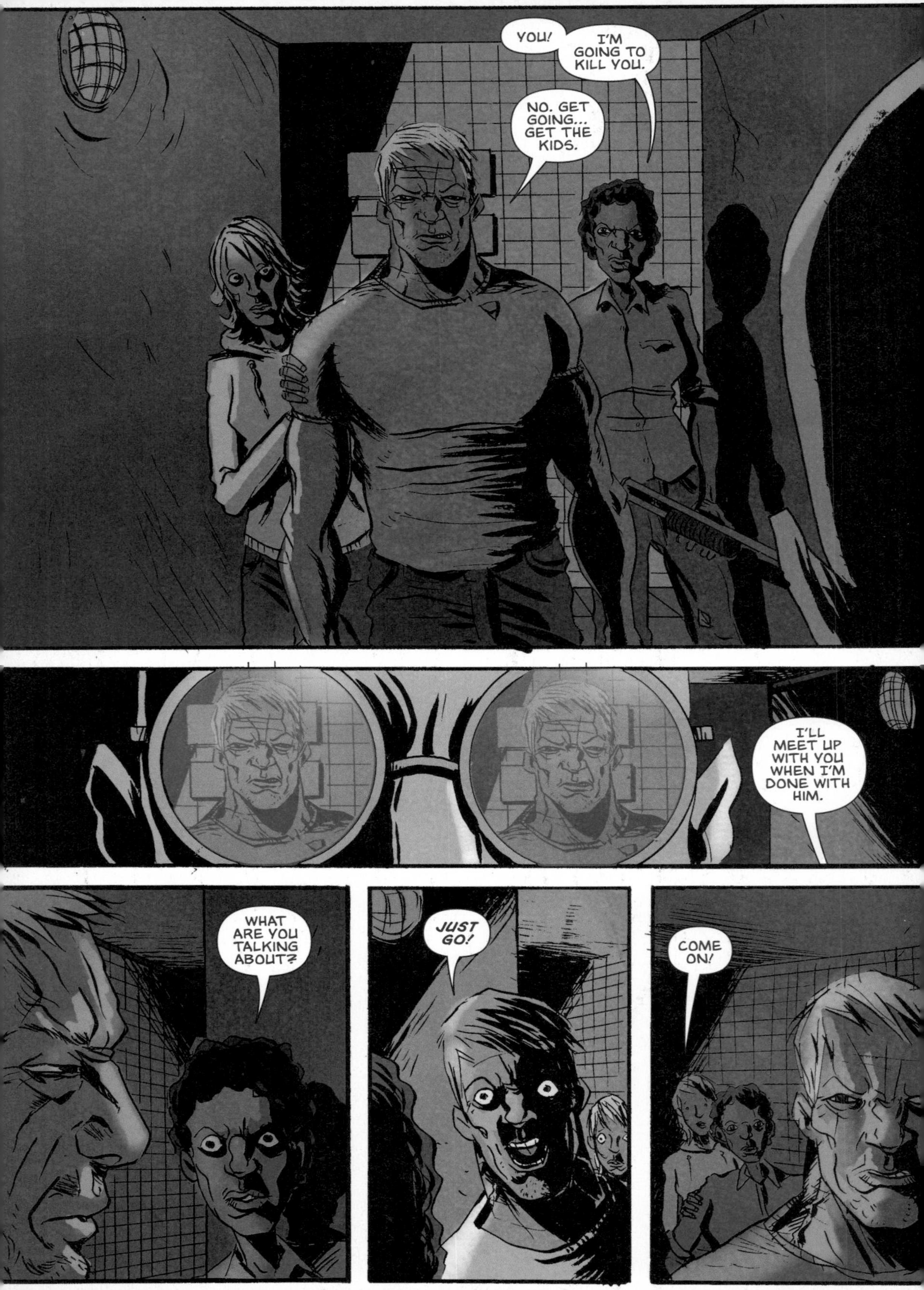
YOU!
I'M GOING TO KILL YOU.
NO. GET GOING... GET THE KIDS.
I'LL MEET UP WITH YOU WHEN I'M DONE WITH HIM.
WHAT ARE YOU TALKING ABOUT?
JUST GO!
COME ON!

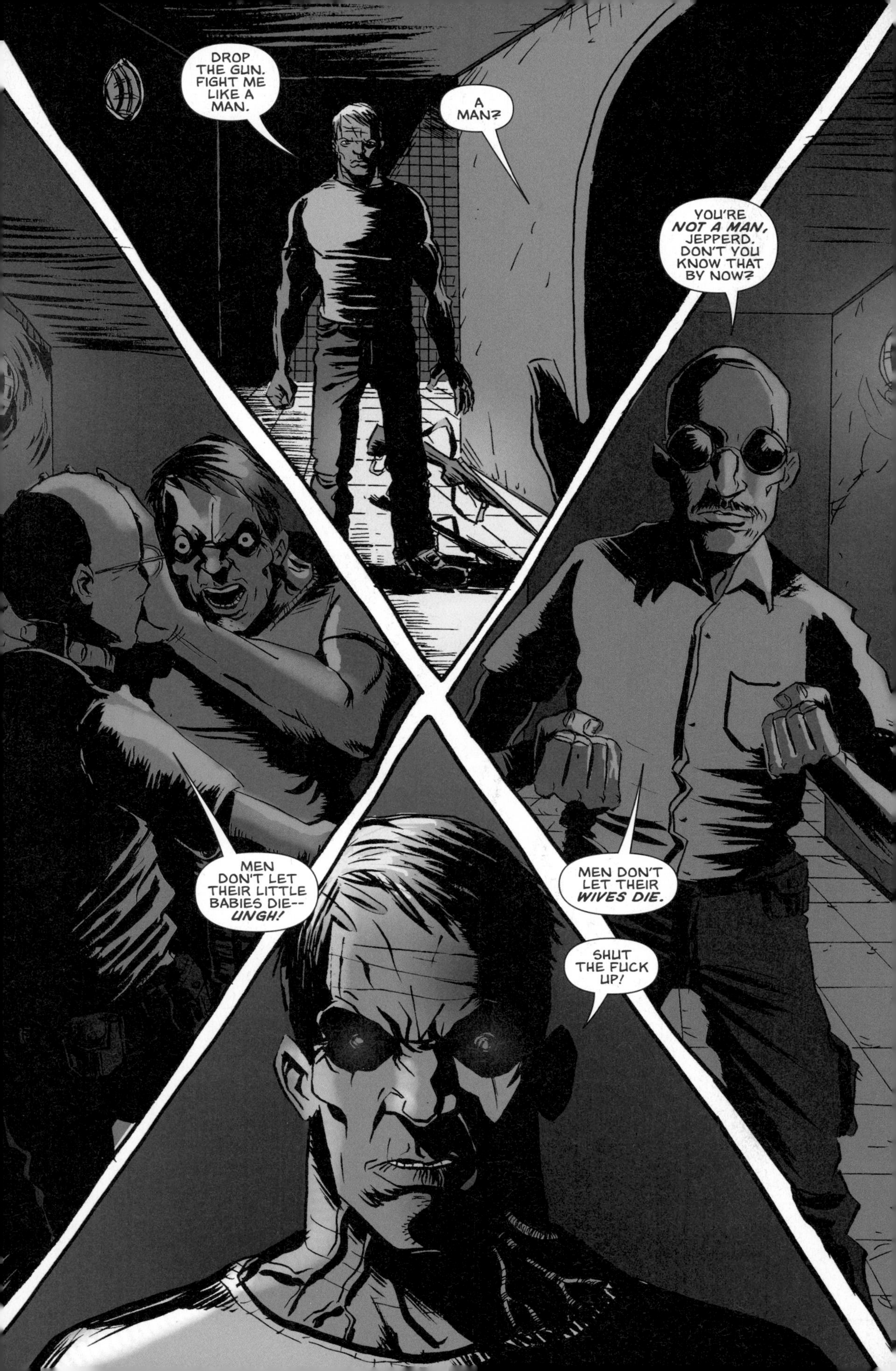
DROP THE GUN. FIGHT ME LIKE A MAN.
A MAN?
YOU'RE NOT A MAN, JEPPERD. DON'T YOU KNOW THAT BY NOW?
MEN DON'T LET THEIR LITTLE BABIES DIE-- UNGH!
MEN DON'T LET THEIR WIVES DIE.
SHUT THE FUCK UP!

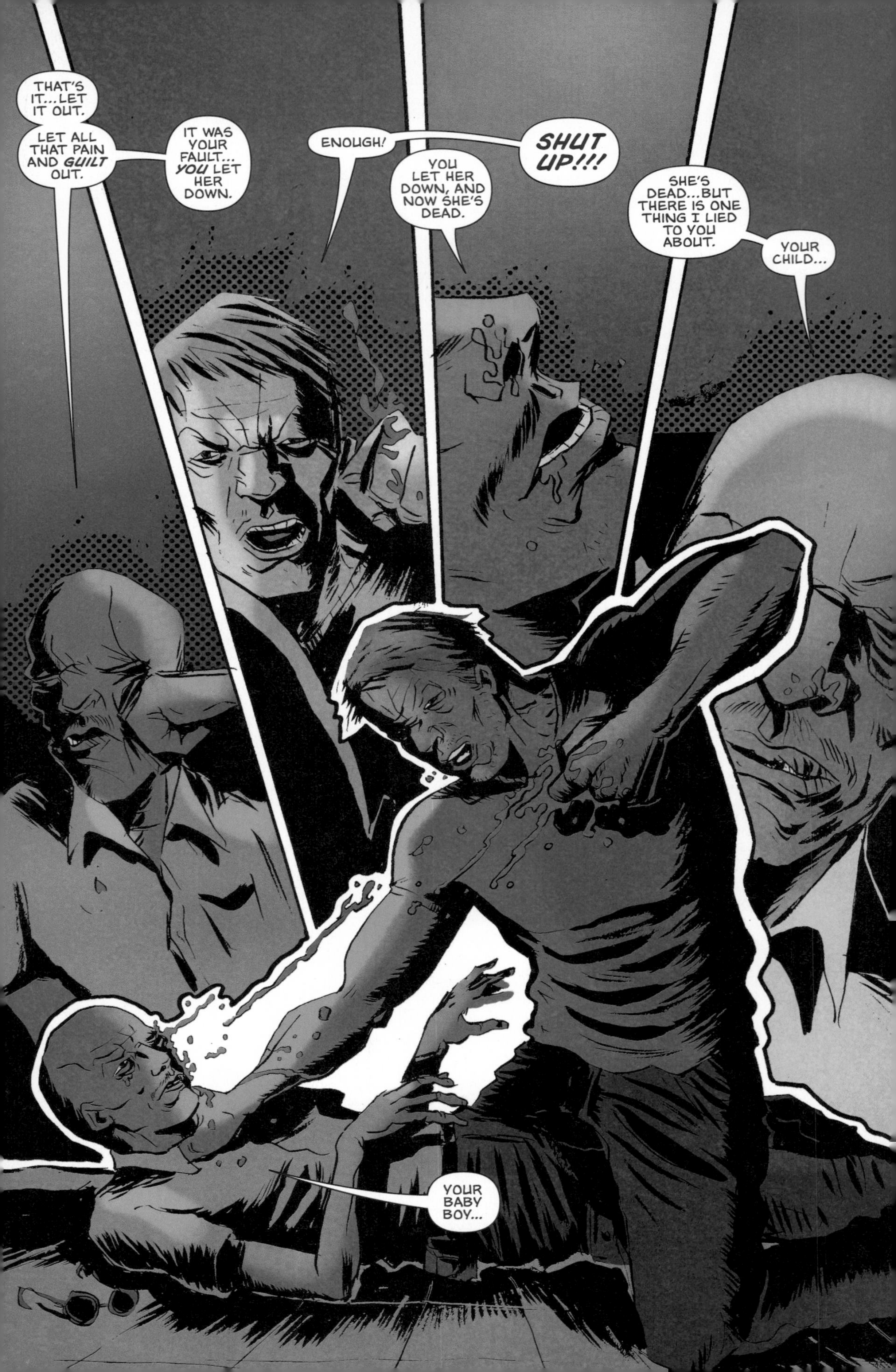
THAT'S IT...LET IT OUT.
LET ALL THAT PAIN AND *GUILT* OUT.
IT WAS YOUR FAULT... *YOU* LET HER DOWN.
ENOUGH!
SHUT UP!!!
YOU LET HER DOWN, AND NOW SHE'S DEAD.
SHE'S DEAD...BUT THERE IS ONE THING I LIED TO YOU ABOUT.
YOUR CHILD...
YOUR BABY BOY...

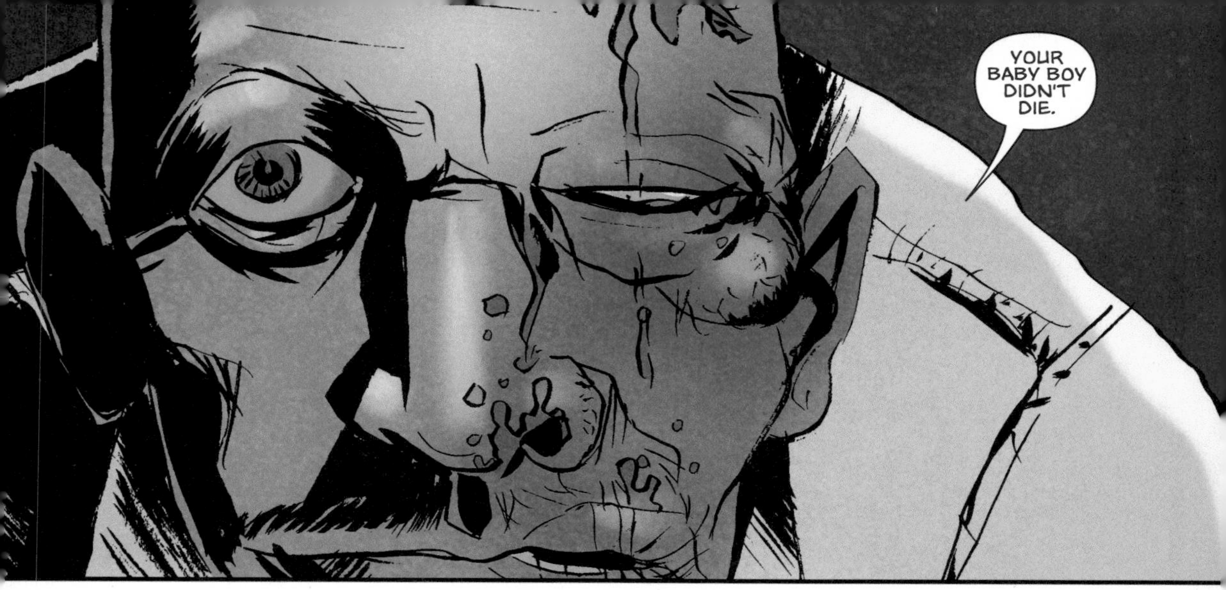
YOUR BABY BOY DIDN'T DIE.
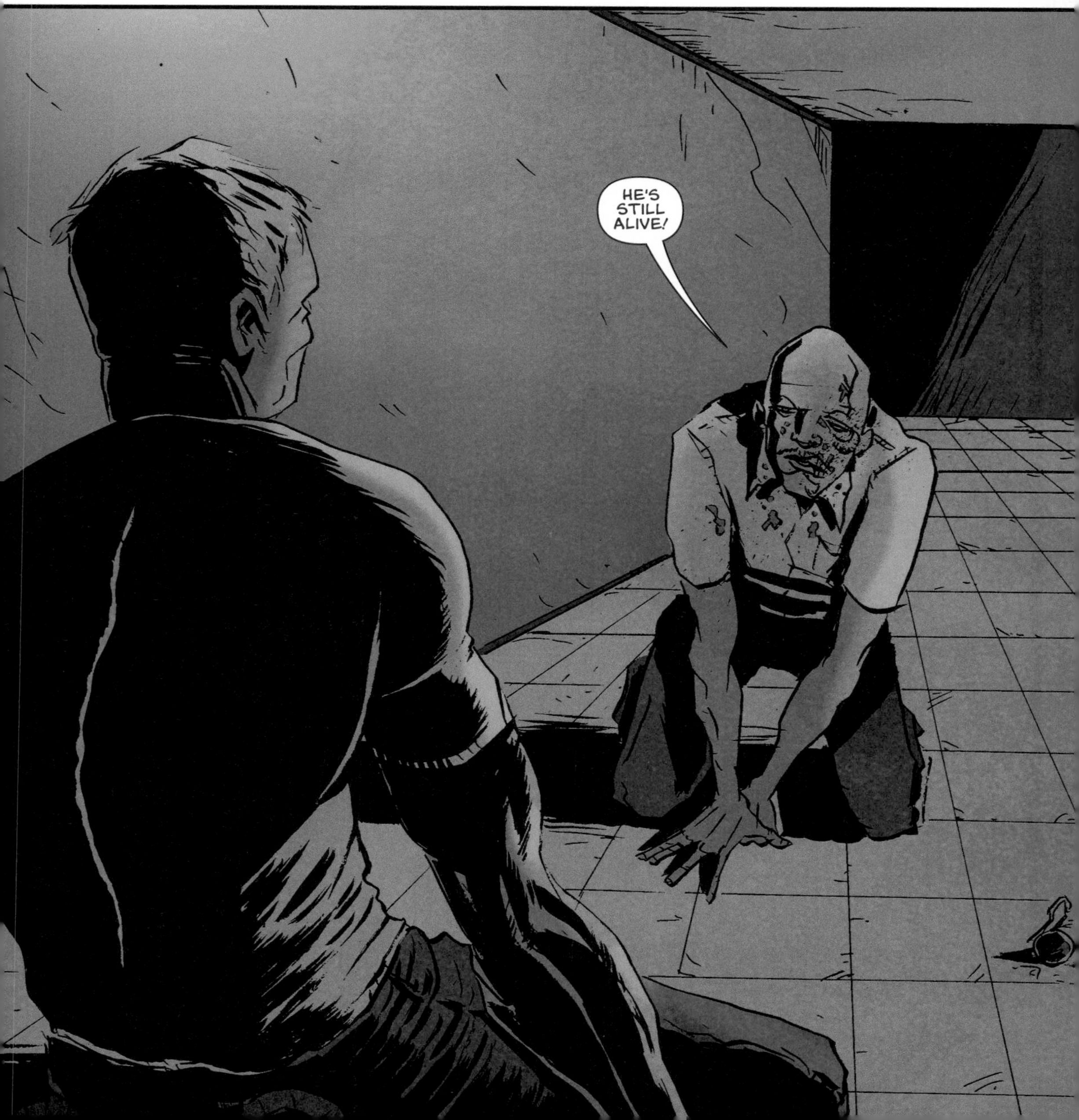
HE'S STILL ALIVE!

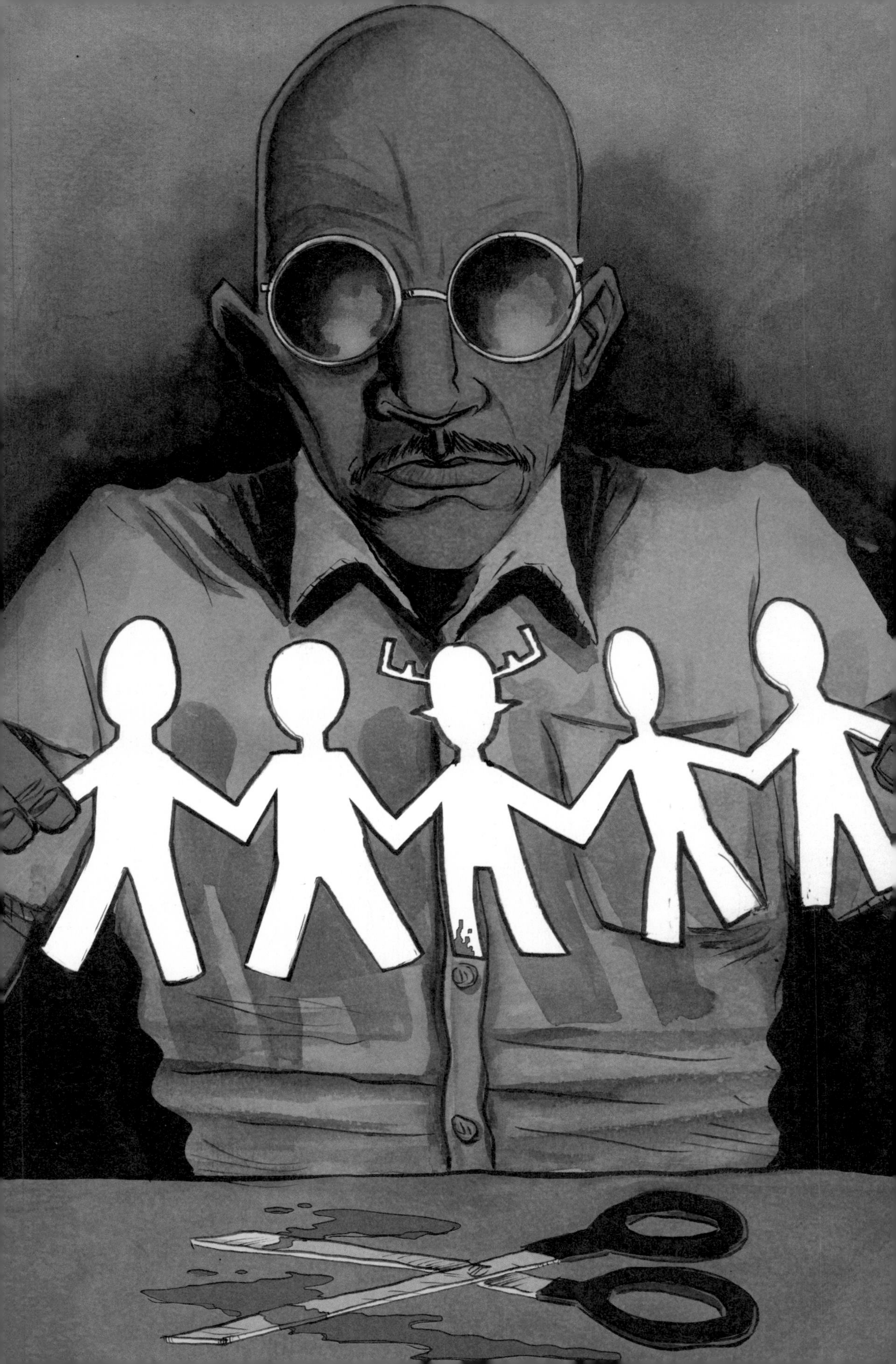

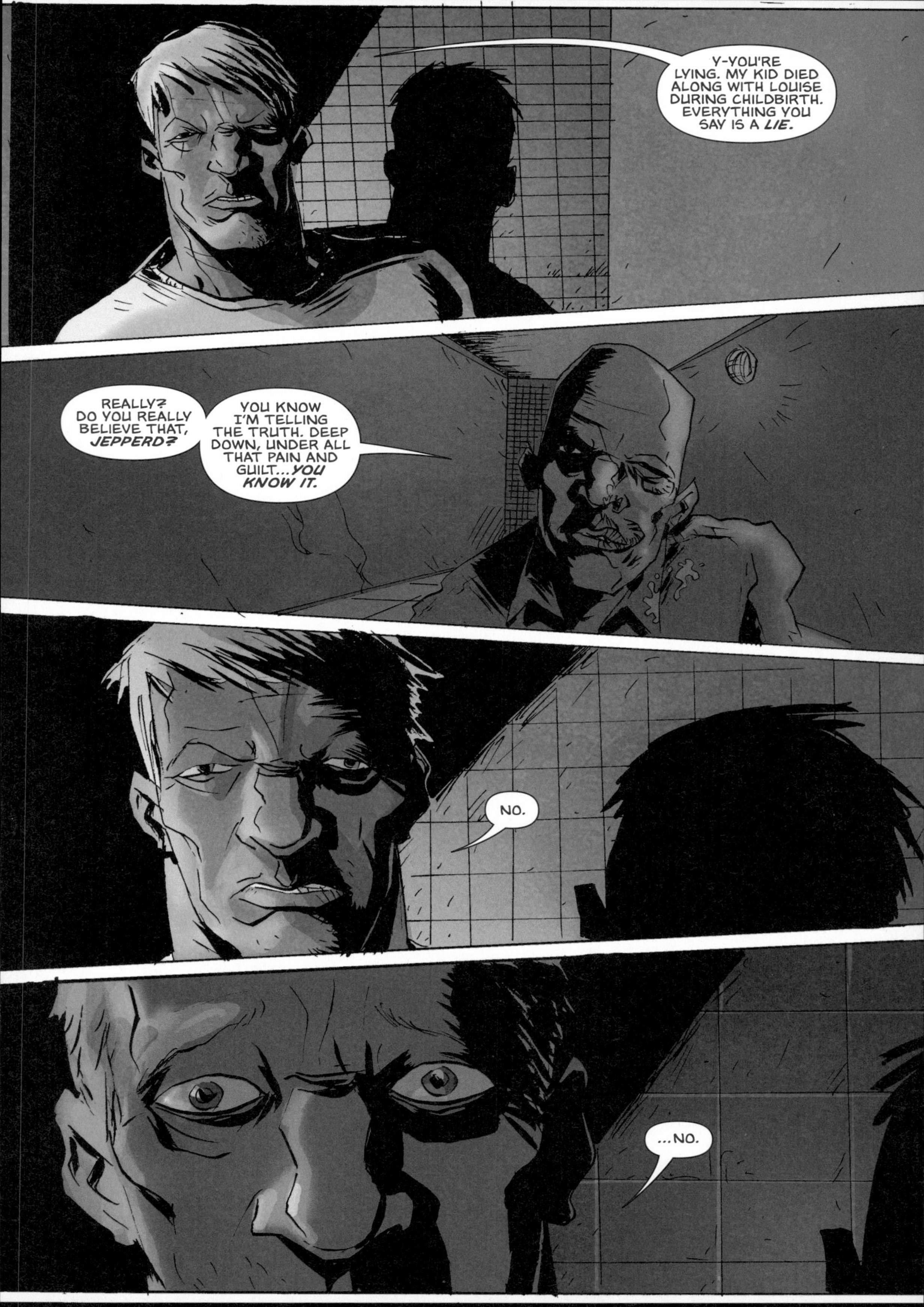
Y-YOU'RE LYING. MY KID DIED ALONG WITH LOUISE DURING CHILDBIRTH. EVERYTHING YOU SAY IS A *LIE.*
REALLY? DO YOU REALLY BELIEVE THAT, *JEPPERD?*
YOU KNOW I'M TELLING THE TRUTH. DEEP DOWN, UNDER ALL THAT PAIN AND GUILT...*YOU KNOW IT.*
NO.
...NO.

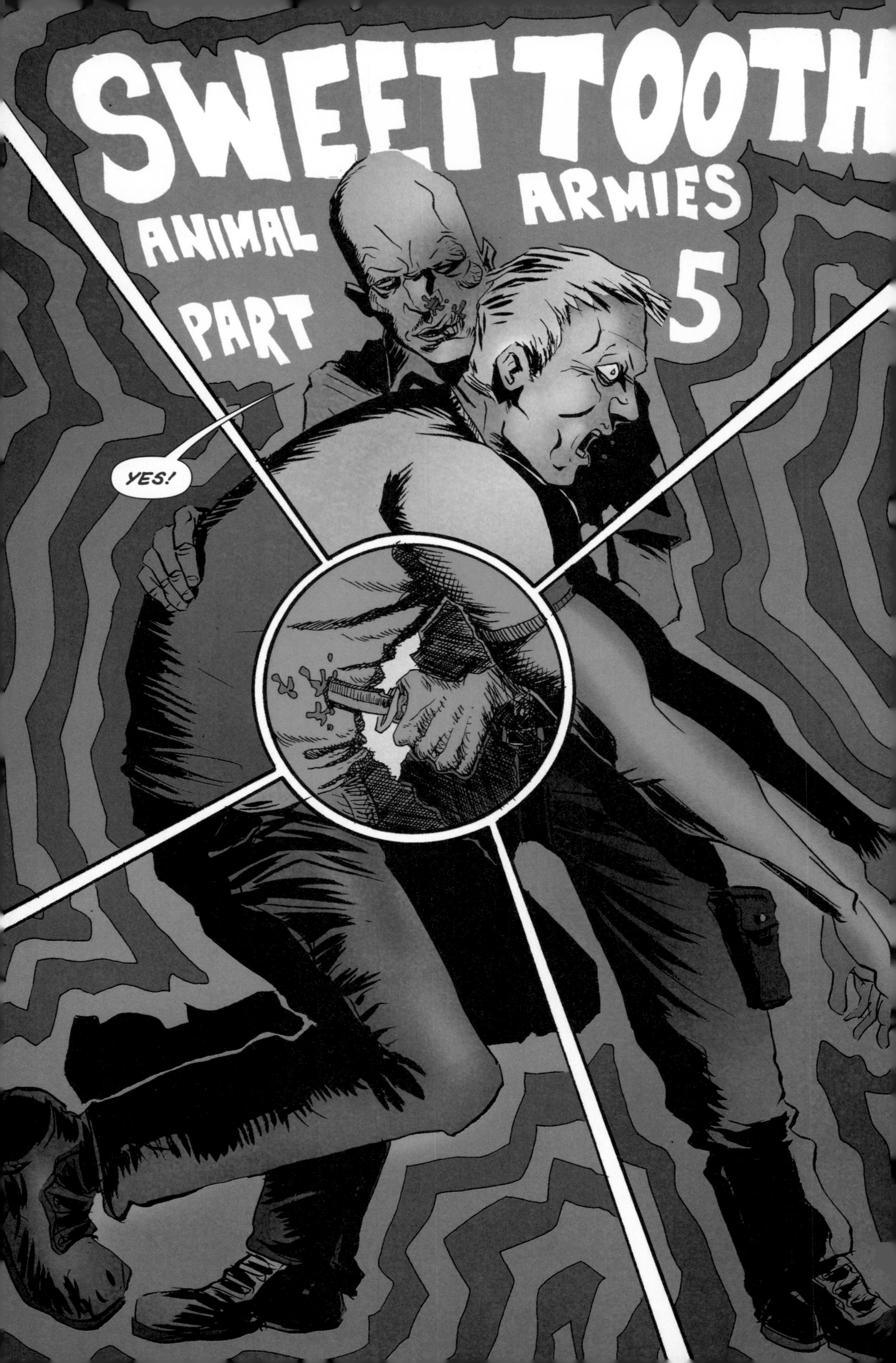
SWEET TOOTH
ANIMAL ARMIES
PART 5
YES!

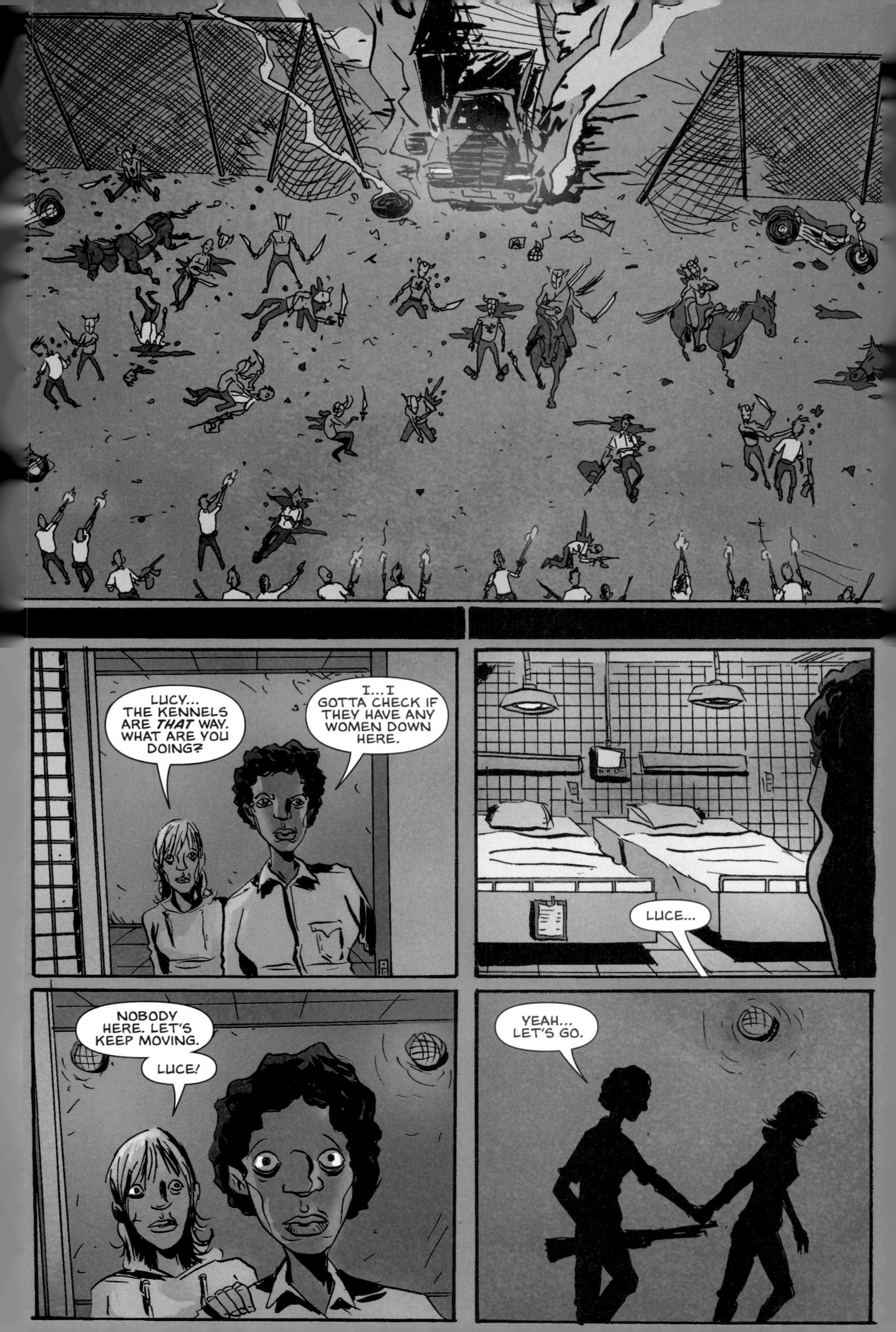
LUCY... THE KENNELS ARE *THAT* WAY. WHAT ARE YOU DOING?
I...I GOTTA CHECK IF THEY HAVE ANY WOMEN DOWN HERE.
LUCE...
NOBODY HERE. LET'S KEEP MOVING.
LUCE!
YEAH... LET'S GO.

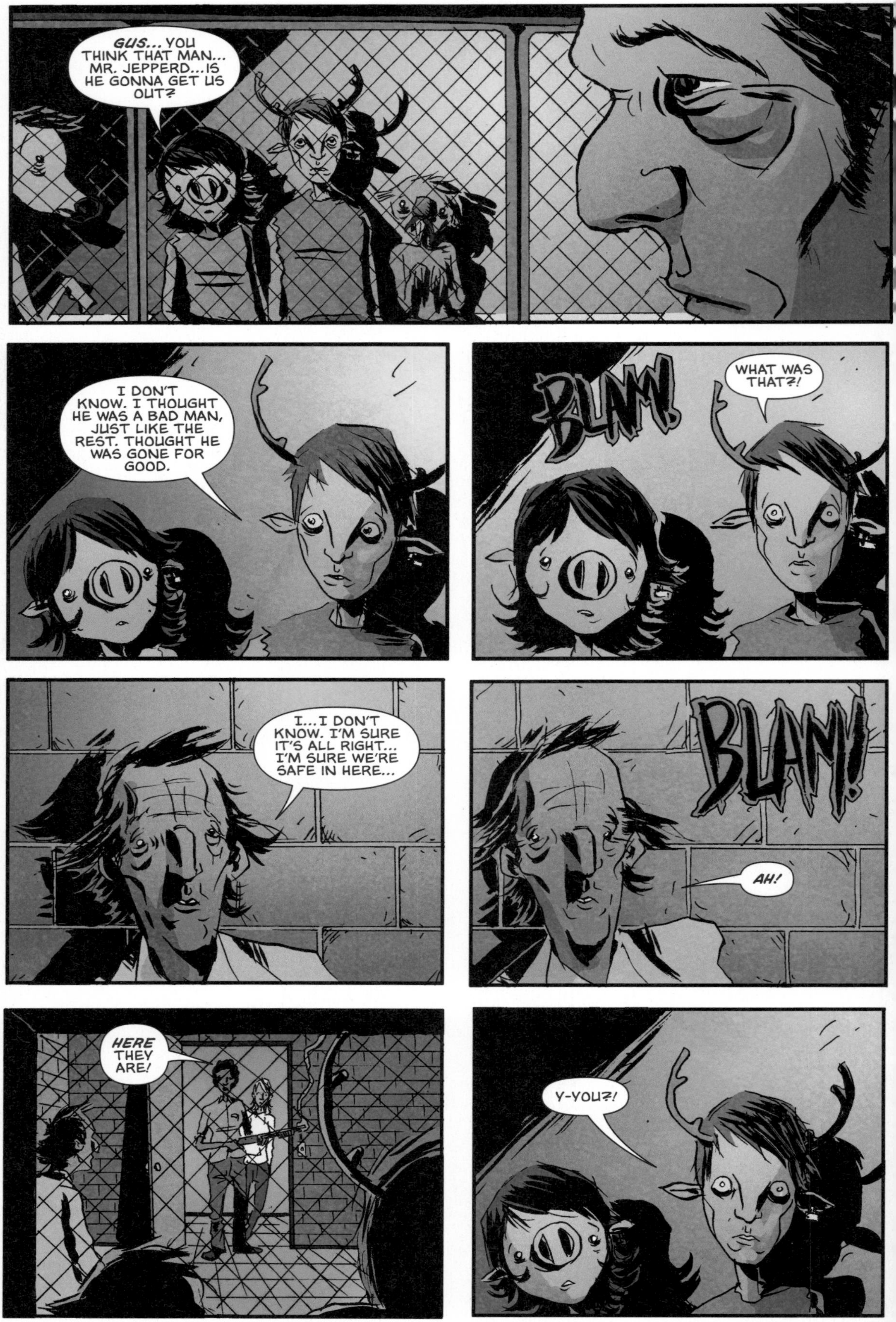
GUS... YOU THINK THAT MAN... MR. JEPPERD...IS HE GONNA GET US OUT?
I DON'T KNOW. I THOUGHT HE WAS A BAD MAN, JUST LIKE THE REST. THOUGHT HE WAS GONE FOR GOOD.
BLAM!
WHAT WAS THAT?!
I...I DON'T KNOW. I'M SURE IT'S ALL RIGHT... I'M SURE WE'RE SAFE IN HERE...
BLAM!
AH!
HERE THEY ARE!
Y-YOU?!

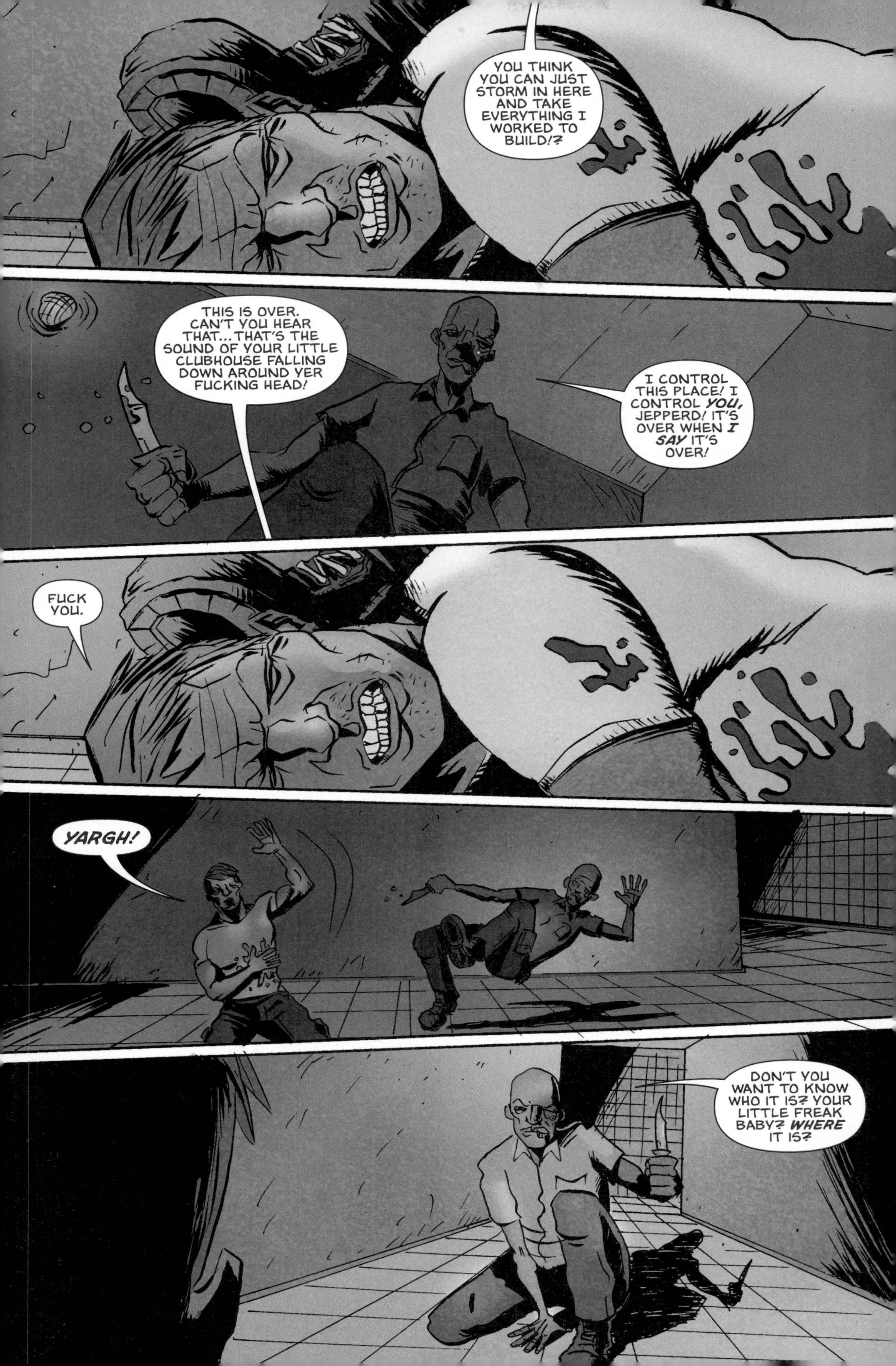
YOU THINK YOU CAN JUST STORM IN HERE AND TAKE EVERYTHING I WORKED TO BUILD!?
THIS IS OVER. CAN'T YOU HEAR THAT...THAT'S THE SOUND OF YOUR LITTLE CLUBHOUSE FALLING DOWN AROUND YER FUCKING HEAD!
I CONTROL THIS PLACE! I CONTROL *YOU*, JEPPERD! IT'S OVER WHEN *I SAY* IT'S OVER!
FUCK YOU.
YARGH!
DON'T YOU WANT TO KNOW WHO IT IS? YOUR LITTLE FREAK BABY? *WHERE* IT IS?

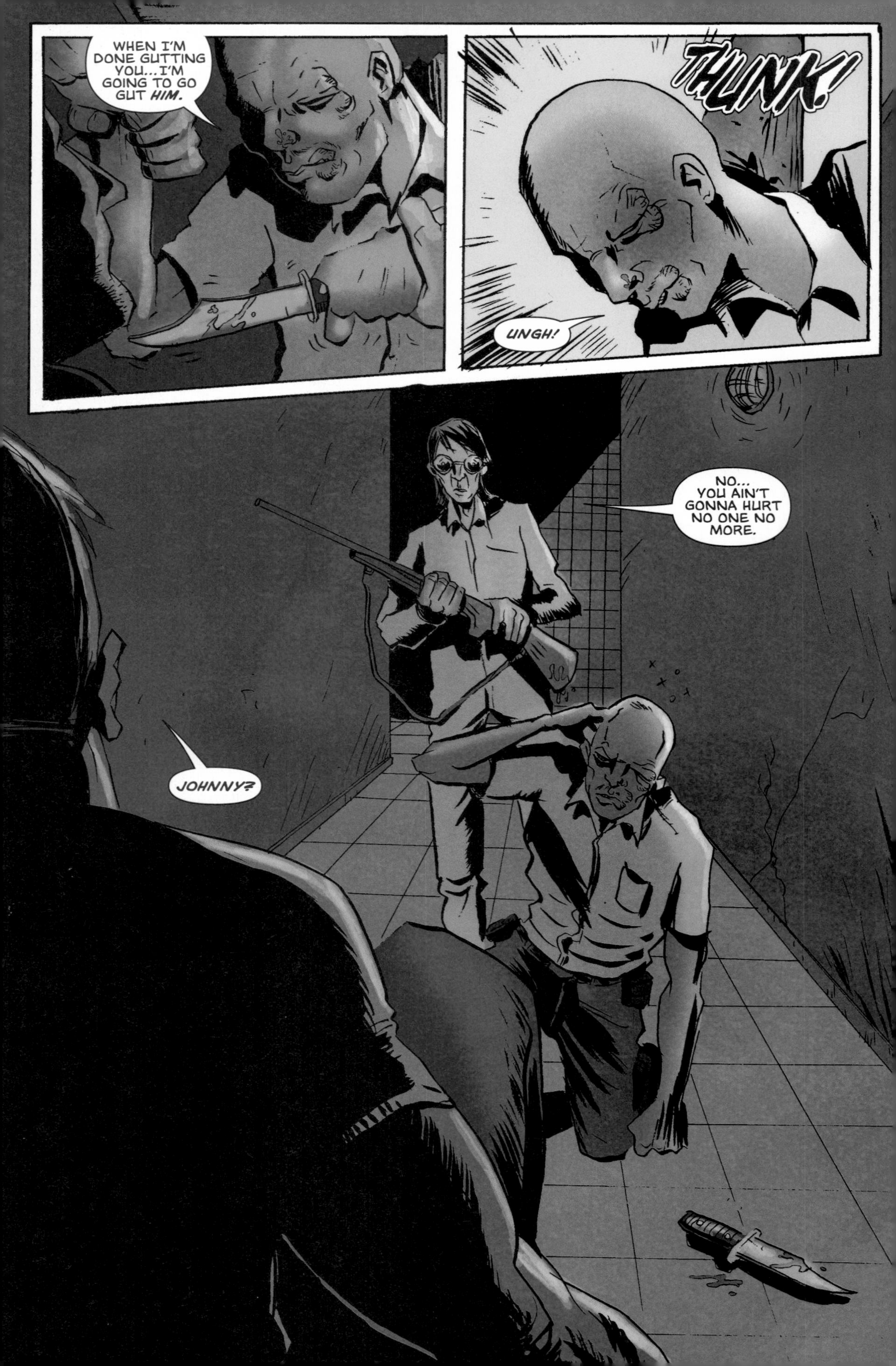
WHEN I'M DONE GUTTING YOU...I'M GOING TO GO GUT HIM.
THUNK!
UNGH!
NO... YOU AIN'T GONNA HURT NO ONE NO MORE.
JOHNNY?

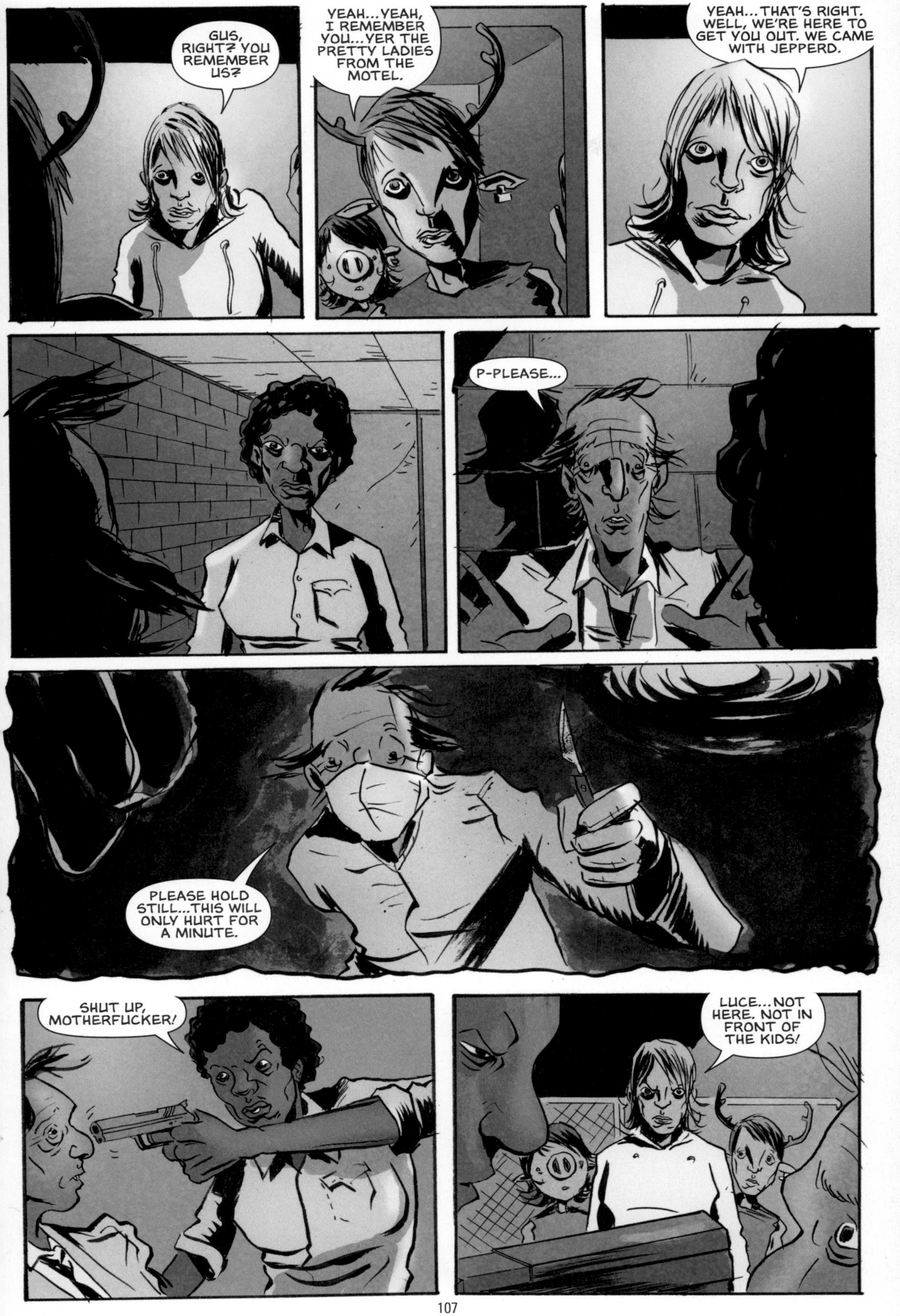
GUS, RIGHT? YOU REMEMBER US?
YEAH...YEAH, I REMEMBER YOU...YER THE PRETTY LADIES FROM THE MOTEL.
YEAH...THAT'S RIGHT. WELL, WE'RE HERE TO GET YOU OUT. WE CAME WITH JEPPERD.
P-PLEASE...
PLEASE HOLD STILL...THIS WILL ONLY HURT FOR A MINUTE.
SHUT UP, MOTHERFUCKER!
LUCE...NOT HERE. NOT IN FRONT OF THE KIDS!

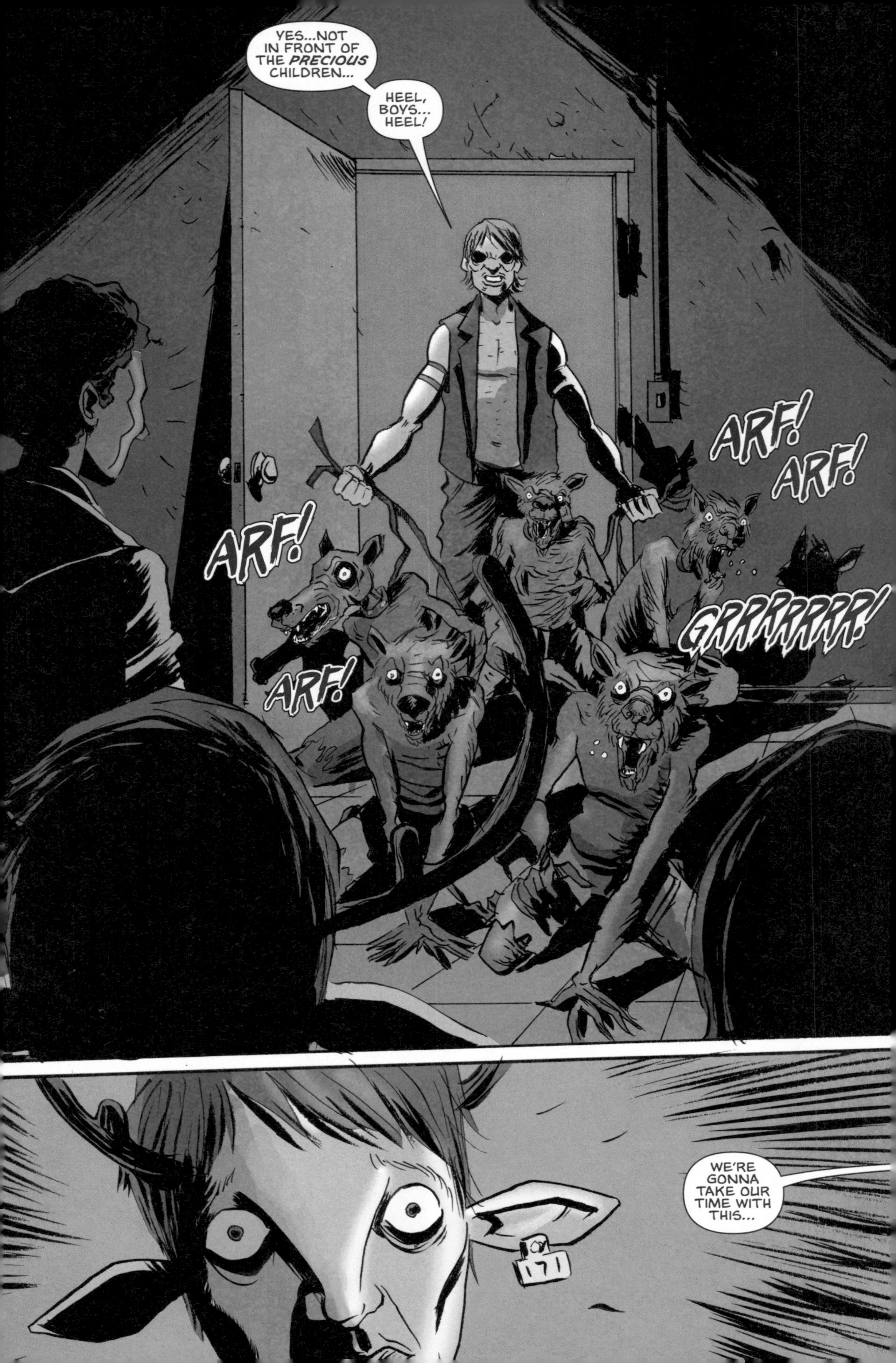
YES...NOT IN FRONT OF THE *PRECIOUS* CHILDREN...
HEEL, BOYS... HEEL!
ARF! ARF!
ARF!
ARF!
GRRRRRRR!
ARF!
WE'RE GONNA TAKE OUR TIME WITH THIS...

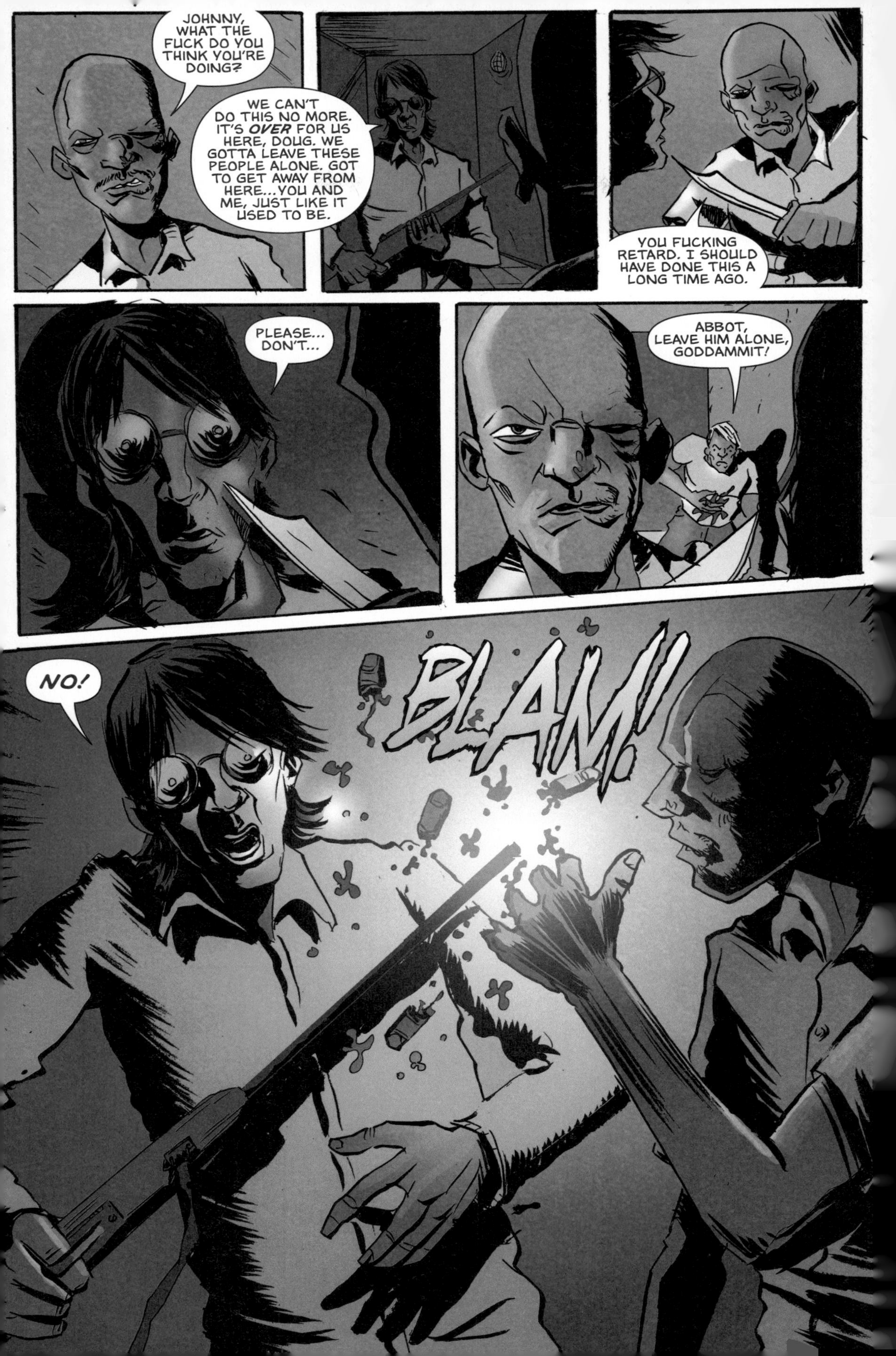

JOHNNY, WHAT THE FUCK DO YOU THINK YOU'RE DOING?
WE CAN'T DO THIS NO MORE. IT'S *OVER* FOR US HERE, DOUG. WE GOTTA LEAVE THESE PEOPLE ALONE. GOT TO GET AWAY FROM HERE...YOU AND ME, JUST LIKE IT USED TO BE.
YOU FUCKING RETARD. I SHOULD HAVE DONE THIS A LONG TIME AGO.
PLEASE... DON'T...
ABBOT, LEAVE HIM ALONE, GODDAMMIT!
NO!
BLAM!

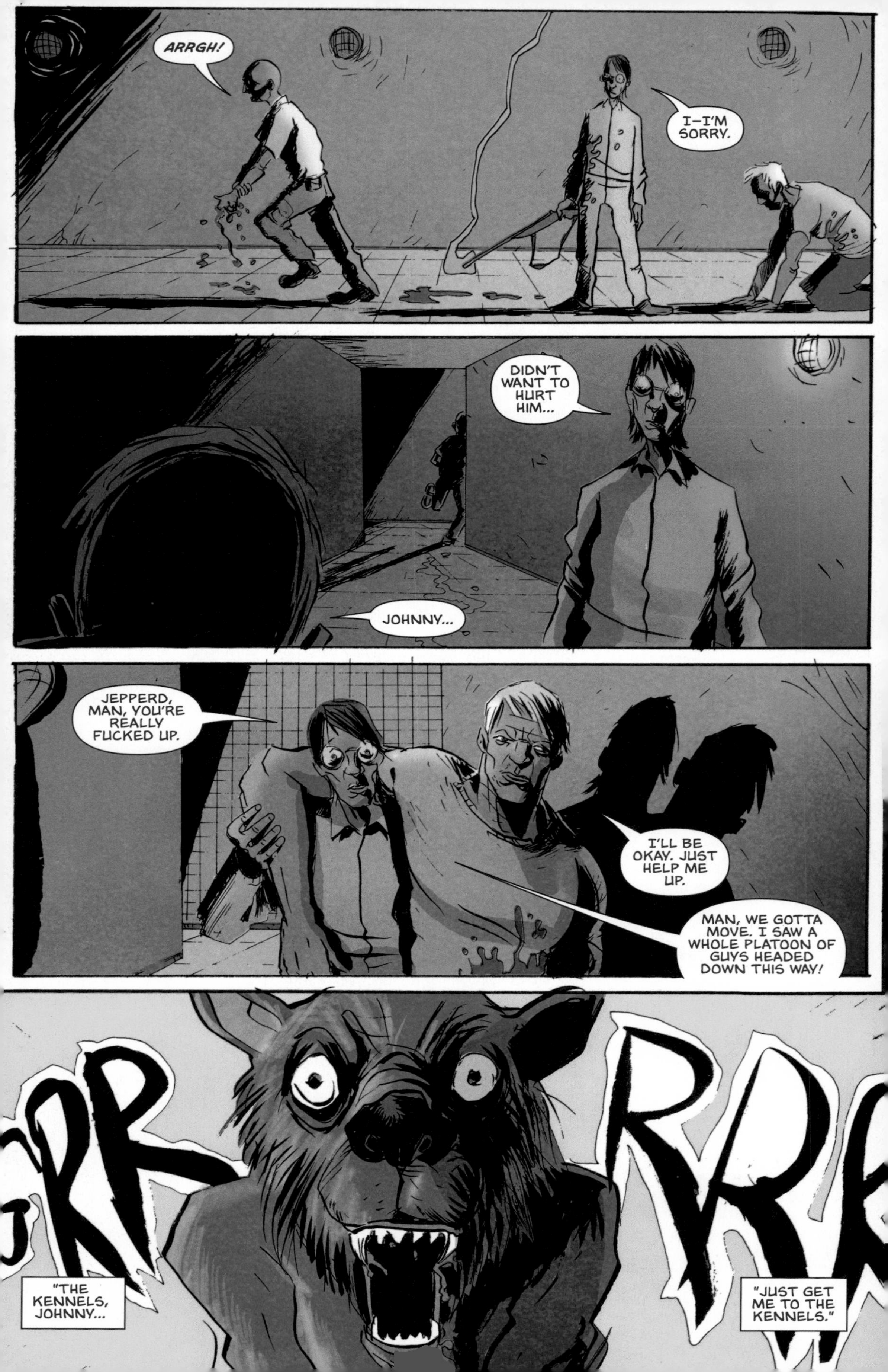
ARRGH!
I—I'M SORRY.
DIDN'T WANT TO HURT HIM...
JOHNNY...
JEPPERD, MAN, YOU'RE REALLY FUCKED UP.
I'LL BE OKAY. JUST HELP ME UP.
MAN, WE GOTTA MOVE. I SAW A WHOLE PLATOON OF GUYS HEADED DOWN THIS WAY!
"THE KENNELS, JOHNNY...
"JUST GET ME TO THE KENNELS."

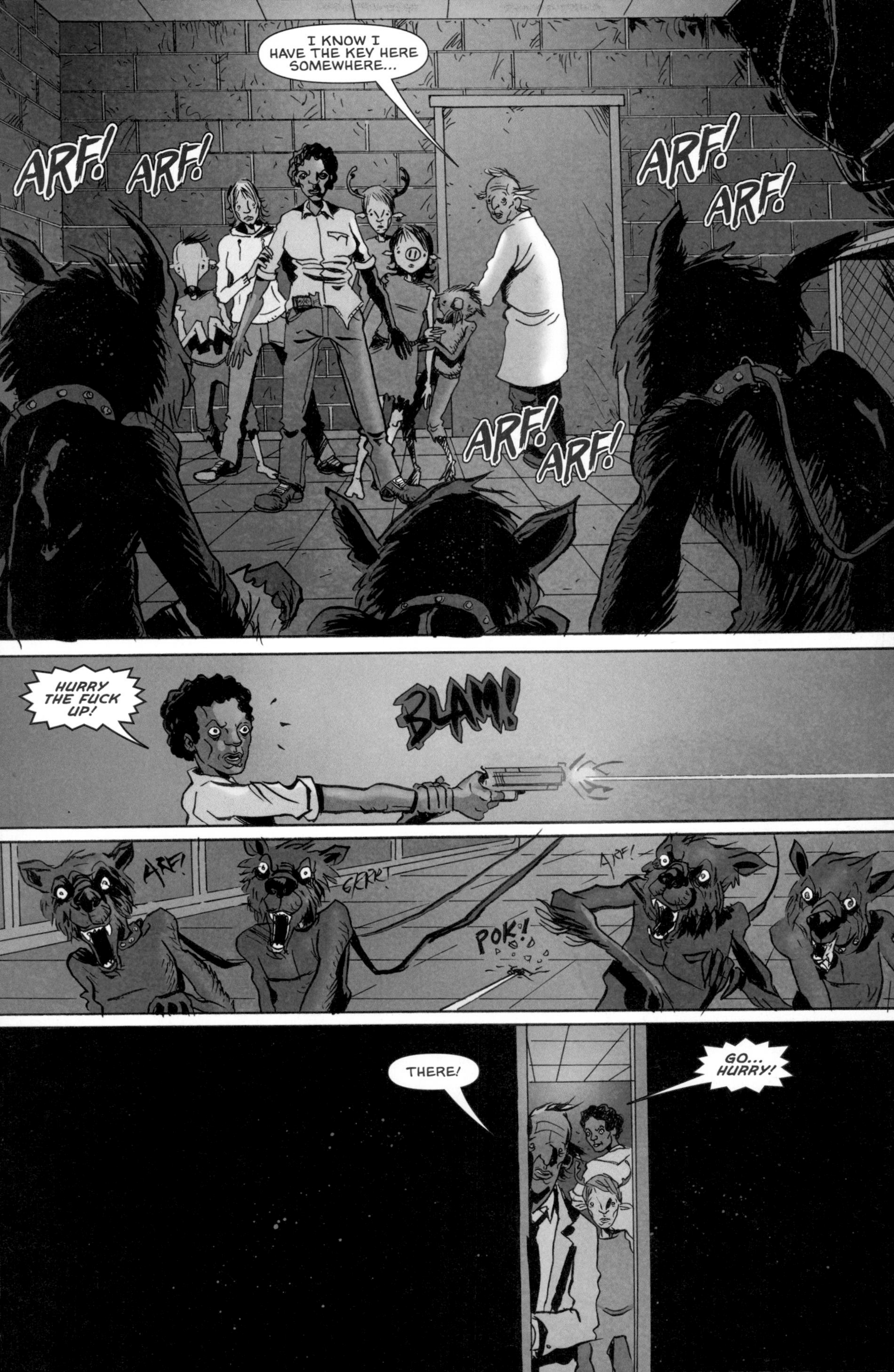
I KNOW I HAVE THE KEY HERE SOMEWHERE...
ARF! ARF!
ARF! ARF!
ARF! ARF!
HURRY THE FUCK UP!
BLAM!
ARF!
GRRR!
ARF!
POK!
THERE!
GO... HURRY!

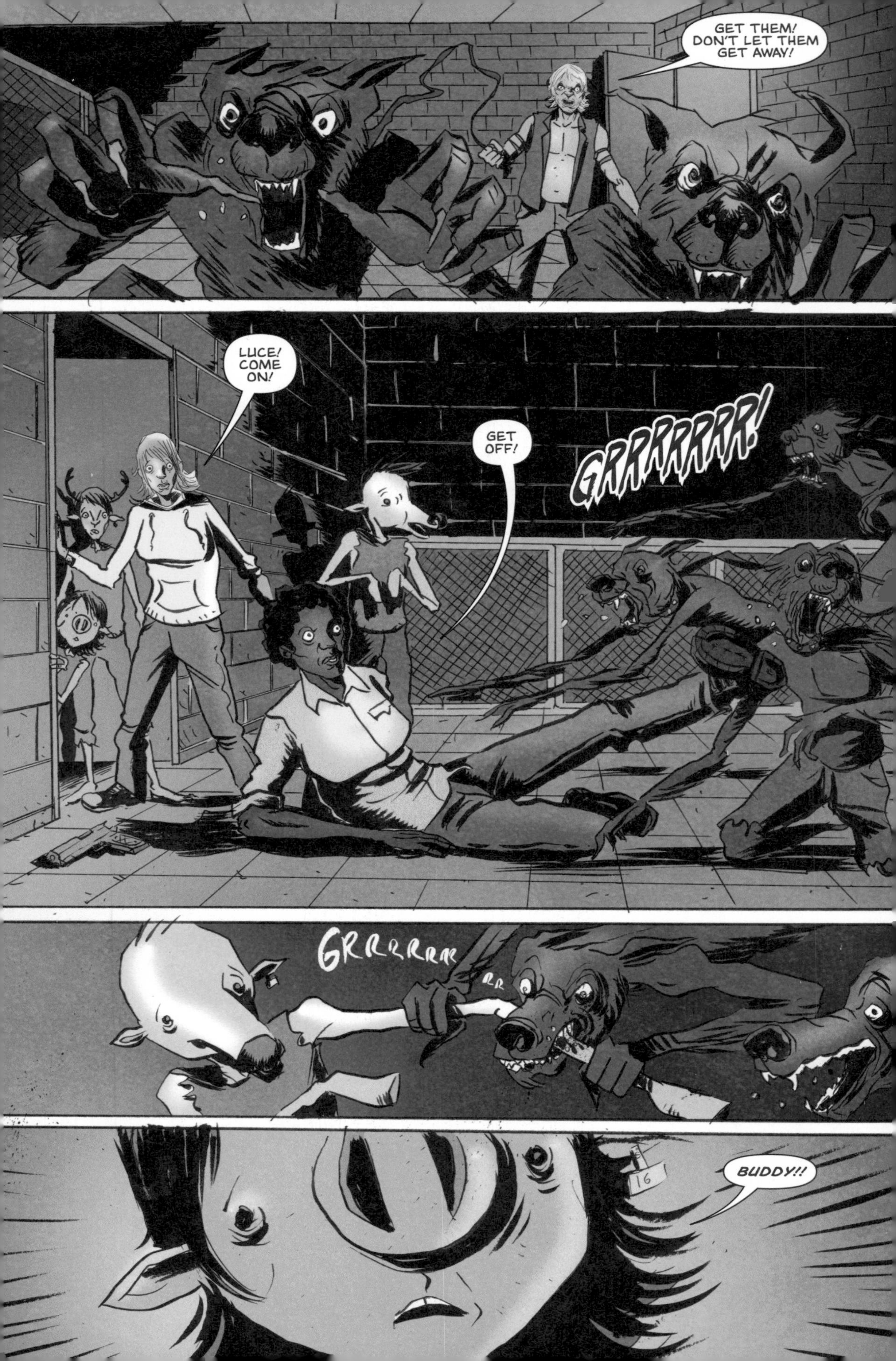
GET THEM! DON'T LET THEM GET AWAY!
LUCE! COME ON!
GET OFF!
GRRRRRRR!
GRRRRRRR
RR
16
BUDDY!!

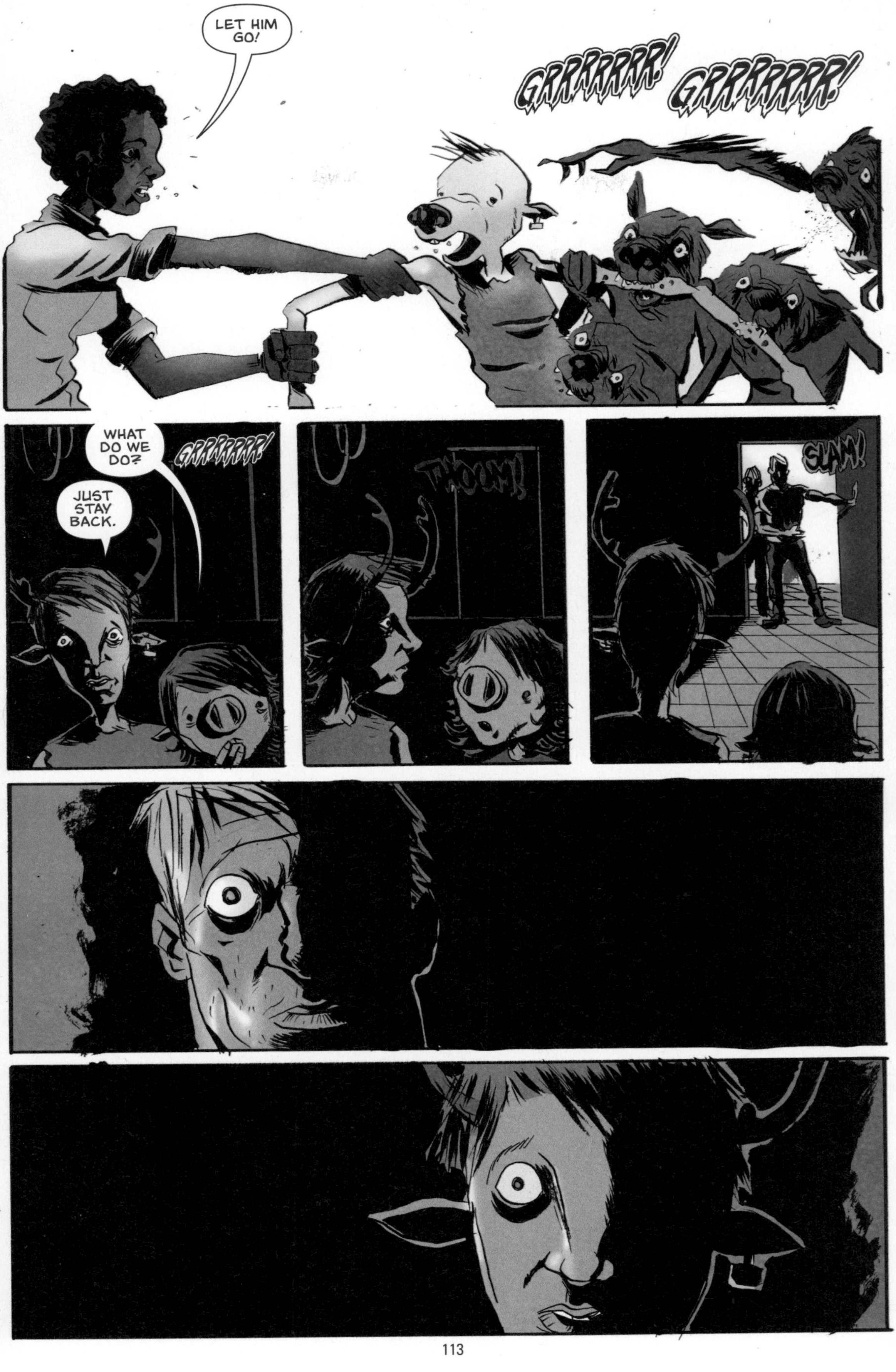
LET HIM GO!
GRRRRRRR! GRRRRRRR!
WHAT DO WE DO?
GRRRRRRR!
JUST STAY BACK.
THOOM!
SLAM!

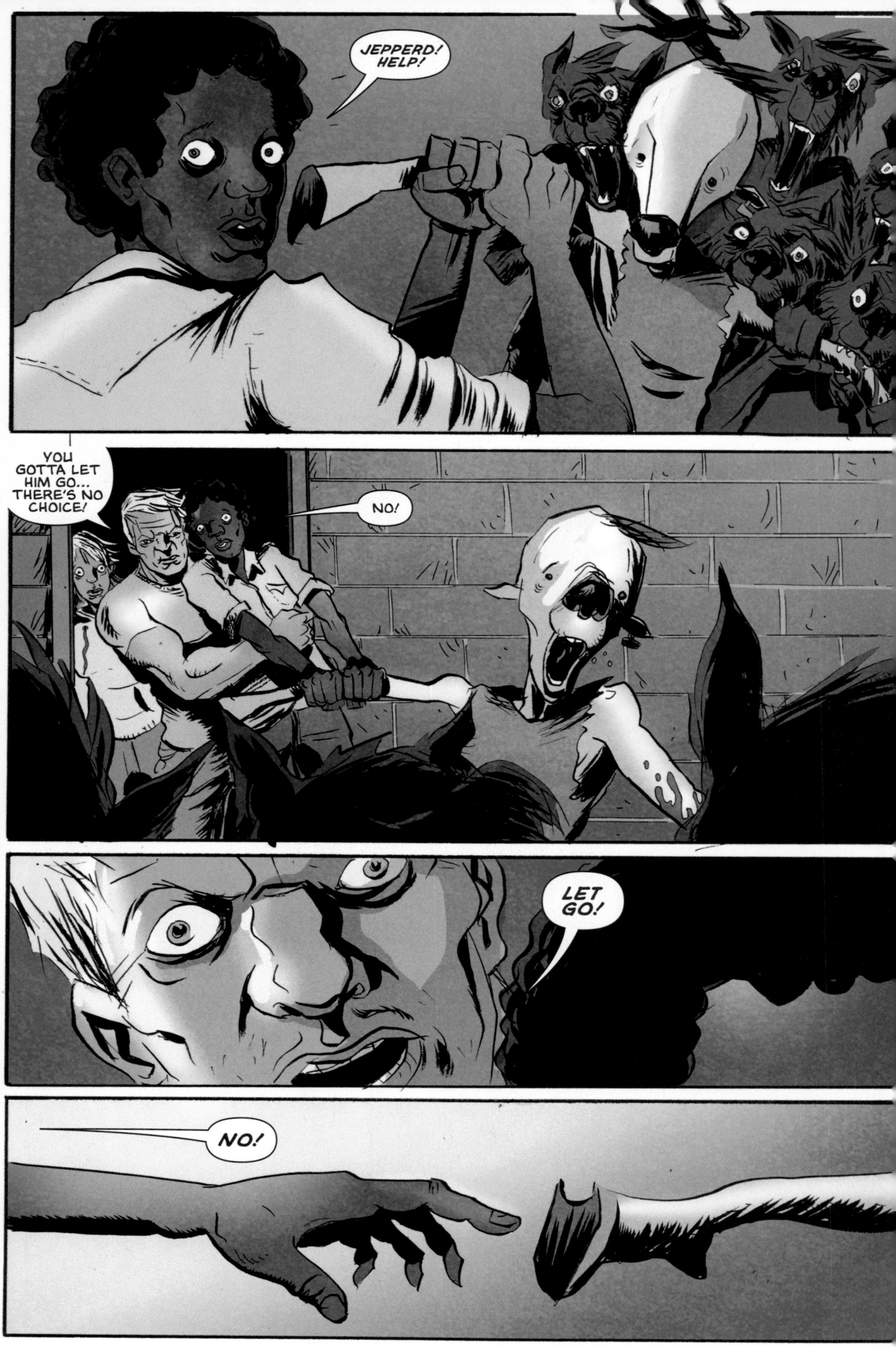
JEPPERD! HELP!
YOU GOTTA LET HIM GO... THERE'S NO CHOICE!
NO!
LET GO!
NO!

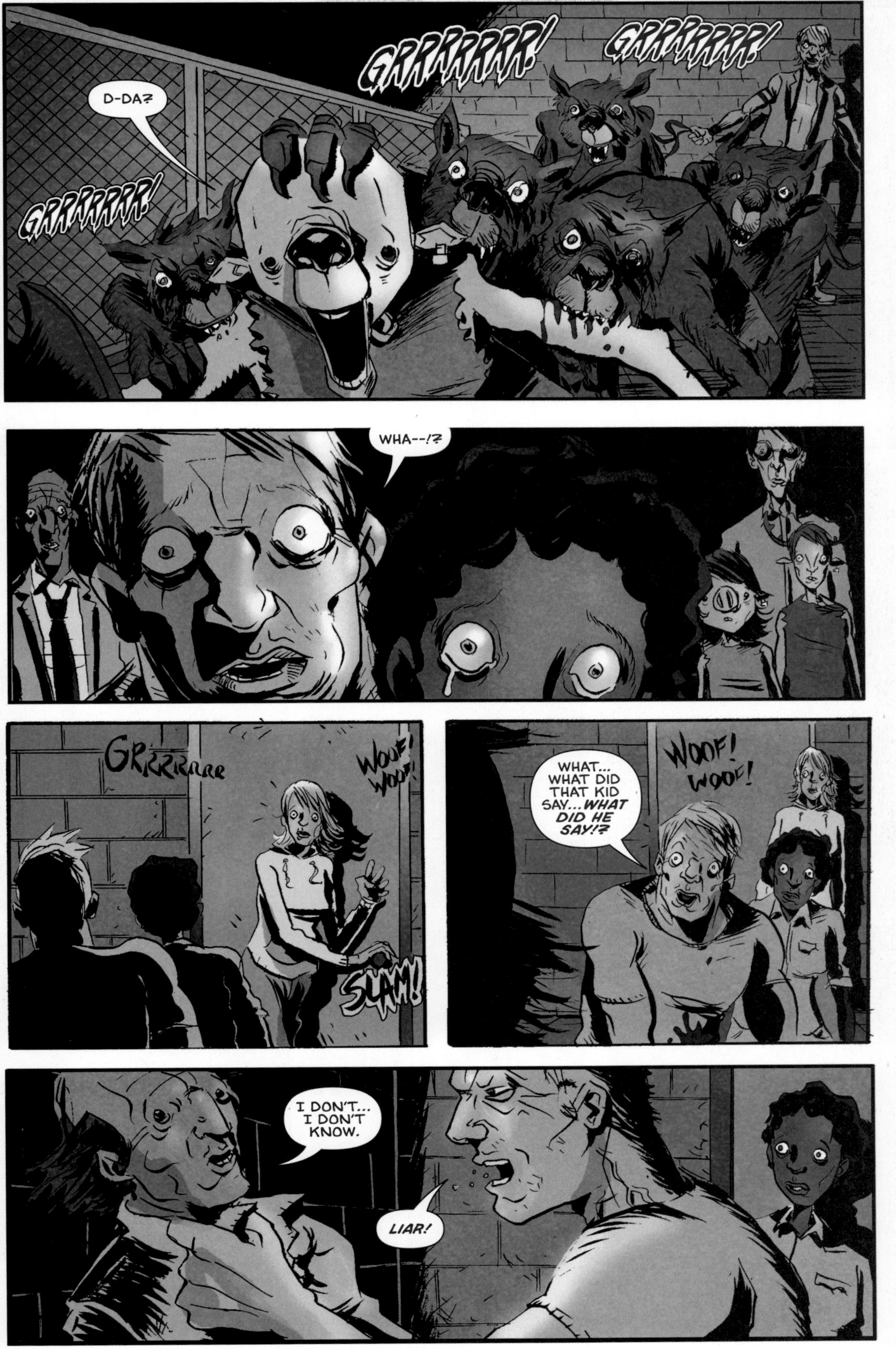
GRRRRRRR!
GRRRRRRR!
D-DA?
GRRRRRRR!
WHA--!?
GRRRRRRR
WOOF! WOOF!
SLAM!
WOOF! WOOF!
WHAT... WHAT DID THAT KID SAY...WHAT DID HE SAY!?
I DON'T... I DON'T KNOW.
LIAR!

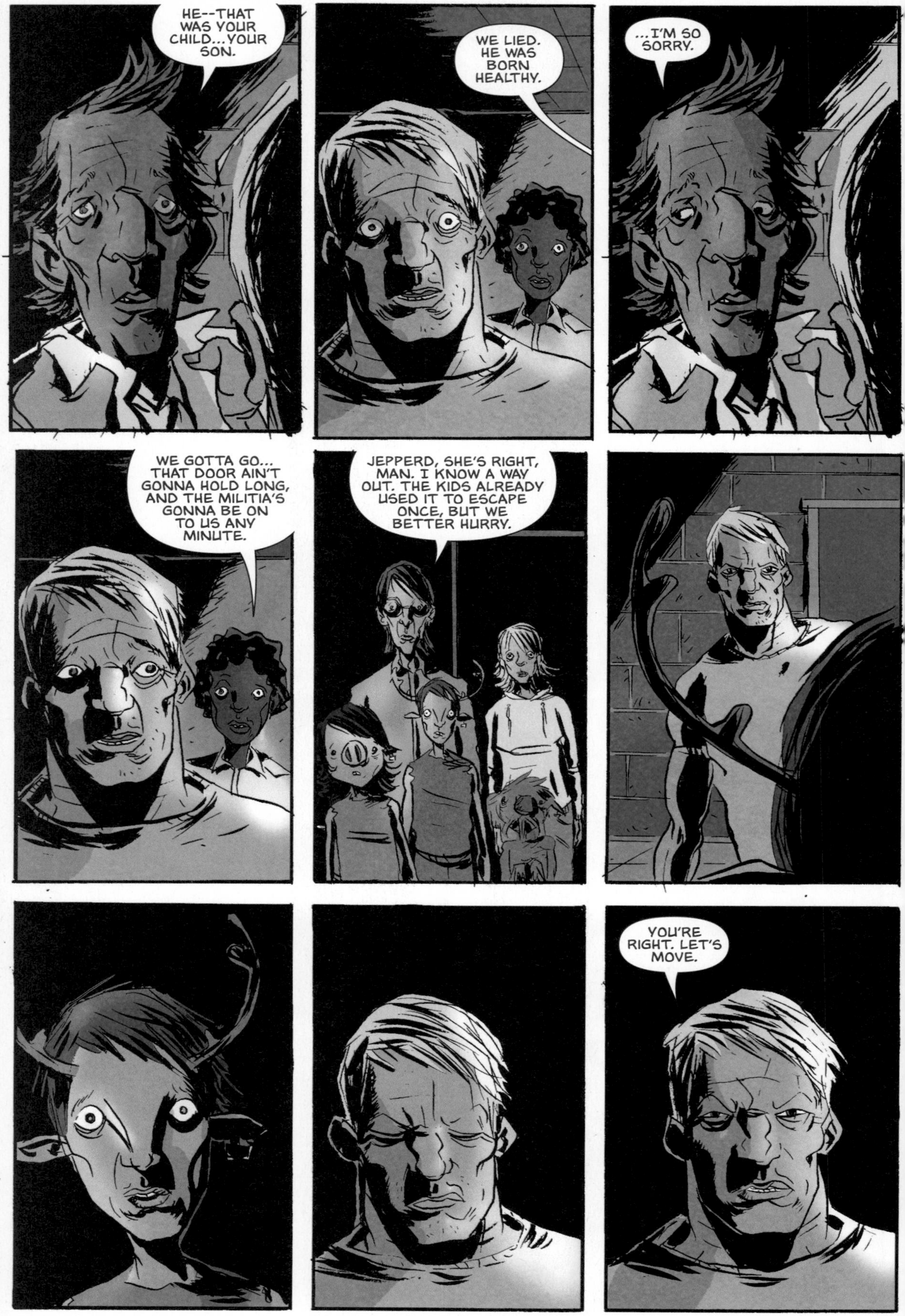
HE--THAT WAS YOUR CHILD...YOUR SON.
WE LIED. HE WAS BORN HEALTHY.
...I'M SO SORRY.
WE GOTTA GO... THAT DOOR AIN'T GONNA HOLD LONG, AND THE MILITIA'S GONNA BE ON TO US ANY MINUTE.
JEPPERD, SHE'S RIGHT, MAN. I KNOW A WAY OUT. THE KIDS ALREADY USED IT TO ESCAPE ONCE, BUT WE BETTER HURRY.
YOU'RE RIGHT. LET'S MOVE.

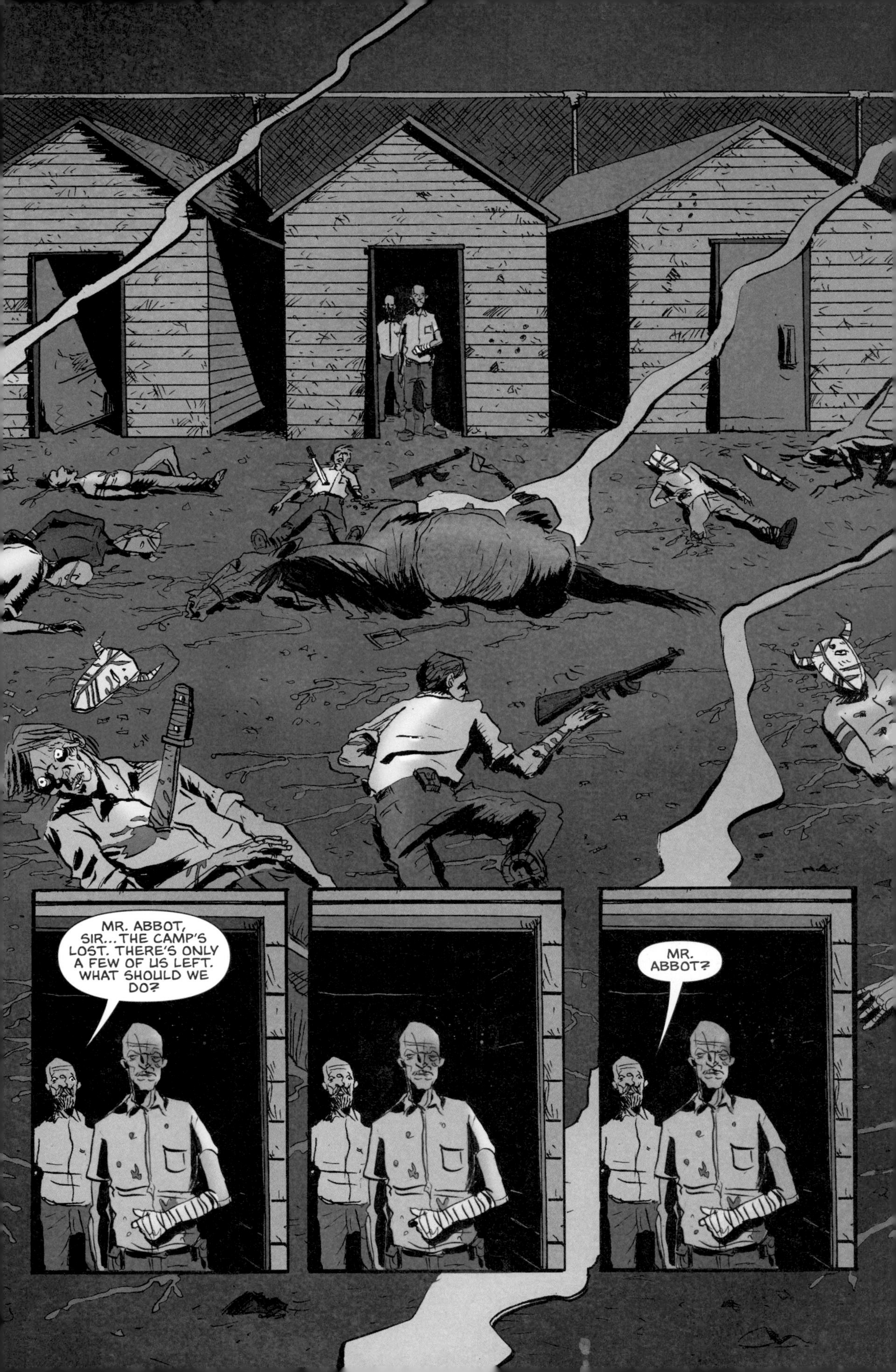
MR. ABBOT, SIR... THE CAMP'S LOST. THERE'S ONLY A FEW OF US LEFT. WHAT SHOULD WE DO?
MR. ABBOT?

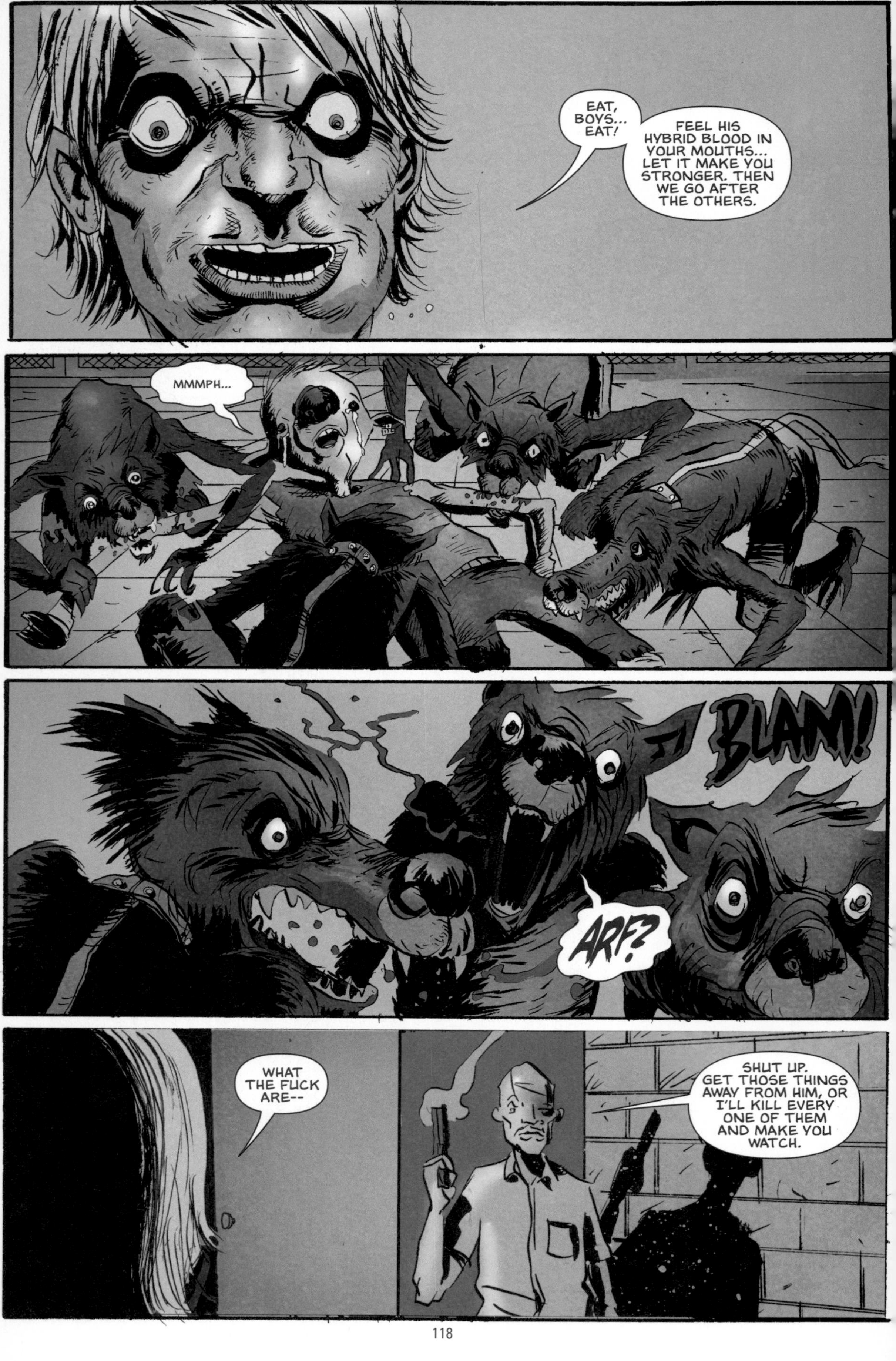
EAT, BOYS... EAT!
FEEL HIS HYBRID BLOOD IN YOUR MOUTHS... LET IT MAKE YOU STRONGER. THEN WE GO AFTER THE OTHERS.
MMMPH...
BLAM!
ARF?
WHAT THE FUCK ARE--
SHUT UP. GET THOSE THINGS AWAY FROM HIM, OR I'LL KILL EVERY ONE OF THEM AND MAKE YOU WATCH.

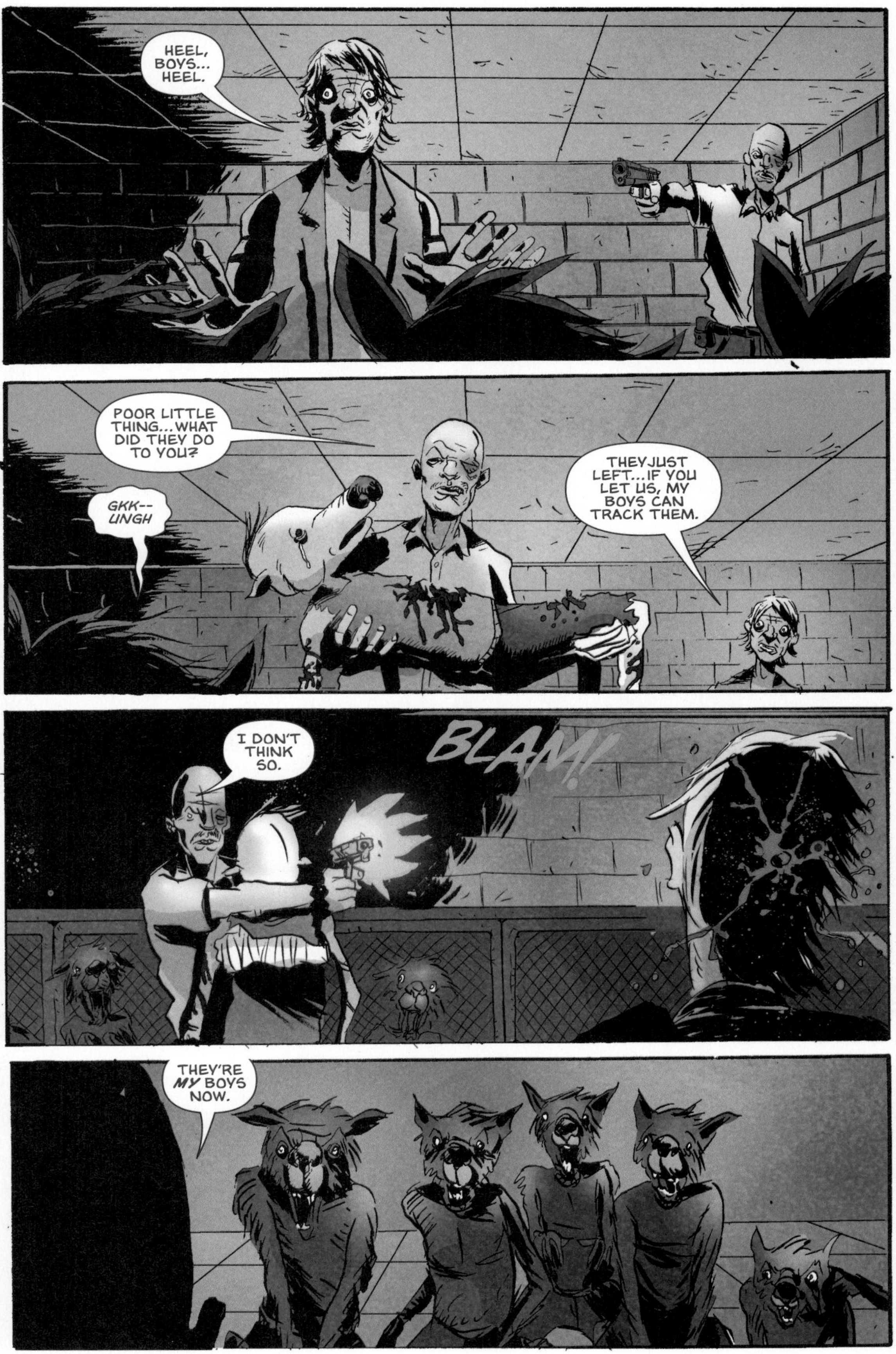

HEEL, BOYS... HEEL.
POOR LITTLE THING...WHAT DID THEY DO TO YOU?
GKK--UNGH
THEY JUST LEFT...IF YOU LET US, MY BOYS CAN TRACK THEM.
I DON'T THINK SO.
BLAM!
THEY'RE *MY* BOYS NOW.

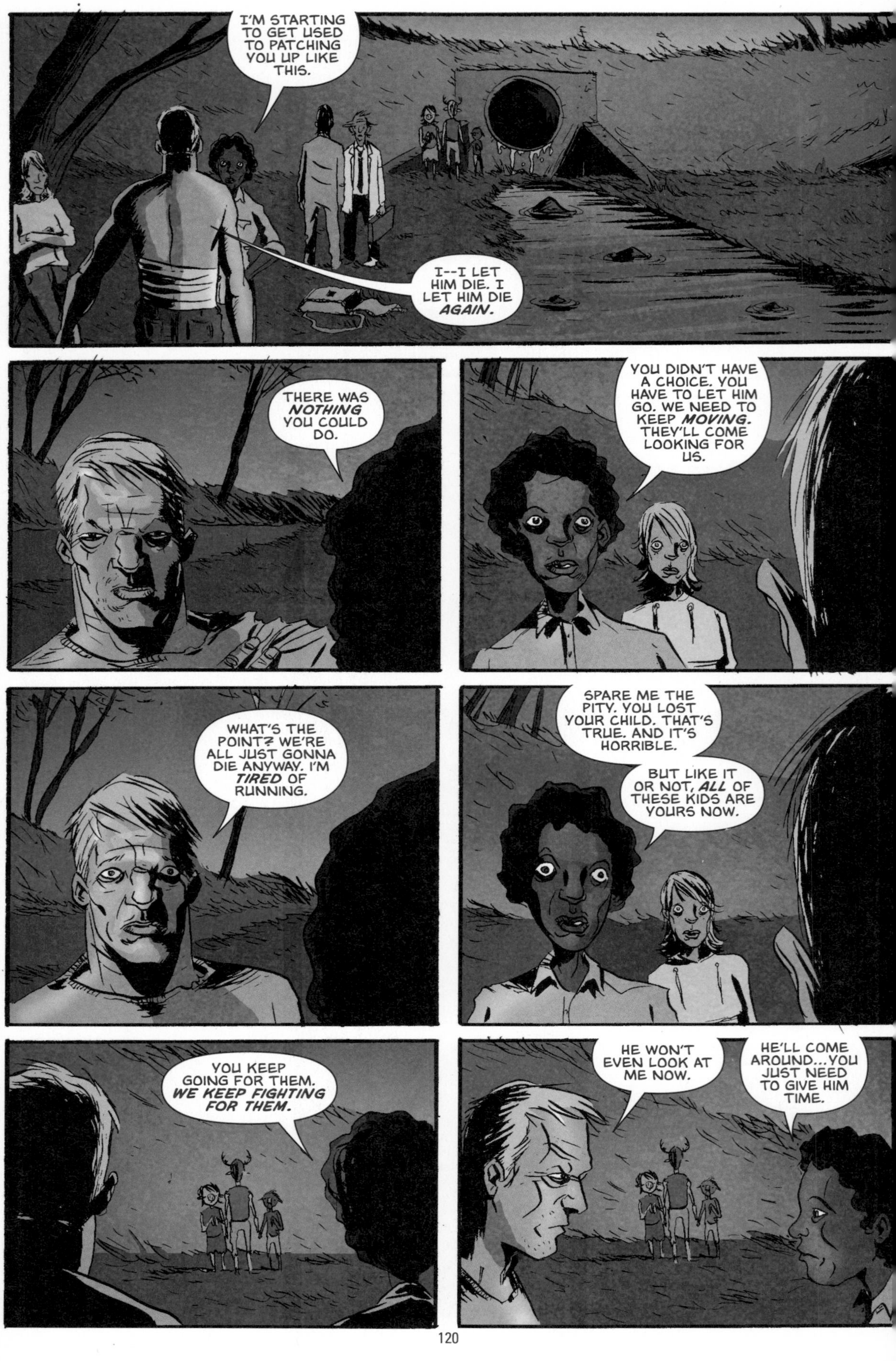
I'M STARTING TO GET USED TO PATCHING YOU UP LIKE THIS.
I--I LET HIM DIE. I LET HIM DIE *AGAIN.*
THERE WAS *NOTHING* YOU COULD DO.
YOU DIDN'T HAVE A CHOICE. YOU HAVE TO LET HIM GO. WE NEED TO KEEP *MOVING.* THEY'LL COME LOOKING FOR US.
WHAT'S THE POINT? WE'RE ALL JUST GONNA DIE ANYWAY. I'M *TIRED* OF RUNNING.
SPARE ME THE PITY. YOU LOST YOUR CHILD. THAT'S TRUE. AND IT'S HORRIBLE.
BUT LIKE IT OR NOT, *ALL* OF THESE KIDS ARE YOURS NOW.
YOU KEEP GOING FOR THEM. *WE KEEP FIGHTING FOR THEM.*
HE WON'T EVEN LOOK AT ME NOW.
HE'LL COME AROUND...YOU JUST NEED TO GIVE HIM TIME.

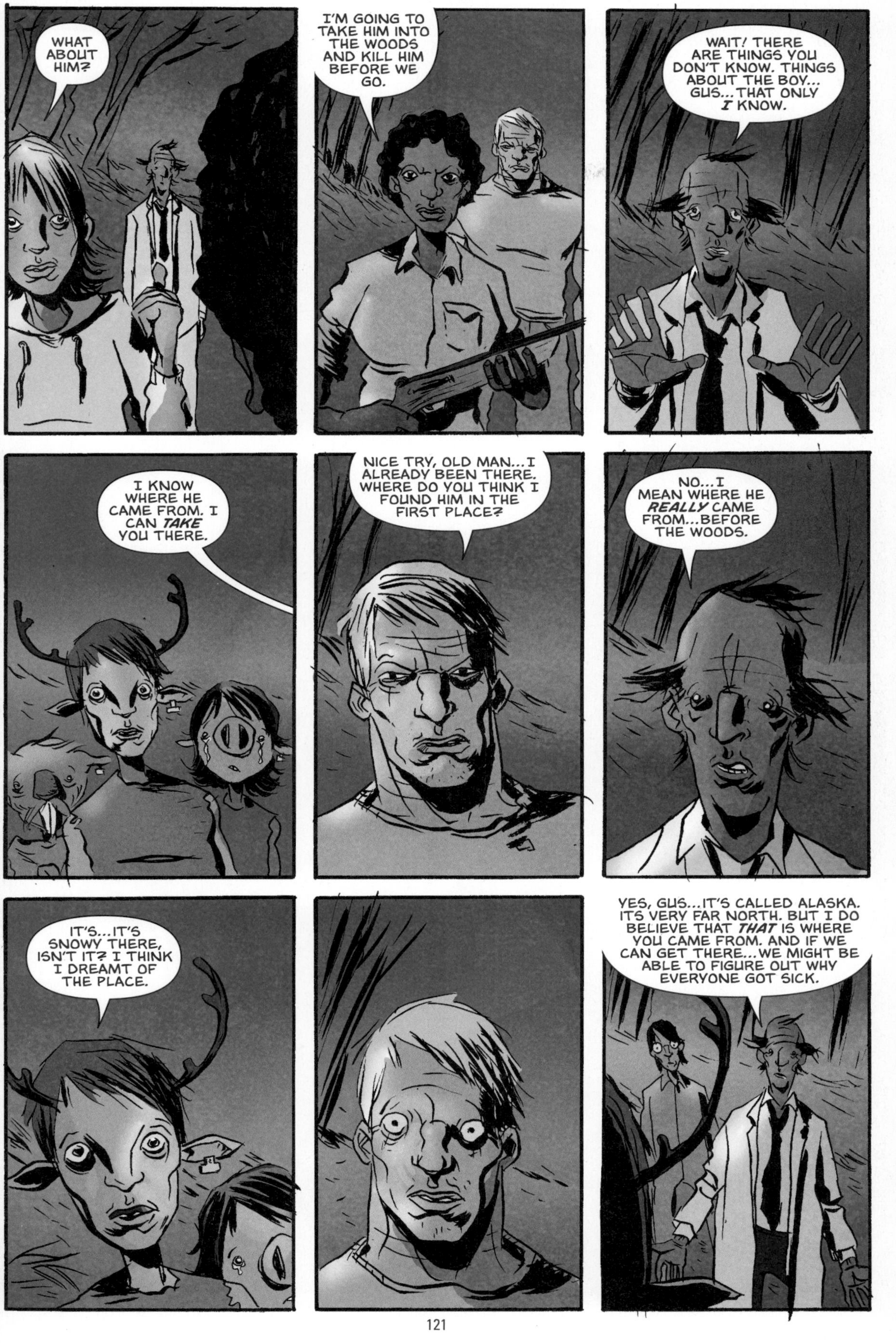
WHAT ABOUT HIM?
I'M GOING TO TAKE HIM INTO THE WOODS AND KILL HIM BEFORE WE GO.
WAIT! THERE ARE THINGS YOU DON'T KNOW. THINGS ABOUT THE BOY... GUS...THAT ONLY *I* KNOW.
I KNOW WHERE HE CAME FROM. I CAN *TAKE* YOU THERE.
NICE TRY, OLD MAN...I ALREADY BEEN THERE. WHERE DO YOU THINK I FOUND HIM IN THE FIRST PLACE?
NO...I MEAN WHERE HE *REALLY* CAME FROM...BEFORE THE WOODS.
IT'S...IT'S SNOWY THERE, ISN'T IT? I THINK I DREAMT OF THE PLACE.
YES, GUS...IT'S CALLED ALASKA. ITS VERY FAR NORTH. BUT I DO BELIEVE THAT *THAT* IS WHERE YOU CAME FROM. AND IF WE CAN GET THERE...WE MIGHT BE ABLE TO FIGURE OUT WHY EVERYONE GOT SICK.

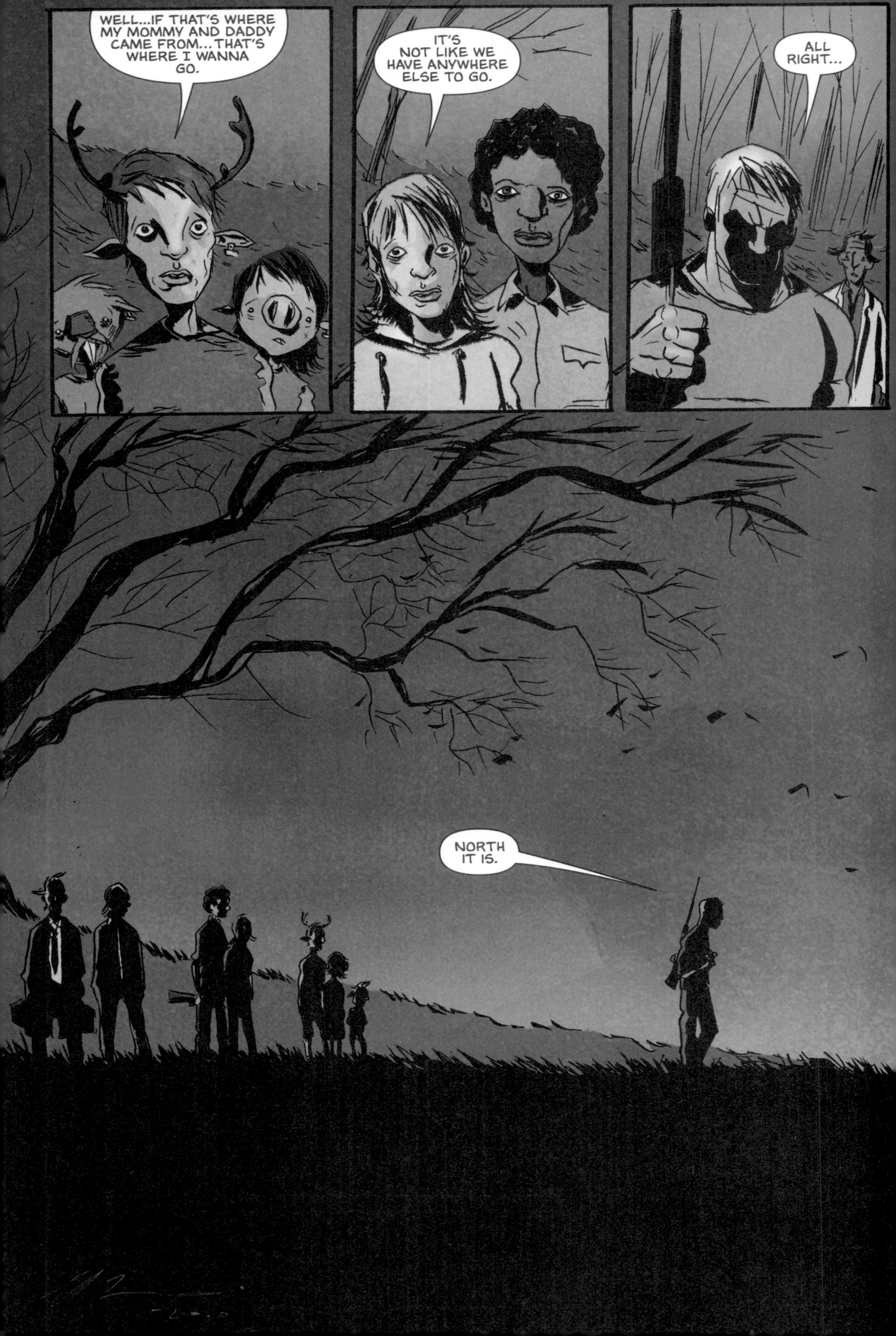
WELL...IF THAT'S WHERE MY MOMMY AND DADDY CAME FROM...THAT'S WHERE I WANNA GO.
IT'S NOT LIKE WE HAVE ANYWHERE ELSE TO GO.
ALL RIGHT...
NORTH IT IS.

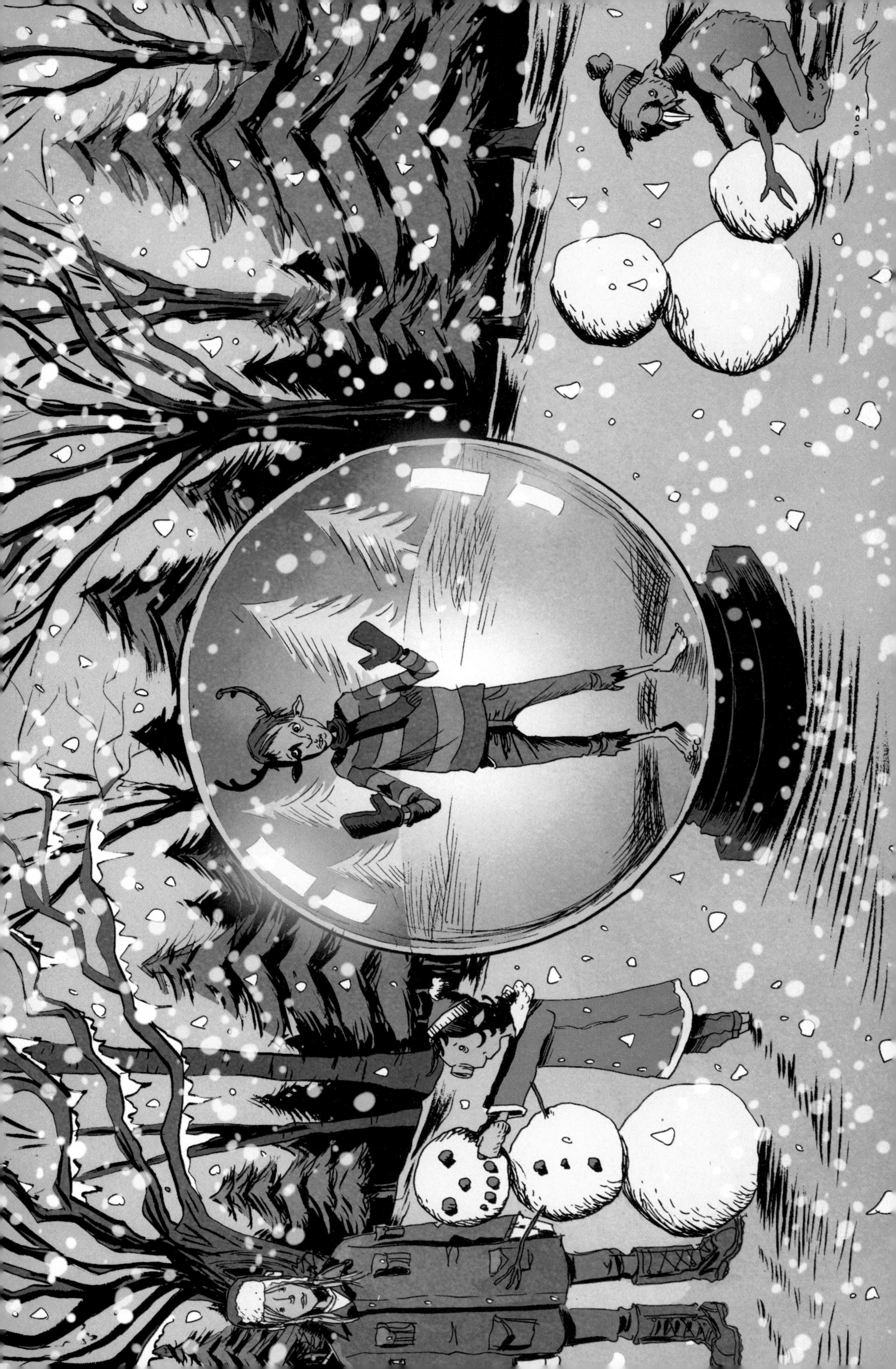

THE FURTHER ADVENTURES OF THE BOY AND THE BIG MAN

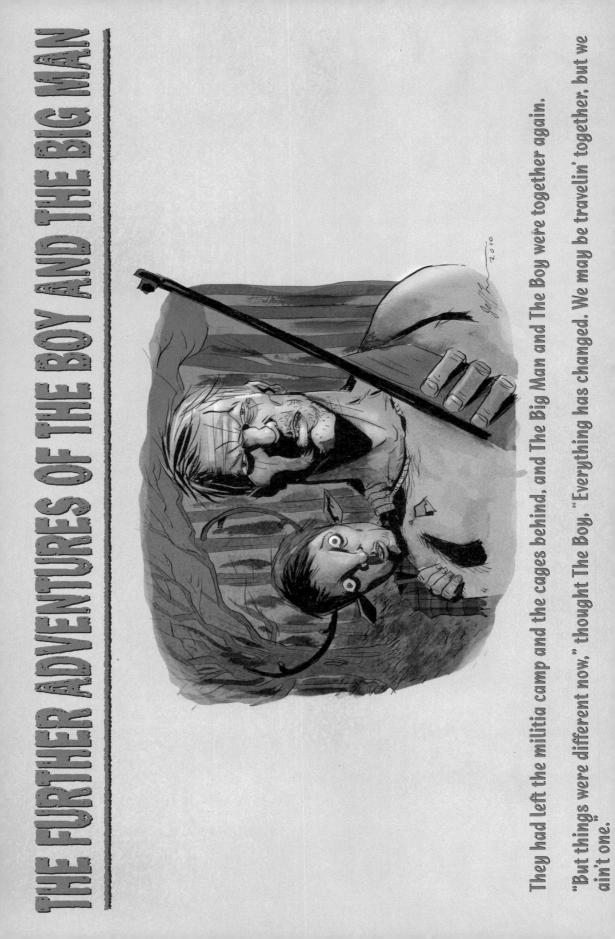

They had left the militia camp and the cages behind, and The Big Man and The Boy were together again.

"But things were different now," thought The Boy. "Everything has changed. We may be travelin' together, but we ain't one."

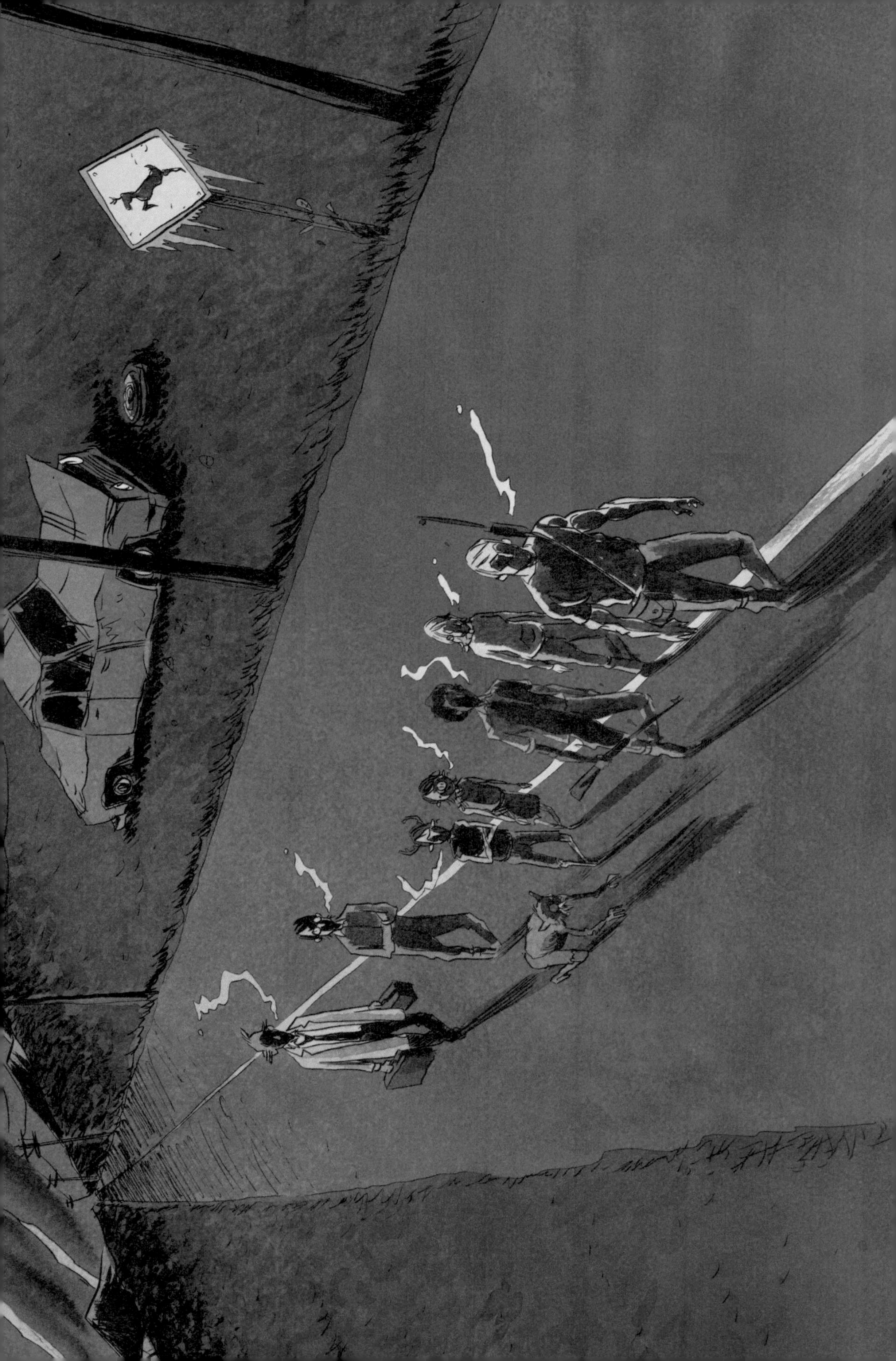

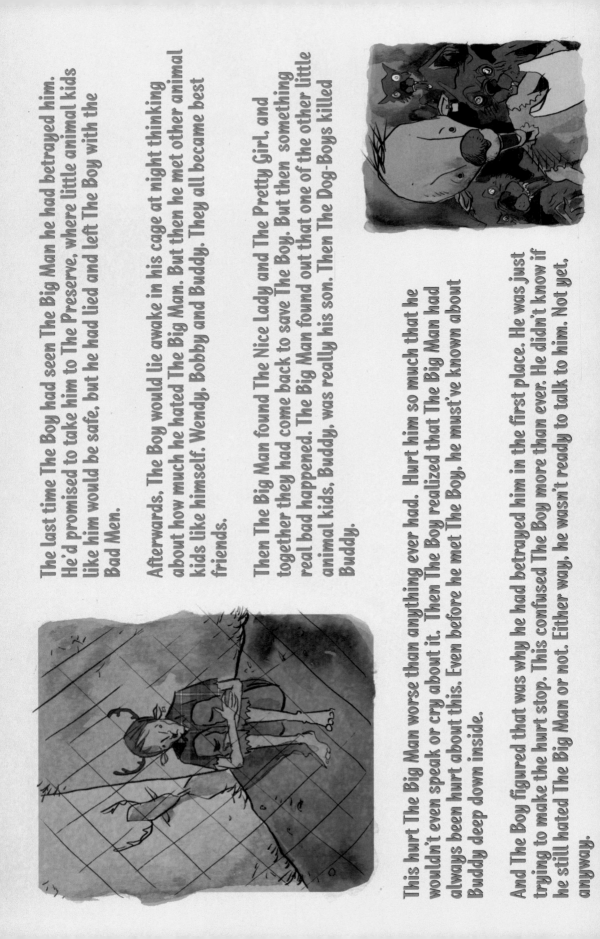

The last time The Boy had seen The Big Man he had betrayed him. He'd promised to take him to The Preserve, where little animal kids like him would be safe, but he had lied and left The Boy with the Bad Men.

Afterwards, The Boy would lie awake in his cage at night thinking about how much he hated The Big Man. But then he met other animal kids like himself. Wendy. Bobby and Buddy. They all became best friends.

Then The Big Man found The Nice Lady and The Pretty Girl, and together they had come back to save The Boy. But then something real bad happened. The Big Man found out that one of the other little animal kids, Buddy, was really his son. Then The Dog-Boys killed Buddy.

This hurt The Big Man worse than anything ever had. Hurt him so much that he wouldn't even speak or cry about it. Then The Boy realized that The Big Man had always been hurt about this. Even before he met The Boy, he must've known about Buddy deep down inside.

And The Boy figured that was why he had betrayed him in the first place. He was just trying to make the hurt stop. This confused The Boy more than ever. He didn't know if he still hated The Big Man or not. Either way, he wasn't ready to talk to him. Not yet, anyway.

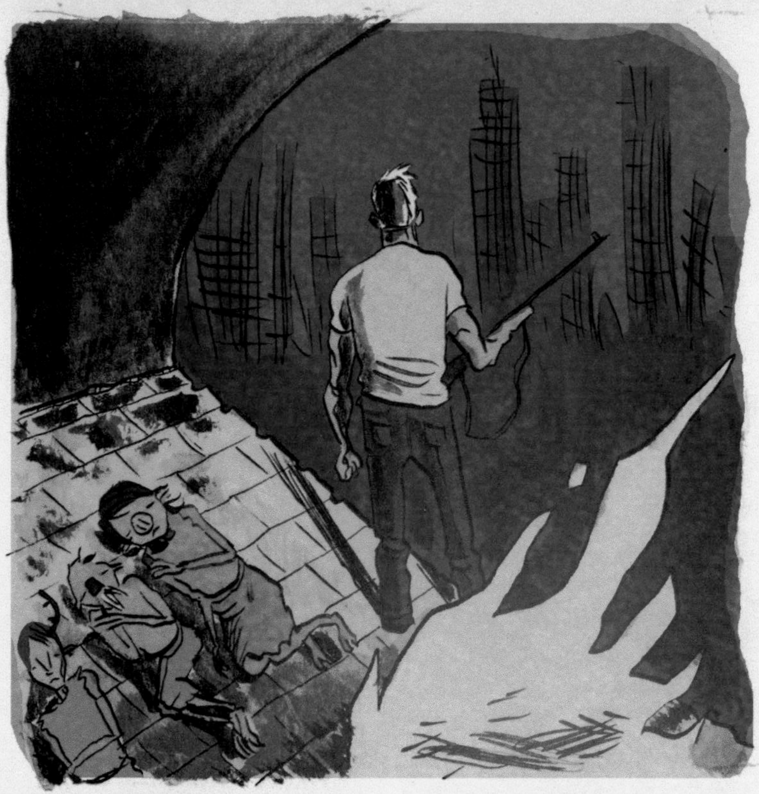

So The Boy never looked at The Big Man, and The Big Man never looked at The Boy, and they all just kept walking north. It had started to get real cold too. The Nice Lady told them they were heading to a place called Alaska, and that it would get even colder.

She said they'd have to find warmer clothes and supplies. She and The Big Man argued, but finally he agreed, and they went into the outskirts of The City. It was real dangerous, and they had to camp under bridges, and The Big Man never slept. He just stayed up all night keeping watch.

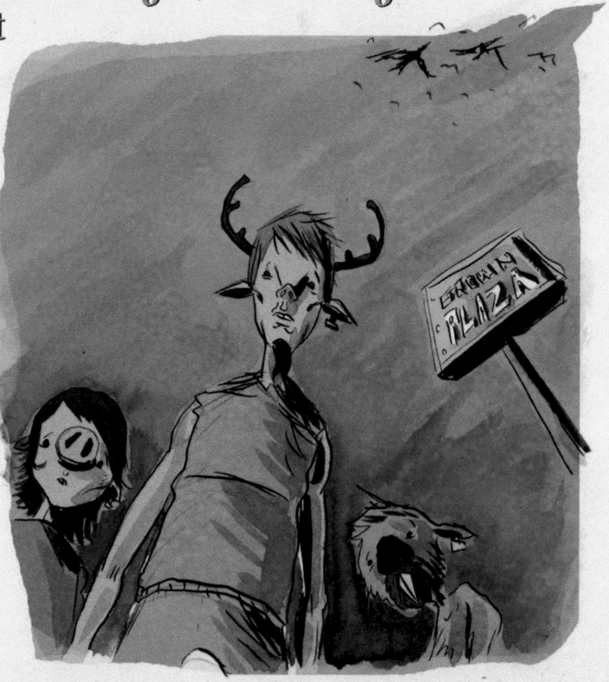
BROWN
PLAZA

Finally on the third day they found the place they had been looking for. A place called "The Mall."

The Pretty Girl explained to the Boy and his friends that The Mall was a building where "you could buy anything you needed." The Boy and his friends were excited to see what was inside.

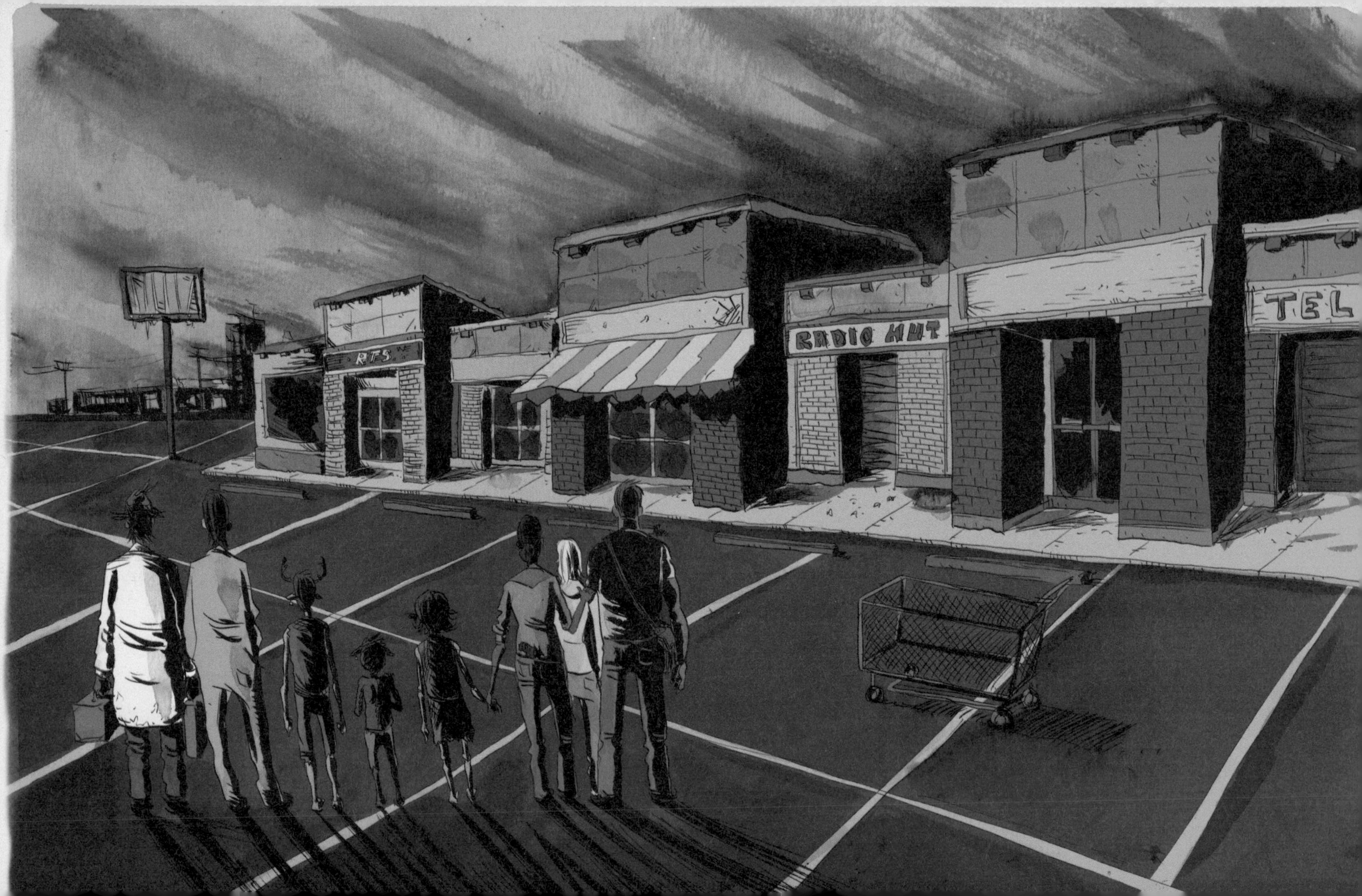
ARTS
RADIO HUT
TEL

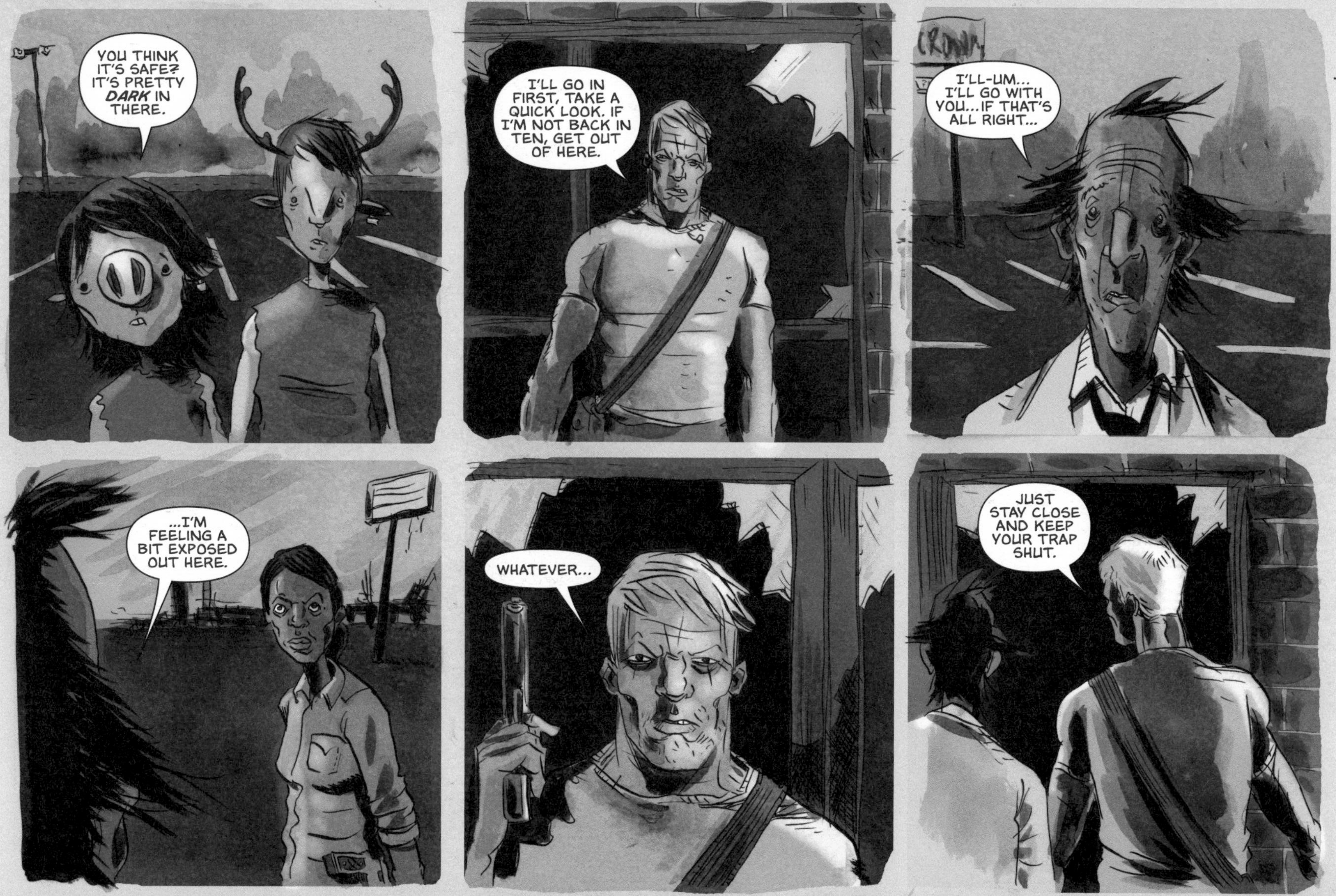
YOU THINK IT'S SAFE? IT'S PRETTY *DARK* IN THERE.
I'LL GO IN FIRST, TAKE A QUICK LOOK. IF I'M NOT BACK IN TEN, GET OUT OF HERE.
I'LL-UM... I'LL GO WITH YOU...IF THAT'S ALL RIGHT...
...I'M FEELING A BIT EXPOSED OUT HERE.
WHATEVER...
JUST STAY CLOSE AND KEEP YOUR TRAP SHUT.

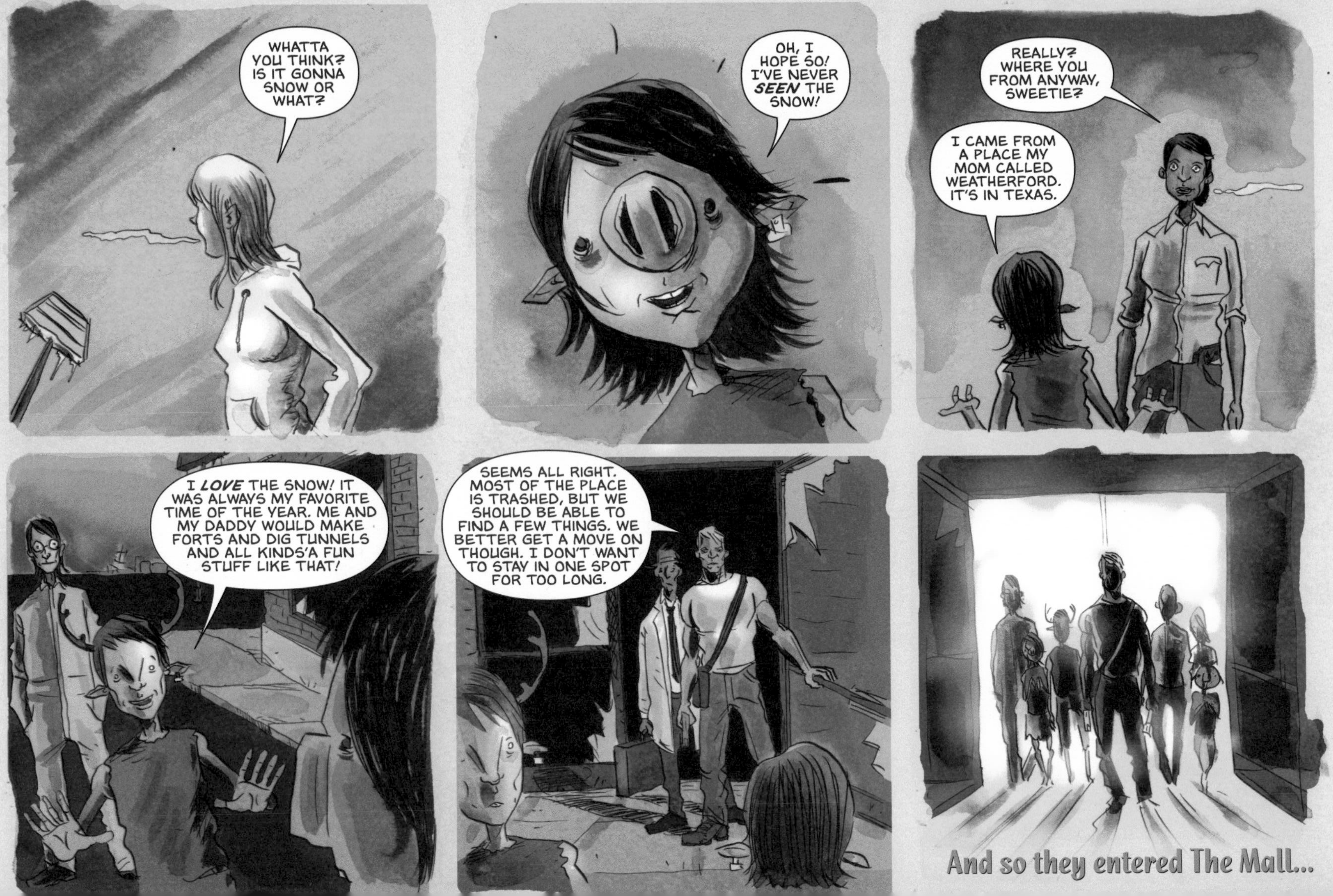
WHATTA YOU THINK? IS IT GONNA SNOW OR WHAT?
OH, I HOPE SO! I'VE NEVER *SEEN* THE SNOW!
REALLY? WHERE YOU FROM ANYWAY, SWEETIE?
I CAME FROM A PLACE MY MOM CALLED WEATHERFORD. IT'S IN TEXAS.
I *LOVE* THE SNOW! IT WAS ALWAYS MY FAVORITE TIME OF THE YEAR. ME AND MY DADDY WOULD MAKE FORTS AND DIG TUNNELS AND ALL KINDS'A FUN STUFF LIKE THAT!
SEEMS ALL RIGHT. MOST OF THE PLACE IS TRASHED, BUT WE SHOULD BE ABLE TO FIND A FEW THINGS. WE BETTER GET A MOVE ON THOUGH. I DON'T WANT TO STAY IN ONE SPOT FOR TOO LONG.
And so they entered The Mall...

It turned out to be just another big building full of junk. The Boy didn't like going into places like this, 'cause it just reminded him of all the people who had once been alive but now were dead. And even if The Boy's Daddy had been right, even if all the people had been sinners and had died 'cause God had wanted them to, The Boy still felt sad for them.

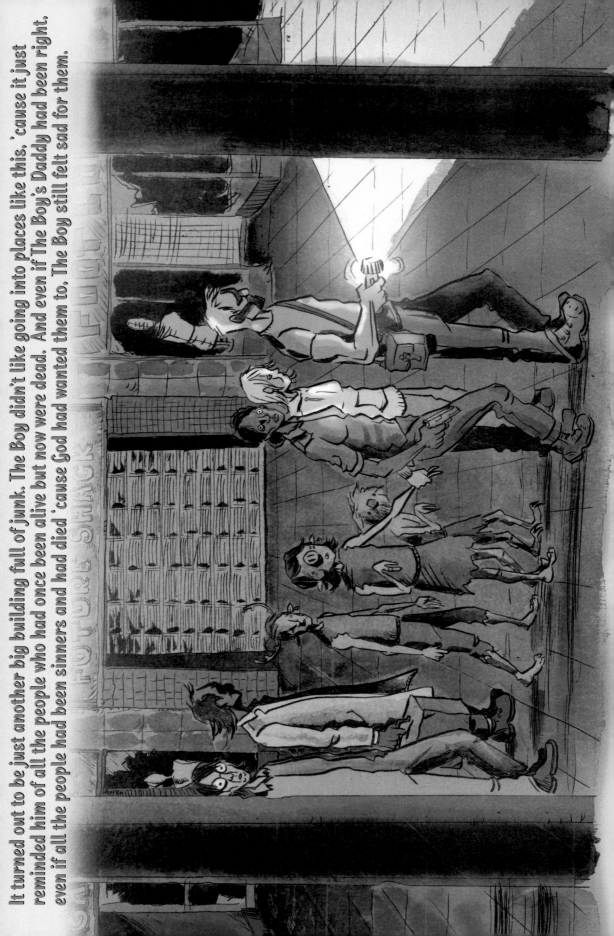

But soon they found what they were looking for...

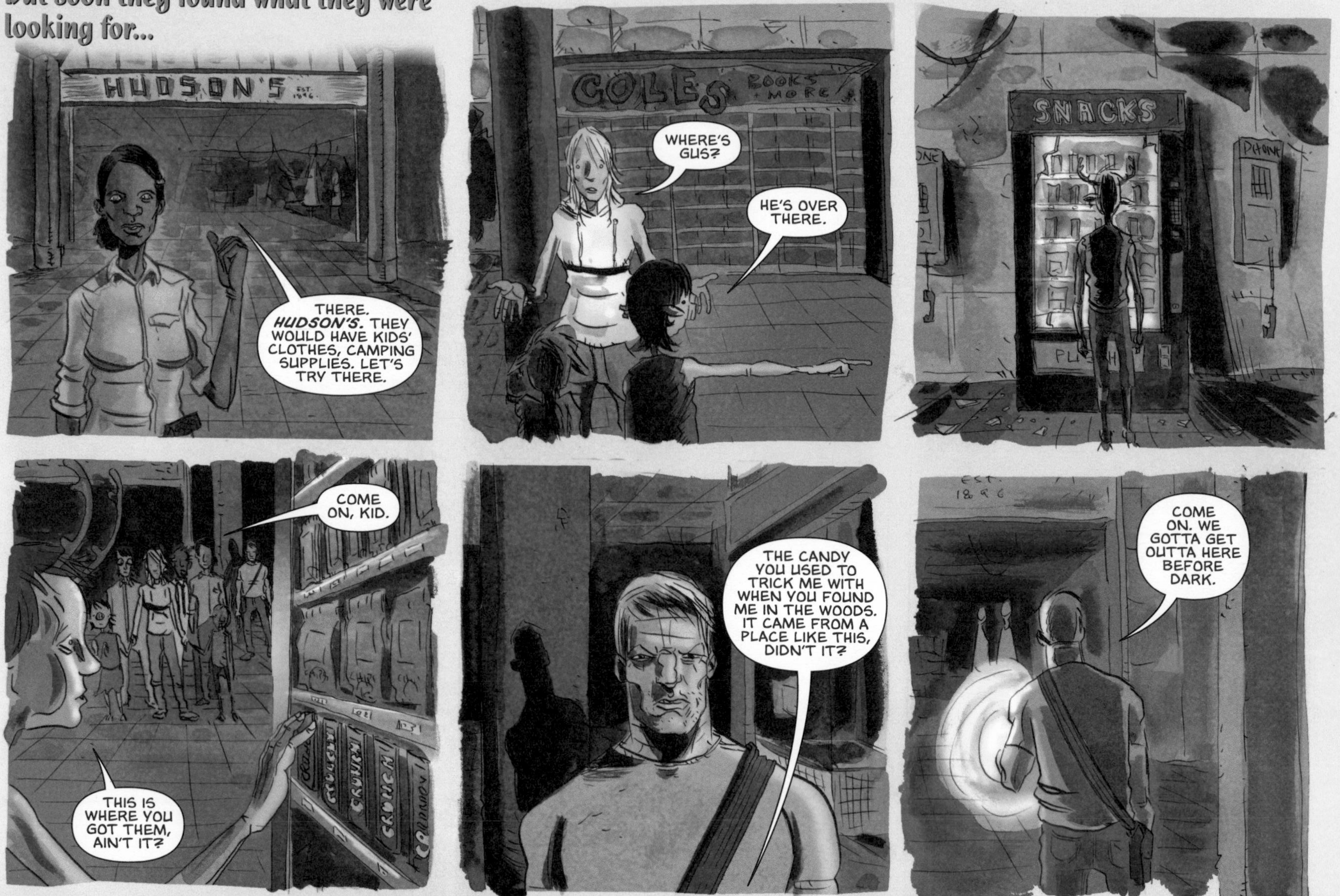
HUDSON'S EST. 1976.
THERE. *HUDSON'S.* THEY WOULD HAVE KIDS' CLOTHES, CAMPING SUPPLIES. LET'S TRY THERE.
COLE'S BOOKS + MORE
WHERE'S GUS?
HE'S OVER THERE.
SNACKS
PHONE
COME ON, KID.
THIS IS WHERE YOU GOT THEM, AIN'T IT?
THE CANDY YOU USED TO TRICK ME WITH WHEN YOU FOUND ME IN THE WOODS. IT CAME FROM A PLACE LIKE THIS, DIDN'T IT?
COME ON. WE GOTTA GET OUTTA HERE BEFORE DARK.

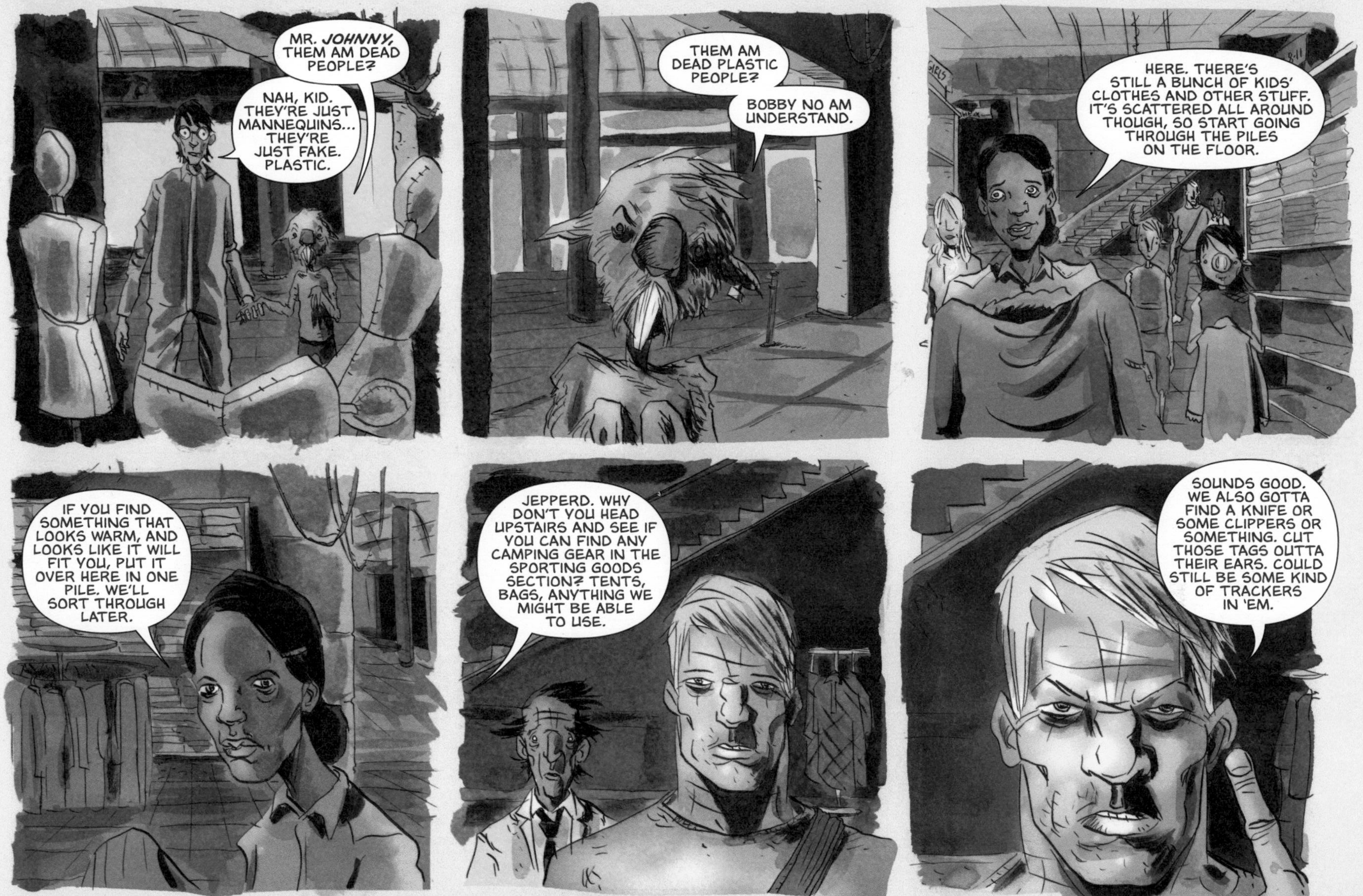
MR. JOHNNY, THEM AM DEAD PEOPLE?
NAH, KID. THEY'RE JUST MANNEQUINS... THEY'RE JUST FAKE. PLASTIC.
THEM AM DEAD PLASTIC PEOPLE?
BOBBY NO AM UNDERSTAND.
HERE. THERE'S STILL A BUNCH OF KIDS' CLOTHES AND OTHER STUFF. IT'S SCATTERED ALL AROUND THOUGH, SO START GOING THROUGH THE PILES ON THE FLOOR.
IF YOU FIND SOMETHING THAT LOOKS WARM, AND LOOKS LIKE IT WILL FIT YOU, PUT IT OVER HERE IN ONE PILE. WE'LL SORT THROUGH LATER.
JEPPERD. WHY DON'T YOU HEAD UPSTAIRS AND SEE IF YOU CAN FIND ANY CAMPING GEAR IN THE SPORTING GOODS SECTION? TENTS, BAGS, ANYTHING WE MIGHT BE ABLE TO USE.
SOUNDS GOOD. WE ALSO GOTTA FIND A KNIFE OR SOME CLIPPERS OR SOMETHING. CUT THOSE TAGS OUTTA THEIR EARS. COULD STILL BE SOME KIND OF TRACKERS IN 'EM.

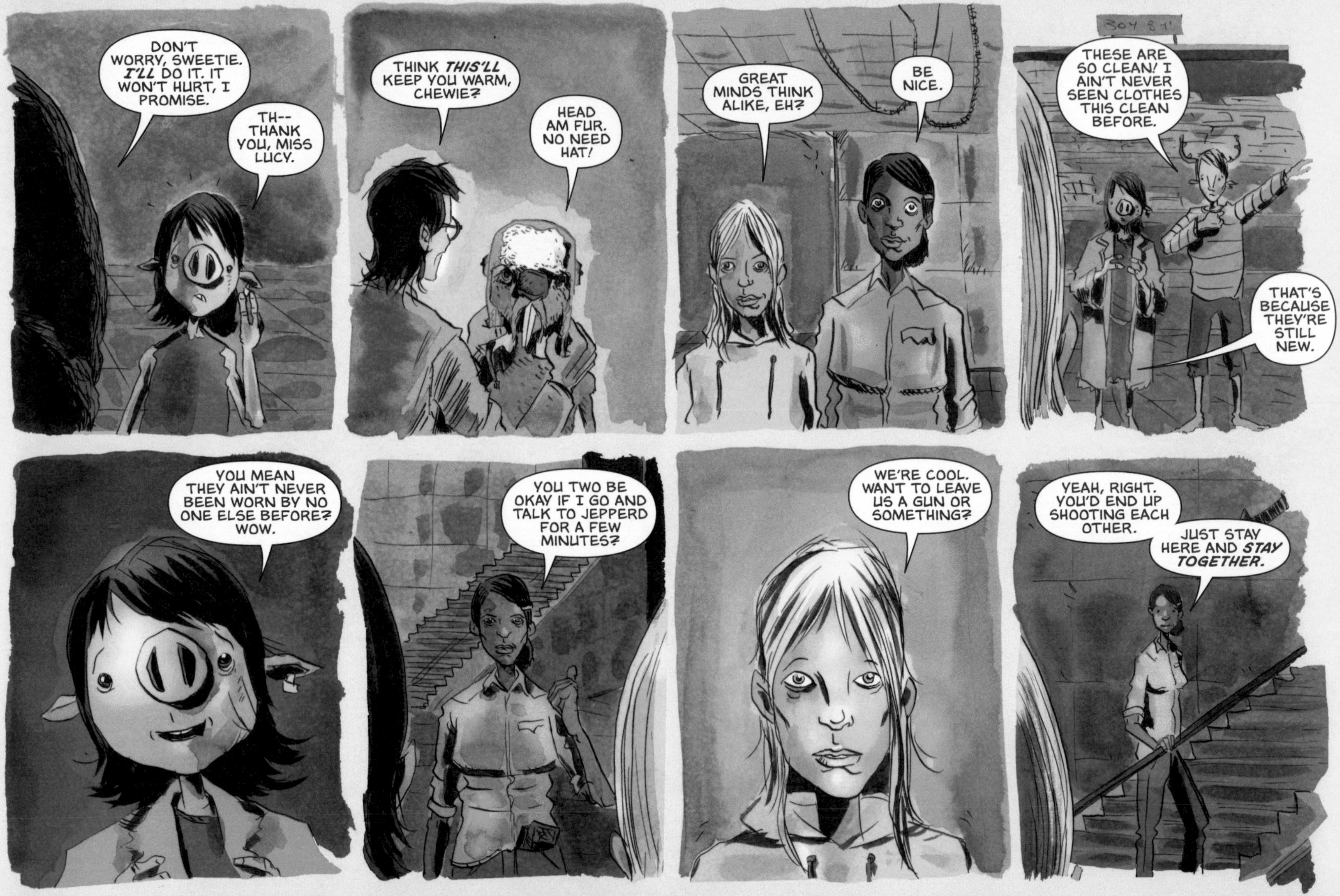
DON'T WORRY, SWEETIE. *I'LL* DO IT. IT WON'T HURT, I PROMISE.
TH-- THANK YOU, MISS LUCY.
THINK *THIS'LL* KEEP YOU WARM, CHEWIE?
HEAD AM FUR. NO NEED HAT!
GREAT MINDS THINK ALIKE, EH?
BE NICE.
THESE ARE SO CLEAN! I AIN'T NEVER SEEN CLOTHES THIS CLEAN BEFORE.
THAT'S BECAUSE THEY'RE STILL NEW.
YOU MEAN THEY AIN'T NEVER BEEN WORN BY NO ONE ELSE BEFORE? WOW.
YOU TWO BE OKAY IF I GO AND TALK TO JEPPERD FOR A FEW MINUTES?
WE'RE COOL. WANT TO LEAVE US A GUN OR SOMETHING?
YEAH, RIGHT. YOU'D END UP SHOOTING EACH OTHER.
JUST STAY HERE AND *STAY TOGETHER.*

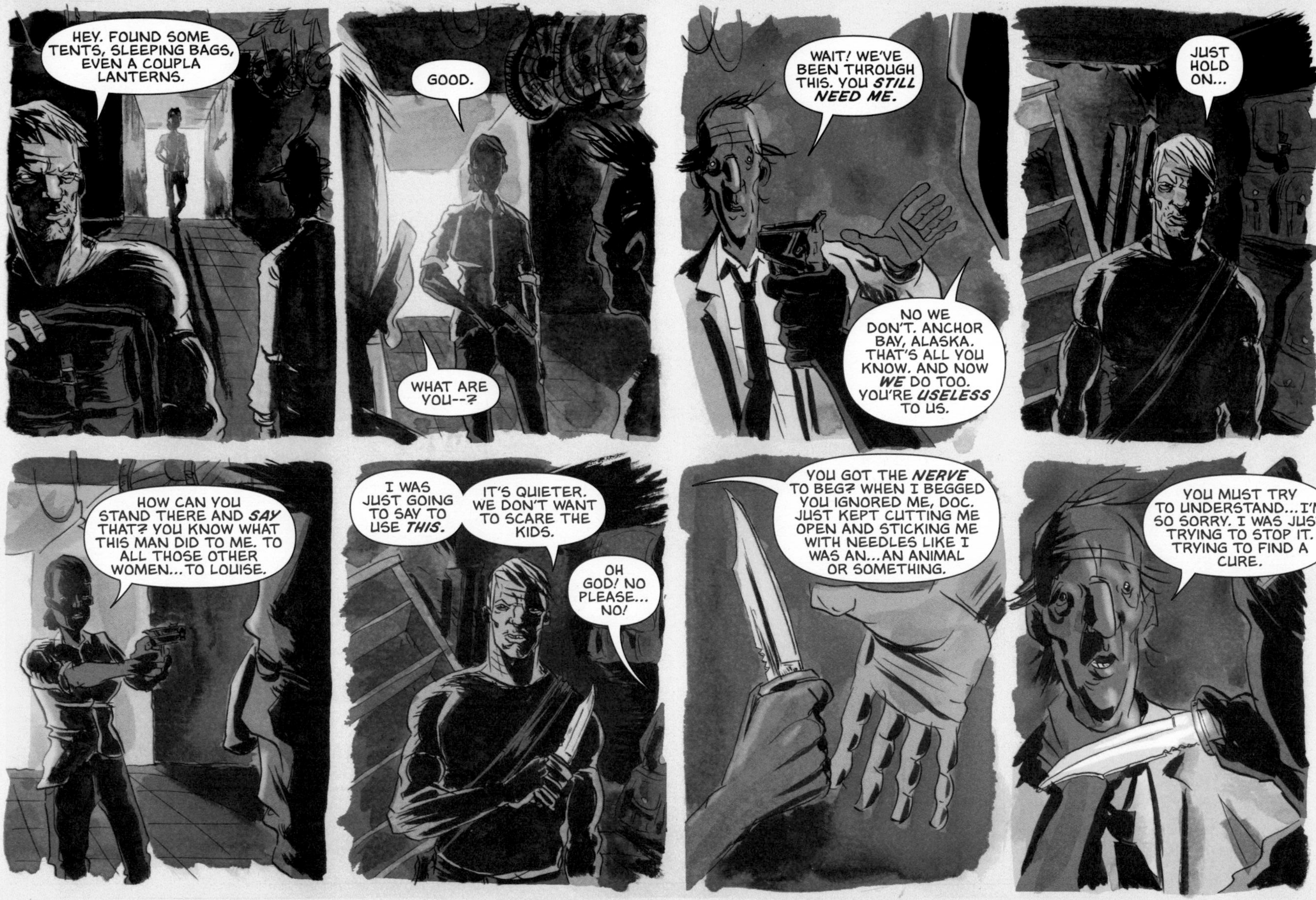
HEY. FOUND SOME TENTS, SLEEPING BAGS, EVEN A COUPLA LANTERNS.
GOOD.
WHAT ARE YOU--?
WAIT! WE'VE BEEN THROUGH THIS. YOU *STILL NEED ME.*
NO WE DON'T. ANCHOR BAY, ALASKA. THAT'S ALL YOU KNOW. AND NOW *WE* DO TOO. YOU'RE *USELESS* TO US.
JUST HOLD ON...
HOW CAN YOU STAND THERE AND *SAY* THAT? YOU KNOW WHAT THIS MAN DID TO ME. TO ALL THOSE OTHER WOMEN... TO LOUISE.
I WAS JUST GOING TO SAY TO USE *THIS.*
IT'S QUIETER. WE DON'T WANT TO SCARE THE KIDS.
OH GOD! NO PLEASE... NO!
YOU GOT THE *NERVE* TO BEG? WHEN I BEGGED YOU IGNORED ME, DOC. JUST KEPT CUTTING ME OPEN AND STICKING ME WITH NEEDLES LIKE I WAS AN... AN ANIMAL OR SOMETHING.
YOU MUST TRY TO UNDERSTAND... I'M SO SORRY. I WAS JUST TRYING TO STOP IT. TRYING TO FIND A CURE.

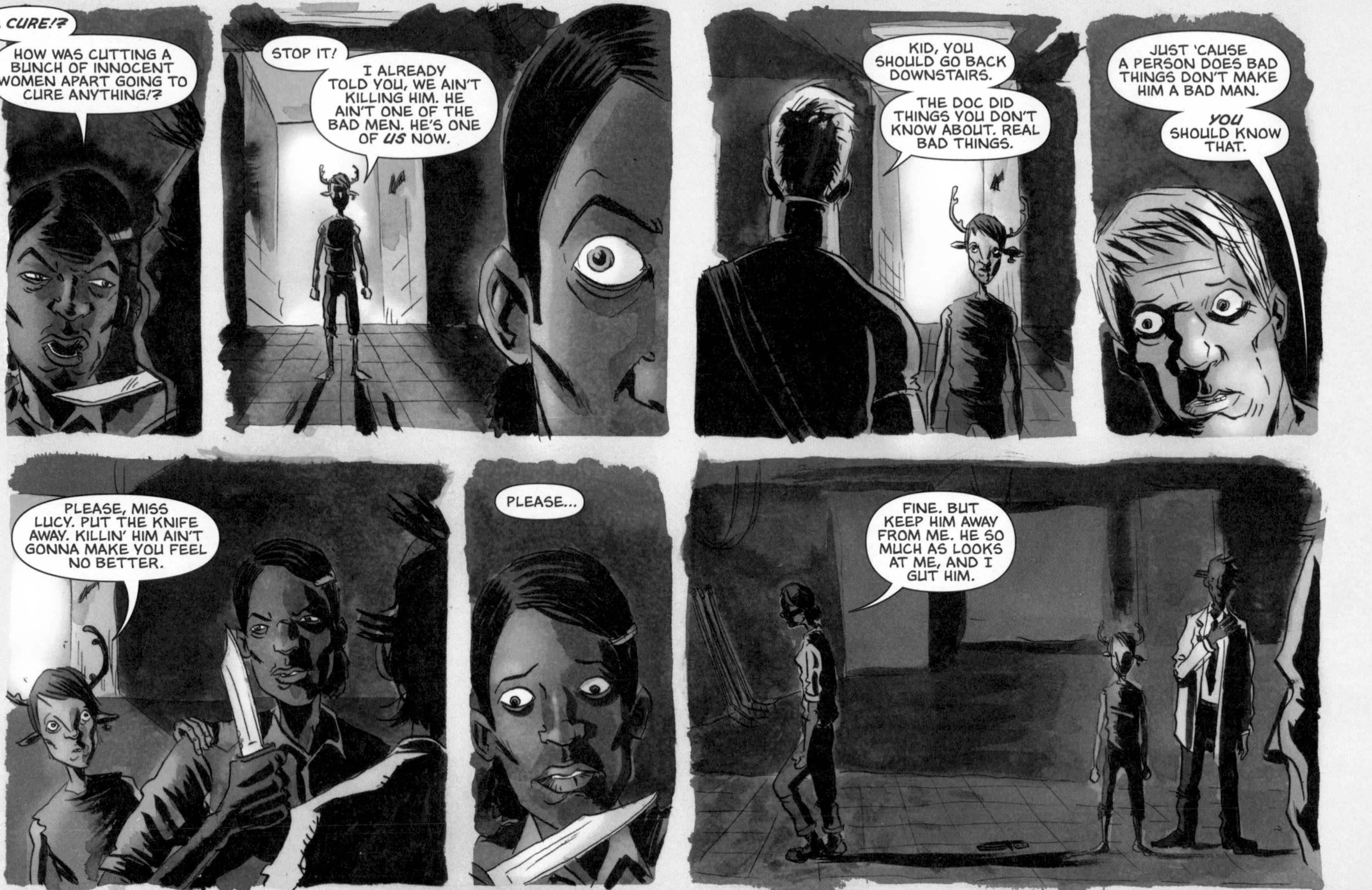
A *CURE!?*
HOW WAS CUTTING A BUNCH OF INNOCENT WOMEN APART GOING TO CURE ANYTHING!?
STOP IT!
I ALREADY TOLD YOU, WE AIN'T KILLING HIM. HE AIN'T ONE OF THE BAD MEN. HE'S ONE OF *US* NOW.
KID, YOU SHOULD GO BACK DOWNSTAIRS.
THE DOC DID THINGS YOU DON'T KNOW ABOUT. REAL BAD THINGS.
JUST 'CAUSE A PERSON DOES BAD THINGS DON'T MAKE HIM A BAD MAN.
YOU SHOULD KNOW THAT.
PLEASE, MISS LUCY. PUT THE KNIFE AWAY. KILLIN' HIM AIN'T GONNA MAKE YOU FEEL NO BETTER.
PLEASE...
FINE. BUT KEEP HIM AWAY FROM ME. HE SO MUCH AS LOOKS AT ME, AND I GUT HIM.

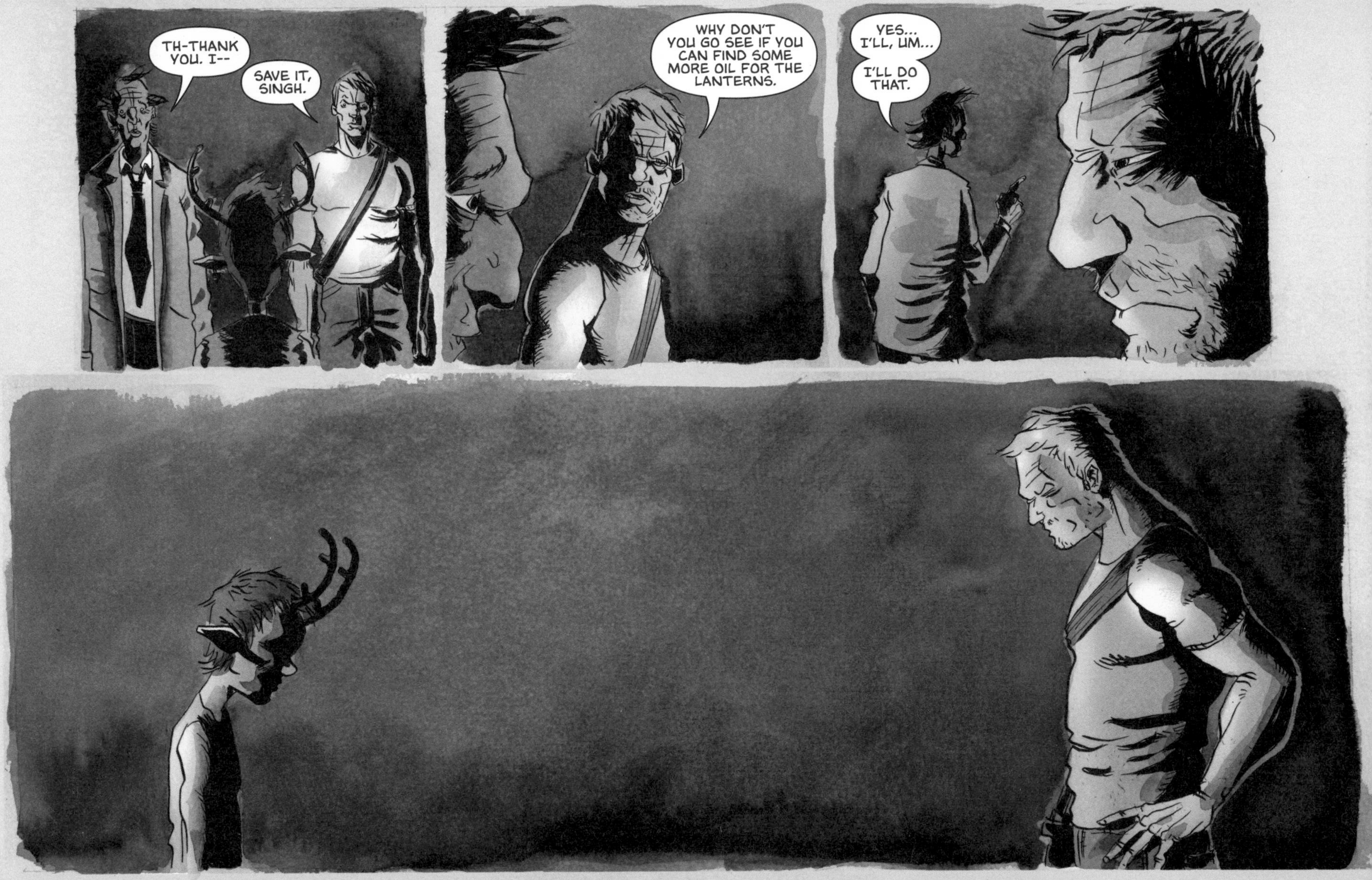
TH-THANK YOU. I--
SAVE IT, SINGH.
WHY DON'T YOU GO SEE IF YOU CAN FIND SOME MORE OIL FOR THE LANTERNS.
YES... I'LL, UM...
I'LL DO THAT.

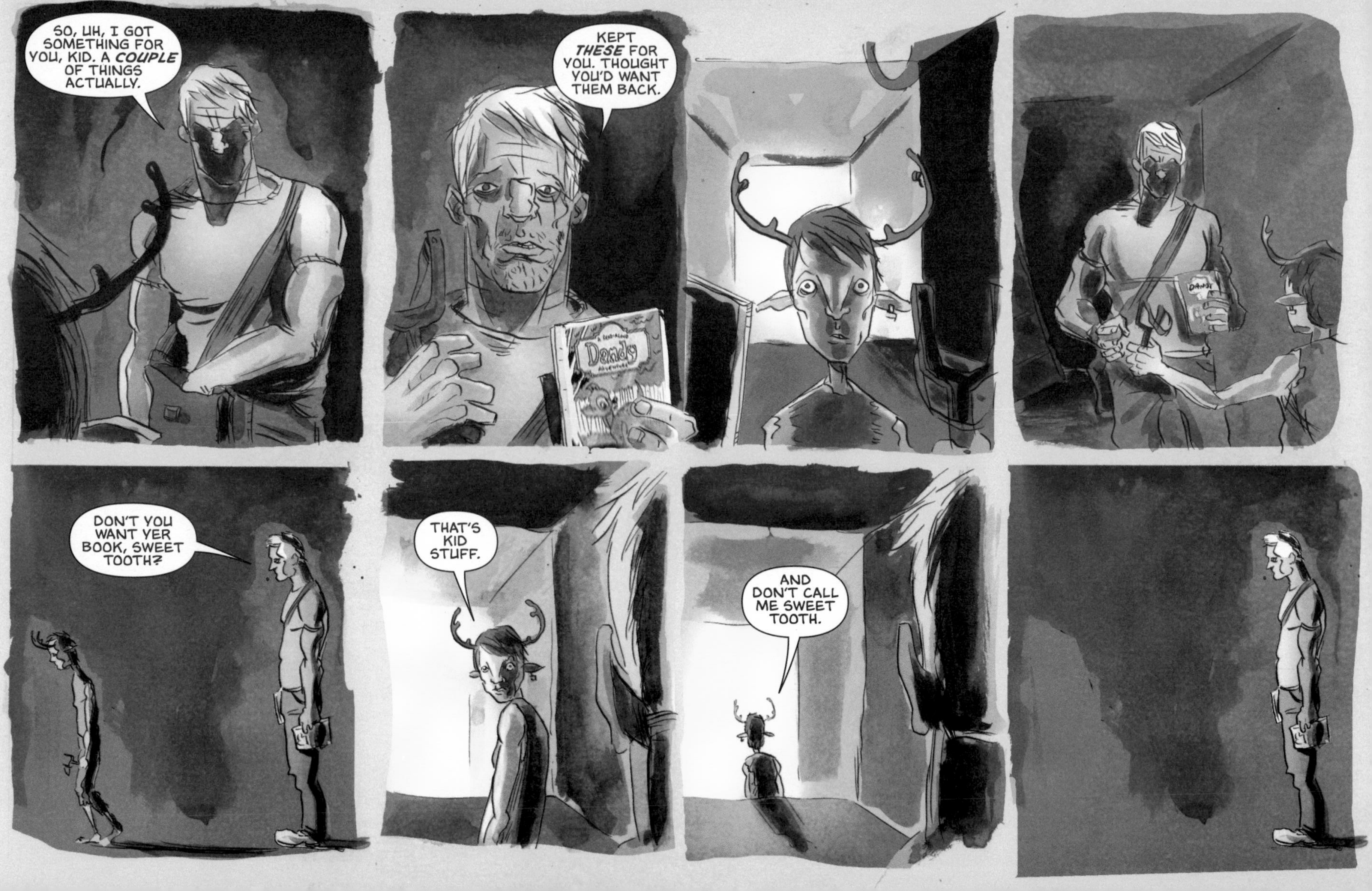
SO, UH, I GOT SOMETHING FOR YOU, KID. A *COUPLE* OF THINGS ACTUALLY.
KEPT *THESE* FOR YOU. THOUGHT YOU'D WANT THEM BACK.
A READ-ALONG Dandy ADVENTURE
DON'T YOU WANT YER BOOK, SWEET TOOTH?
THAT'S KID STUFF.
AND DON'T CALL ME SWEET TOOTH.

The Big Man decided it was too close to dark to leave, so they would stay the night. The children were excited and wondered why they couldn't just stay there forever. The Big Man said it wasn't safe to stay in one spot, no matter how nice it was. He said the militia was still out there and that sooner or later they'd come looking for them.

Besides, The Boy wanted to keep going to Alaska. He wanted to see where he had come from.

That night they slept in warm tents with lots of blankets and everything. But as comfortable as it was, The Boy couldn't fall asleep. He just lay there staring up at the tent. The Boy thought of everything that had happened since he had left the woods. They had all had so many bad things happen to them, he just couldn't see how he would ever feel truly safe or happy again. Eventually he drifted off, but he didn't dream that night.

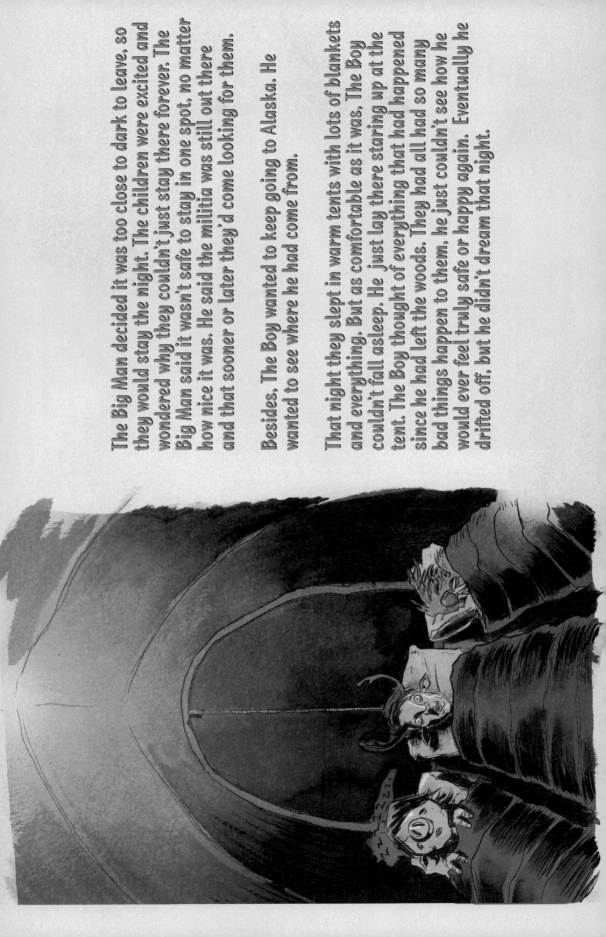

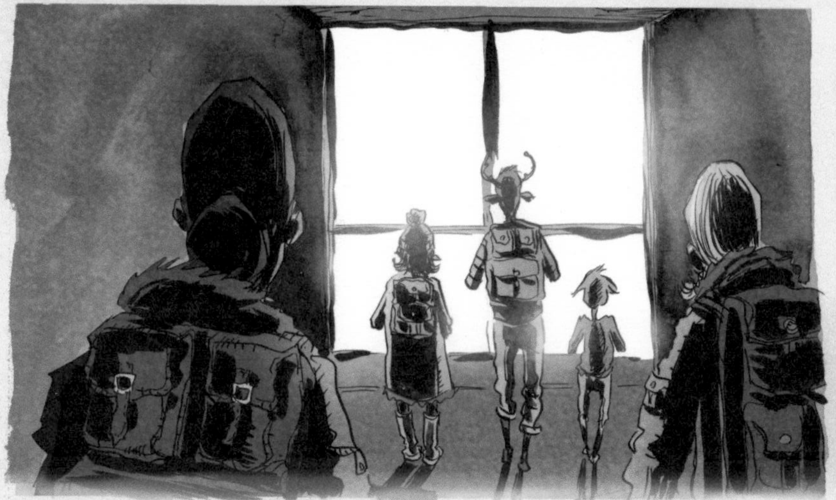

The next morning they packed up what they could carry and moved out.

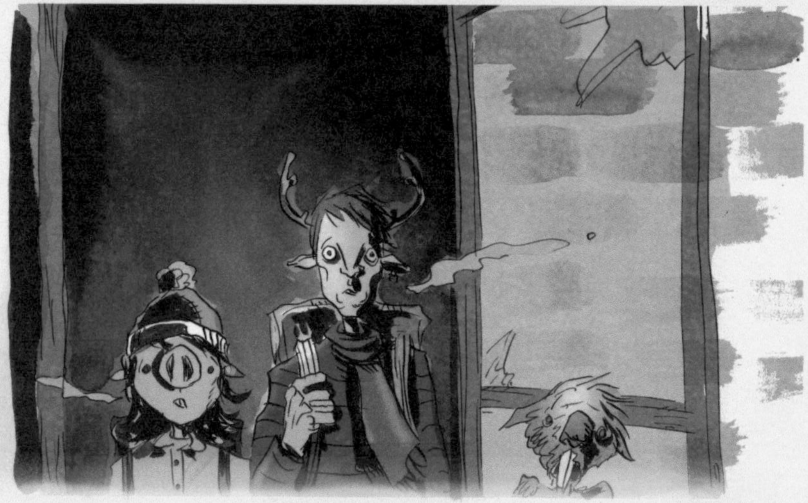

But nothing could prepare them for what they saw when they left the Mall.

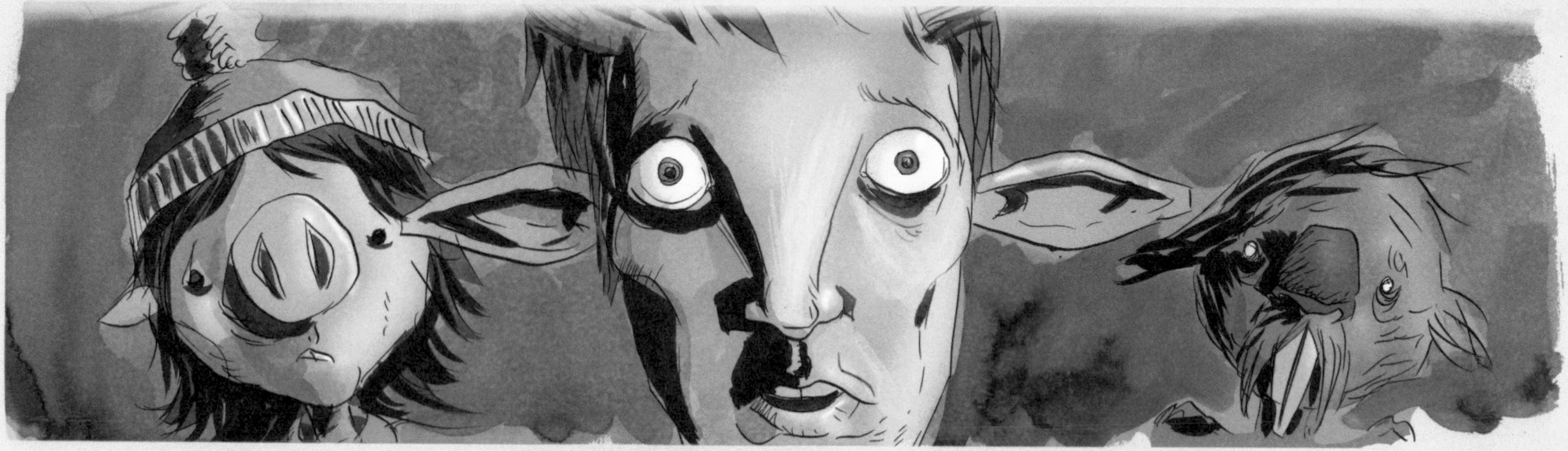

It had come in the night. Silent. And it had changed everything...

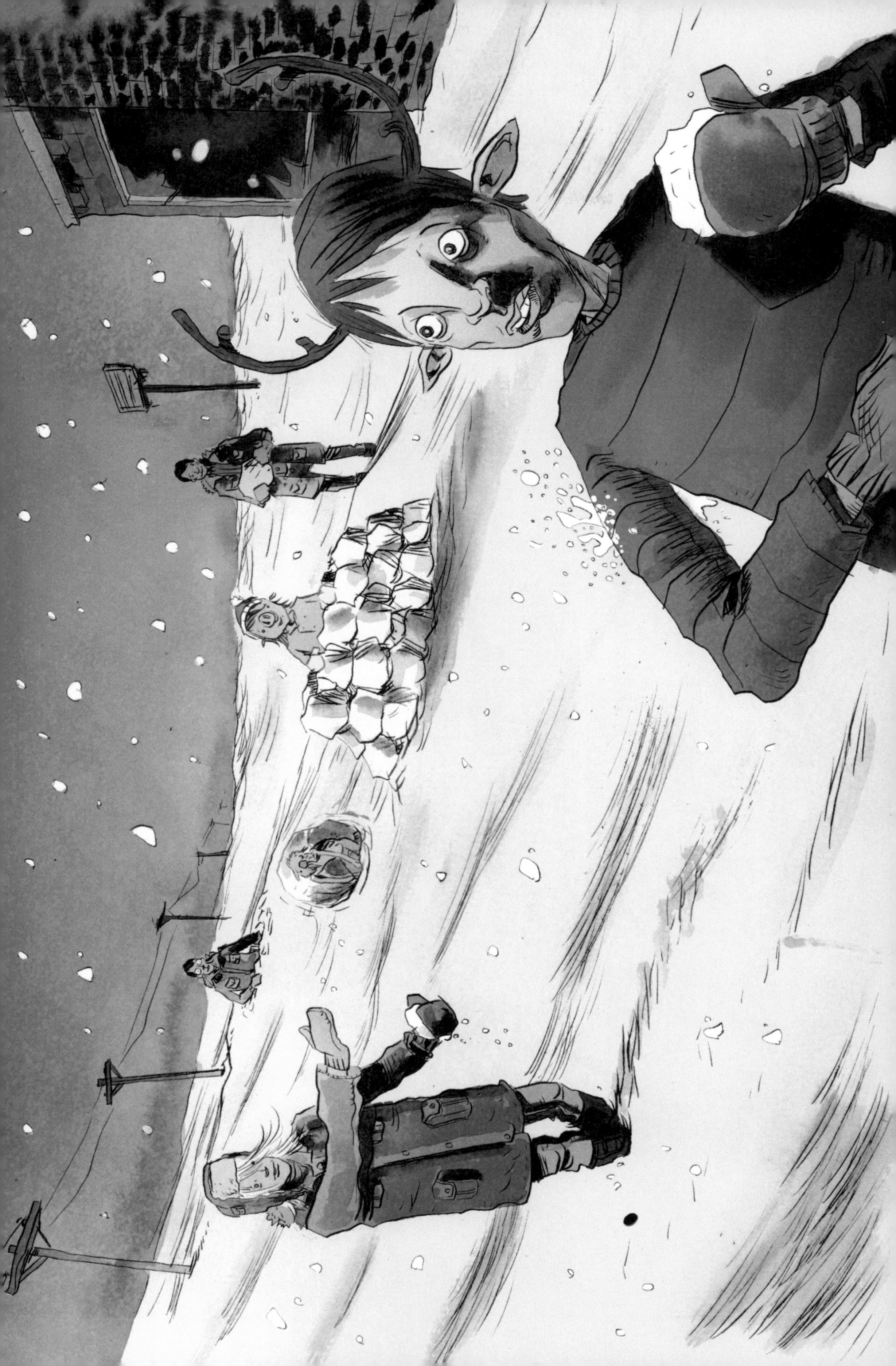

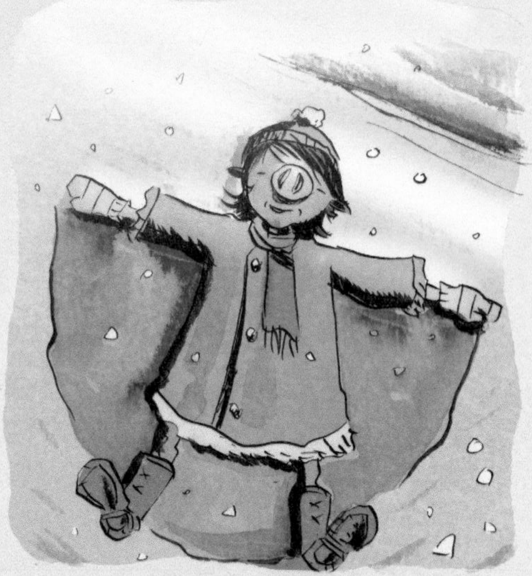

Snow.

It had come while they slept, and it was as deep as their shins and soft and bright and clean! They ran around and jumped in it and ate it and laughed. The Nice Lady showed them how they could all see angels in the snow if they lay on their backs and flapped their arms and legs. The Boy liked seeing angels.

Then The Man With The Funny Eyes and The Pretty Girl started digging big holes in the snow and making walls. They called them "forts." All the girls made one fort, and The Man With The Funny Eyes and Bobby and The Boy made another. They made snowballs and had a war. Not a real war with killing and blood like they had seen at the camp, just a pretend one.

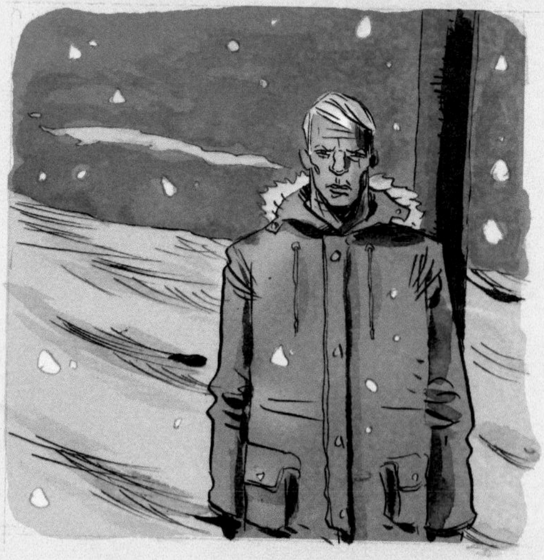

They all laughed and smiled. The Boy looked over and even thought he saw a smile on The Big Man's face. . . but it was so bright out he couldn't be sure.

Finally The Pretty Girl and Wendy started to make a Snowman. The kids had never seen one of those before. They made eyes and a nose and a mouth out of stones.

They liked the Snowman, but Johnny said something was missing...

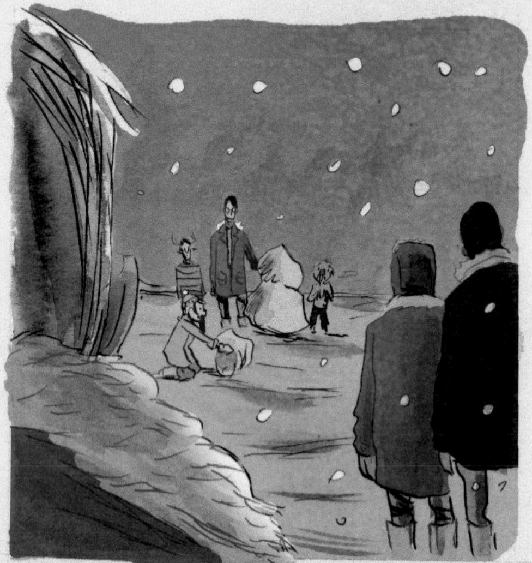

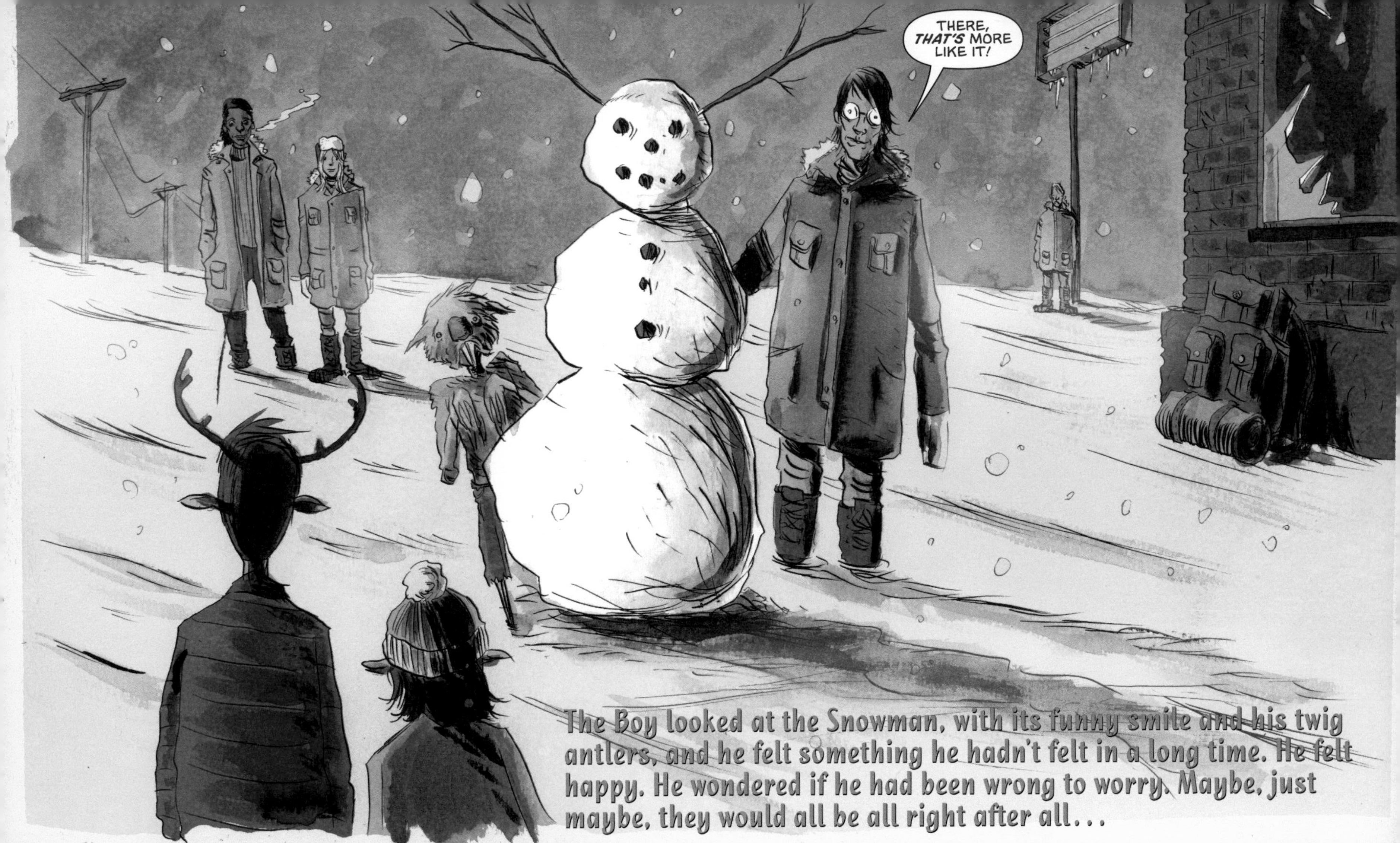
THERE, THAT'S MORE LIKE IT!
The Boy looked at the Snowman, with its funny smile and his twig antlers, and he felt something he hadn't felt in a long time. He felt happy. He wondered if he had been wrong to worry. Maybe, just maybe, they would all be all right after all. . .

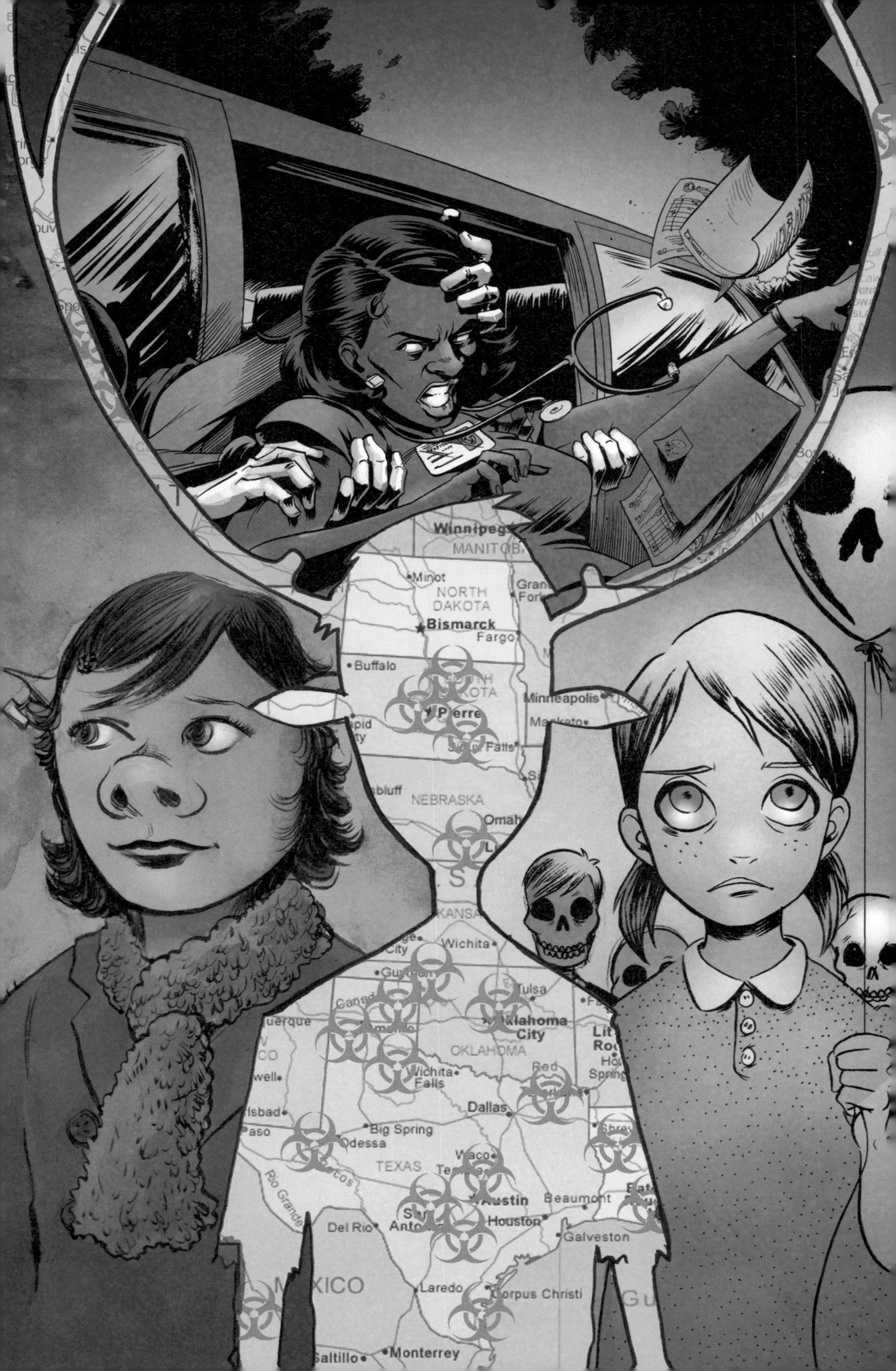
Winnipeg
MANITOBA
Minot
NORTH
DAKOTA
Bismarck
Fargo
Buffalo
Minneapolis
Mankato
NEBRASKA
Omaha
Wichita
Tulsa
Oklahoma
City
OKLAHOMA
Wichita
Falls
Dallas
Big Spring
Odessa
TEXAS
Waco
Austin
Beaumont
Houston
Del Rio
Galveston
Laredo
Corpus Christi
Saltillo
Monterrey
Rio Grande

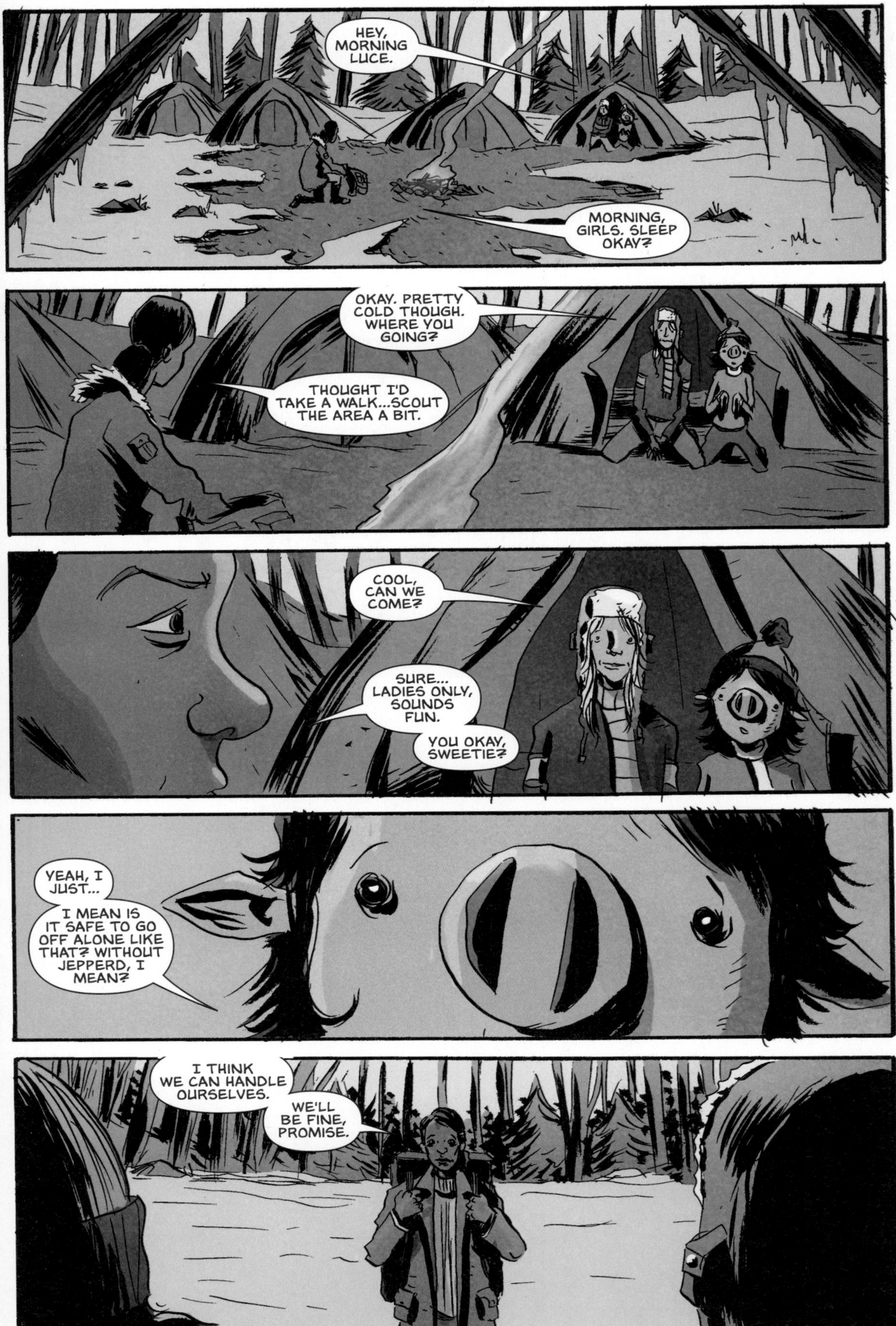
HEY, MORNING LUCE.
MORNING, GIRLS. SLEEP OKAY?
OKAY. PRETTY COLD THOUGH. WHERE YOU GOING?
THOUGHT I'D TAKE A WALK...SCOUT THE AREA A BIT.
COOL, CAN WE COME?
SURE... LADIES ONLY, SOUNDS FUN.
YOU OKAY, SWEETIE?
YEAH, I JUST...
I MEAN IS IT SAFE TO GO OFF ALONE LIKE THAT? WITHOUT JEPPERD, I MEAN?
I THINK WE CAN HANDLE OURSELVES.
WE'LL BE FINE, PROMISE.

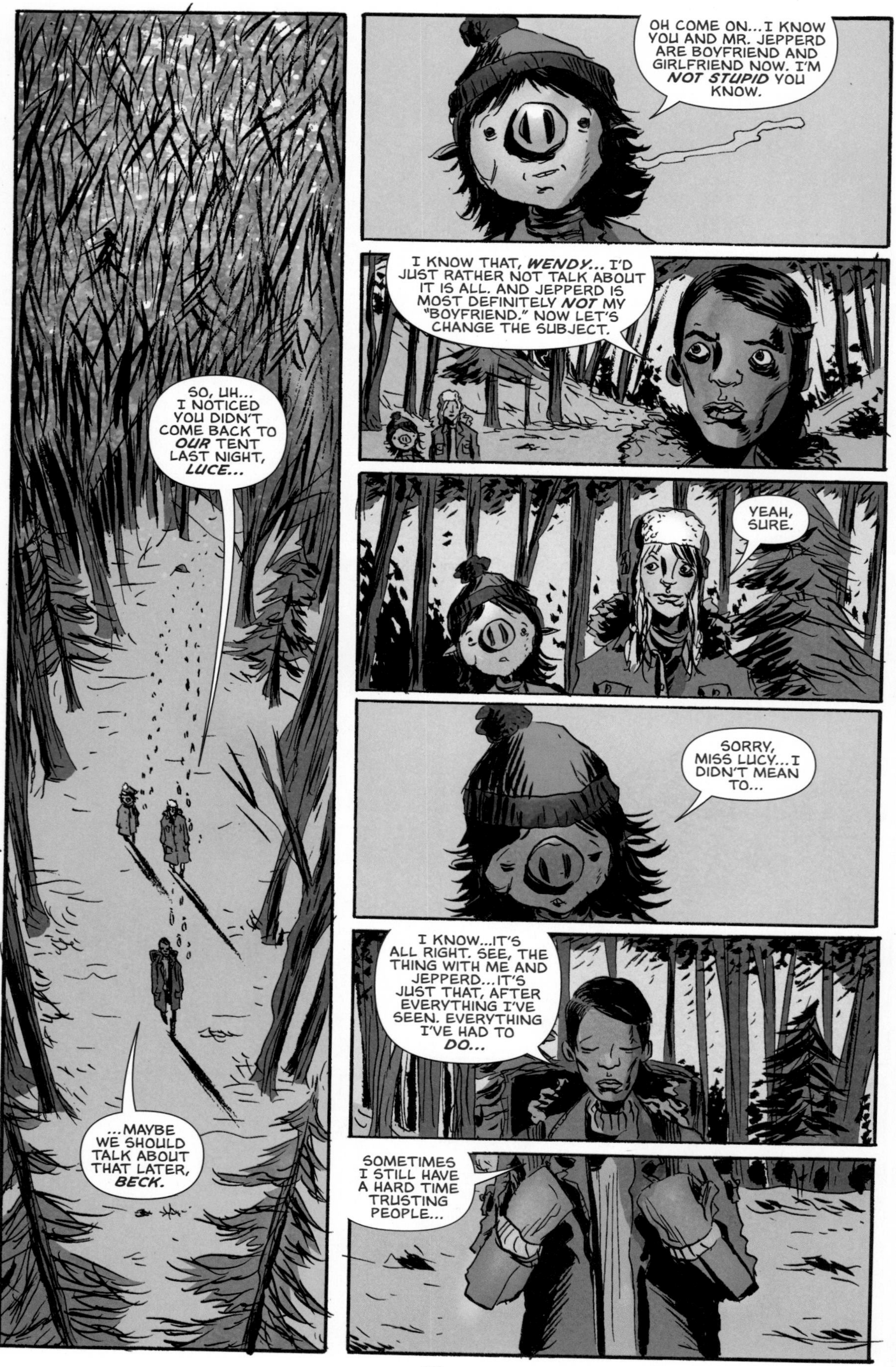
SO, UH... I NOTICED YOU DIDN'T COME BACK TO OUR TENT LAST NIGHT, LUCE...
...MAYBE WE SHOULD TALK ABOUT THAT LATER, BECK.
OH COME ON... I KNOW YOU AND MR. JEPPERD ARE BOYFRIEND AND GIRLFRIEND NOW. I'M NOT STUPID YOU KNOW.
I KNOW THAT, WENDY... I'D JUST RATHER NOT TALK ABOUT IT IS ALL. AND JEPPERD IS MOST DEFINITELY NOT MY "BOYFRIEND." NOW LET'S CHANGE THE SUBJECT.
YEAH, SURE.
SORRY, MISS LUCY... I DIDN'T MEAN TO...
I KNOW... IT'S ALL RIGHT. SEE, THE THING WITH ME AND JEPPERD... IT'S JUST THAT, AFTER EVERYTHING I'VE SEEN. EVERYTHING I'VE HAD TO DO...
SOMETIMES I STILL HAVE A HARD TIME TRUSTING PEOPLE...

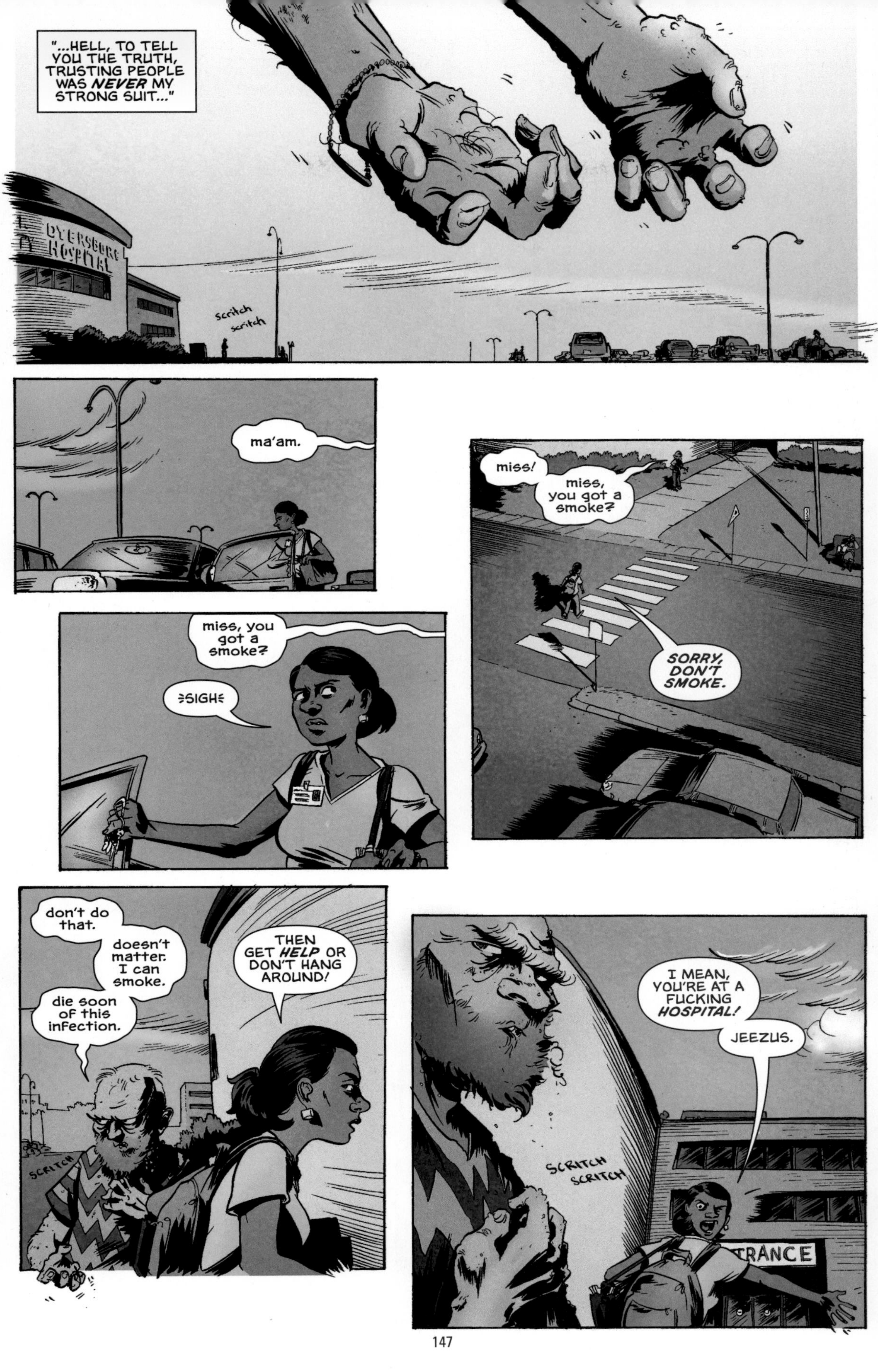
"...HELL, TO TELL YOU THE TRUTH, TRUSTING PEOPLE WAS NEVER MY STRONG SUIT..."
DYERSBURG HOSPITAL
scritch scritch
ma'am.
miss!
miss, you got a smoke?
SORRY, DON'T SMOKE.
miss, you got a smoke?
SIGH
don't do that.
doesn't matter. I can smoke.
die soon of this infection.
THEN GET HELP OR DON'T HANG AROUND!
SCRITCH
I MEAN, YOU'RE AT A FUCKING HOSPITAL!
JEEZUS.
SCRITCH SCRITCH
TRANCE

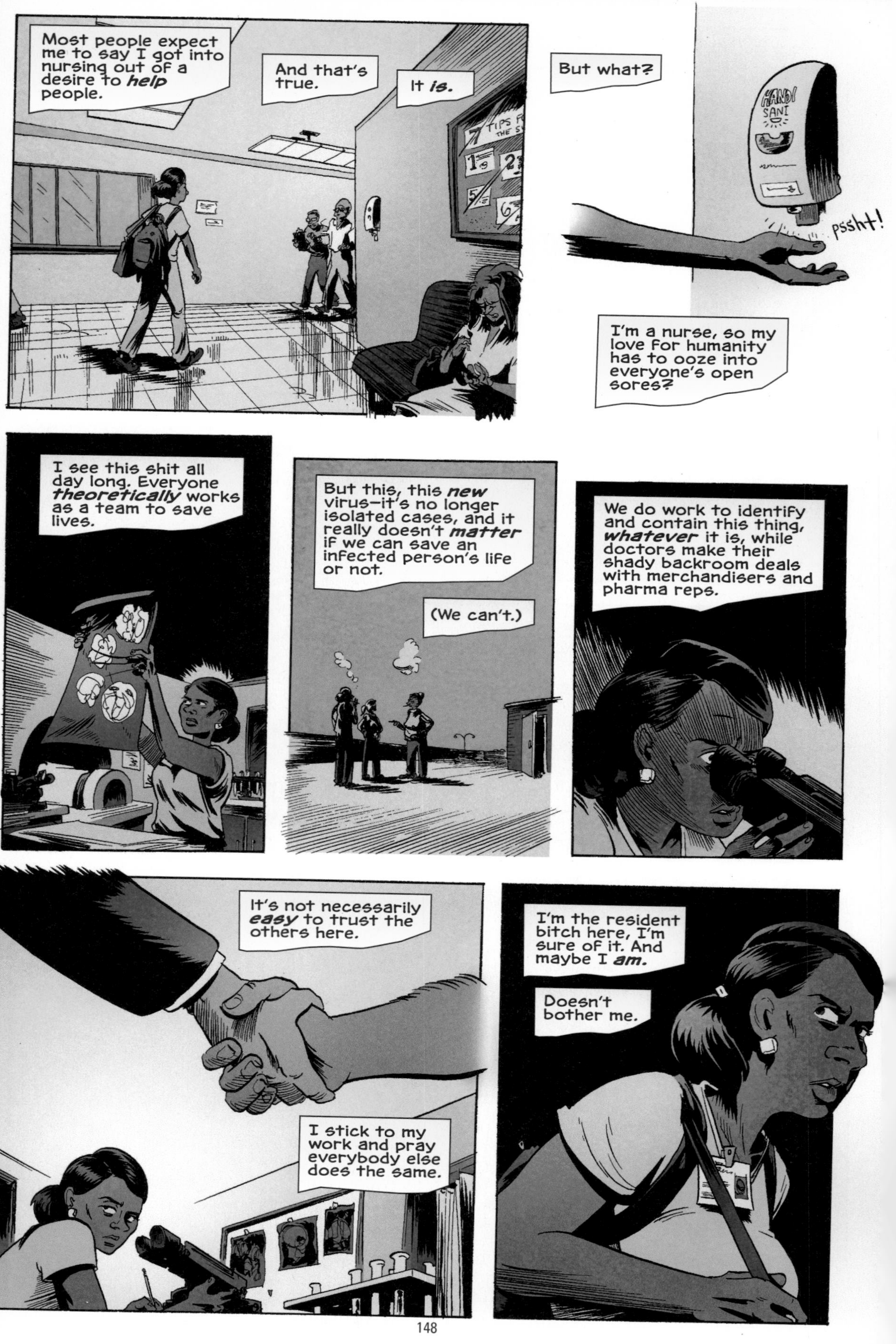
Most people expect me to say I got into nursing out of a desire to *help* people.
And that's true.
It *is.*
TIPS F THE S
But what?
HANDI SANI
psssht!
I'm a nurse, so my love for humanity has to ooze into everyone's open sores?
I see this shit all day long. Everyone *theoretically* works as a team to save lives.
But this, this *new* virus—it's no longer isolated cases, and it really doesn't *matter* if we can save an infected person's life or not.
(We can't.)
We do work to identify and contain this thing, *whatever* it is, while doctors make their shady backroom deals with merchandisers and pharma reps.
It's not necessarily *easy* to trust the others here.
I stick to my work and pray everybody else does the same.
I'm the resident bitch here, I'm sure of it. And maybe I *am.*
Doesn't bother me.

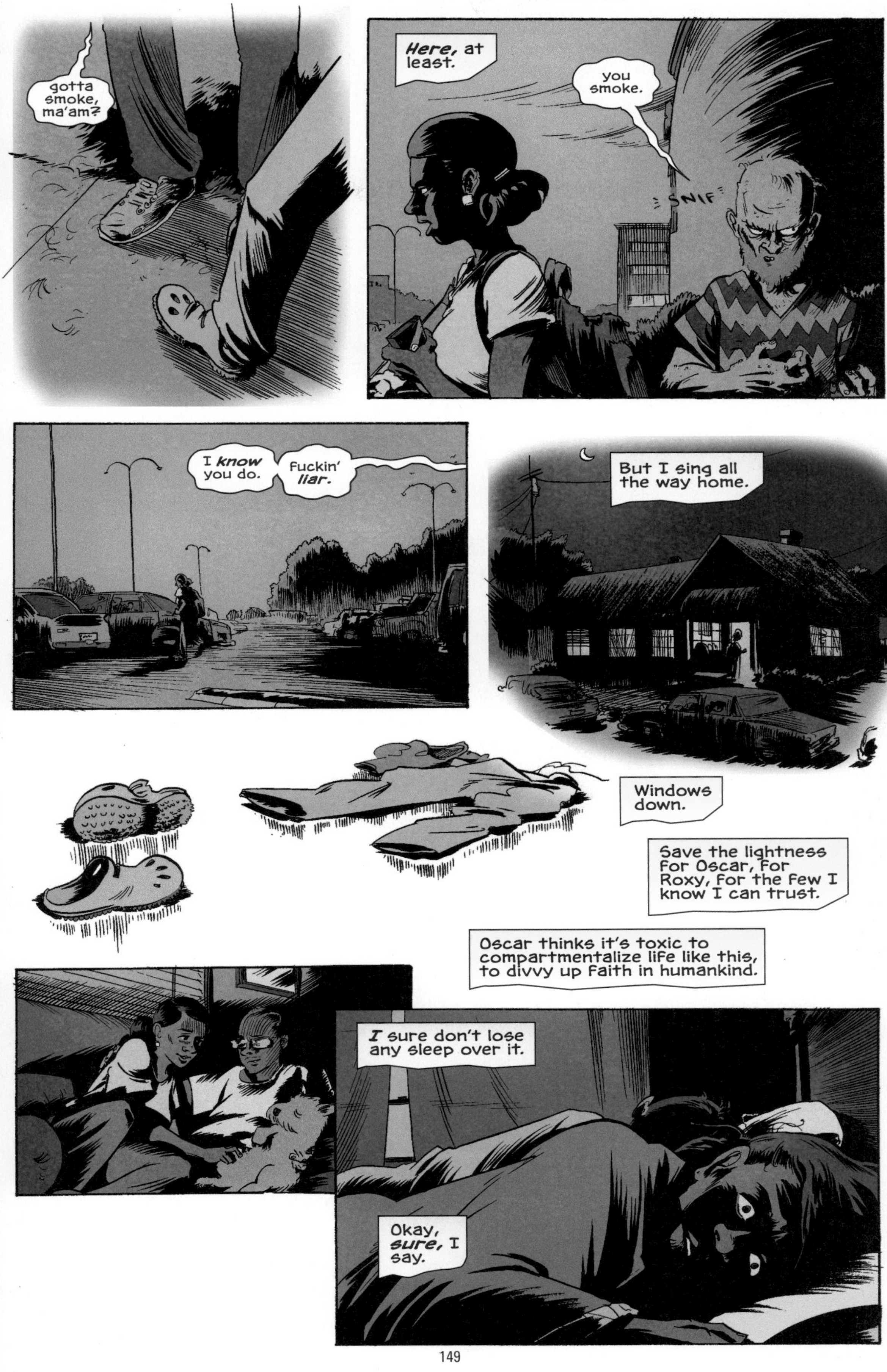
gotta smoke, ma'am?
Here, at least.
you smoke.
SNIF
I *know* you do.
Fuckin' *liar.*
But I sing all the way home.
Windows down.
Save the lightness for Oscar, for Roxy, for the few I know I can trust.
Oscar thinks it's toxic to compartmentalize life like this, to divvy up faith in humankind.
I sure don't lose any sleep over it.
Okay, *sure,* I say.

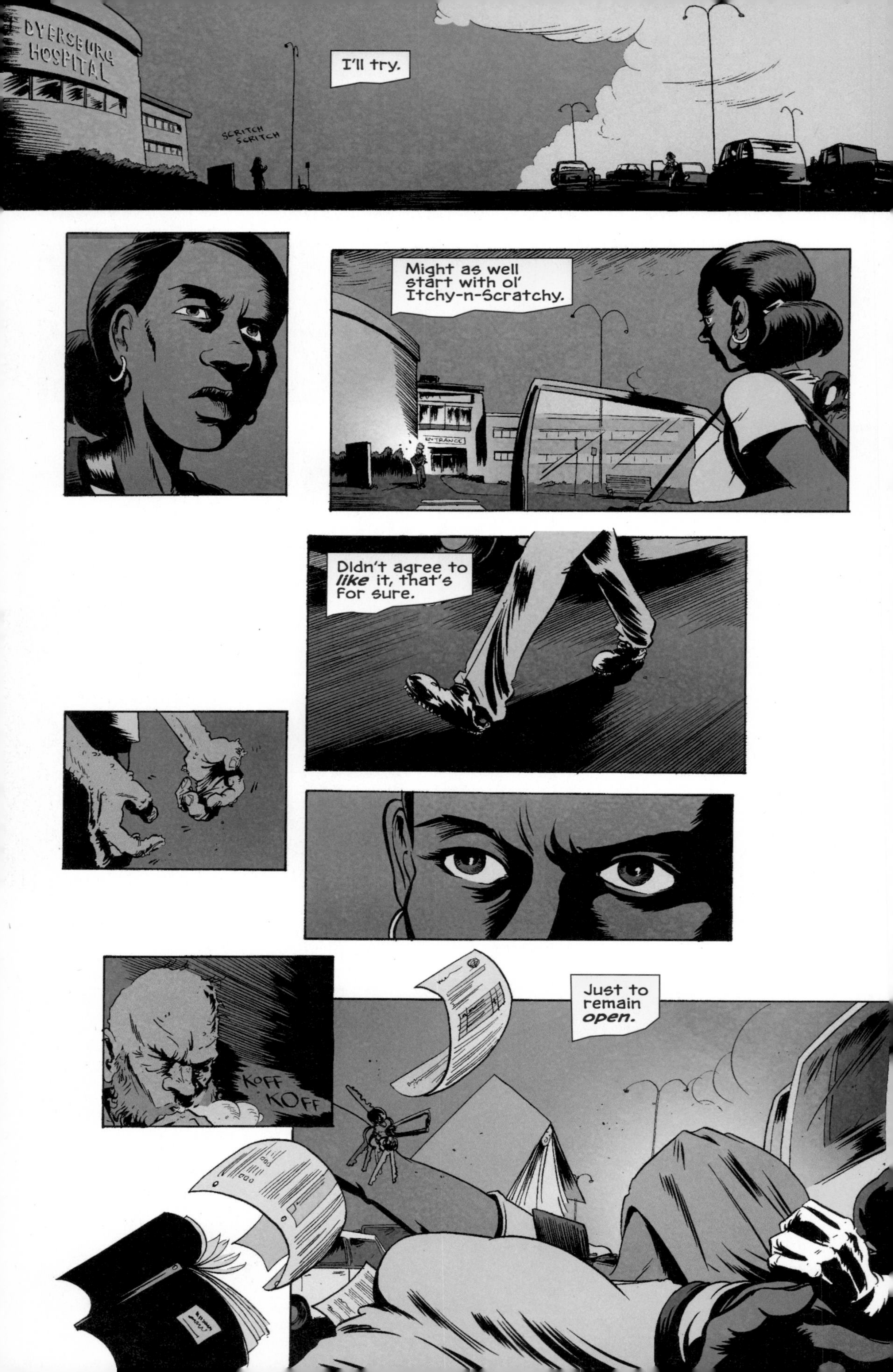
DYERSBURG HOSPITAL
I'll try.
SCRITCH SCRITCH
Might as well start with ol' Itchy-n-Scratchy.
ENTRANCE
Didn't agree to *like* it, that's for sure.
KOFF KOFF
Just to remain *open.*

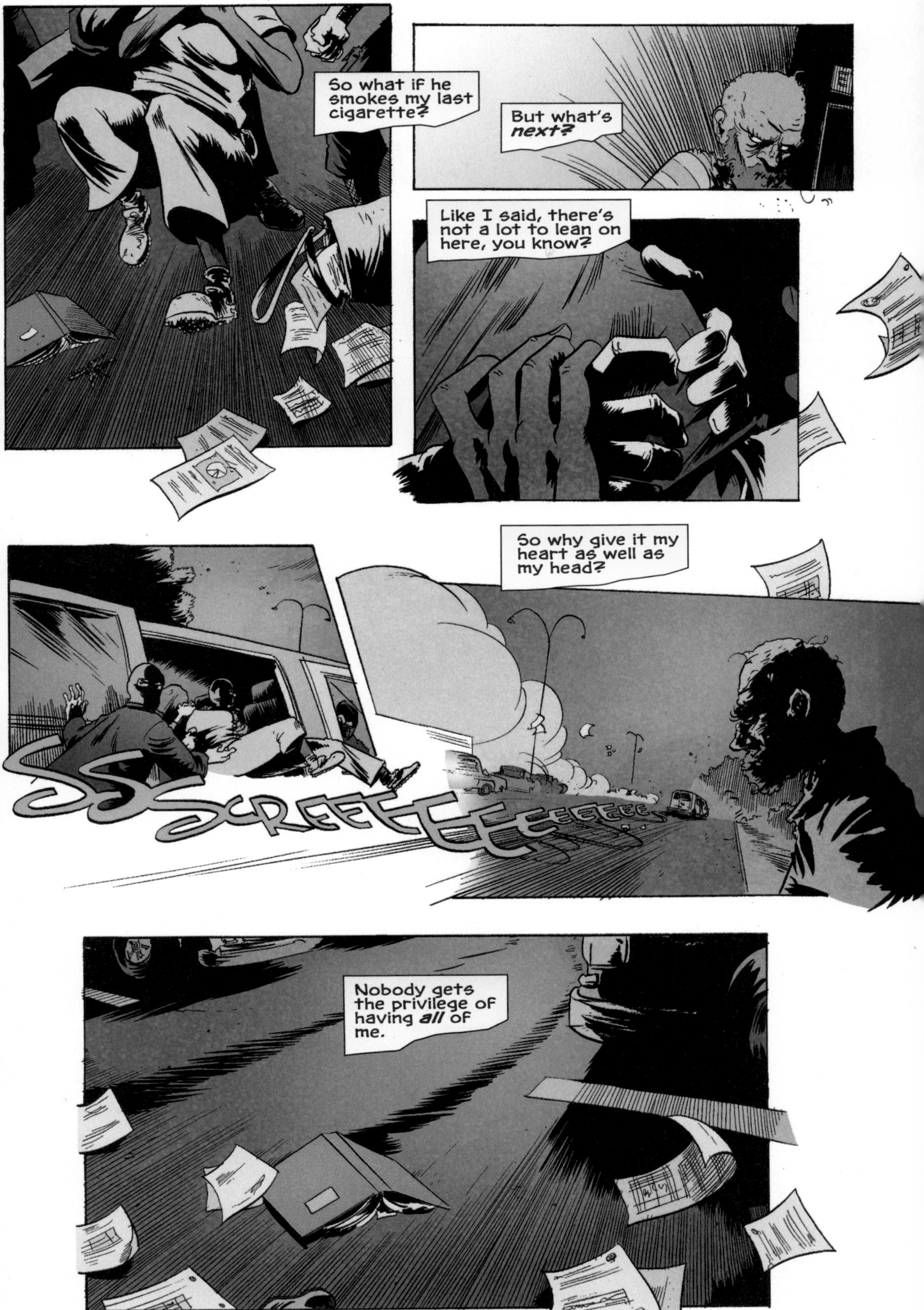

So what if he smokes my last cigarette?
But what's *next?*
Like I said, there's not a lot to lean on here, you know?
So why give it my heart as well as my head?
SSSCREEEEEEEEEEEEEE
Nobody gets the privilege of having *all* of me.

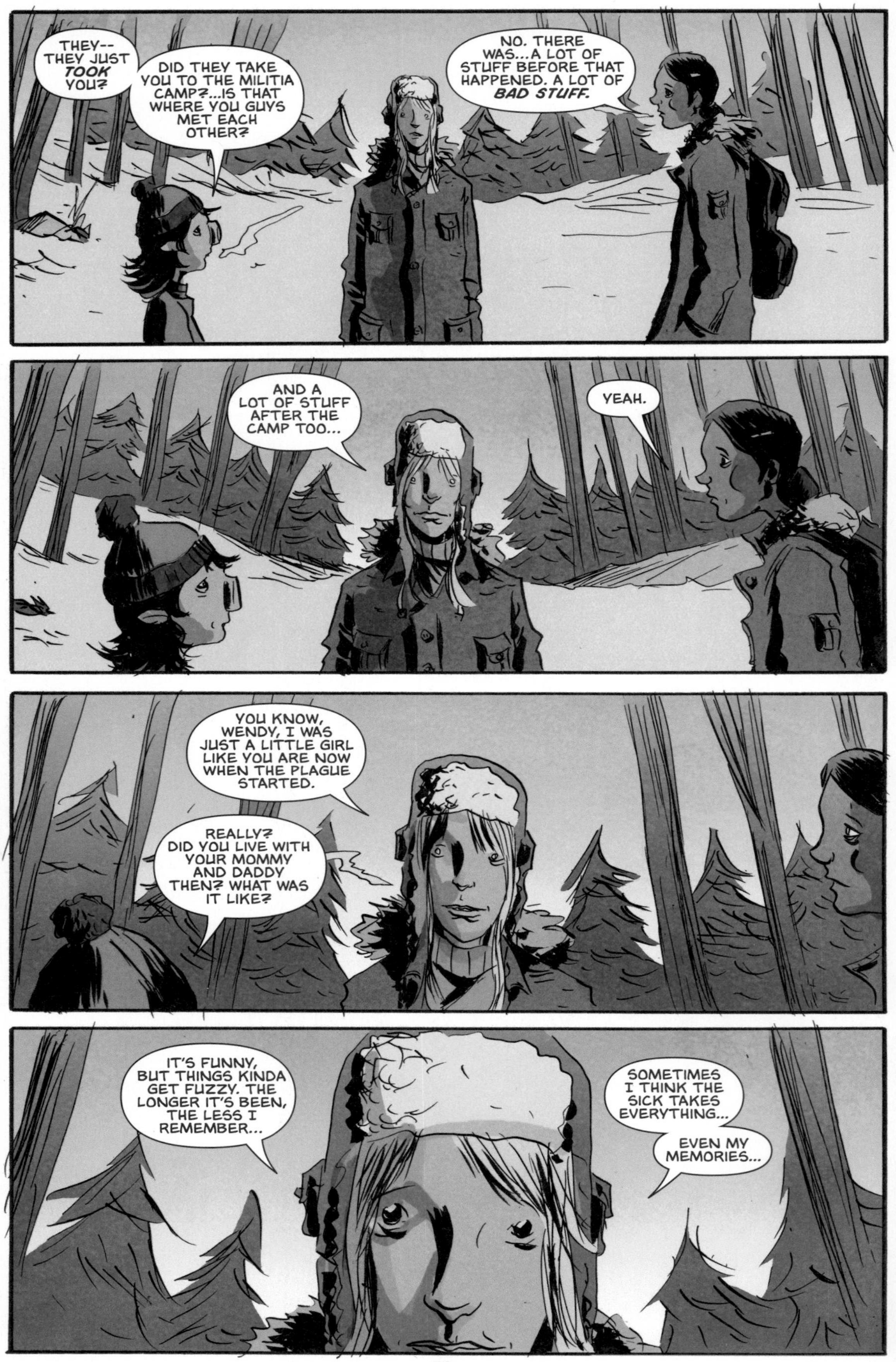
THEY-- THEY JUST *TOOK* YOU?
DID THEY TAKE YOU TO THE MILITIA CAMP?...IS THAT WHERE YOU GUYS MET EACH OTHER?
NO. THERE WAS...A LOT OF STUFF BEFORE THAT HAPPENED. A LOT OF ***BAD STUFF.***
AND A LOT OF STUFF AFTER THE CAMP TOO...
YEAH.
YOU KNOW, WENDY, I WAS JUST A LITTLE GIRL LIKE YOU ARE NOW WHEN THE PLAGUE STARTED.
REALLY? DID YOU LIVE WITH YOUR MOMMY AND DADDY THEN? WHAT WAS IT LIKE?
IT'S FUNNY, BUT THINGS KINDA GET FUZZY. THE LONGER IT'S BEEN, THE LESS I REMEMBER...
SOMETIMES I THINK THE SICK TAKES EVERYTHING...
EVEN MY MEMORIES...

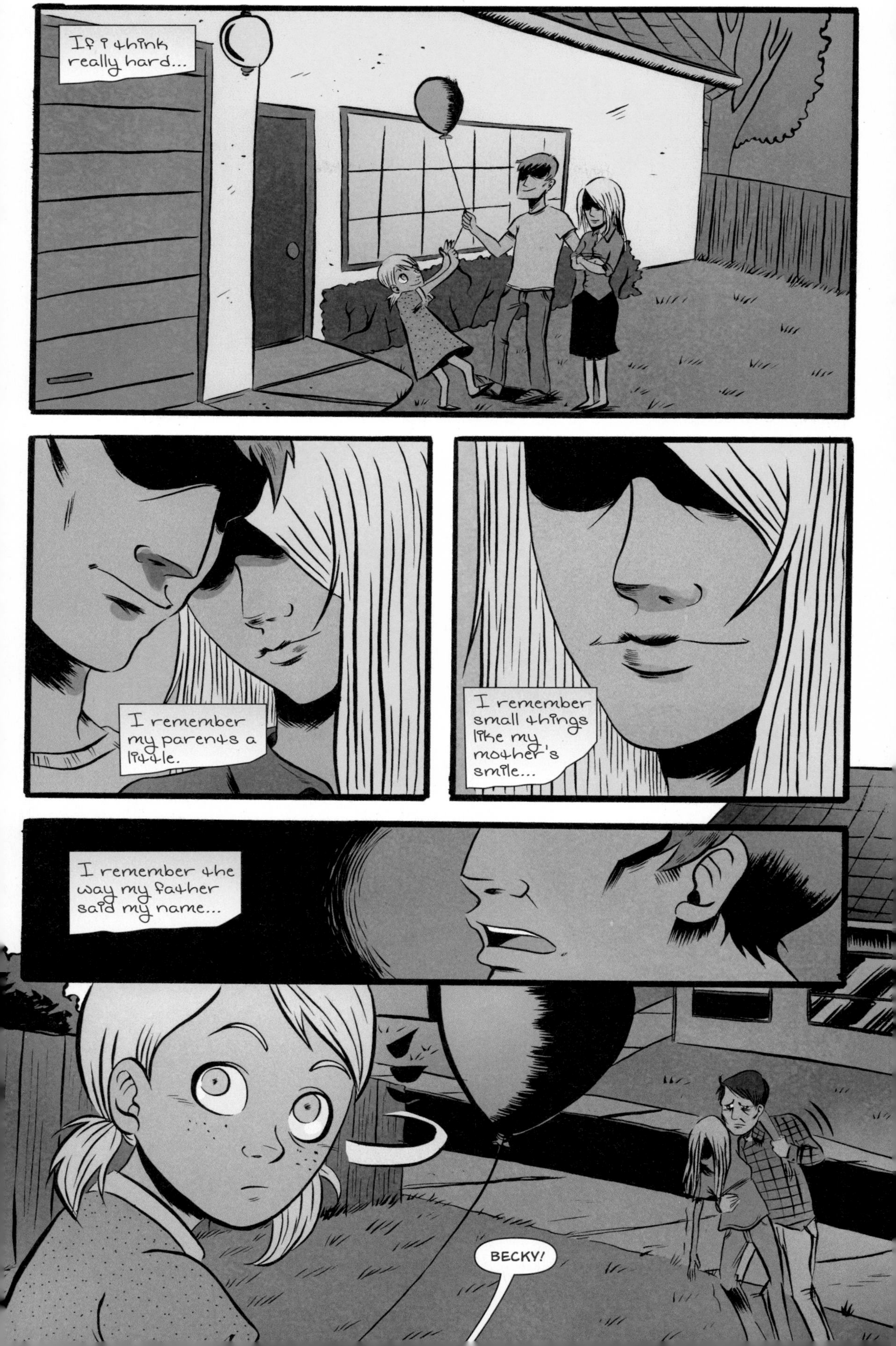

If i think really hard...
I remember my parents a little.
I remember small things like my mother's smile...
I remember the way my father said my name...
BECKY!

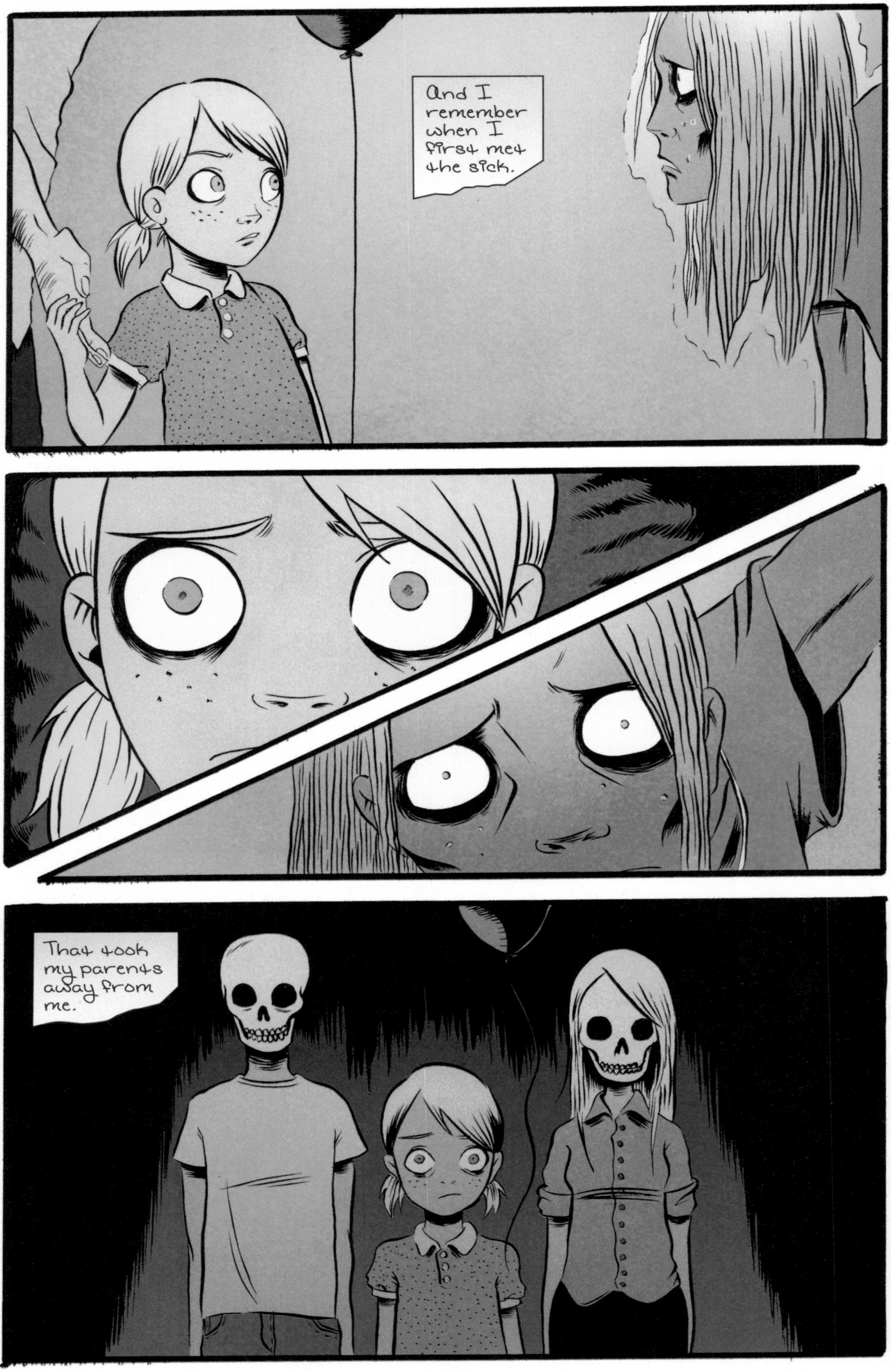
And I remember when I first met the sick.
That took my parents away from me.

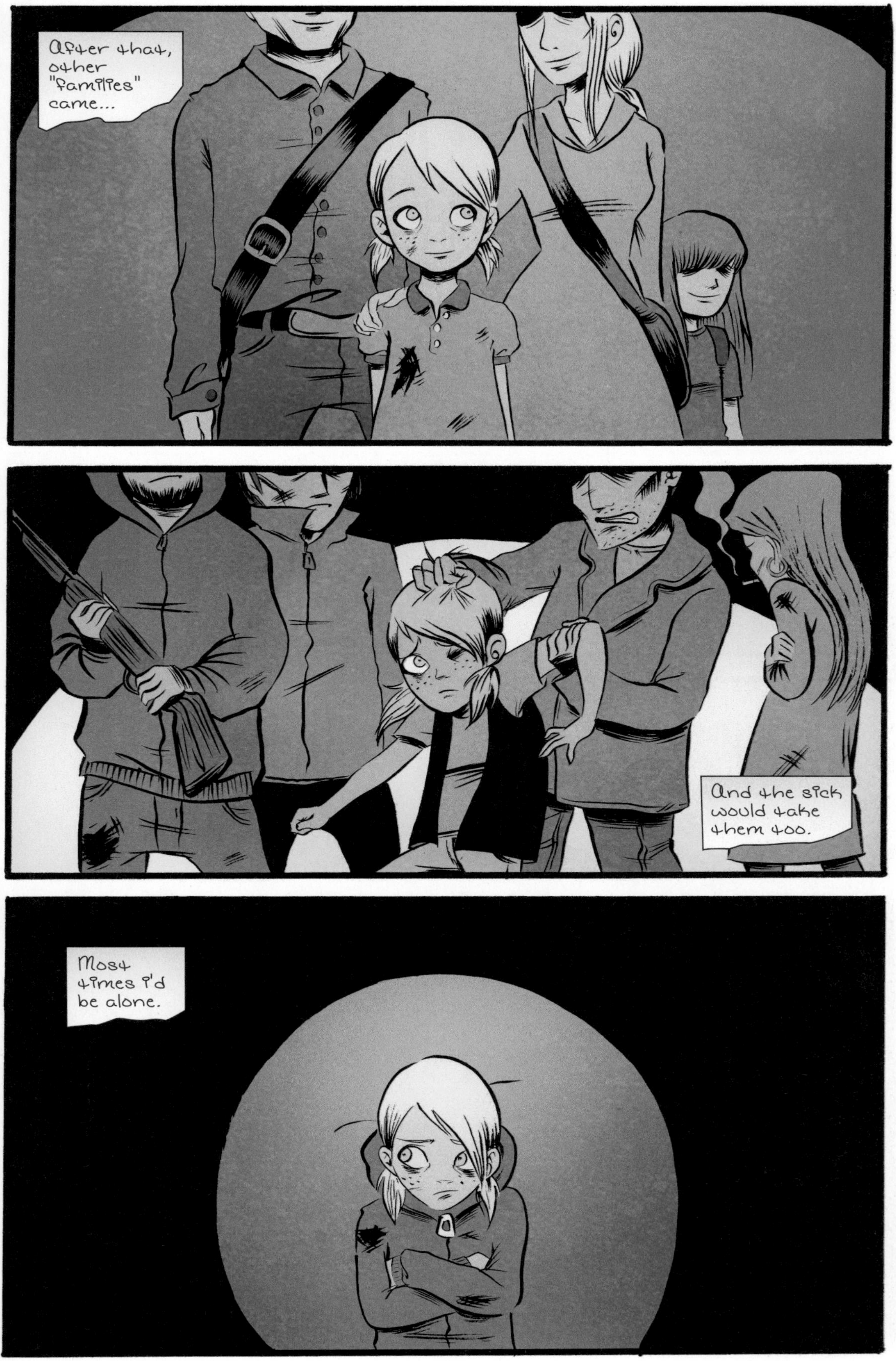
After that, other "families" came...
And the sick would take them too.
Most times I'd be alone.

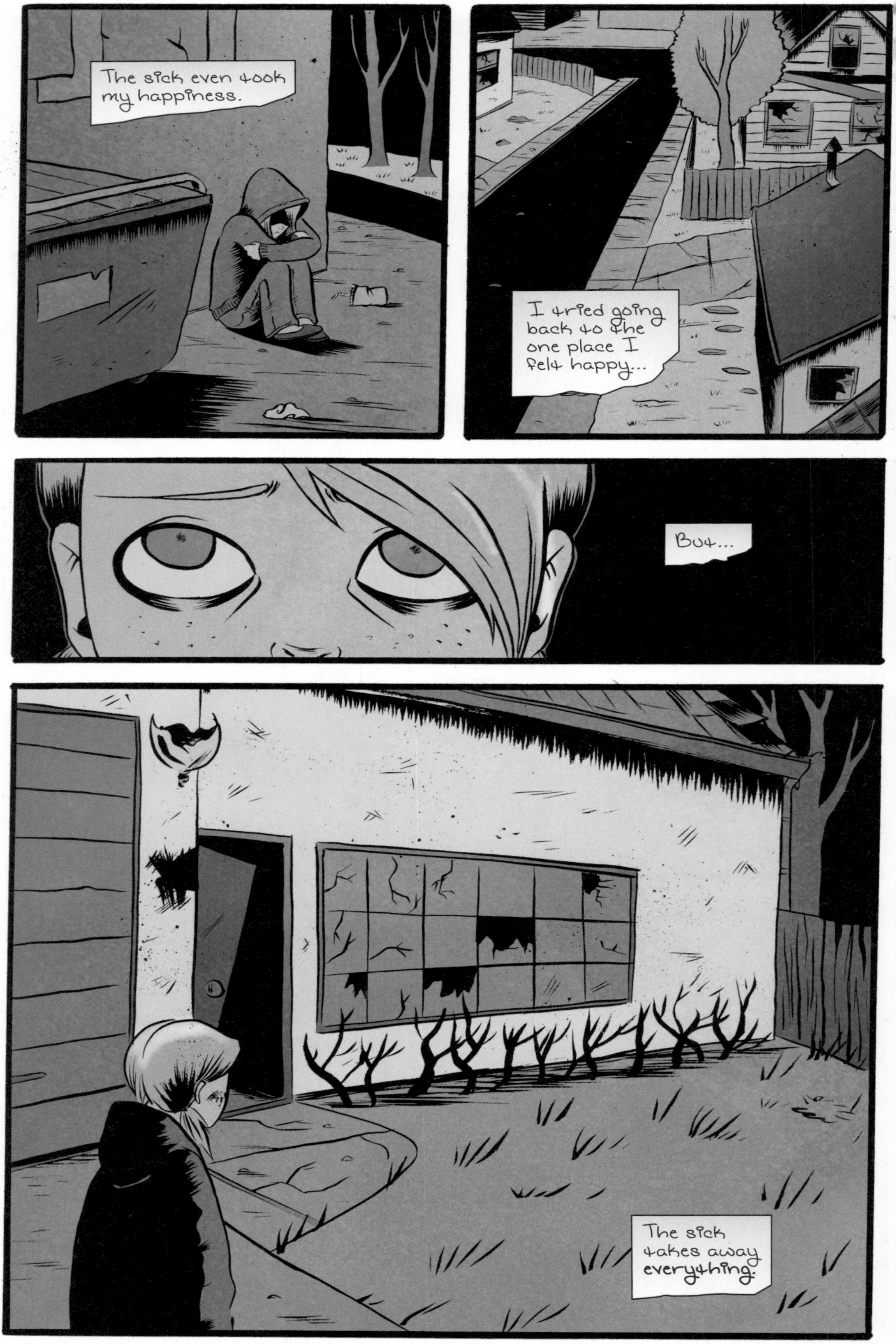
The sick even took my happiness.
I tried going back to the one place I felt happy...
But...
The sick takes away everything.

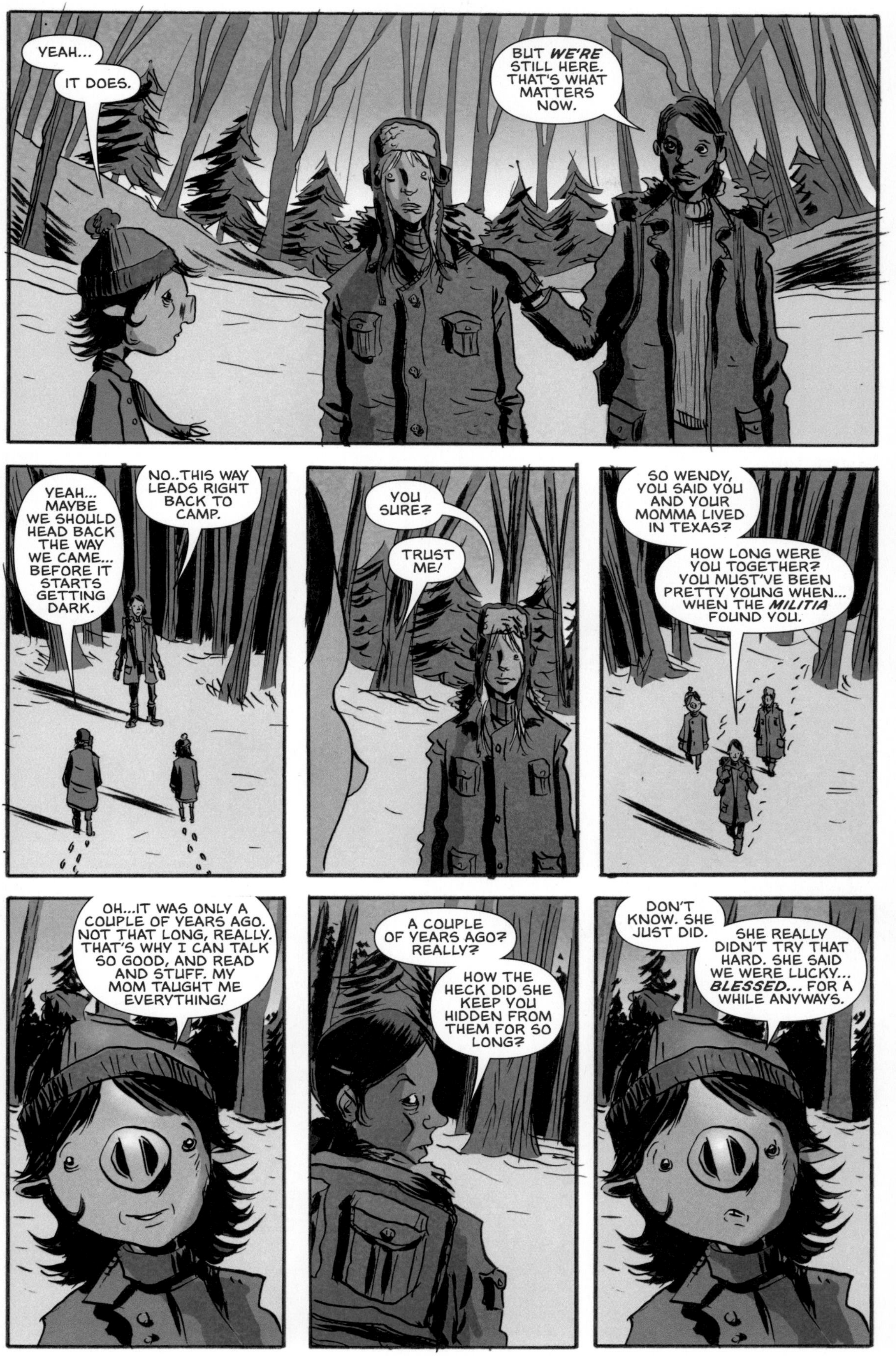
YEAH...
IT DOES.
BUT WE'RE STILL HERE. THAT'S WHAT MATTERS NOW.
YEAH... MAYBE WE SHOULD HEAD BACK THE WAY WE CAME... BEFORE IT STARTS GETTING DARK.
NO..THIS WAY LEADS RIGHT BACK TO CAMP.
YOU SURE?
TRUST ME!
SO WENDY, YOU SAID YOU AND YOUR MOMMA LIVED IN TEXAS?
HOW LONG WERE YOU TOGETHER? YOU MUST'VE BEEN PRETTY YOUNG WHEN... WHEN THE MILITIA FOUND YOU.
OH...IT WAS ONLY A COUPLE OF YEARS AGO. NOT THAT LONG, REALLY. THAT'S WHY I CAN TALK SO GOOD, AND READ AND STUFF. MY MOM TAUGHT ME EVERYTHING!
A COUPLE OF YEARS AGO? REALLY?
HOW THE HECK DID SHE KEEP YOU HIDDEN FROM THEM FOR SO LONG?
DON'T KNOW. SHE JUST DID.
SHE REALLY DIDN'T TRY THAT HARD. SHE SAID WE WERE LUCKY... BLESSED... FOR A WHILE ANYWAYS.

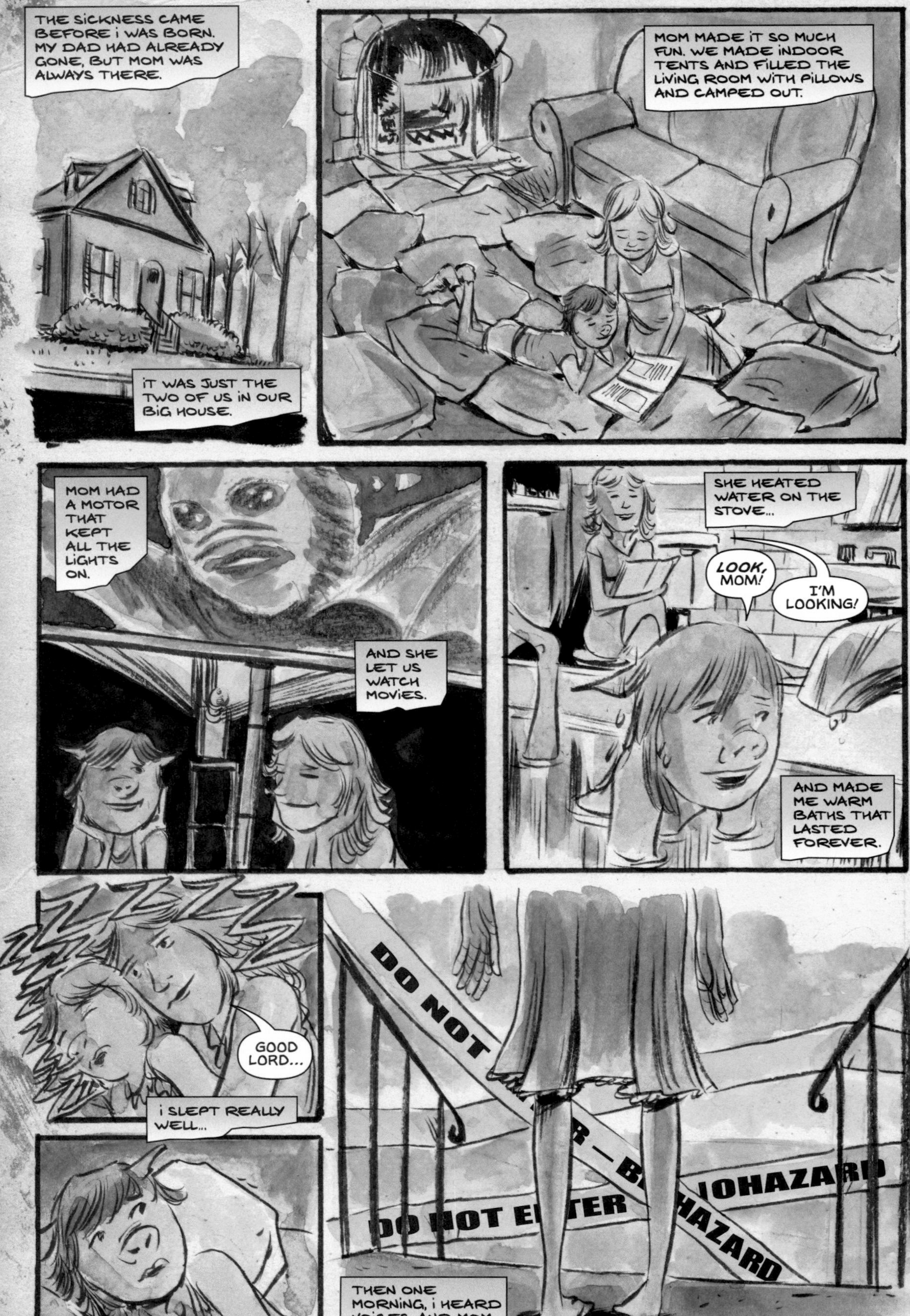
THE SICKNESS CAME BEFORE I WAS BORN. MY DAD HAD ALREADY GONE, BUT MOM WAS ALWAYS THERE.
IT WAS JUST THE TWO OF US IN OUR BIG HOUSE.
MOM MADE IT SO MUCH FUN. WE MADE INDOOR TENTS AND FILLED THE LIVING ROOM WITH PILLOWS AND CAMPED OUT.
MOM HAD A MOTOR THAT KEPT ALL THE LIGHTS ON.
AND SHE LET US WATCH MOVIES.
SHE HEATED WATER ON THE STOVE...
LOOK, MOM!
I'M LOOKING!
AND MADE ME WARM BATHS THAT LASTED FOREVER.
GOOD LORD...
I SLEPT REALLY WELL...
DO NOT
BIOHAZARD
DO NOT ENTER
HAZARD
THEN ONE MORNING, I HEARD VOICES, AND MOM WAS GONE.

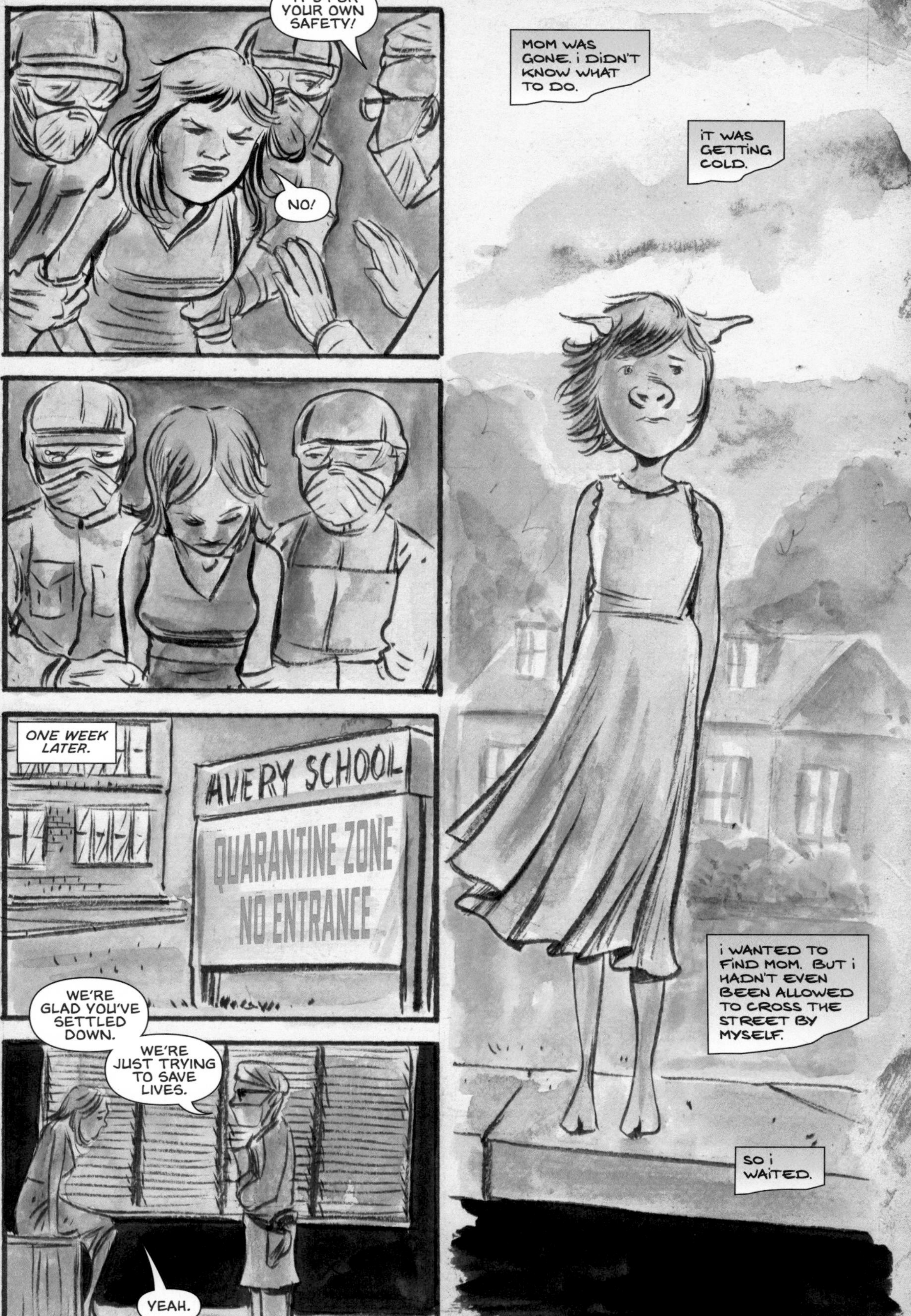
IT'S FOR YOUR OWN SAFETY!
NO!
ONE WEEK LATER.
AVERY SCHOOL
QUARANTINE ZONE NO ENTRANCE
WE'RE GLAD YOU'VE SETTLED DOWN.
WE'RE JUST TRYING TO SAVE LIVES.
YEAH.
MOM WAS GONE. i DIDN'T KNOW WHAT TO DO.
iT WAS GETTING COLD.
i WANTED TO FIND MOM. BUT i HADN'T EVEN BEEN ALLOWED TO CROSS THE STREET BY MYSELF.
SO i WAITED.

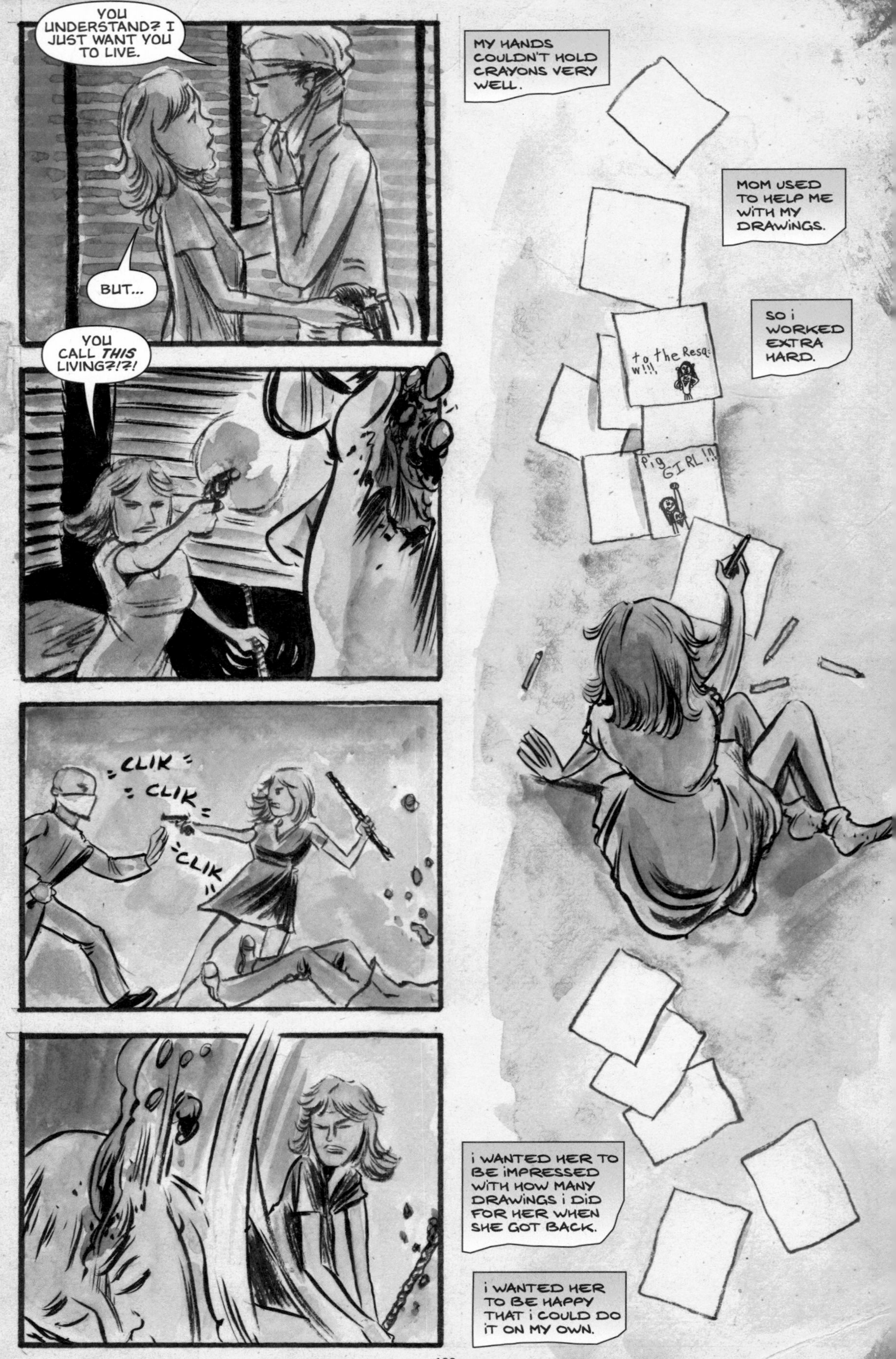

YOU UNDERSTAND? I JUST WANT YOU TO LIVE.
BUT...
YOU CALL *THIS* LIVING?!?!
CLIK
CLIK
CLIK
MY HANDS COULDN'T HOLD CRAYONS VERY WELL.
MOM USED TO HELP ME WITH MY DRAWINGS.
SO I WORKED EXTRA HARD.
to the Resqu w!!!
Pig GIRL!!!
I WANTED HER TO BE IMPRESSED WITH HOW MANY DRAWINGS I DID FOR HER WHEN SHE GOT BACK.
I WANTED HER TO BE HAPPY THAT I COULD DO IT ON MY OWN.

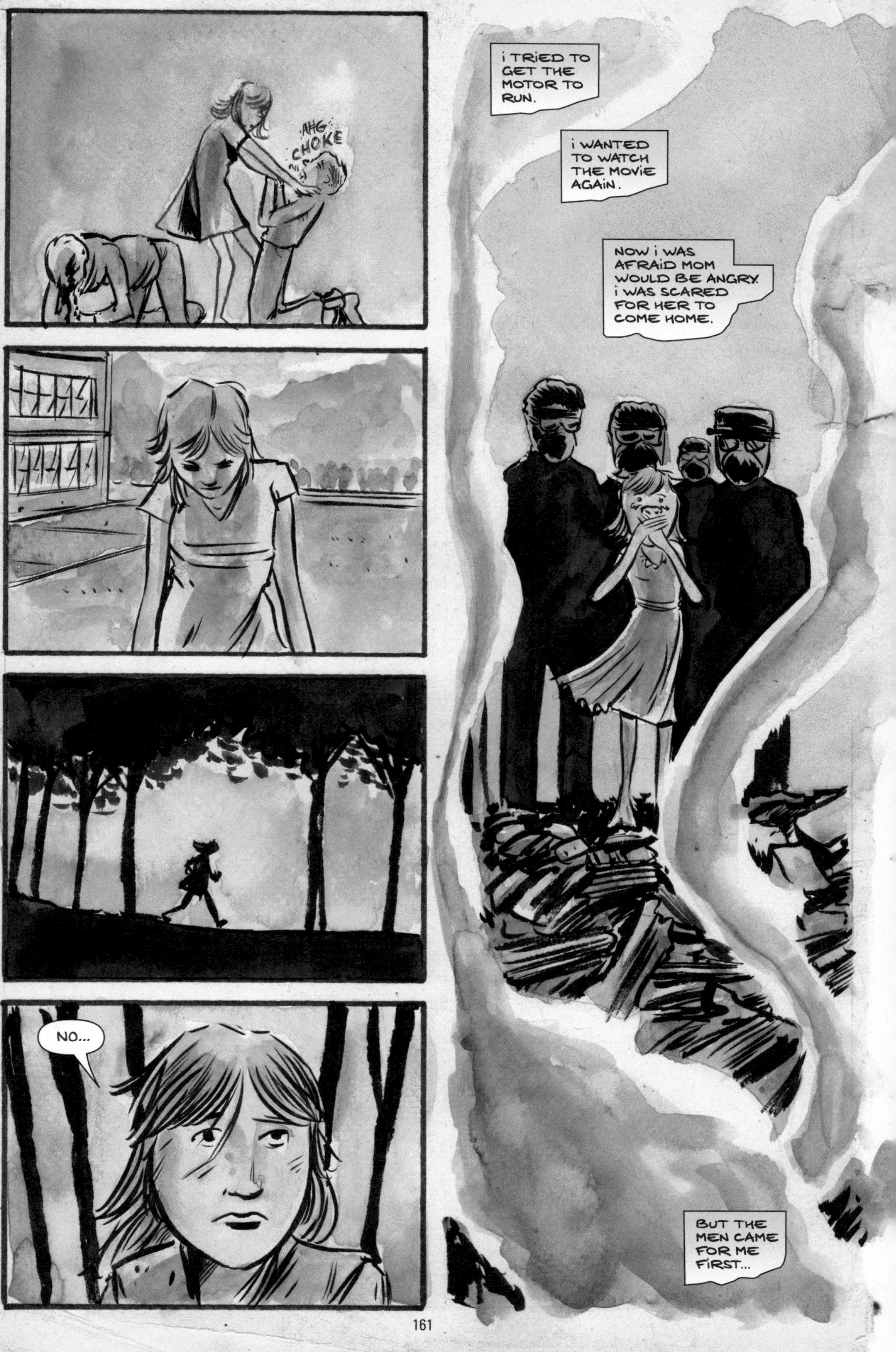
AHG
CHOKE
NO...
i TRIED TO GET THE MOTOR TO RUN.
i WANTED TO WATCH THE MOVIE AGAIN.
NOW i WAS AFRAID MOM WOULD BE ANGRY. i WAS SCARED FOR HER TO COME HOME.
BUT THE MEN CAME FOR ME FIRST...

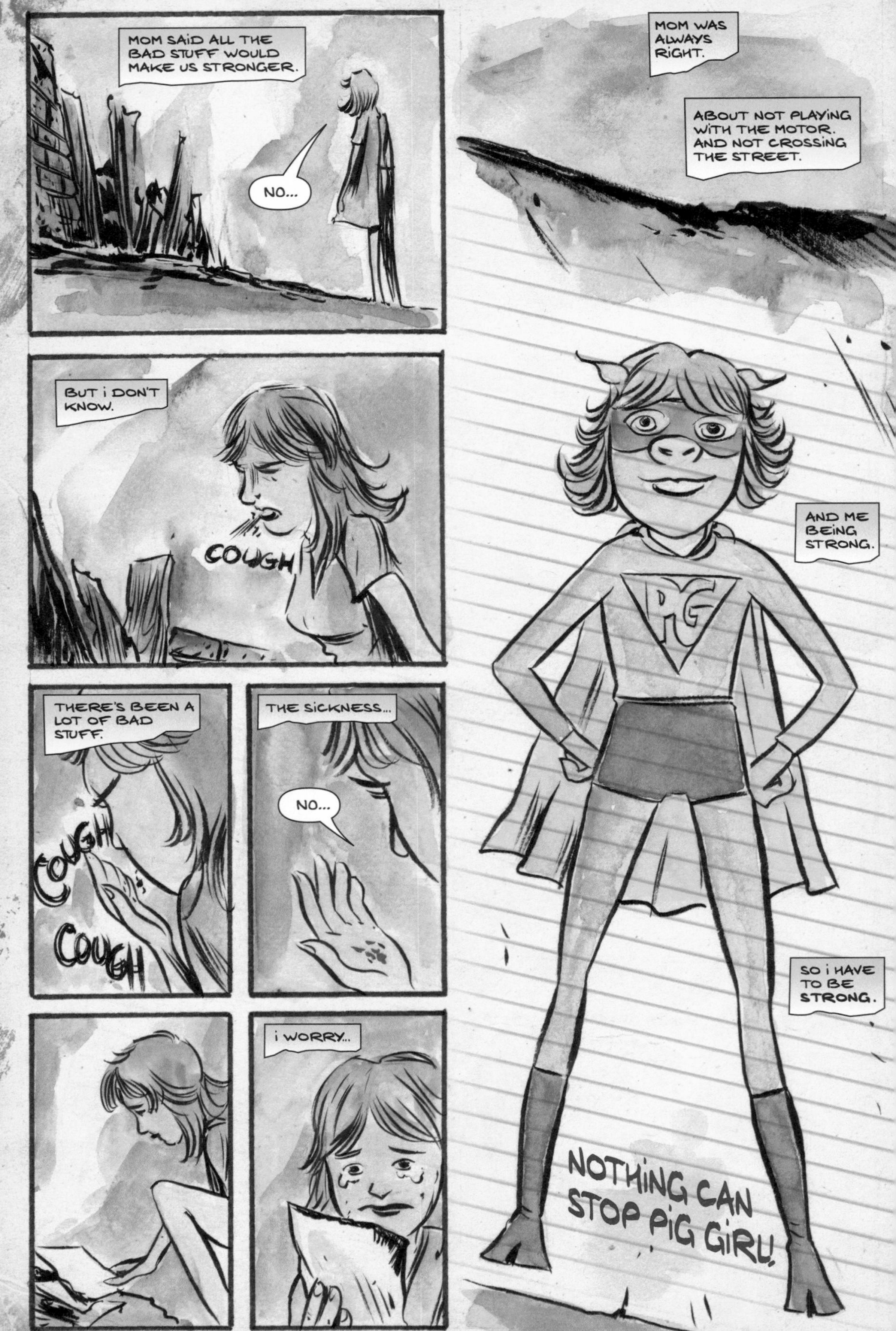
MOM SAID ALL THE BAD STUFF WOULD MAKE US STRONGER.
NO...
BUT I DON'T KNOW.
COUGH
THERE'S BEEN A LOT OF BAD STUFF.
COUGH
COUGH
THE SICKNESS...
NO...
I WORRY...
MOM WAS ALWAYS RIGHT.
ABOUT NOT PLAYING WITH THE MOTOR. AND NOT CROSSING THE STREET.
AND ME BEING STRONG.
PG
SO I HAVE TO BE STRONG.
NOTHING CAN STOP PIG GIRL!

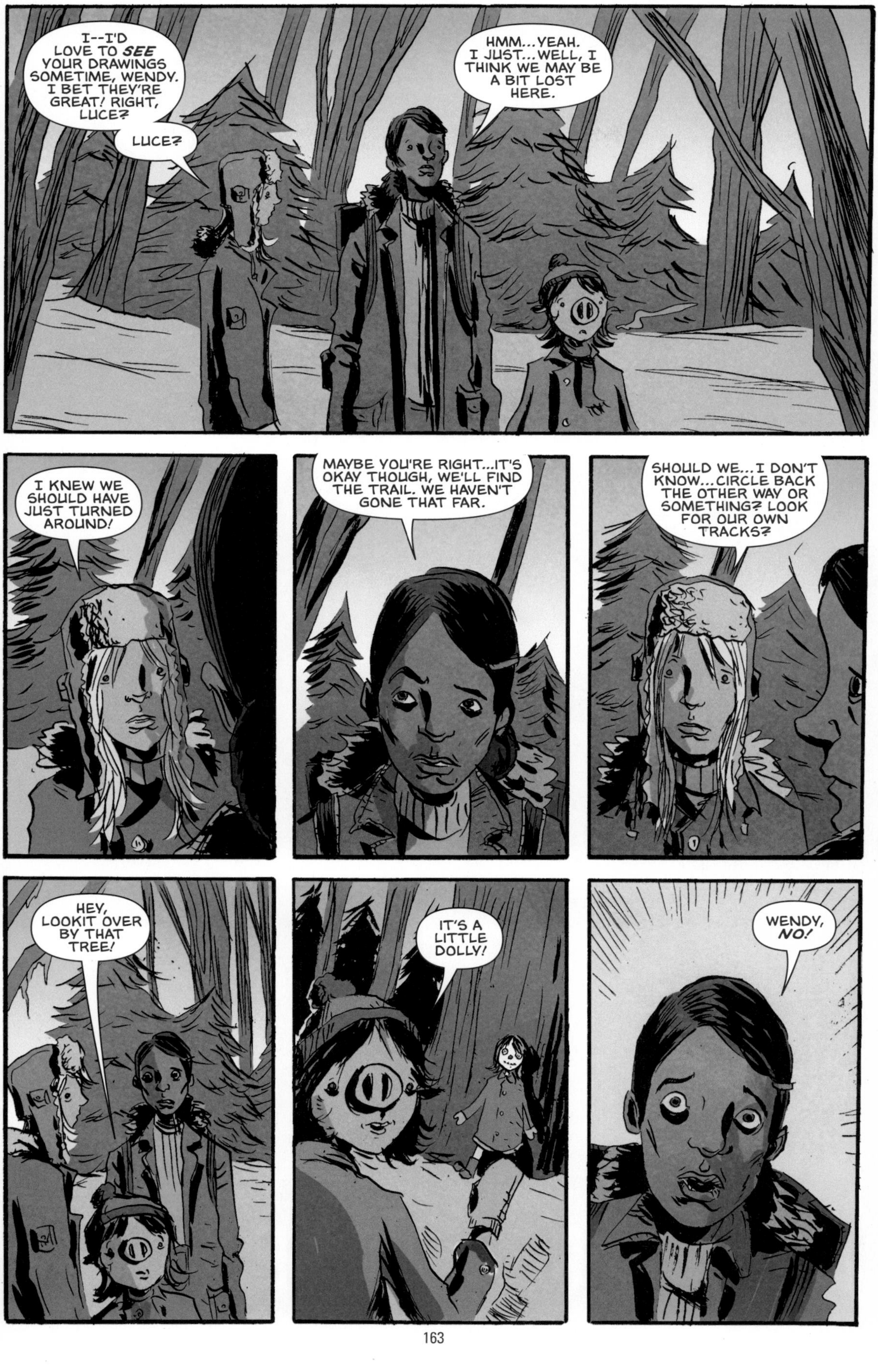
I--I'D LOVE TO SEE YOUR DRAWINGS SOMETIME, WENDY. I BET THEY'RE GREAT! RIGHT, LUCE?
LUCE?
HMM...YEAH. I JUST...WELL, I THINK WE MAY BE A BIT LOST HERE.
I KNEW WE SHOULD HAVE JUST TURNED AROUND!
MAYBE YOU'RE RIGHT...IT'S OKAY THOUGH, WE'LL FIND THE TRAIL. WE HAVEN'T GONE THAT FAR.
SHOULD WE...I DON'T KNOW...CIRCLE BACK THE OTHER WAY OR SOMETHING? LOOK FOR OUR OWN TRACKS?
HEY, LOOKIT OVER BY THAT TREE!
IT'S A LITTLE DOLLY!
WENDY, NO!

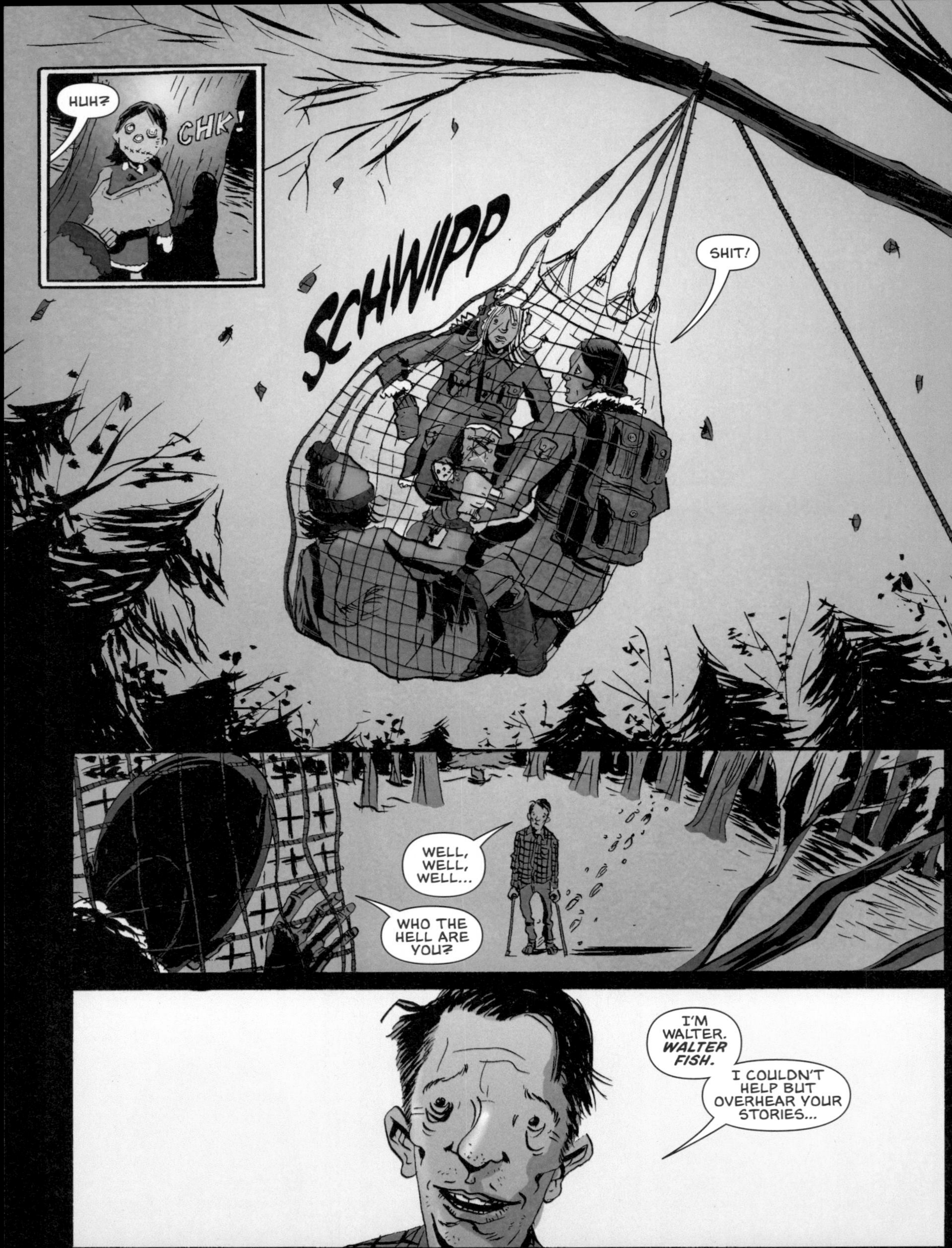
HUH?
CHK!
SCHWIPP
SHIT!
WELL, WELL, WELL...
WHO THE HELL ARE YOU?
I'M WALTER. *WALTER FISH.*
I COULDN'T HELP BUT OVERHEAR YOUR STORIES...

ENDANGERED SPECIES PRELUDE: LOST TRAILS

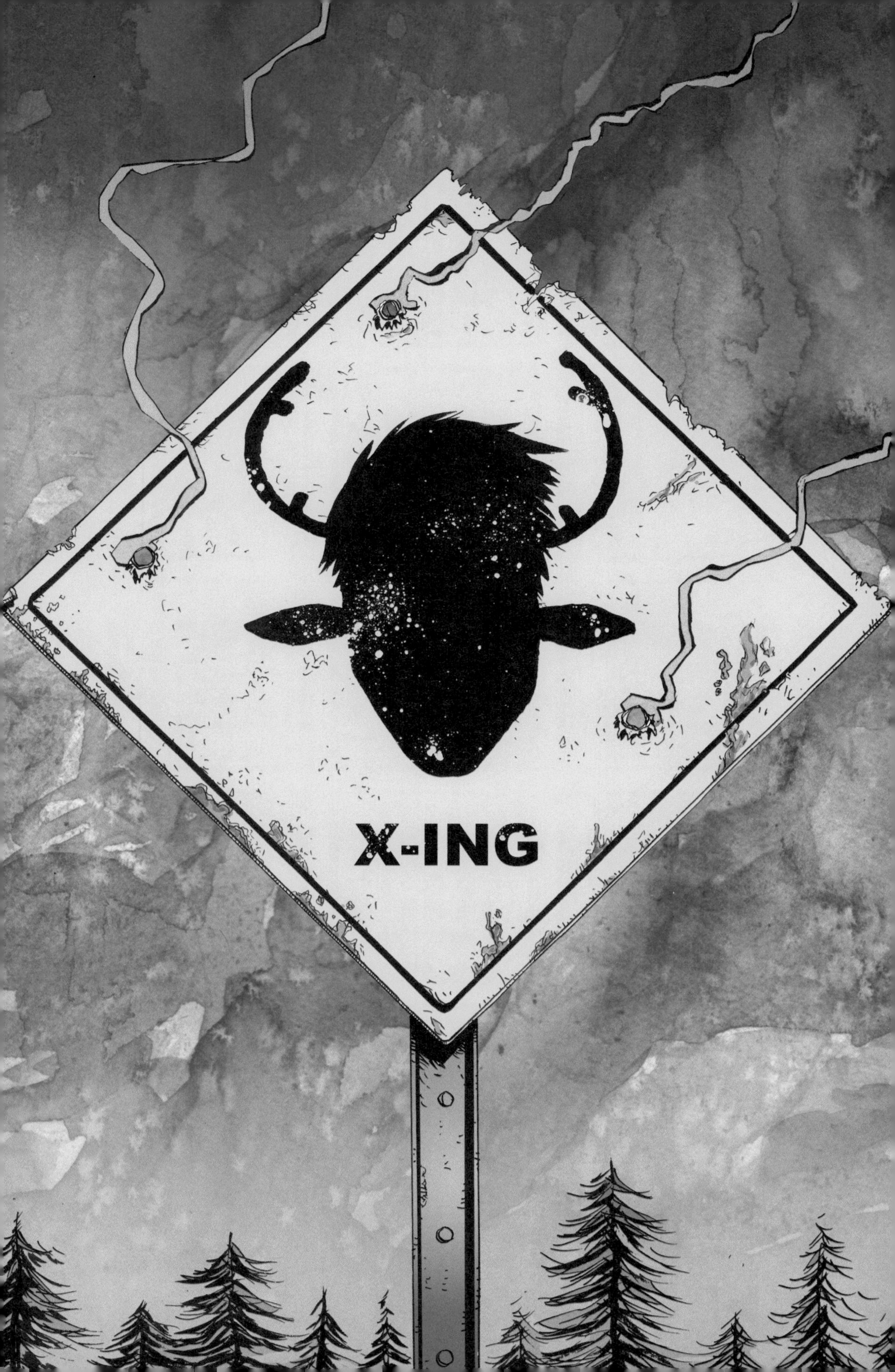
X-ING

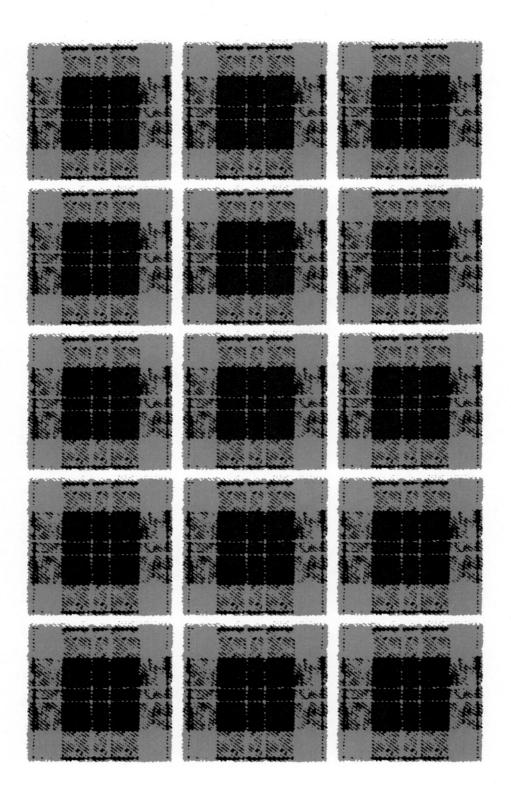

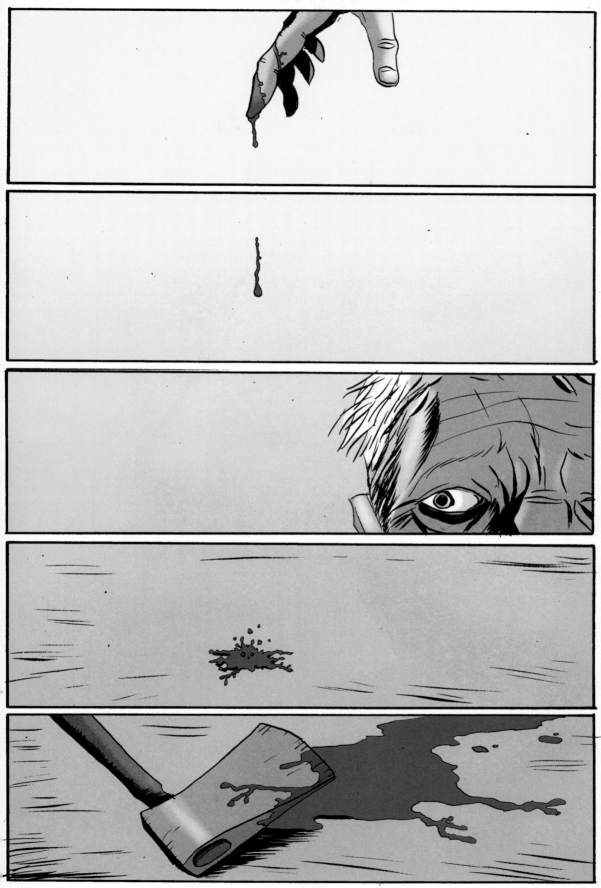

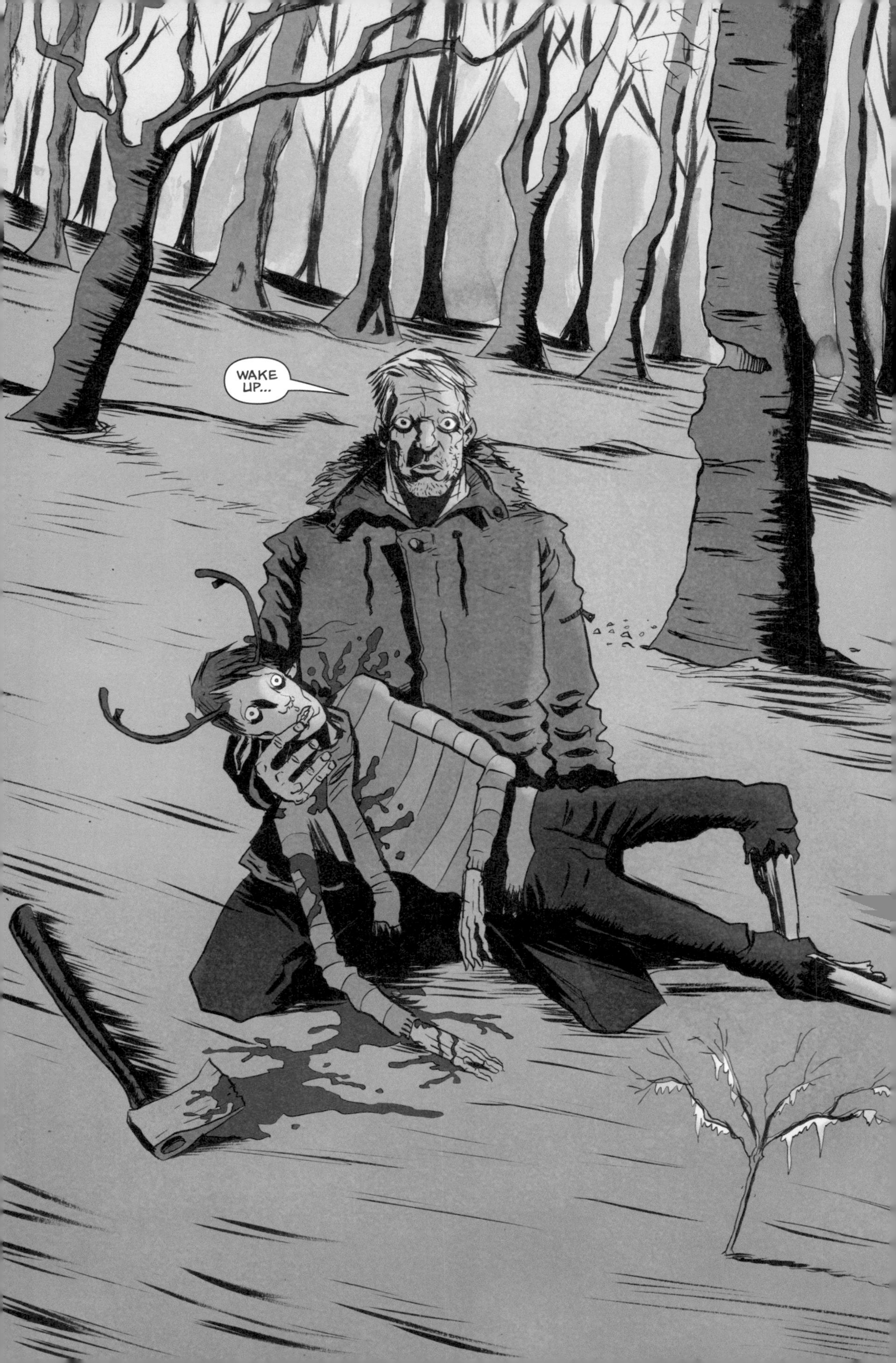
WAKE UP...

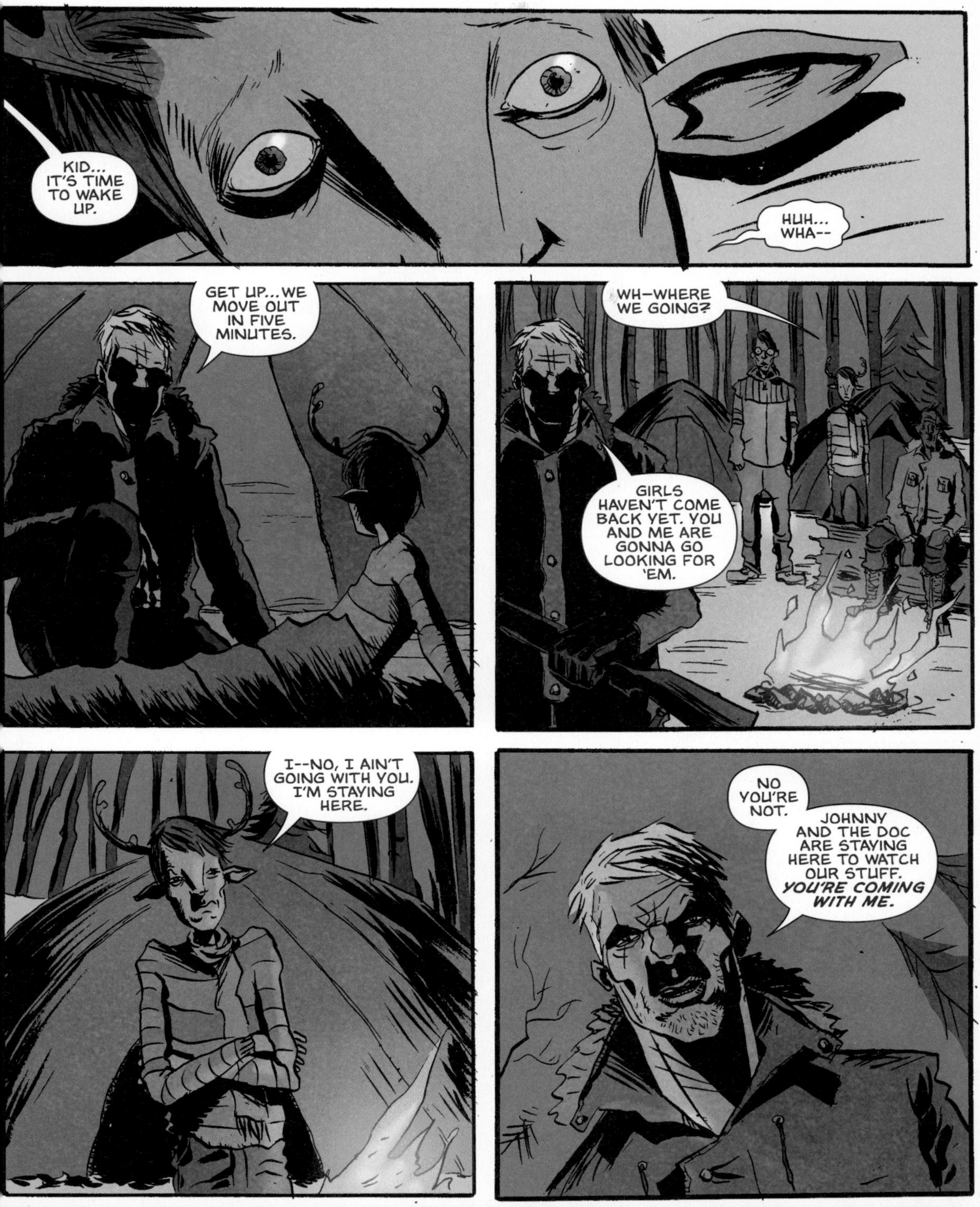
KID... IT'S TIME TO WAKE UP.
HUH... WHA--
GET UP...WE MOVE OUT IN FIVE MINUTES.
WH-WHERE WE GOING?
GIRLS HAVEN'T COME BACK YET. YOU AND ME ARE GONNA GO LOOKING FOR 'EM.
I--NO, I AIN'T GOING WITH YOU. I'M STAYING HERE.
NO YOU'RE NOT.
JOHNNY AND THE DOC ARE STAYING HERE TO WATCH OUR STUFF. *YOU'RE COMING WITH ME.*
LET'S MOVE.

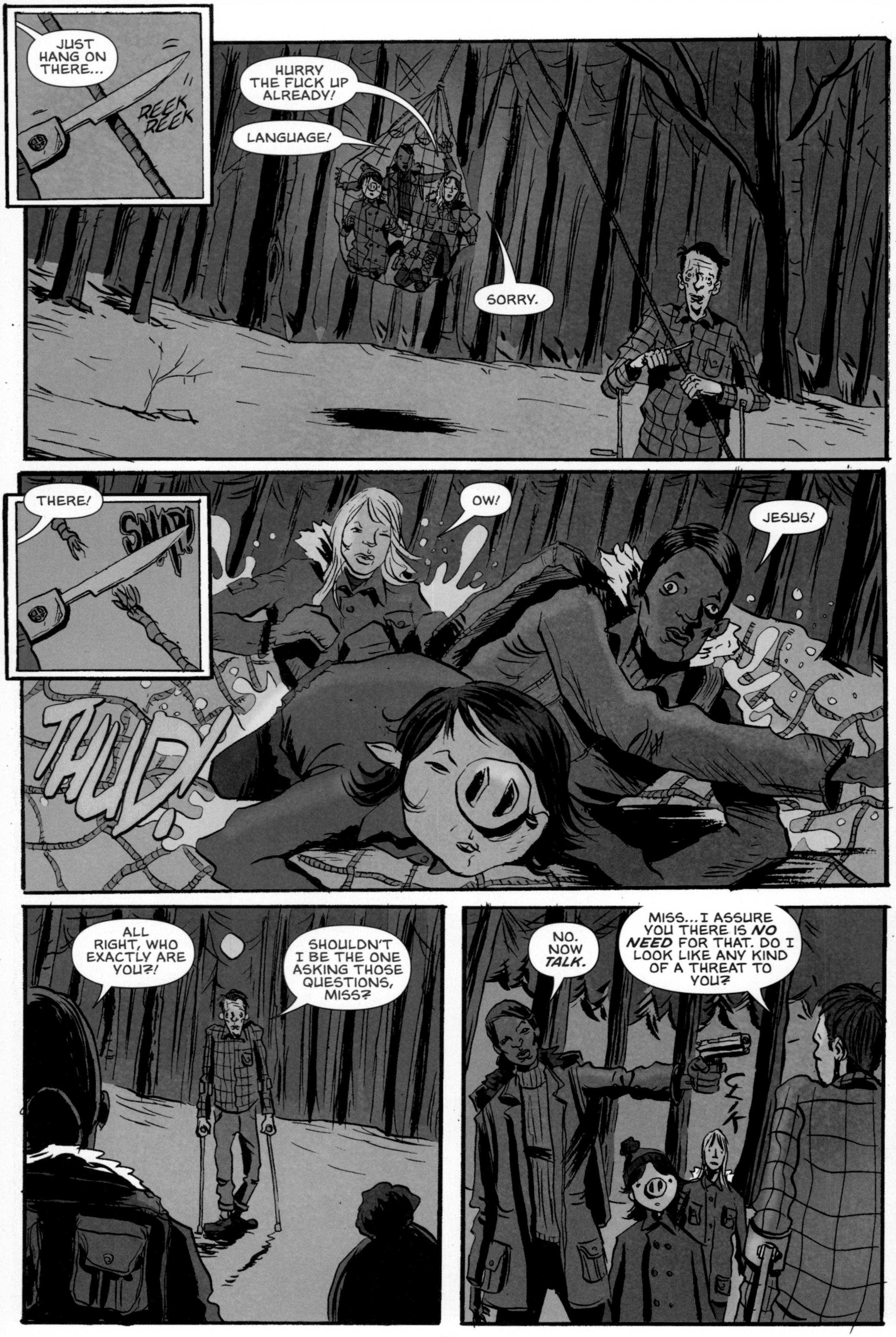
JUST HANG ON THERE...
DEEK DEEK
HURRY THE FUCK UP ALREADY!
LANGUAGE!
SORRY.
THERE!
SNAP!
OW!
JESUS!
THUD!
ALL RIGHT, WHO EXACTLY ARE YOU?!
SHOULDN'T I BE THE ONE ASKING THOSE QUESTIONS, MISS?
NO. NOW TALK.
MISS... I ASSURE YOU THERE IS NO NEED FOR THAT. DO I LOOK LIKE ANY KIND OF A THREAT TO YOU?
CLIK

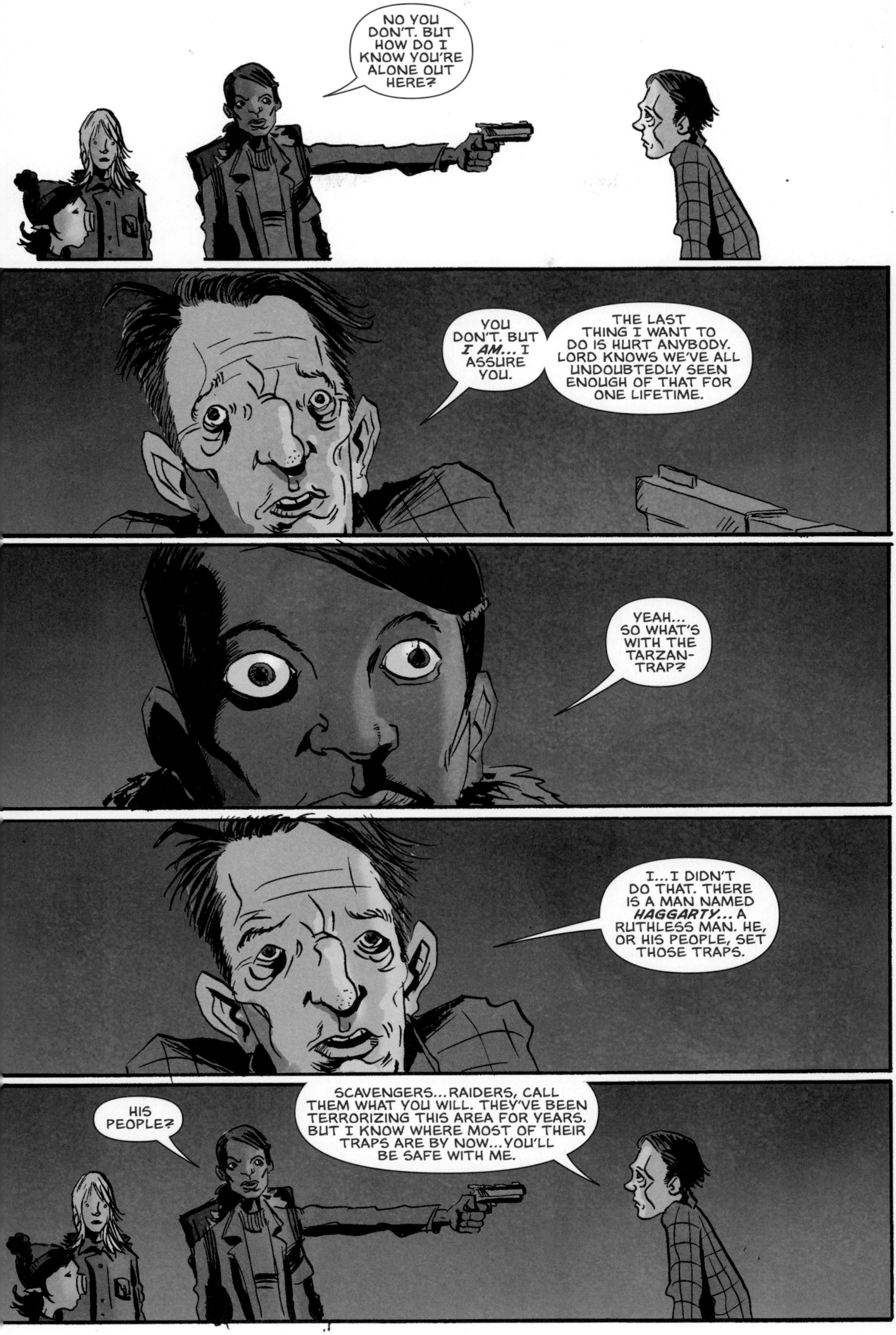
NO YOU DON'T. BUT HOW DO I KNOW YOU'RE ALONE OUT HERE?
YOU DON'T. BUT *I AM...* I ASSURE YOU.
THE LAST THING I WANT TO DO IS HURT ANYBODY. LORD KNOWS WE'VE ALL UNDOUBTEDLY SEEN ENOUGH OF THAT FOR ONE LIFETIME.
YEAH... SO WHAT'S WITH THE TARZAN-TRAP?
I...I DIDN'T DO THAT. THERE IS A MAN NAMED *HAGGARTY...* A RUTHLESS MAN. HE, OR HIS PEOPLE, SET THOSE TRAPS.
HIS PEOPLE?
SCAVENGERS...RAIDERS, CALL THEM WHAT YOU WILL. THEY'VE BEEN TERRORIZING THIS AREA FOR YEARS. BUT I KNOW WHERE MOST OF THEIR TRAPS ARE BY NOW...YOU'LL BE SAFE WITH ME.

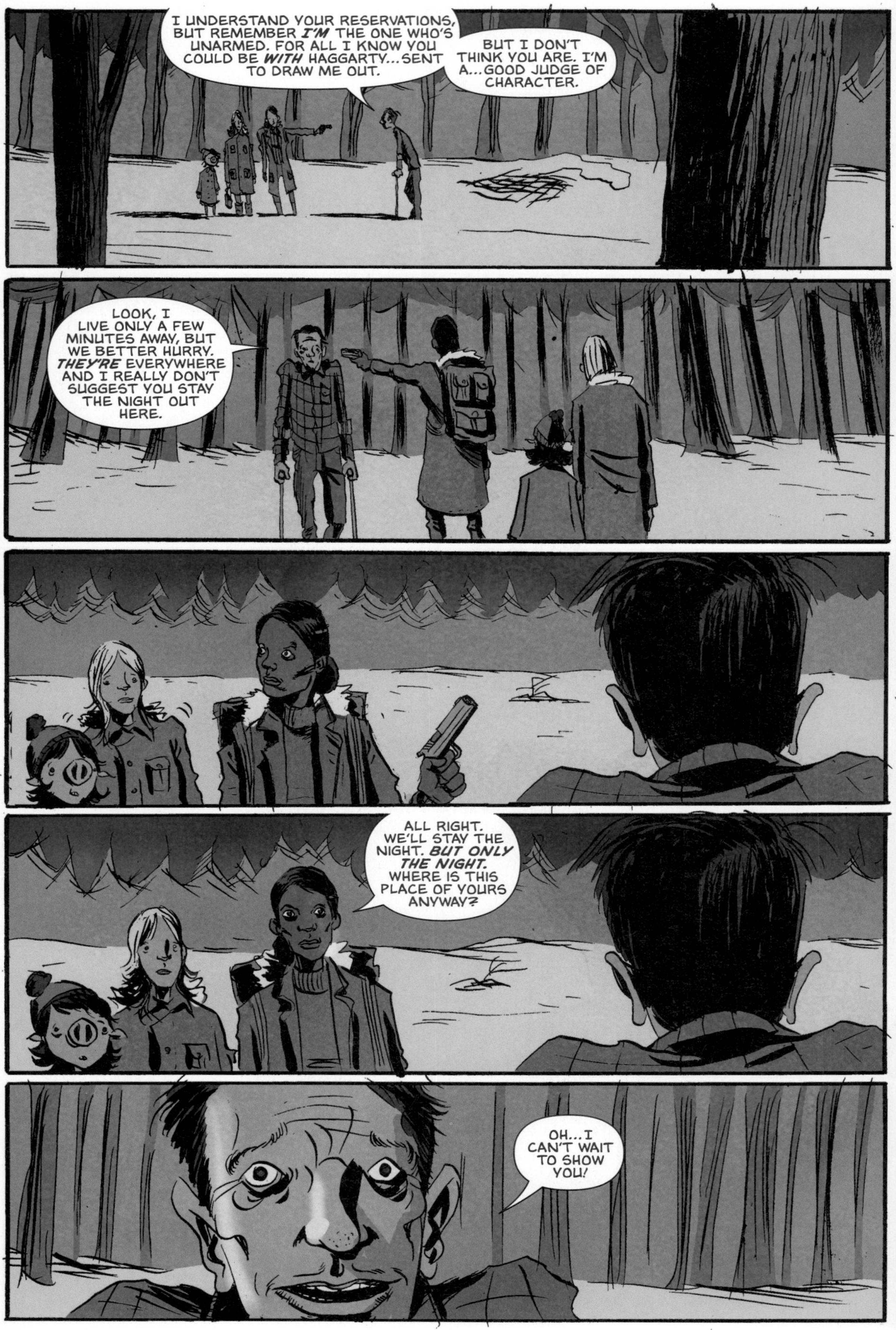
I UNDERSTAND YOUR RESERVATIONS, BUT REMEMBER *I'M* THE ONE WHO'S UNARMED. FOR ALL I KNOW YOU COULD BE *WITH* HAGGARTY... SENT TO DRAW ME OUT.
BUT I DON'T THINK YOU ARE. I'M A... GOOD JUDGE OF CHARACTER.
LOOK, I LIVE ONLY A FEW MINUTES AWAY, BUT WE BETTER HURRY. *THEY'RE* EVERYWHERE AND I REALLY DON'T SUGGEST YOU STAY THE NIGHT OUT HERE.
ALL RIGHT. WE'LL STAY THE NIGHT. *BUT ONLY THE NIGHT.* WHERE IS THIS PLACE OF YOURS ANYWAY?
OH... I CAN'T WAIT TO SHOW YOU!

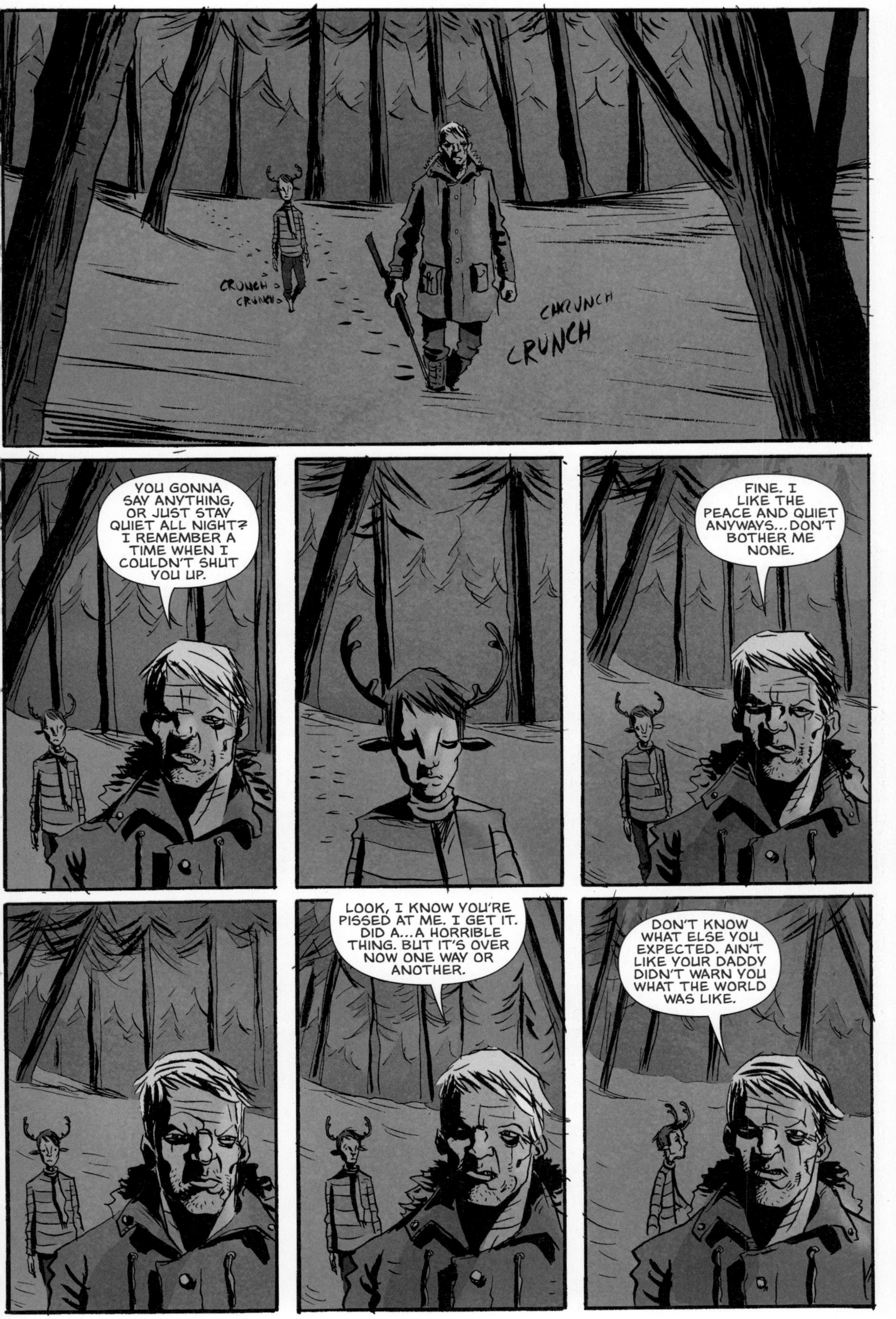
CRUNCH
CRUNCH
CHRUNCH
CRUNCH
YOU GONNA SAY ANYTHING, OR JUST STAY QUIET ALL NIGHT? I REMEMBER A TIME WHEN I COULDN'T SHUT YOU UP.
FINE. I LIKE THE PEACE AND QUIET ANYWAYS... DON'T BOTHER ME NONE.
LOOK, I KNOW YOU'RE PISSED AT ME. I GET IT. DID A... A HORRIBLE THING. BUT IT'S OVER NOW ONE WAY OR ANOTHER.
DON'T KNOW WHAT ELSE YOU EXPECTED. AIN'T LIKE YOUR DADDY DIDN'T WARN YOU WHAT THE WORLD WAS LIKE.

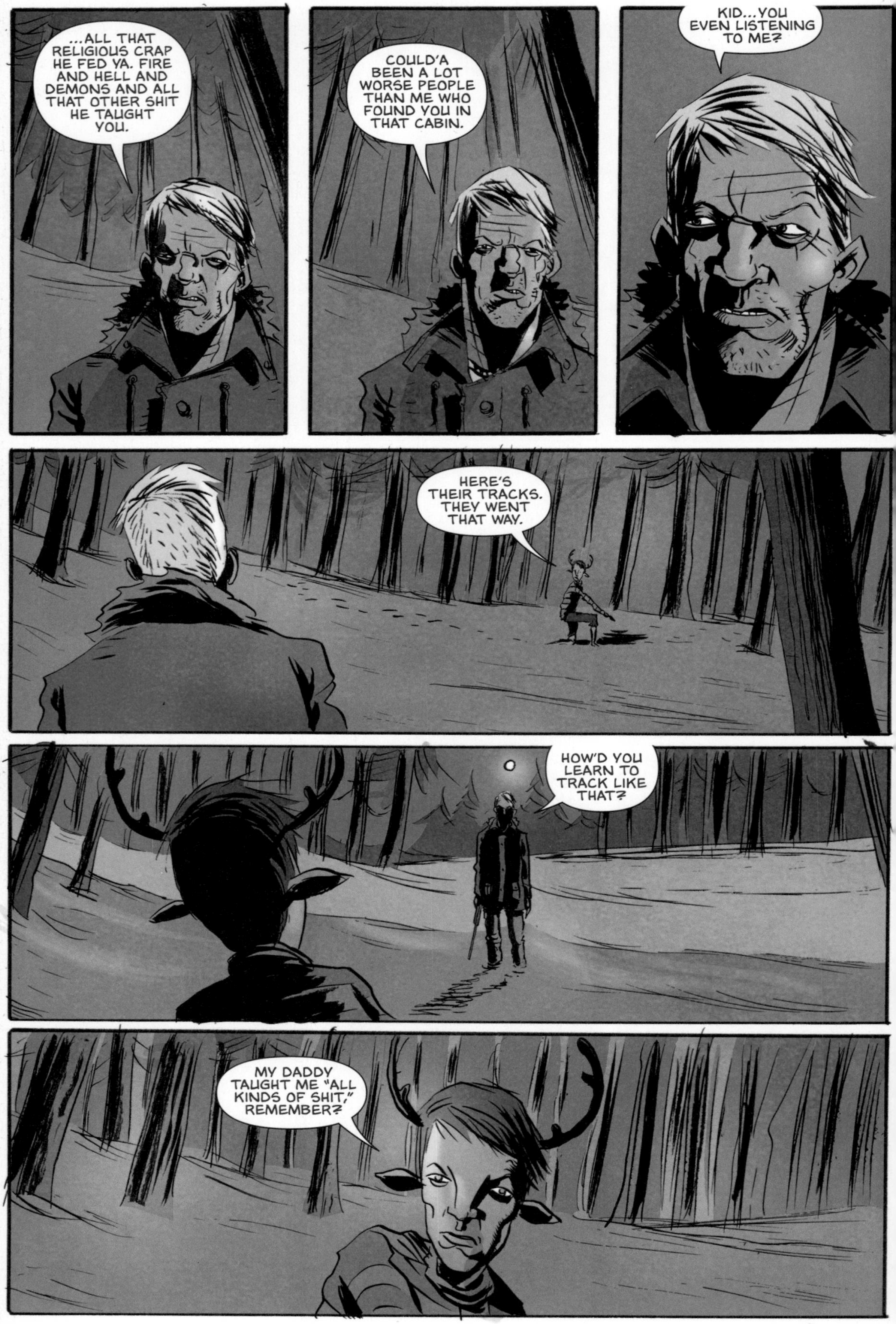
...ALL THAT RELIGIOUS CRAP HE FED YA. FIRE AND HELL AND DEMONS AND ALL THAT OTHER SHIT HE TAUGHT YOU.
COULD'A BEEN A LOT WORSE PEOPLE THAN ME WHO FOUND YOU IN THAT CABIN.
KID...YOU EVEN LISTENING TO ME?
HERE'S THEIR TRACKS. THEY WENT THAT WAY.
HOW'D YOU LEARN TO TRACK LIKE THAT?
MY DADDY TAUGHT ME "ALL KINDS OF SHIT," REMEMBER?

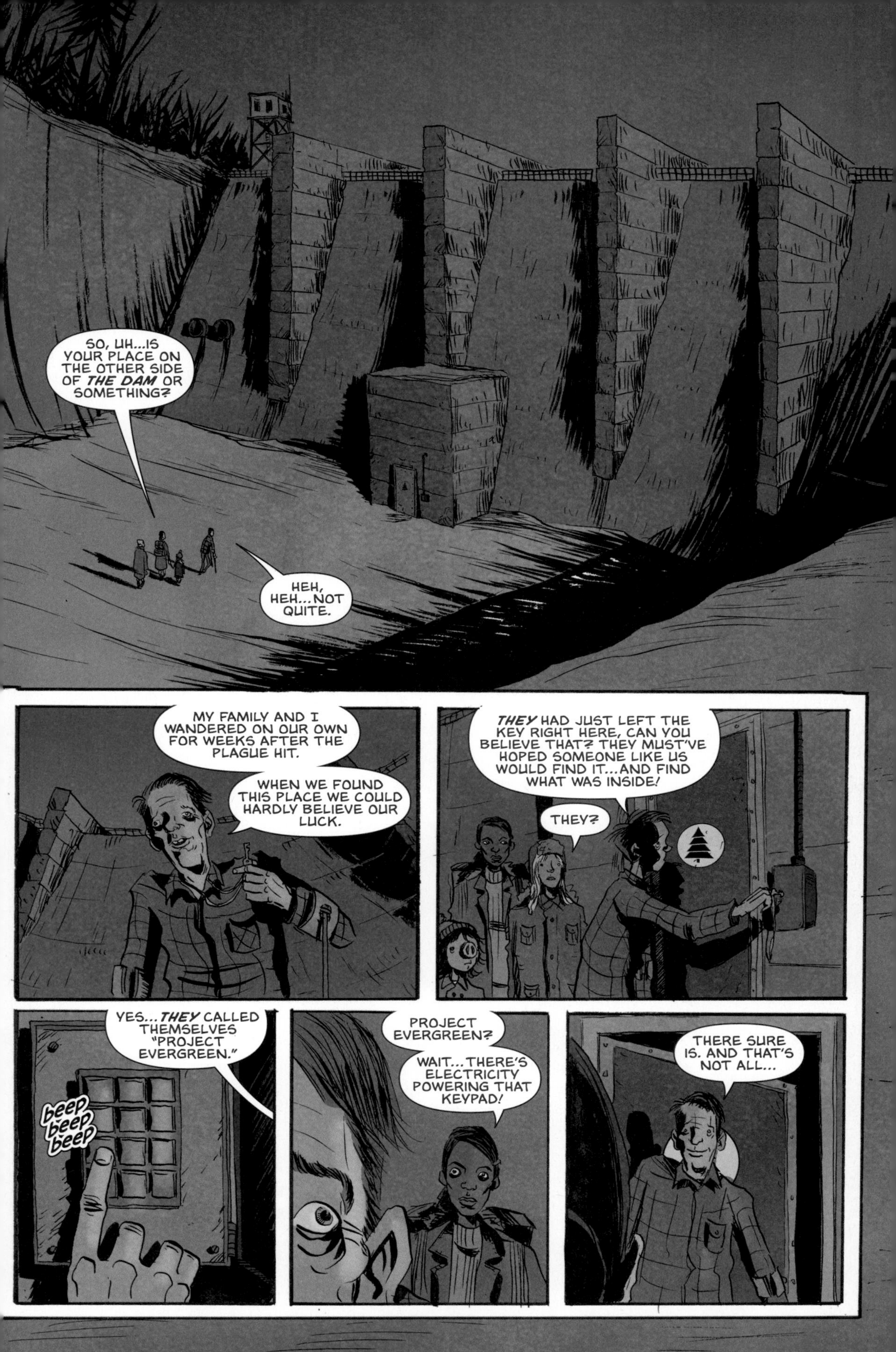
SO, UH...IS YOUR PLACE ON THE OTHER SIDE OF *THE DAM* OR SOMETHING?
HEH, HEH...NOT QUITE.
MY FAMILY AND I WANDERED ON OUR OWN FOR WEEKS AFTER THE PLAGUE HIT.
WHEN WE FOUND THIS PLACE WE COULD HARDLY BELIEVE OUR LUCK.
THEY HAD JUST LEFT THE KEY RIGHT HERE, CAN YOU BELIEVE THAT? THEY MUST'VE HOPED SOMEONE LIKE US WOULD FIND IT...AND FIND WHAT WAS INSIDE!
THEY?
YES...*THEY* CALLED THEMSELVES "PROJECT EVERGREEN."
beep beep beep
PROJECT EVERGREEN?
WAIT...THERE'S ELECTRICITY POWERING THAT KEYPAD!
THERE SURE IS. AND THAT'S NOT ALL...

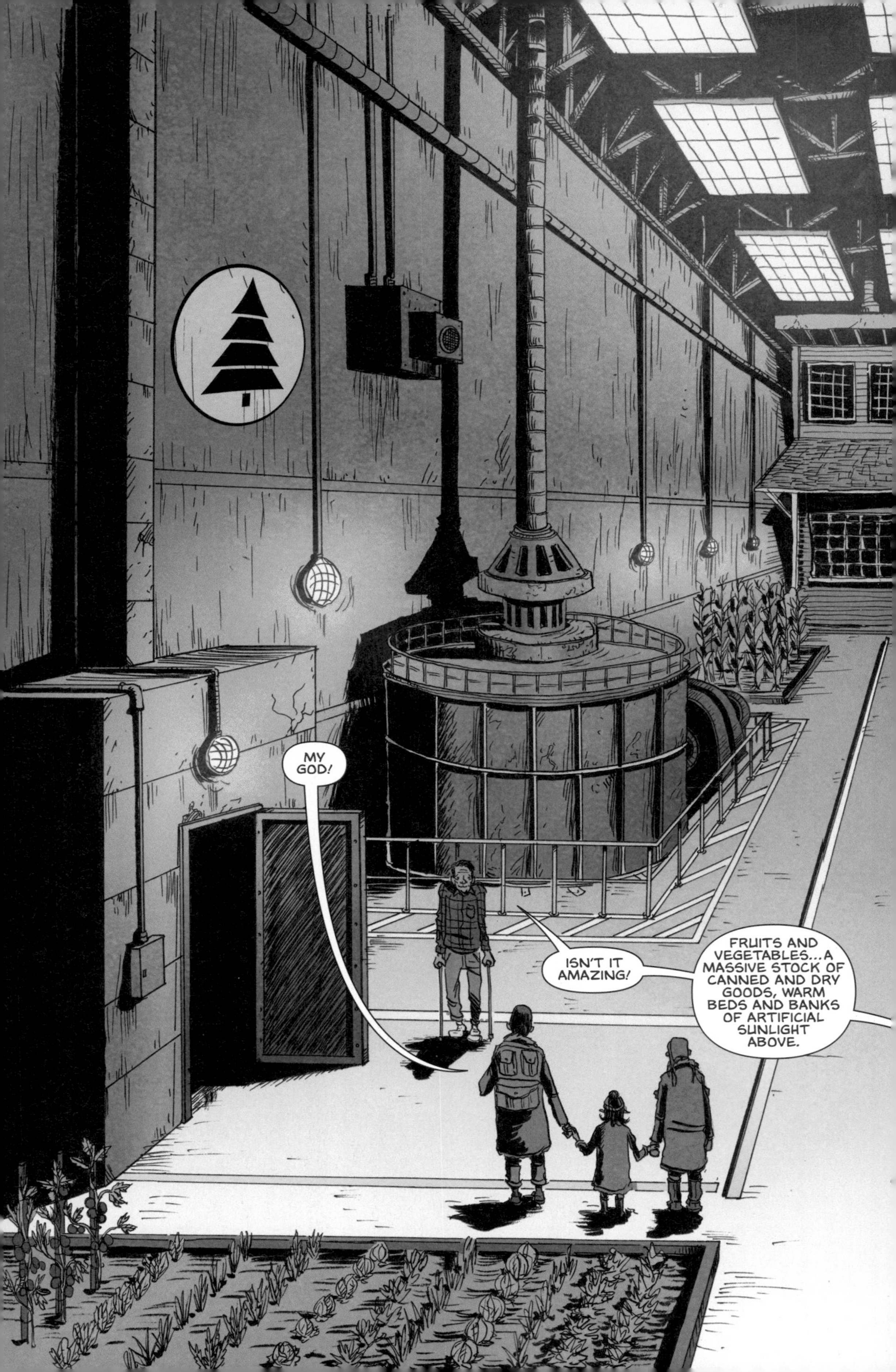
MY GOD!
ISN'T IT AMAZING!
FRUITS AND VEGETABLES...A MASSIVE STOCK OF CANNED AND DRY GOODS, WARM BEDS AND BANKS OF ARTIFICIAL SUNLIGHT ABOVE.

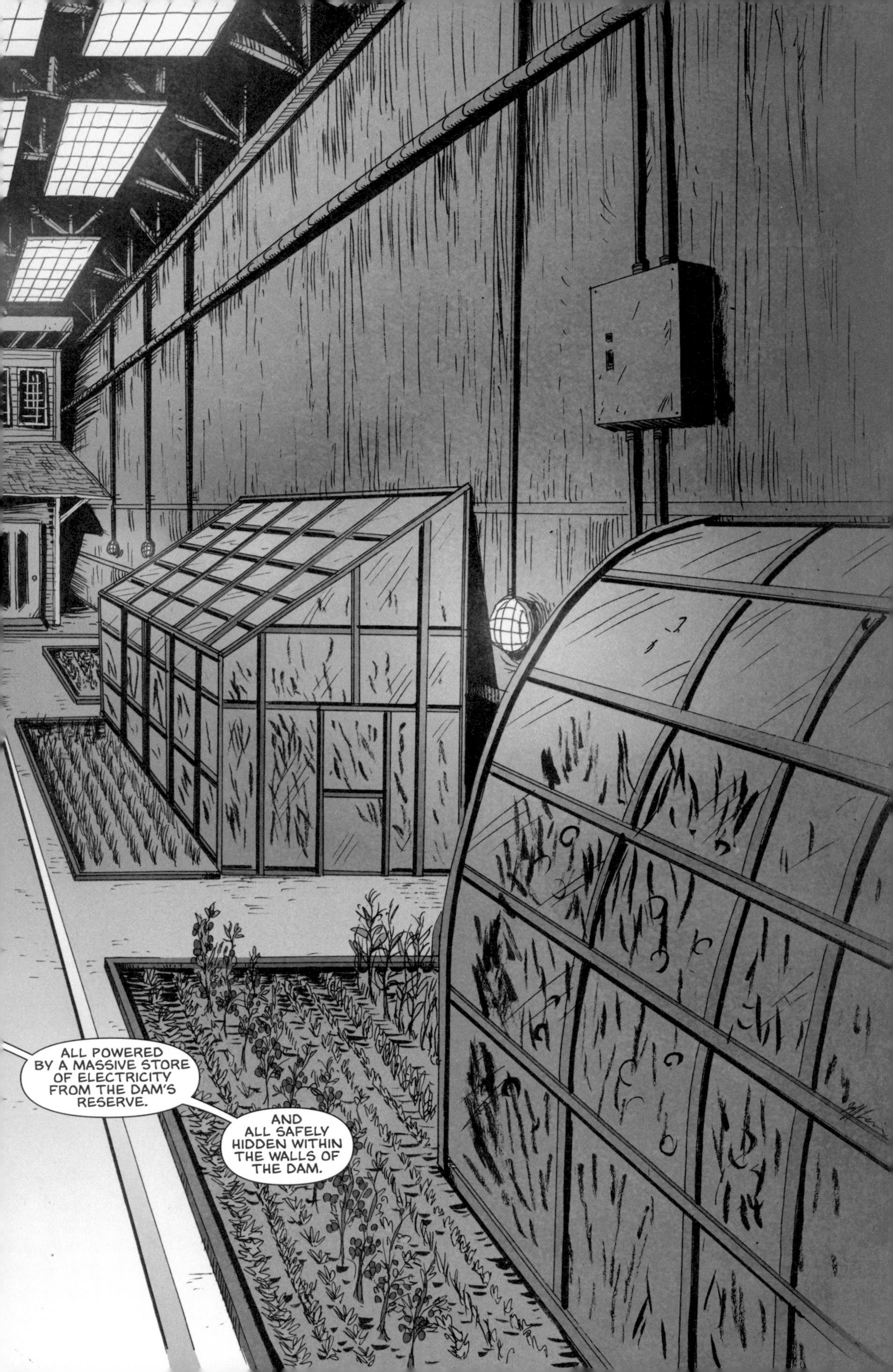
ALL POWERED BY A MASSIVE STORE OF ELECTRICITY FROM THE DAM'S RESERVE.
AND ALL SAFELY HIDDEN WITHIN THE WALLS OF THE DAM.

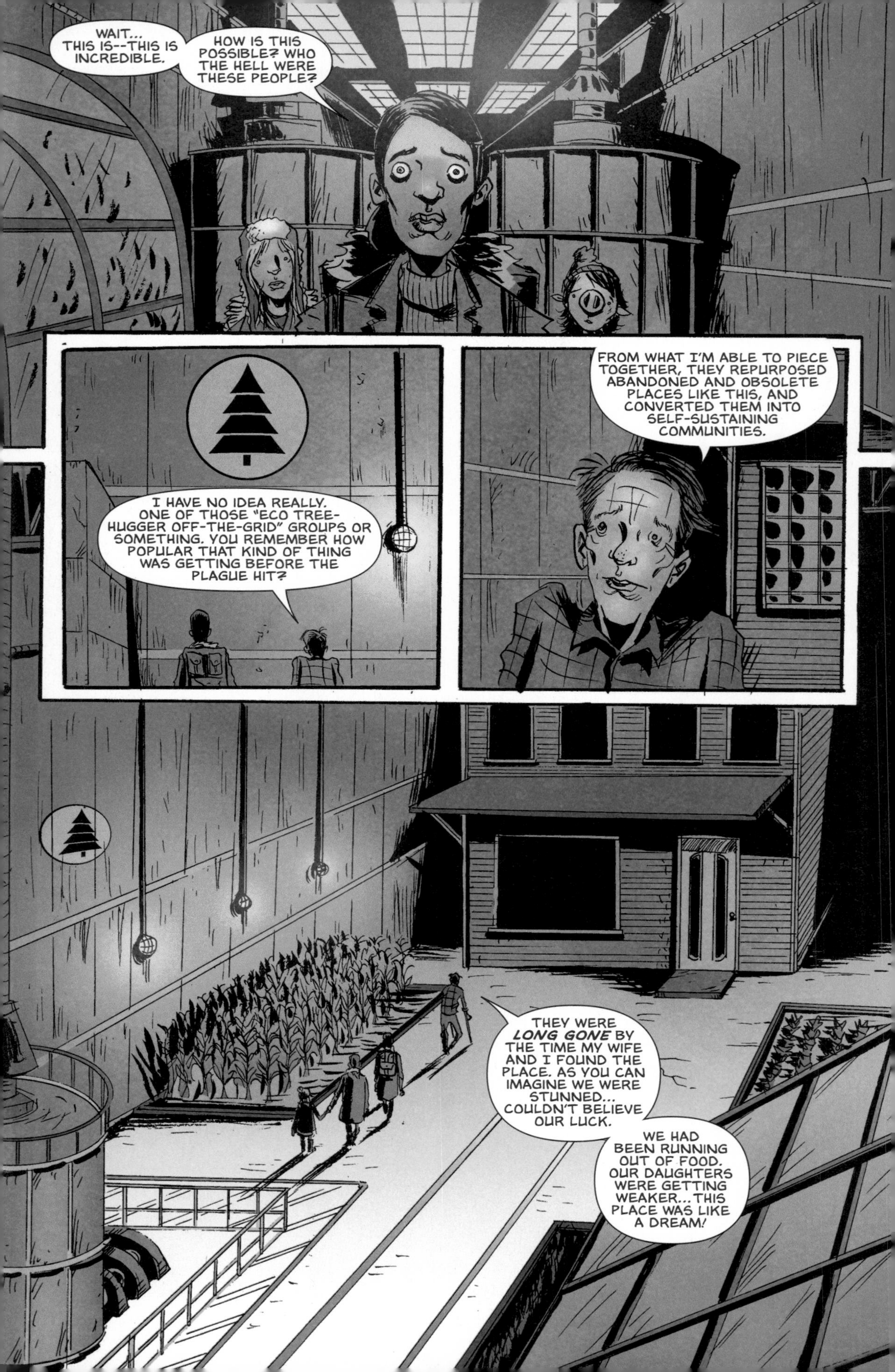
WAIT... THIS IS--THIS IS INCREDIBLE.
HOW IS THIS POSSIBLE? WHO THE HELL WERE THESE PEOPLE?
I HAVE NO IDEA REALLY. ONE OF THOSE "ECO TREE-HUGGER OFF-THE-GRID" GROUPS OR SOMETHING. YOU REMEMBER HOW POPULAR THAT KIND OF THING WAS GETTING BEFORE THE PLAGUE HIT?
FROM WHAT I'M ABLE TO PIECE TOGETHER, THEY REPURPOSED ABANDONED AND OBSOLETE PLACES LIKE THIS, AND CONVERTED THEM INTO SELF-SUSTAINING COMMUNITIES.
THEY WERE *LONG GONE* BY THE TIME MY WIFE AND I FOUND THE PLACE. AS YOU CAN IMAGINE WE WERE STUNNED... COULDN'T BELIEVE OUR LUCK.
WE HAD BEEN RUNNING OUT OF FOOD. OUR DAUGHTERS WERE GETTING WEAKER... THIS PLACE WAS LIKE A DREAM!

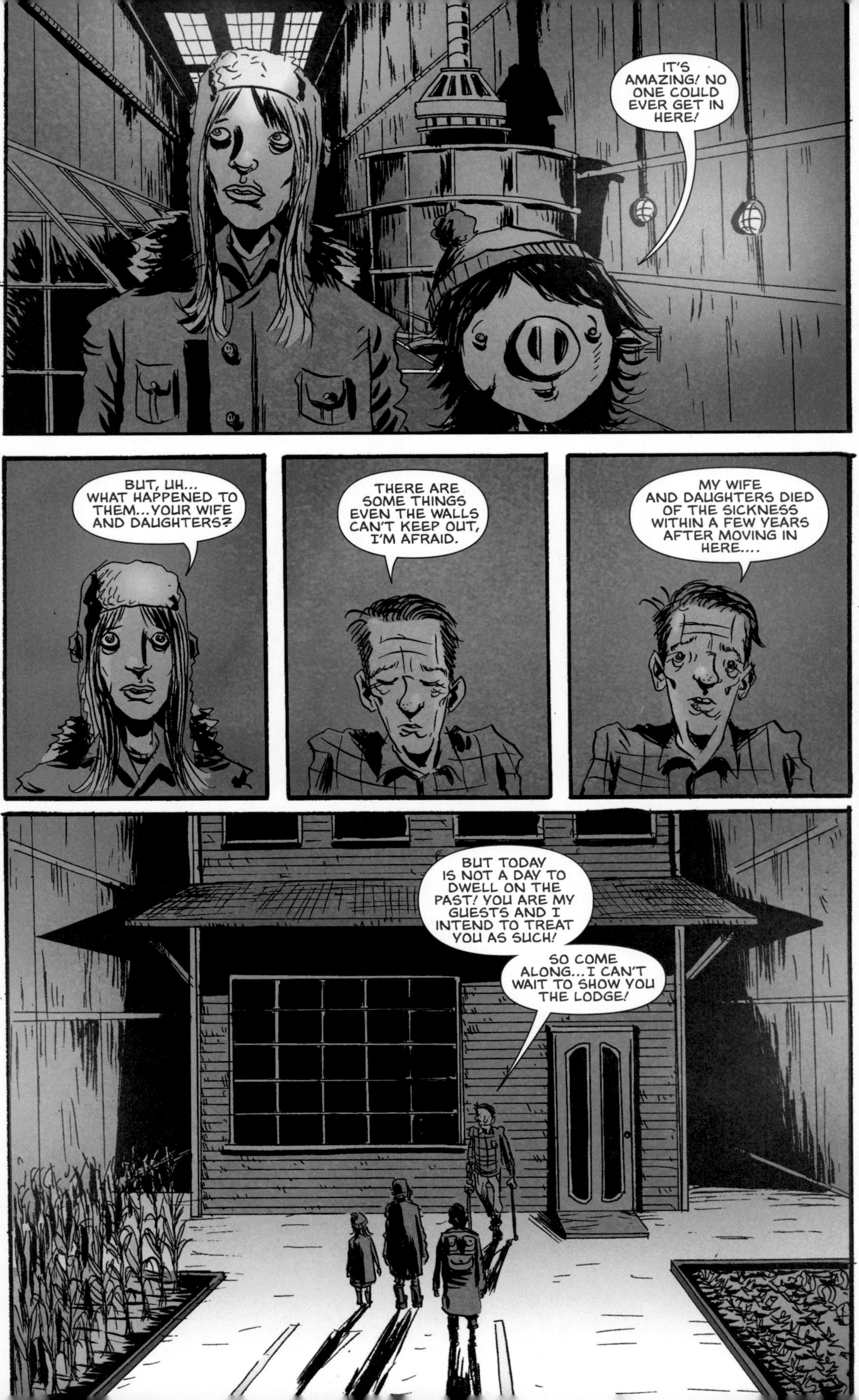
IT'S AMAZING! NO ONE COULD EVER GET IN HERE!
BUT, UH... WHAT HAPPENED TO THEM...YOUR WIFE AND DAUGHTERS?
THERE ARE SOME THINGS EVEN THE WALLS CAN'T KEEP OUT, I'M AFRAID.
MY WIFE AND DAUGHTERS DIED OF THE SICKNESS WITHIN A FEW YEARS AFTER MOVING IN HERE....
BUT TODAY IS NOT A DAY TO DWELL ON THE PAST! YOU ARE MY GUESTS AND I INTEND TO TREAT YOU AS SUCH!
SO COME ALONG...I CAN'T WAIT TO SHOW YOU THE LODGE!

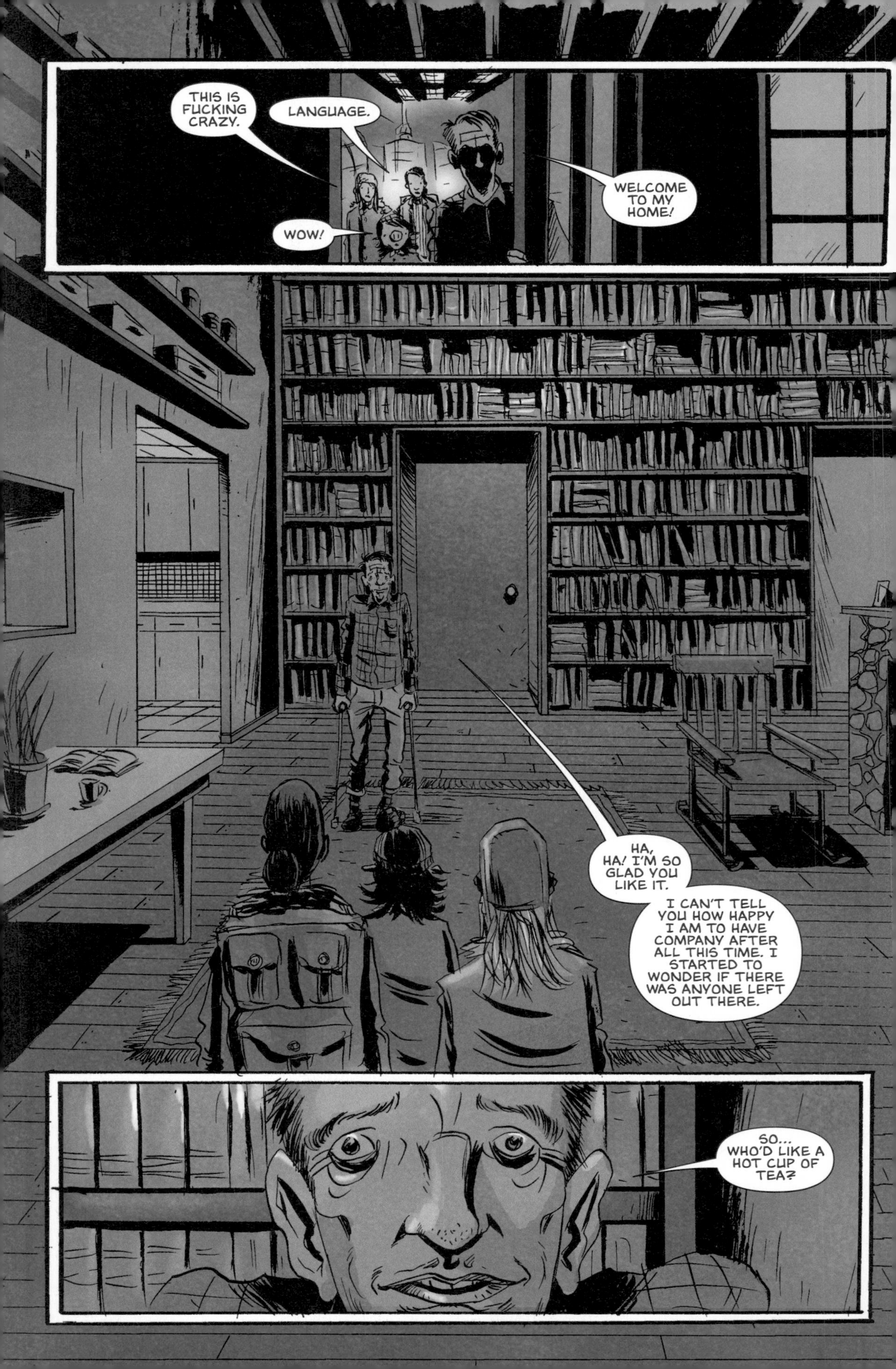
THIS IS FUCKING CRAZY.
LANGUAGE.
WOW!
WELCOME TO MY HOME!
HA, HA! I'M SO GLAD YOU LIKE IT.
I CAN'T TELL YOU HOW HAPPY I AM TO HAVE COMPANY AFTER ALL THIS TIME. I STARTED TO WONDER IF THERE WAS ANYONE LEFT OUT THERE.
SO... WHO'D LIKE A HOT CUP OF TEA?

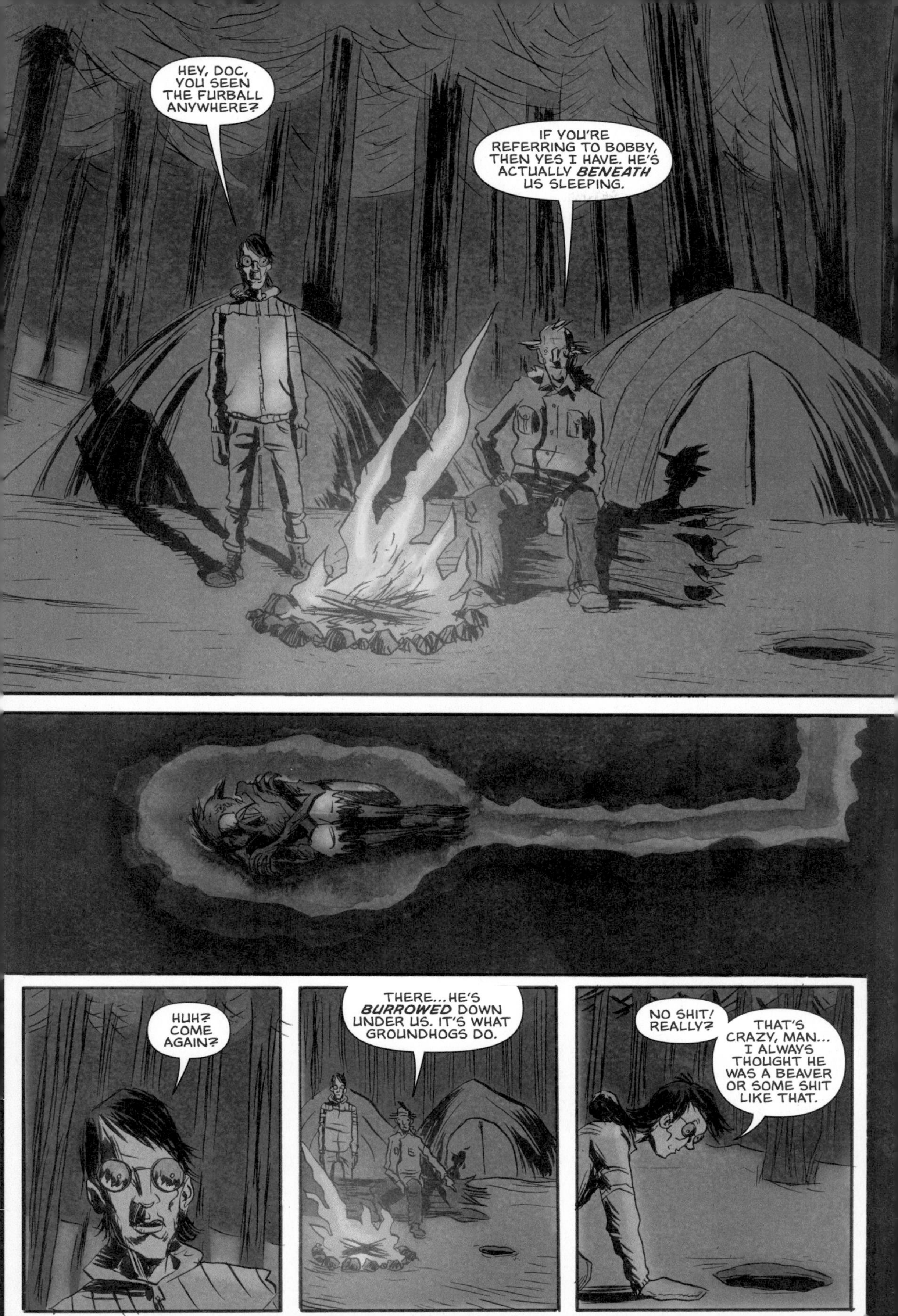
HEY, DOC, YOU SEEN THE FURBALL ANYWHERE?
IF YOU'RE REFERRING TO BOBBY, THEN YES I HAVE. HE'S ACTUALLY BENEATH US SLEEPING.
HUH? COME AGAIN?
THERE...HE'S BURROWED DOWN UNDER US. IT'S WHAT GROUNDHOGS DO.
NO SHIT! REALLY?
THAT'S CRAZY, MAN... I ALWAYS THOUGHT HE WAS A BEAVER OR SOME SHIT LIKE THAT.

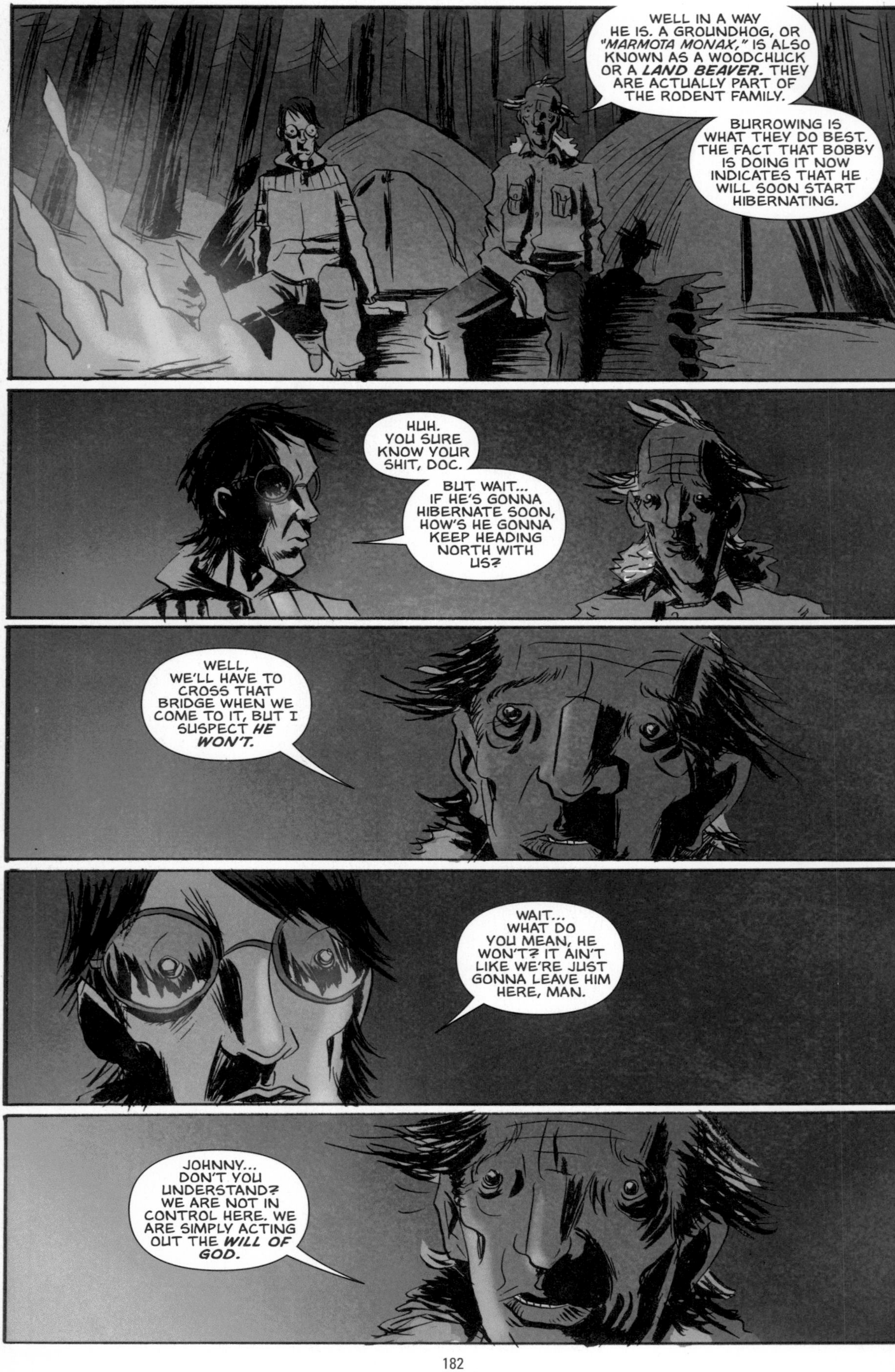
WELL IN A WAY HE IS. A GROUNDHOG, OR "MARMOTA MONAX," IS ALSO KNOWN AS A WOODCHUCK OR A LAND BEAVER. THEY ARE ACTUALLY PART OF THE RODENT FAMILY.
BURROWING IS WHAT THEY DO BEST. THE FACT THAT BOBBY IS DOING IT NOW INDICATES THAT HE WILL SOON START HIBERNATING.
HUH. YOU SURE KNOW YOUR SHIT, DOC.
BUT WAIT... IF HE'S GONNA HIBERNATE SOON, HOW'S HE GONNA KEEP HEADING NORTH WITH US?
WELL, WE'LL HAVE TO CROSS THAT BRIDGE WHEN WE COME TO IT, BUT I SUSPECT HE WON'T.
WAIT... WHAT DO YOU MEAN, HE WON'T? IT AIN'T LIKE WE'RE JUST GONNA LEAVE HIM HERE, MAN.
JOHNNY... DON'T YOU UNDERSTAND? WE ARE NOT IN CONTROL HERE. WE ARE SIMPLY ACTING OUT THE WILL OF GOD.

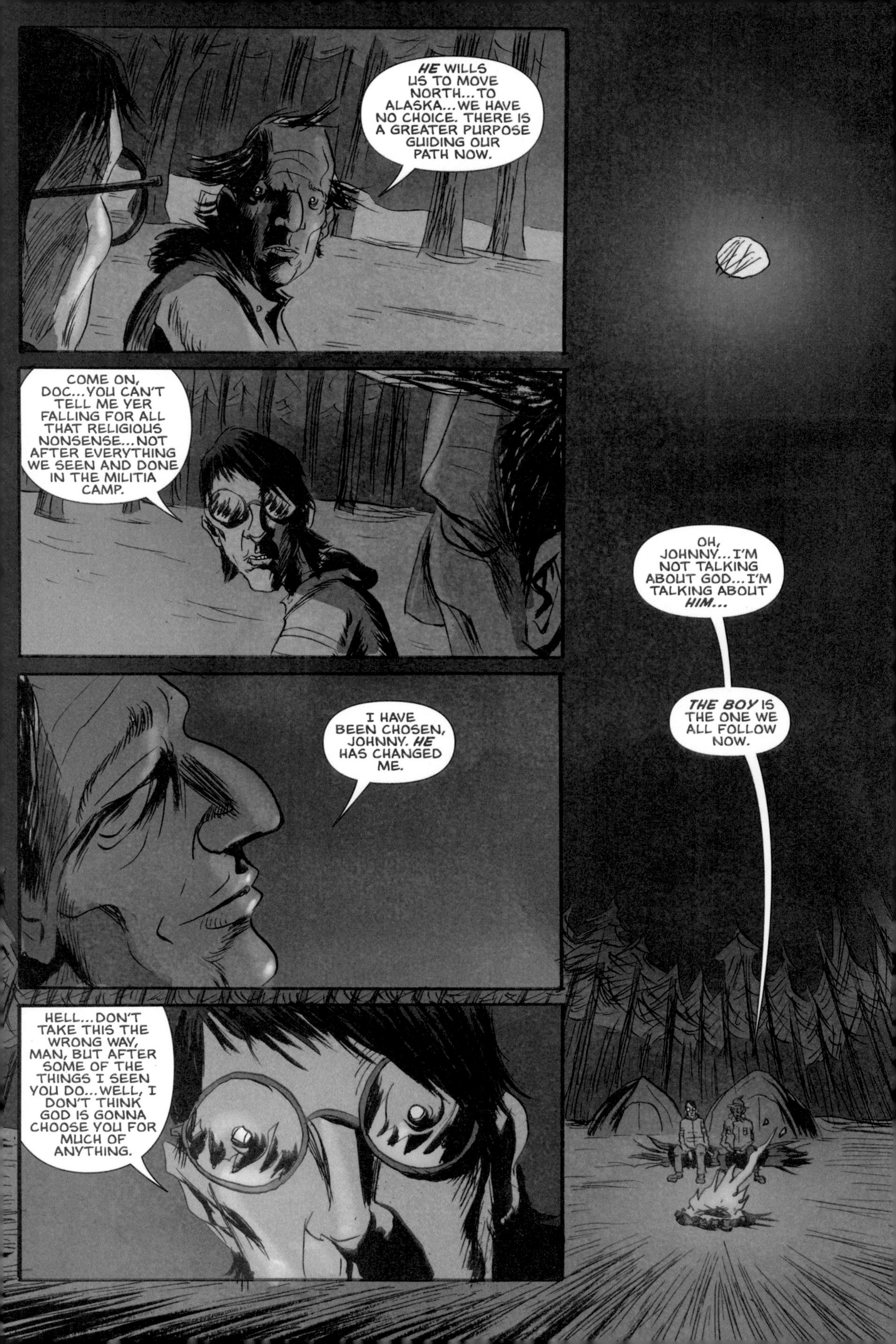
HE WILLS US TO MOVE NORTH...TO ALASKA...WE HAVE NO CHOICE. THERE IS A GREATER PURPOSE GUIDING OUR PATH NOW.
COME ON, DOC...YOU CAN'T TELL ME YER FALLING FOR ALL THAT RELIGIOUS NONSENSE...NOT AFTER EVERYTHING WE SEEN AND DONE IN THE MILITIA CAMP.
I HAVE BEEN CHOSEN, JOHNNY. HE HAS CHANGED ME.
HELL...DON'T TAKE THIS THE WRONG WAY, MAN, BUT AFTER SOME OF THE THINGS I SEEN YOU DO...WELL, I DON'T THINK GOD IS GONNA CHOOSE YOU FOR MUCH OF ANYTHING.
OH, JOHNNY...I'M NOT TALKING ABOUT GOD...I'M TALKING ABOUT HIM...
THE BOY IS THE ONE WE ALL FOLLOW NOW.

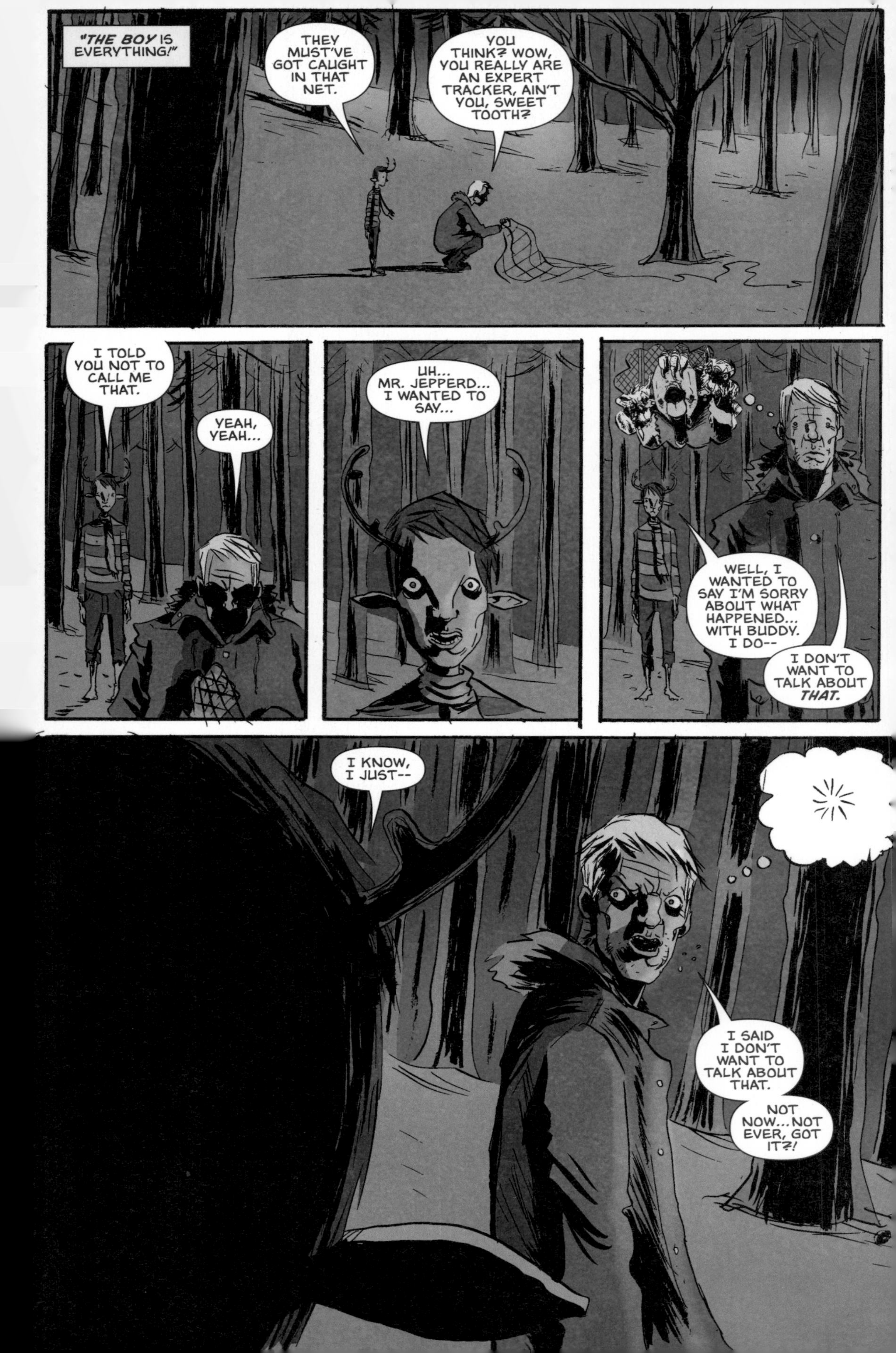
"THE BOY IS EVERYTHING!"
THEY MUST'VE GOT CAUGHT IN THAT NET.
YOU THINK? WOW, YOU REALLY ARE AN EXPERT TRACKER, AIN'T YOU, SWEET TOOTH?
I TOLD YOU NOT TO CALL ME THAT.
YEAH, YEAH...
UH... MR. JEPPERD... I WANTED TO SAY...
WELL, I WANTED TO SAY I'M SORRY ABOUT WHAT HAPPENED... WITH BUDDY. I DO--
I DON'T WANT TO TALK ABOUT THAT.
I KNOW, I JUST--
I SAID I DON'T WANT TO TALK ABOUT THAT.
NOT NOW... NOT EVER, GOT IT?!

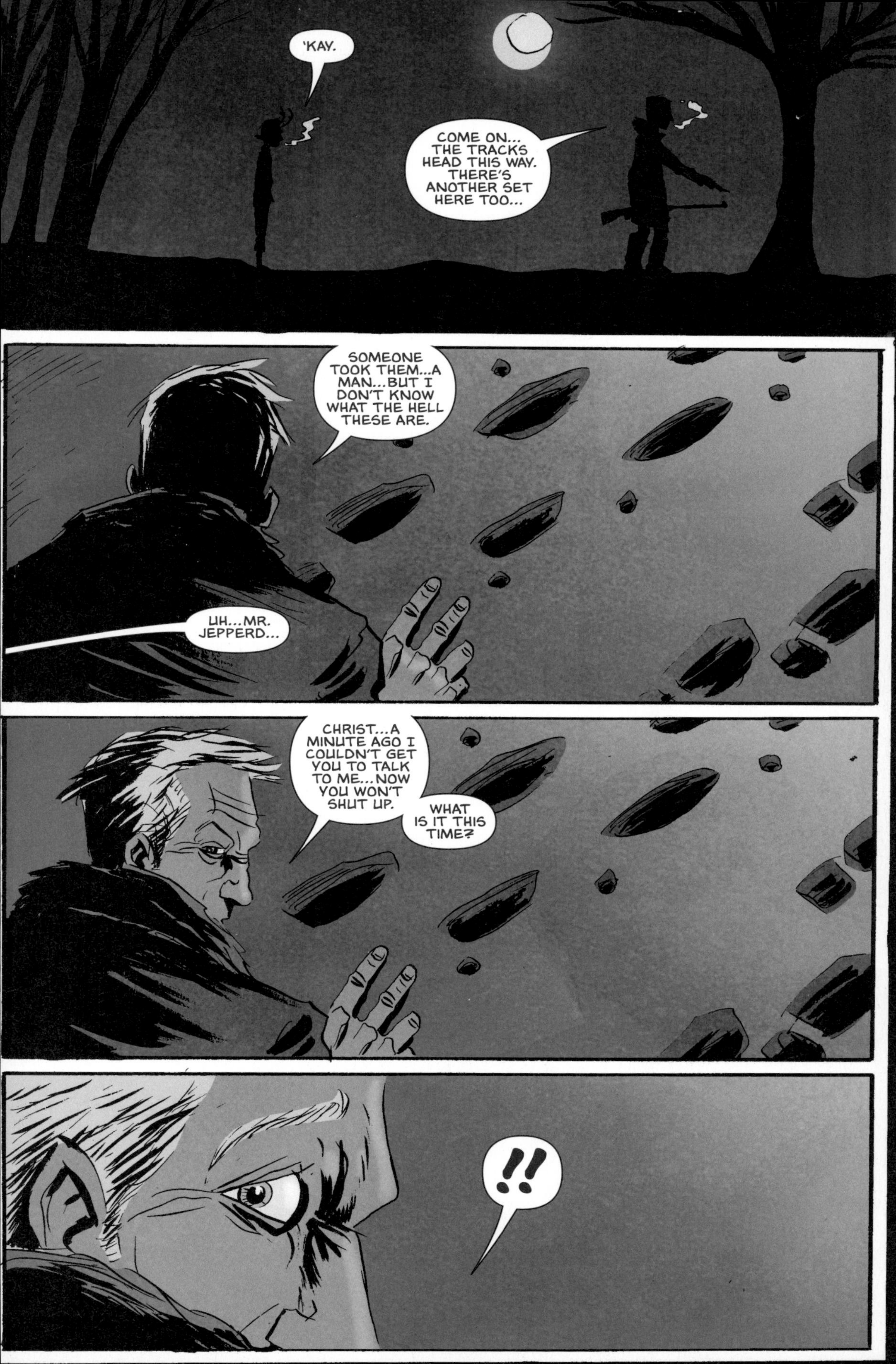

'KAY.
COME ON... THE TRACKS HEAD THIS WAY. THERE'S ANOTHER SET HERE TOO...
SOMEONE TOOK THEM...A MAN...BUT I DON'T KNOW WHAT THE HELL THESE ARE.
UH...MR. JEPPERD...
CHRIST...A MINUTE AGO I COULDN'T GET YOU TO TALK TO ME...NOW YOU WON'T SHUT UP.
WHAT IS IT THIS TIME?
!!

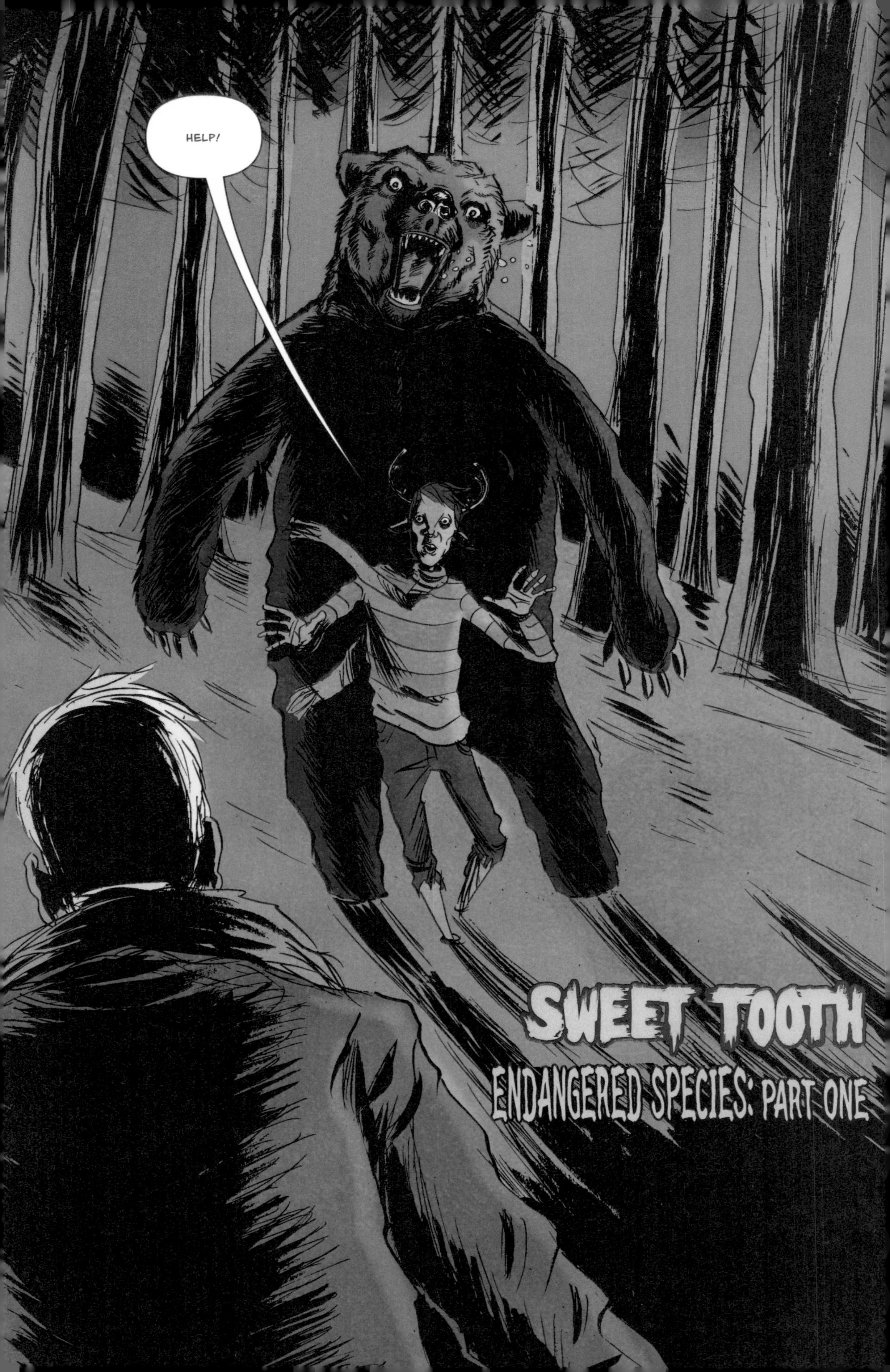
HELP!
SWEET TOOTH
ENDANGERED SPECIES: PART ONE

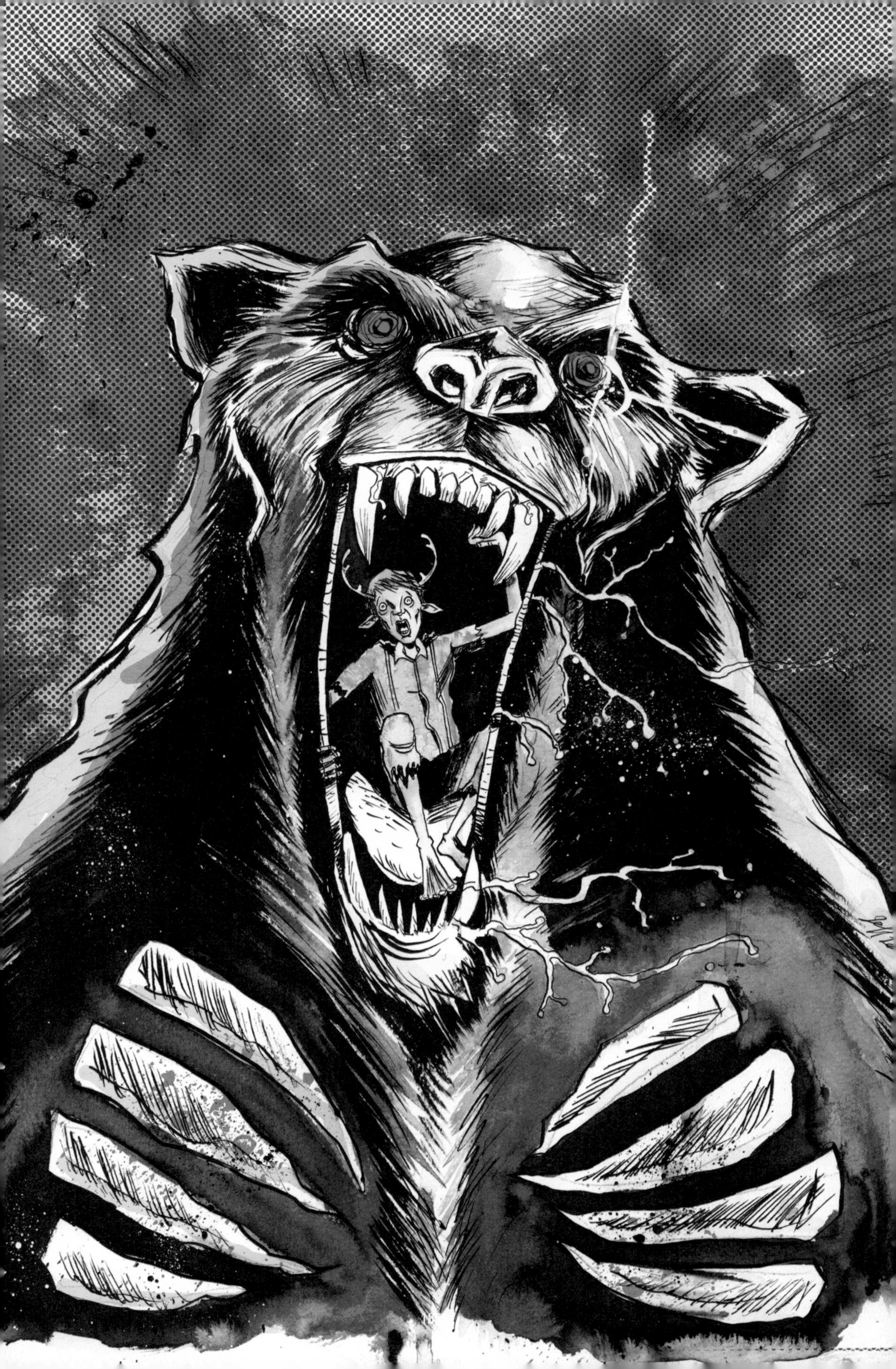

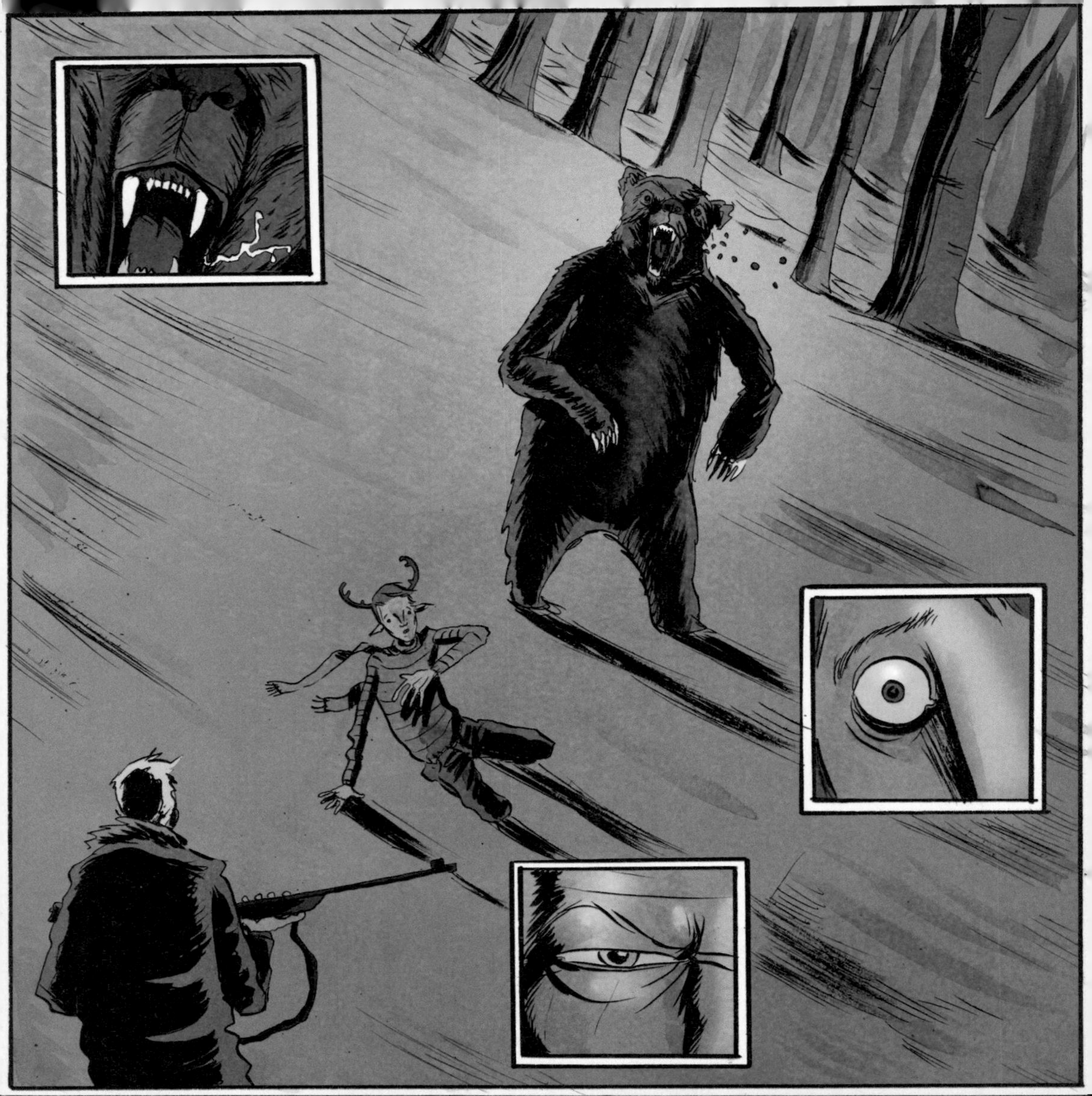

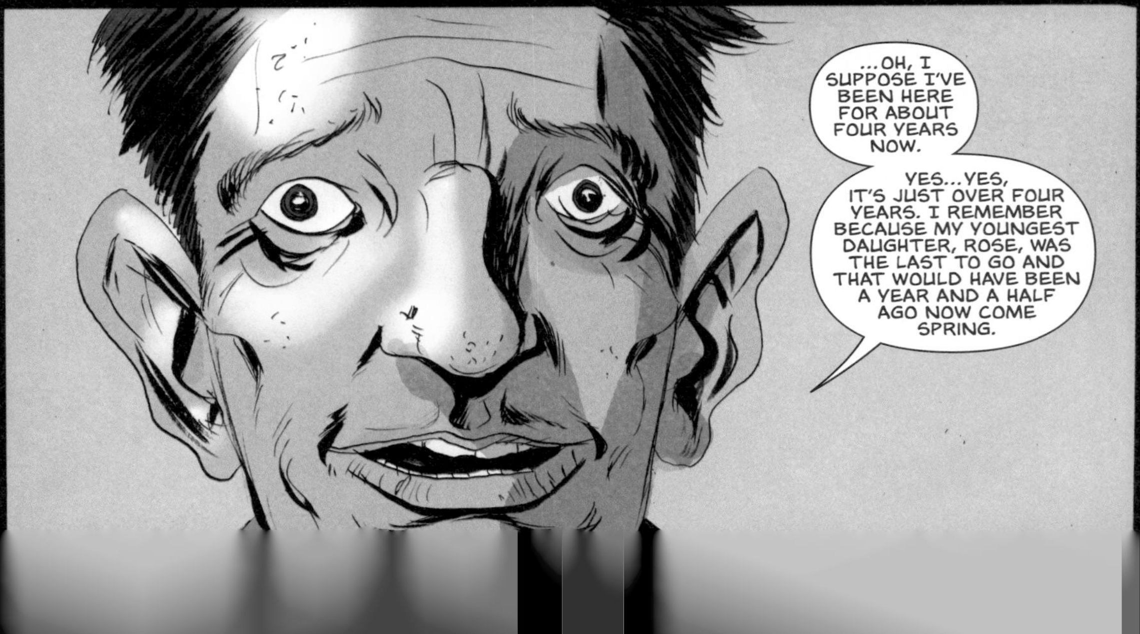
...OH, I SUPPOSE I'VE BEEN HERE FOR ABOUT FOUR YEARS NOW.
YES...YES, IT'S JUST OVER FOUR YEARS. I REMEMBER BECAUSE MY YOUNGEST DAUGHTER, ROSE, WAS THE LAST TO GO AND THAT WOULD HAVE BEEN A YEAR AND A HALF AGO NOW COME SPRING.

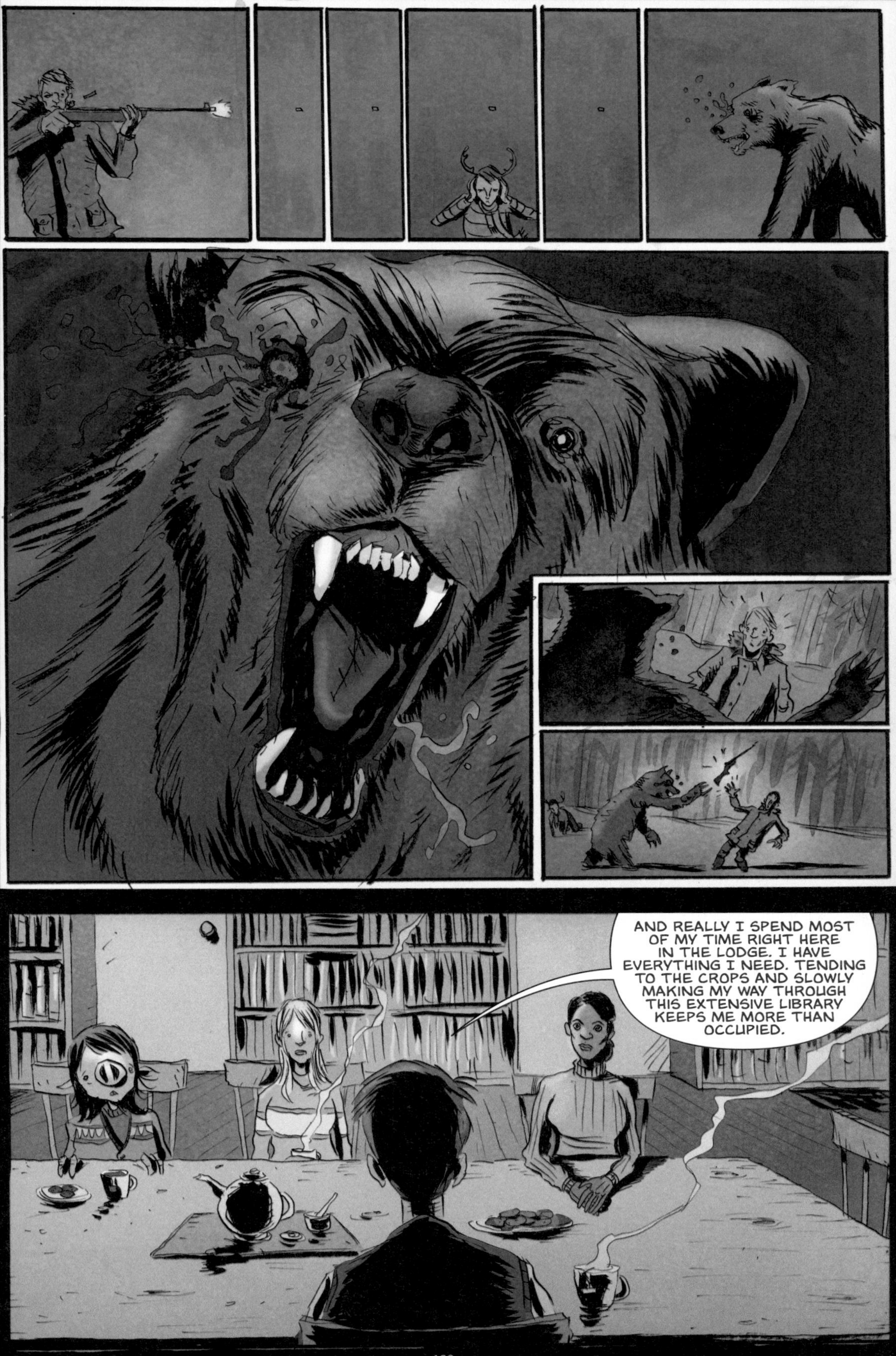
AND REALLY I SPEND MOST OF MY TIME RIGHT HERE IN THE LODGE. I HAVE EVERYTHING I NEED. TENDING TO THE CROPS AND SLOWLY MAKING MY WAY THROUGH THIS EXTENSIVE LIBRARY KEEPS ME MORE THAN OCCUPIED.

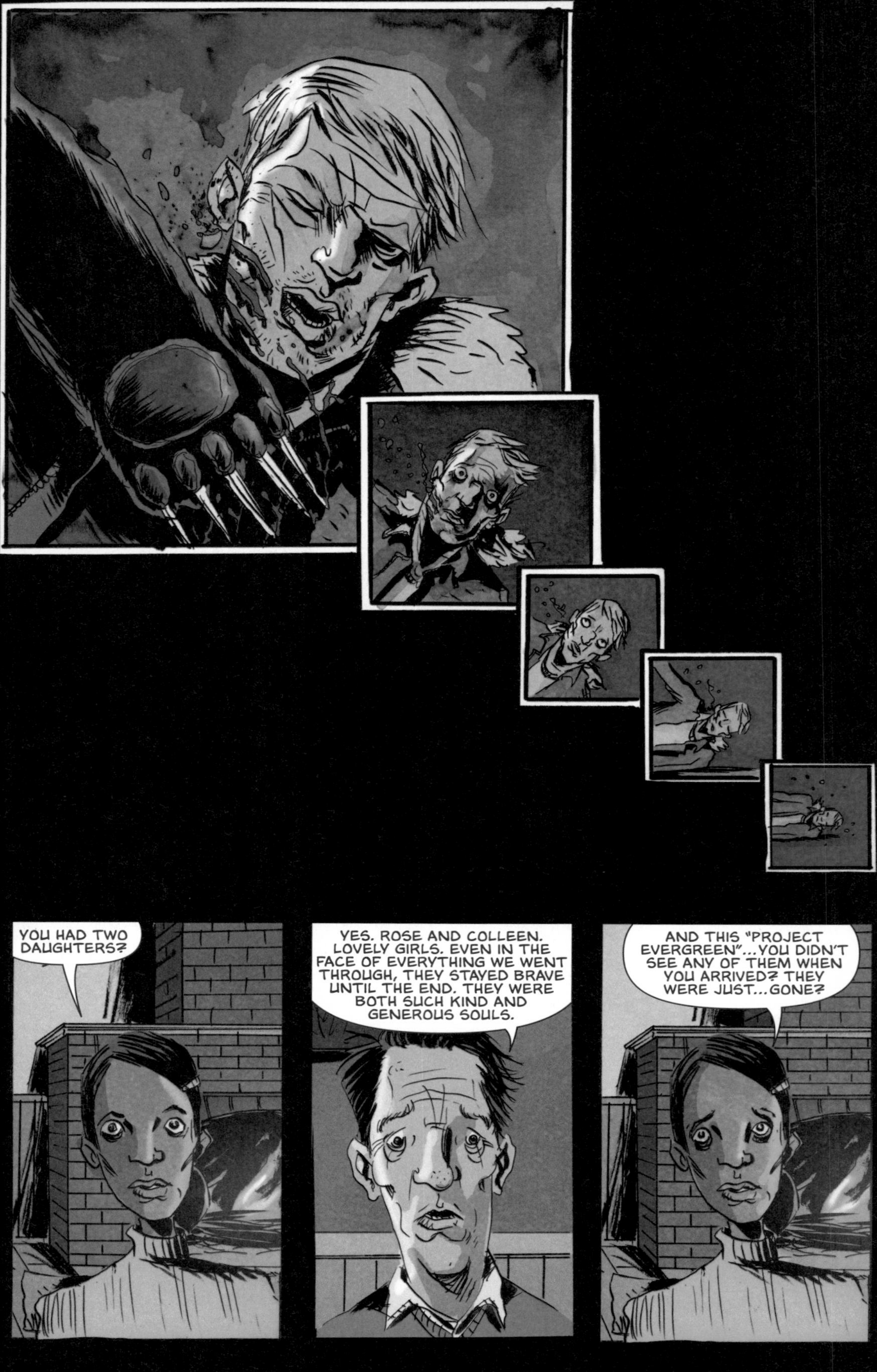
YOU HAD TWO DAUGHTERS?
YES. ROSE AND COLLEEN. LOVELY GIRLS. EVEN IN THE FACE OF EVERYTHING WE WENT THROUGH, THEY STAYED BRAVE UNTIL THE END. THEY WERE BOTH SUCH KIND AND GENEROUS SOULS.
AND THIS "PROJECT EVERGREEN"...YOU DIDN'T SEE ANY OF THEM WHEN YOU ARRIVED? THEY WERE JUST...GONE?

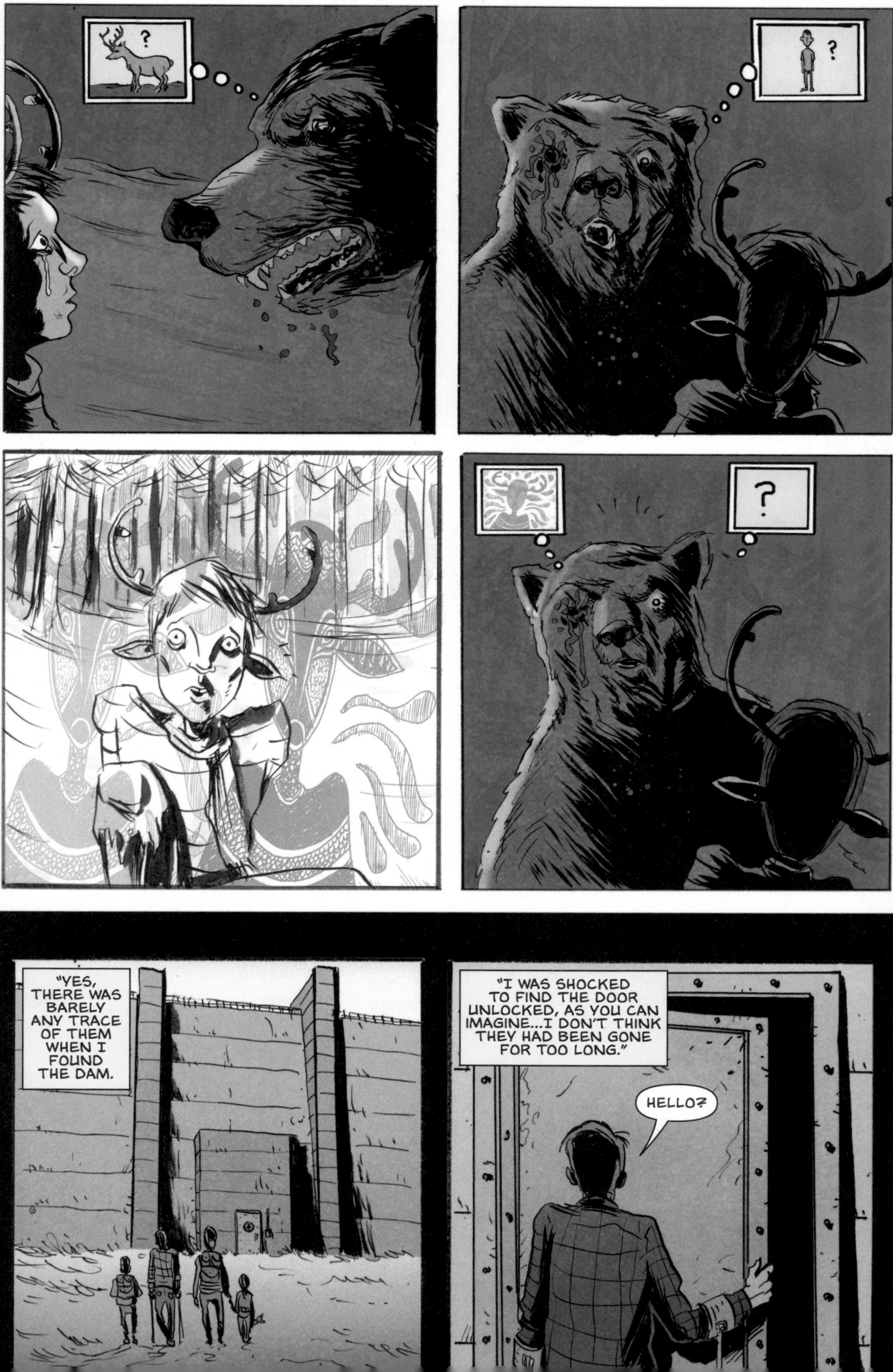
?
?
?
"YES, THERE WAS BARELY ANY TRACE OF THEM WHEN I FOUND THE DAM.
"I WAS SHOCKED TO FIND THE DOOR UNLOCKED, AS YOU CAN IMAGINE...I DON'T THINK THEY HAD BEEN GONE FOR TOO LONG."
HELLO?

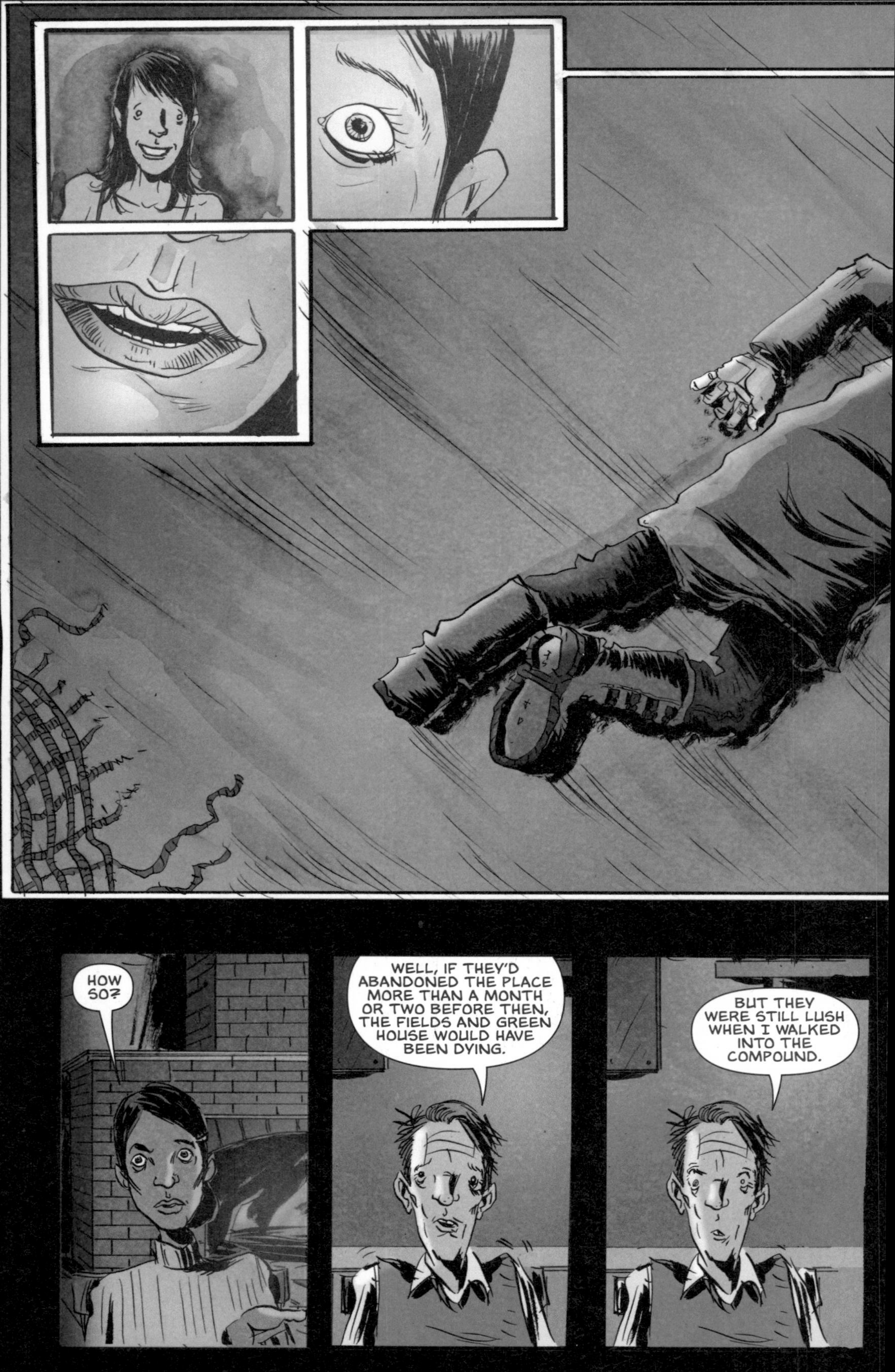
HOW SO?
WELL, IF THEY'D ABANDONED THE PLACE MORE THAN A MONTH OR TWO BEFORE THEN, THE FIELDS AND GREEN HOUSE WOULD HAVE BEEN DYING.
BUT THEY WERE STILL LUSH WHEN I WALKED INTO THE COMPOUND.

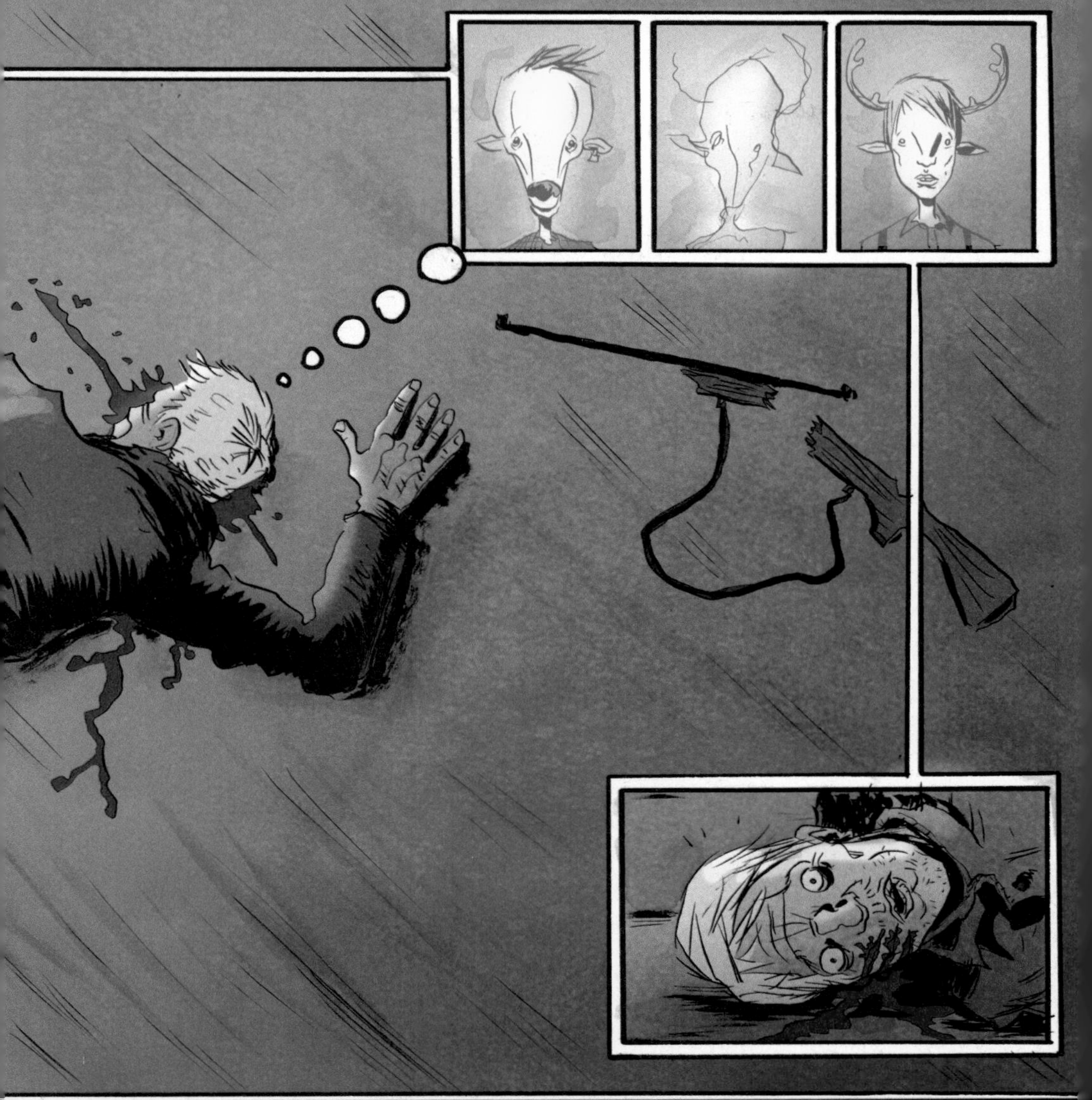
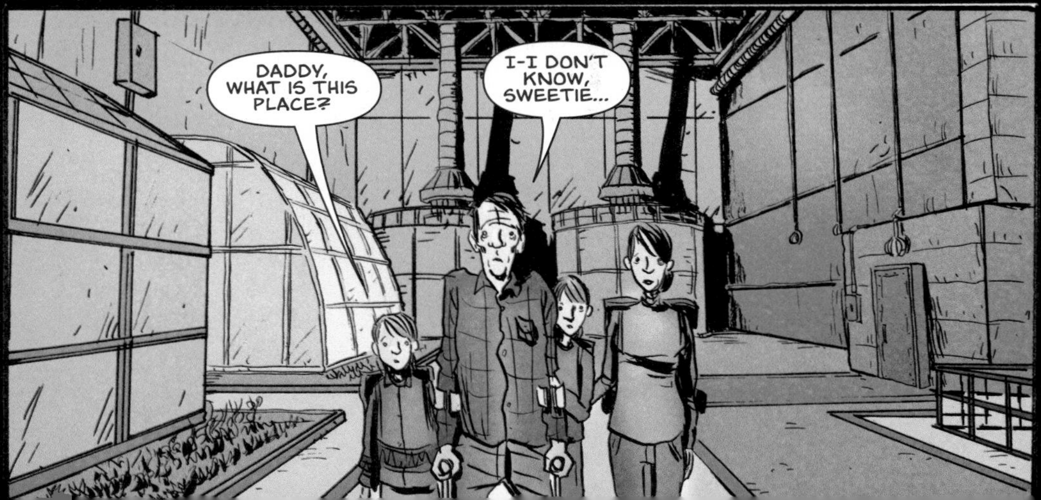
DADDY, WHAT IS THIS PLACE?
I-I DON'T KNOW, SWEETIE...

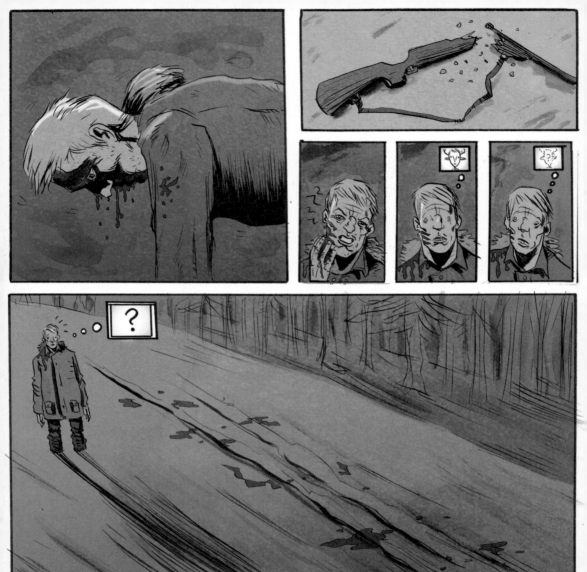

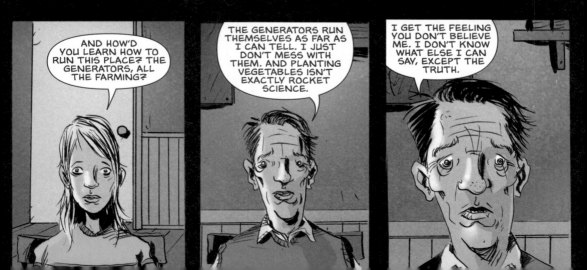

AND HOW'D YOU LEARN HOW TO RUN THIS PLACE? THE GENERATORS, ALL THE FARMING?

THE GENERATORS RUN THEMSELVES AS FAR AS I CAN TELL. I JUST DON'T MESS WITH THEM. AND PLANTING VEGETABLES ISN'T EXACTLY ROCKET SCIENCE.

I GET THE FEELING YOU DON'T BELIEVE ME. I DON'T KNOW WHAT ELSE I CAN SAY, EXCEPT THE TRUTH.

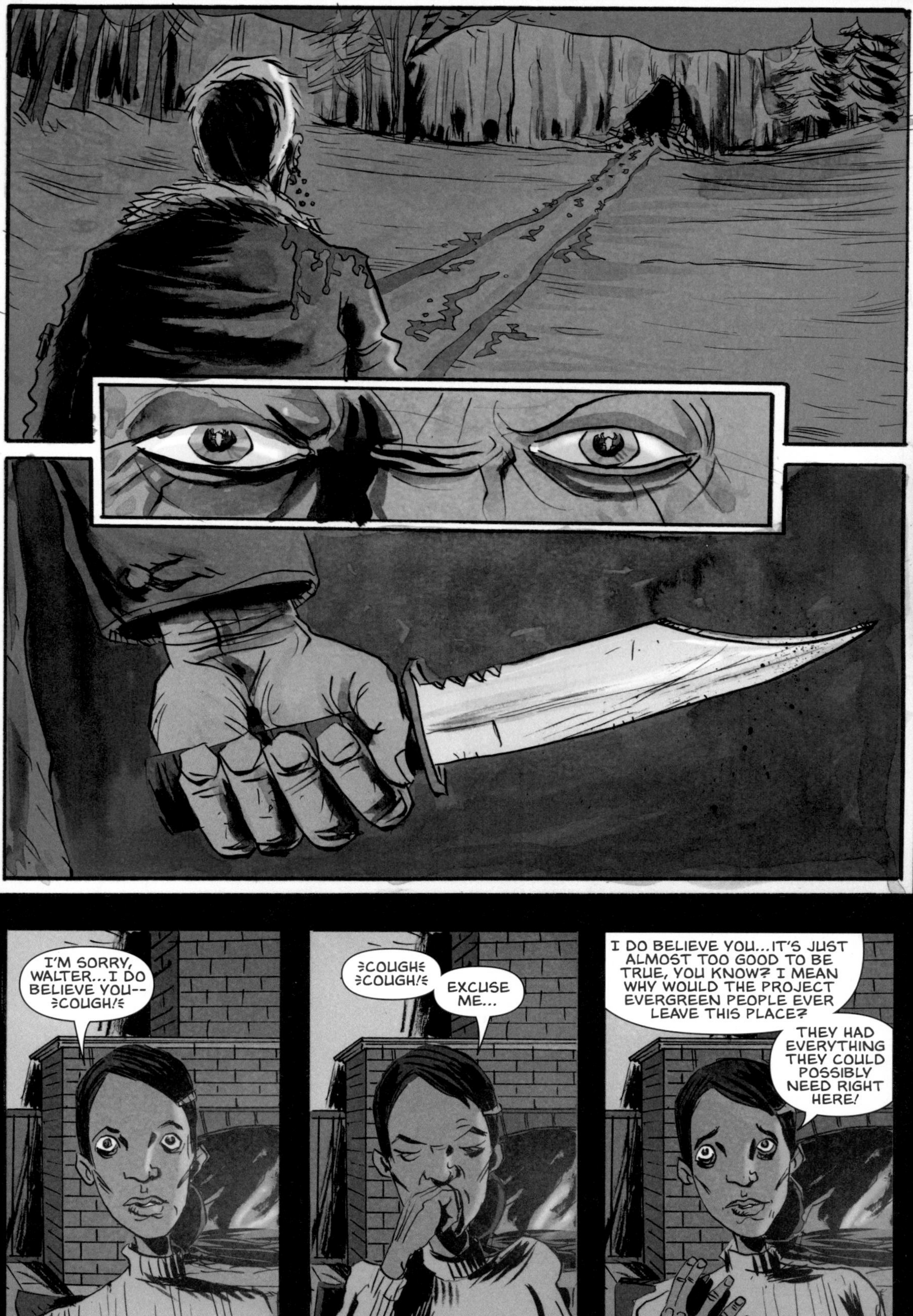
I'M SORRY, WALTER... I DO BELIEVE YOU-- ≶COUGH!≶
≶COUGH≶ ≶COUGH!≶
EXCUSE ME...
I DO BELIEVE YOU...IT'S JUST ALMOST TOO GOOD TO BE TRUE, YOU KNOW? I MEAN WHY WOULD THE PROJECT EVERGREEN PEOPLE EVER LEAVE THIS PLACE?
THEY HAD EVERYTHING THEY COULD POSSIBLY NEED RIGHT HERE!

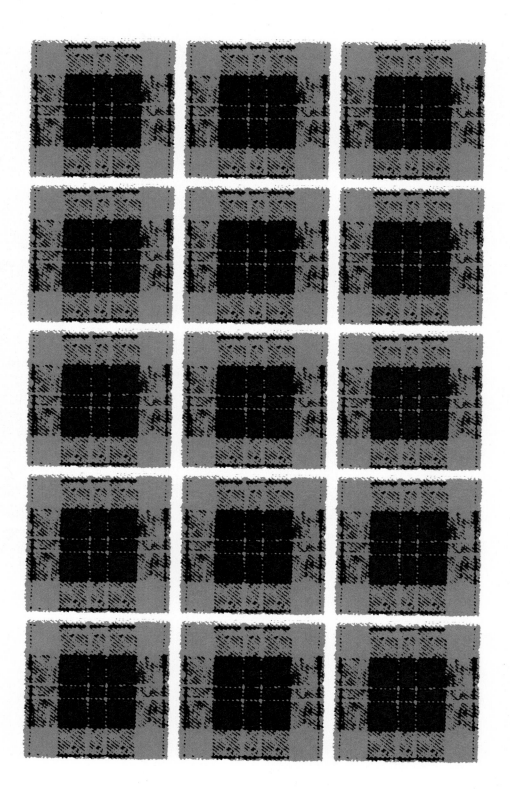

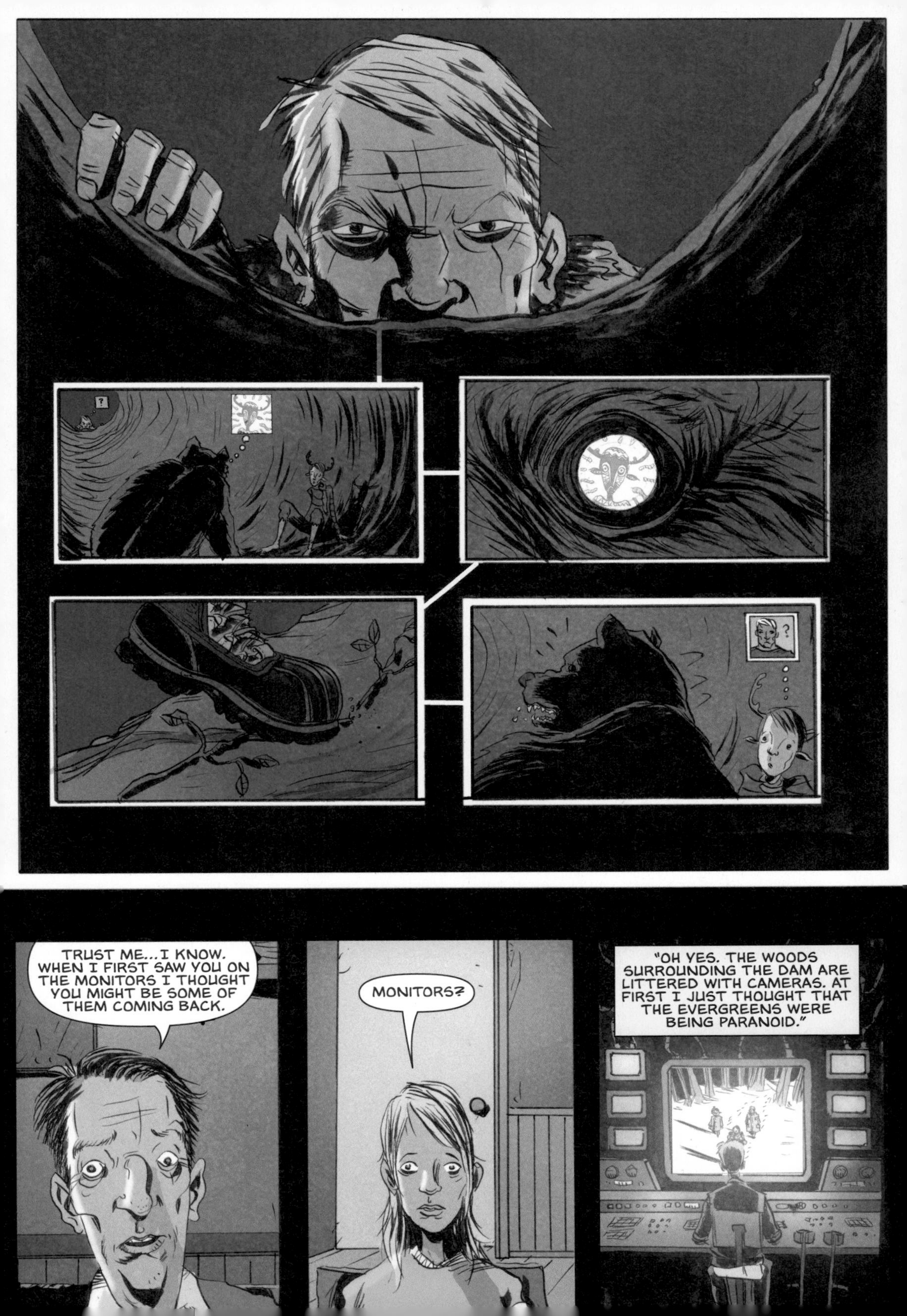
?
?
TRUST ME... I KNOW. WHEN I FIRST SAW YOU ON THE MONITORS I THOUGHT YOU MIGHT BE SOME OF THEM COMING BACK.
MONITORS?
"OH YES. THE WOODS SURROUNDING THE DAM ARE LITTERED WITH CAMERAS. AT FIRST I JUST THOUGHT THAT THE EVERGREENS WERE BEING PARANOID."

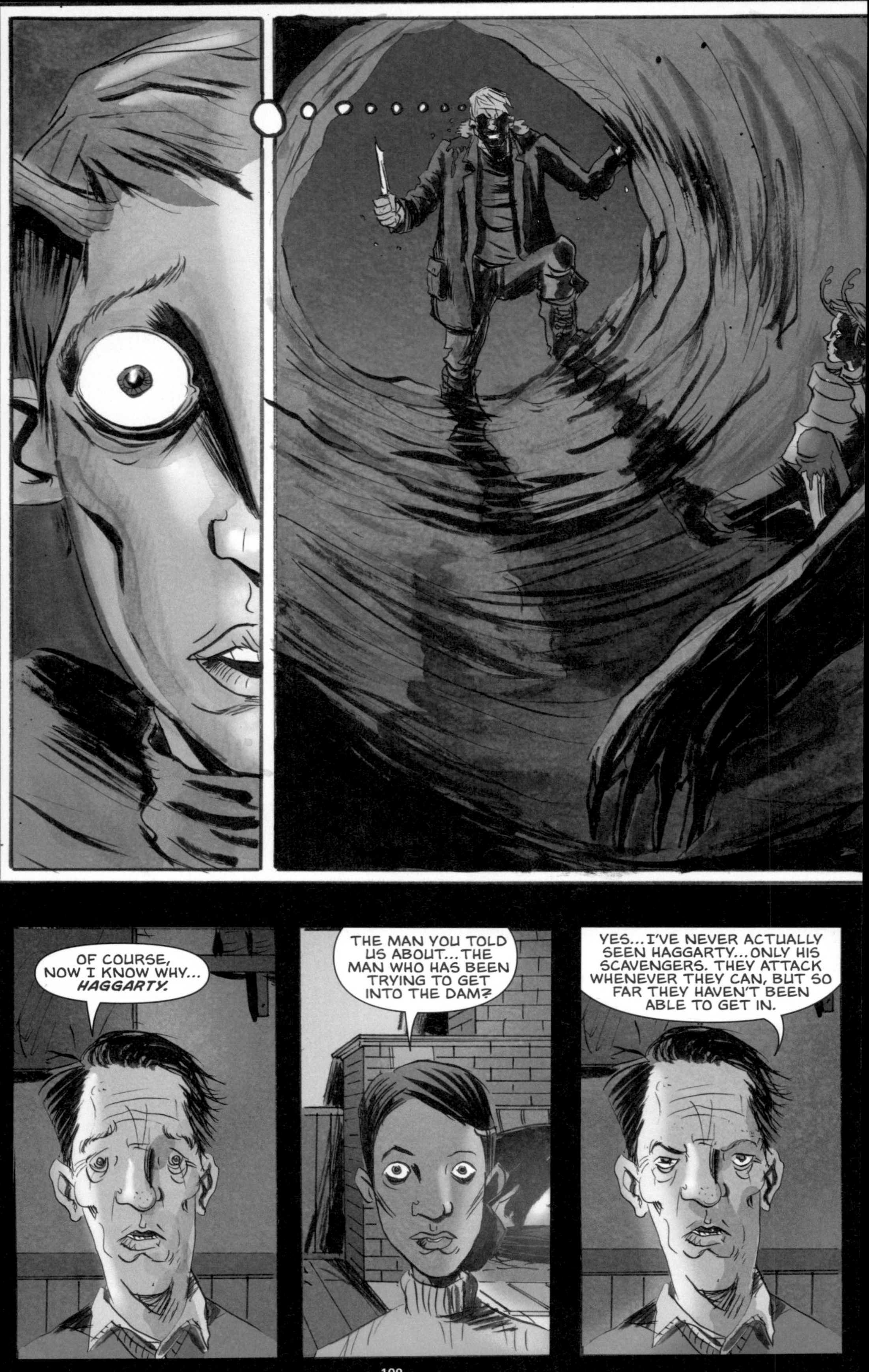
OF COURSE, NOW I KNOW WHY... HAGGARTY.
THE MAN YOU TOLD US ABOUT... THE MAN WHO HAS BEEN TRYING TO GET INTO THE DAM?
YES... I'VE NEVER ACTUALLY SEEN HAGGARTY... ONLY HIS SCAVENGERS. THEY ATTACK WHENEVER THEY CAN, BUT SO FAR THEY HAVEN'T BEEN ABLE TO GET IN.

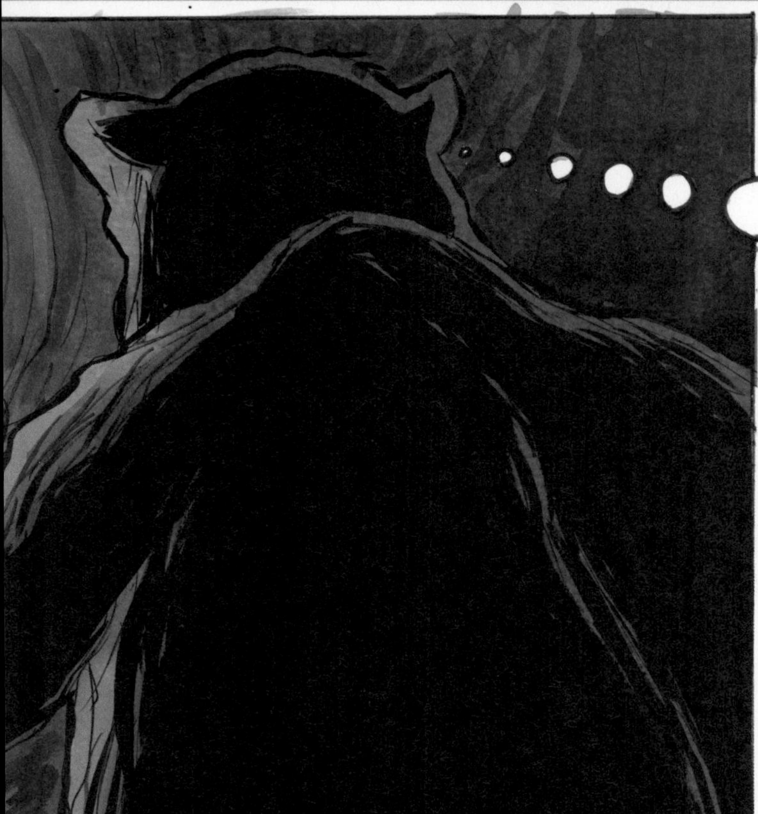

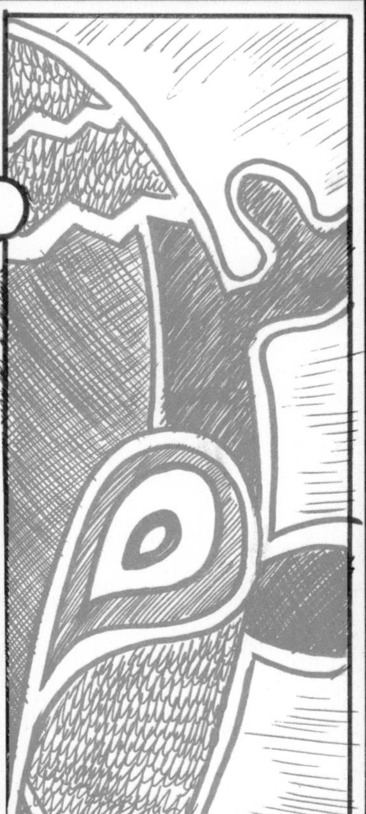

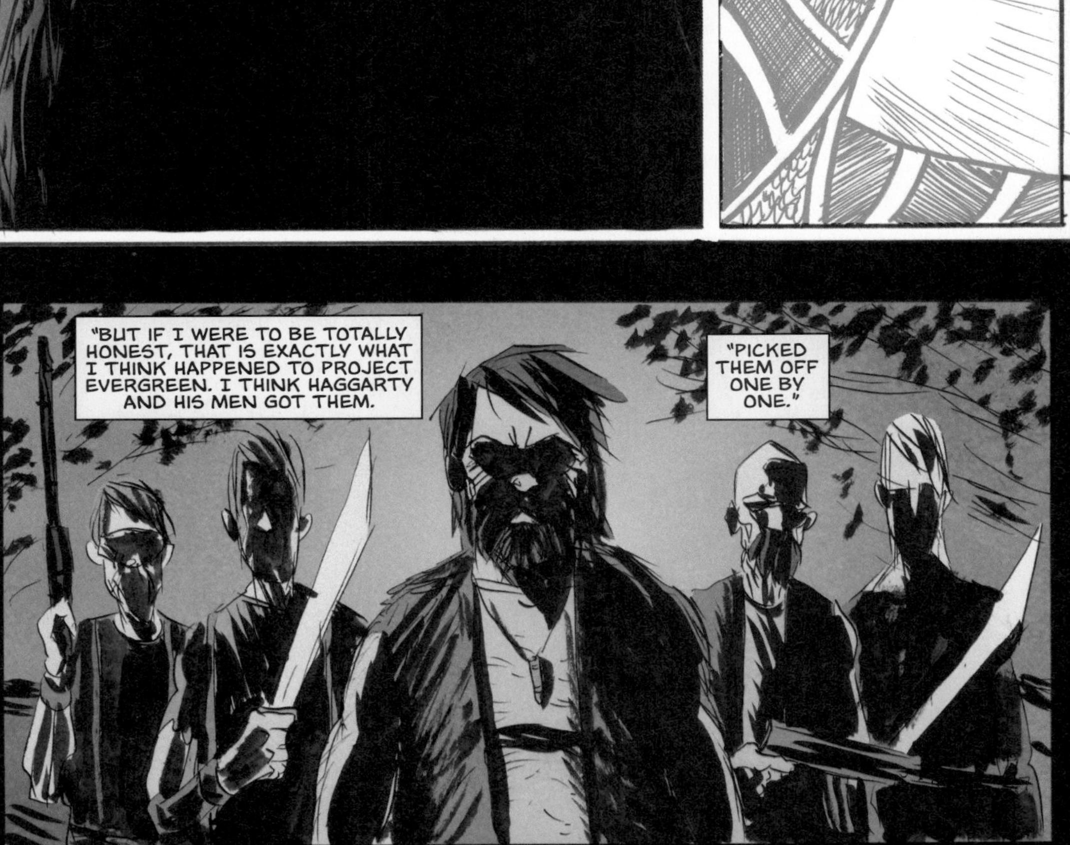
"BUT IF I WERE TO BE TOTALLY HONEST, THAT IS EXACTLY WHAT I THINK HAPPENED TO PROJECT EVERGREEN. I THINK HAGGARTY AND HIS MEN GOT THEM.
"PICKED THEM OFF ONE BY ONE."

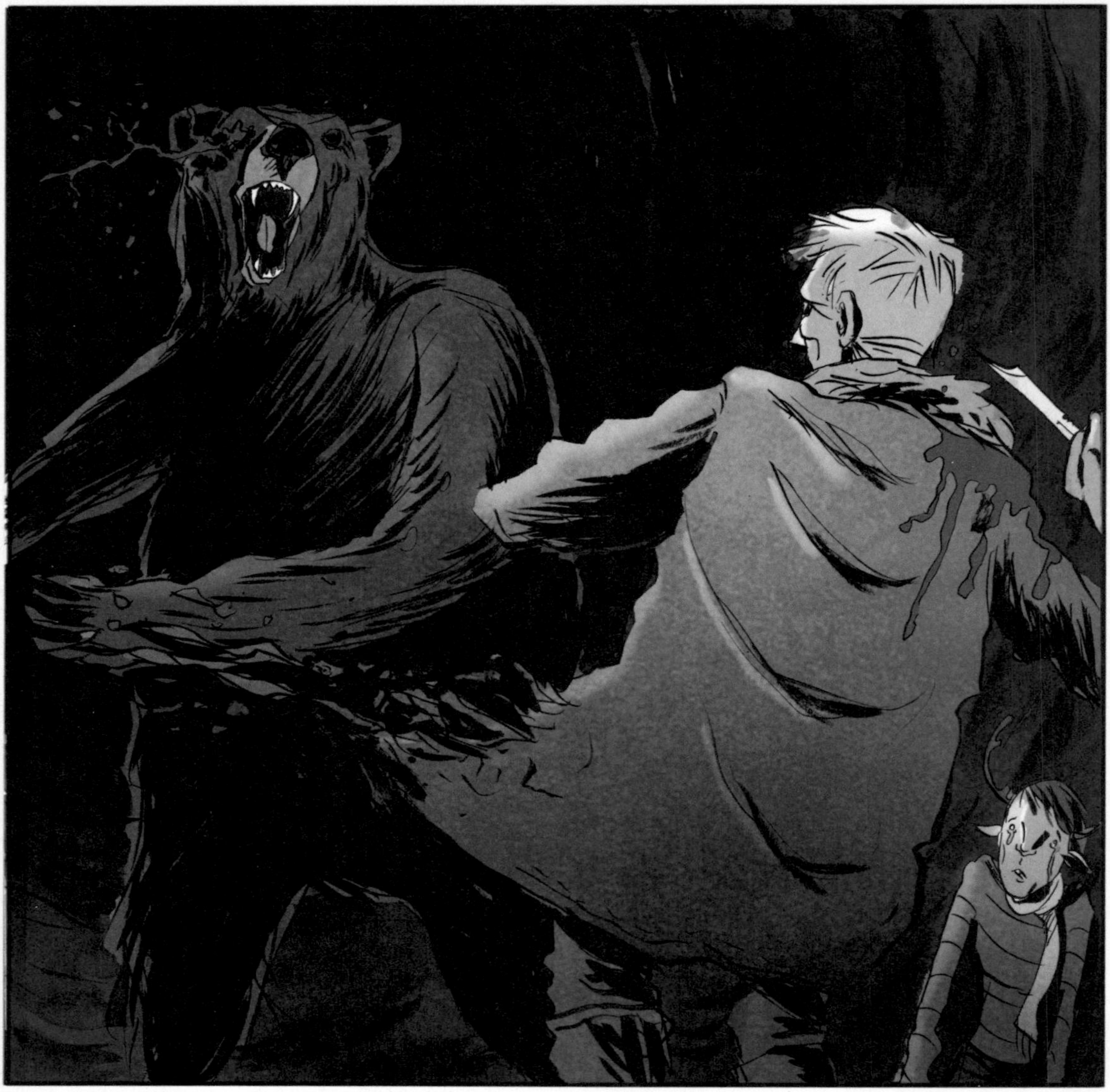

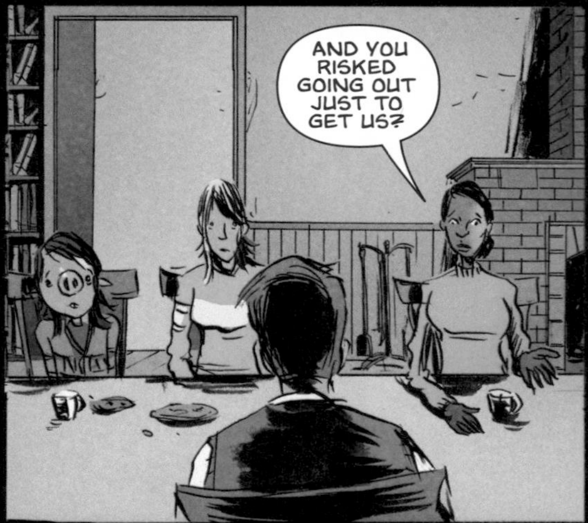
AND YOU RISKED GOING OUT JUST TO GET US?

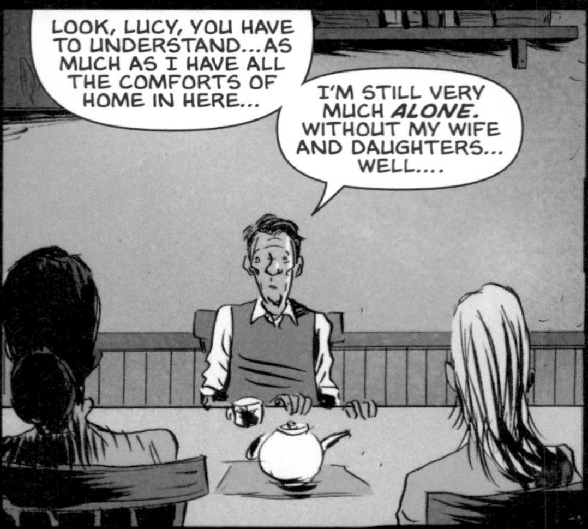
LOOK, LUCY, YOU HAVE TO UNDERSTAND...AS MUCH AS I HAVE ALL THE COMFORTS OF HOME IN HERE...
I'M STILL VERY MUCH *ALONE.* WITHOUT MY WIFE AND DAUGHTERS... WELL....

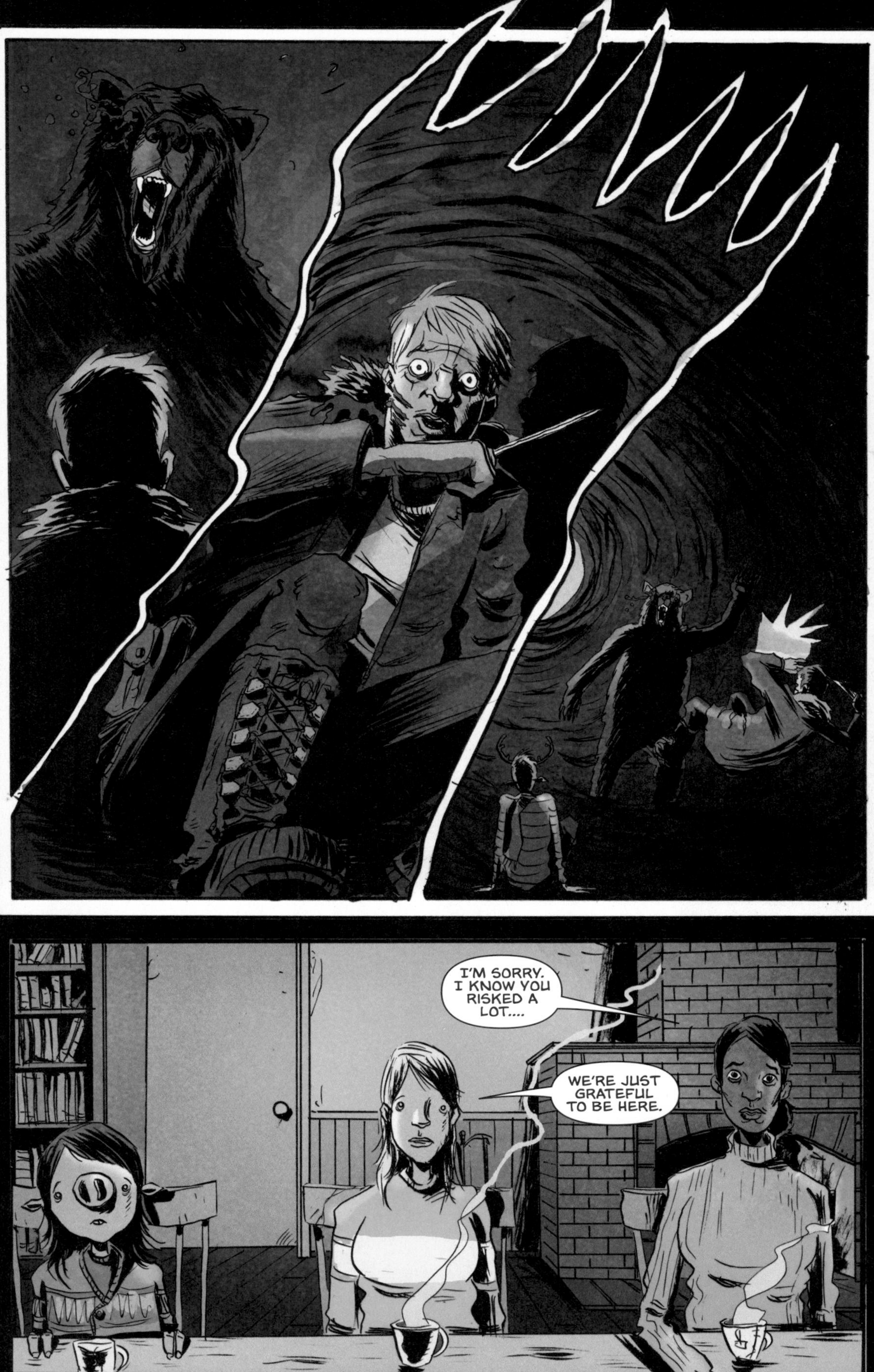
I'M SORRY. I KNOW YOU RISKED A LOT....
WE'RE JUST GRATEFUL TO BE HERE.

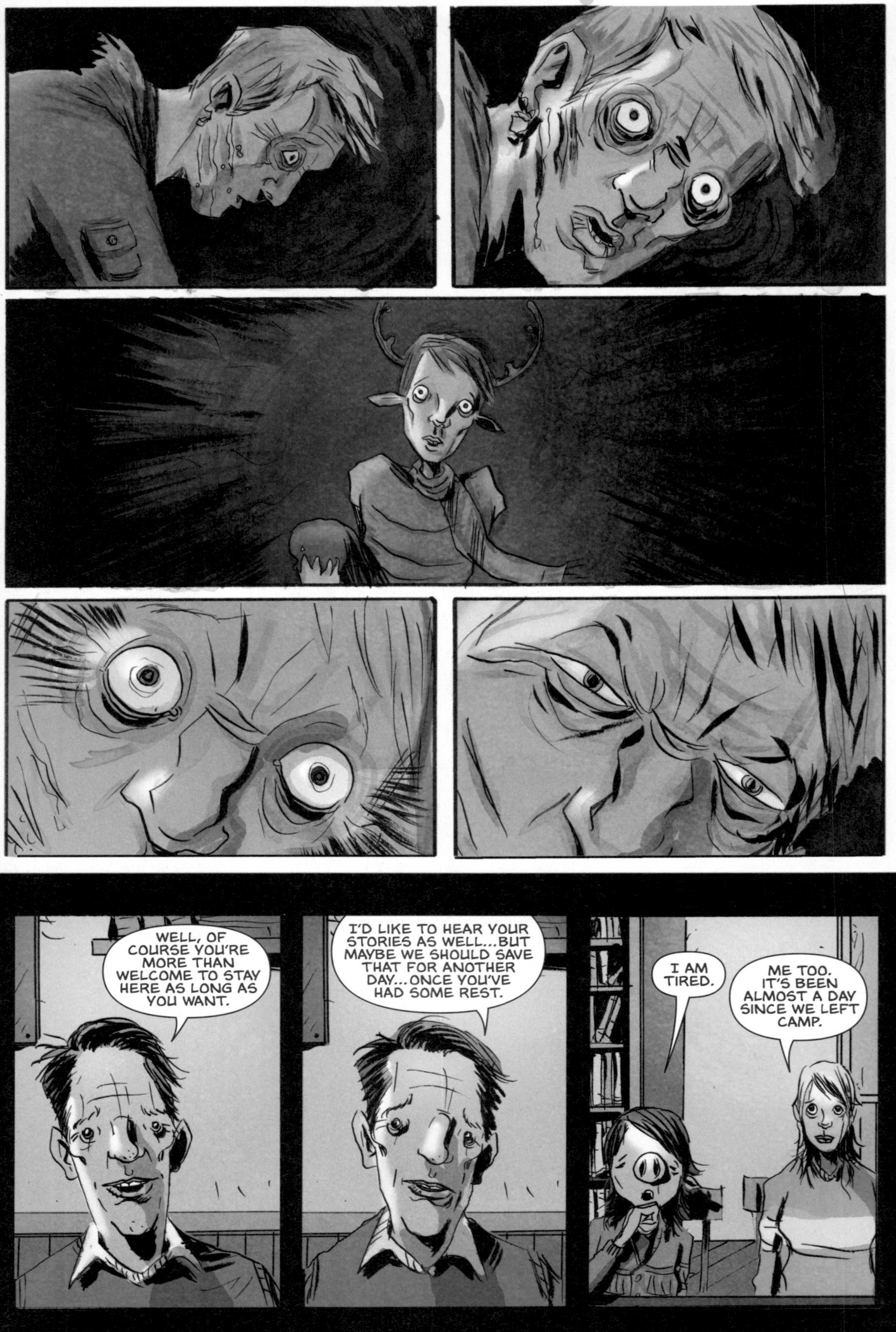
WELL, OF COURSE YOU'RE MORE THAN WELCOME TO STAY HERE AS LONG AS YOU WANT.
I'D LIKE TO HEAR YOUR STORIES AS WELL...BUT MAYBE WE SHOULD SAVE THAT FOR ANOTHER DAY...ONCE YOU'VE HAD SOME REST.
I AM TIRED.
ME TOO. IT'S BEEN ALMOST A DAY SINCE WE LEFT CAMP.

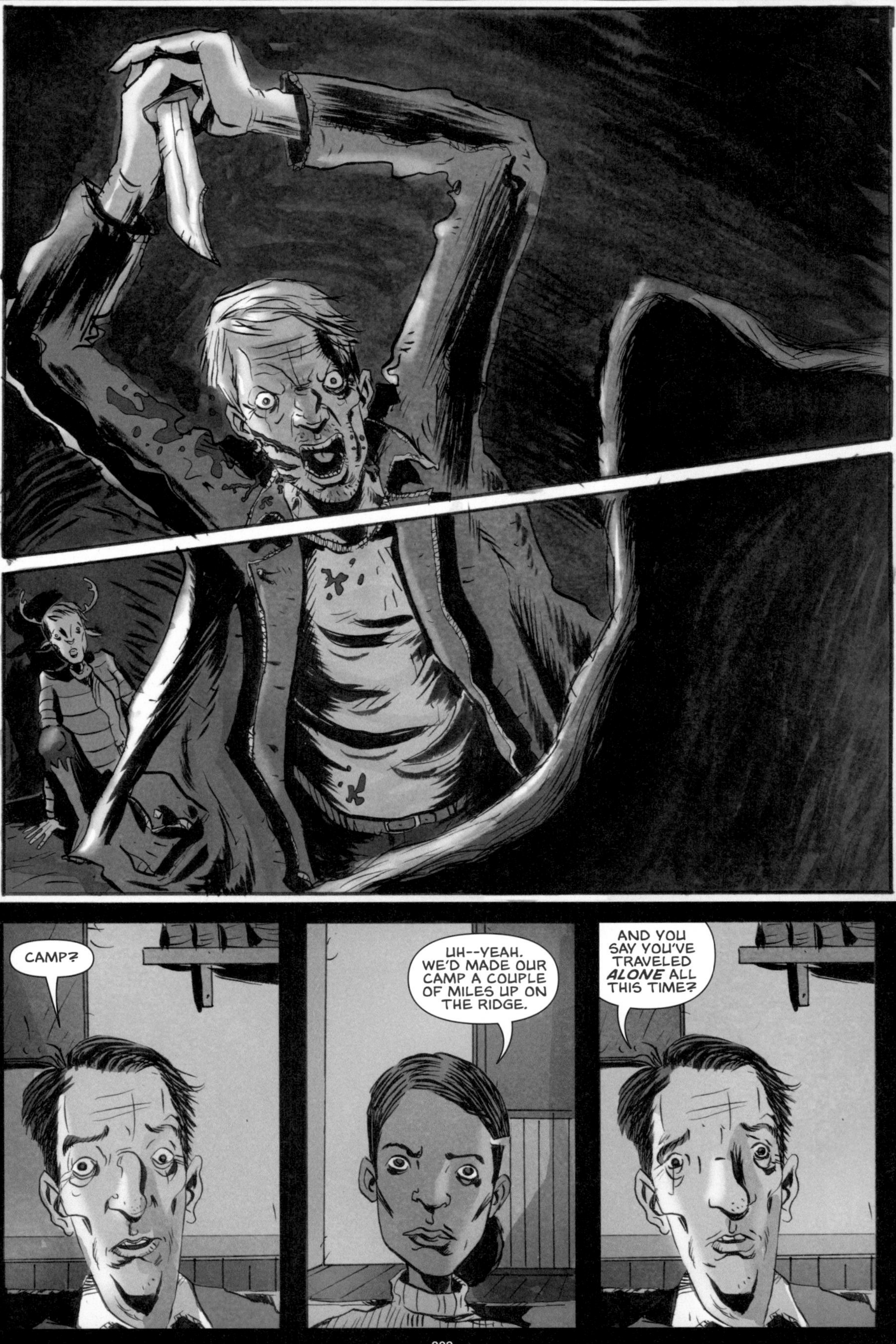
CAMP?
UH--YEAH. WE'D MADE OUR CAMP A COUPLE OF MILES UP ON THE RIDGE.
AND YOU SAY YOU'VE TRAVELED ALONE ALL THIS TIME?

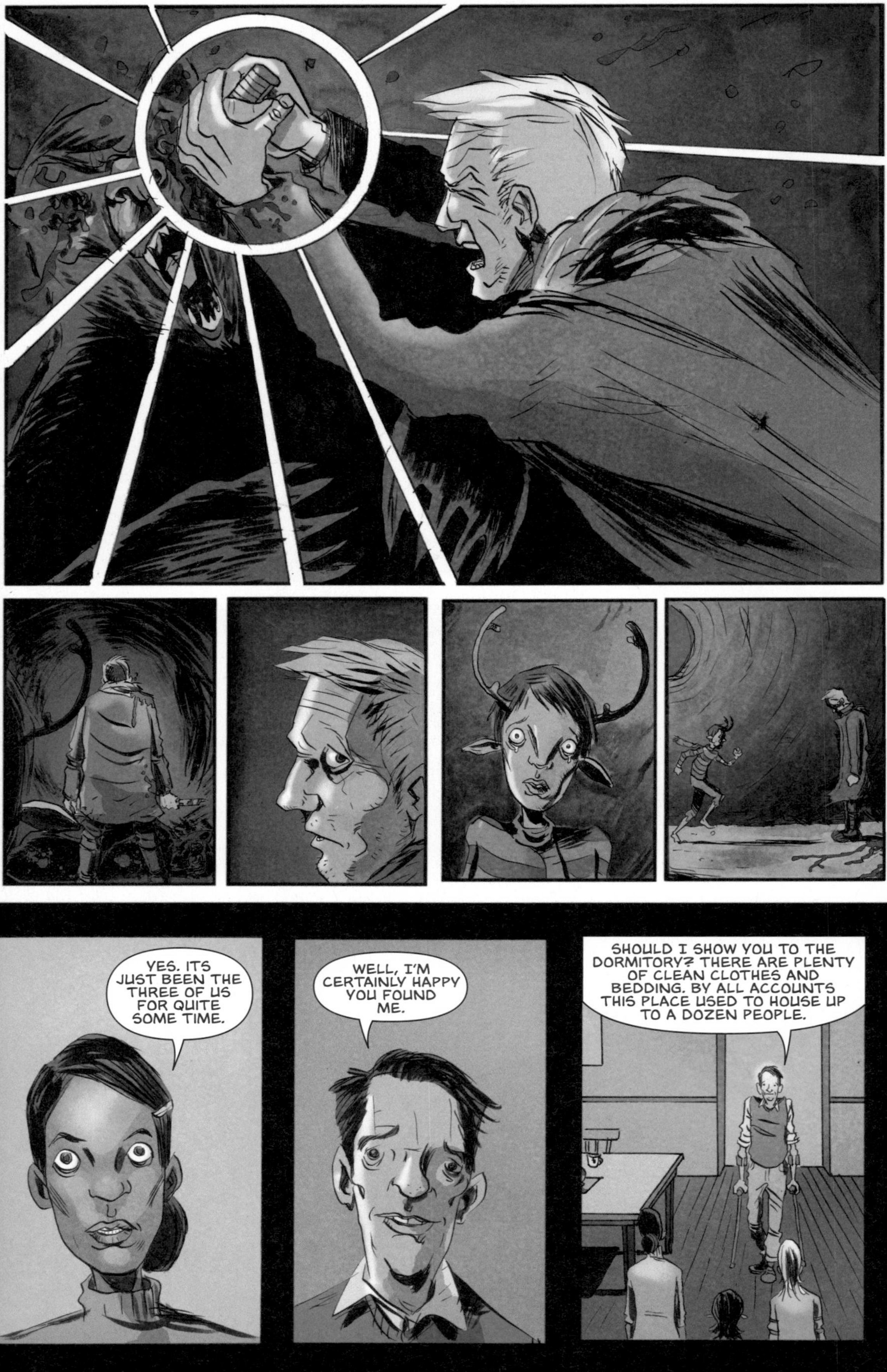
YES. ITS JUST BEEN THE THREE OF US FOR QUITE SOME TIME.
WELL, I'M CERTAINLY HAPPY YOU FOUND ME.
SHOULD I SHOW YOU TO THE DORMITORY? THERE ARE PLENTY OF CLEAN CLOTHES AND BEDDING. BY ALL ACCOUNTS THIS PLACE USED TO HOUSE UP TO A DOZEN PEOPLE.

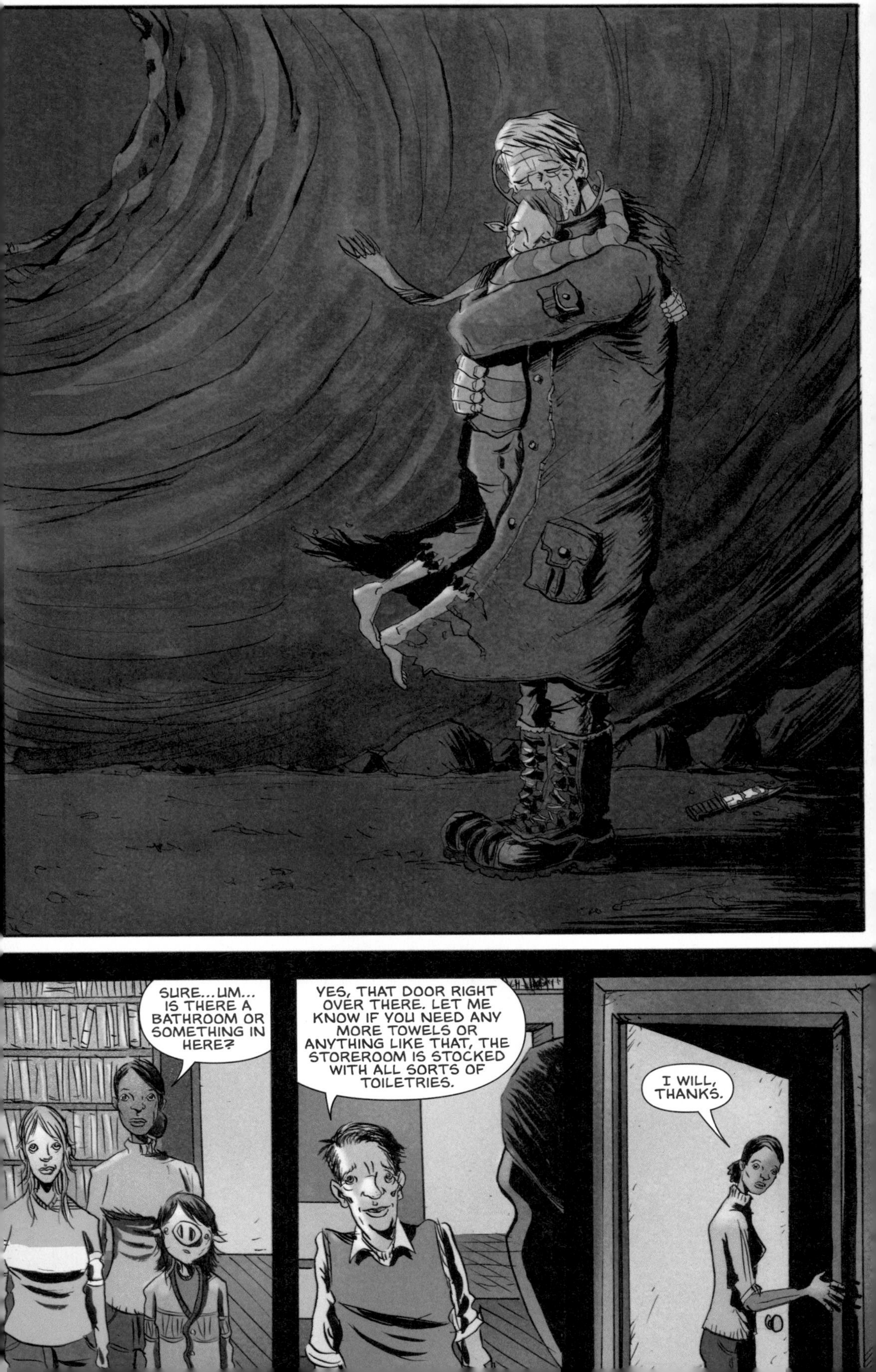

SURE... UM... IS THERE A BATHROOM OR SOMETHING IN HERE?
YES, THAT DOOR RIGHT OVER THERE. LET ME KNOW IF YOU NEED ANY MORE TOWELS OR ANYTHING LIKE THAT, THE STOREROOM IS STOCKED WITH ALL SORTS OF TOILETRIES.
I WILL, THANKS.

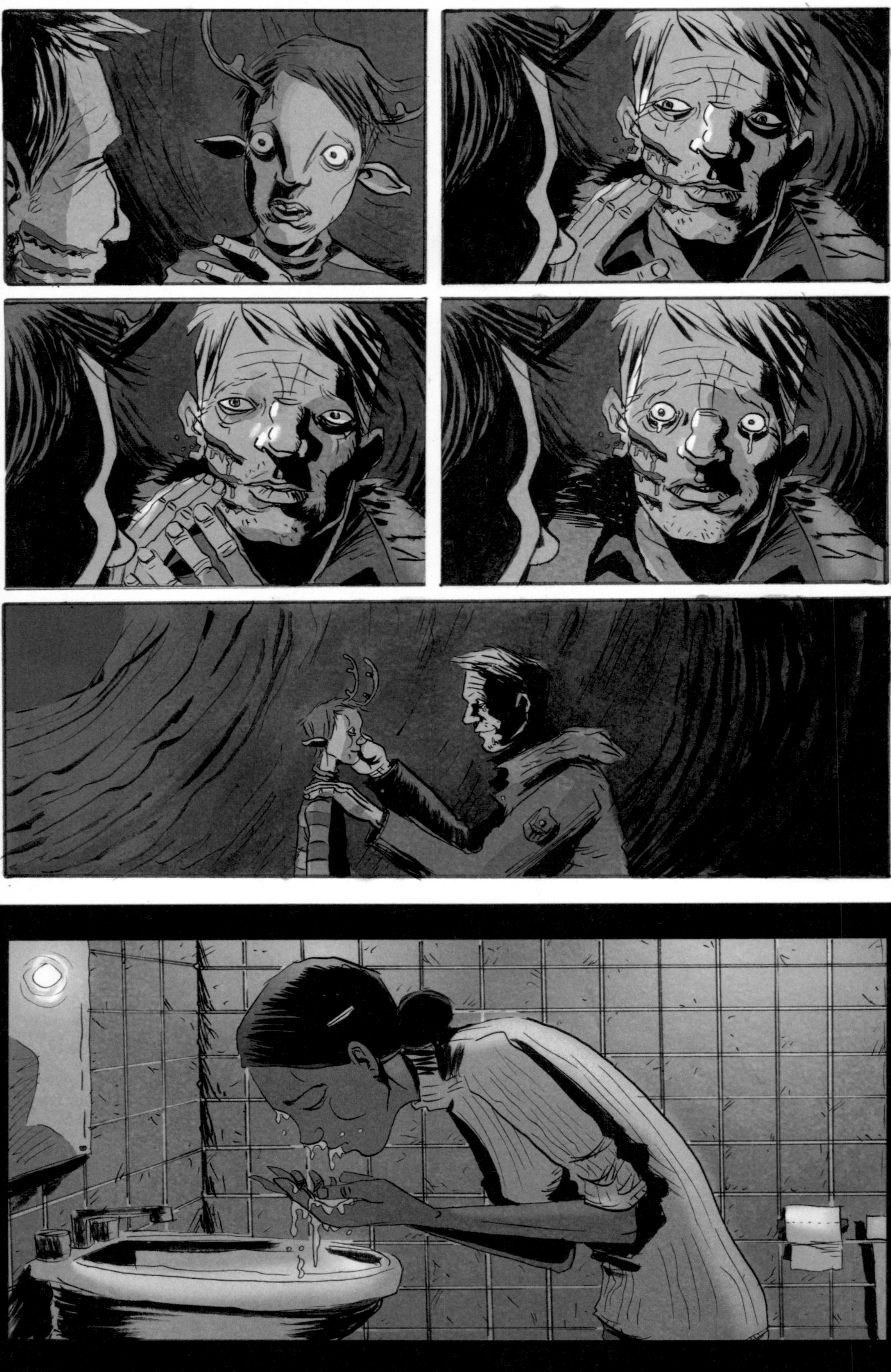

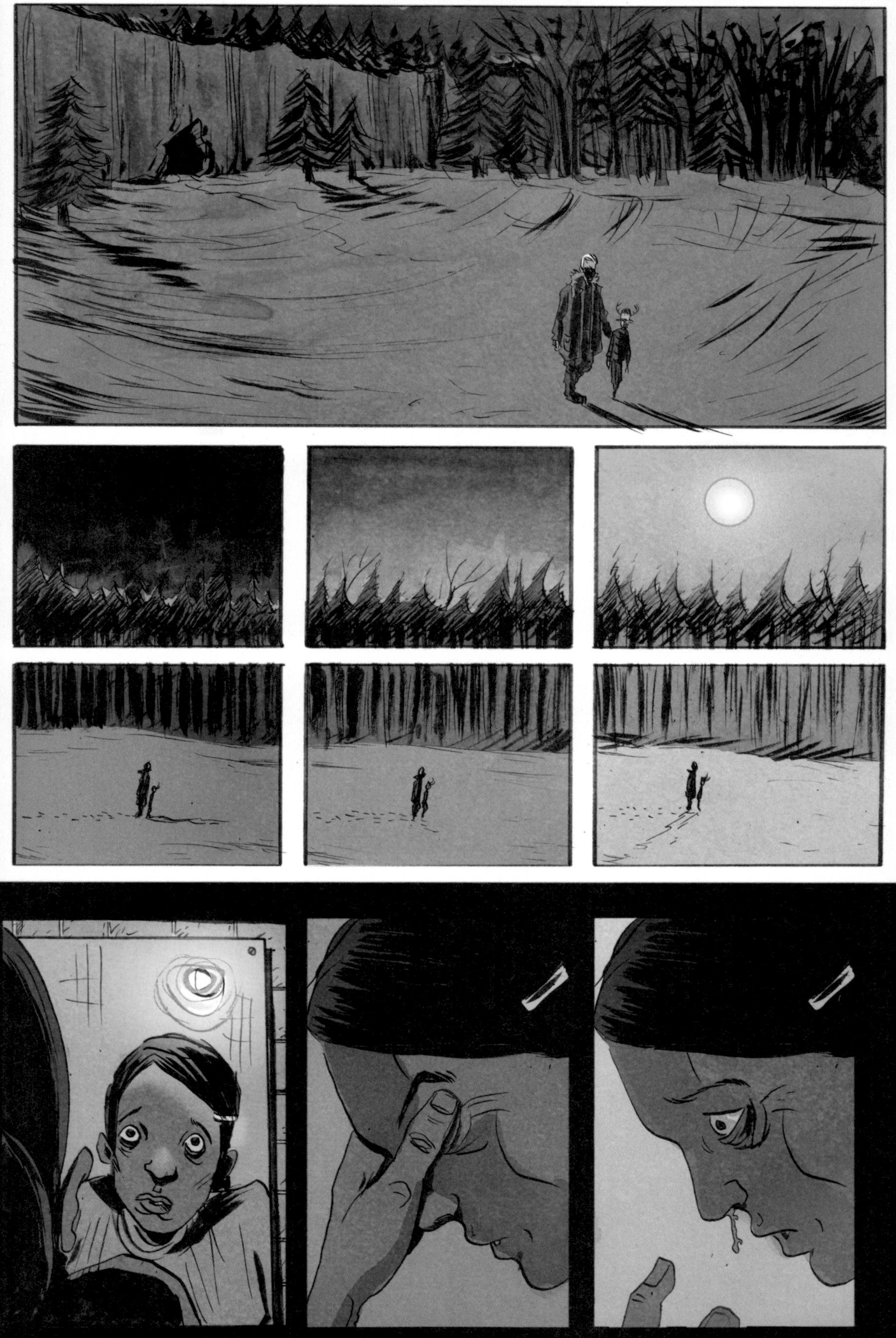

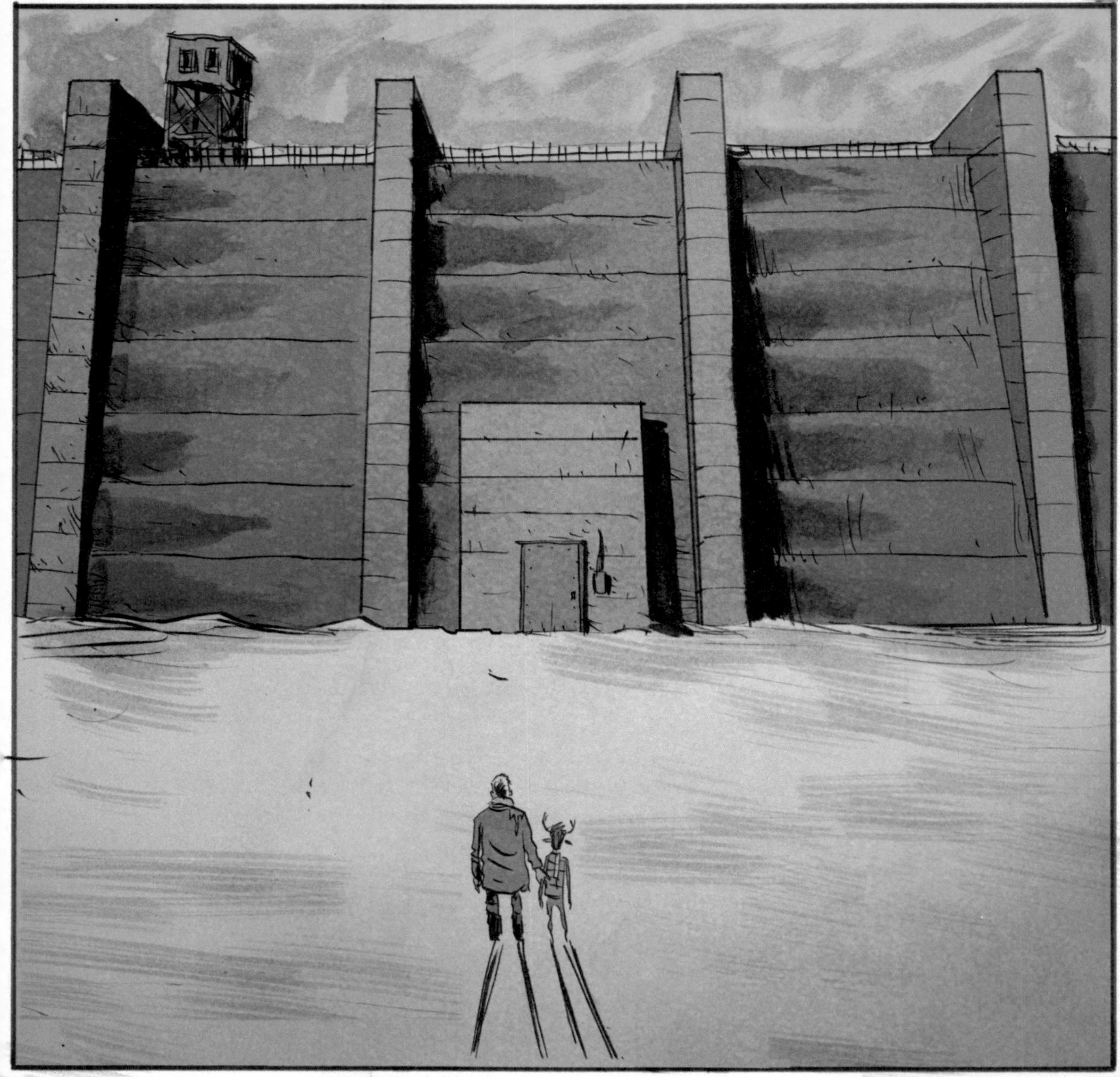

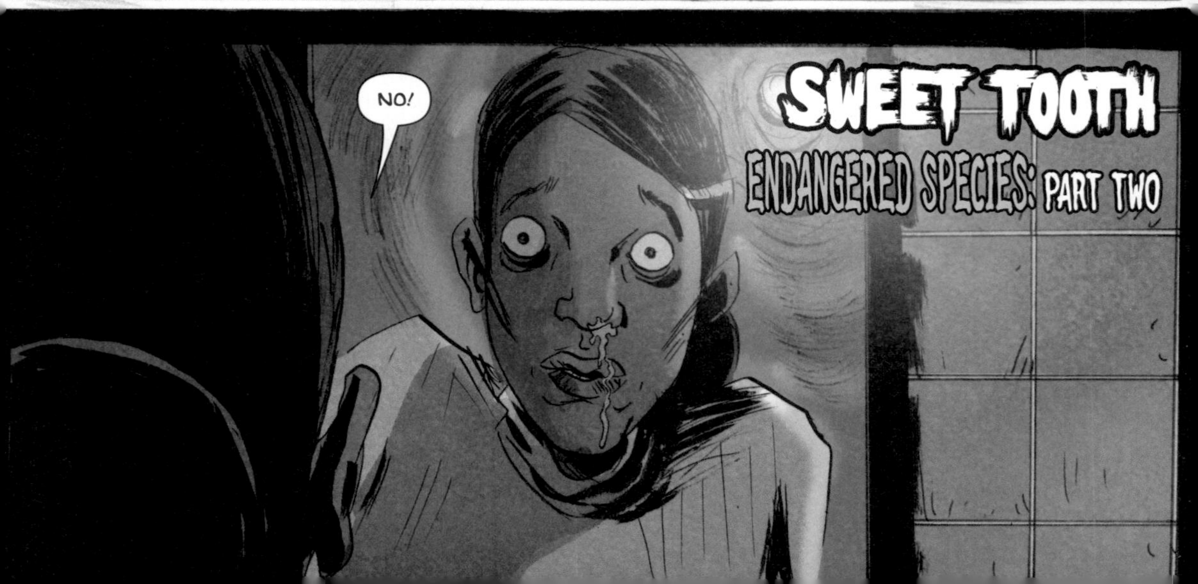
NO!
SWEET TOOTH
ENDANGERED SPECIES: PART TWO

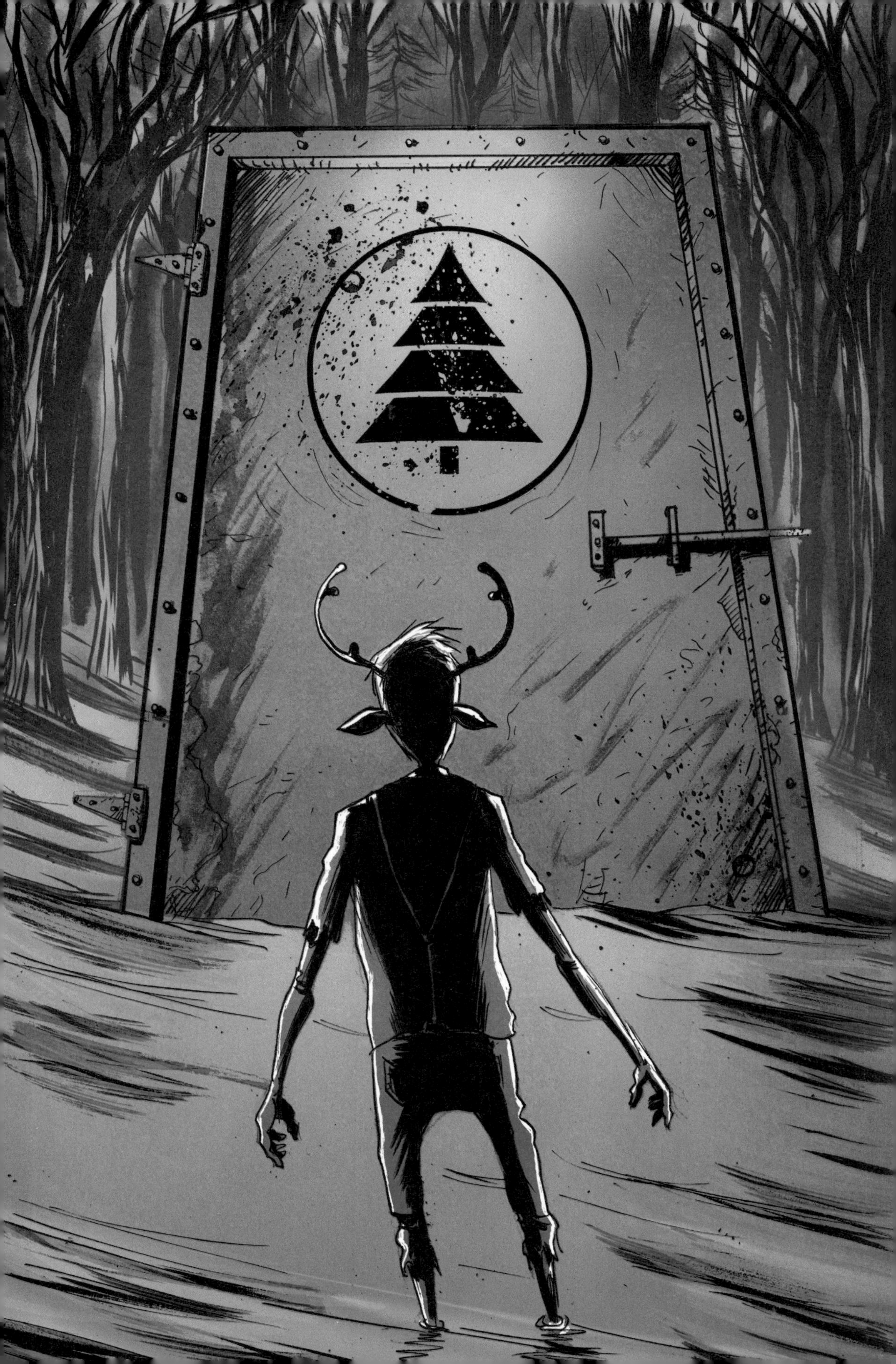

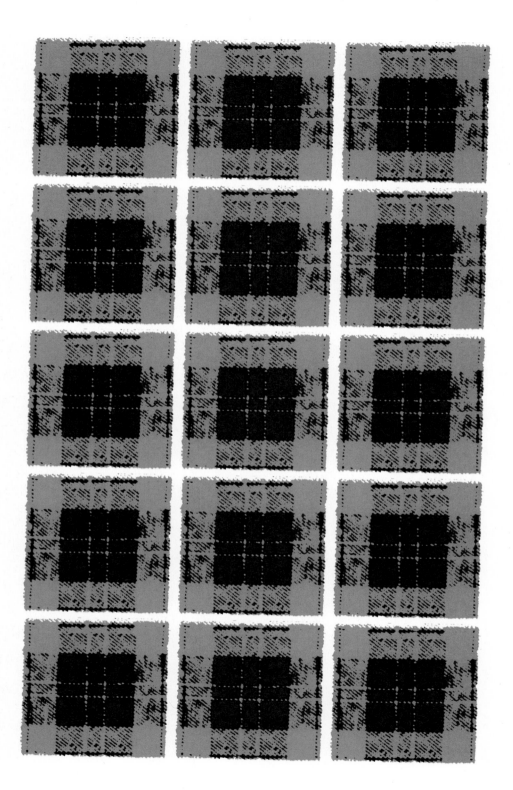

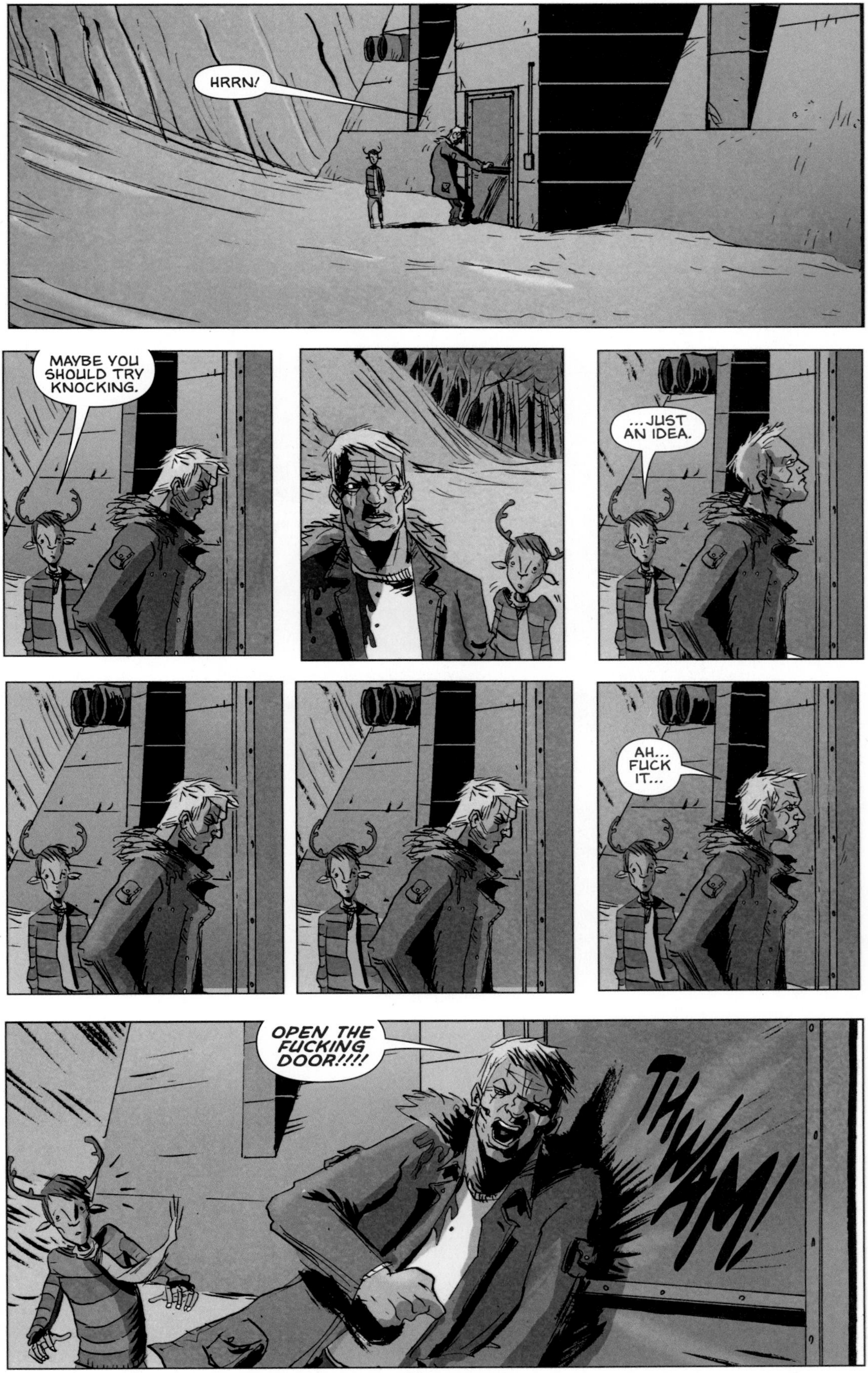
HRRN!
MAYBE YOU SHOULD TRY KNOCKING.
...JUST AN IDEA.
AH... FUCK IT...
OPEN THE FUCKING DOOR!!!!
THWAM!

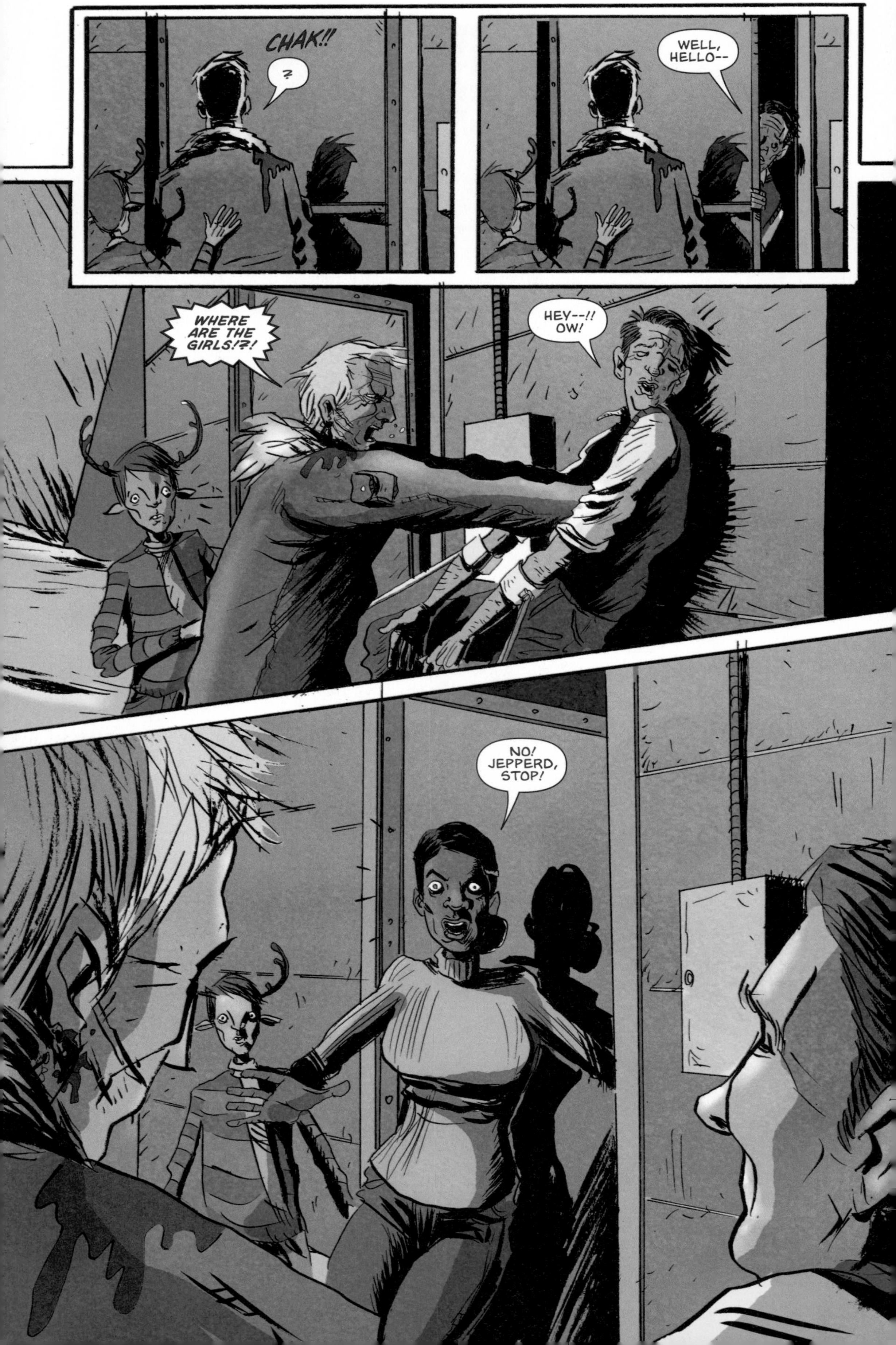
CHAK!!
?
WELL, HELLO--
WHERE ARE THE GIRLS!?!
HEY--!! OW!
NO! JEPPERD, STOP!

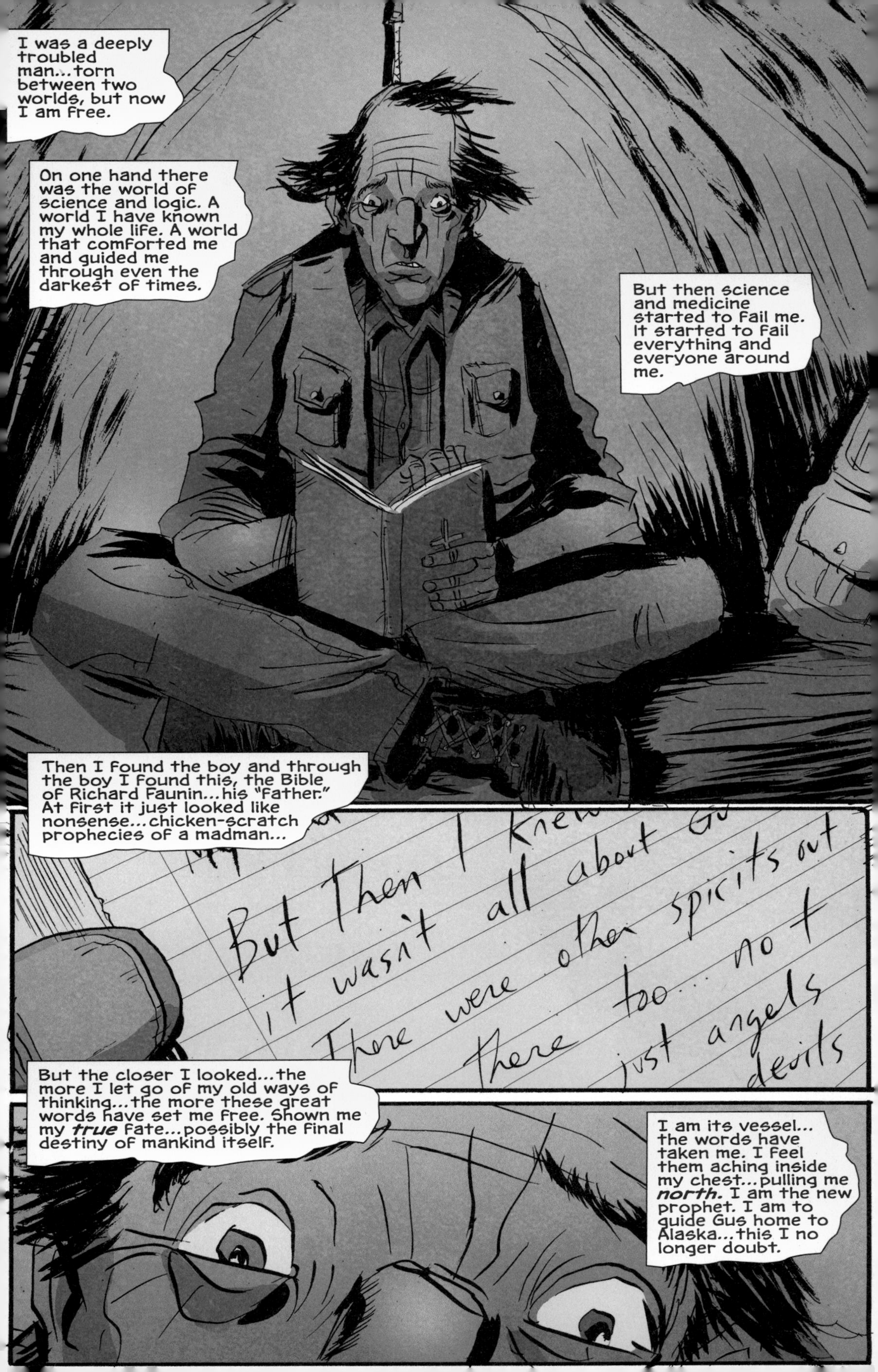

I was a deeply troubled man...torn between two worlds, but now I am free.
On one hand there was the world of science and logic. A world I have known my whole life. A world that comforted me and guided me through even the darkest of times.
But then science and medicine started to fail me. It started to fail everything and everyone around me.
Then I found the boy and through the boy I found this, the Bible of Richard Faunin...his "Father." At first it just looked like nonsense...chicken-scratch prophecies of a madman...
But Then I
it wasn't all about
There were other spirits out
There too... not
just angels
devils
But the closer I looked...the more I let go of my old ways of thinking...the more these great words have set me free. Shown me my *true* fate...possibly the final destiny of mankind itself.
I am its vessel... the words have taken me. I feel them aching inside my chest...pulling me *north*. I am the new prophet. I am to guide Gus home to Alaska...this I no longer doubt.

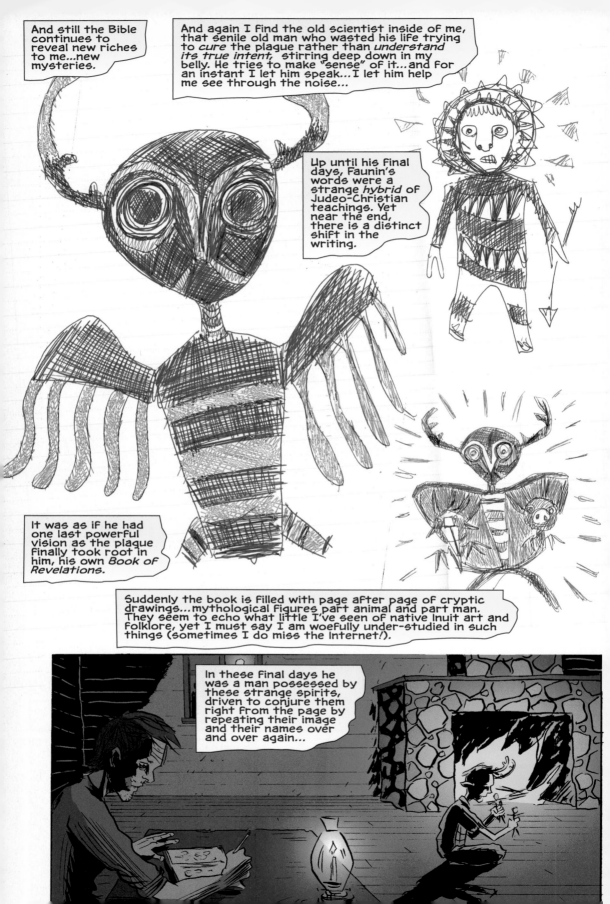

And still the Bible continues to reveal new riches to me...new mysteries.

And again I find the old scientist inside of me, that senile old man who wasted his life trying to *cure* the plague rather than *understand its true intent*, stirring deep down in my belly. He tries to make "sense" of it...and for an instant I let him speak...I let him help me see through the noise...

Up until his final days, Faunin's words were a strange *hybrid* of Judeo-Christian teachings. Yet near the end, there is a distinct shift in the writing.

It was as if he had one last powerful vision as the plague finally took root in him, his own *Book of Revelations*.

Suddenly the book is filled with page after page of cryptic drawings...mythological figures part animal and part man. They seem to echo what little I've seen of native Inuit art and folklore, yet I must say I am woefully under-studied in such things (sometimes I do miss the Internet!).

In these final days he was a man possessed by these strange spirits, driven to conjure them right from the page by repeating their image and their names over and over again...

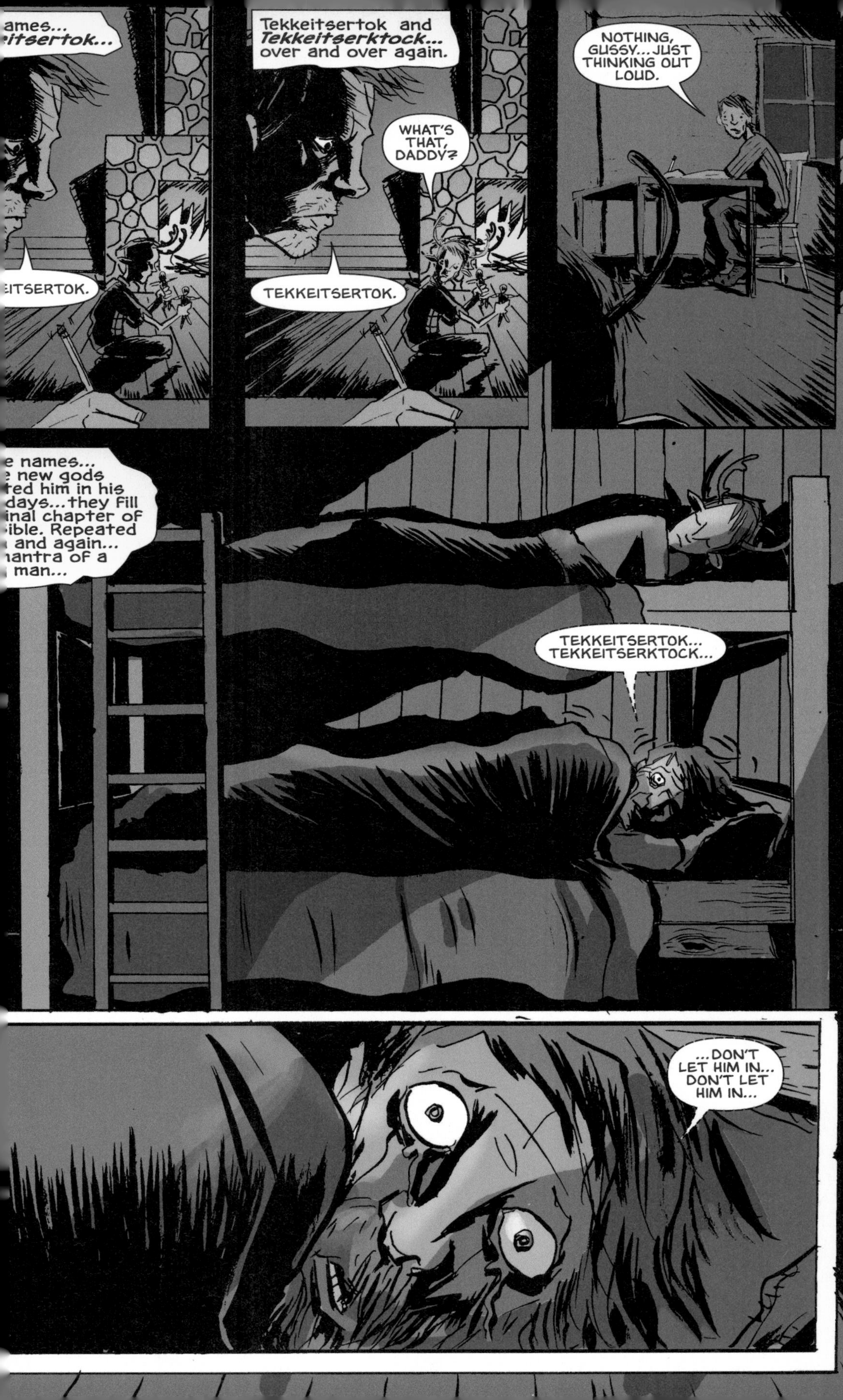
ames... itsertok...
Tekkeitsertok and Tekkeitserktock... over and over again.
EITSERTOK.
WHAT'S THAT, DADDY?
TEKKEITSERTOK.
NOTHING, GUSSY... JUST THINKING OUT LOUD.
e names... e new gods ted him in his days... they fill inal chapter of ible. Repeated and again... mantra of a man...
TEKKEITSERTOK... TEKKEITSERKTOCK...
...DON'T LET HIM IN... DON'T LET HIM IN...

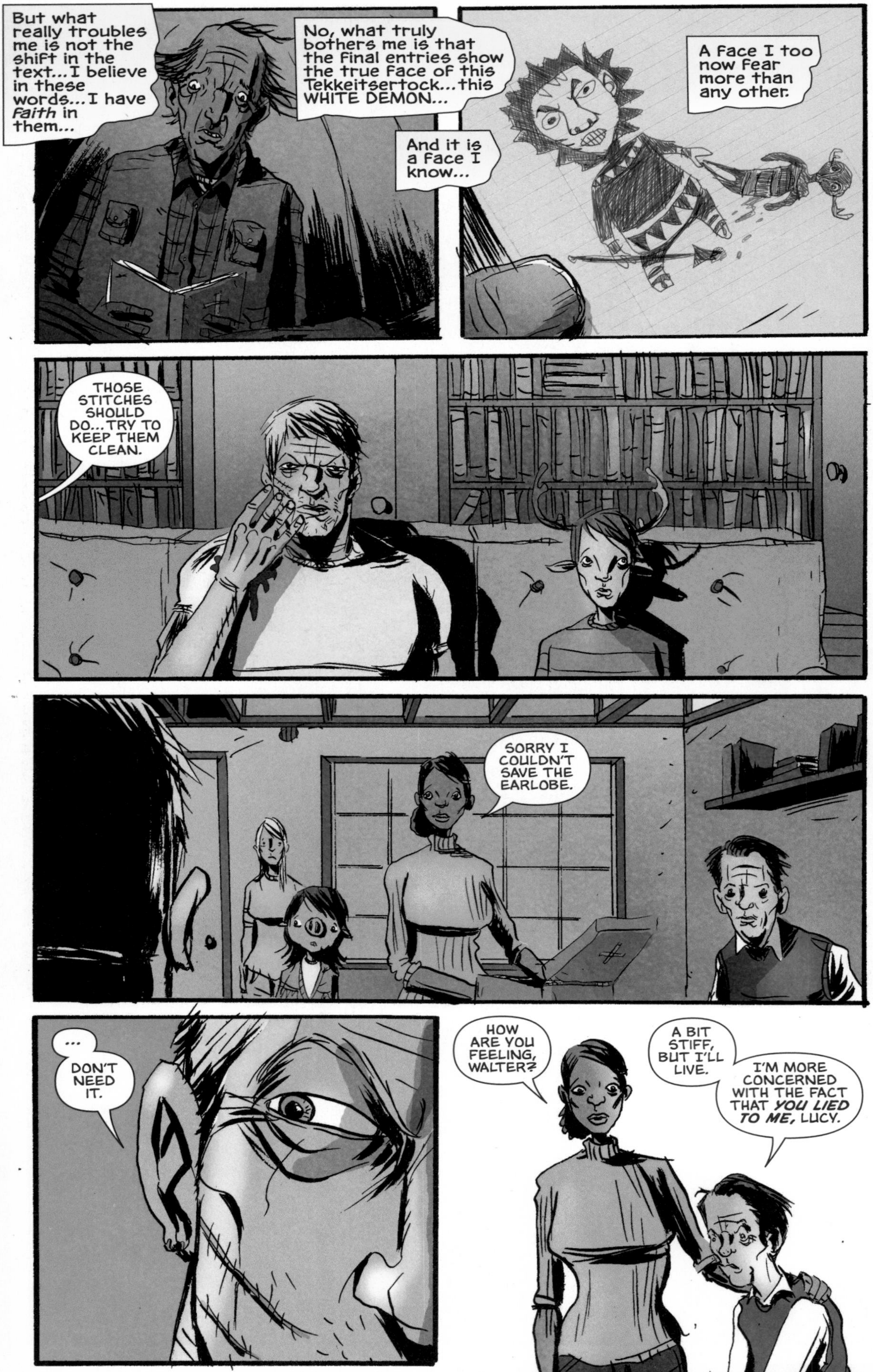
But what really troubles me is not the shift in the text... I believe in these words... I have *faith* in them...
No, what truly bothers me is that the final entries show the true face of this Tekkeitsertock... this WHITE DEMON...
And it is a face I know...
A face I too now fear more than any other.
THOSE STITCHES SHOULD DO... TRY TO KEEP THEM CLEAN.
SORRY I COULDN'T SAVE THE EARLOBE.
...
DON'T NEED IT.
HOW ARE YOU FEELING, WALTER?
A BIT STIFF, BUT I'LL LIVE.
I'M MORE CONCERNED WITH THE FACT THAT *YOU LIED TO ME,* LUCY.

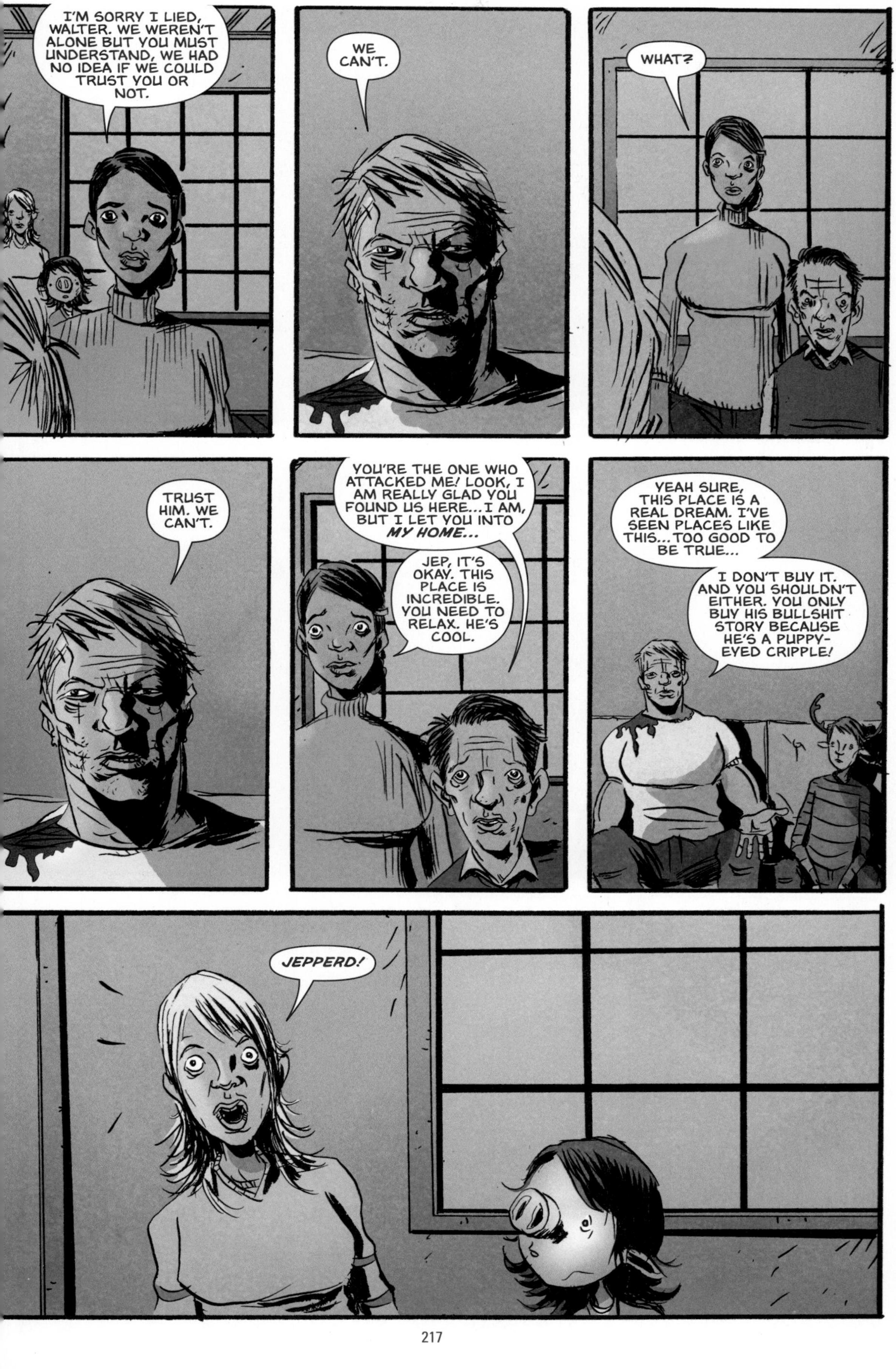

I'M SORRY I LIED, WALTER. WE WEREN'T ALONE BUT YOU MUST UNDERSTAND, WE HAD NO IDEA IF WE COULD TRUST YOU OR NOT.
WE CAN'T.
WHAT?
TRUST HIM. WE CAN'T.
YOU'RE THE ONE WHO ATTACKED ME! LOOK, I AM REALLY GLAD YOU FOUND US HERE...I AM, BUT I LET YOU INTO MY HOME...
JEP, IT'S OKAY. THIS PLACE IS INCREDIBLE. YOU NEED TO RELAX. HE'S COOL.
YEAH SURE, THIS PLACE IS A REAL DREAM. I'VE SEEN PLACES LIKE THIS...TOO GOOD TO BE TRUE...
I DON'T BUY IT. AND YOU SHOULDN'T EITHER. YOU ONLY BUY HIS BULLSHIT STORY BECAUSE HE'S A PUPPY-EYED CRIPPLE!
JEPPERD!

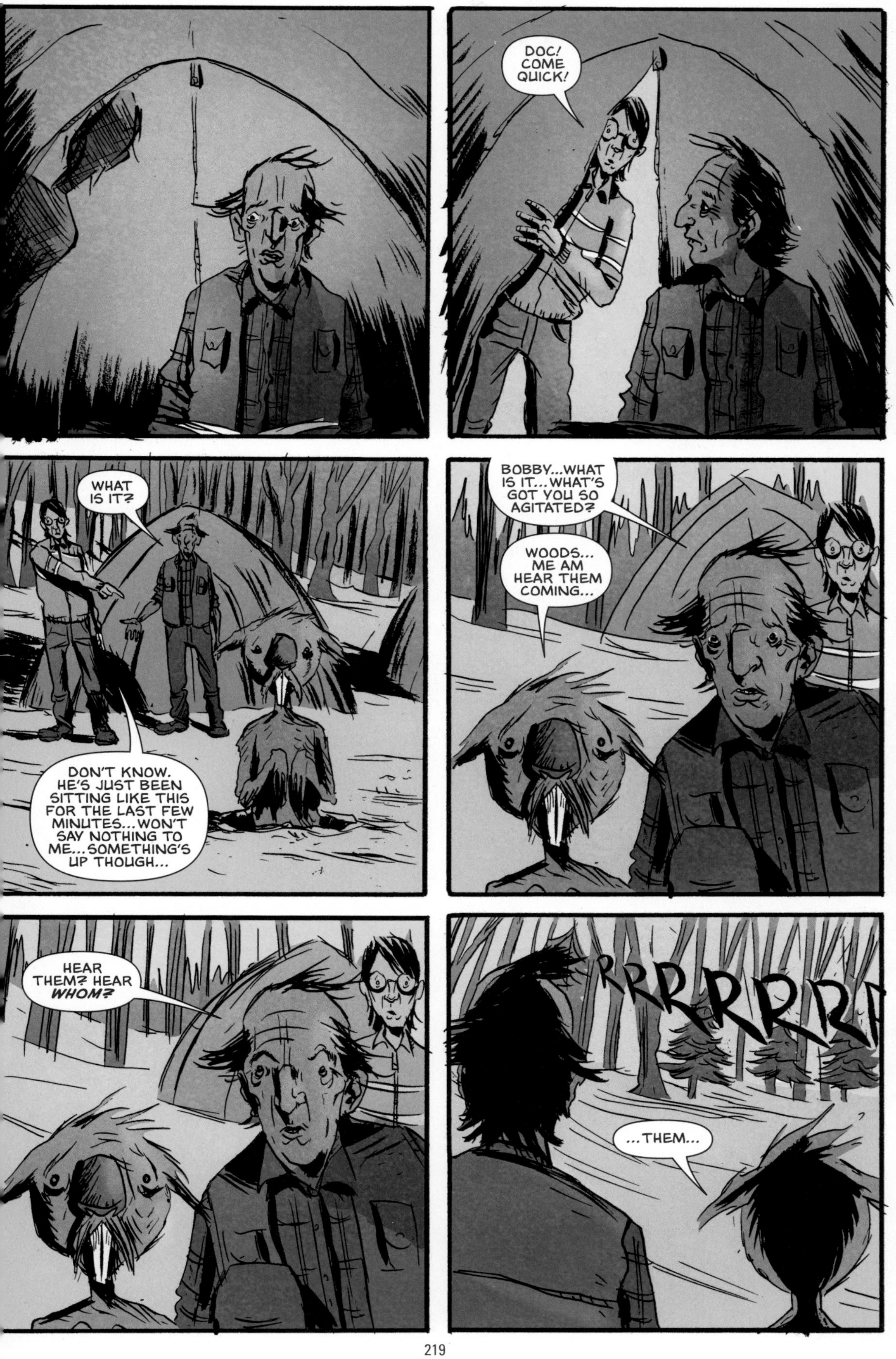
DOC! COME QUICK!
WHAT IS IT?
DON'T KNOW. HE'S JUST BEEN SITTING LIKE THIS FOR THE LAST FEW MINUTES...WON'T SAY NOTHING TO ME...SOMETHING'S UP THOUGH...
BOBBY...WHAT IS IT...WHAT'S GOT YOU SO AGITATED?
WOODS... ME AM HEAR THEM COMING...
HEAR THEM? HEAR *WHOM?*
RRRRRRRR
...THEM...

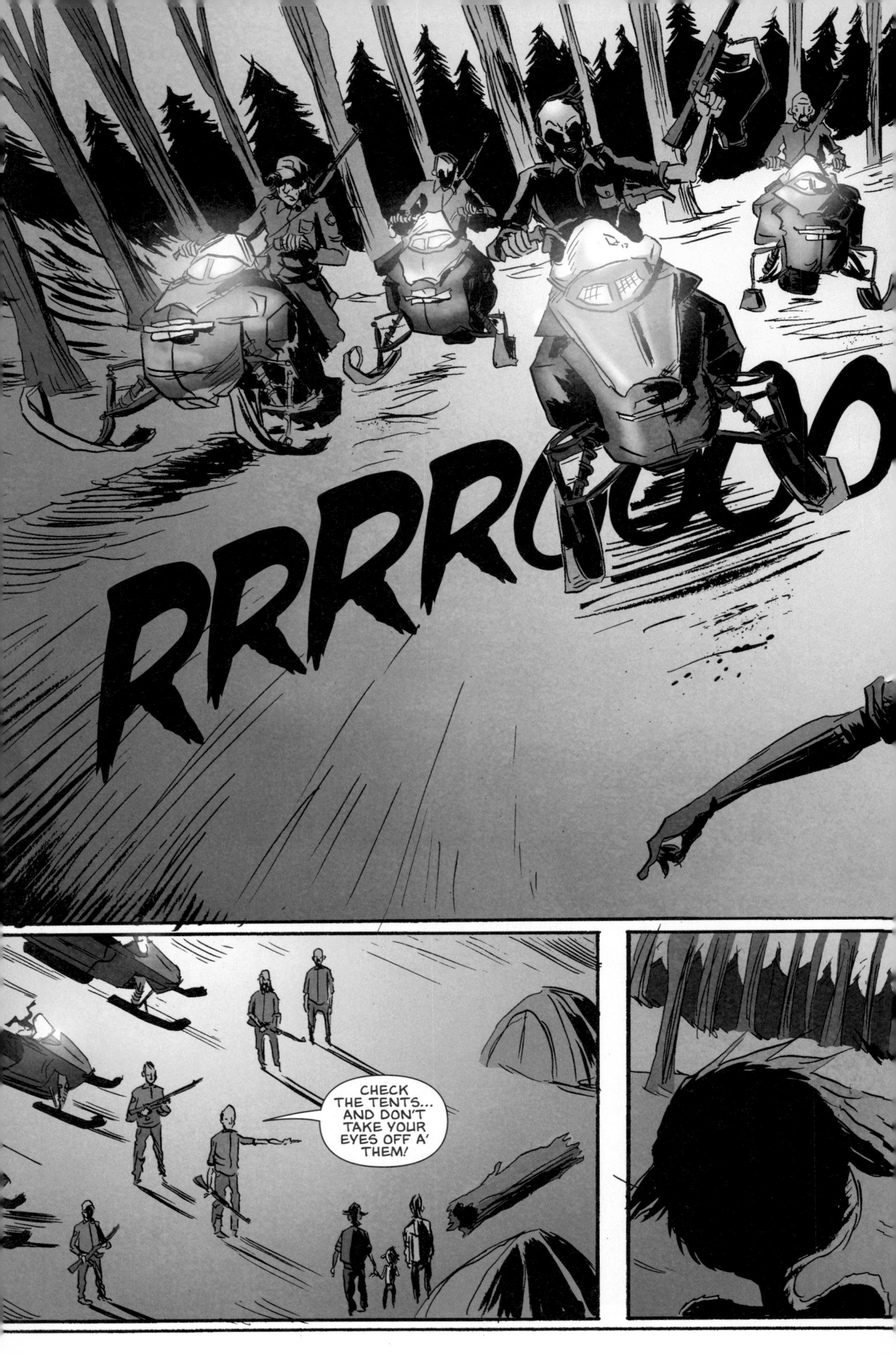
CHECK THE TENTS... AND DON'T TAKE YOUR EYES OFF A' THEM!

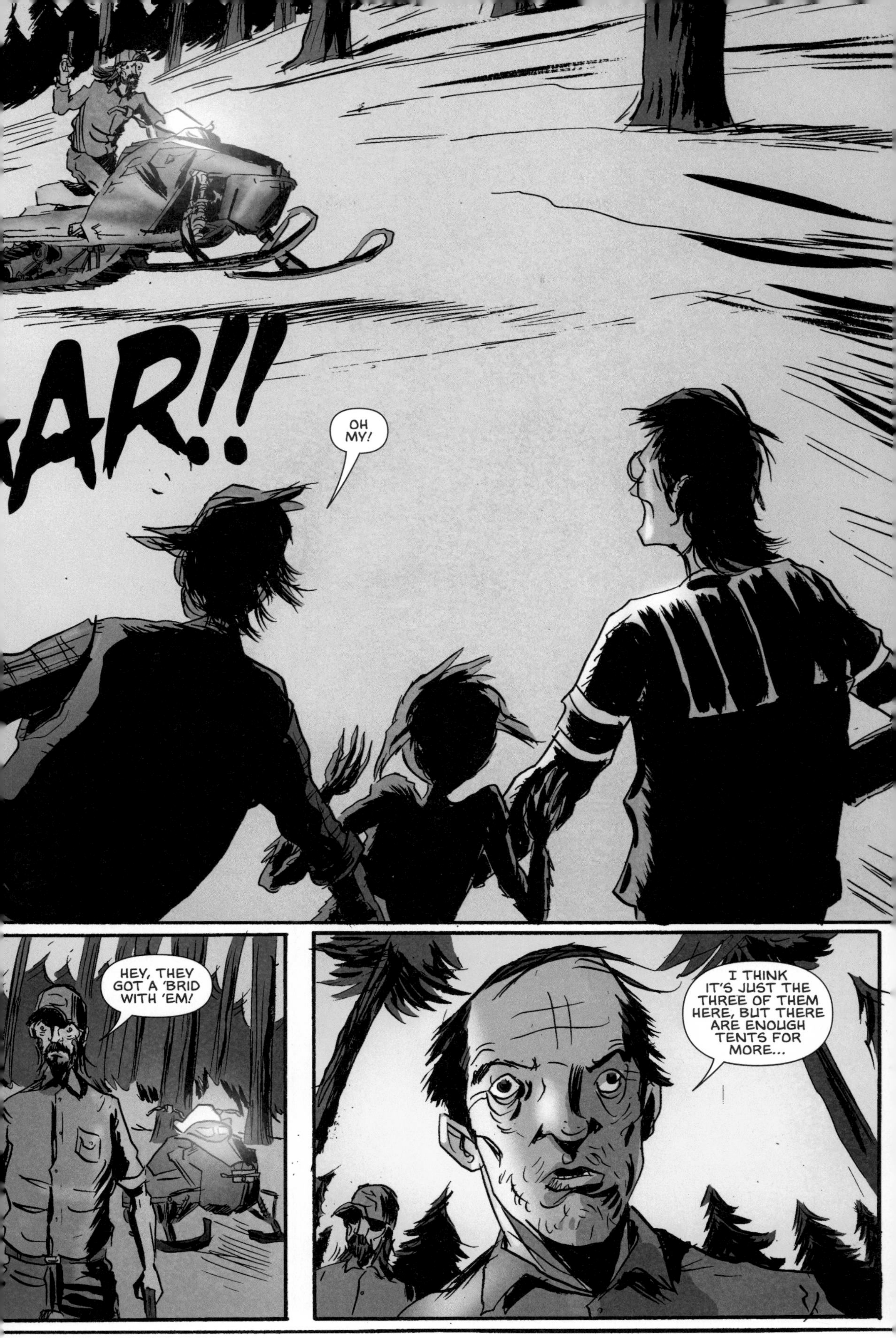
AR!!
OH MY!
HEY, THEY GOT A 'BRID WITH 'EM!
I THINK IT'S JUST THE THREE OF THEM HERE, BUT THERE ARE ENOUGH TENTS FOR MORE...

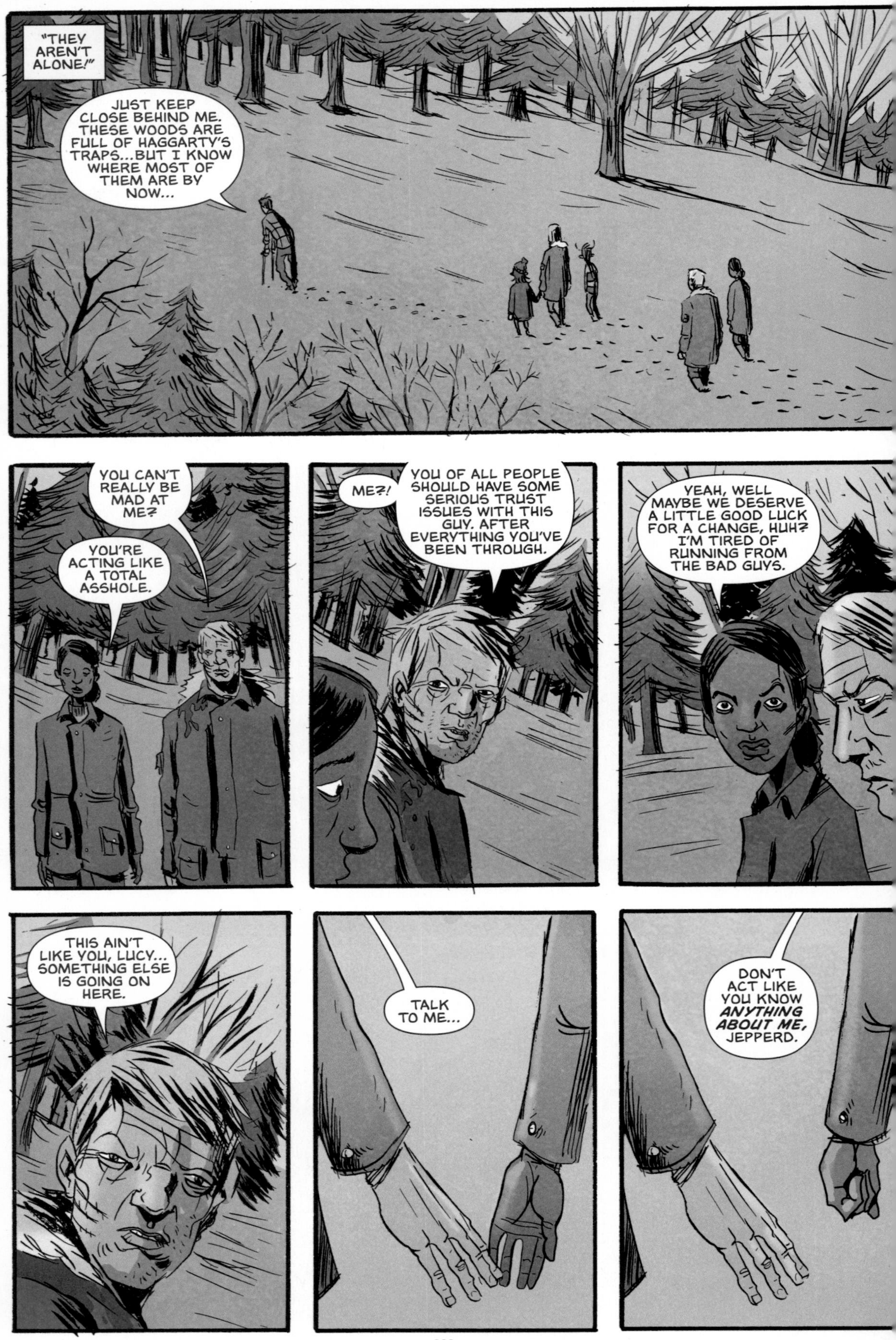
"THEY AREN'T ALONE!"
JUST KEEP CLOSE BEHIND ME. THESE WOODS ARE FULL OF HAGGARTY'S TRAPS...BUT I KNOW WHERE MOST OF THEM ARE BY NOW...
YOU CAN'T REALLY BE MAD AT ME?
YOU'RE ACTING LIKE A TOTAL ASSHOLE.
ME?!
YOU OF ALL PEOPLE SHOULD HAVE SOME SERIOUS TRUST ISSUES WITH THIS GUY. AFTER EVERYTHING YOU'VE BEEN THROUGH.
YEAH, WELL MAYBE WE DESERVE A LITTLE GOOD LUCK FOR A CHANGE, HUH? I'M TIRED OF RUNNING FROM THE BAD GUYS.
THIS AIN'T LIKE YOU, LUCY... SOMETHING ELSE IS GOING ON HERE.
TALK TO ME...
DON'T ACT LIKE YOU KNOW ***ANYTHING ABOUT ME,*** JEPPERD.

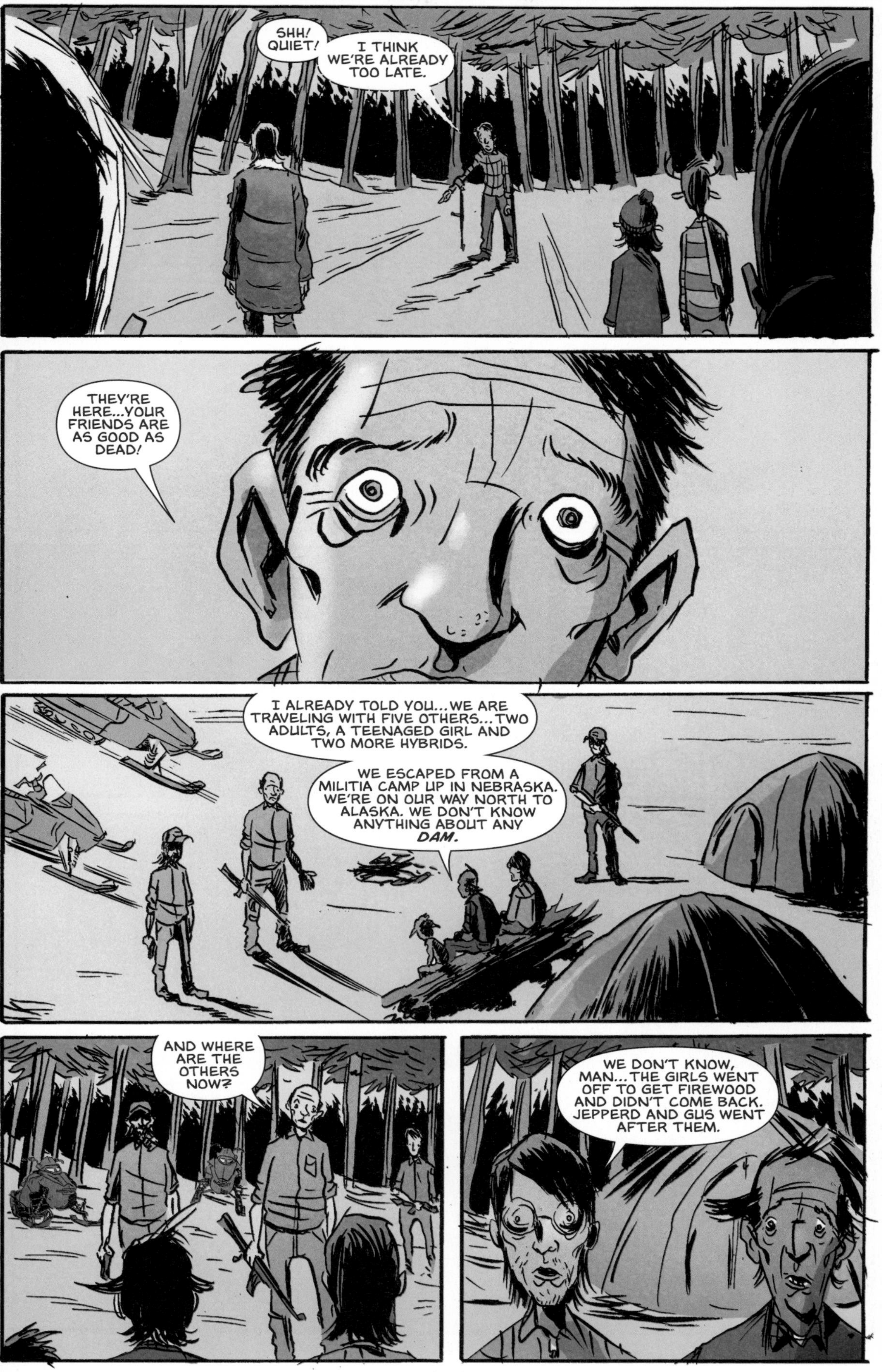
SHH! QUIET!
I THINK WE'RE ALREADY TOO LATE.
THEY'RE HERE...YOUR FRIENDS ARE AS GOOD AS DEAD!
I ALREADY TOLD YOU...WE ARE TRAVELING WITH FIVE OTHERS...TWO ADULTS, A TEENAGED GIRL AND TWO MORE HYBRIDS.
WE ESCAPED FROM A MILITIA CAMP UP IN NEBRASKA. WE'RE ON OUR WAY NORTH TO ALASKA. WE DON'T KNOW ANYTHING ABOUT ANY *DAM.*
AND WHERE ARE THE OTHERS NOW?
WE DON'T KNOW, MAN...THE GIRLS WENT OFF TO GET FIREWOOD AND DIDN'T COME BACK. JEPPERD AND GUS WENT AFTER THEM.

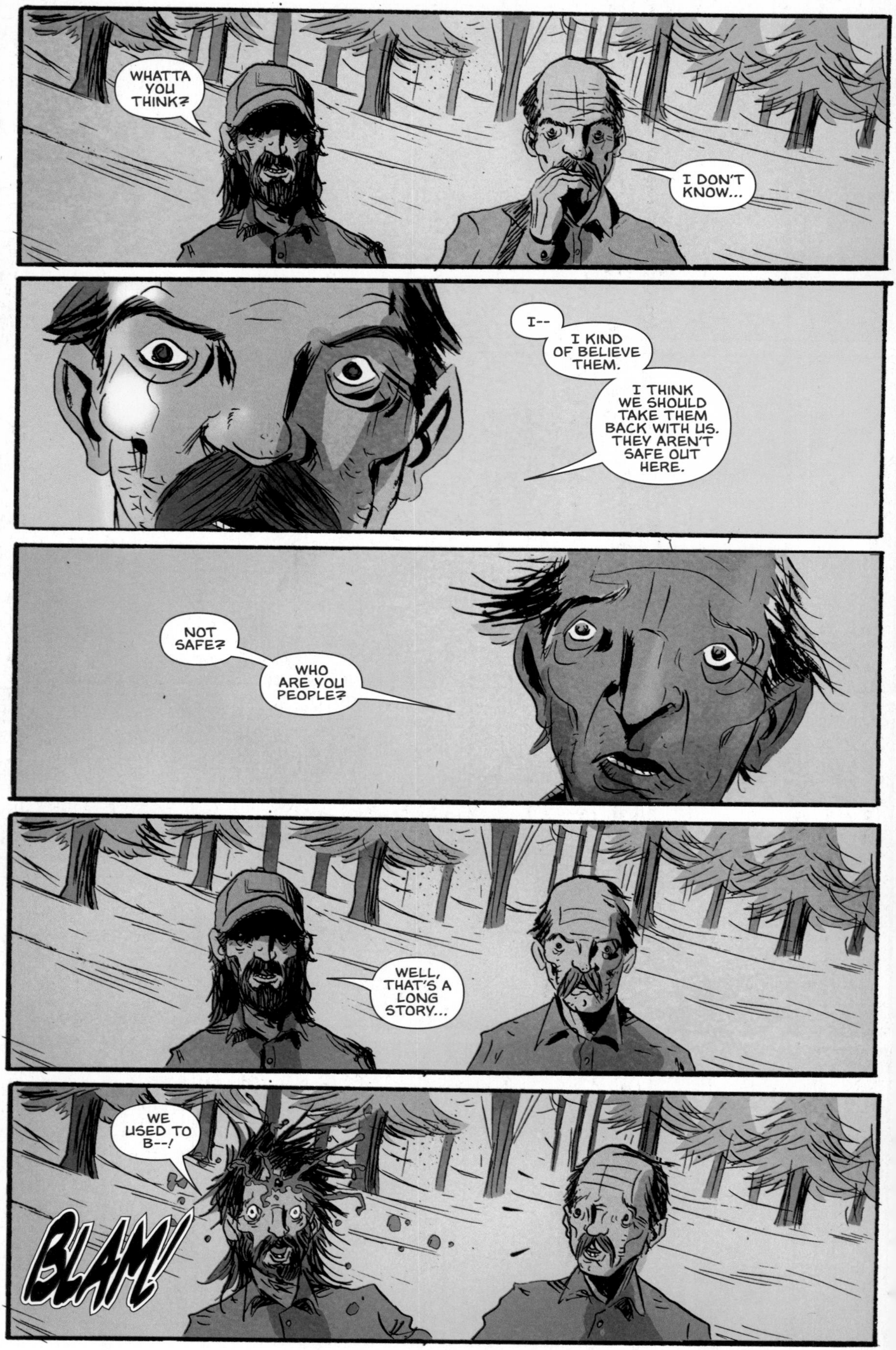
WHATTA YOU THINK?
I DON'T KNOW...
I--
I KIND OF BELIEVE THEM.
I THINK WE SHOULD TAKE THEM BACK WITH US. THEY AREN'T SAFE OUT HERE.
NOT SAFE?
WHO ARE YOU PEOPLE?
WELL, THAT'S A LONG STORY...
WE USED TO B--!
BLAM!

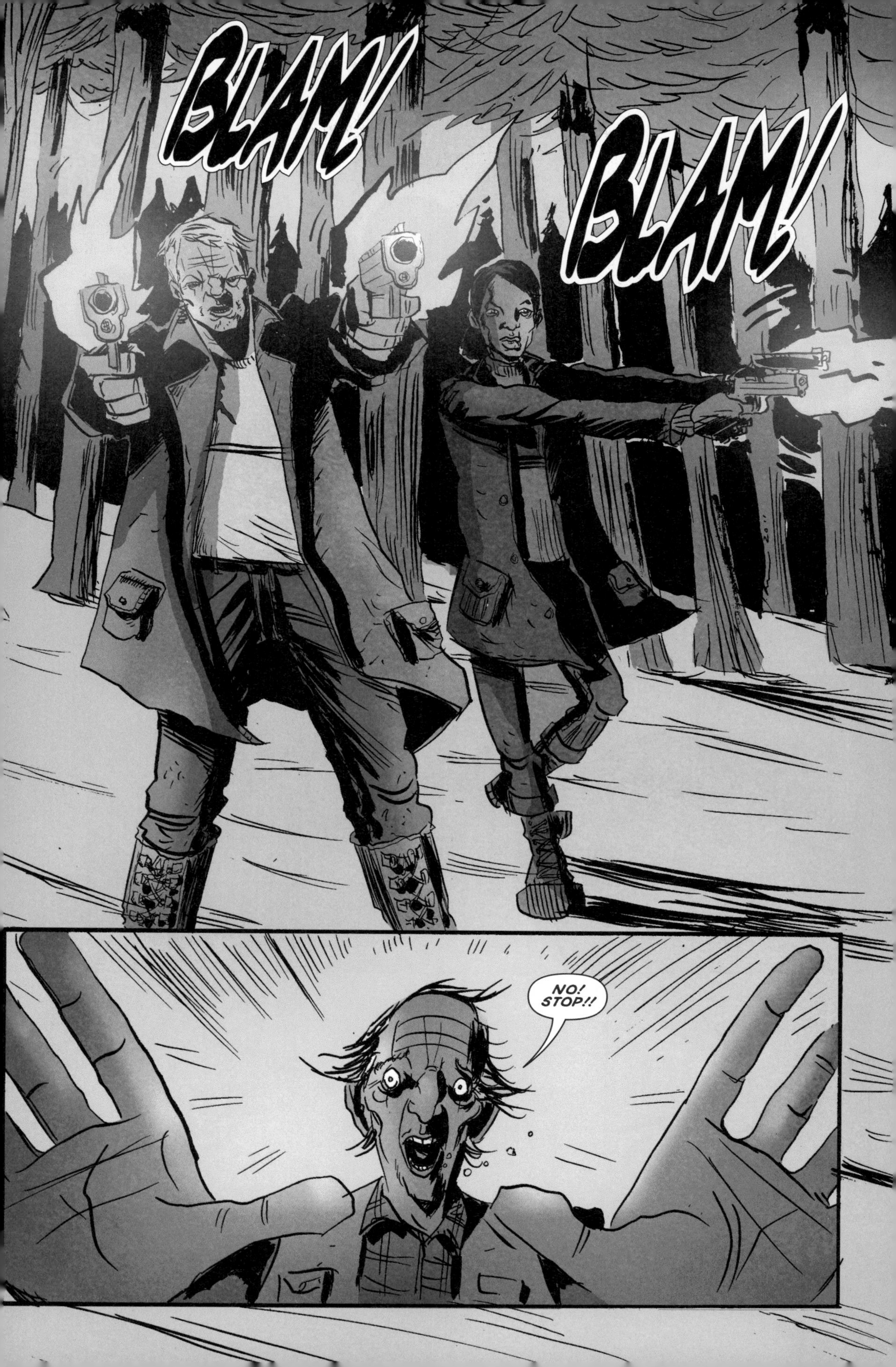
BLAM!
BLAM!
NO! STOP!!

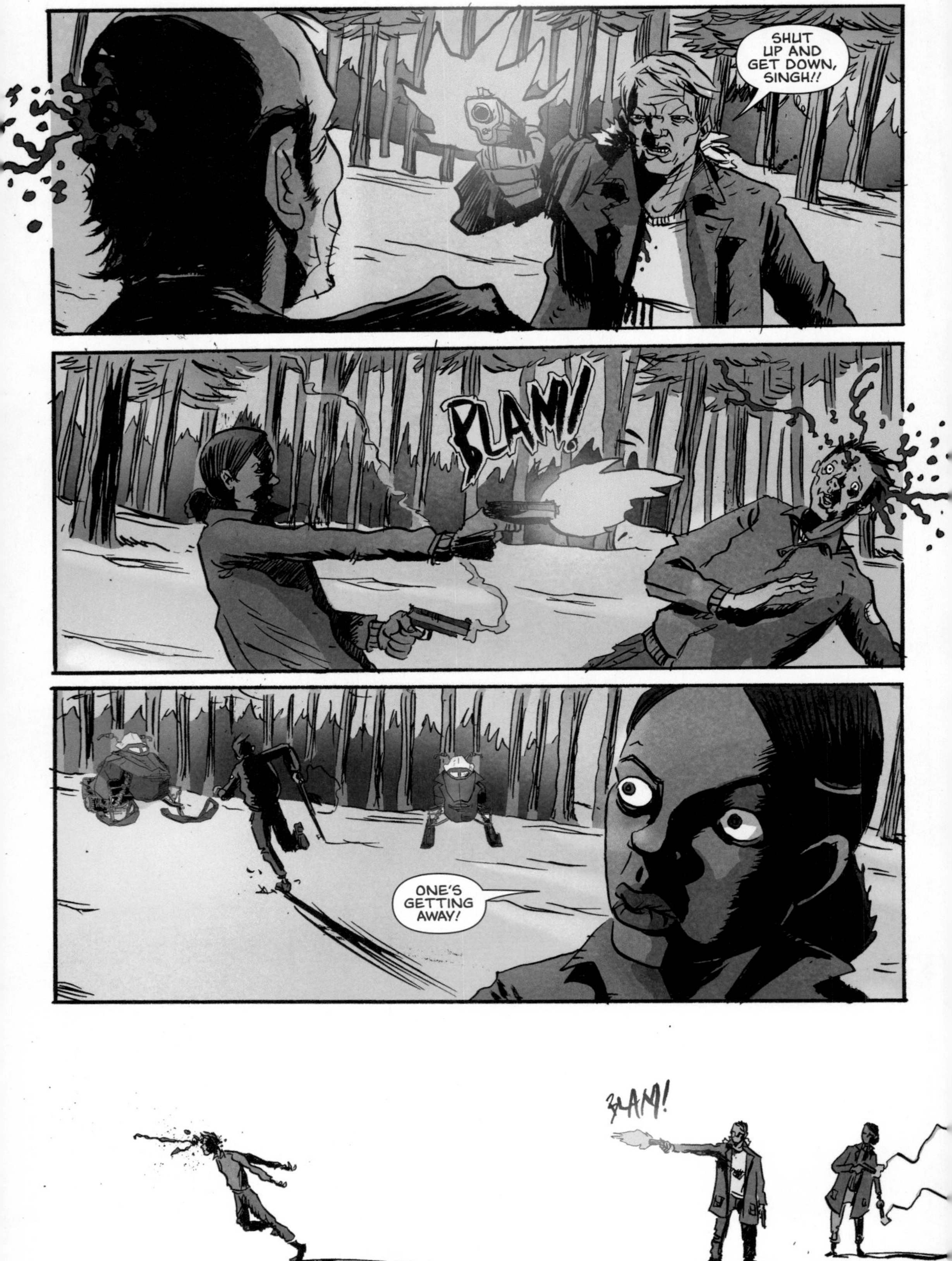
SHUT UP AND GET DOWN, SINGH!!
BLAM!
ONE'S GETTING AWAY!
BLAM!

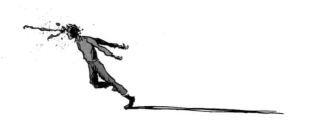

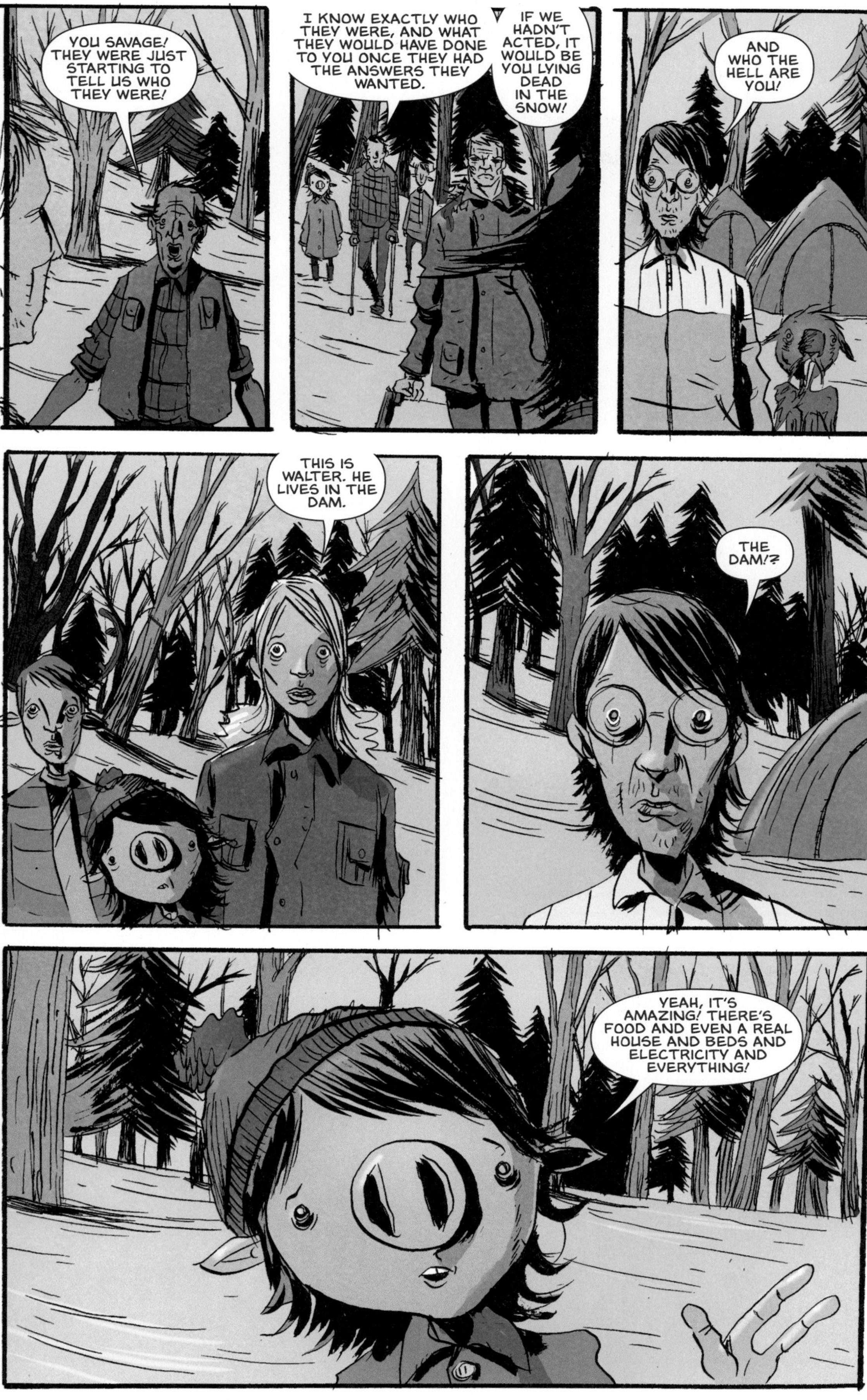
YOU SAVAGE! THEY WERE JUST STARTING TO TELL US WHO THEY WERE!
I KNOW EXACTLY WHO THEY WERE, AND WHAT THEY WOULD HAVE DONE TO YOU ONCE THEY HAD THE ANSWERS THEY WANTED.
IF WE HADN'T ACTED, IT WOULD BE YOU LYING DEAD IN THE SNOW!
AND WHO THE HELL ARE YOU!
THIS IS WALTER. HE LIVES IN THE DAM.
THE DAM!?
YEAH, IT'S AMAZING! THERE'S FOOD AND EVEN A REAL HOUSE AND BEDS AND ELECTRICITY AND EVERYTHING!

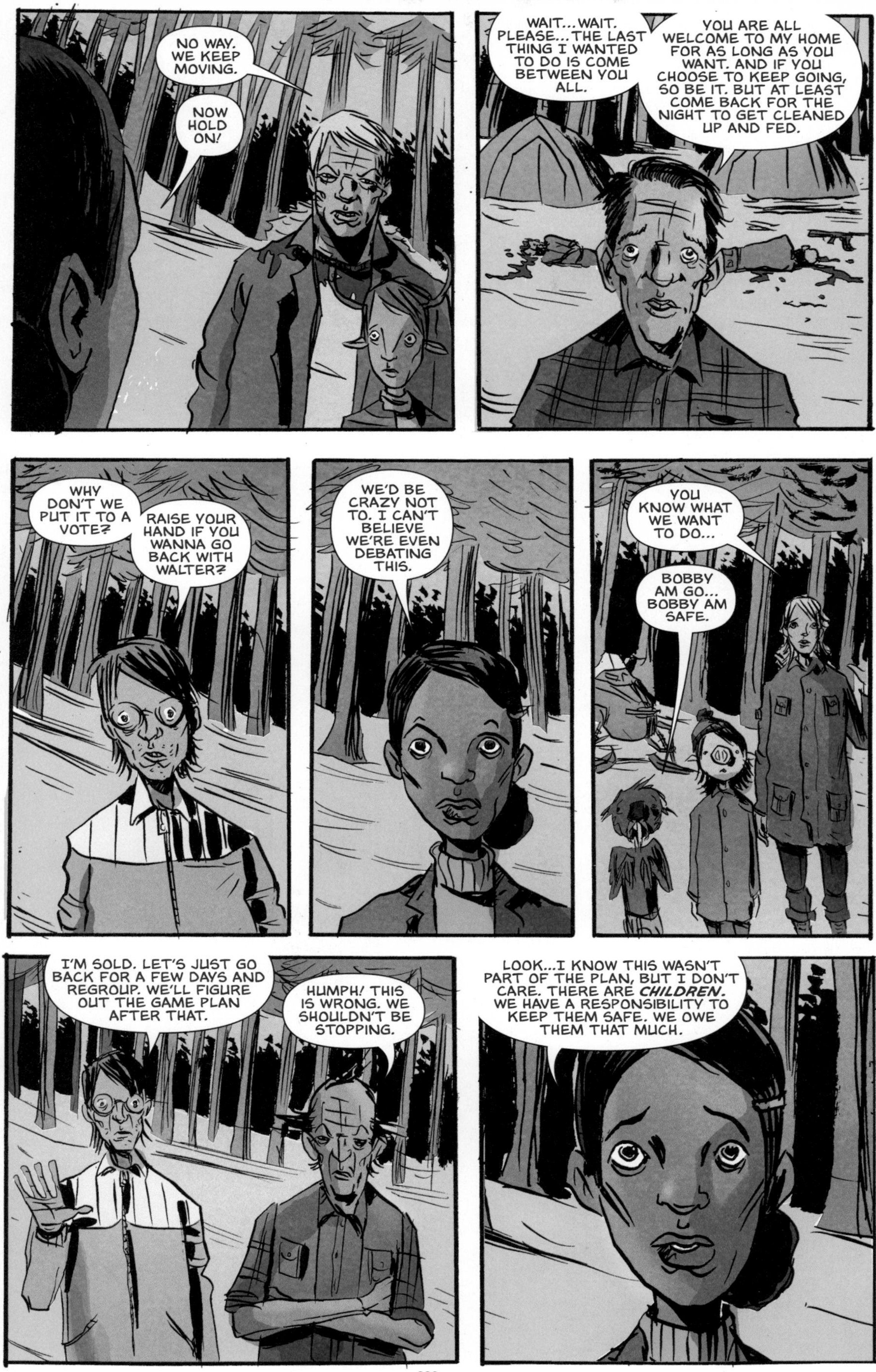
NO WAY. WE KEEP MOVING.
NOW HOLD ON!
WAIT...WAIT. PLEASE...THE LAST THING I WANTED TO DO IS COME BETWEEN YOU ALL.
YOU ARE ALL WELCOME TO MY HOME FOR AS LONG AS YOU WANT. AND IF YOU CHOOSE TO KEEP GOING, SO BE IT. BUT AT LEAST COME BACK FOR THE NIGHT TO GET CLEANED UP AND FED.
WHY DON'T WE PUT IT TO A VOTE?
RAISE YOUR HAND IF YOU WANNA GO BACK WITH WALTER?
WE'D BE CRAZY NOT TO. I CAN'T BELIEVE WE'RE EVEN DEBATING THIS.
YOU KNOW WHAT WE WANT TO DO...
BOBBY AM GO... BOBBY AM SAFE.
I'M SOLD. LET'S JUST GO BACK FOR A FEW DAYS AND REGROUP. WE'LL FIGURE OUT THE GAME PLAN AFTER THAT.
HUMPH! THIS IS WRONG. WE SHOULDN'T BE STOPPING.
LOOK...I KNOW THIS WASN'T PART OF THE PLAN, BUT I DON'T CARE. THERE ARE *CHILDREN*. WE HAVE A RESPONSIBILITY TO KEEP THEM SAFE. WE OWE THEM THAT MUCH.

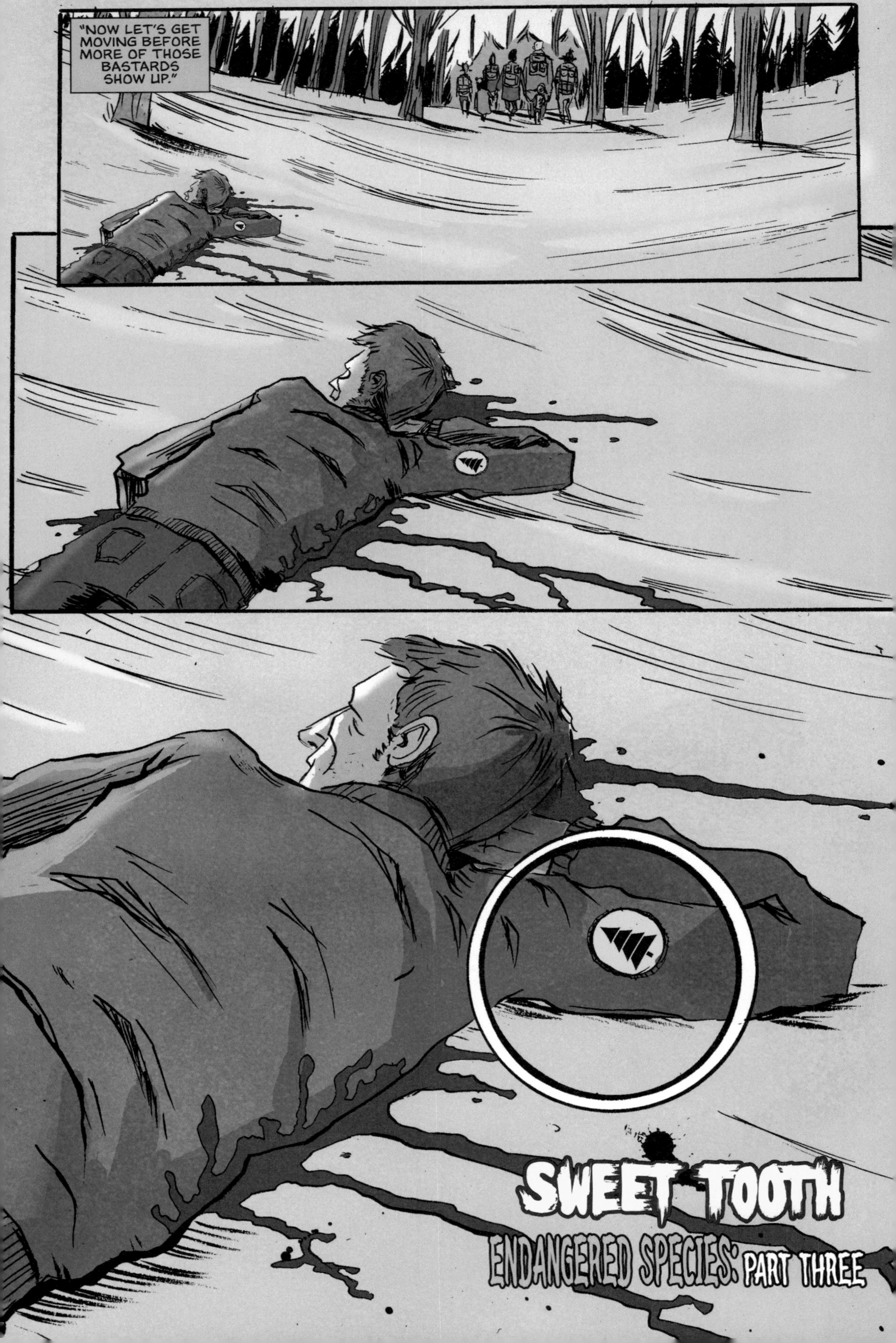
"NOW LET'S GET MOVING BEFORE MORE OF THOSE BASTARDS SHOW UP."
SWEET TOOTH
ENDANGERED SPECIES: PART THREE

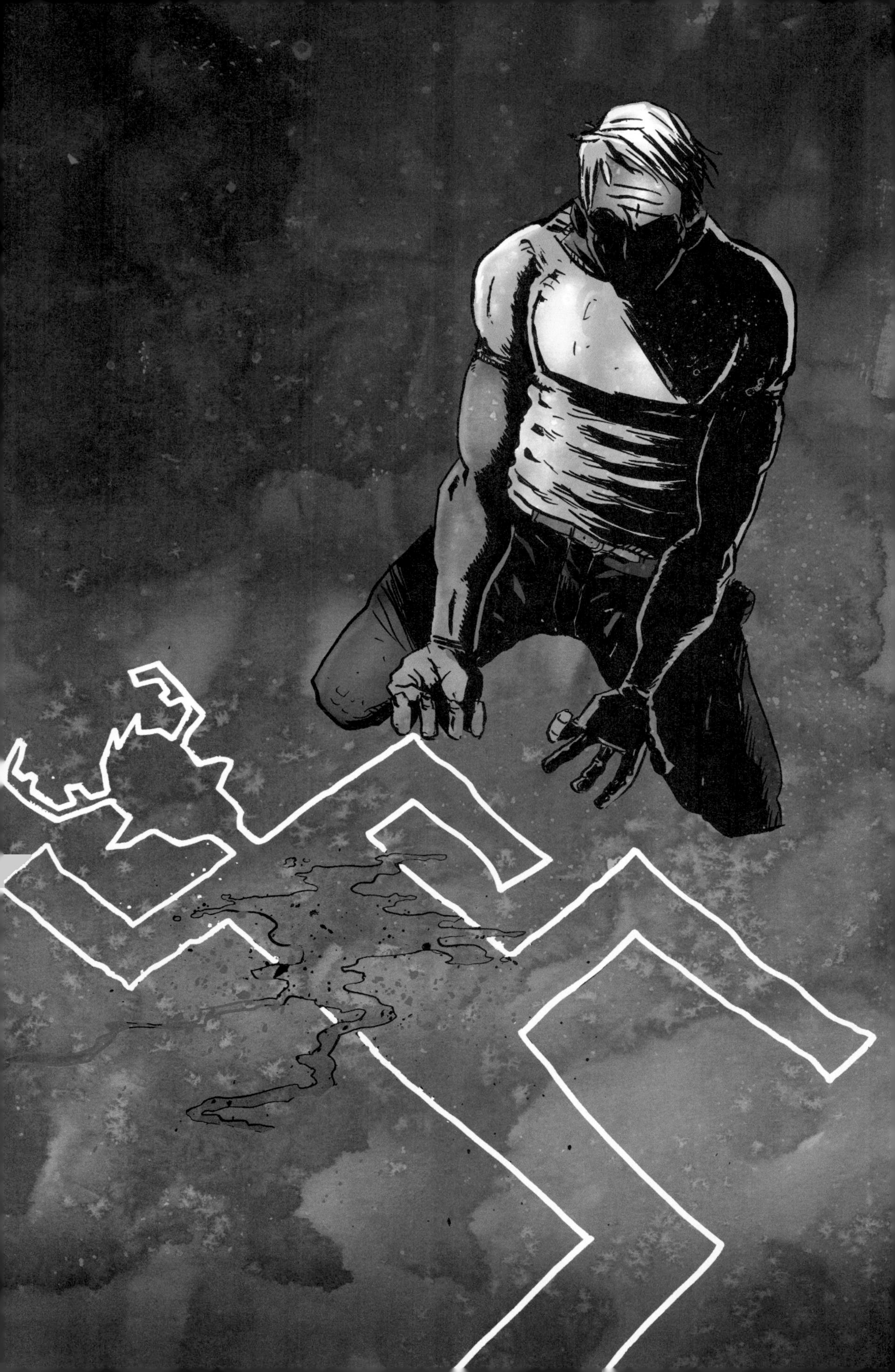

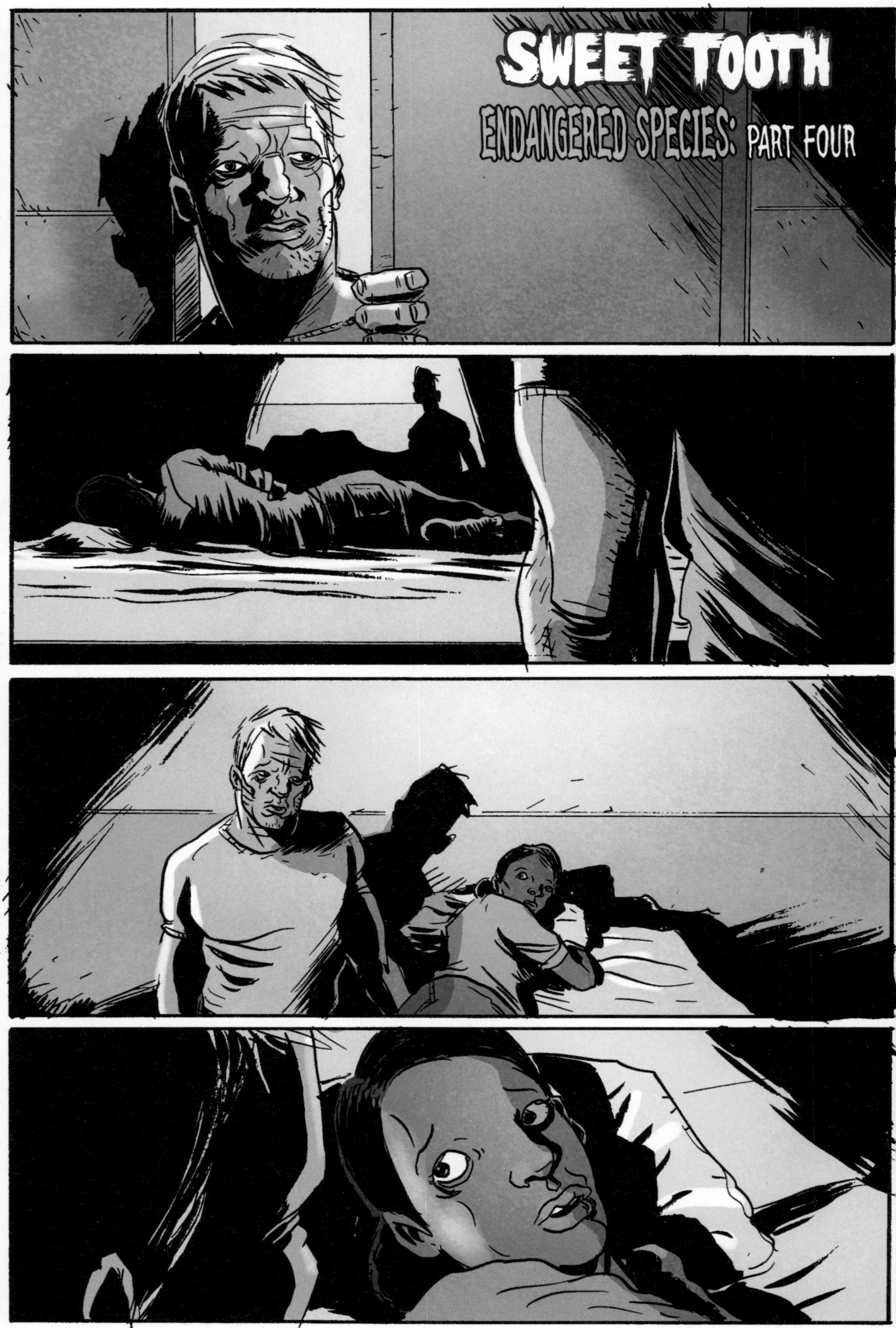
SWEET TOOTH
ENDANGERED SPECIES: PART FOUR

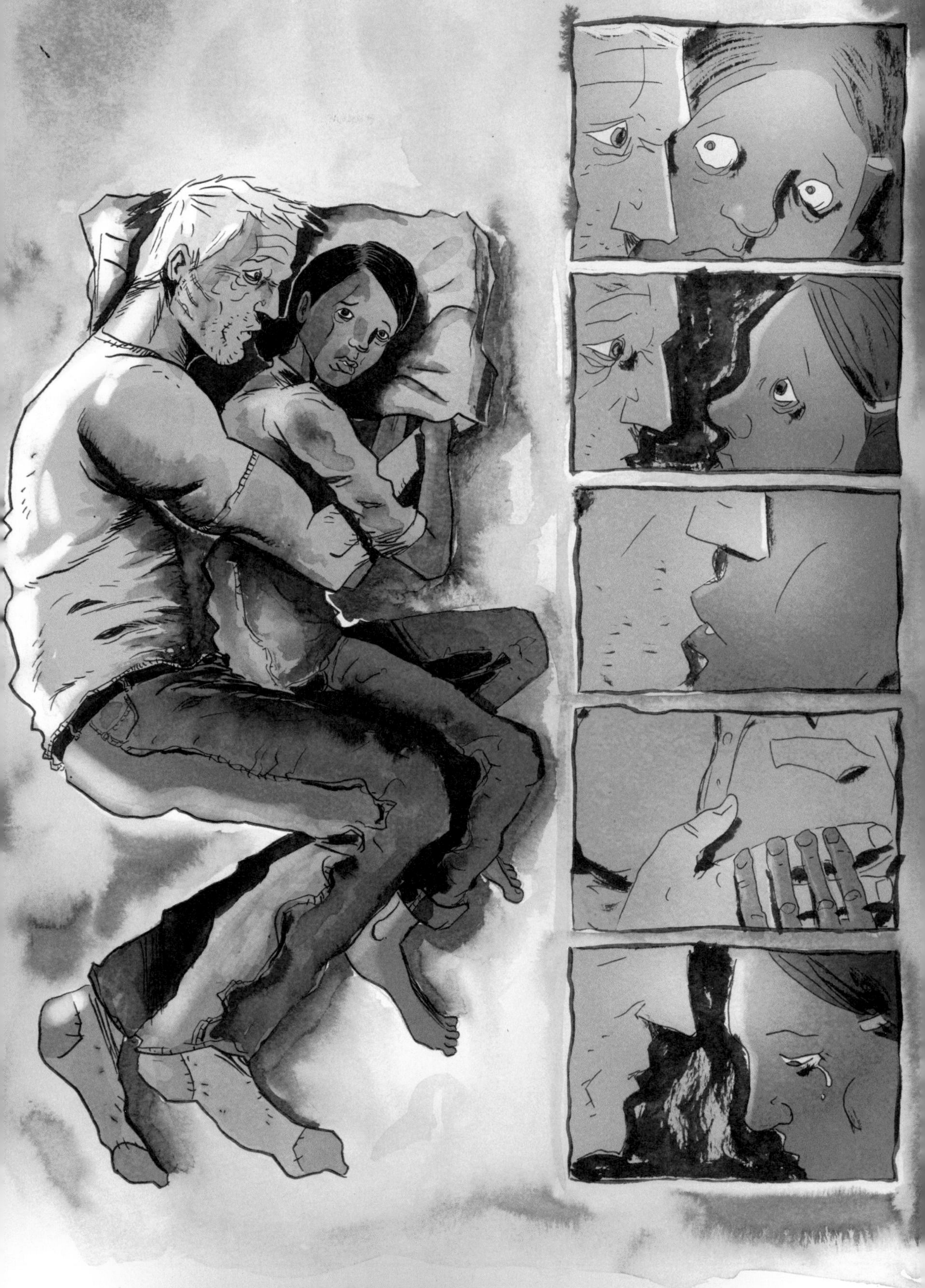

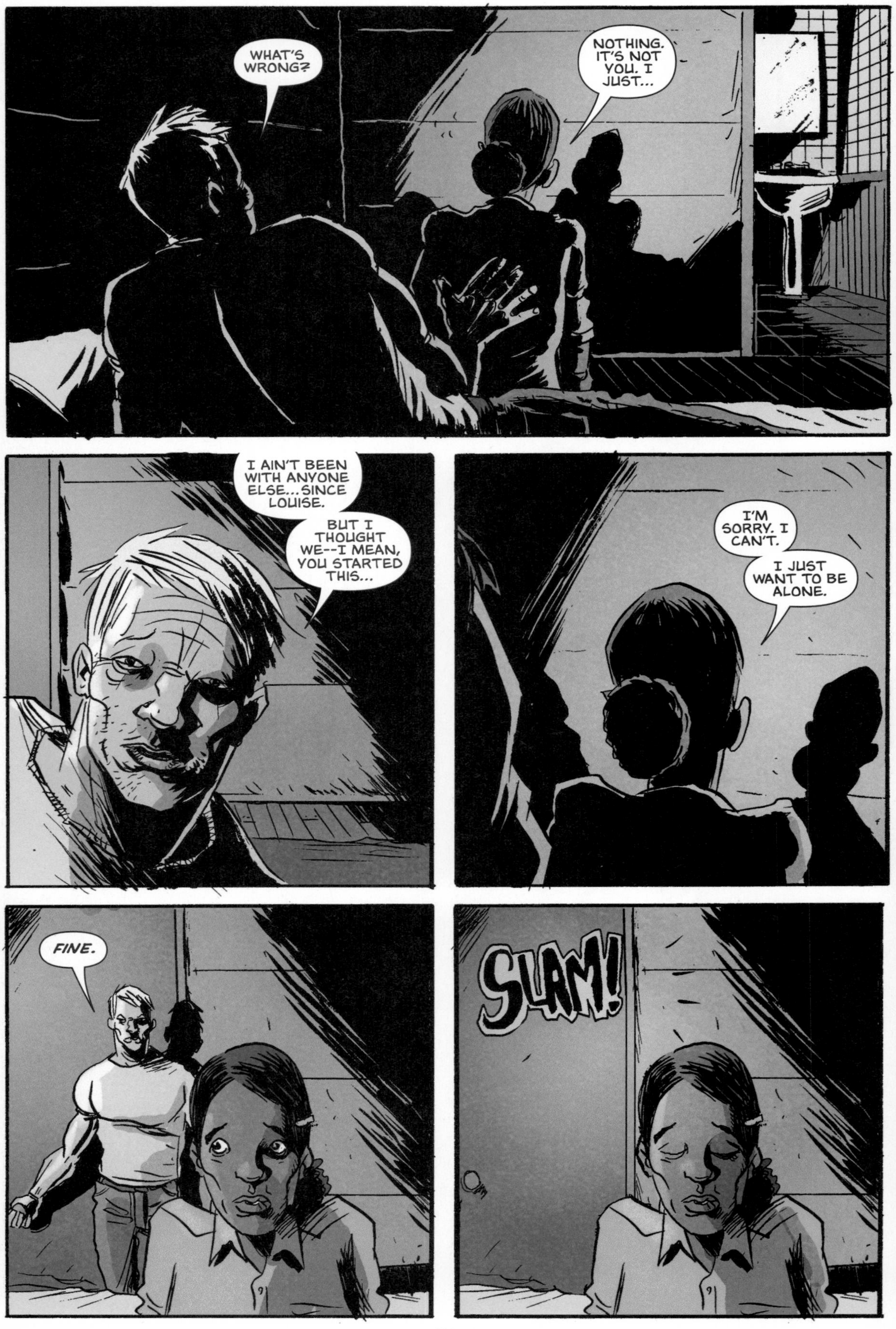
WHAT'S WRONG?
NOTHING. IT'S NOT YOU. I JUST...
I AIN'T BEEN WITH ANYONE ELSE...SINCE LOUISE.
BUT I THOUGHT WE--I MEAN, YOU STARTED THIS...
I'M SORRY. I CAN'T.
I JUST WANT TO BE ALONE.
FINE.
SLAM!

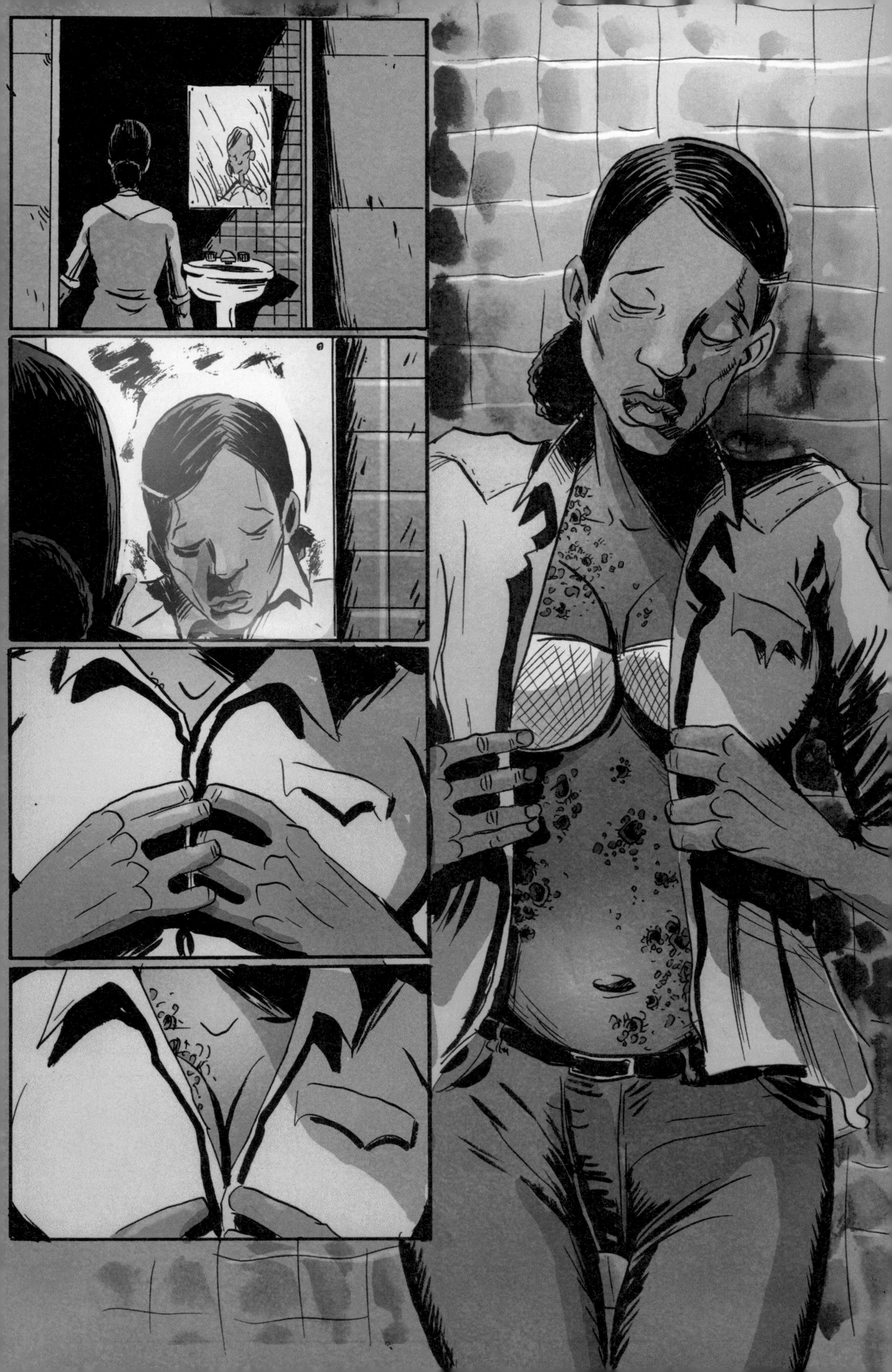

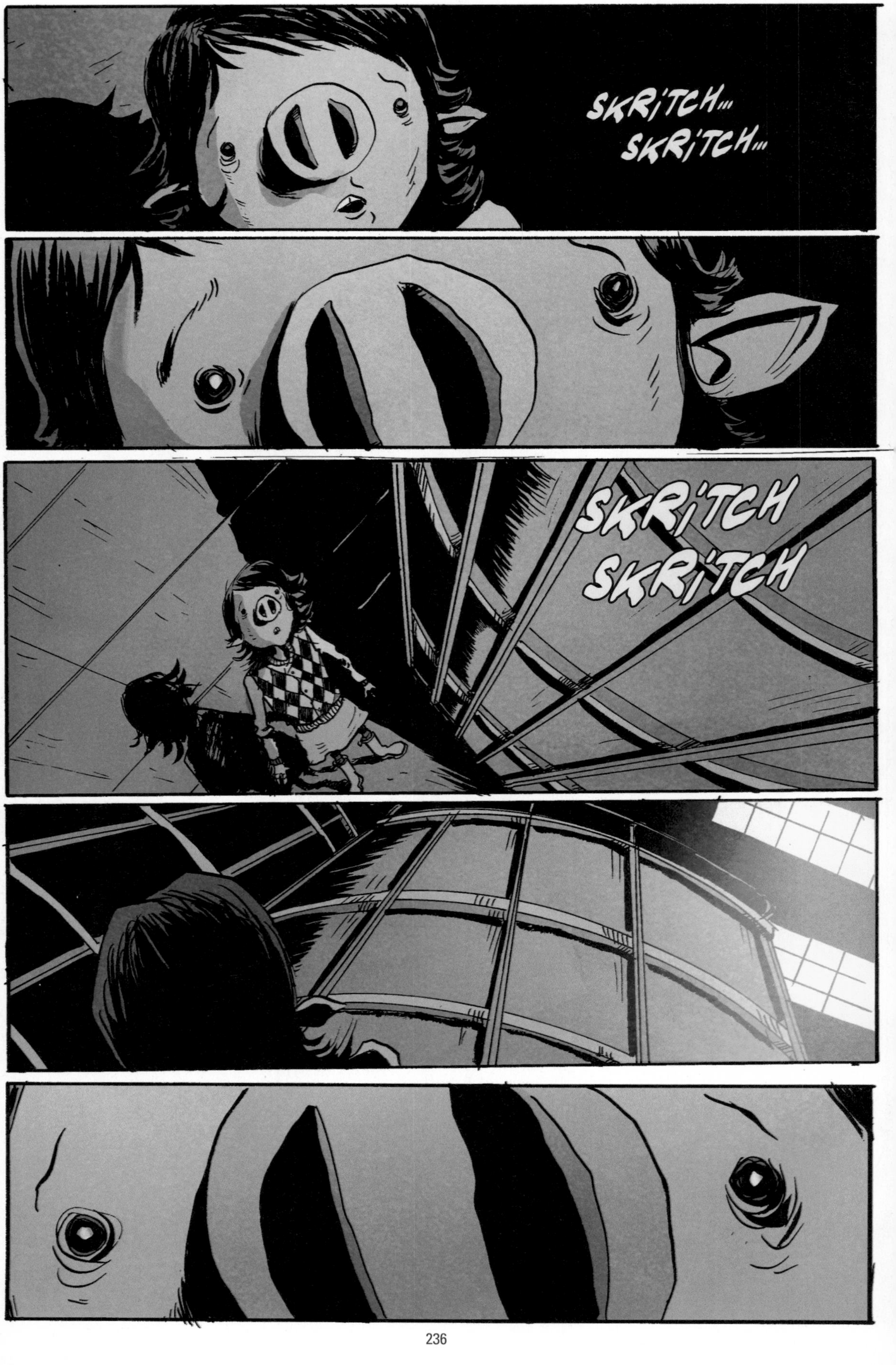
SKRITCH...
SKRITCH...
SKRITCH
SKRITCH

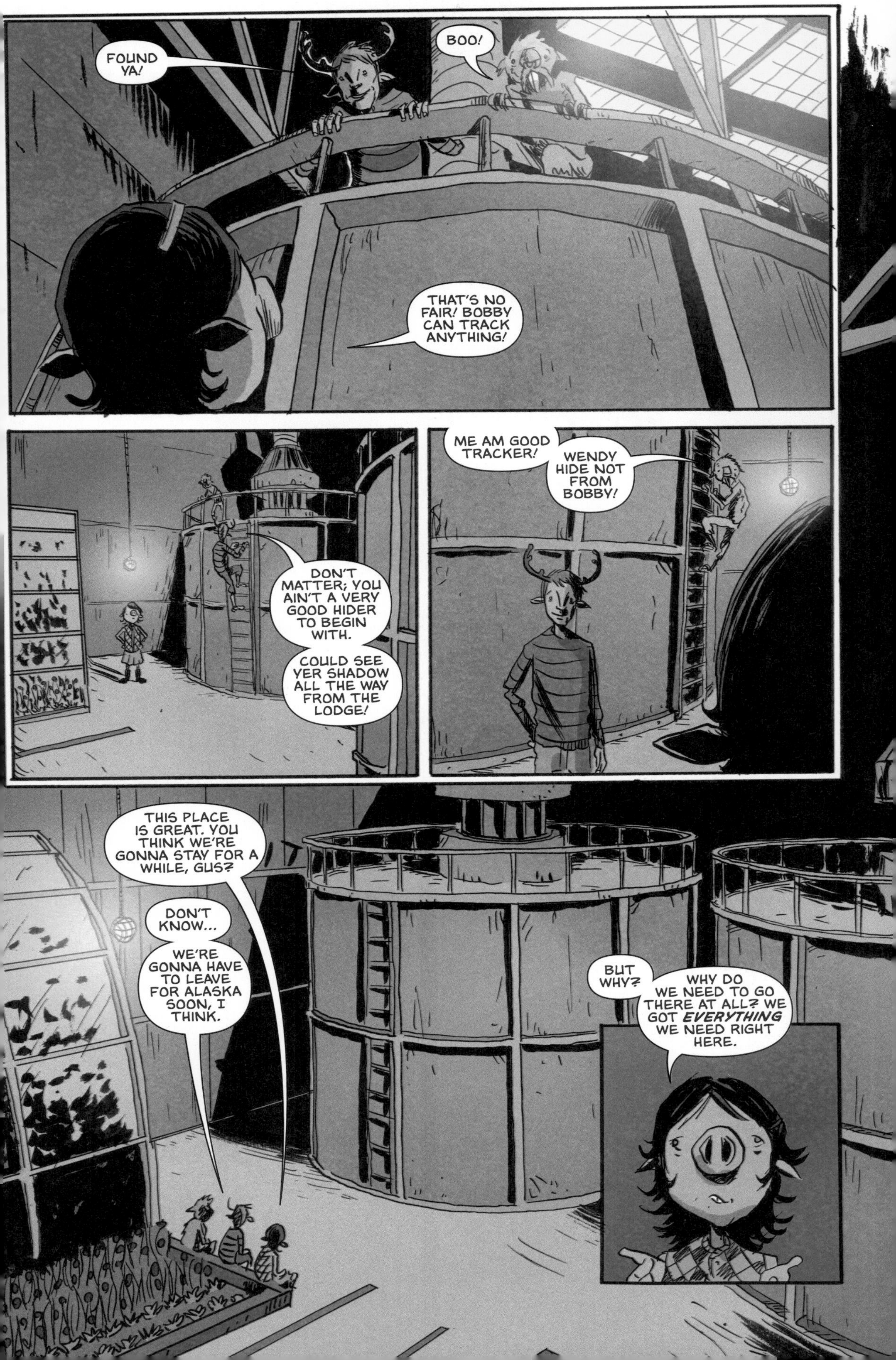
FOUND YA!
BOO!
THAT'S NO FAIR! BOBBY CAN TRACK ANYTHING!
DON'T MATTER; YOU AIN'T A VERY GOOD HIDER TO BEGIN WITH.
COULD SEE YER SHADOW ALL THE WAY FROM THE LODGE!
ME AM GOOD TRACKER!
WENDY HIDE NOT FROM BOBBY!
THIS PLACE IS GREAT. YOU THINK WE'RE GONNA STAY FOR A WHILE, GUS?
DON'T KNOW...
WE'RE GONNA HAVE TO LEAVE FOR ALASKA SOON, I THINK.
BUT WHY?
WHY DO WE NEED TO GO THERE AT ALL? WE GOT *EVERYTHING* WE NEED RIGHT HERE.

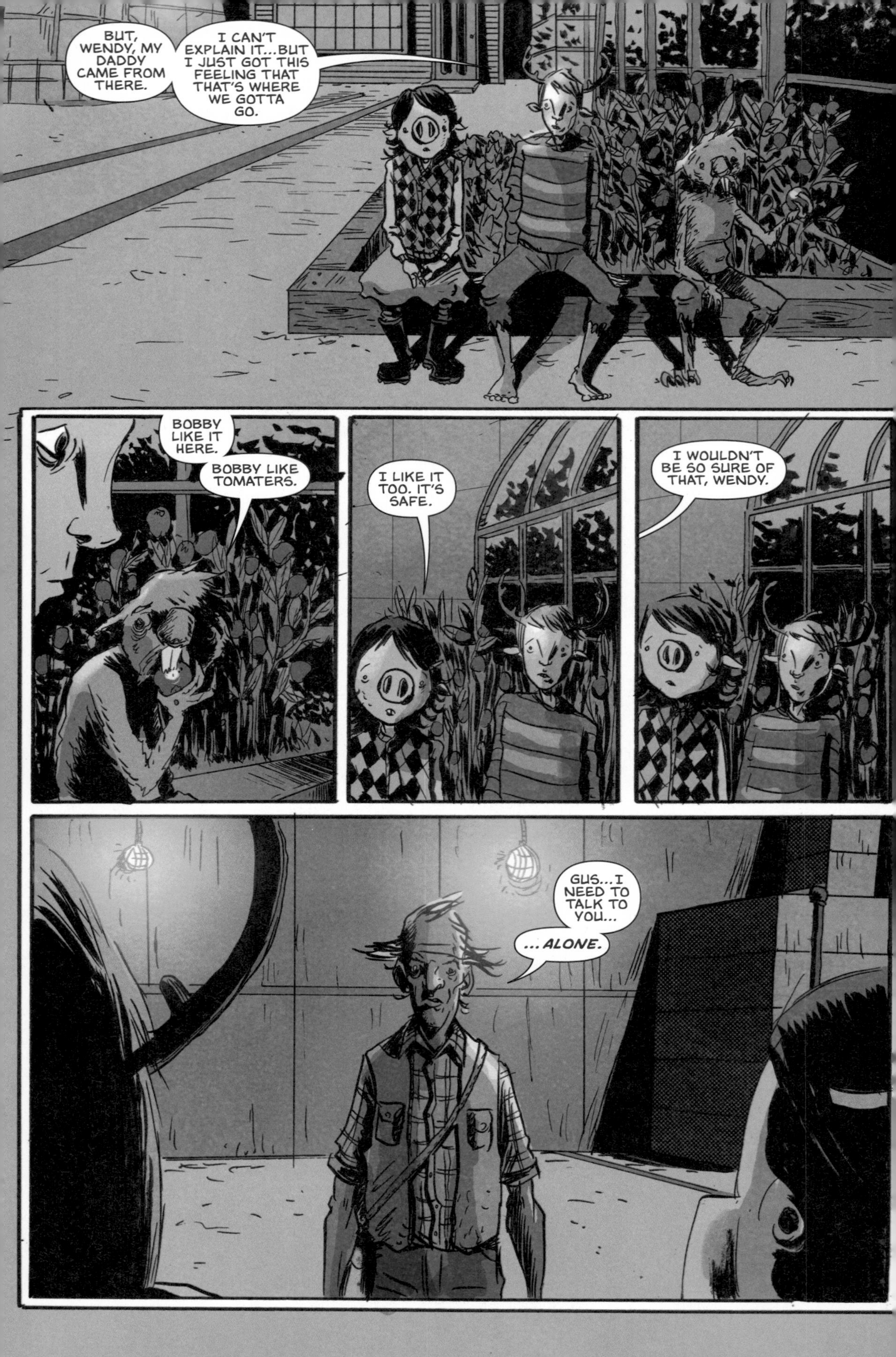
BUT, WENDY, MY DADDY CAME FROM THERE.
I CAN'T EXPLAIN IT...BUT I JUST GOT THIS FEELING THAT THAT'S WHERE WE GOTTA GO.
BOBBY LIKE IT HERE.
BOBBY LIKE TOMATERS.
I LIKE IT TOO. IT'S SAFE.
I WOULDN'T BE SO SURE OF THAT, WENDY.
GUS...I NEED TO TALK TO YOU...
...ALONE.

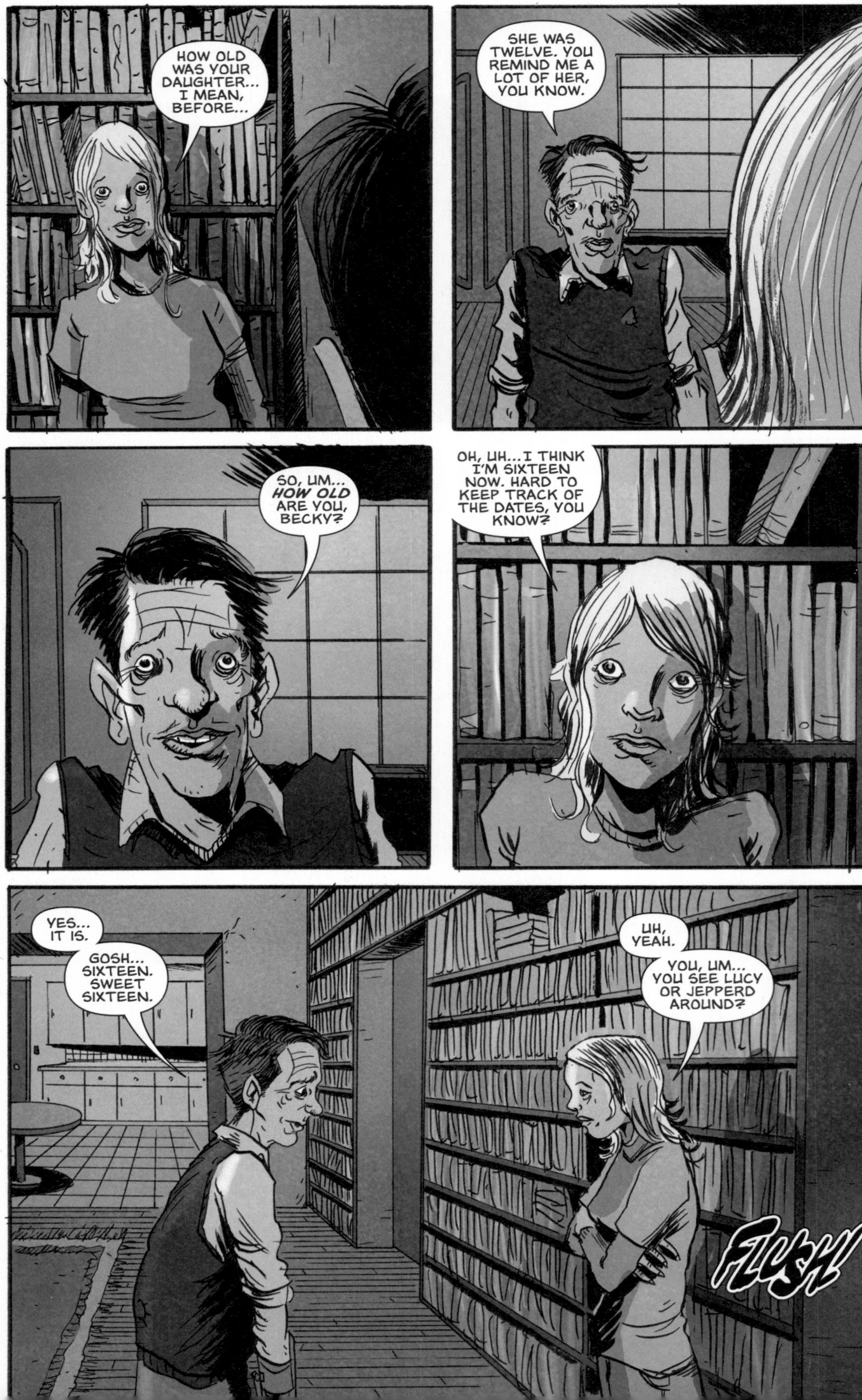
HOW OLD WAS YOUR DAUGHTER... I MEAN, BEFORE...
SHE WAS TWELVE. YOU REMIND ME A LOT OF HER, YOU KNOW.
SO, UM... *HOW OLD* ARE YOU, BECKY?
OH, UH... I THINK I'M SIXTEEN NOW. HARD TO KEEP TRACK OF THE DATES, YOU KNOW?
YES... IT IS.
GOSH... SIXTEEN. SWEET SIXTEEN.
UH, YEAH.
YOU, UM... YOU SEE LUCY OR JEPPERD AROUND?
FLUSH!

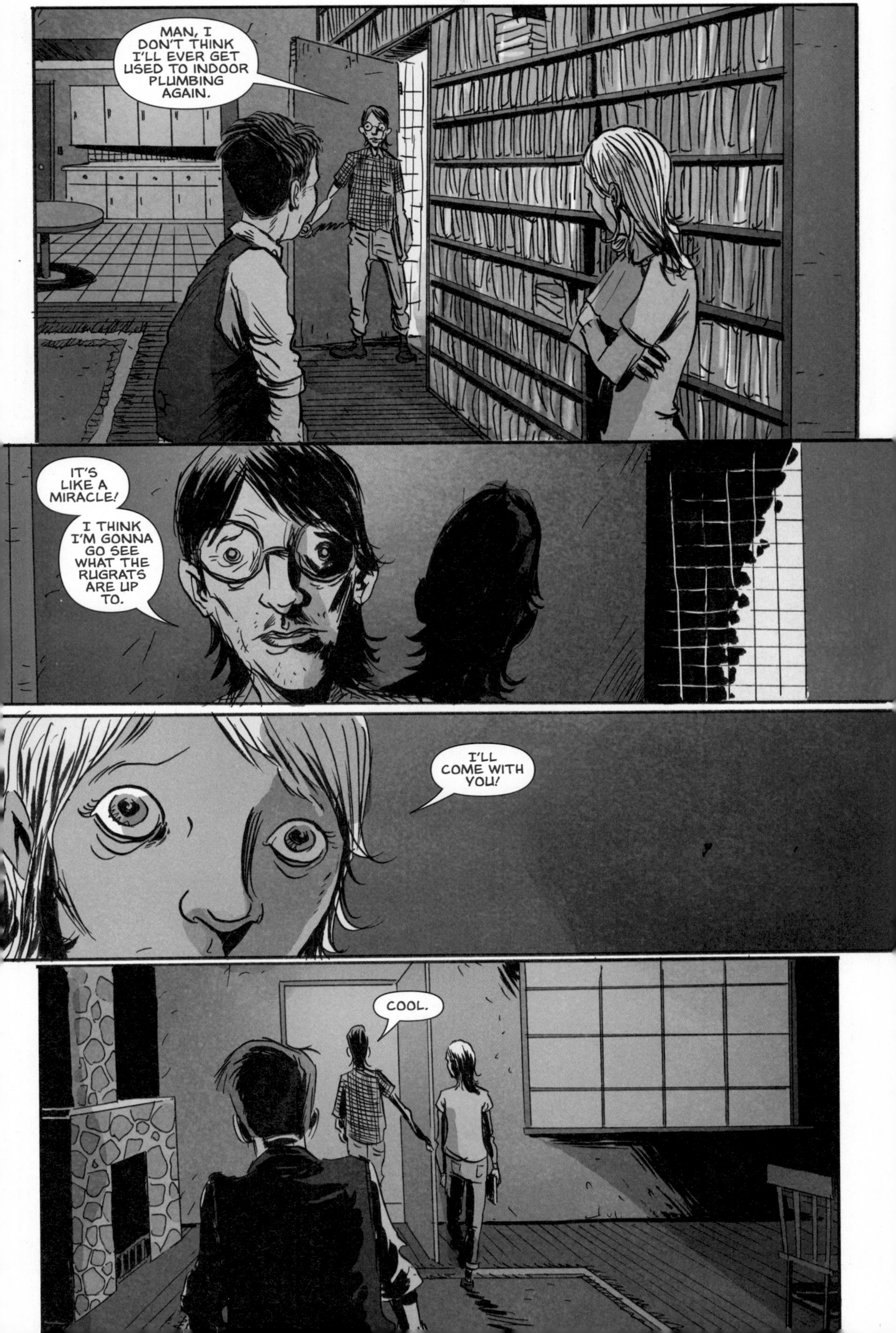
MAN, I DON'T THINK I'LL EVER GET USED TO INDOOR PLUMBING AGAIN.
IT'S LIKE A MIRACLE!
I THINK I'M GONNA GO SEE WHAT THE RUGRATS ARE UP TO.
I'LL COME WITH YOU!
COOL.

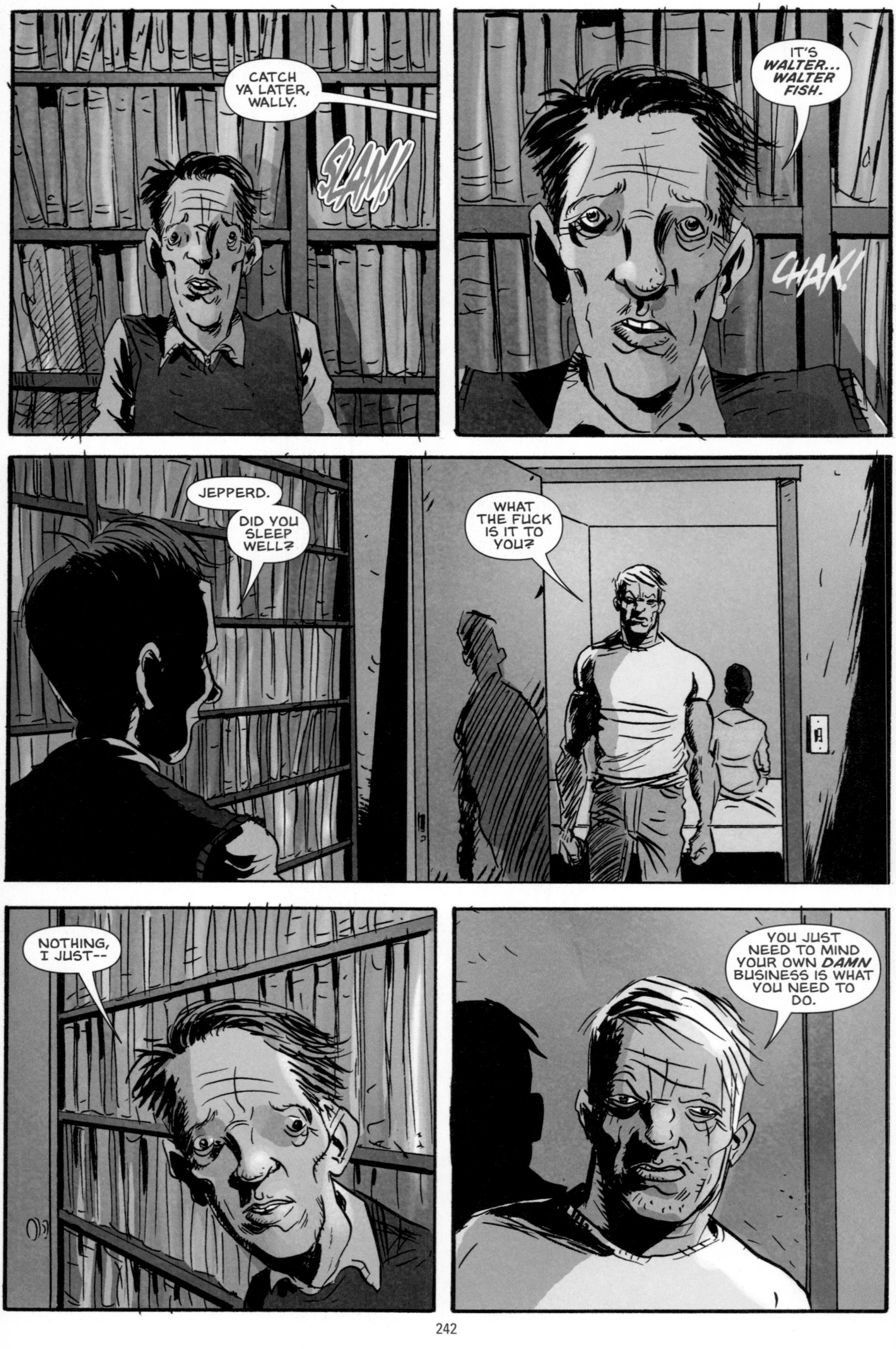

CATCH YA LATER, WALLY.
SLAM!
IT'S WALTER... WALTER FISH.
CHAK!
JEPPERD.
DID YOU SLEEP WELL?
WHAT THE FUCK IS IT TO YOU?
NOTHING, I JUST--
YOU JUST NEED TO MIND YOUR OWN DAMN BUSINESS IS WHAT YOU NEED TO DO.

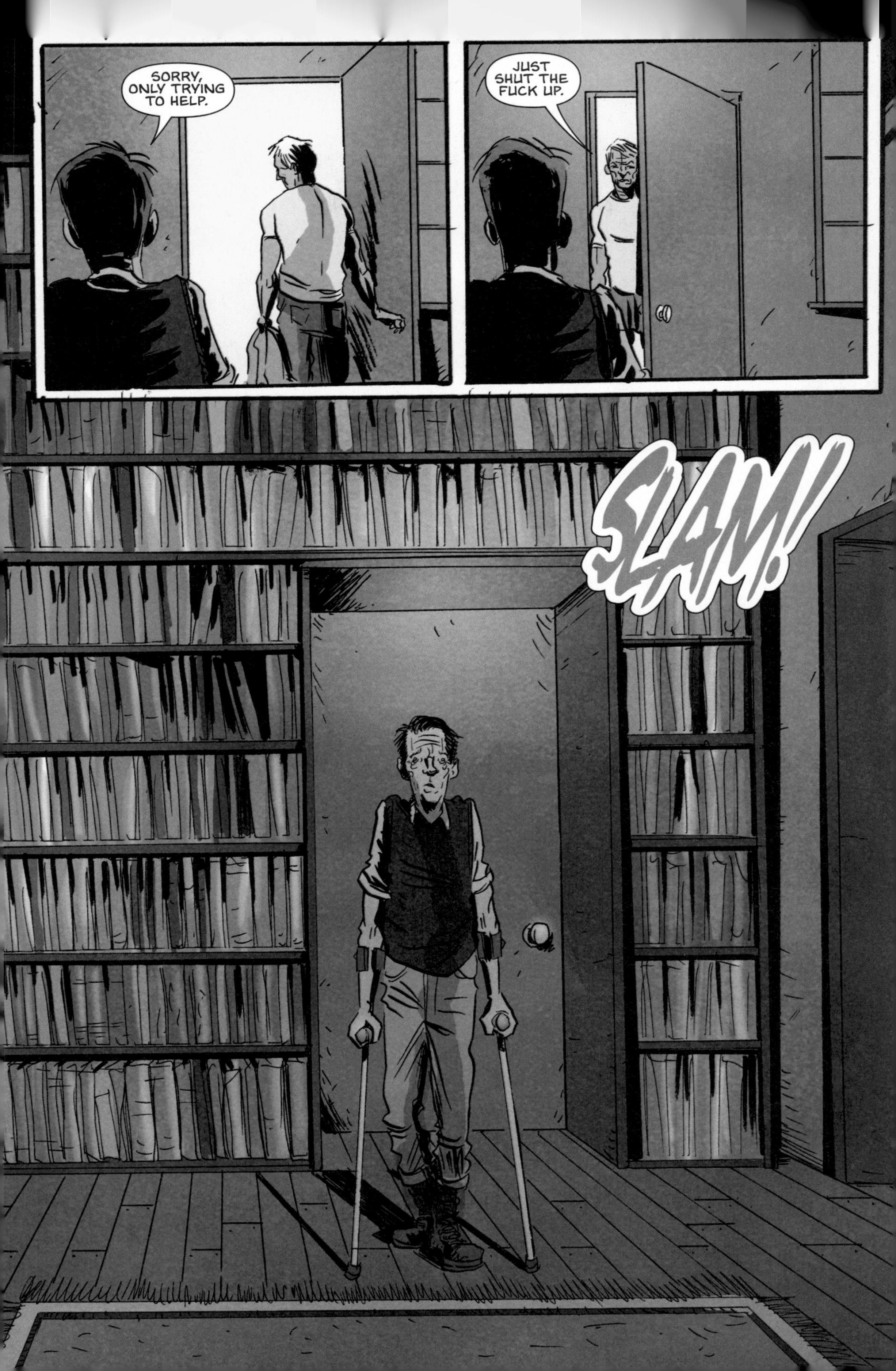
SORRY, ONLY TRYING TO HELP.
JUST SHUT THE FUCK UP.
SLAM!

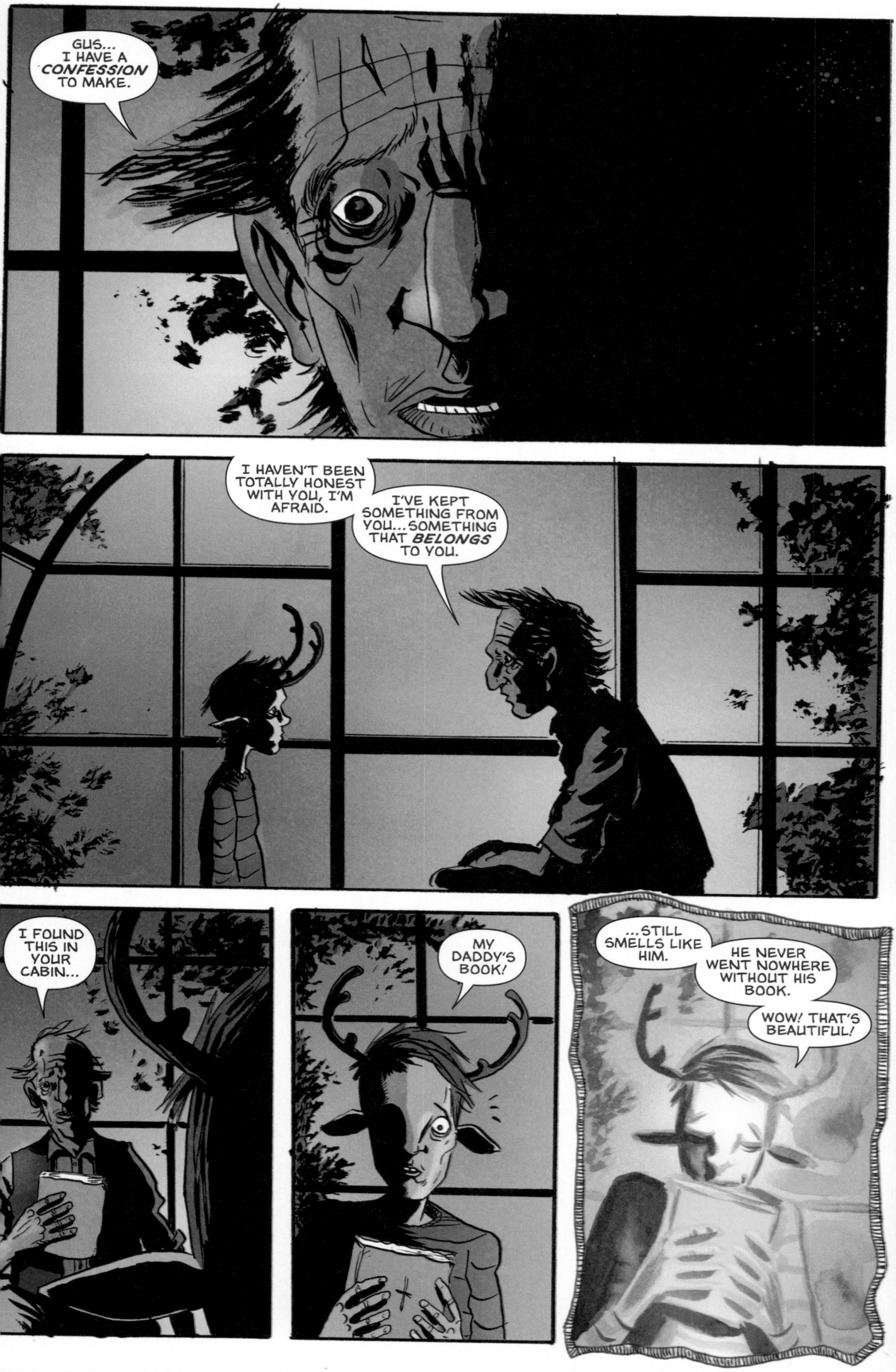
GUS... I HAVE A *CONFESSION* TO MAKE.
I HAVEN'T BEEN TOTALLY HONEST WITH YOU, I'M AFRAID.
I'VE KEPT SOMETHING FROM YOU... SOMETHING THAT *BELONGS* TO YOU.
I FOUND THIS IN YOUR CABIN...
MY DADDY'S BOOK!
...STILL SMELLS LIKE HIM.
HE NEVER WENT NOWHERE WITHOUT HIS BOOK.
WOW! THAT'S BEAUTIFUL!

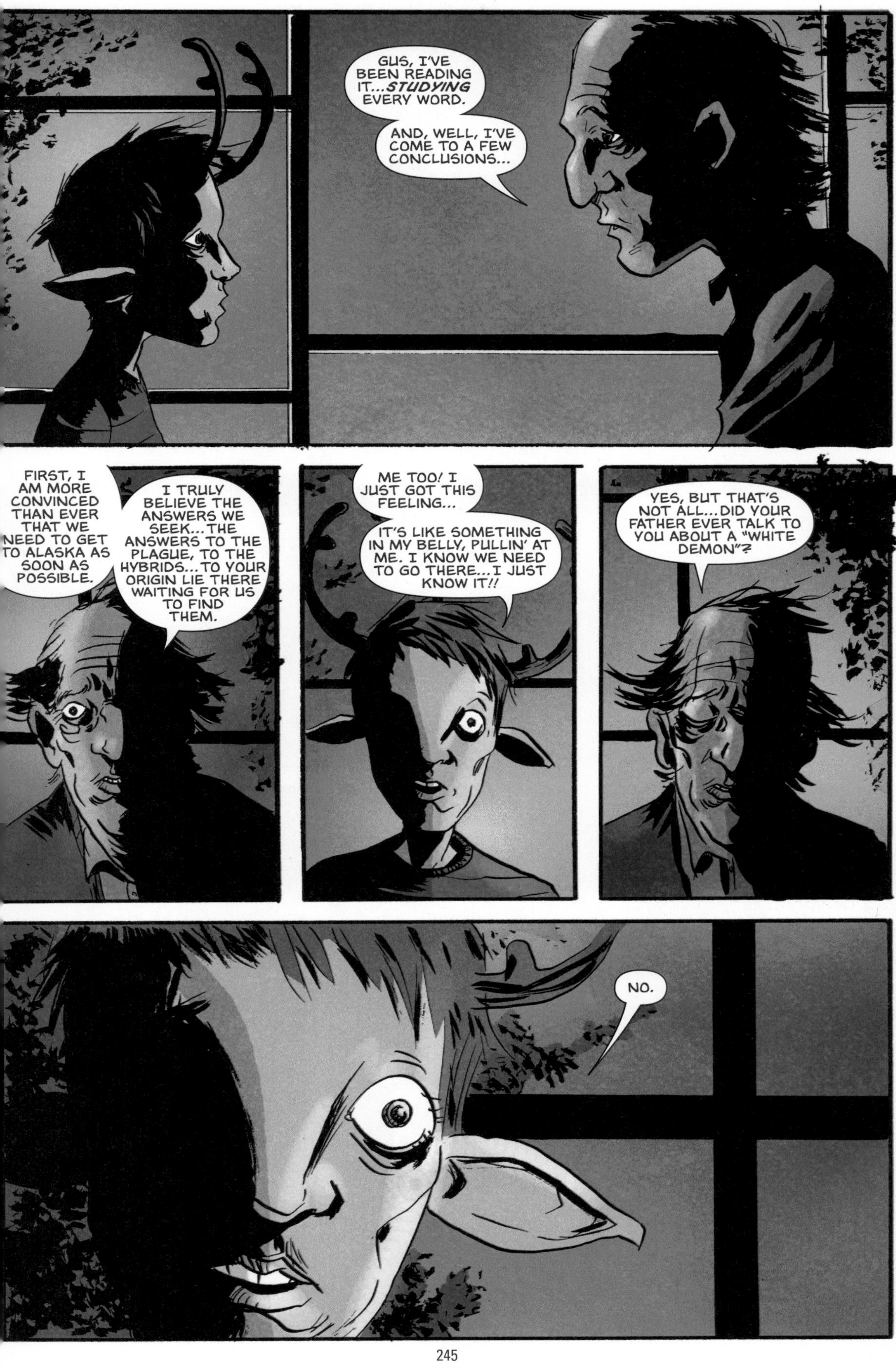
GUS, I'VE BEEN READING IT...STUDYING EVERY WORD.
AND, WELL, I'VE COME TO A FEW CONCLUSIONS...
FIRST, I AM MORE CONVINCED THAN EVER THAT WE NEED TO GET TO ALASKA AS SOON AS POSSIBLE.
I TRULY BELIEVE THE ANSWERS WE SEEK...THE ANSWERS TO THE PLAGUE, TO THE HYBRIDS...TO YOUR ORIGIN LIE THERE WAITING FOR US TO FIND THEM.
ME TOO! I JUST GOT THIS FEELING...
IT'S LIKE SOMETHING IN MY BELLY, PULLIN' AT ME. I KNOW WE NEED TO GO THERE...I JUST KNOW IT!!
YES, BUT THAT'S NOT ALL...DID YOUR FATHER EVER TALK TO YOU ABOUT A "WHITE DEMON"?
NO.

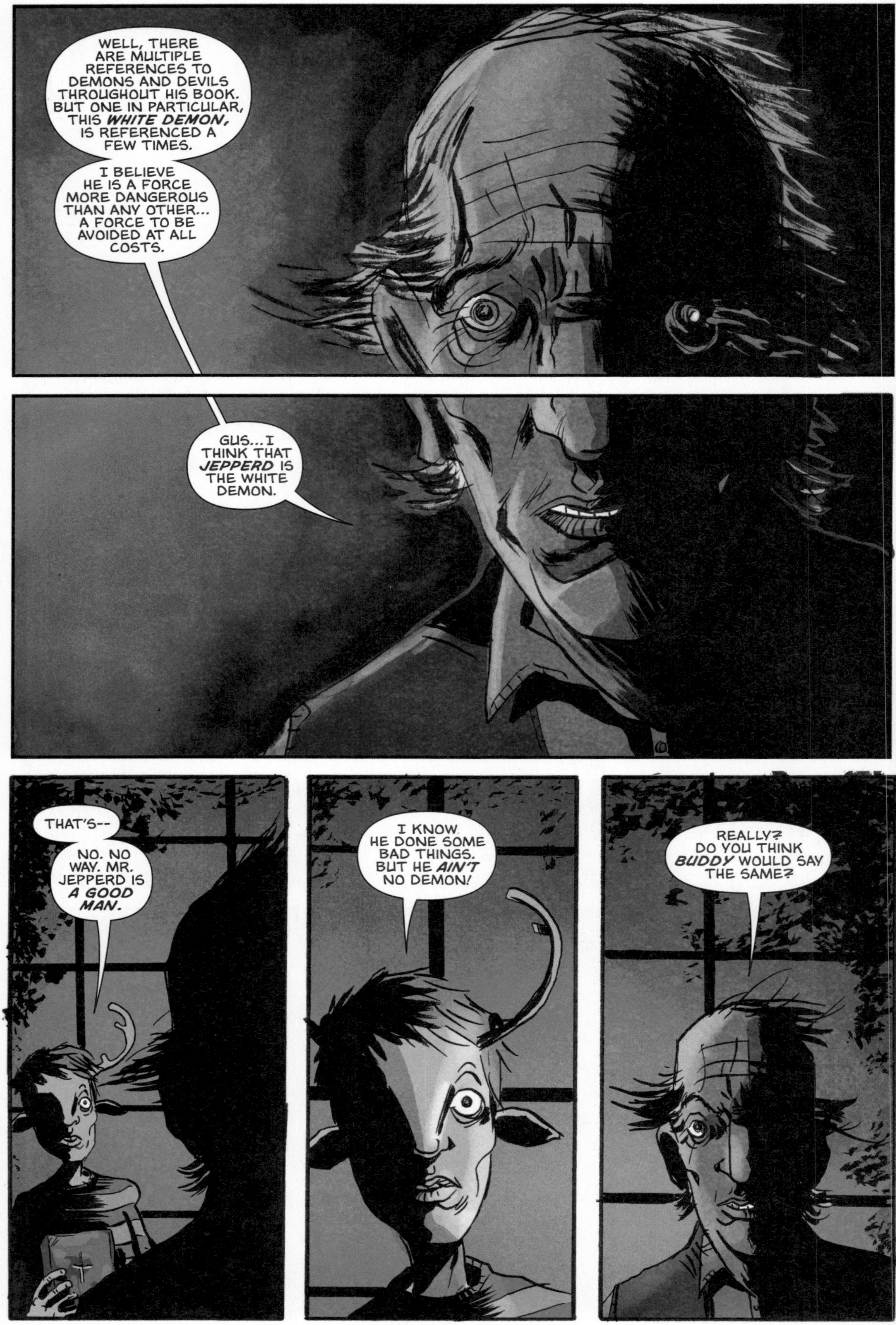
WELL, THERE ARE MULTIPLE REFERENCES TO DEMONS AND DEVILS THROUGHOUT HIS BOOK. BUT ONE IN PARTICULAR, THIS *WHITE DEMON,* IS REFERENCED A FEW TIMES.
I BELIEVE HE IS A FORCE MORE DANGEROUS THAN ANY OTHER... A FORCE TO BE AVOIDED AT ALL COSTS.
GUS... I THINK THAT *JEPPERD* IS THE WHITE DEMON.
THAT'S--
NO. NO WAY. MR. JEPPERD IS ***A GOOD MAN.***
I KNOW. HE DONE SOME BAD THINGS. BUT HE *AIN'T* NO DEMON!
REALLY? DO YOU THINK ***BUDDY*** WOULD SAY THE SAME?

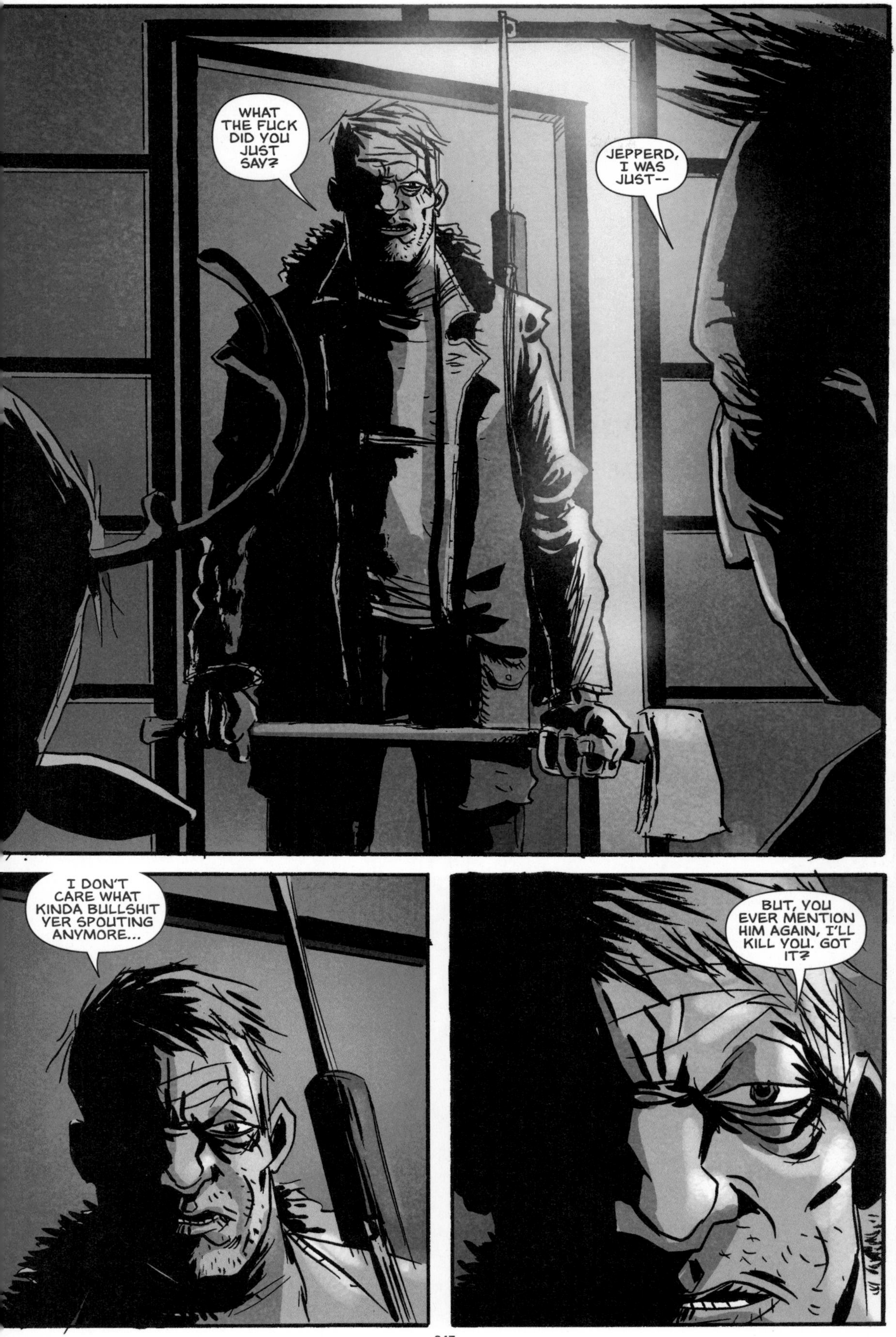
WHAT THE FUCK DID YOU JUST SAY?
JEPPERD, I WAS JUST--
I DON'T CARE WHAT KINDA BULLSHIT YER SPOUTING ANYMORE...
BUT, YOU EVER MENTION HIM AGAIN, I'LL KILL YOU. GOT IT?

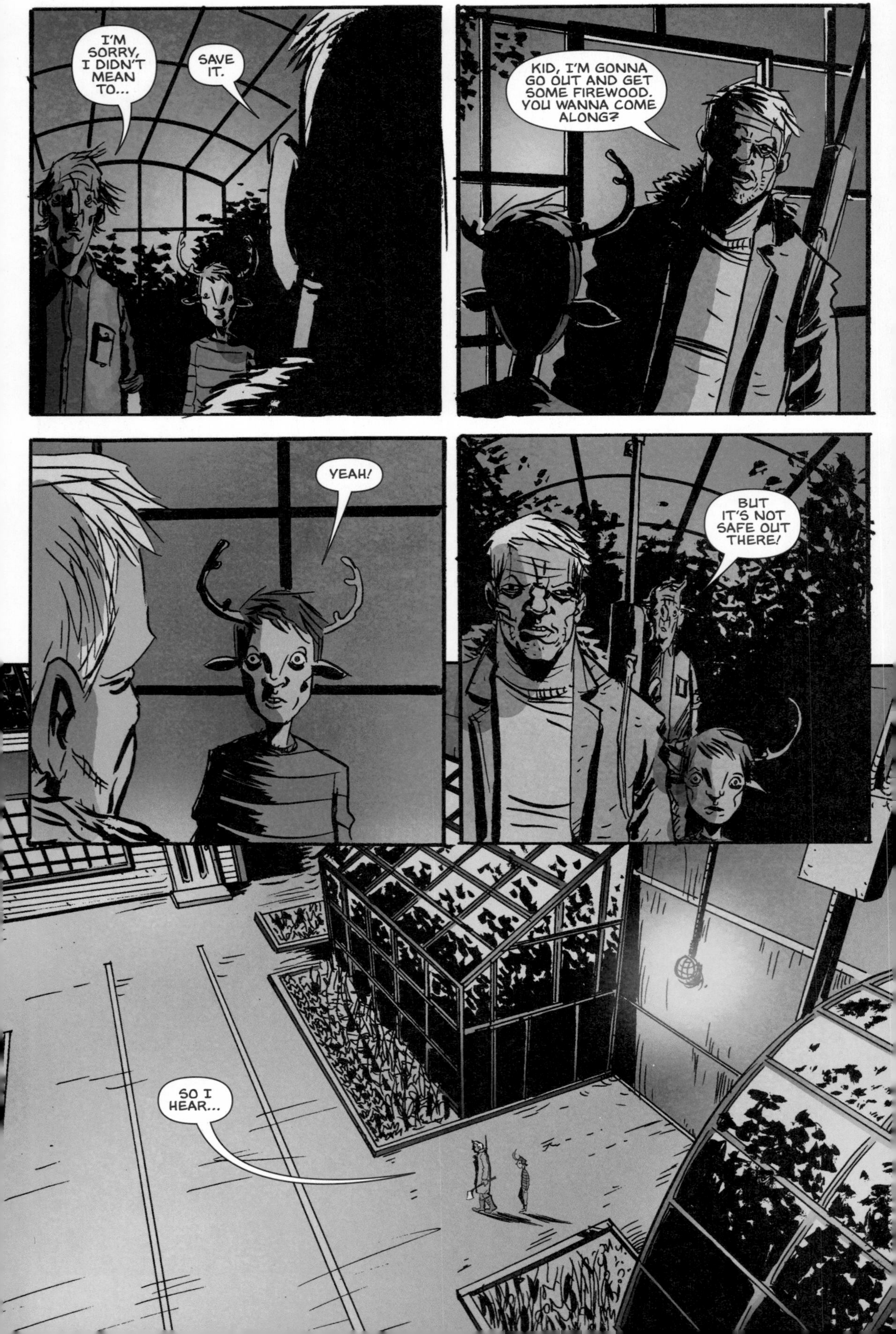

I'M SORRY, I DIDN'T MEAN TO...
SAVE IT.
KID, I'M GONNA GO OUT AND GET SOME FIREWOOD. YOU WANNA COME ALONG?
YEAH!
BUT IT'S NOT SAFE OUT THERE!
SO I HEAR...

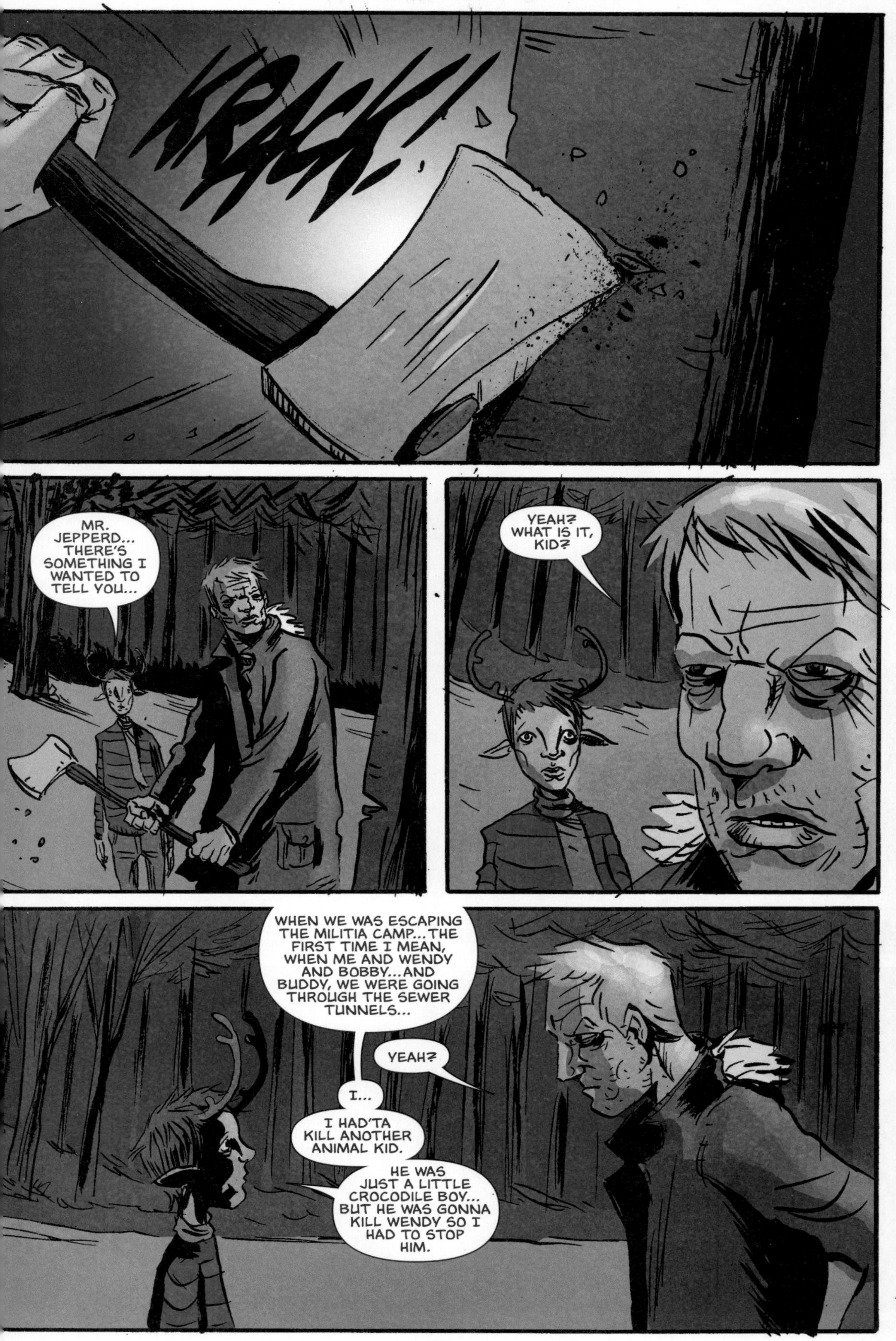
KRACK!
MR. JEPPERD... THERE'S SOMETHING I WANTED TO TELL YOU...
YEAH? WHAT IS IT, KID?
WHEN WE WAS ESCAPING THE MILITIA CAMP... THE FIRST TIME I MEAN, WHEN ME AND WENDY AND BOBBY...AND BUDDY, WE WERE GOING THROUGH THE SEWER TUNNELS...
YEAH?
I...
I HAD'TA KILL ANOTHER ANIMAL KID.
HE WAS JUST A LITTLE CROCODILE BOY... BUT HE WAS GONNA KILL WENDY SO I HAD TO STOP HIM.

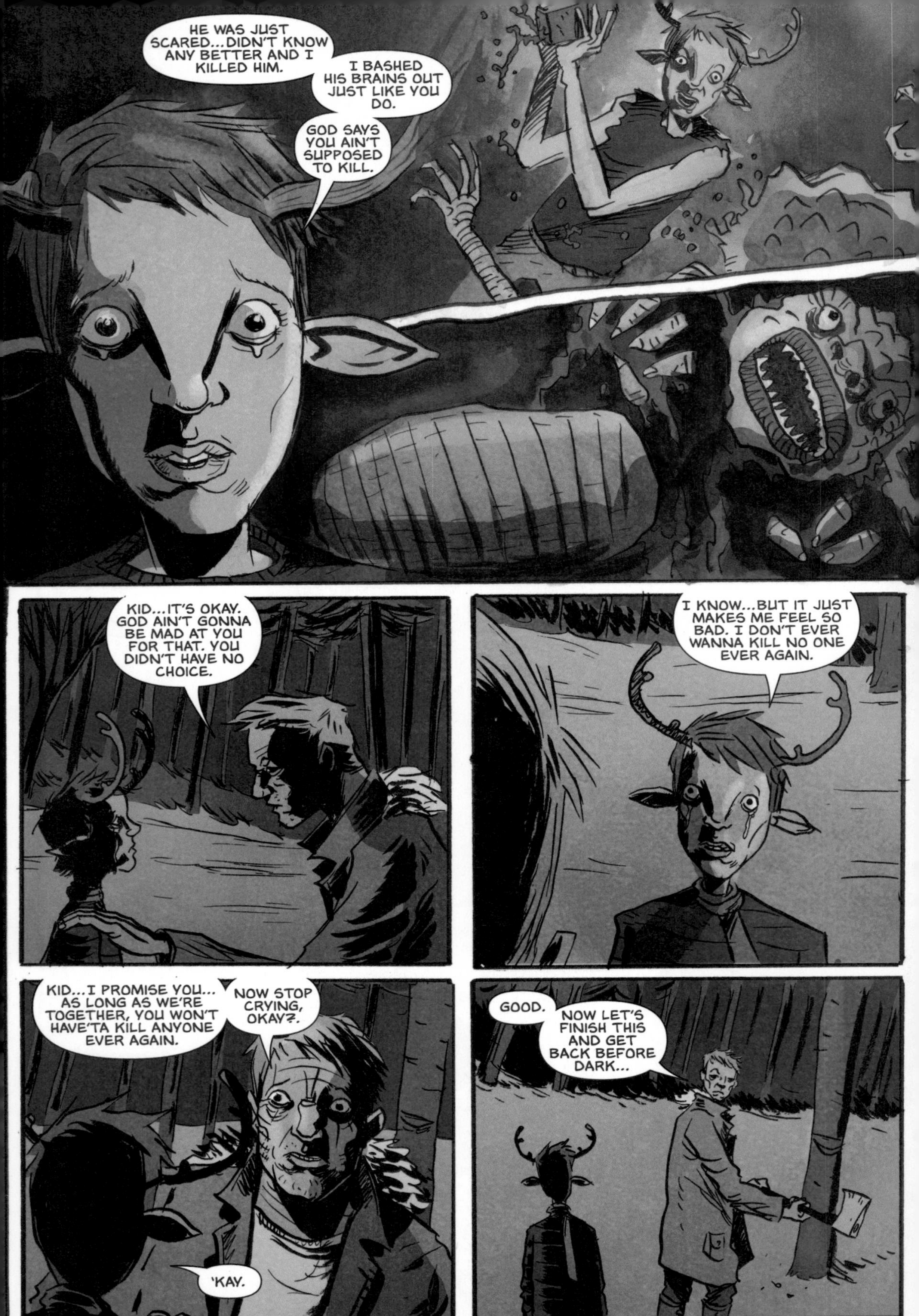
HE WAS JUST SCARED...DIDN'T KNOW ANY BETTER AND I KILLED HIM.
I BASHED HIS BRAINS OUT JUST LIKE YOU DO.
GOD SAYS YOU AIN'T SUPPOSED TO KILL.
KID...IT'S OKAY. GOD AIN'T GONNA BE MAD AT YOU FOR THAT. YOU DIDN'T HAVE NO CHOICE.
I KNOW...BUT IT JUST MAKES ME FEEL SO BAD. I DON'T EVER WANNA KILL NO ONE EVER AGAIN.
KID...I PROMISE YOU... AS LONG AS WE'RE TOGETHER, YOU WON'T HAVE'TA KILL ANYONE EVER AGAIN.
NOW STOP CRYING, OKAY?.
'KAY.
GOOD.
NOW LET'S FINISH THIS AND GET BACK BEFORE DARK...

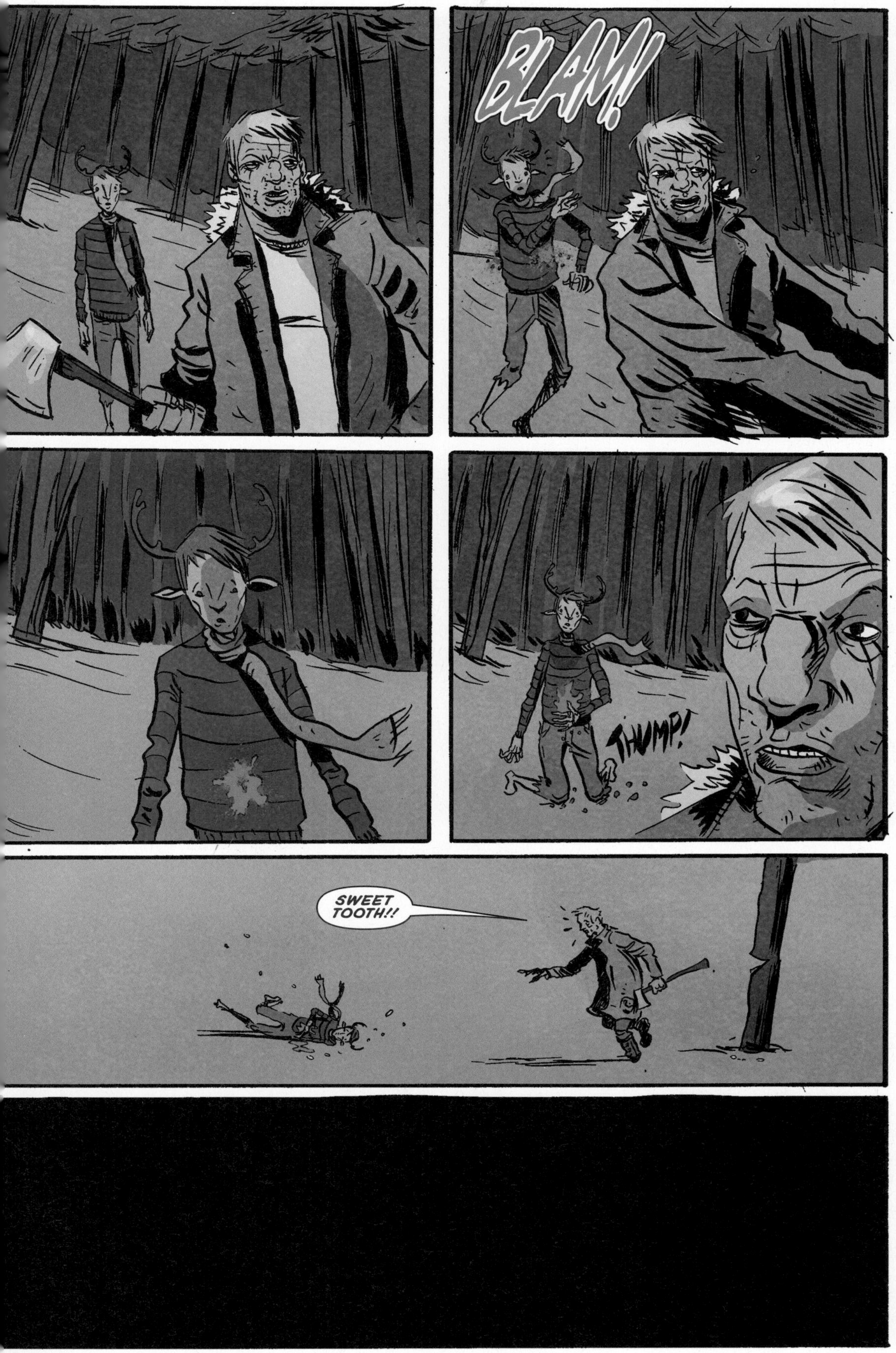
BLAM!
THUMP!
SWEET TOOTH!!

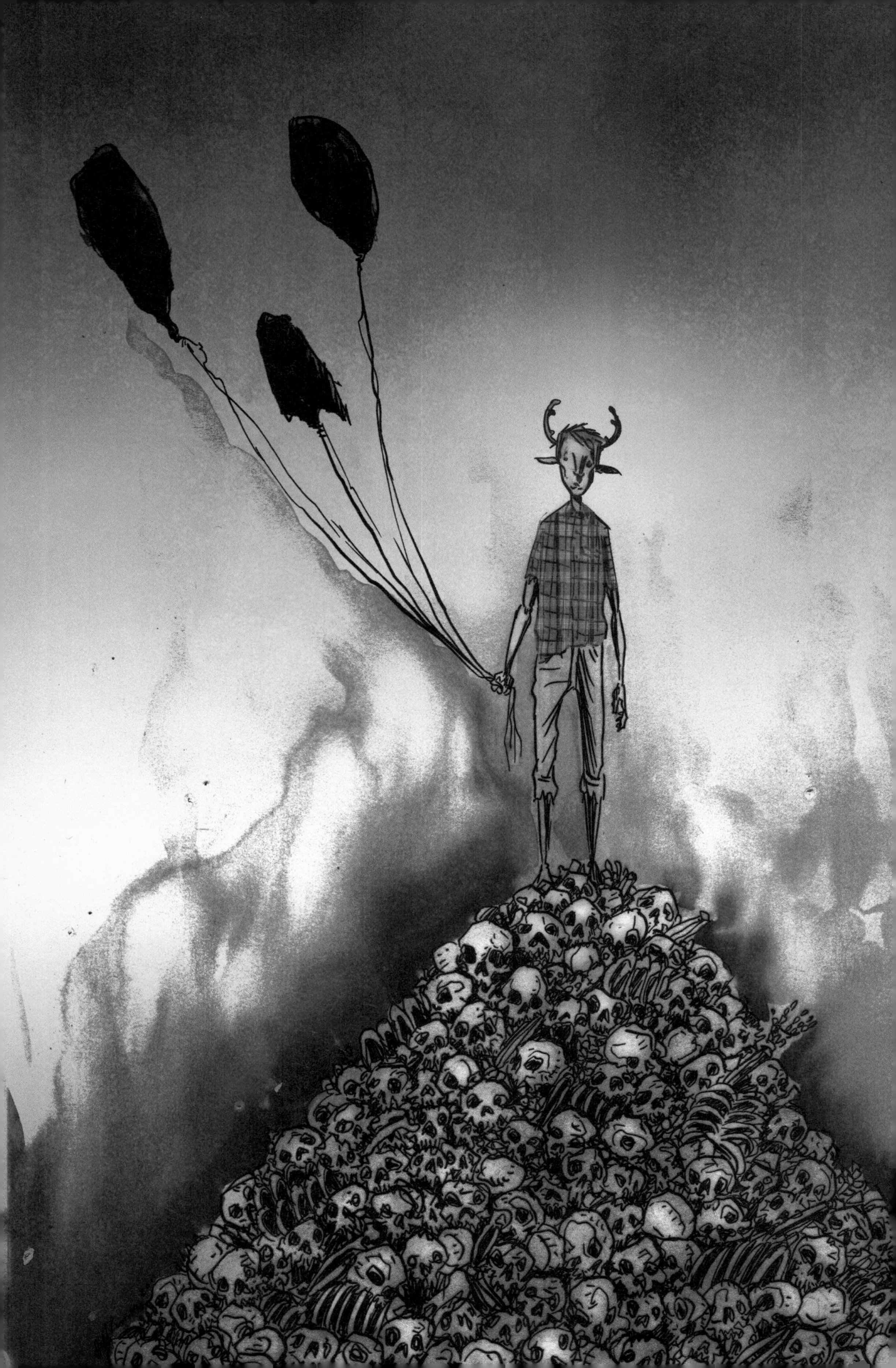

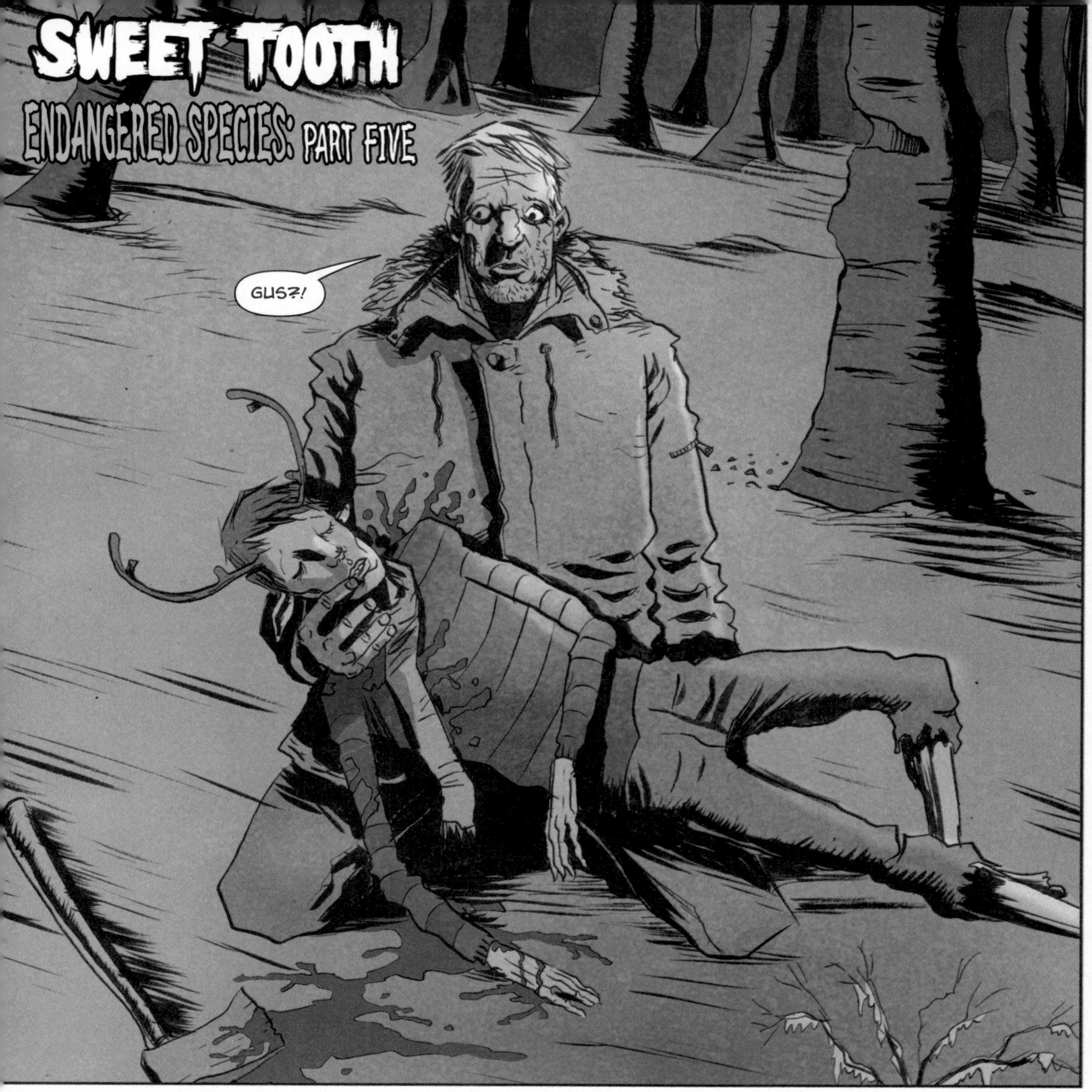
SWEET TOOTH
ENDANGERED SPECIES: PART FIVE
GUS?!

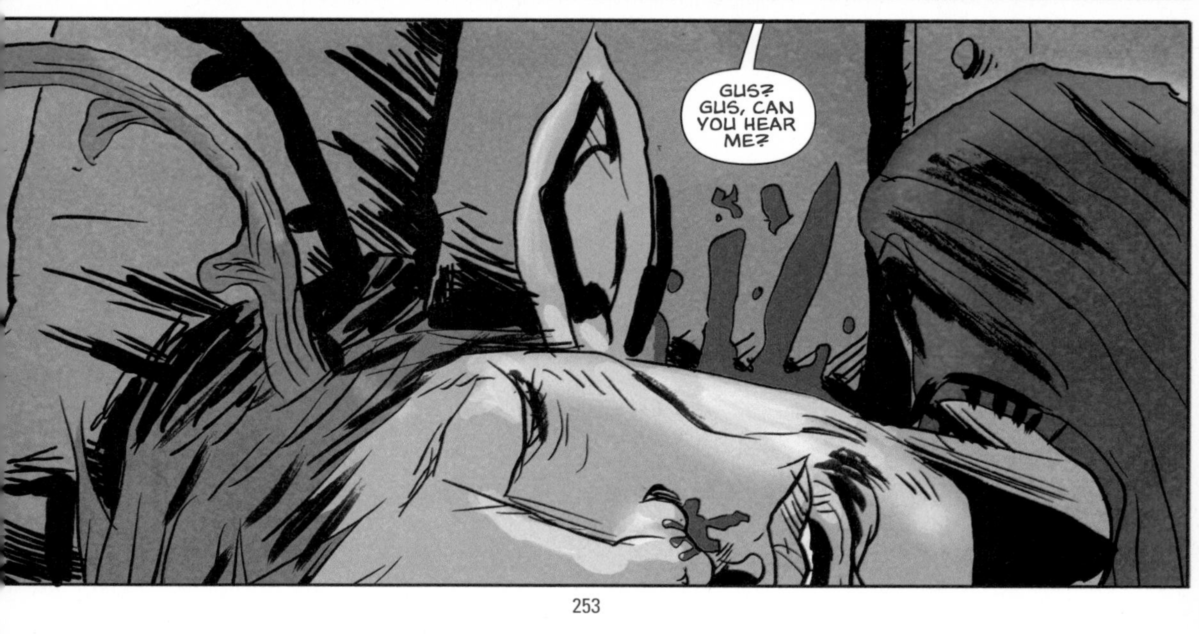
GUS? GUS, CAN YOU HEAR ME?

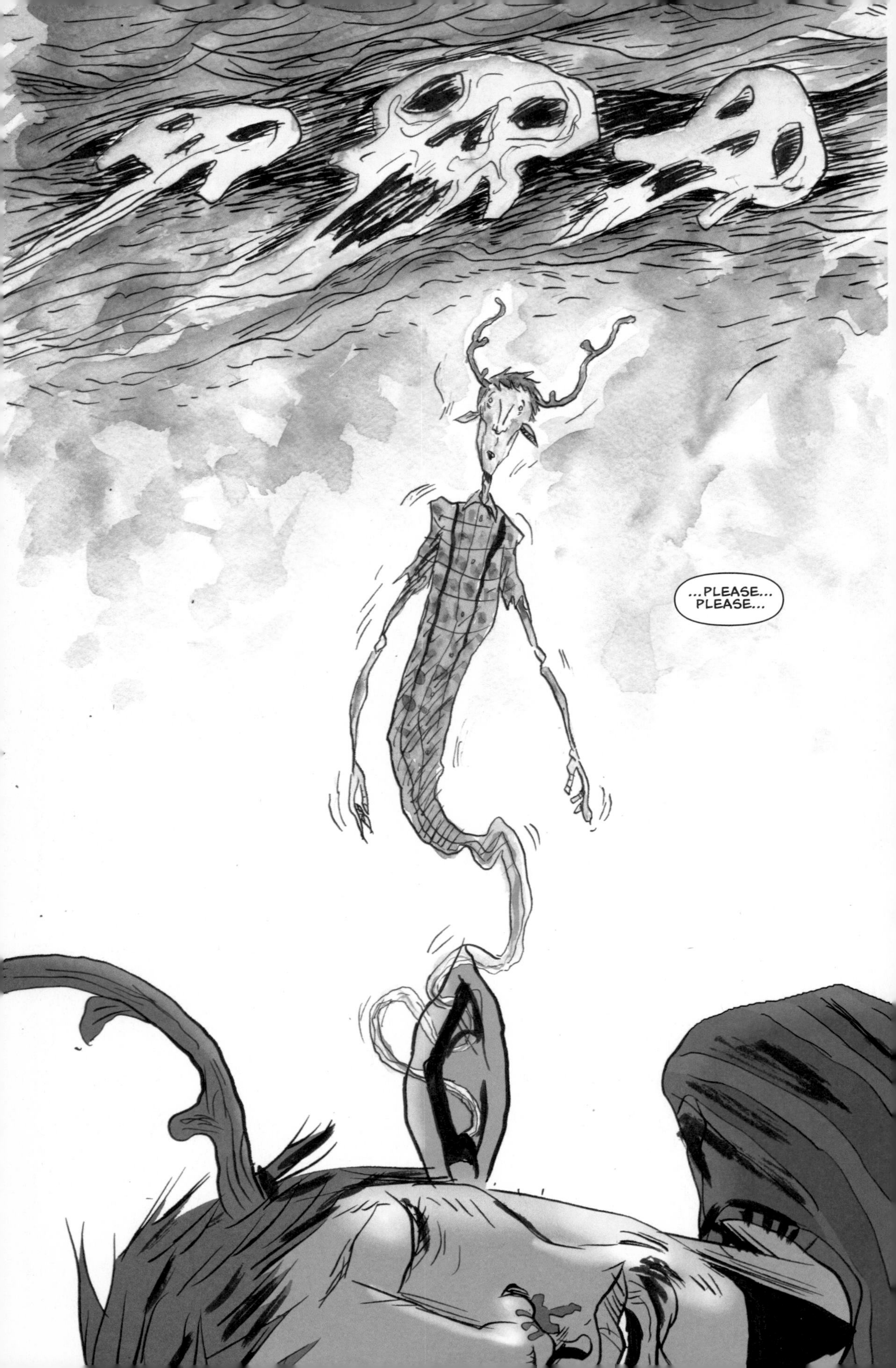
...PLEASE...
PLEASE...

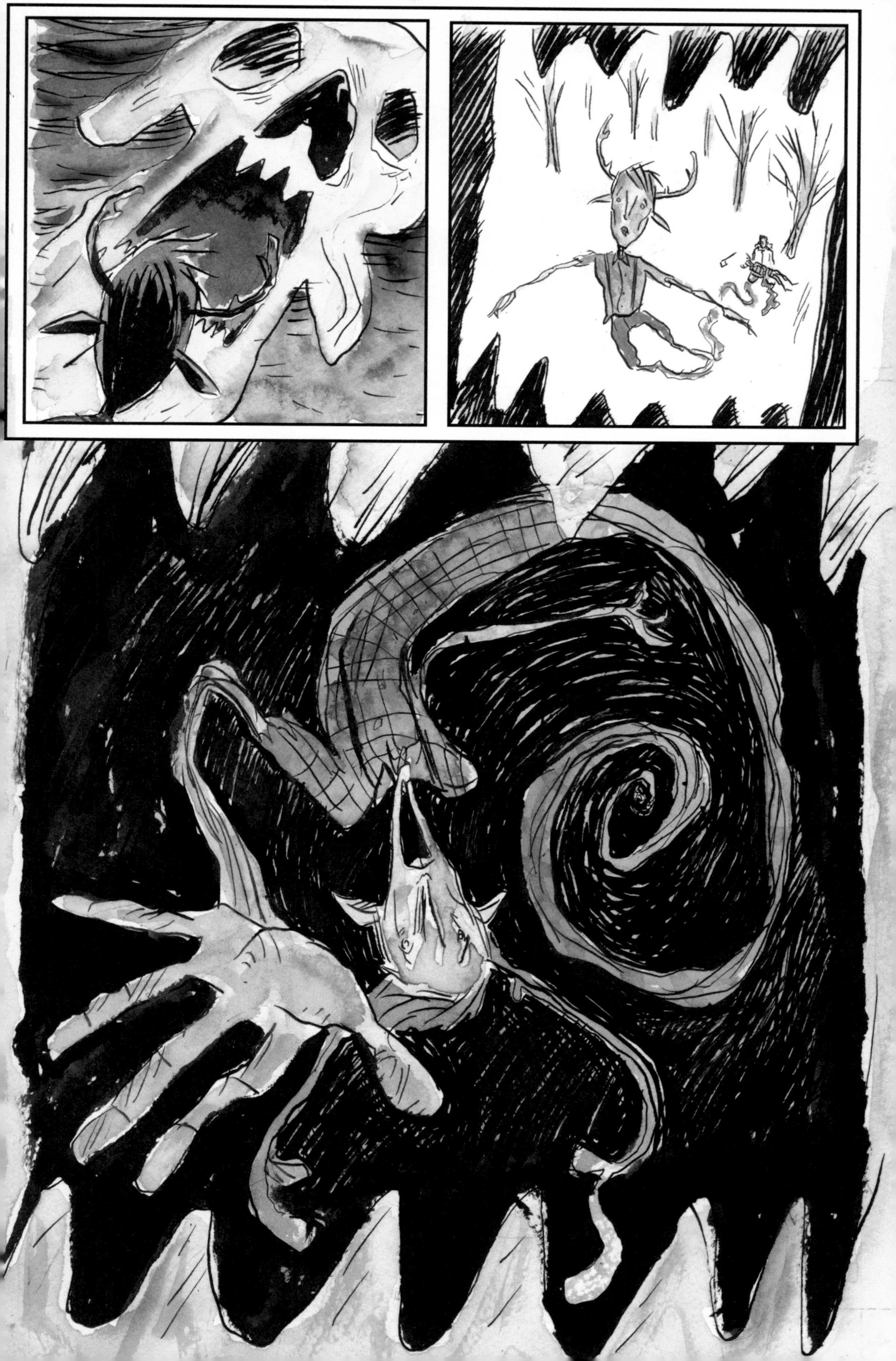

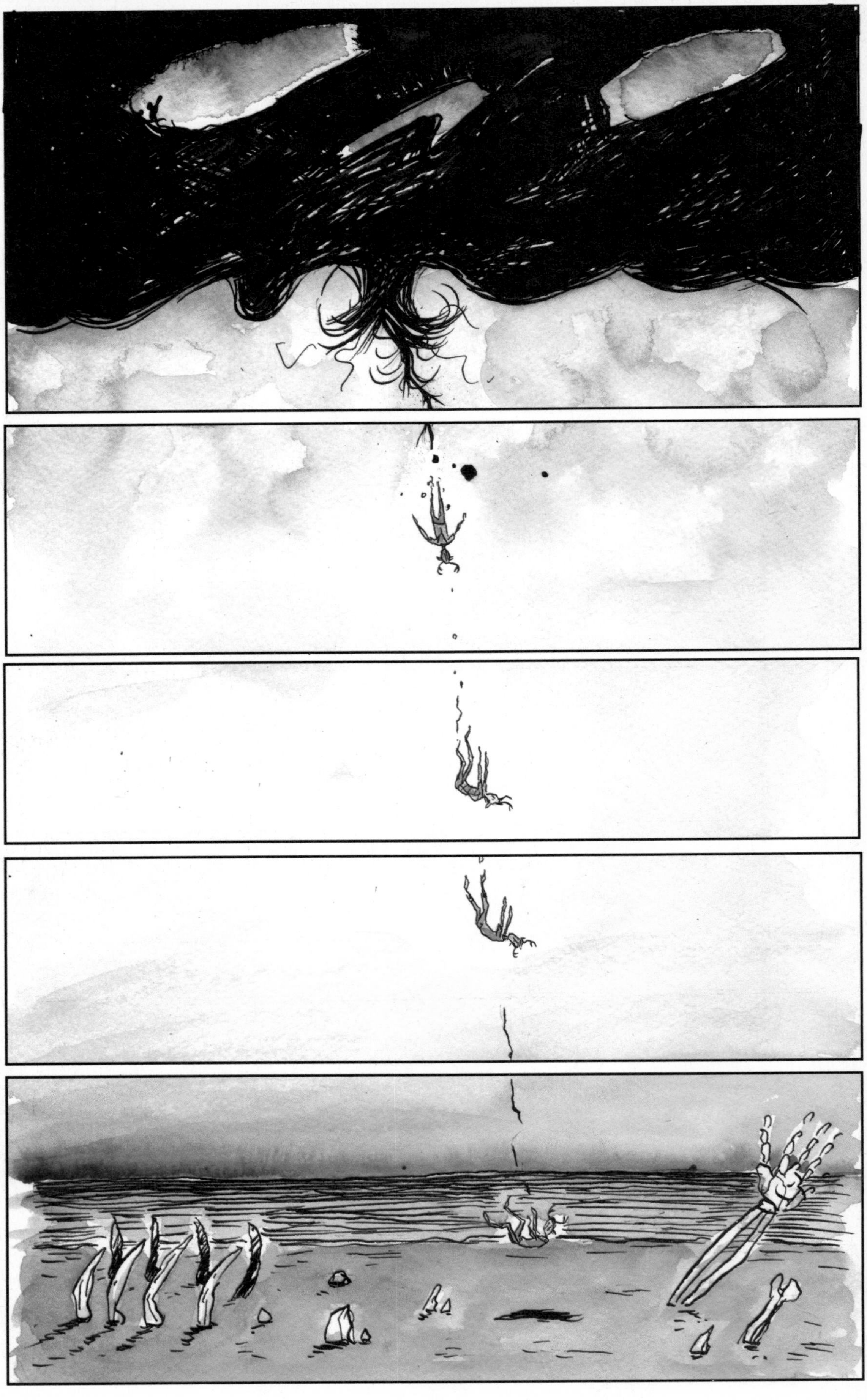

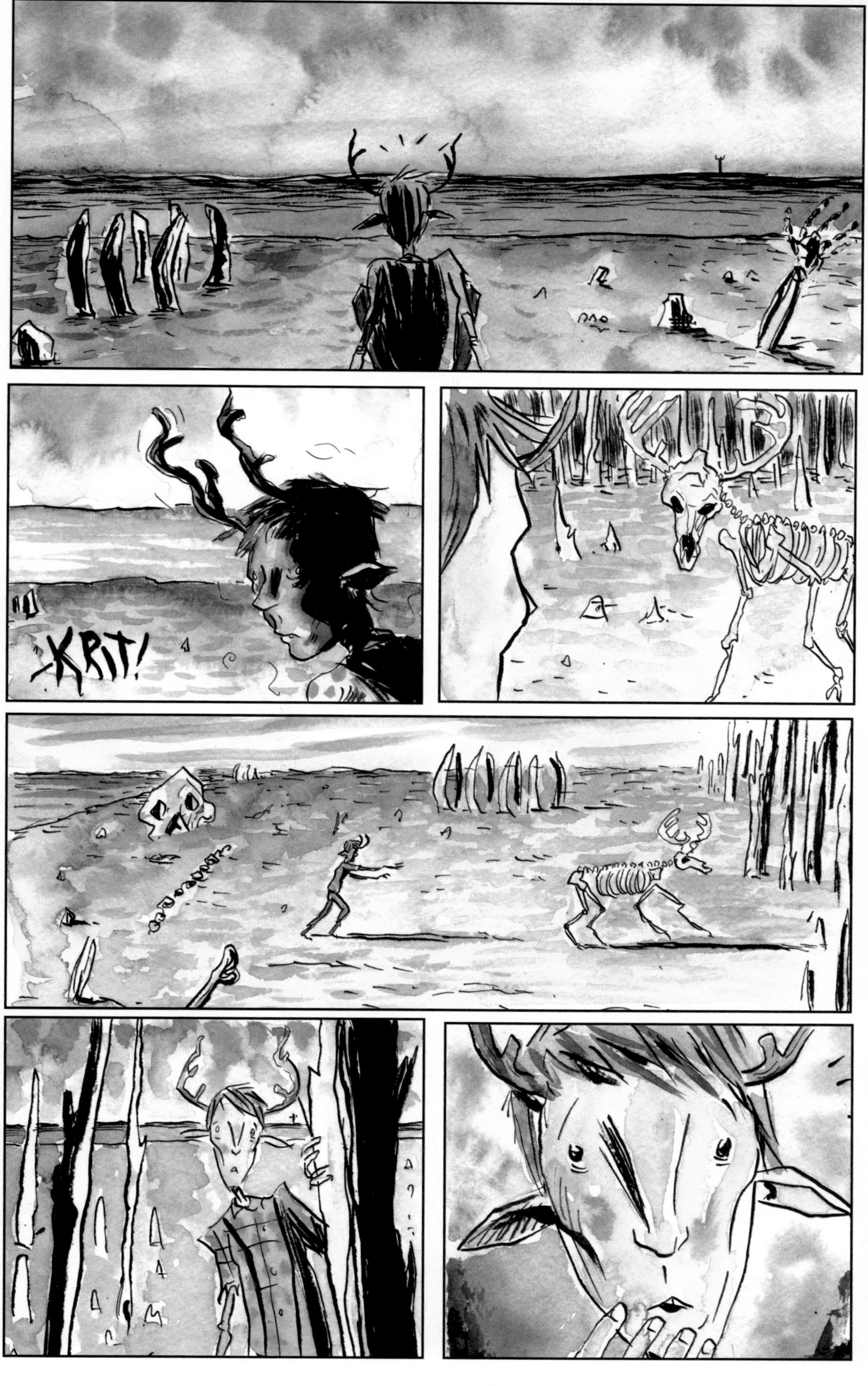
KRIT!

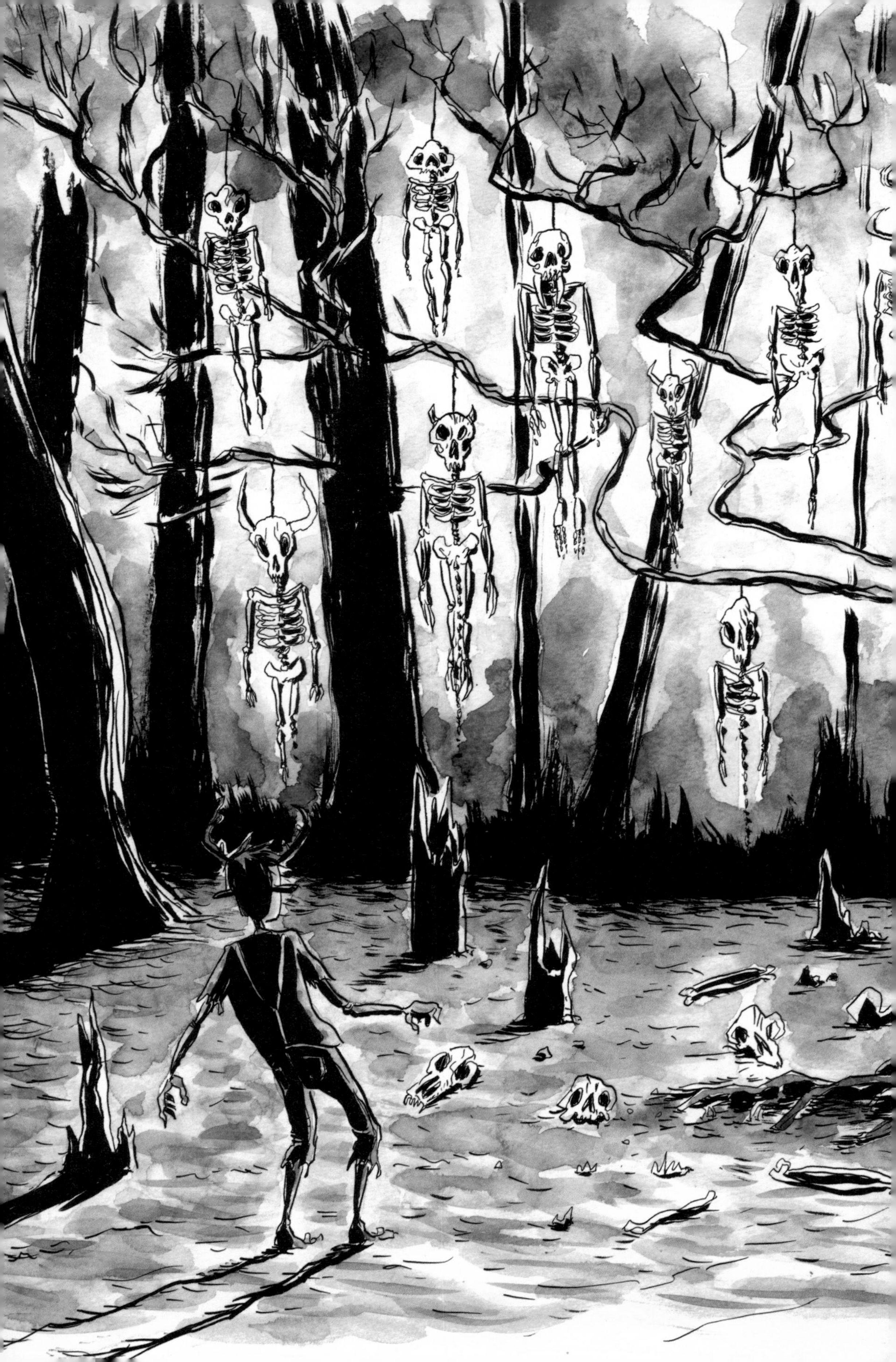

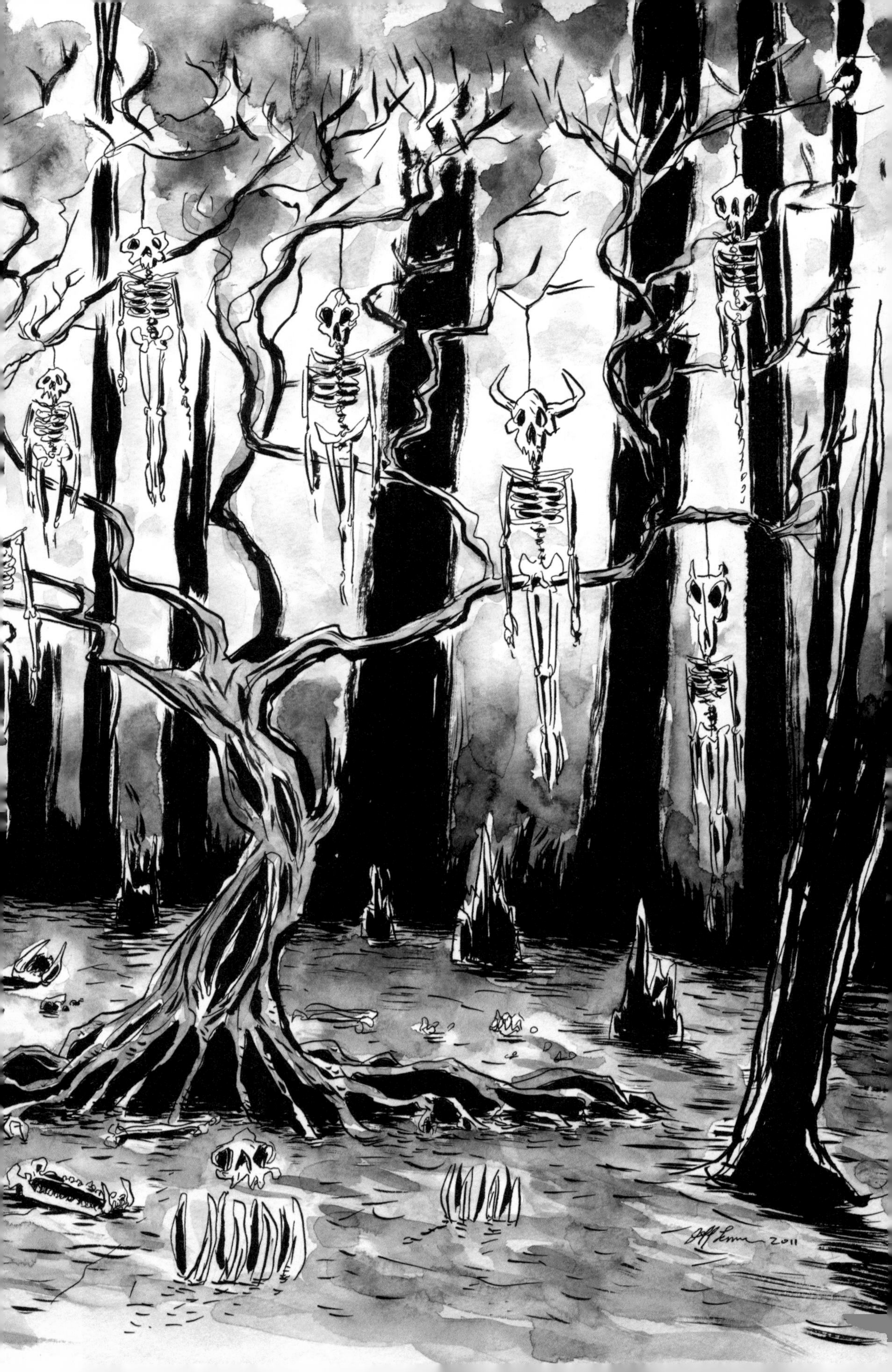

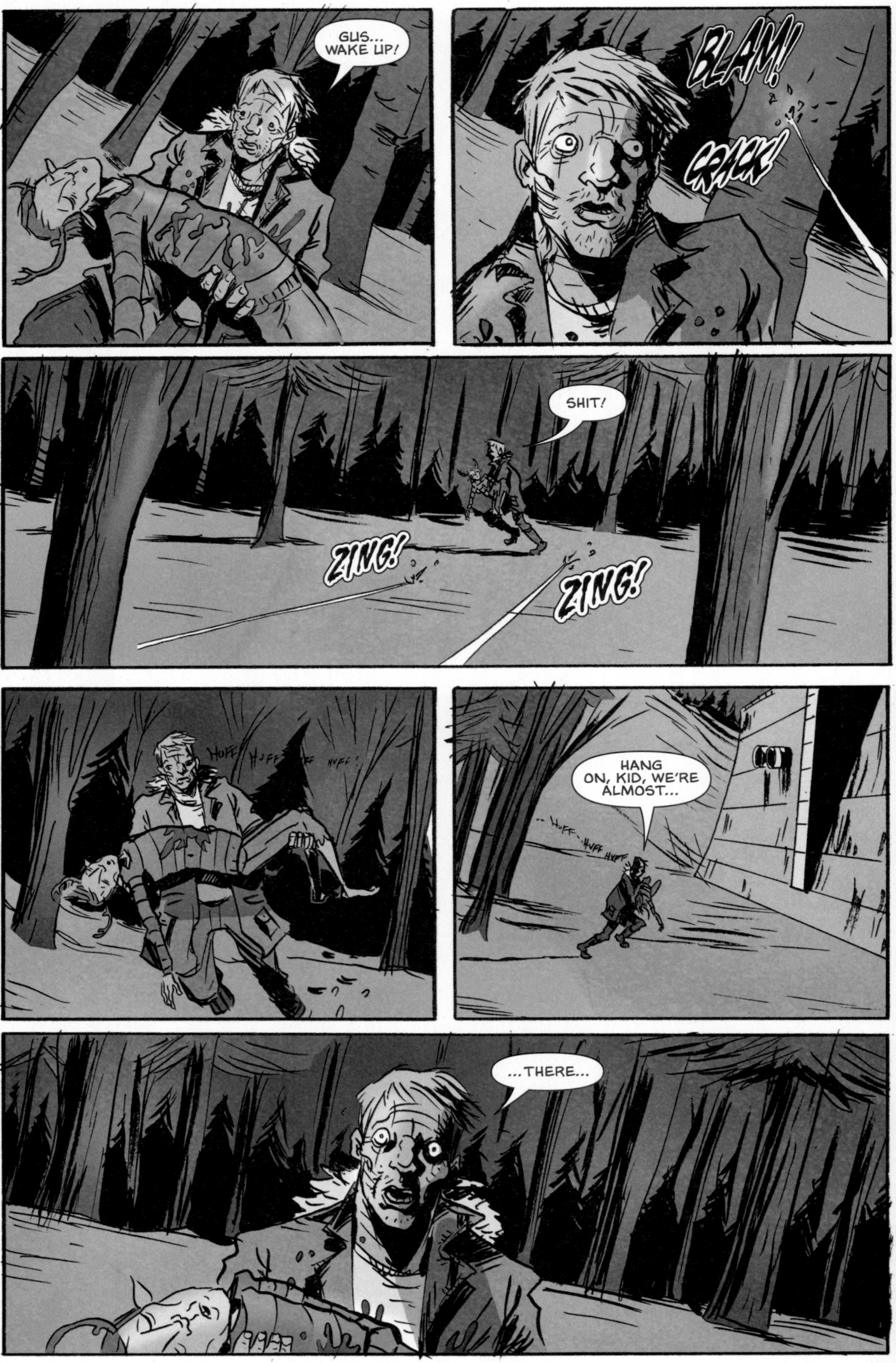
GUS... WAKE UP!
BLAM!
CRACK!
SHIT!
ZING!
ZING!
HUFF HUFF HUFF HUFF!
HANG ON, KID, WE'RE ALMOST...
HUFF HUFF HUFF
...THERE...

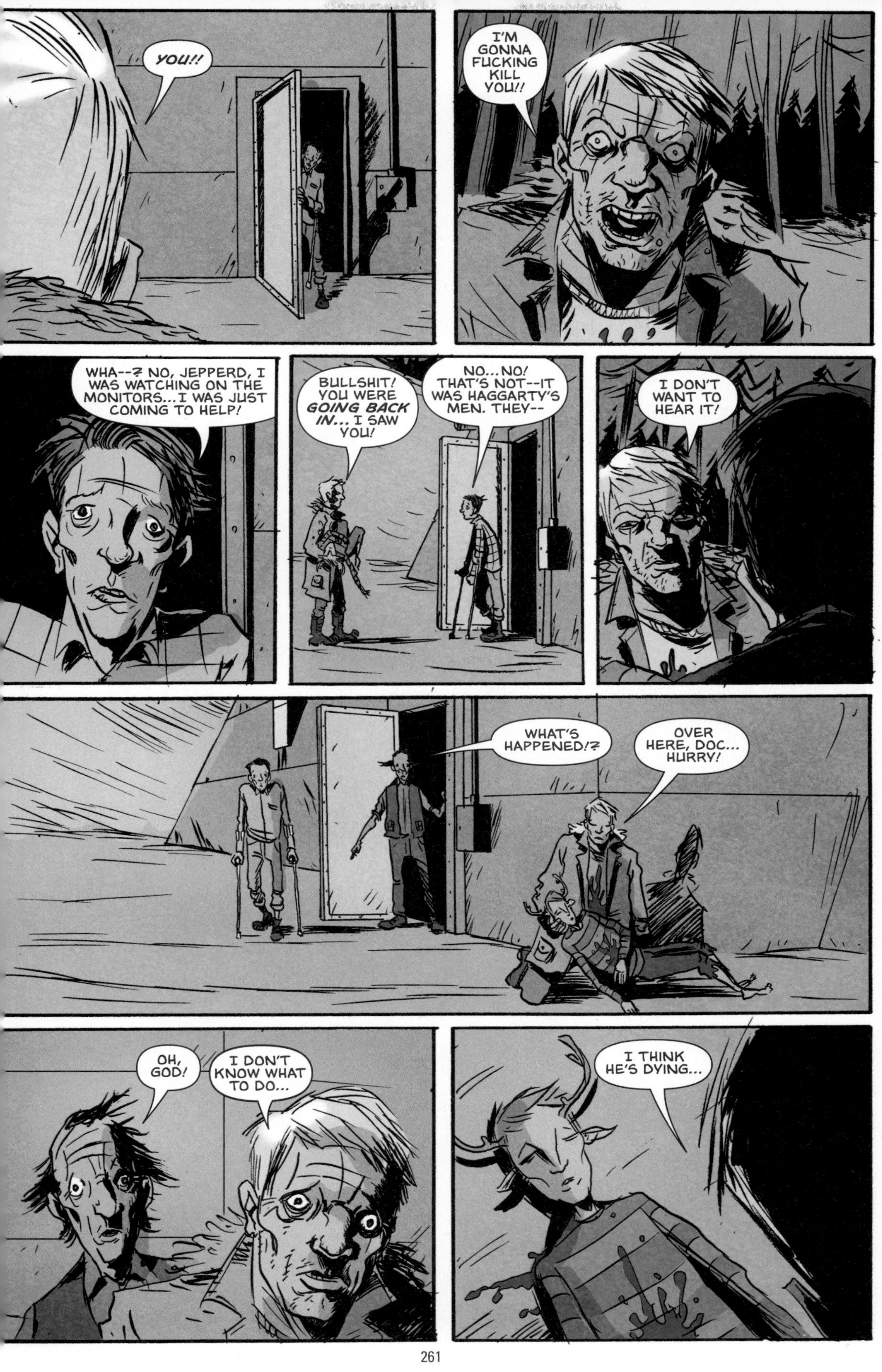
YOU!!
I'M GONNA FUCKING KILL YOU!!
WHA--?! NO, JEPPERD, I WAS WATCHING ON THE MONITORS... I WAS JUST COMING TO HELP!
BULLSHIT! YOU WERE GOING BACK IN... I SAW YOU!
NO... NO! THAT'S NOT--IT WAS HAGGARTY'S MEN. THEY--
I DON'T WANT TO HEAR IT!
WHAT'S HAPPENED!?
OVER HERE, DOC... HURRY!
OH, GOD!
I DON'T KNOW WHAT TO DO...
I THINK HE'S DYING...

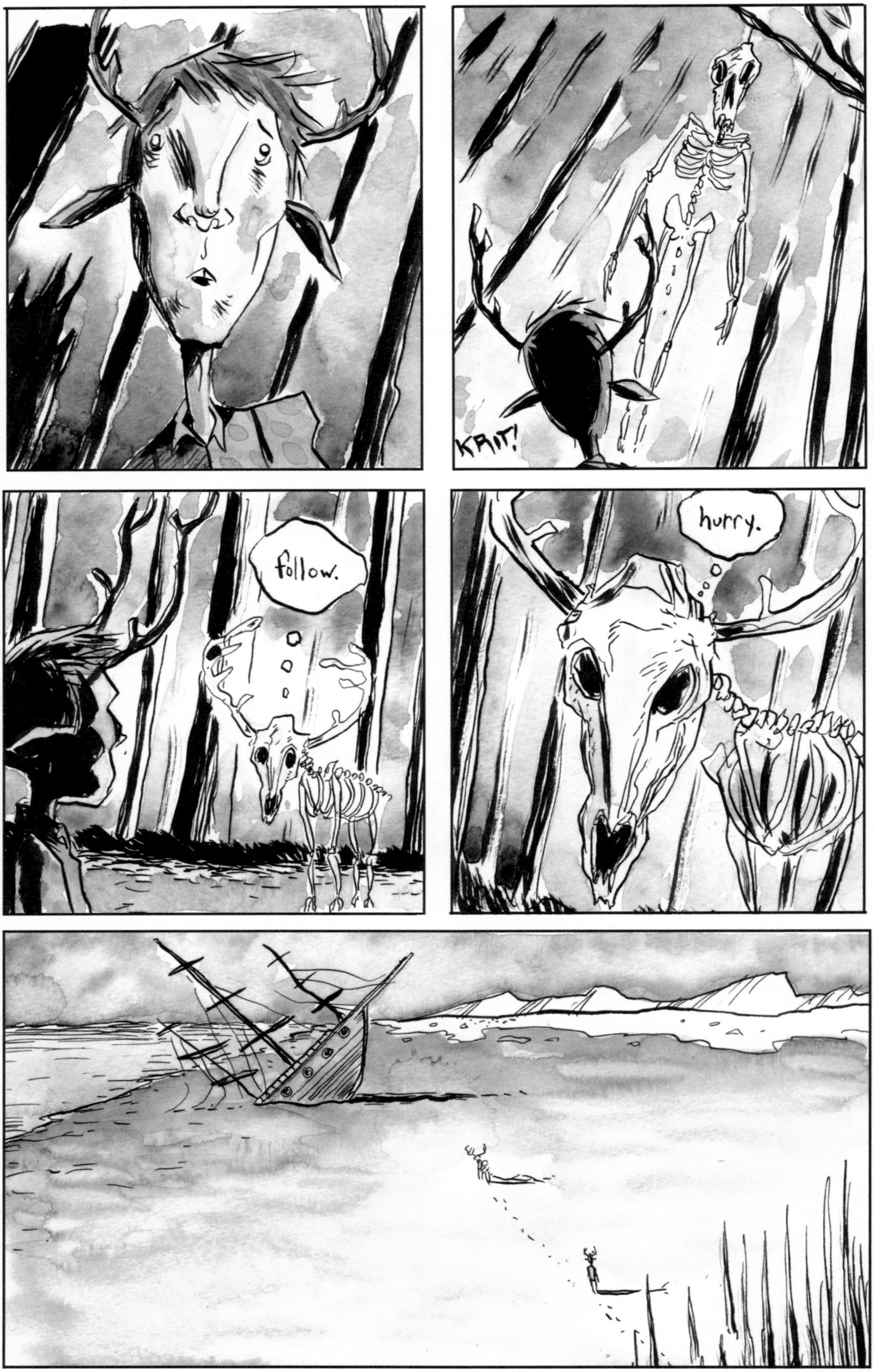
KRIT!
follow.
hurry.

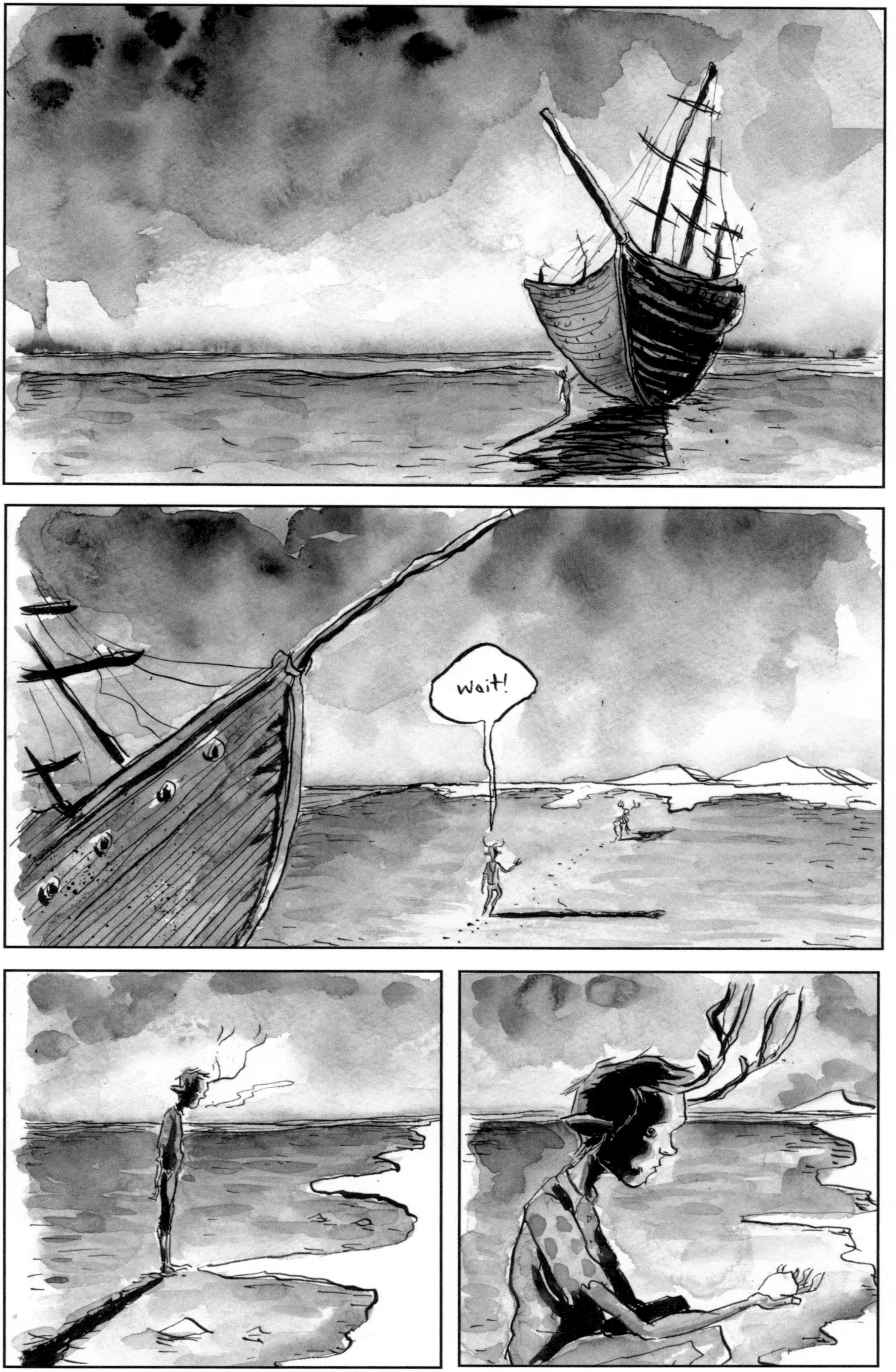
wait!

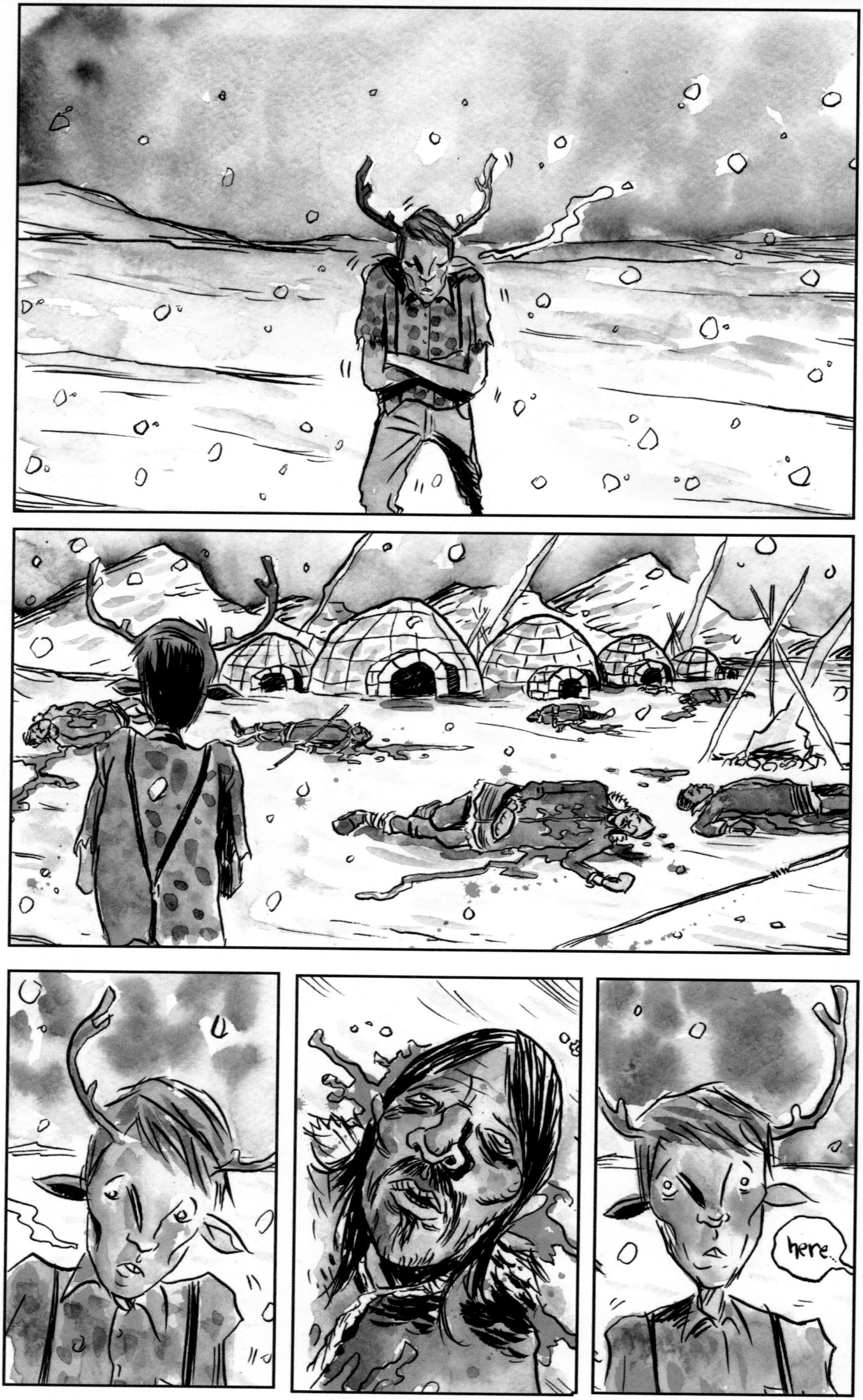
here...

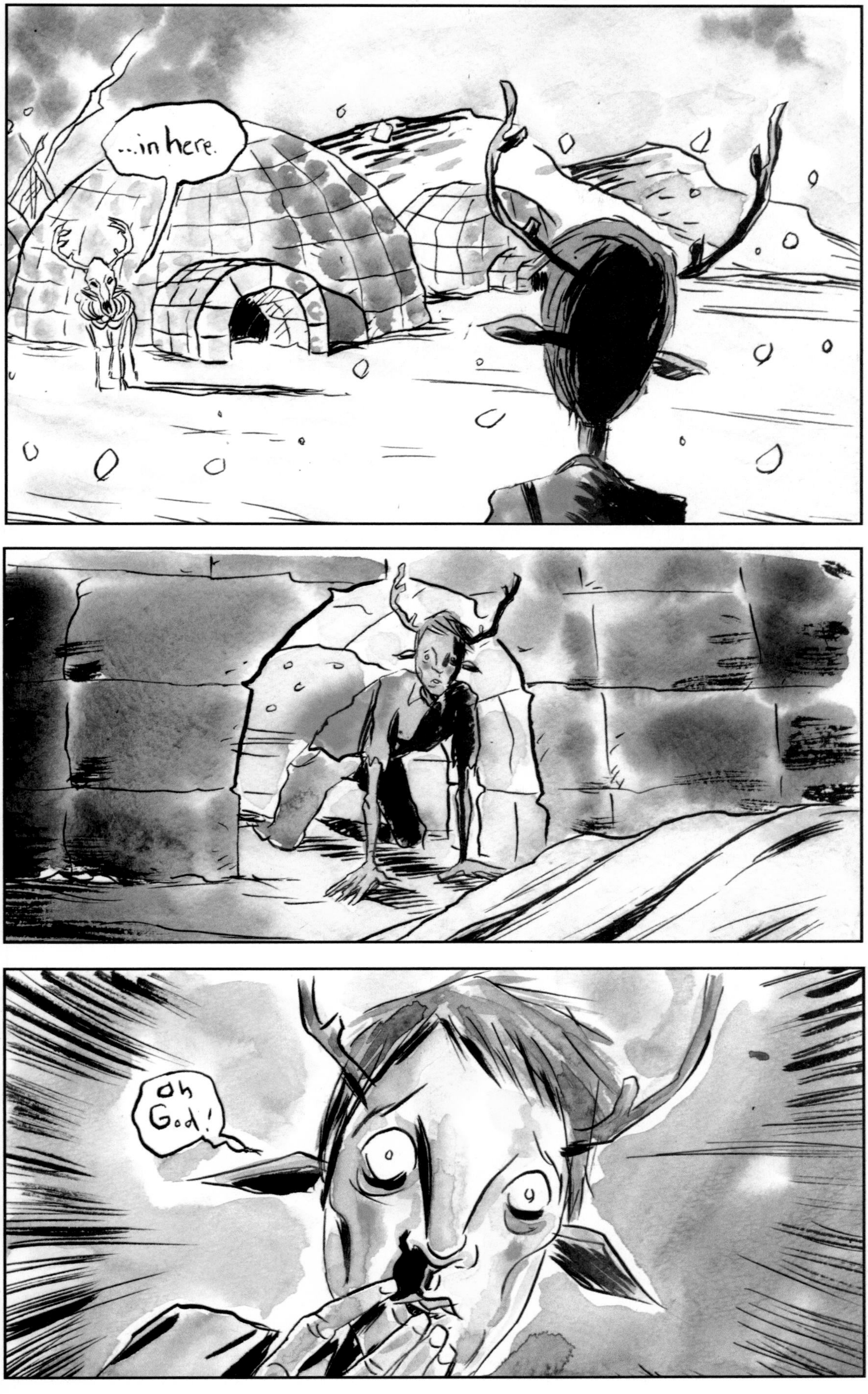
...in here.
Oh God!

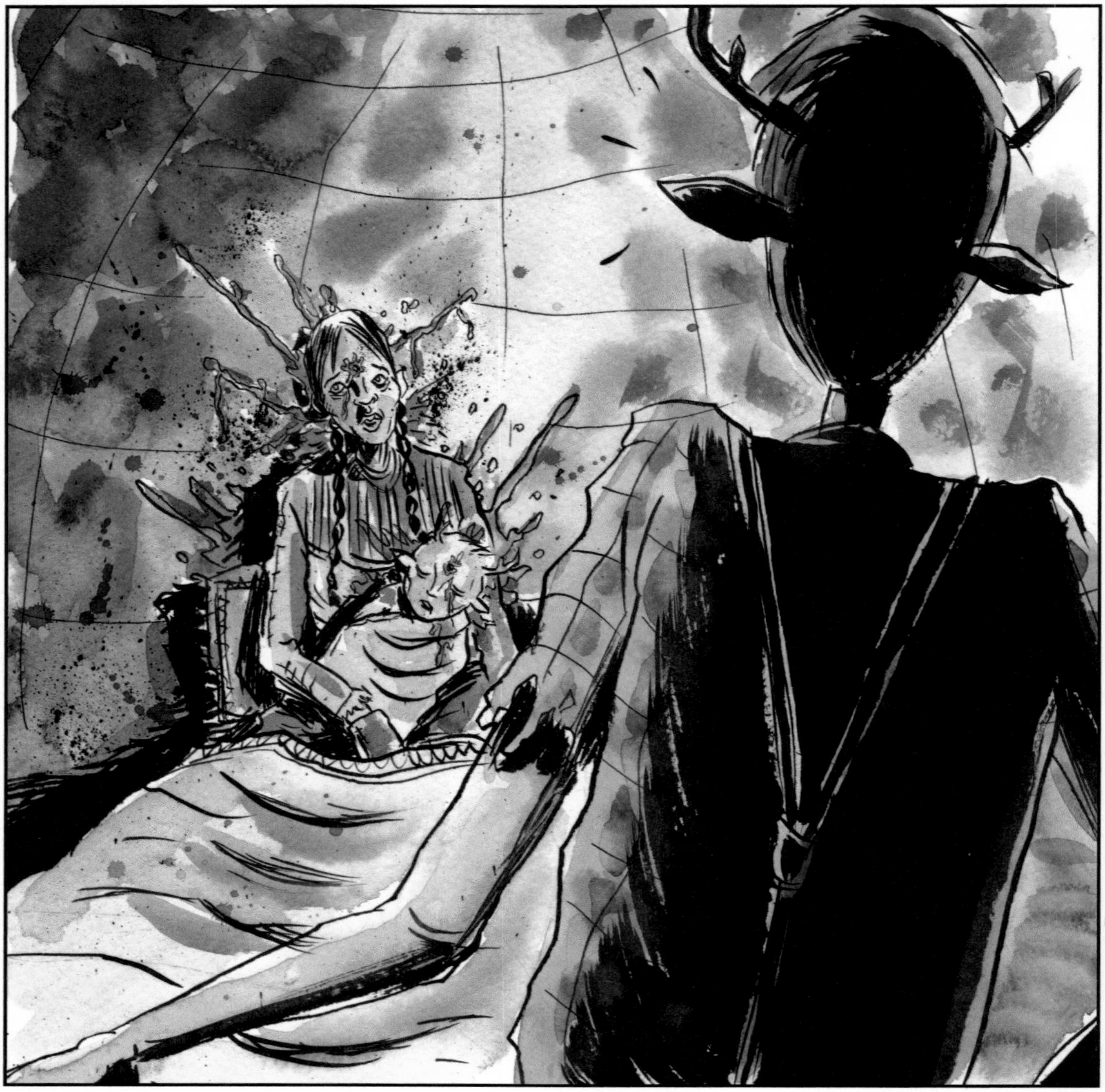

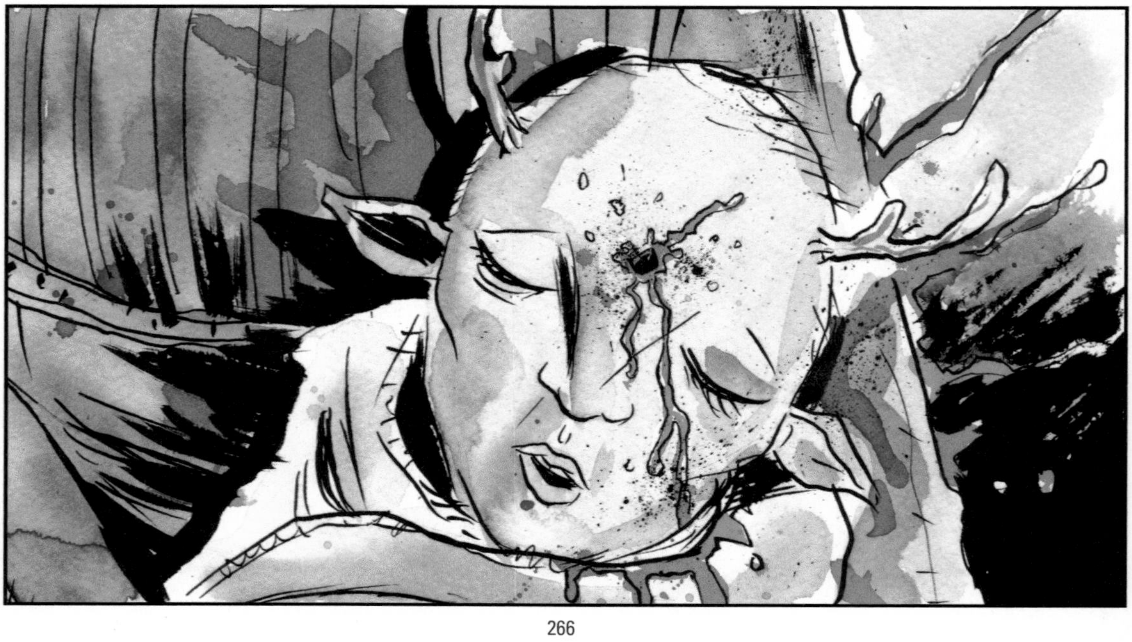

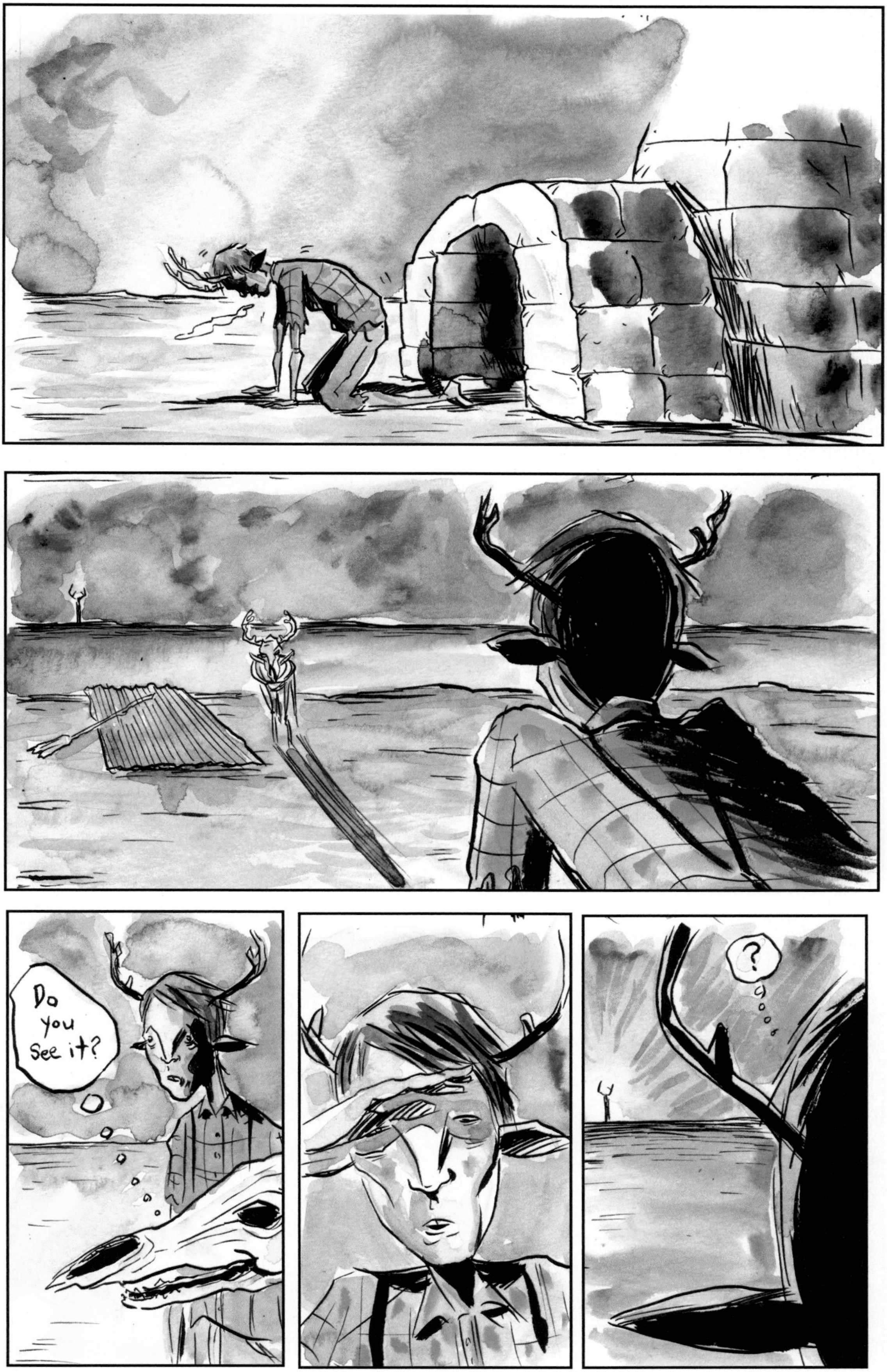
Do you see it?
?

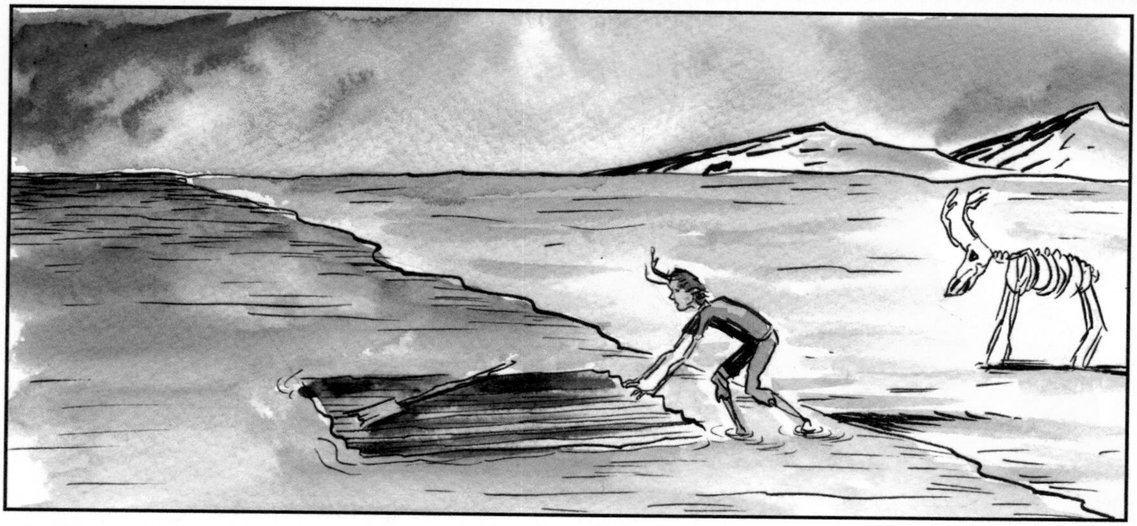

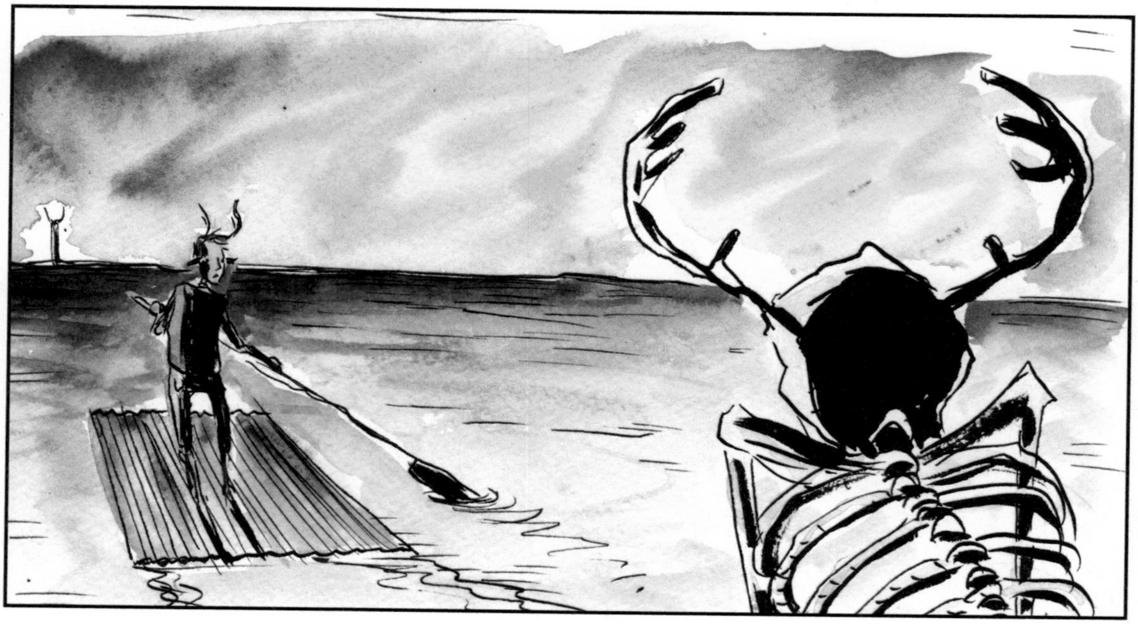

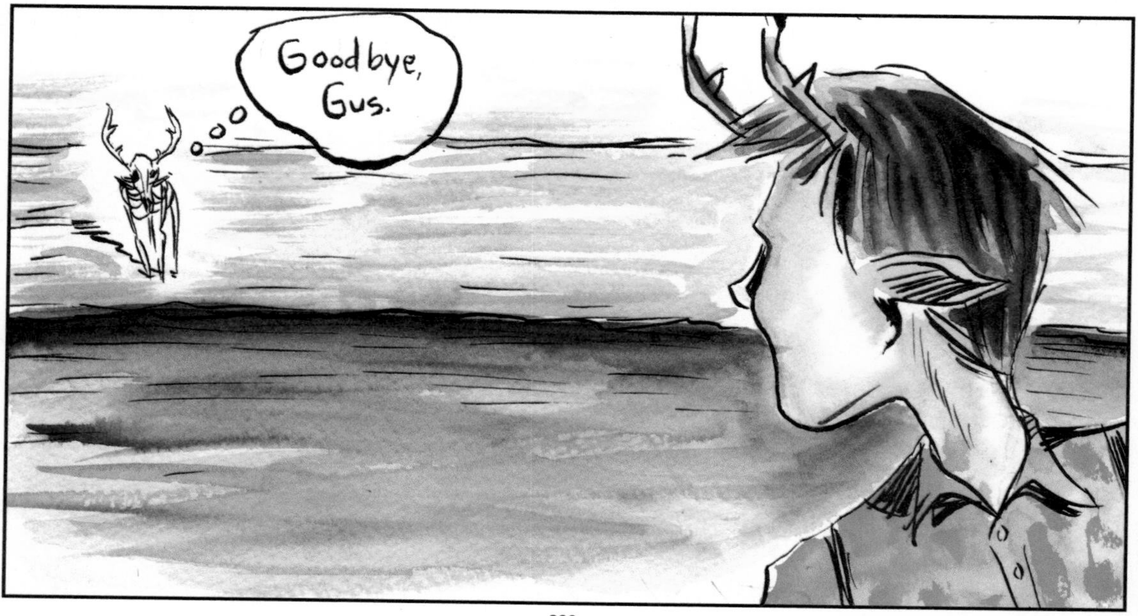
Goodbye, Gus.

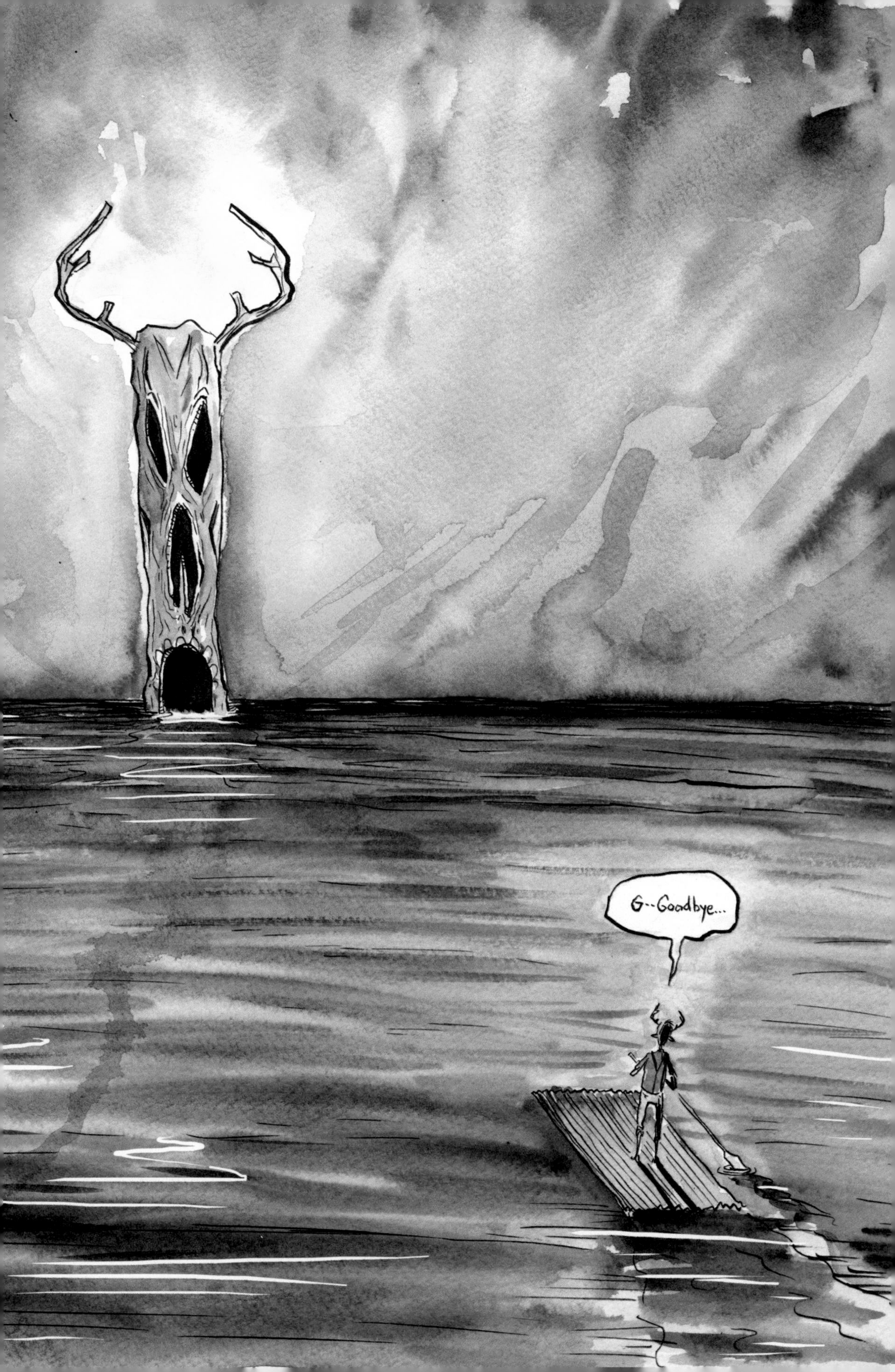
G--Goodbye...

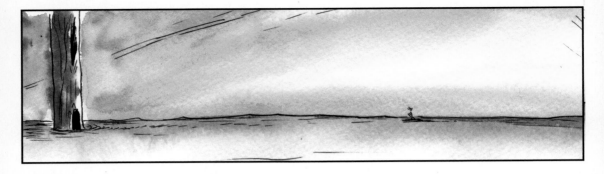

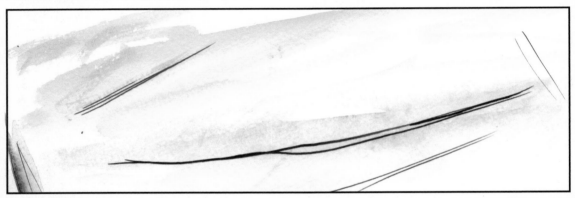

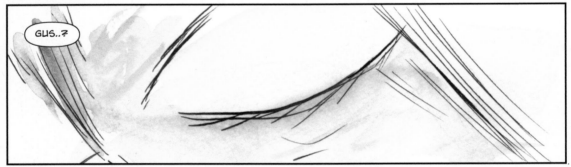

GUS..?

GUS, CAN YOU HEAR ME?

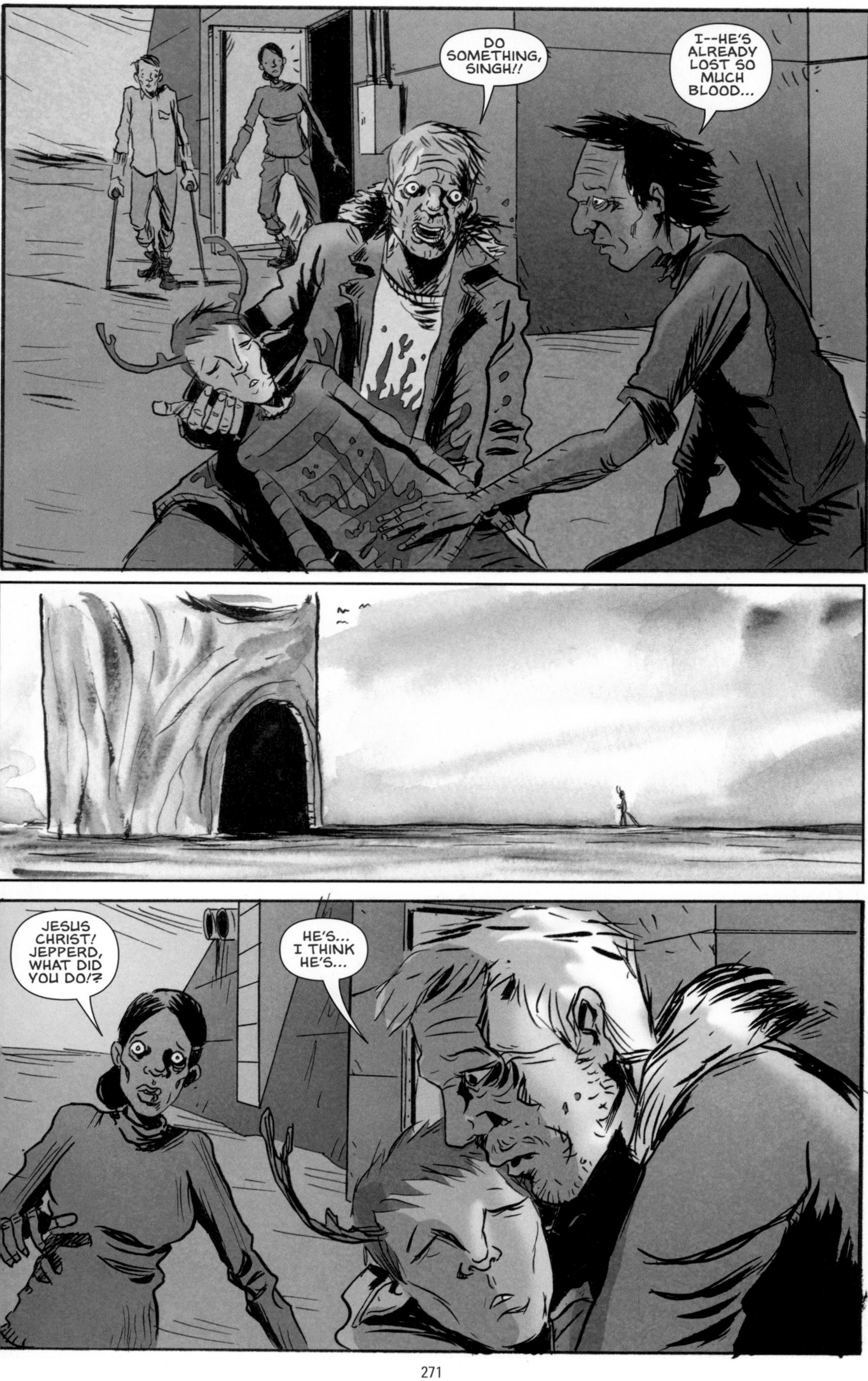
DO SOMETHING, SINGH!!
I--HE'S ALREADY LOST SO MUCH BLOOD...
JESUS CHRIST! JEPPERD, WHAT DID YOU DO!?
HE'S... I THINK HE'S...

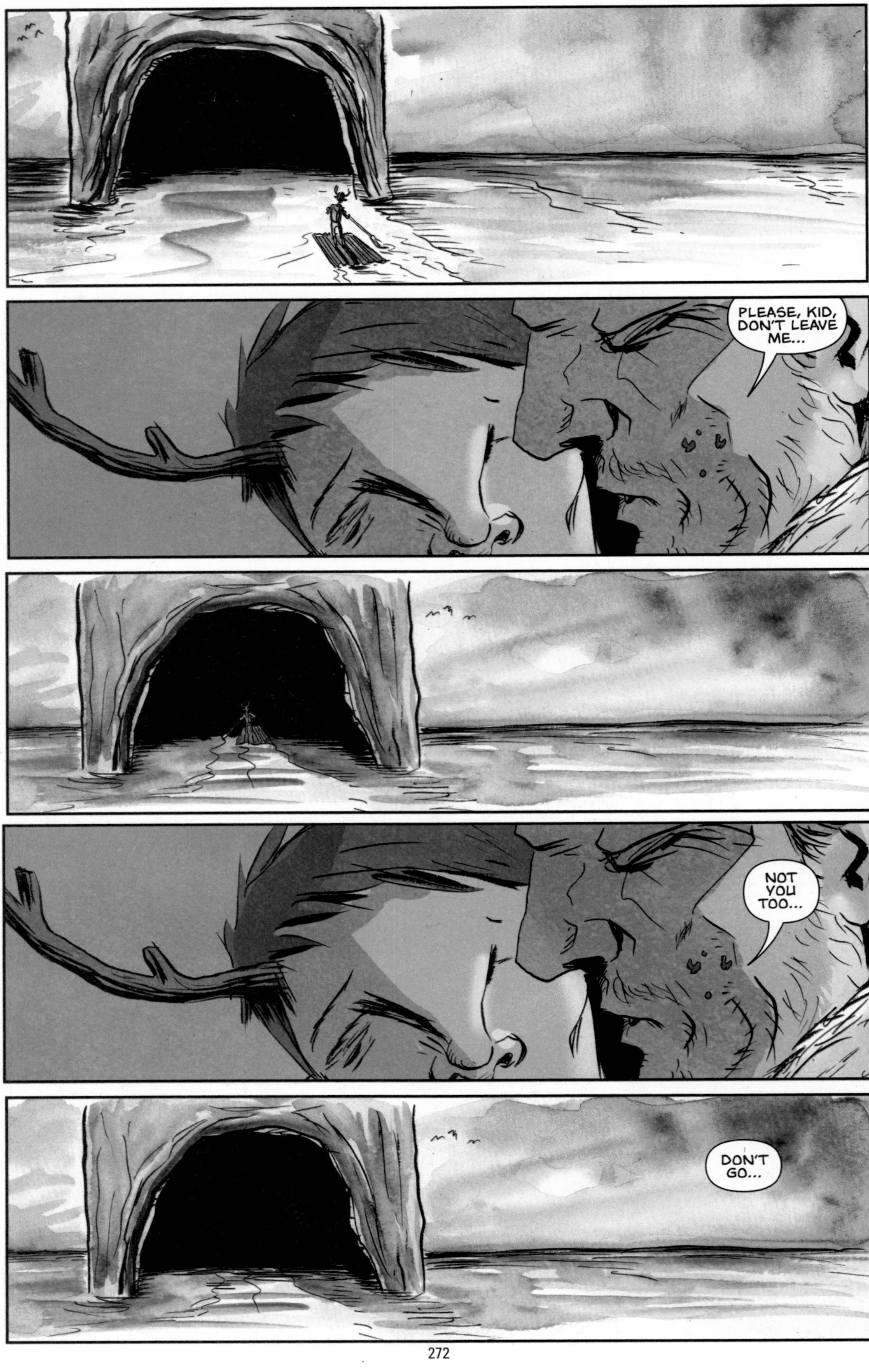
PLEASE, KID, DON'T LEAVE ME...
NOT YOU TOO...
DON'T GO...

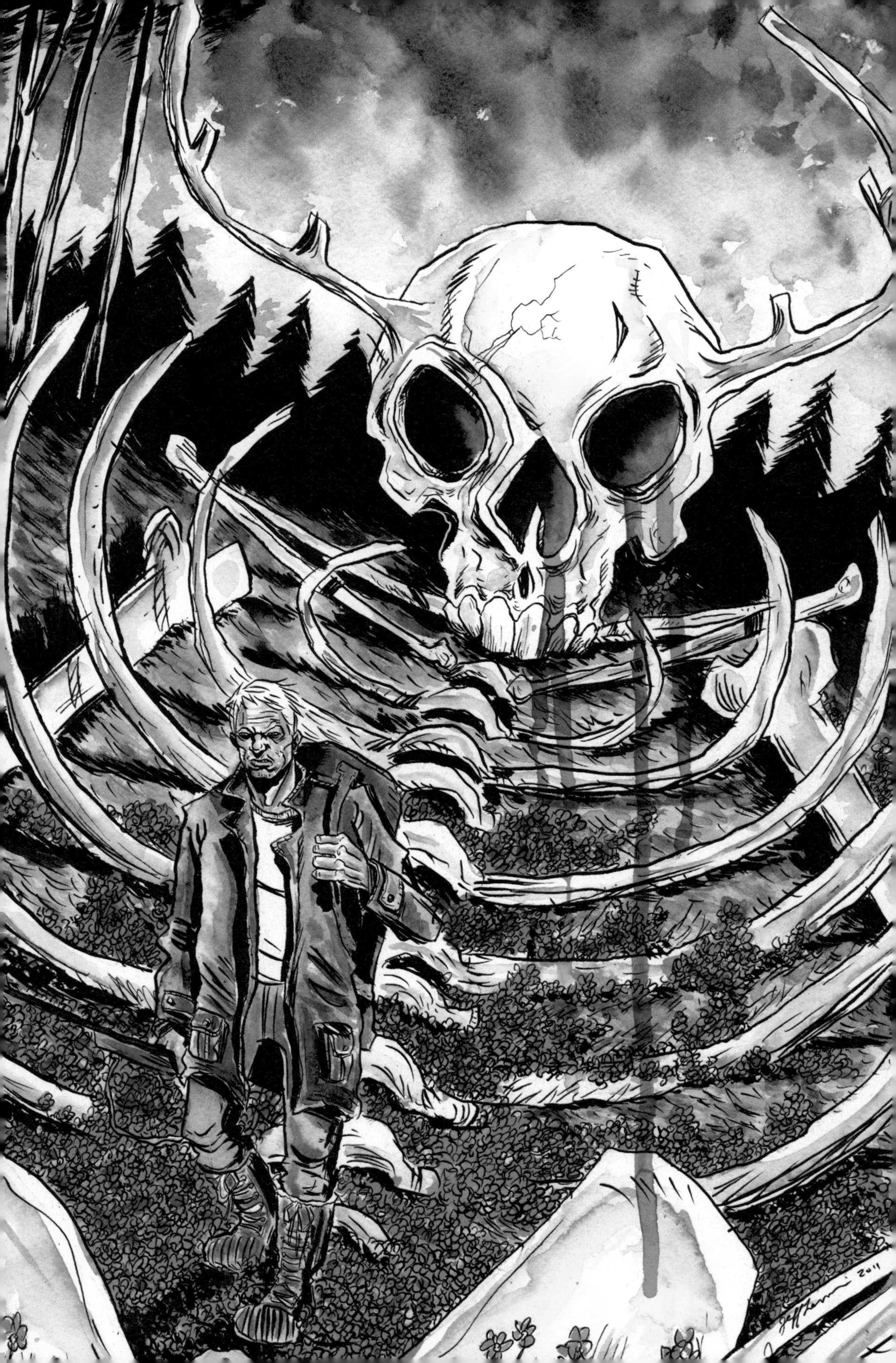

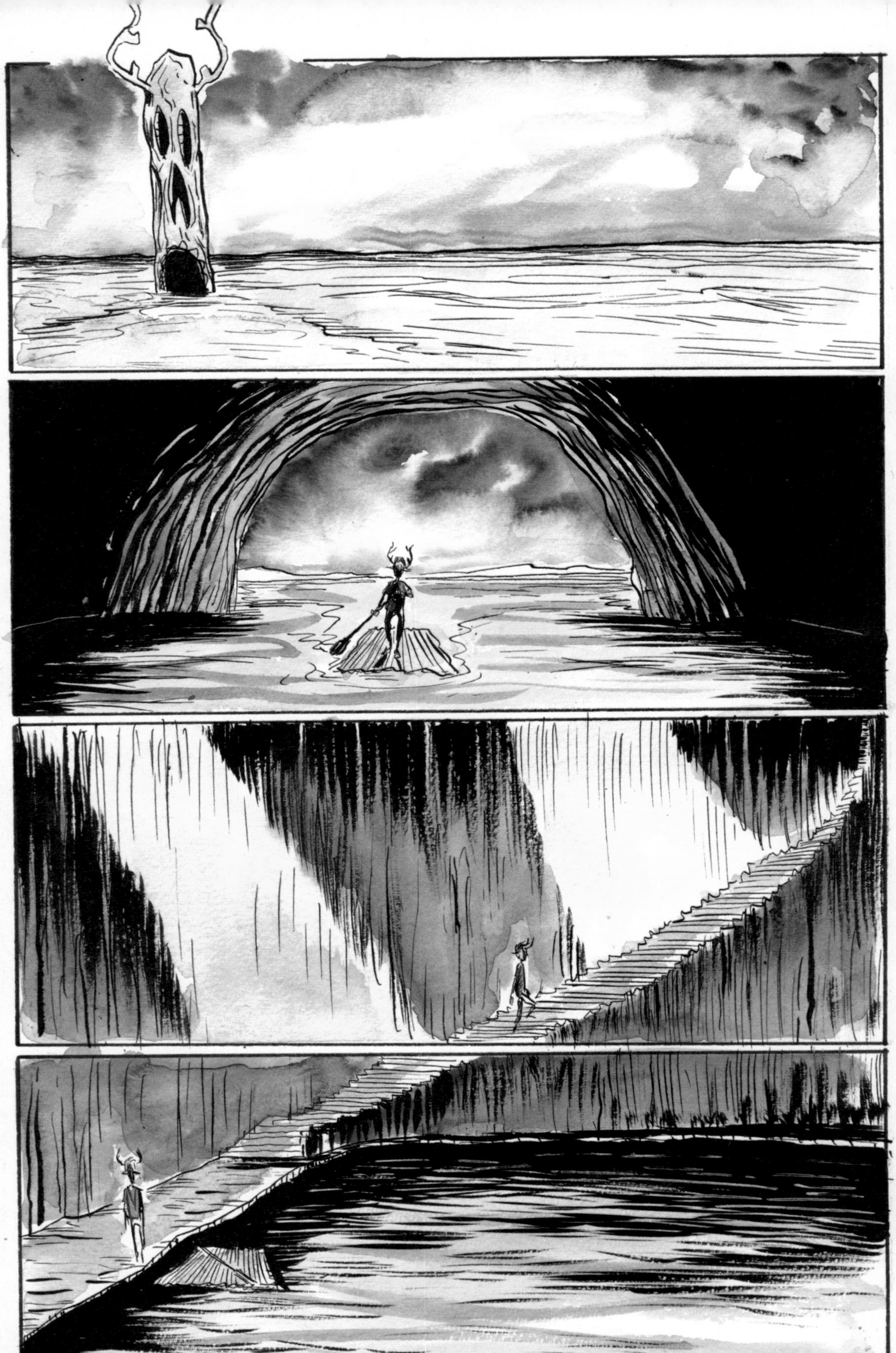
"ALMOST..."

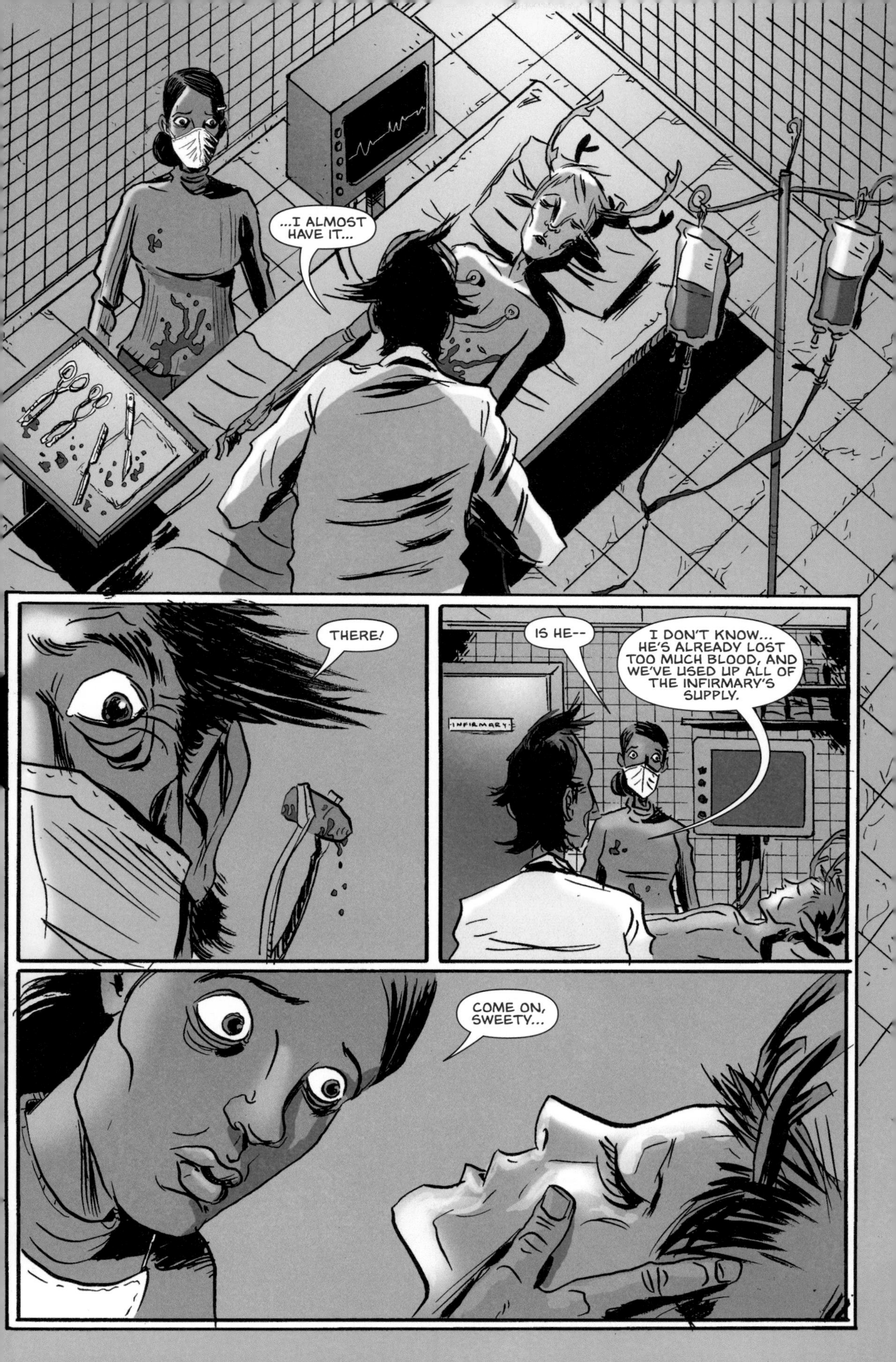
...I ALMOST HAVE IT...
THERE!
IS HE--
I DON'T KNOW... HE'S ALREADY LOST TOO MUCH BLOOD, AND WE'VE USED UP ALL OF THE INFIRMARY'S SUPPLY.
INFIRMARY
COME ON, SWEETY...

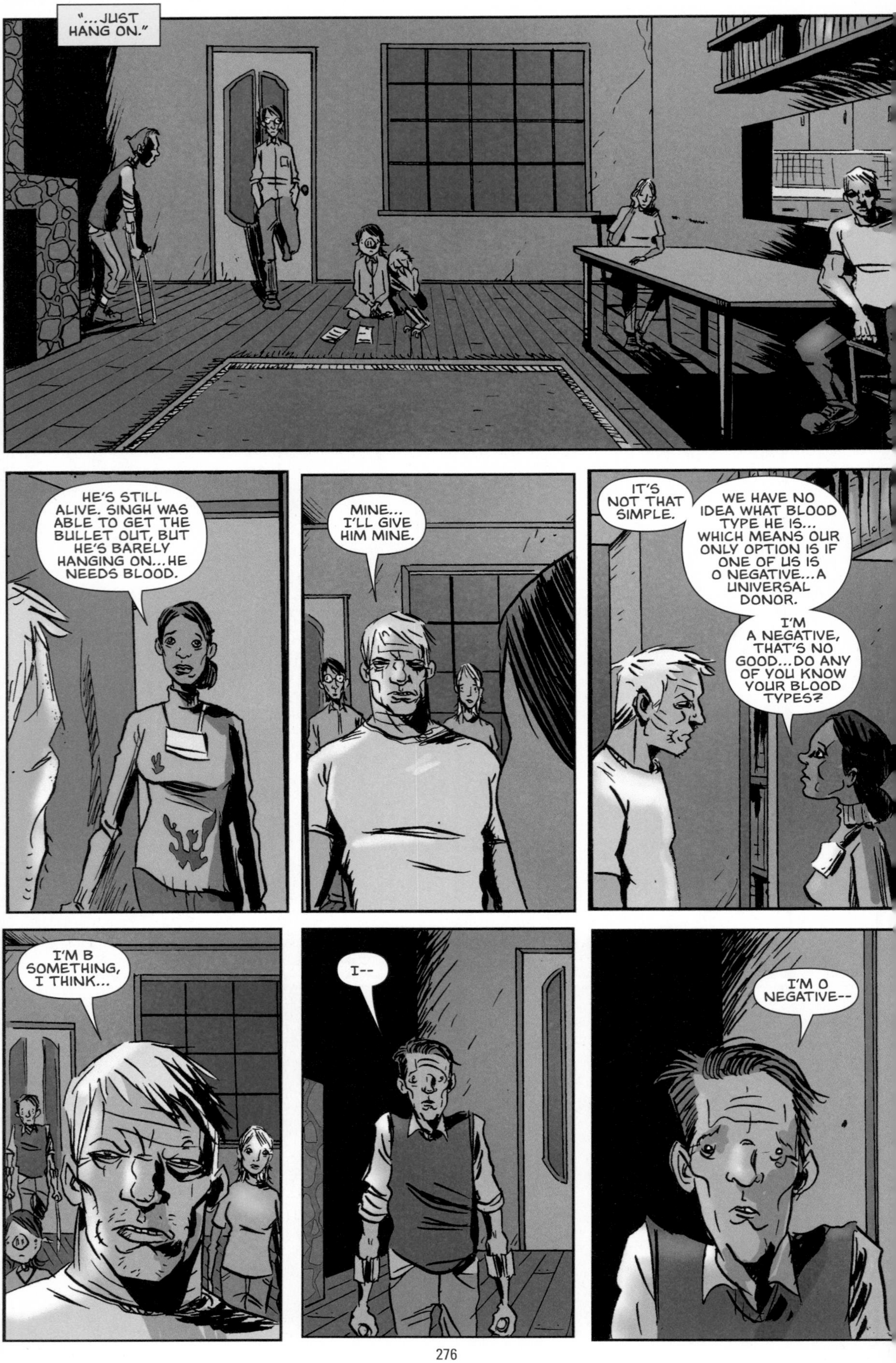
"...JUST HANG ON."
HE'S STILL ALIVE. SINGH WAS ABLE TO GET THE BULLET OUT, BUT HE'S BARELY HANGING ON...HE NEEDS BLOOD.
MINE... I'LL GIVE HIM MINE.
IT'S NOT THAT SIMPLE.
WE HAVE NO IDEA WHAT BLOOD TYPE HE IS... WHICH MEANS OUR ONLY OPTION IS IF ONE OF US IS O NEGATIVE...A UNIVERSAL DONOR.
I'M A NEGATIVE, THAT'S NO GOOD...DO ANY OF YOU KNOW YOUR BLOOD TYPES?
I'M B SOMETHING, I THINK...
I--
I'M O NEGATIVE--

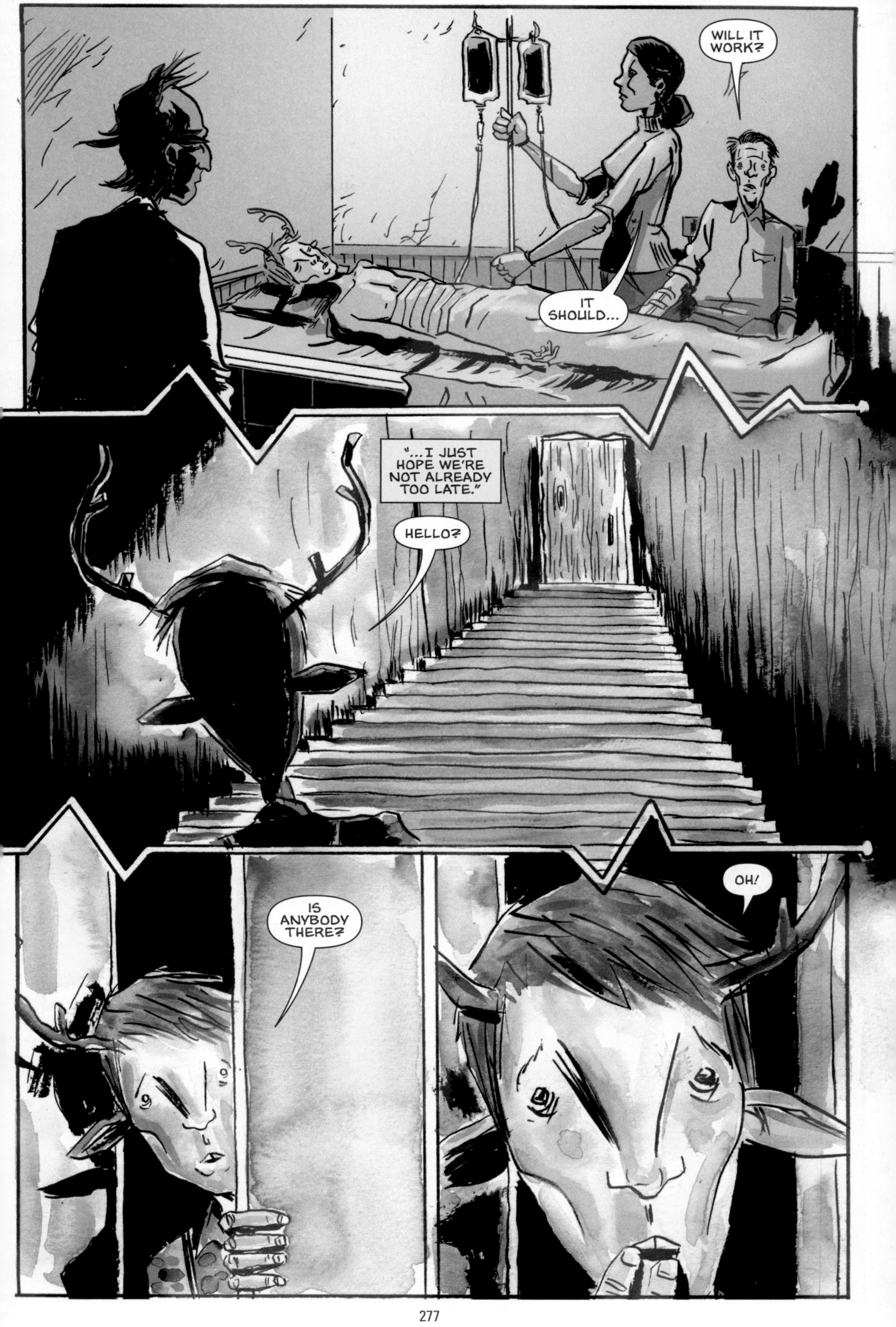
WILL IT WORK?
IT SHOULD...
"...I JUST HOPE WE'RE NOT ALREADY TOO LATE."
HELLO?
IS ANYBODY THERE?
OH!

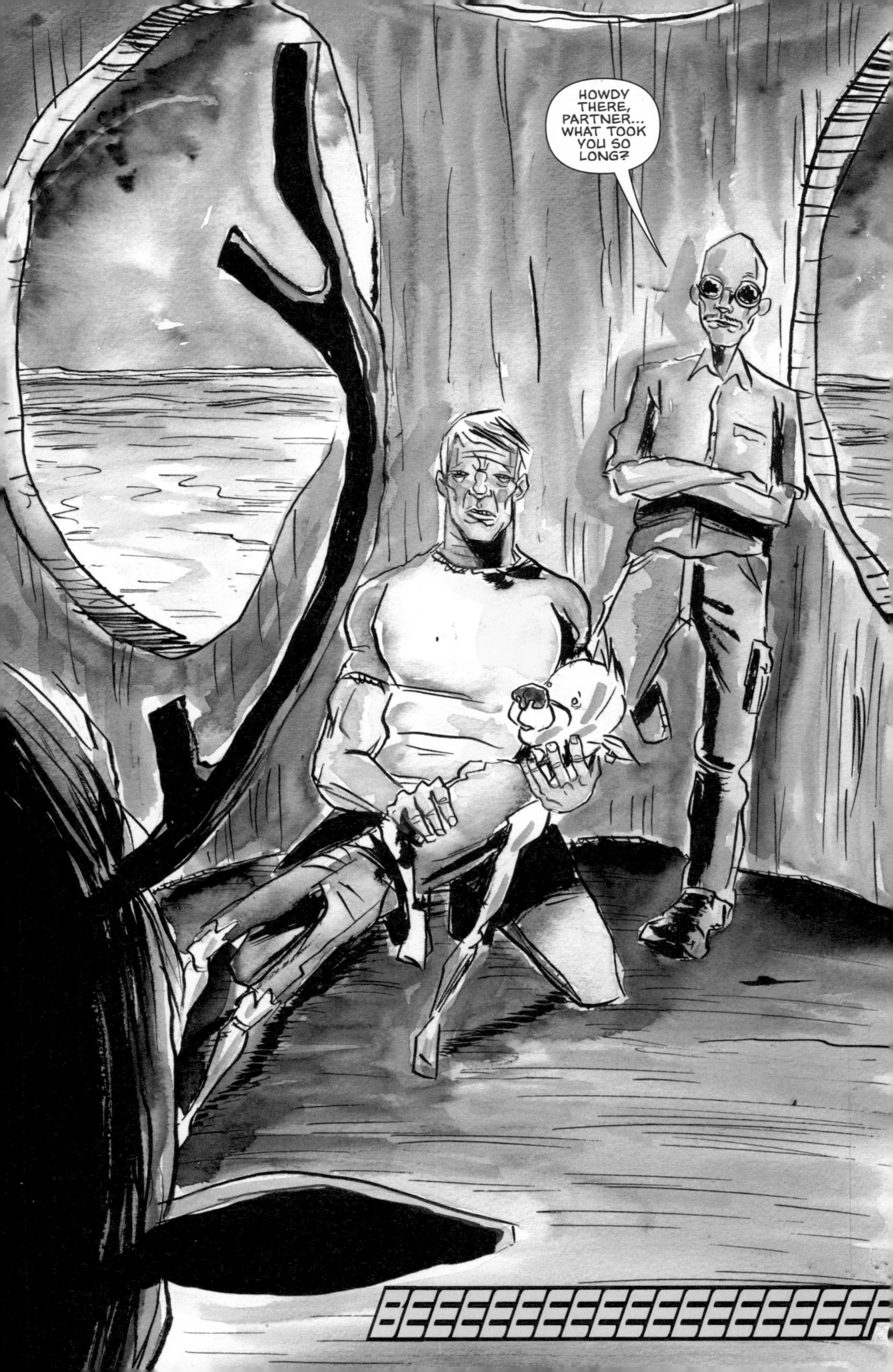
HOWDY THERE, PARTNER... WHAT TOOK YOU SO LONG?
BEEEEEEEEEEEEEEEEEEEEP

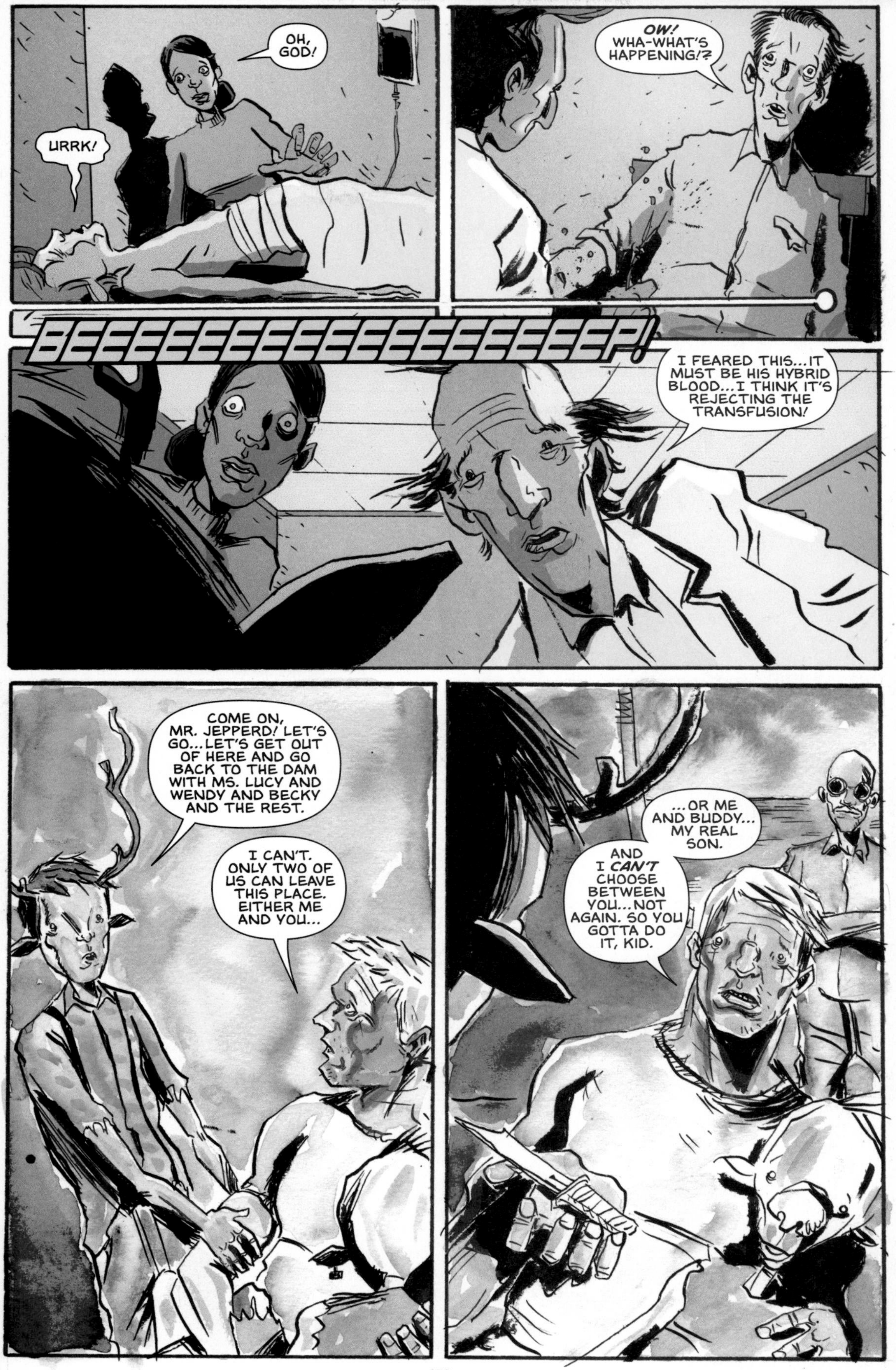
OH, GOD!
URRK!
OW! WHA-WHAT'S HAPPENING!?
BEEEEEEEEEEEEEEEEEEEEEEP!
I FEARED THIS...IT MUST BE HIS HYBRID BLOOD...I THINK IT'S REJECTING THE TRANSFUSION!
COME ON, MR. JEPPERD! LET'S GO...LET'S GET OUT OF HERE AND GO BACK TO THE DAM WITH MS. LUCY AND WENDY AND BECKY AND THE REST.
I CAN'T. ONLY TWO OF US CAN LEAVE THIS PLACE. EITHER ME AND YOU...
...OR ME AND BUDDY... MY REAL SON.
AND I CAN'T CHOOSE BETWEEN YOU...NOT AGAIN. SO YOU GOTTA DO IT, KID.

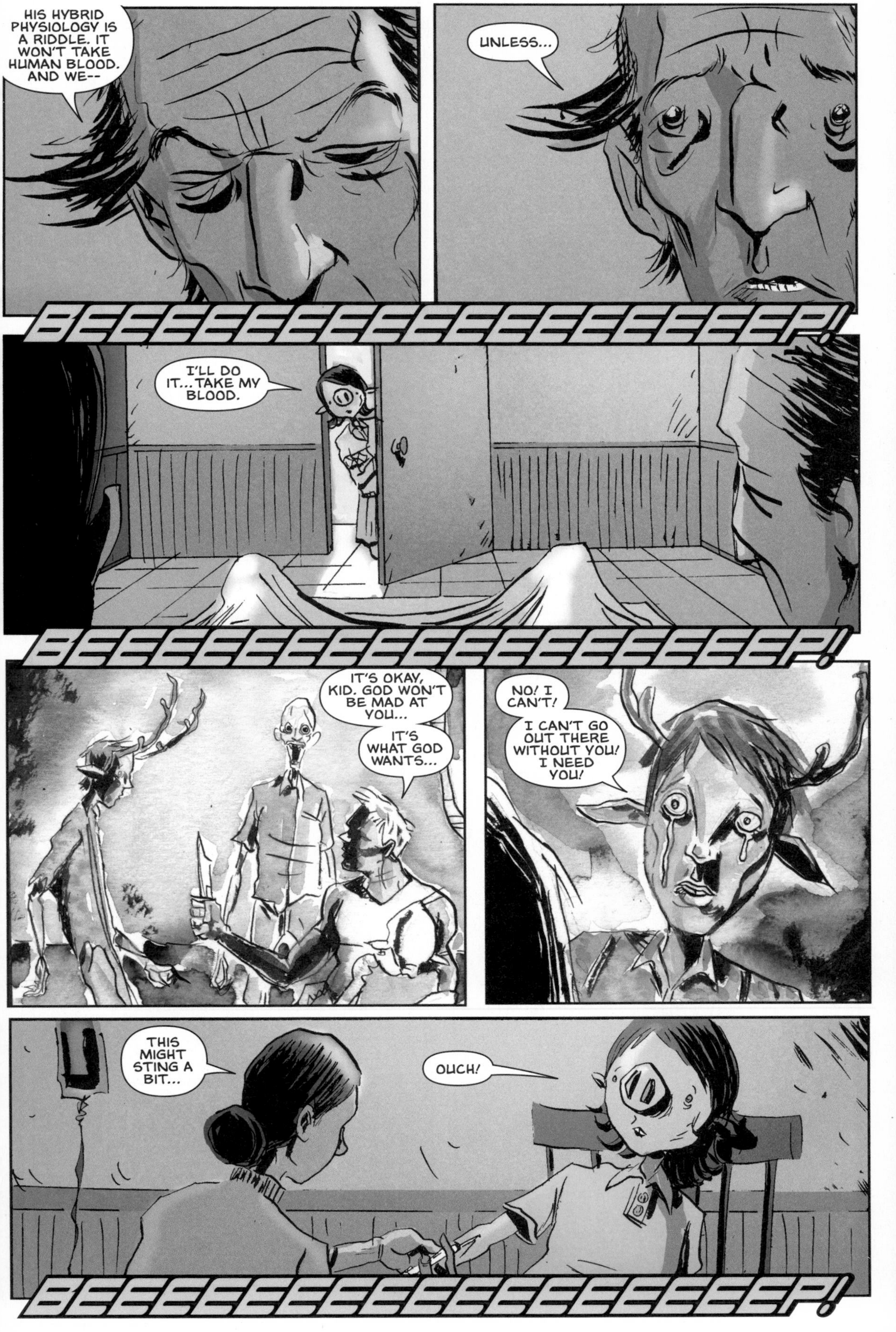
HIS HYBRID PHYSIOLOGY IS A RIDDLE. IT WON'T TAKE HUMAN BLOOD. AND WE--
UNLESS...
BEEEEEEEEEEEEEEEEEEEEEP!
I'LL DO IT...TAKE MY BLOOD.
BEEEEEEEEEEEEEEEEEEEEEEEP!
IT'S OKAY, KID. GOD WON'T BE MAD AT YOU...
IT'S WHAT GOD WANTS...
NO! I CAN'T!
I CAN'T GO OUT THERE WITHOUT YOU! I NEED YOU!
THIS MIGHT STING A BIT...
OUCH!
BEEEEEEEEEEEEEEEEEEEEEEP!

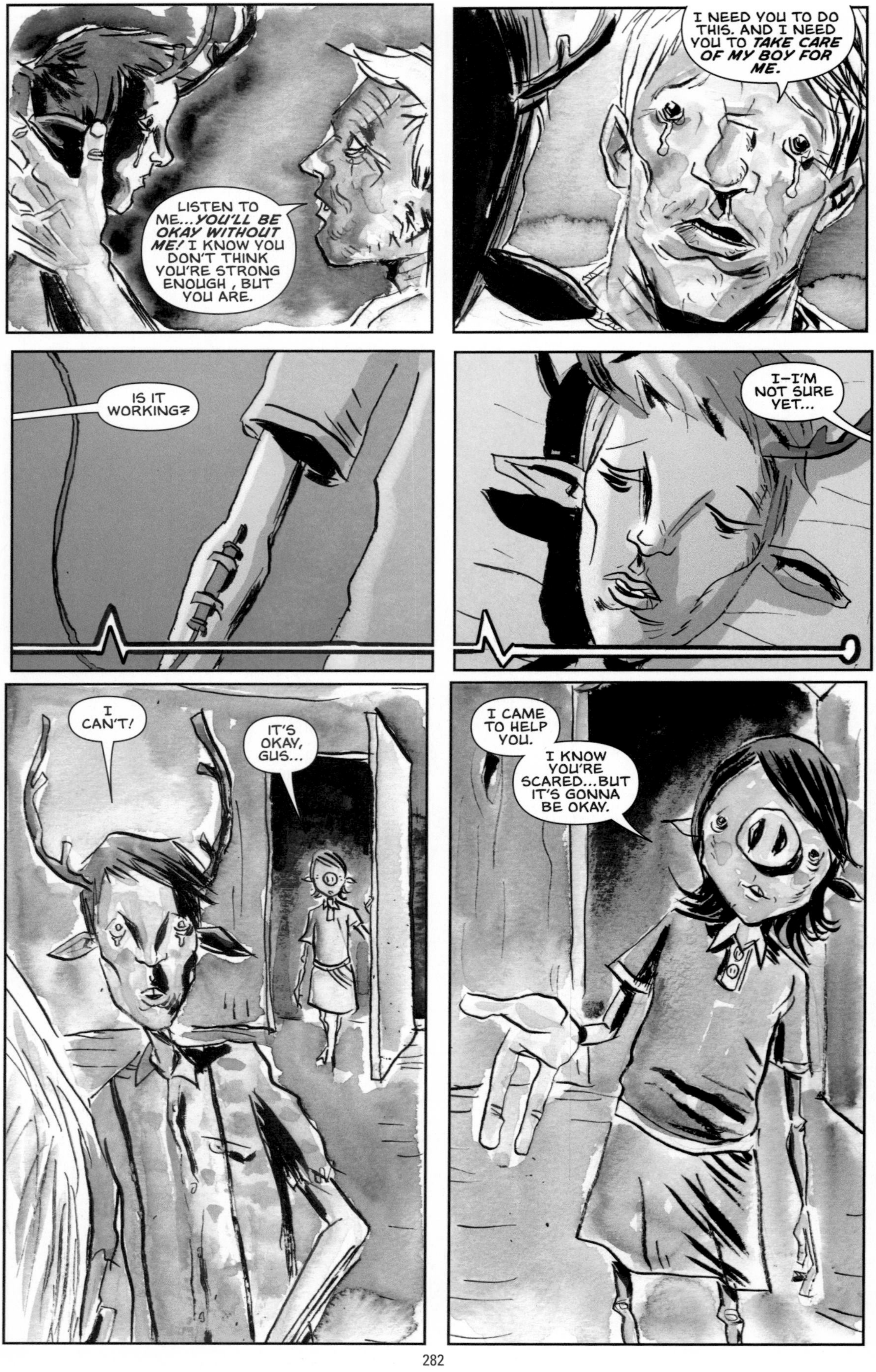
LISTEN TO ME... *YOU'LL BE OKAY WITHOUT ME!* I KNOW YOU DON'T THINK YOU'RE STRONG ENOUGH , BUT YOU ARE.
I NEED YOU TO DO THIS. AND I NEED YOU TO *TAKE CARE OF MY BOY FOR ME.*
IS IT WORKING?
I—I'M NOT SURE YET...
I CAN'T!
IT'S OKAY, GUS...
I CAME TO HELP YOU.
I KNOW YOU'RE SCARED...BUT IT'S GONNA BE OKAY.

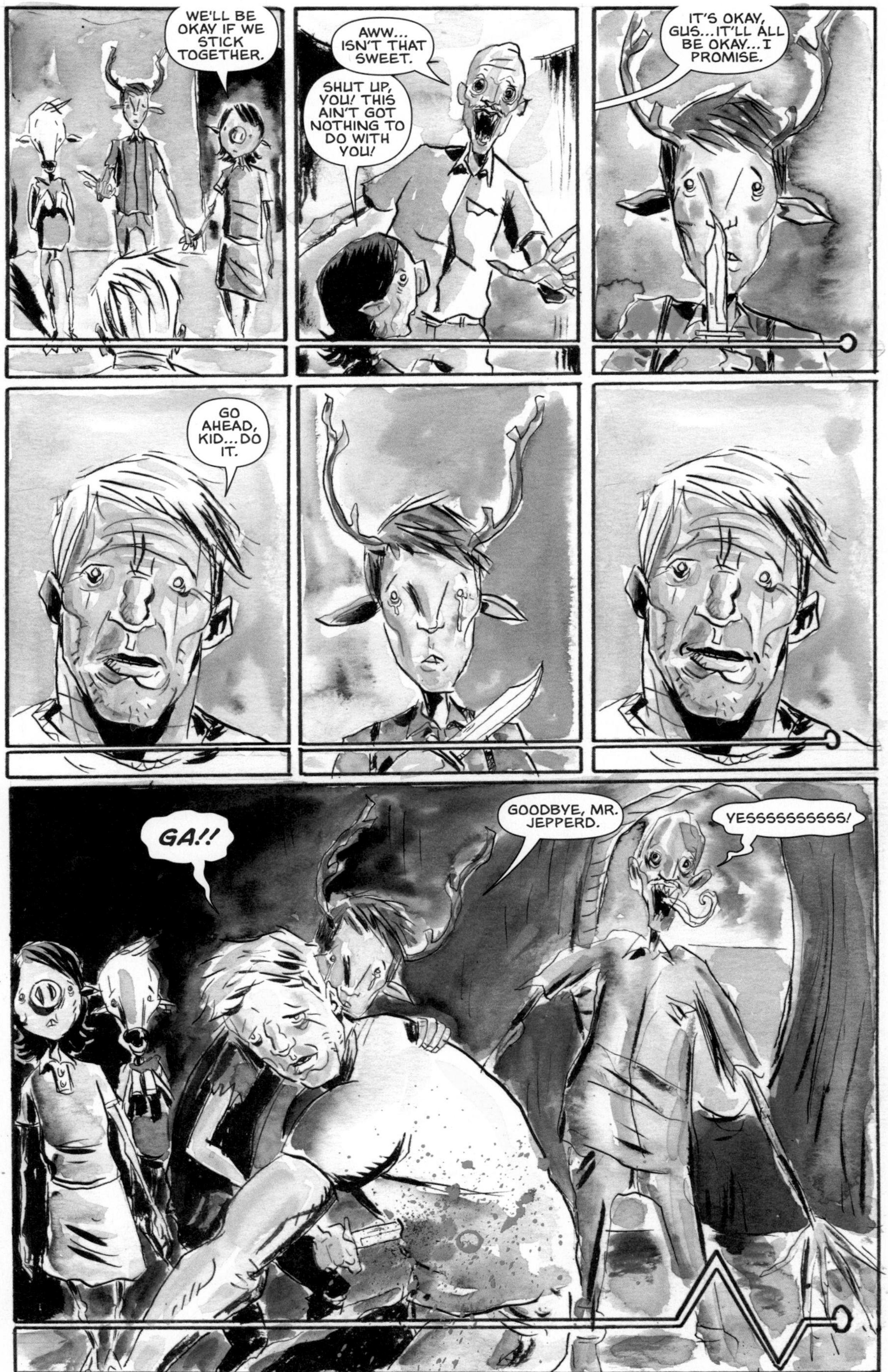
WE'LL BE OKAY IF WE STICK TOGETHER.
AWW... ISN'T THAT SWEET.
SHUT UP, YOU! THIS AIN'T GOT NOTHING TO DO WITH YOU!
IT'S OKAY, GUS...IT'LL ALL BE OKAY...I PROMISE.
GO AHEAD, KID...DO IT.
GA!!
GOODBYE, MR. JEPPERD.
YESSSSSSSSSS!

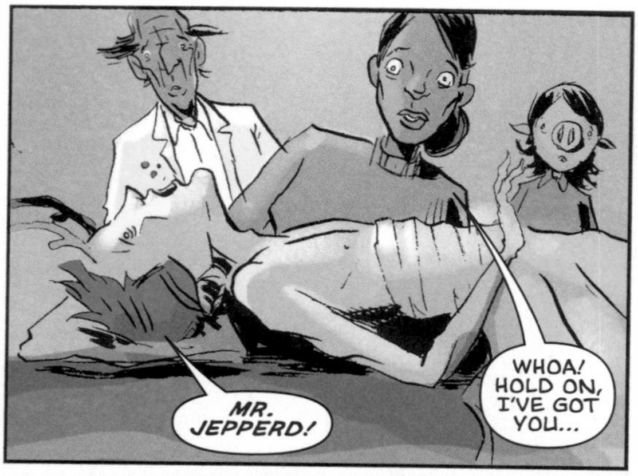
MR. JEPPERD!
WHOA! HOLD ON, I'VE GOT YOU...
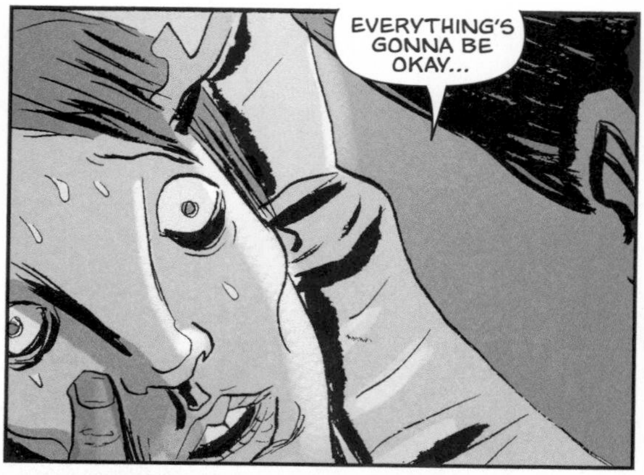
EVERYTHING'S GONNA BE OKAY...
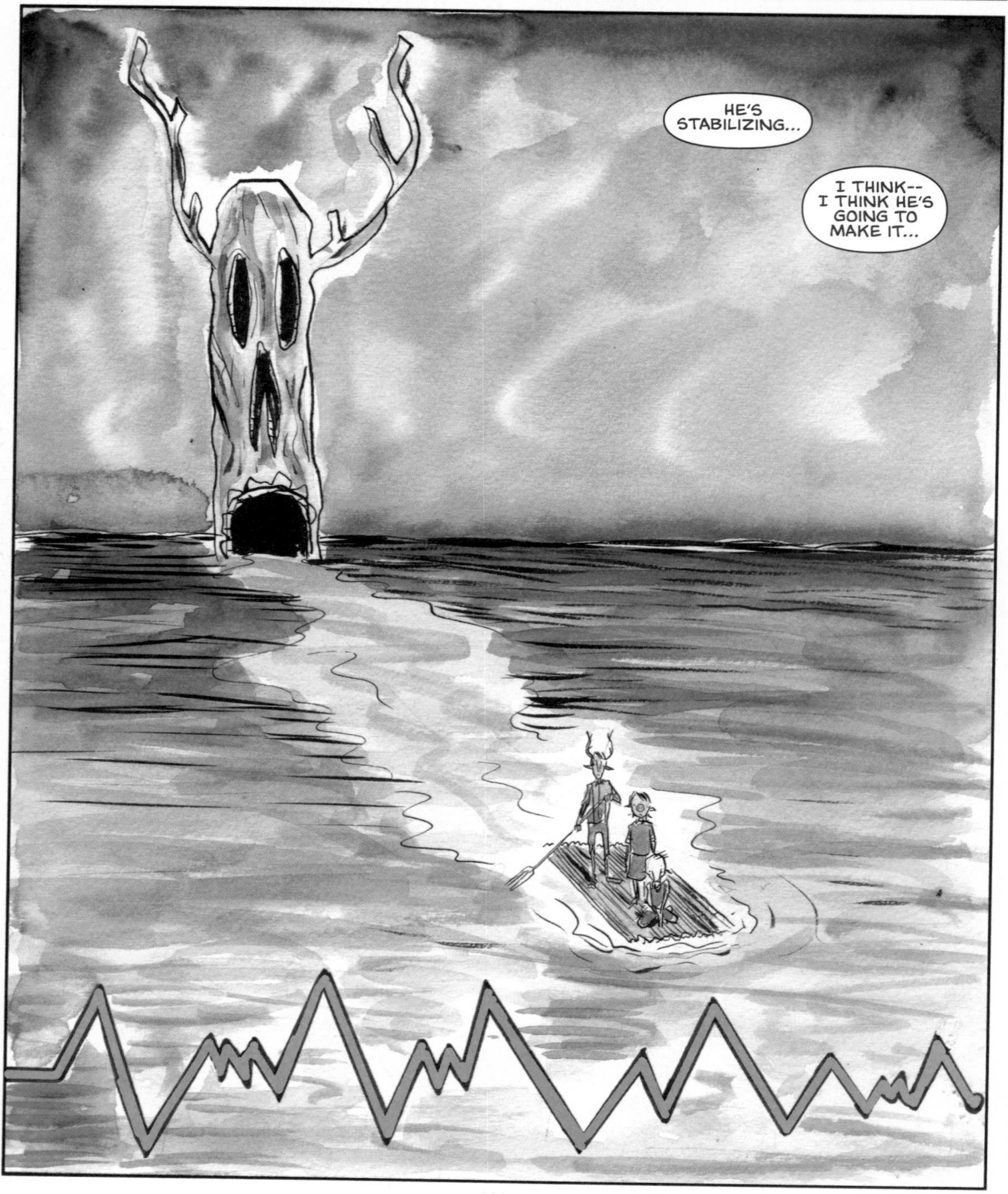
HE'S STABILIZING...
I THINK-- I THINK HE'S GOING TO MAKE IT...

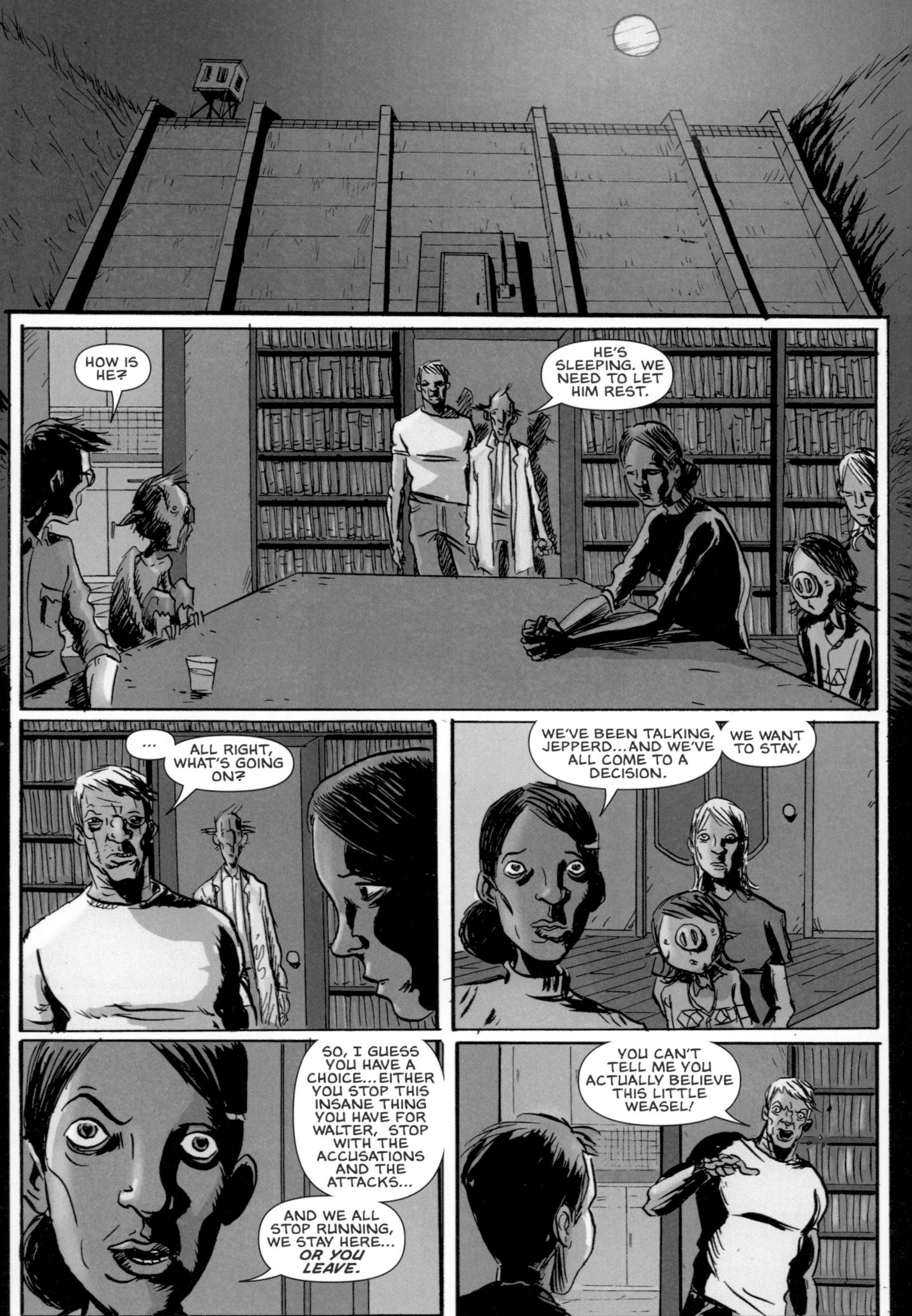
HOW IS HE?
HE'S SLEEPING. WE NEED TO LET HIM REST.
...
ALL RIGHT, WHAT'S GOING ON?
WE'VE BEEN TALKING, JEPPERD...AND WE'VE ALL COME TO A DECISION.
WE WANT TO STAY.
SO, I GUESS YOU HAVE A CHOICE...EITHER YOU STOP THIS INSANE THING YOU HAVE FOR WALTER, STOP WITH THE ACCUSATIONS AND THE ATTACKS...
AND WE ALL STOP RUNNING, WE STAY HERE... *OR YOU LEAVE.*
YOU CAN'T TELL ME YOU ACTUALLY BELIEVE THIS LITTLE WEASEL!

286

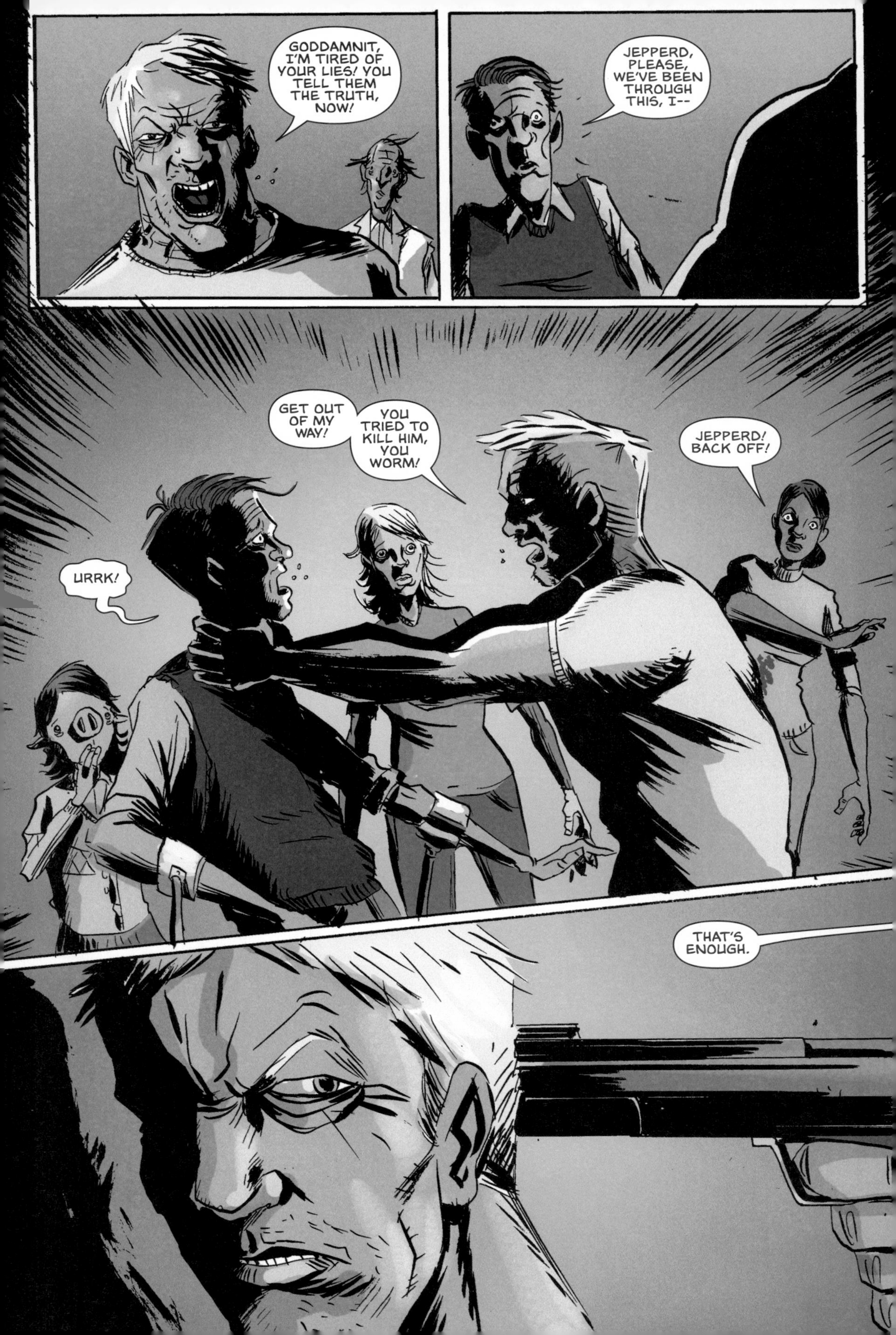
GODDAMNIT, I'M TIRED OF YOUR LIES! YOU TELL THEM THE TRUTH, NOW!
JEPPERD, PLEASE, WE'VE BEEN THROUGH THIS, I--
GET OUT OF MY WAY!
YOU TRIED TO KILL HIM, YOU WORM!
JEPPERD! BACK OFF!
URRK!
THAT'S ENOUGH.

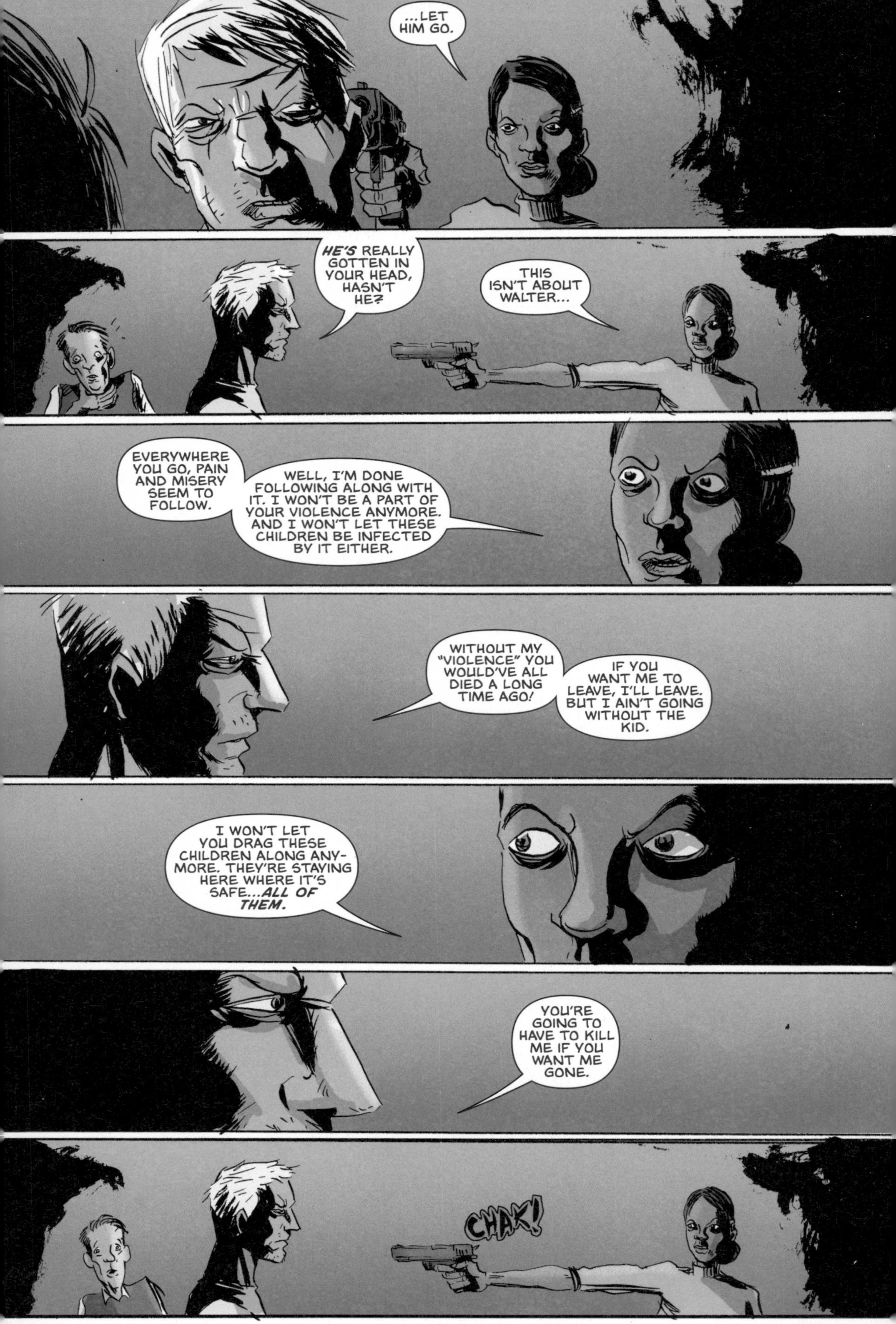
...LET HIM GO.
HE'S REALLY GOTTEN IN YOUR HEAD, HASN'T HE?
THIS ISN'T ABOUT WALTER...
EVERYWHERE YOU GO, PAIN AND MISERY SEEM TO FOLLOW.
WELL, I'M DONE FOLLOWING ALONG WITH IT. I WON'T BE A PART OF YOUR VIOLENCE ANYMORE. AND I WON'T LET THESE CHILDREN BE INFECTED BY IT EITHER.
WITHOUT MY "VIOLENCE" YOU WOULD'VE ALL DIED A LONG TIME AGO!
IF YOU WANT ME TO LEAVE, I'LL LEAVE. BUT I AIN'T GOING WITHOUT THE KID.
I WON'T LET YOU DRAG THESE CHILDREN ALONG ANY-MORE. THEY'RE STAYING HERE WHERE IT'S SAFE...*ALL OF THEM.*
YOU'RE GOING TO HAVE TO KILL ME IF YOU WANT ME GONE.
CHAK!

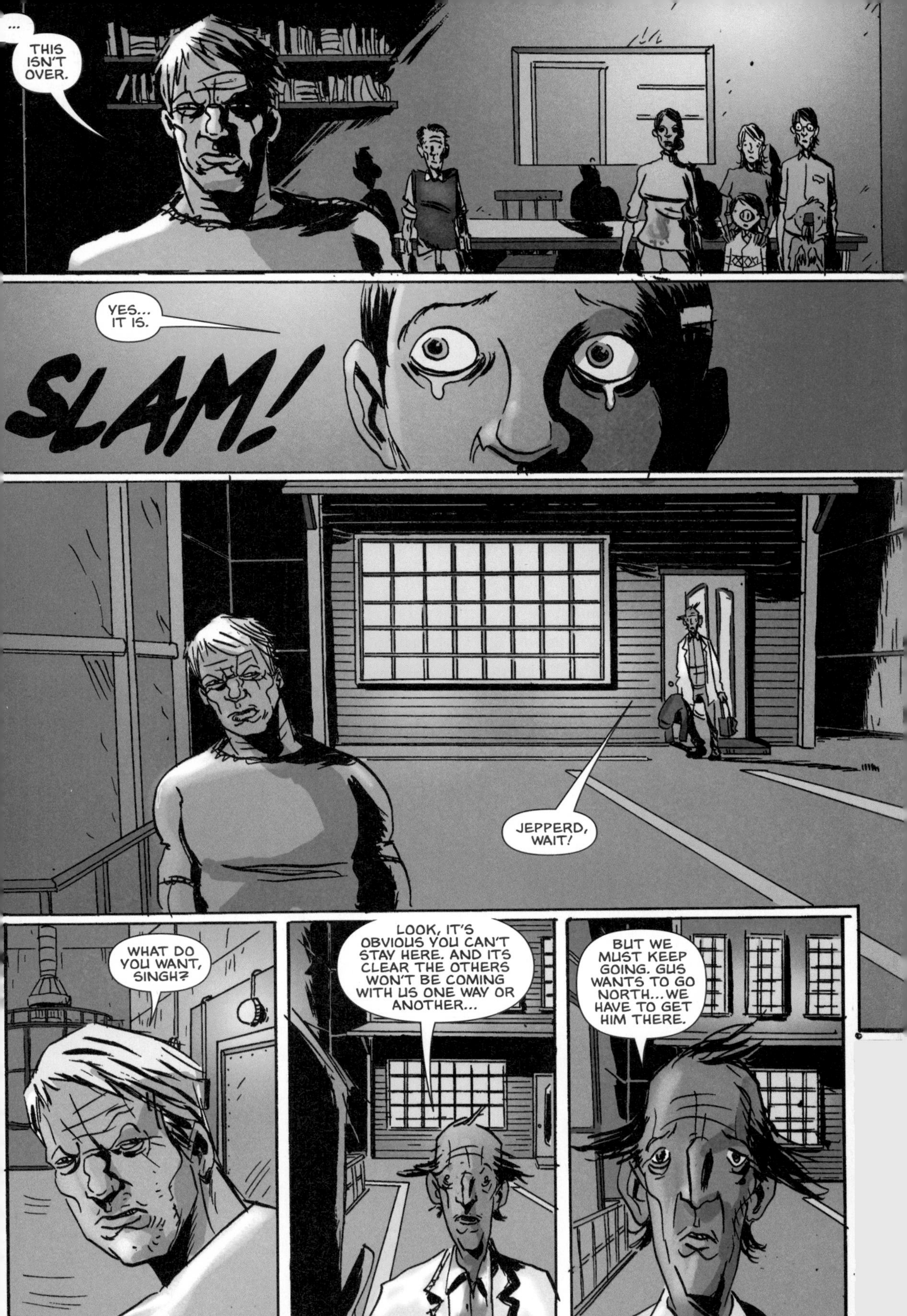
...
THIS ISN'T OVER.
YES... IT IS.
SLAM!
JEPPERD, WAIT!
WHAT DO YOU WANT, SINGH?
LOOK, IT'S OBVIOUS YOU CAN'T STAY HERE. AND ITS CLEAR THE OTHERS WON'T BE COMING WITH US ONE WAY OR ANOTHER...
BUT WE MUST KEEP GOING. GUS WANTS TO GO NORTH...WE HAVE TO GET HIM THERE.

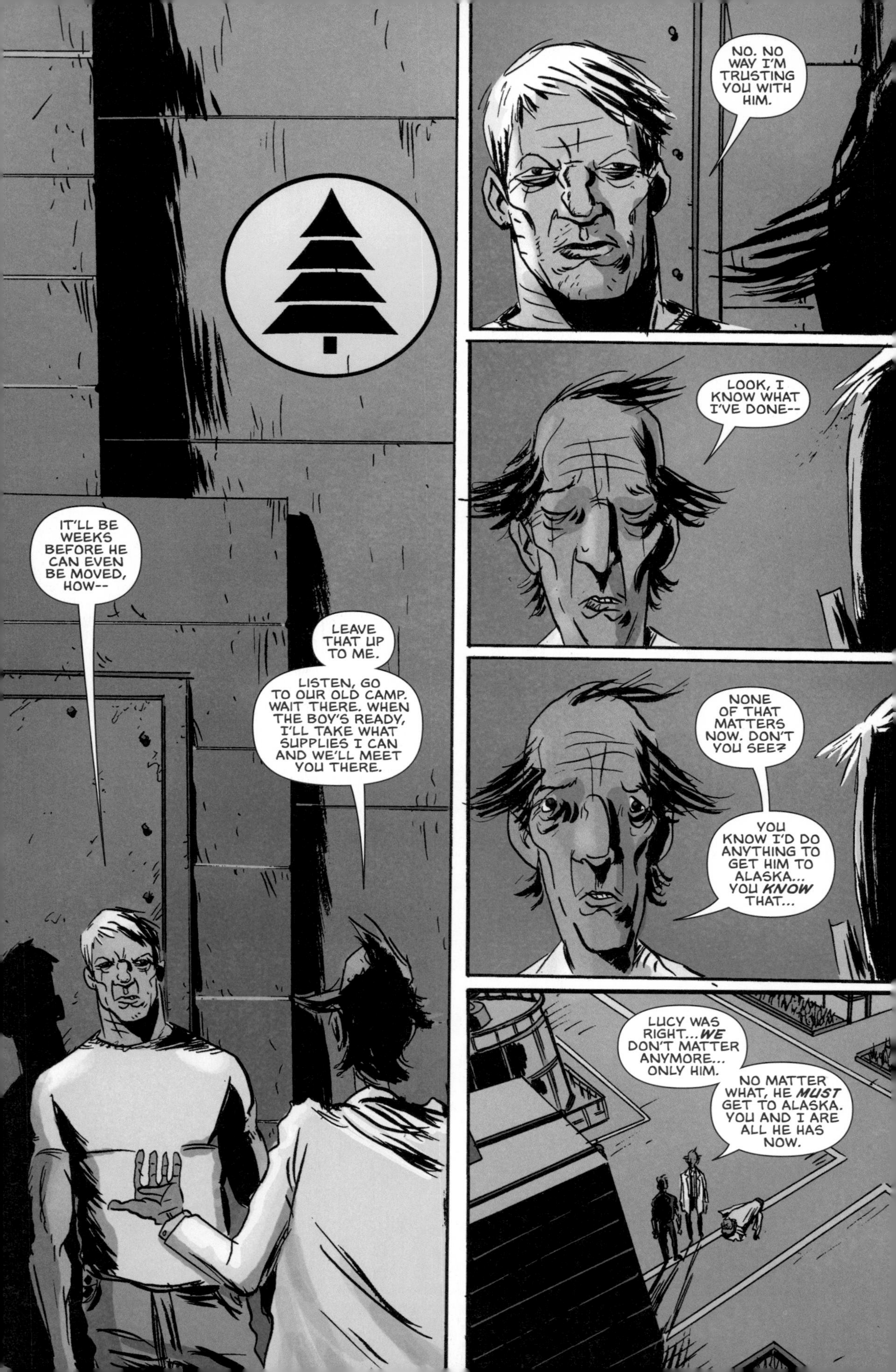
IT'LL BE WEEKS BEFORE HE CAN EVEN BE MOVED, HOW--
LEAVE THAT UP TO ME.
LISTEN, GO TO OUR OLD CAMP. WAIT THERE. WHEN THE BOY'S READY, I'LL TAKE WHAT SUPPLIES I CAN AND WE'LL MEET YOU THERE.
NO. NO WAY I'M TRUSTING YOU WITH HIM.
LOOK, I KNOW WHAT I'VE DONE--
NONE OF THAT MATTERS NOW. DON'T YOU SEE?
YOU KNOW I'D DO ANYTHING TO GET HIM TO ALASKA... YOU *KNOW* THAT...
LUCY WAS RIGHT... *WE* DON'T MATTER ANYMORE... ONLY HIM.
NO MATTER WHAT, HE *MUST* GET TO ALASKA. YOU AND I ARE ALL HE HAS NOW.

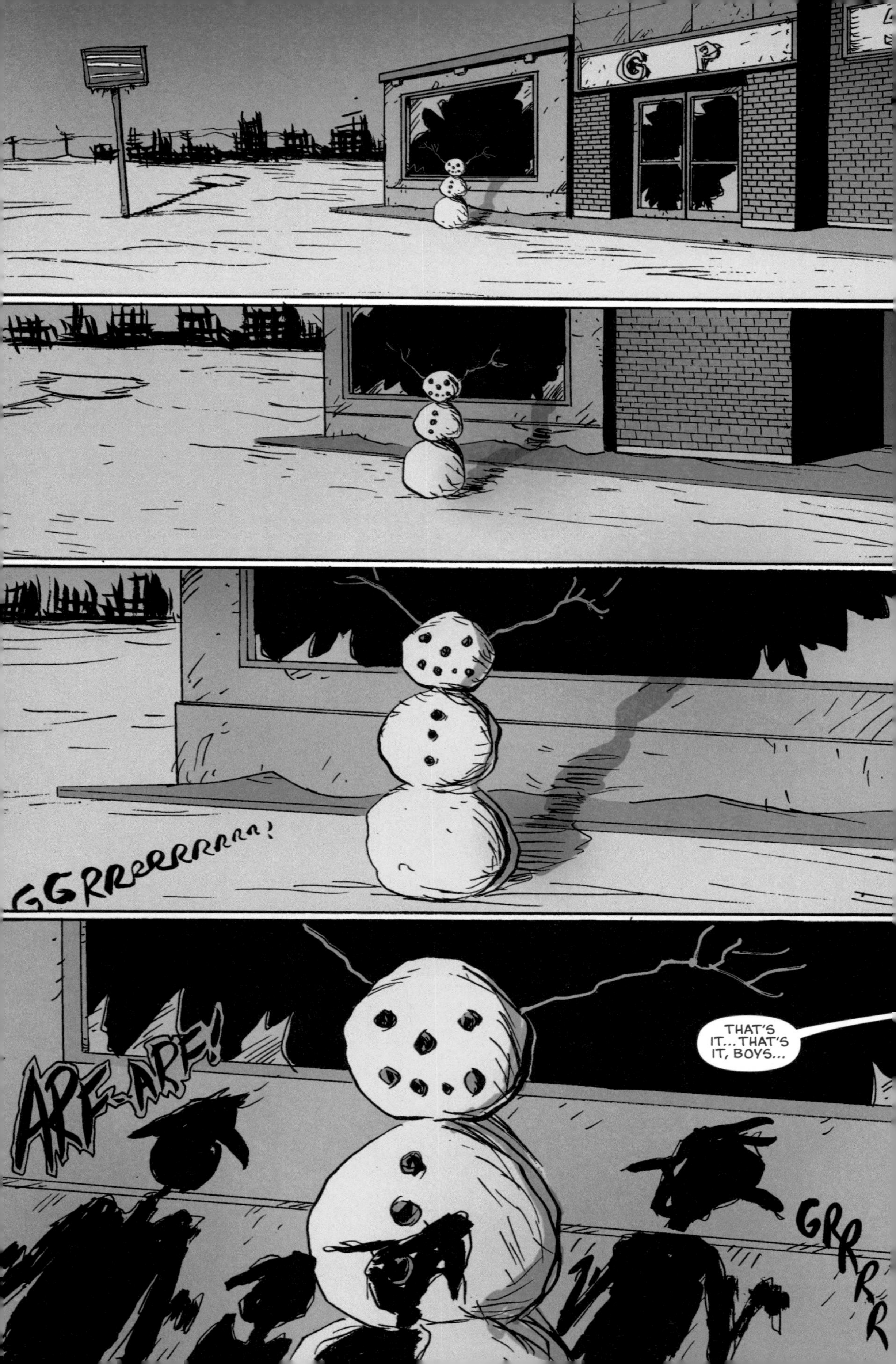
GGRRRRRRRRRR!
ARF-ARF!
THAT'S IT... THAT'S IT, BOYS...
GRRRR

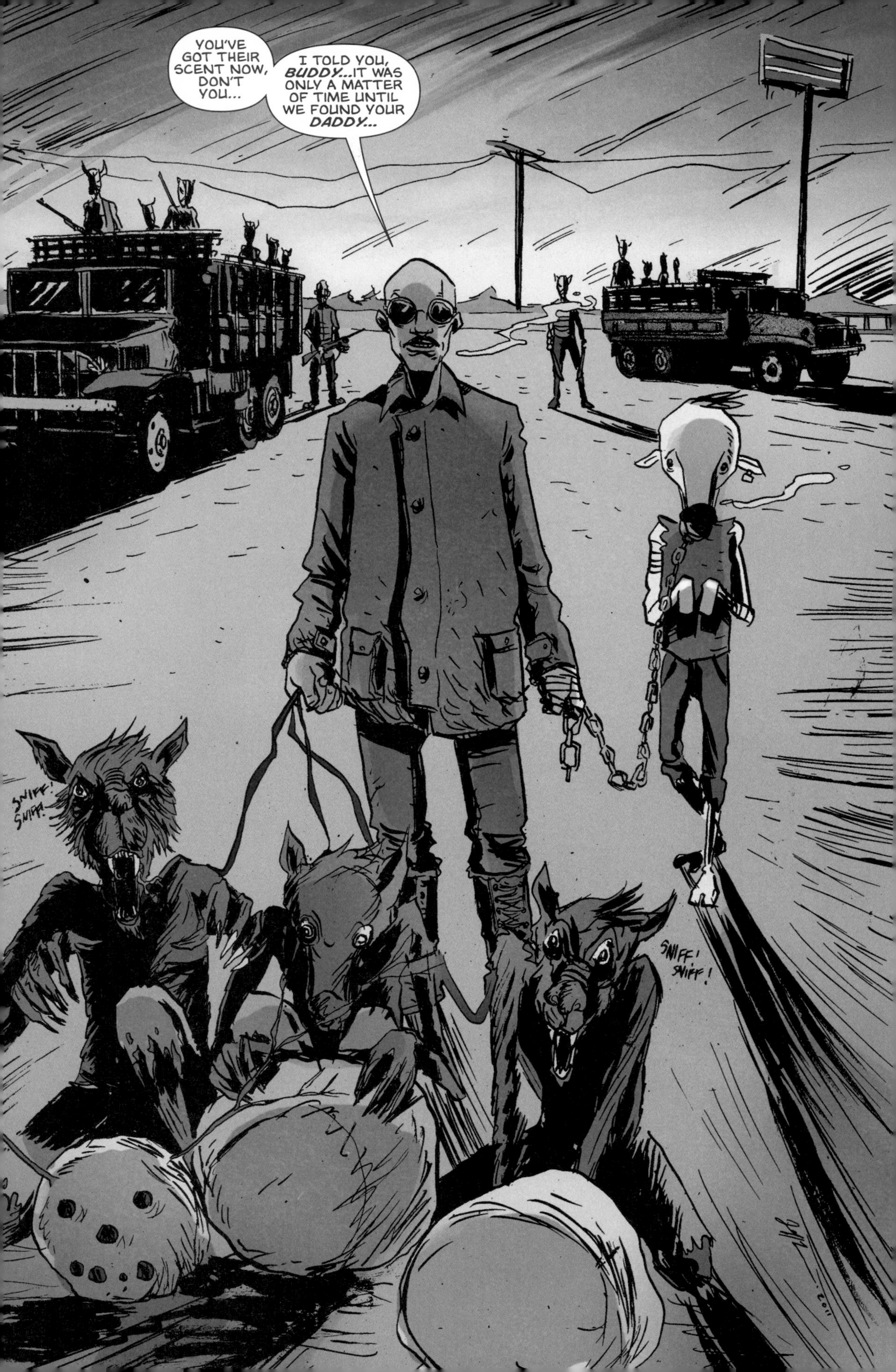
YOU'VE GOT THEIR SCENT NOW, DON'T YOU...
I TOLD YOU, *BUDDY*...IT WAS ONLY A MATTER OF TIME UNTIL WE FOUND YOUR *DADDY*...
SNIFF! SNIFF!
SNIFF! SNIFF!

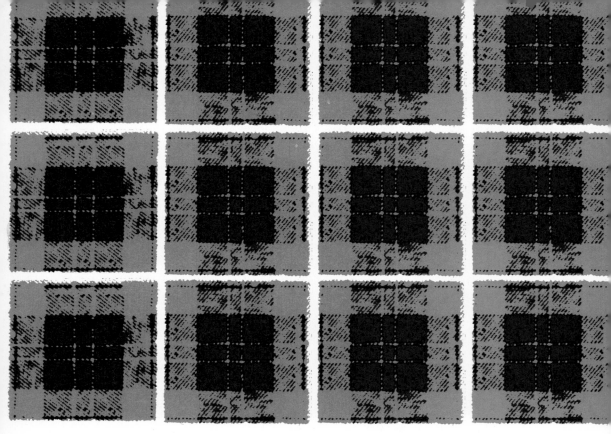

SWEET TOOTH
PINUP GALLERY

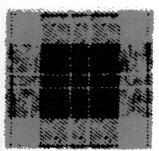

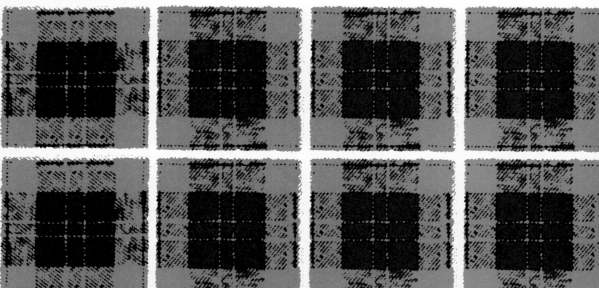

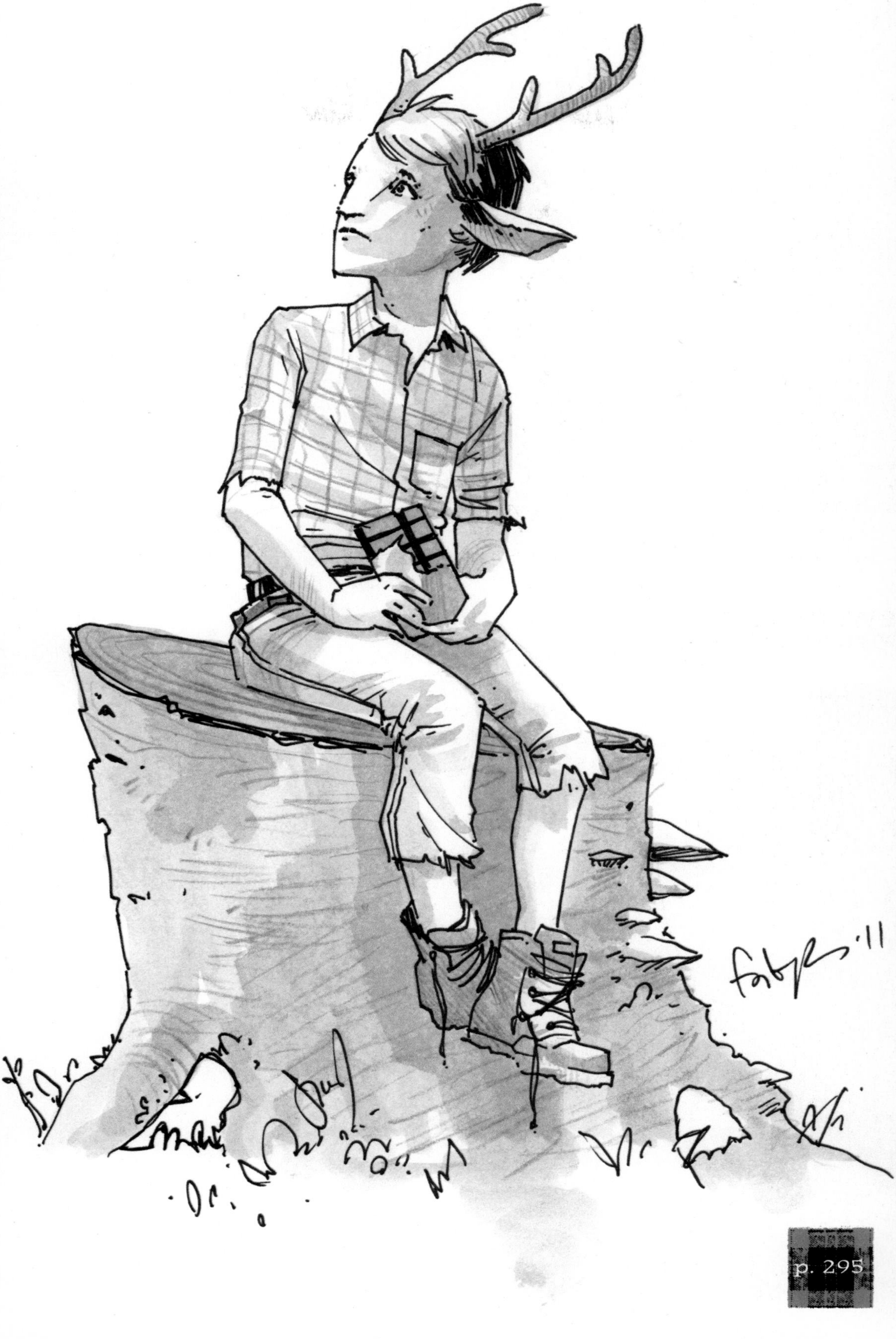

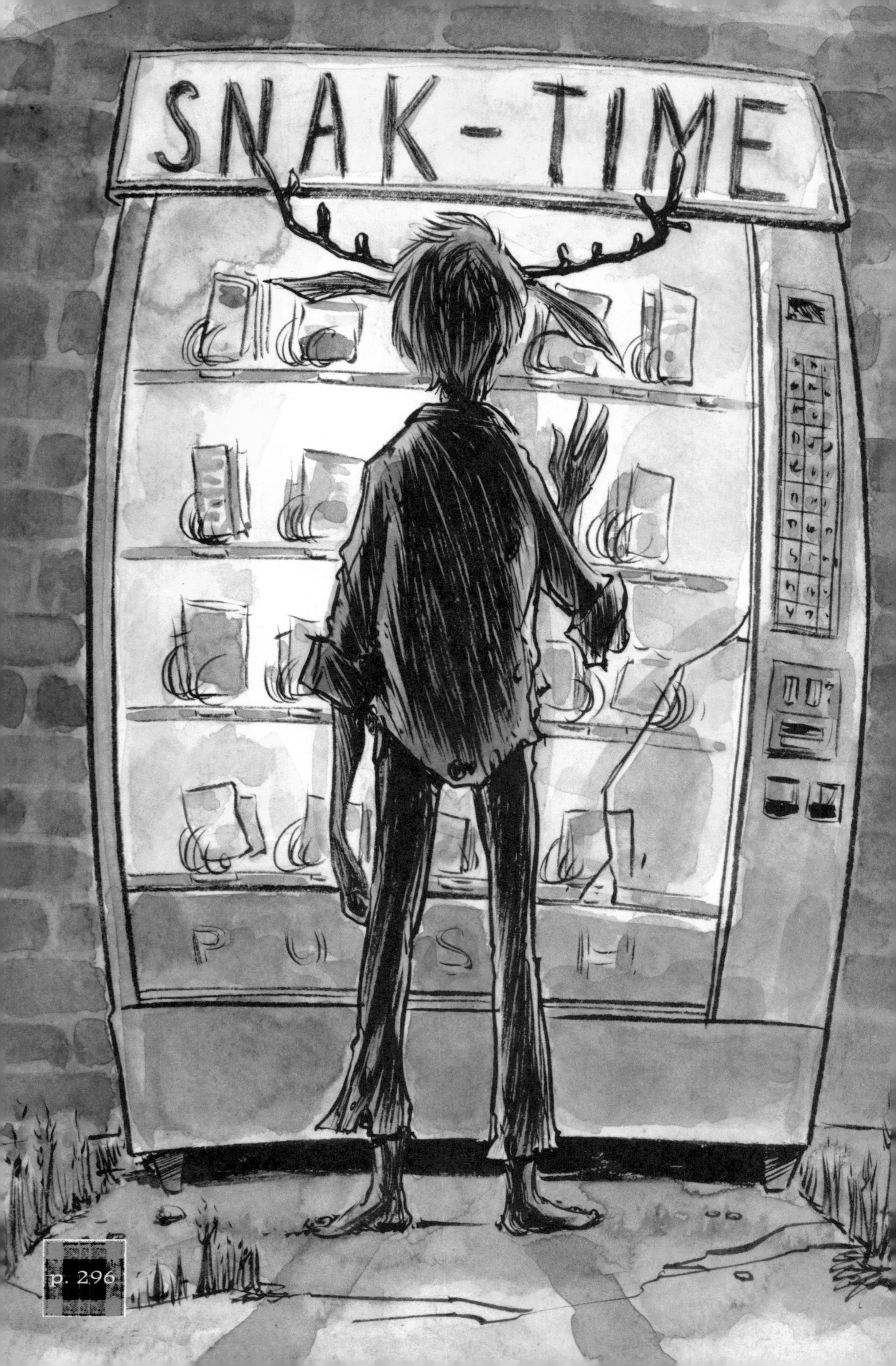
SNAK-TIME
PUSH

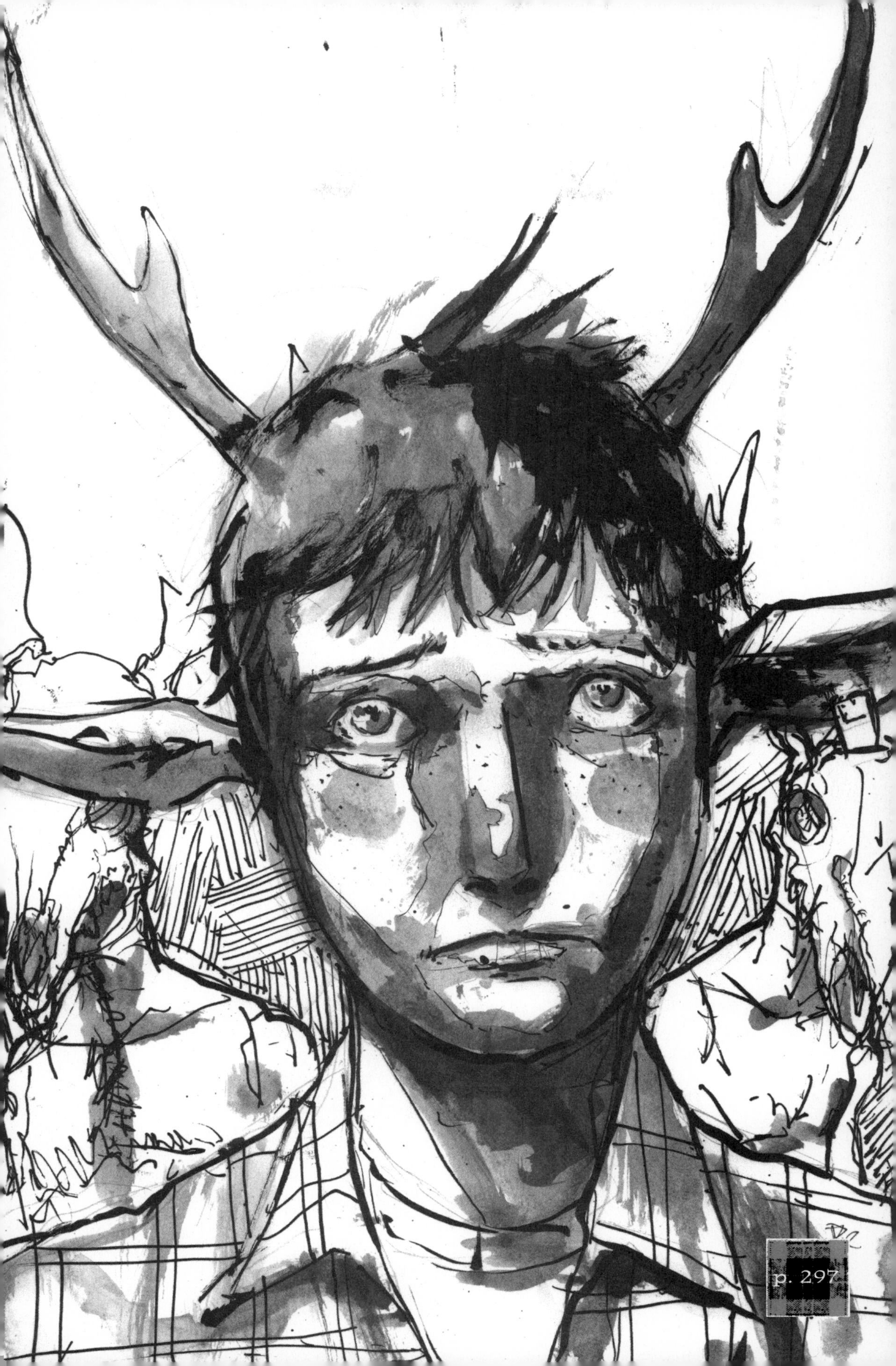

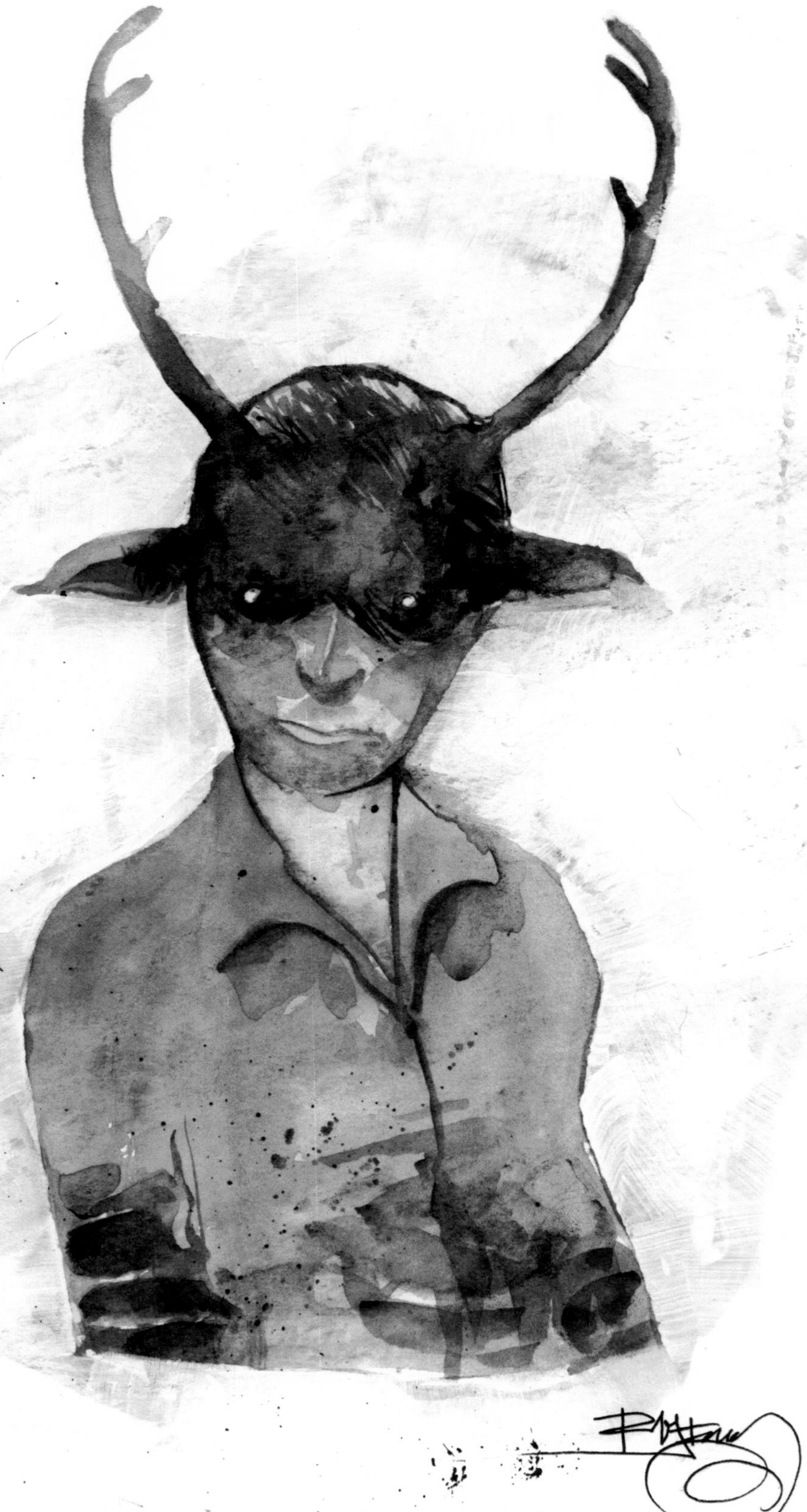

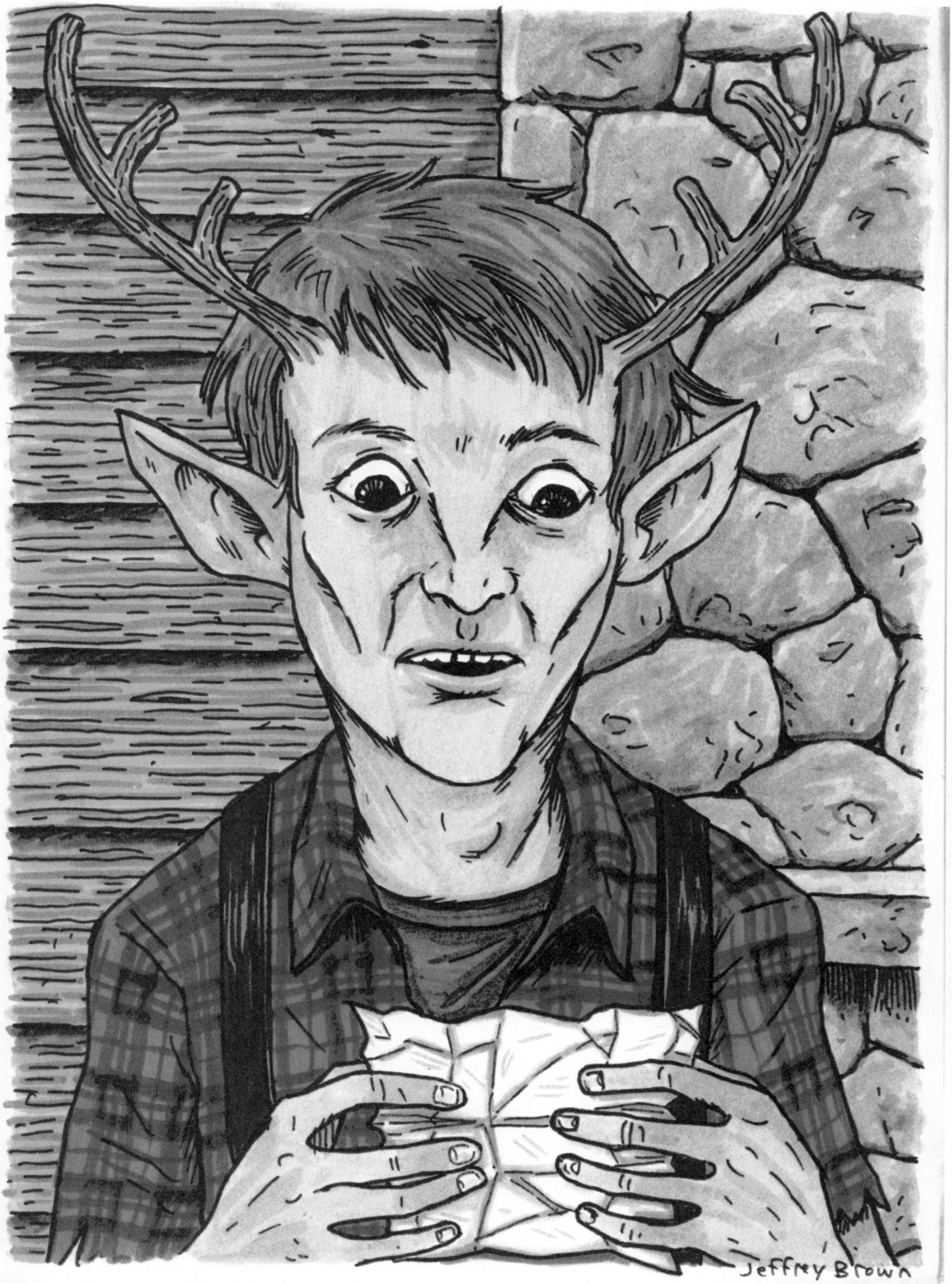
Jeffrey Brown

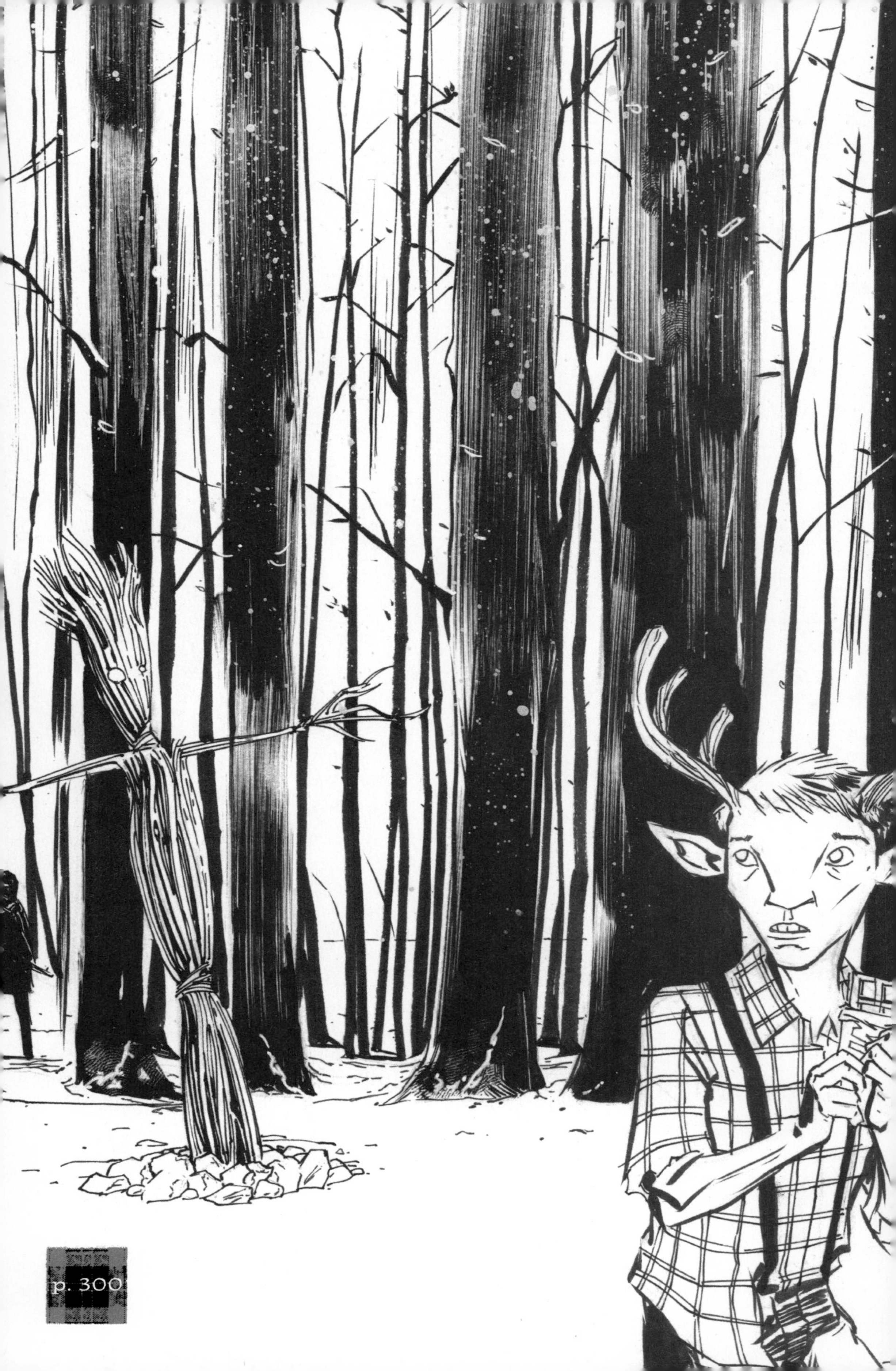

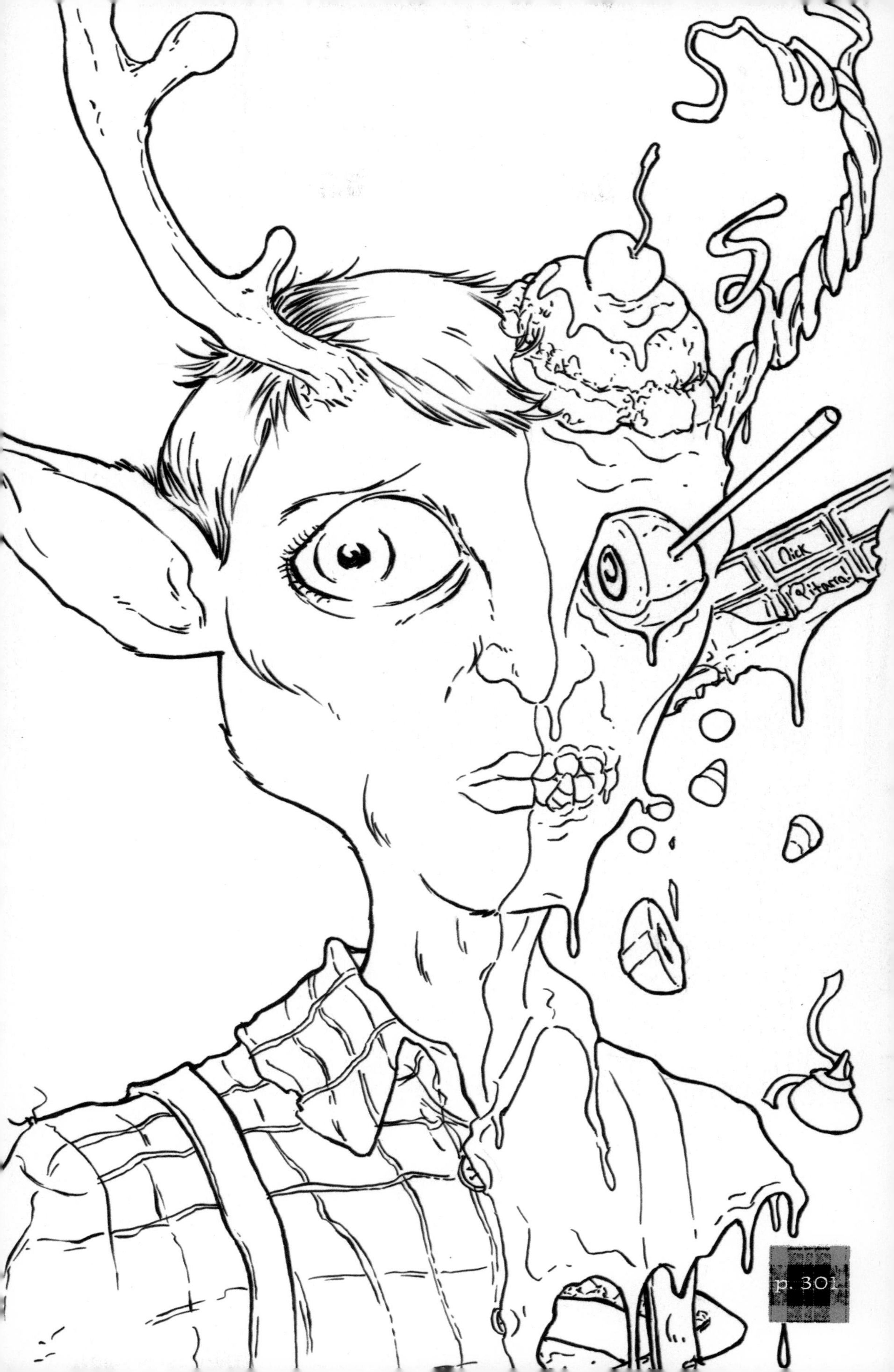
Nick
Pitarra!

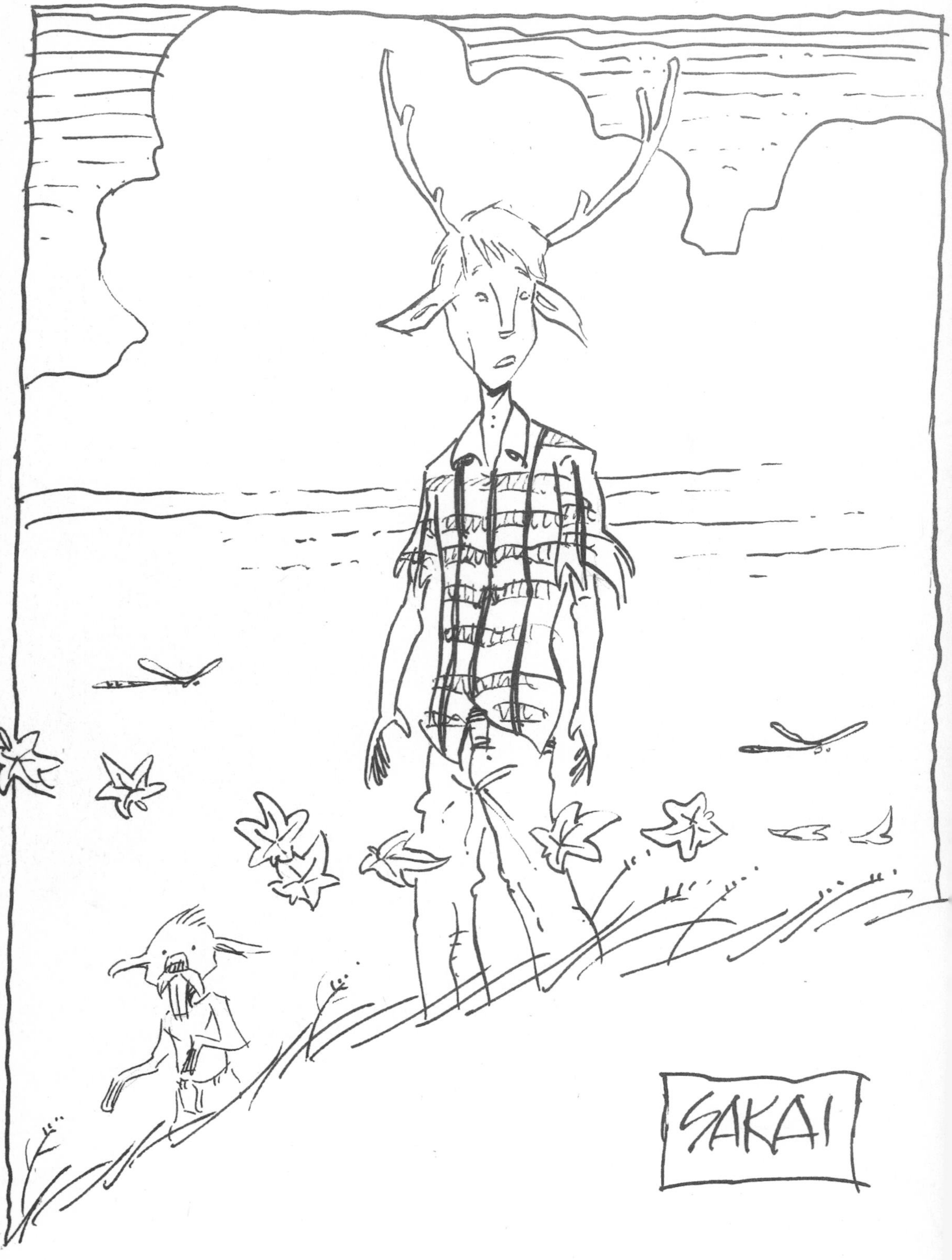
SAKAI

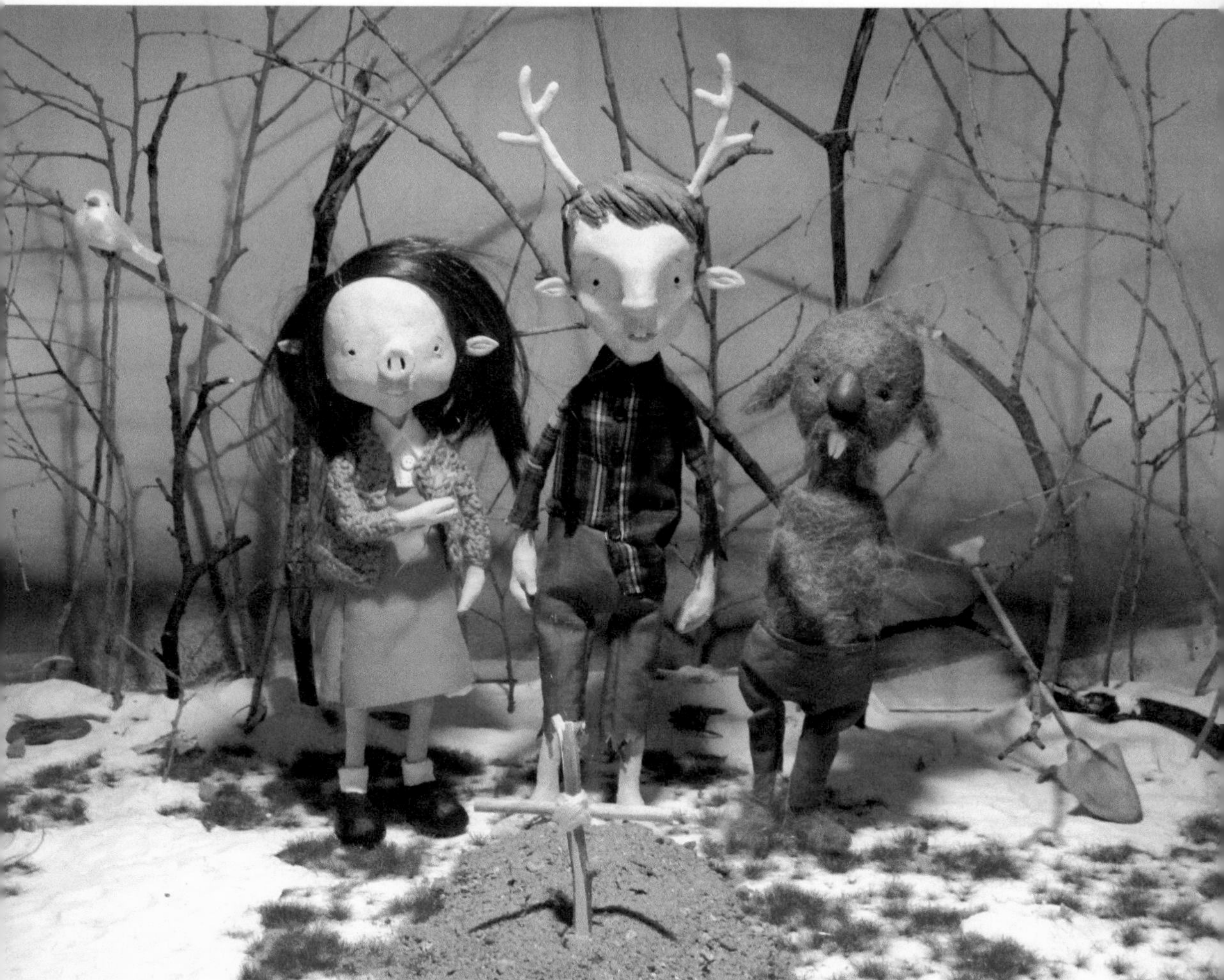

p. 303